JUNIOR CYCLE BUSINESS STUDIES

Be Business

Caroline McHale

GILL EDUCATION

*To my beautiful parents, Margaret and Peter McHale, who instilled in me
a love for education and the importance of being enterprising.*

Gill Education
Hume Avenue
Park West
Dublin 12
www.gilleducation.ie

Gill Education is an imprint of M.H. Gill & Co.

© Caroline McHale 2016

ISBN: 978-0-7171-69849

All rights reserved. No part of this publication may be copied, reproduced or transmitted in any form or by any means without written permission of the publishers or else under the terms of any licence permitting limited copying issued by the Irish Copyright Licensing Agency.

Illustrations: Derry Dillon and Aptara

At the time of going to press, all web addresses were active and contained information relevant to the topics in this book. Gill Education does not, however, accept responsibility for the content or views contained on these websites. Content, views and addresses may change beyond the publisher or author's control. Students should always be supervised when reviewing websites.

For permission to reproduce photographs, the author and publisher gratefully acknowledge the following:

Adam Pacitti; The Advertising Archives; Alamy; Alone; An Garda Síochána; An Post; Andy Kenny Fitness; ASAI; ASTI; Bank of Ireland; Bord na Móna; CIE; Coillte; Collins; DAA; David Andrew; David Fennell; Department of Finance; Department of the Taoiseach; Done Deal; Enterprise Ireland; Environmental Protection Agency; Erasmus+; Ervia; ESB; Facebook; Financial Services Ombudsman; FreeTrade Ireland; getirelandactive.ie; Getty Images; Global Goals www.globalgoals.org; GOAL; Iarnród Éireann; IDA Ireland; Inpho; INPHO; Irish Second-Level Students' Union; iStock; Jack & Jill Children's Foundation; Jen Patton; Largo Foods; LauraLynn; LUAS; MABS; Met Éireann; Music Generation; Netwatch; The Office of the Revenue Commissioners; One4All; Premier Lotteries Ireland Limited; Press Association; Rolling News; RTÉ; St Vincent de Paul; Susan Hayes; Tidy Towns; Trócaire: Hannah Evans of Trócaire with Enestina Muyeye from Dedza, Malawi; TUI; Twitter; USIT; YouTube; The Zip Yard. The eBay Inc. logo is a trademark of eBay Inc. Used with permission. Thanks to staff and students from Presentation De La Salle, Bagenalstown, Co. Carlow.

The author and publisher have made every effort to trace all copyright holders, but if any have been inadvertently overlooked we would be pleased to make the necessary arrangement at the first opportunity.

The paper used in this book is made from the wood pulp of managed forests. For every tree felled, at least one tree is planted, thereby renewing natural resources.

17020083VP

Table of Contents

Introduction		v
Using this Book		vi
Assessment Focus		x

STRAND 1	PERSONAL FINANCE	1
Unit 1.1	Personal Resources	5
Unit 1.2	Personal Income and Expenditure	21
Unit 1.3	Personal Financial Life Cycle	38
Unit 1.4	Key Personal Taxes	48
Unit 1.5	Personal Saving and Borrowing	65
Unit 1.6	Personal Insurance	84
Unit 1.7	Rights and Responsibilities of Consumers	100
Unit 1.8	Services, Consumer Agencies, Financial Institutions	111
Unit 1.9	Ethics and Sustainable Consumption	121
Unit 1.10	Globalisation and Technology	135
Unit 1.11	Wage Slip and Personal Tax Liability	143
Unit 1.12	Budgeting	151
Unit 1.13	Income, Expenditure and Bank Statements	174

STRAND 2	ENTERPRISE	191
Unit 2.1	Financial, Social and Cultural Enterprise Roles	202
Unit 2.2	Enterprise and the Entrepreneur	216
Unit 2.3	Employment, Work and Volunteerism	228
Unit 2.4	Rights and Responsibilities: Employers and Employees	239

Unit 2.5	Organisations' Positive and Negative Impacts on Communities	248
Unit 2.6	Digital Technology: Benefits and Costs	257
Unit 2.7	Market Research	267
Unit 2.8	Marketing Mix	282
Unit 2.9	Business Plan	294
Unit 2.10	Key Business Documents	303
Unit 2.11	Cash Budget	328
Unit 2.12	Cash Book, Ledger and Trial Balance	345
Unit 2.13	Final Accounts	360

STRAND 3	**OUR ECONOMY**	**397**
Unit 3.1	Scarcity and Choice	401
Unit 3.2	Circular Flow of Income	412
Unit 3.3	Supply and Demand	424
Unit 3.4	Government Revenue and Government Expenditure	438
Unit 3.5	Taxation	449
Unit 3.6	Positive and Negative Economic Growth and Sustainability	459
Unit 3.7	Globalisation of Trade	470
Unit 3.8	European Union – Benefits and Challenges	484
Unit 3.9	Economic Indicators	493
Unit 3.10	Economic Issues	508
Unit 3.11	Economic Policy	513

Key Terms Glossary	521
Classroom-based Assessment Guidelines	532
Templates	546

Introduction

Be Business is a three-year textbook designed to meet all the requirements of the new **Junior Cycle Business Studies Specification**. There are thirty-seven learning outcomes in the Specification, which focus on improving students' understanding of the business environment and on developing skills for life, work and further study through the three interconnected strands: **Personal Finance**, **Enterprise** and **Our Economy**.

To give further emphasis to the integrated nature of learning, the outcomes for each strand are grouped by reference to three elements:

- Managing my resources
- Exploring business
- Using skills for business.

Each element focuses on new knowledge, skills and values.

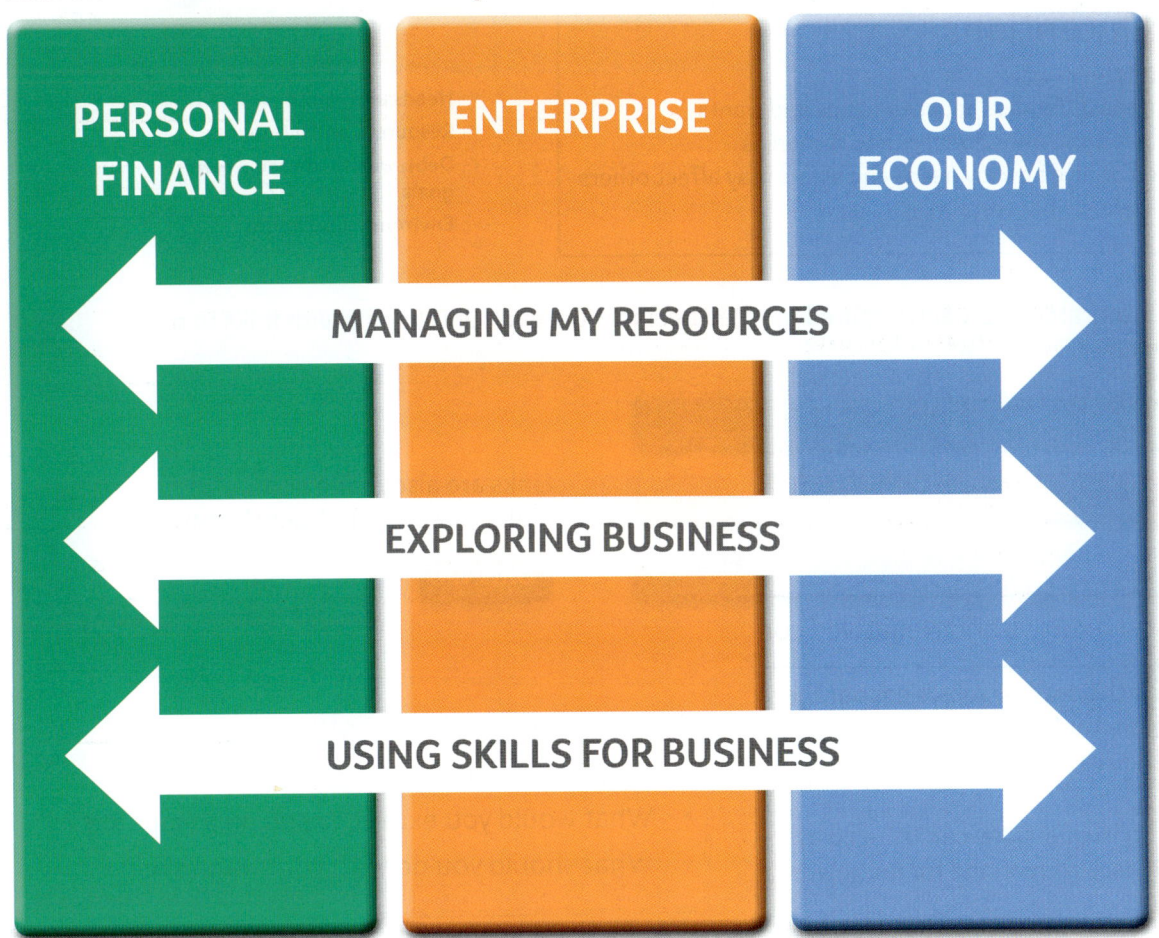

PERSONAL FINANCE   **ENTERPRISE**   **OUR ECONOMY**

MANAGING MY RESOURCES

EXPLORING BUSINESS

USING SKILLS FOR BUSINESS

In line with the Specification, *Be Business* ensures that over the three years of Junior Cycle, students have a wide and varied experience of activities that stimulate, engage, inspire and challenge.

Using this Book

The **Learning Outcomes** are referenced for the teacher and student at the beginning of each strand. Each **unit is linked** to a learning outcome to ensure alignment with the Specification and to facilitate easy progress-tracking.

The learning outcomes have been unpacked into easy-to-follow **Learning Intentions** for the student. With a strong AfL focus, these intentions involve the learner in the whole process of learning and ongoing assessment.

Units are framed by relevant **Learning Intentions** and **Key Concepts**.

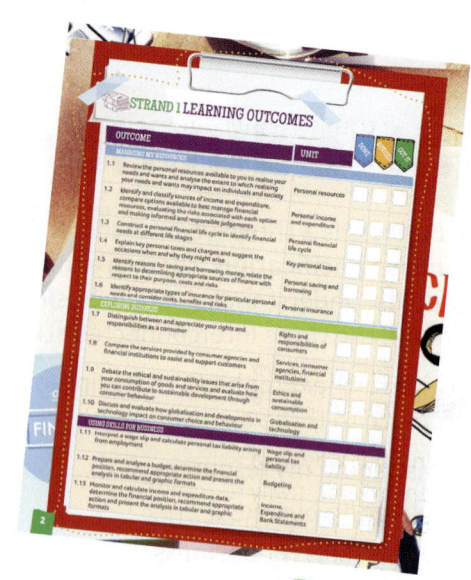

Learning Intentions
At the end of this unit I will:
- Understand the difference between needs and wants
- Be able to recognise my influences and resources
- Be able to recognise how my needs and wants may affect others
- Be able to explain what sustainability is

Key Concepts
- ✓ Needs and wants
- ✓ Resources and influences
- ✓ Debt, wealth, decisions and goals
- ✓ Environmental issues

In line with the integrated approach required for the Specification, each unit begins with links to other learning outcomes:

- 1.3 Personal financial life cycle
- 2.8 Marketing mix
- 3.1 Scarcity and choice

Links are also made and highlighted throughout the text:

Unit 1.4

'3Ts' exercises at the start of topics encourage students to explore their prior knowledge and to predict before they read/listen/watch.

Regular **Checking In** questions can be used as a form of ongoing assessment and for homework.

'3Ts' = Think, Turn, Talk
- What is a wage slip?
- What would you expect to see on a wage slip?
- What should you do with your wage slip?

CHECKING IN...
1. Describe the difference between a need and a want.
2. What is a personal resource? Give three examples.
3. What is a material resource? Give three examples.

USING THIS BOOK

Time to think encourages students to think about the bigger picture and relate topics to their own lives.

Time to think

In what ways are you environmentally friendly? Explain why you make these choices.

Working with Others tasks offer the opportunity for creative pair and group work.

WORKING WITH OTHERS

- You have received €30 for your birthday. You need to buy some new clothes for a school trip, but have just read on social media that your favourite shop imports all its cheap clothes from a supplier who uses sweat shops. What will you do? Work with a partner to come up with two possible choices. Discuss their likely outcomes on people, profits (businesses) and the planet. Set out those impacts in a table.

Choice 1	Positive impact	Negative impact

Choice 2	Positive impact	Negative impact

- Share your choices with others. You may change your decision after listening to their thoughts. It is important that you are open to, and able to reflect upon, new information. You can make use of the decision tree template, which you can find at the back of this book.

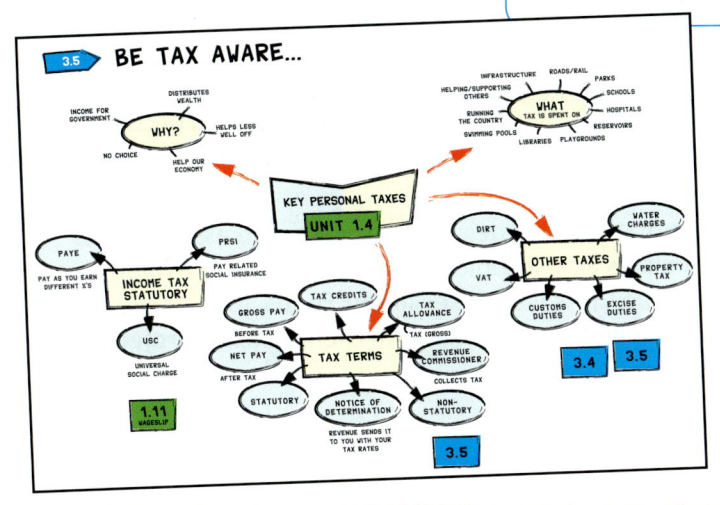

Easy-to-follow **mind maps** at the end of each unit are a great revision tool and provide vital links to other learning outcomes.

The **Be Prepared** sections facilitate students to evaluate their learning and support their progression.

Be Prepared: My Support Sheets

Completing the activities here will help you to reflect on and reinforce your learning before you move on to the next unit.
- Write down the **key terms** in this unit and make sure you understand them. See if they match the ones at the back of the book.
- List the key **concepts/themes** in this unit.
- List the **three most interesting points** about this unit.

Students are encouraged to note the **key terms**, **concepts/themes** and **interesting points**. This exercise results in an excellent **revision tool** that is created in their own words. The **Business Studies Key Terms** glossary at the back of the book can assist with this activity.

Business in Action Idea!

For your Enterprise in Action, create a business plan for a business of your choice.

Choose from one of the following options:
1. Invent an imaginary for-profit organisation, with a name and either a product/service that you are familiar with and create a Business Plan, similar to Ciara Cupcakes.
2. Write a business plan on a business you are familiar with.

Success criteria:
- Title – including an innovative business name and logo
- Nine sections as shown in this unit
- Show an understanding of each section
- Use of business terms you have learned in your Business Studies course
- Use of visuals
- Use of technology, if appropriate

Business in Action (group) and **Presentation** (individual) ideas are given at the end of each unit. Many of these activities are scaffolded with **success criteria** to prompt the student to fully address the task and to encourage self- and peer assessment.

vii

BE BUSINESS

QUESTION TIME

1. Describe something you planned for, perhaps going to a concert or attending a game abroad. What did you do? Did your plan change? If so describe the changes.

General contextual **questions** bring topics together.

EVALUATE MY LEARNING

Describe
- Did I/we meet our learning intentions?
- What went well? What are my/our strengths?

Assess
- Was the unit and its activities useful?
- How did I/we work with others?
- Were there challenges?

Recommend
- How might I improve?
- What skills and learning might I apply to new situations?
- What are my new goals now?

Evaluation should be ongoing. Initially evaluate yourself, working with others, your class, and where appropriate the visitor to the classroom.

With reflection as a form of learning, students are encouraged to **evaluate** their learning after each unit. This will help them to focus on enhancing their learning and experiences. These important questions may be challenging initially; however, they will support students in improving their understanding and help them to become independent learners.

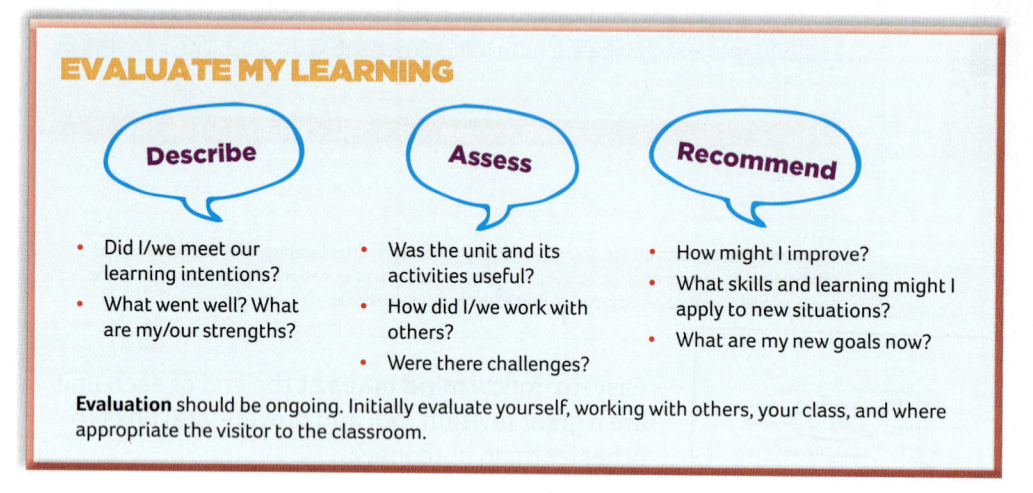

As they work through each chapter, students will generate material for their **classroom-based assessments (CBAs)** – **Business in Action** and **Presentation** – and make links across topics in preparation for the **final examination**. Certain learning outcomes are necessary for the CBAs (see **Assessment Focus**, p. x). At the end of relevant units in the book, students are prompted to consider if the unit will form their topic for **project** or **presentation**.

CBA 1 Business in Action:
Will I use this unit for my topic for **Economics in Action** or **Finance in Action**?

You need to be preparing for your CBAs
- Exceptional
- Above expectations
- In line with expectations
- Yet to meet expectations

Other features to help the student in *Be Business*

Be Business encourages students to put themselves at the centre of the learning – **'Be creative'**, **'Be Numerate'**, **'Be Literate'**, etc. signpost to students the skills they are learning.

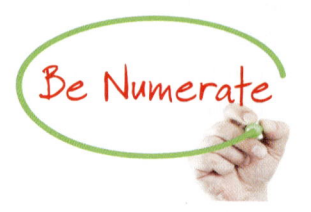

Be Numerate   Be Literate   Be Aware   Be a Researcher

USING THIS BOOK

Top Tip!

Prepare an **audit of your resources**. This involves making a list of both your financial (money) and your non-financial (people, personal qualities) resources and updating it regularly. It is a great habit to form.

Top Tips! give useful advice and help throughout the units.

Concise and student-friendly **explanations/definitions** of key words/terms are given throughout.

When you owe money to another person or to a company, you are in debt. The **debt** is the amount that you owe.

WORKBOOK

The *Be Business* **Workbook** provides valuable additional material to practice and consolidate learning.

- Anticipation and key word exercises
- Unit-by-unit additional questions (also given by theme)
- Lots of activities to support ongoing assessment
- Opportunities to engage actively and collaboratively.

TEACHER RESOURCES

The **Teacher's Resource Book** provides valuable additional material to encourage active learning and group work.

- Templates
- Guidance on how to approach the Specification
- Appropriate assessment tools
- A variety of practical teaching ideas and strategies
- Ideas on how to structure a lesson.

- The **GillExplore.ie** resources platform gives easy access to all digital material and other supporting teacher's resources.
    - Excel accounts
    - Unit PowerPoints
    - Supports for planning
    - Videos/Podcasts
    - Weblinks and YouTube references.

ix

Assessment Focus

Business Studies Assessment for the Junior Cycle Profile of Achievement (JCPA) will have the following components:

1. **Two classroom-based assessments** (CBAs), one to be carried out in second year and the other in third year, to be evaluated by the class teacher.

2. A **written assessment task** (AT), based on the second CBA. This will be submitted to the State Examinations Commission (SEC) for marking.

3. A **final written exam**, of not more than two hours, to be taken in June of third year.

Remember:

All assessment components are at **common level**.

All assessment and exam **formats may change** from year to year.

1. CLASSROOM-BASED ASSESSMENTS (CBAS)

CBAs will provide opportunities to demonstrate understanding and skills. The project should be undertaken over **four weeks** within a timeframe provided by the NCCA.

Classroom-based assessments	Format	Student preparation	Completed
CBA 1 **Business in Action**	Group project based on one of three options: 1. Enterprise in action 2. Economics in action 3. Finance in action	During a maximum of four weeks with support/guidance from teacher	Towards the end of Year 2
CBA 2 **Presentation**	Individual presentation and investigation on a business-related topic	During a maximum of three weeks, with support/guidance from teacher	Year 3

Grading of CBAs

- Exceptional
- Above expectations
- In line with expectations
- Yet to meet expectations

ASSESSMENT FOCUS

CBA 1: BUSINESS IN ACTION

Students are given three options from which to choose a Business in Action project:

1. Enterprise in Action	An opportunity to engage in an enterprising activity
2. Economics in Action	An opportunity to choose an economic trend, development, change or policy that is impacting positively or negatively on the Irish economy and society
4. Finance in Action	An opportunity to identify and research a financial challenge for a consumer or an organisation (profit or not-for-profit)

Business in Action is a **group project**. It comprises four areas of activity: *conducting research; evaluating information; developing action plans;* and *reporting findings*. Students should collaborate with classmates in order to complete the project, but teachers should ensure that each student makes an individual contribution to the project, and produces their own evidence to meet the Features of Quality for this assessment.

Student preparation	Four weeks
Submitted	May in Year 2
Group activity	One group report
Individual activity	Each team member must submit an individual reflection sheet
Word count	1,200 to 1,500 words (approximately five pages)

Project Option 1: Enterprise in Action

Students are given an opportunity to engage in an enterprising activity. They can choose from the following:

1. Students can develop a product or service. The product or service can be one they devise or create themselves (which they identify as having a potential market), or one that already exists (which they identify as having the potential to expand its market).
2. Students can organise an enterprise event or activity (for-profit or not-for-profit). It can be a once-off event or one that is organised over a longer period of time. It can be undertaken for economic, social or cultural purposes.

As part of this action project students will:

1. Carry out **market research** in order to assess the feasibility of their idea.
2. **Evaluate their research** findings.
3. Develop a business **action plan** based on their research findings which will describe elements of the marketing mix to be applied and financial information for the enterprise.
4. Provide their chosen product, service, enterprise event or activity to their **target market**, where possible.

5. Record the **inputs** and **outputs** of the enterprise.
6. Make a recommendation as to the **viability** of the enterprise.

The main learning outcomes to be assessed through Business in Action in this option are:

Personal Finance	Enterprise	Our Economy
1.2, 1.10	2.6, 2.7, 2.8, 2.9, 2.11	3.10

Project Option 2: Economics in Action

Students are given an opportunity to choose an economic trend, development, change or policy that is impacting positively or negatively on the Irish economy and society.

As part of this action project students will:

1. Carry out **research** on their chosen economic issue.
2. **Evaluate their research** findings. The economic evaluation will include identifying and assessing the economic, social and environmental benefits and costs for different key stakeholders.
3. Demonstrate use of **relevant economic indicators** and graphic representations to support their research findings.
4. Develop an **action plan** outlining an economic policy change that might improve the resulting economic outcomes.

The main learning outcomes to be assessed through Business in Action in this option are:

Personal Finance	Enterprise	Our Economy
1.1	2.5	3.1, 3.2, 3.3, 3.4, 3.5, 3.6

Project Option 3: Finance in Action

Students are given an opportunity to identify and research a financial challenge for a consumer or an organisation (for-profit or not-for-profit).

As part of this action project students will:

1. **Investigate** and **research** a chosen financial challenge.
2. **Evaluate their research** findings. The evaluation will comprise an analysis of the financial position of the consumer or organisation.
3. Suggest some **causes** for the financial challenge and identify the **costs** on different key stakeholders.
4. Support their analysis with **tabular and graphic** representations.
5. Classify and describe the **positive and negative impacts** on the income and expenditure and/or the profit and loss position of a consumer or organisation.

6. Develop **an action plan** to address the financial challenge based on their evaluation of the research findings.

The main learning outcomes to be assessed through Business in Action in this option are:

Personal Finance	Enterprise	Our Economy
1.1, 1.2, 1.3, 1.4, 1.5, 1.8	2.10, 2.11, 2.12, 2.13	3.1, 3.5

CBA 2 PRESENTATION

This classroom-based assessment has two priorities: to give students the opportunity to apply their knowledge, skills and understanding to real-life settings, and to develop their communication skills. The Presentation allows students to: develop their self-awareness as learners; to evaluate evidence and reflect on their values; to demonstrate how they can communicate competently using a range of tools prevalent in the business environment; and to make considered decisions and recommendations.

The Presentation is an **individual** project. There are three areas of activity:

- Investigating
- Making informed judgements
- Communicating.

Students may collaborate with classmates in gathering relevant information, but teachers should ensure that each student is able to individually produce evidence to meet the Features of Quality for this assessment.

The main learning outcomes to be assessed through the Presentation are:

Personal Finance	Enterprise	Our Economy
1.3, 1.7, 1.9, 1.10	2.1, 2.2, 2.4, 2.5, 2.6	3.1, 3.5, 3.9, 3.10

As a guideline, the presentation should last up to **three minutes** per student, including time set aside for engagement with the audience. Teacher support for the student's communication, in the form of questions or interventions, may be part of the presentation. A student may speak with or without notes, and a reading of a prepared script is permitted.

Students can use a range of different support materials and tools, such as stimulus material, digital technology, tabular or graphic representations, posters or storyboards, taking into account a school's unique context and the abilities and interests of the individual students. The use of different materials to support the oral presentation is encouraged and rewarded when used to scaffold the presentation where appropriate.

2. ASSESSMENT TASK

The assessment task is a written task completed by students during class time. It is not marked by the class teacher, but is sent to the State Examinations Commission (SEC) for marking as part of the state-certified examination in Business Studies. The assessment task is specified by the NCCA and is related to the learning outcomes on which the second classroom-based assessment is based – the Presentation. It is worth 10% of total marks. This assessment task will be submitted to the SEC to be marked along with the state certified examination in the subject.

	Format	Student preparation	Completed
The assessment task (AT)	Students complete a specified written task which is sent to the SEC for marking	The assessment task will link to the Presentation (CBA 2)	Following completion of the second classroom-based assessment in Year 3

The assessment task will assess the students in aspects of their learning, including:

1. Ability to evaluate new knowledge or understanding that has emerged through the experience of the presentation
2. Capacity to reflect on the skills developed in undertaking the Presentation
3. Ability to reflect on how their value system has been influenced through the experience of the Presentation.

The assessment task is offered at a common level. It consists of two stages: first, discussing and evaluating individual presentations; and second, reflecting on and writing about experiences as presenters. The assessment task takes place over a double class period or two single class periods, a minimum of eighty minutes. The first class period is used for preparation purposes. The second class period is used for writing up their response. The student response is written into a **pro-forma booklet** and the school forwards the completed student booklets for the assessment task in accordance with arrangements set out by the SEC.

The mark awarded for the assessment task will be aggregated by the SEC with the mark awarded for the examination to determine the overall grade for the state-certified final examination in Business Studies.

3. STATE-CERTIFIED EXAMINATION

The final written examination will be no longer than two hours and is worth 90% of total marks. Completed at the end of third year, it will be a common paper. Examinations will be set, administered, marked and resulted by the SEC.

All elements of assessment will be recorded in the **Junior Cycle Profile of Achievement (JCPA)**.

See pp. 532–545 for guidelines on completing CBA1 and CBA 2

1 PERSONAL FINANCE

Personal Finance focuses on developing skills, knowledge and values that allow you to make informed decisions to effectively and responsibly manage your financial resources. In this strand you will learn about managing your finances, responsible consumer behaviour and the value of using resources ethically and efficiently for the benefit of individuals and society.

- PERSONAL INCOME AND EXPENDITURE
- PERSONAL FINANCIAL LIFE CYCLE
- KEY PERSONAL TAXES
- PERSONAL RESOURCES
- PERSONAL SAVING AND BORROWING
- PERSONAL INSURANCE
- RIGHTS AND RESPONSIBILITIES OF CONSUMERS
- ETHICS AND SUSTAINABLE CONSUMPTION
- GLOBALISATION AND TECHNOLOGY
- SERVICES, CONSUMER AGENCIES, FINANCIAL INSTITUTIONS
- INCOME, EXPENDITURE AND BANK STATEMENTS
- BUDGETING
- WAGE SLIP AND PERSONAL TAX LIABILITY

STRAND 1 LEARNING OUTCOMES

Engaging with personal finance you should be able to: ✓

OUTCOME	UNIT
MANAGING MY RESOURCES	
1.1 Review the personal resources available to you to realise your needs and wants and analyse the extent to which realising your needs and wants may impact on individuals and society	Personal resources
1.2 Identify and classify sources of income and expenditure, compare options available to best manage financial resources, evaluating the risks associated with each option and making informed and responsible judgements	Personal income and expenditure
1.3 Construct a personal financial life cycle to identify financial needs at different life stages	Personal financial life cycle
1.4 Explain key personal taxes and charges and suggest the occasions when and why they might arise	Key personal taxes
1.5 Identify reasons for saving and borrowing money, relate the reasons to determining appropriate sources of finance with respect to their purpose, costs and risks	Personal saving and borrowing
1.6 Identify appropriate types of insurance for particular personal needs and consider costs, benefits and risks	Personal insurance
EXPLORING BUSINESS	
1.7 Distinguish between and appreciate your rights and responsibilities as a consumer	Rights and responsibilities of consumers
1.8 Compare the services provided by consumer agencies and financial institutions to assist and support customers	Services, consumer agencies, financial institutions
1.9 Debate the ethical and sustainability issues that arise from your consumption of goods and services and evaluate how you can contribute to sustainable development through consumer behaviour	Ethics and sustainable consumption
1.10 Discuss and evaluate how globalisation and developments in technology impact on consumer choice and behaviour	Globalisation and technology
USING SKILLS FOR BUSINESS	
1.11 Interpret a wage slip and calculate personal tax liability arising from employment	Wage slip and personal tax liability
1.12 Prepare and analyse a budget, determine the financial position, recommend appropriate action and present the analysis in tabular and graphic formats	Budgeting
1.13 Monitor and calculate income and expenditure data, determine the financial position, recommend appropriate action and present the analysis in tabular and graphic formats	Income, Expenditure and Bank Statements

INTRODUCTION

Personal Finance is about **your money.** It will help you to develop a set of skills and values for making **informed decisions** about your money. Informed decisions can be made only when you have a good knowledge and understanding of a subject.

You will learn how to **manage your money** and how to be a responsible **consumer** (buyer of goods and services) who uses resources ethically and efficiently for the benefits of yourself, business, society and the planet.

WHY PERSONAL FINANCE?

You need to know how money works, how to earn money and how to manage money. Understanding personal finance will help you to lead a **financially healthy life** in which you are able to make enough money to meet your **needs** and to achieve your **wants.** Your financial needs and wants will change at difference stages of your life cycle.

Understanding personal finance is an **essential life skill.** It will help you to control not just the money in your pocket, but also your purchasing, debt and credit decisions. It will help you to deal with other financial matters such as taxation, insurance, banking, savings, investments and pensions.

1 BE BUSINESS: PERSONAL FINANCE

Being financially healthy requires a watchful and sensible attitude to money and resources. In this strand you will have the opportunity to plan a budget (showing money coming in – income, and money going out – expenditure), to take actions, to record and analyse the outcomes and to make adjustments to your plans.

BE SAVVY

This strand offers you an opportunity to learn about and to research important financial needs and decisions. It will help to take the fear out of finance and prepare you to make sensible and shrewd choices for a financially healthy life.

You can work with others in your class to prepare for your classroom-based assessment (CBA), Business in Action. Also, there may be an area in this strand that interests you and that you may choose for your individual presentation.

Time to think

1. What do you **need** to spend money on?
2. What do you **want** to spend money on?
3. Why is it important to make a budget?
4. What should consumers know before they choose goods or services?

Top Tip!

You will encounter numerous key words for this Business Studies course. Document the key terms in your folder.

Listen to the word, **say** the word, **write** it down and **apply** the word.

1.1 PERSONAL RESOURCES

Review the personal resources available to you to realise your needs and wants and analyse the extent to which realising your needs and wants may impact on individuals and society.

Learning Intentions

At the end of this unit I will:

- Understand the difference between needs and wants
- Be able to recognise my influences and resources
- Be able to recognise how my needs and wants may affect others
- Be able to explain the difference between an asset and a debt, and between wealth and income
- Be able to explain what sustainability is

Making the links with other LOs:

- 1.2 Personal income and expenditure
- 1.3 Personal financial life cycle
- 3.1 Scarcity and choice

Are there other LOs?

Key Concepts

- ✓ Needs and wants
- ✓ Resources and influences
- ✓ Debt, wealth, decisions and goals
- ✓ Environmental issues

Wonderful Worthwhile Websites

www.mymoneysense.com
www.bankofireland.com
www.socialstudiesforkids.com
www.creditunion.ie

NEEDS AND WANTS

A **need** is a basic requirement. It is something you require, something you must have to survive. Our basic needs are air, water, food and shelter.

A **want** is something you desire. You would like to have it – you may even crave or yearn for it, but you can survive without it. For example, you may wish to own an expensive car, but you do not need it. Often our wants are influenced by family, friends and background.

'3Ts' = Think, Turn, Talk

- What are our basic human needs? Which of these needs cost money?
- List THREE items you want to have, even though you do not need them.
- Compare your needs and wants with those of your classmates. Note the similarities and differences.

We have needs and wants as individuals and as members of a household. Our needs and wants also impact on society. It is important that you are aware of how your decisions regarding needs and wants may affect you, specific other people and society as a whole.

You cannot have everything you want because resources (particularly income) are scarce. For more on this topic, see Strand 3: Our Economy. Unit 3.1

5

1.1 BE BUSINESS: PERSONAL FINANCE

WORKING WITH OTHERS

- Discuss what could happen if you spent all your money on your wants and had nothing left for your needs.
- Sometimes a want may become a need. When might this happen?
- Why might we consider our needs and wants from the viewpoints of other people?

RESOURCES

Anything that can help us to reach a goal is a **resource**. Although we tend to think about resources in terms of money and material possessions, we have other really important resources, such as:

Family Friends Time Talents

Energy Health Personal Qualities

It is important to manage and use all your resources to reach your life goals. To achieve all your goals, you need to make the best use of all your resources in the best possible way. The same could be said of managing a business.

Good decision-making is a key element in making the best use of your resources. In fact all the key Junior Cycle skills are important for managing resources, as well as for managing yourself.

It takes just **twenty-one days** to form a habit.

Top Tip!

Prepare an **audit of your resources**. This involves making a list of both your financial (money) and your non-financial (people, personal qualities) resources and updating it regularly. It is a great habit to form.

PERSONAL RESOURCES

You will find many resources within yourself. These are known as personal resources.

1. Abilities

Personal resources are what you do well, i.e. your **abilities, skills** and **talents**. For instance, you may be extremely logical and numerate (good at Maths), which will help you to understand wages, taxation, budgeting and accounts. Perhaps, when working with others, you can help a friend who is not so logical. Other abilities may not come so easily to you and will require hard work and practice to develop them.

> **Did you know?**
> Mozart played the piano for more than twelve hours a day to develop his skills. Practice helps create perfection.

> It takes **10,000 hours** to be **a PRO** at what you do.

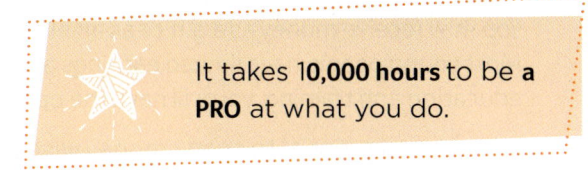

2. Attitudes

Personal resources also include your attitudes, motivations and drive. Your attitudes are your opinions and ideas about life. They affect the way you think, feel, speak and behave.

A positive attitude is probably one of the most valuable resources that you can possess. You will see the glass as being half full rather than half empty. You are likely to have fewer problems and make the most of all your resources.

If you have ever been served in a restaurant by a person who was helpful and positive, you probably had a really enjoyable experience and would happily return to eat there again.

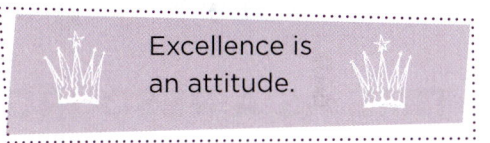

> Excellence is an attitude.

> **WORKING WITH OTHERS**
> Share a story about a positive person you have met. How did that person's positivity affect you? Jot down the main points into your copy/folder.

3. People

Your friends, family, classmates and even the local community are extremely valuable resources. They can support and influence you, helping you to achieve your goals.

Your family members have unconditional love for you and can help you with most aspects of life. Your aunt might be a great organiser who could help you with your research task and managing yourself, as well as managing resources for your classroom-based assessment (CBA). Your friend might be musical and teach you to play the piano. Your local GAA club may need volunteers, and by helping them you may develop important teamwork or communication skills.

1.1 BE BUSINESS: PERSONAL FINANCE

MATERIAL RESOURCES

Your material resources are money and possessions.

1. Money

Money is an integral part of Business Studies. It allows you to get the things you need and to have some financial independence. You need money to buy products/goods and services such as mobile phone credit, sports gear, haircuts or concert tickets.

You may receive money as a gift or as an allowance/pocket money, or perhaps you earn it from work such as babysitting. Most young people have limited earnings and need to make the best use of any money they receive. After you finish education and training, you will have the opportunity to earn more and to spend or save it in numerous ways.

It is always essential to spend money wisely and to save (put aside/not spend) money when you can.

2. Possessions

Possessions are the things that you own for your personal use (e.g. deodorant, an iPod, a bicycle). You may also have shared possessions such as the family pet or internet access.

Possessions help you to achieve your everyday needs. For example, your clothes keep you warm and your mobile phone links you with your friends.

TIME AS A RESOURCE

Time is an important and precious resource that must be managed carefully. You need to set aside time for your school work, your family and your friends. You also need to make time for a healthy lifestyle, with opportunities for plenty of rest, nutritious food and regular exercise.

The key is to ensure a balanced lifestyle. Watching TV all night, or spending hours on Facebook, Instagram and Snapchat, is a misuse of the limited resource of time.

A balanced and healthy lifestyle, with time for friends and family, and working on your education, will ensure that you have the best possible life.

Time is my most important **asset**.

Time to think

1. Why is money a resource?
2. Why is it a good idea to save money?
3. Why are possessions a resource?

Top Tip!

Having read the above, you may wish to update and expand the audit of your resources. Show how each resource might benefit you in life and enable you to achieve your goals.

PERSONAL RESOURCES 1.1

CHECKING IN...

1. Describe the difference between a need and a want.
2. What is a personal resource? Give three examples.
3. What is a material resource? Give three examples.

INFLUENCES

When studying your needs and wants, you should be aware of the many factors that influence you. These include personal, social, economic, environmental, psychological and government influences.

1. PERSONAL INFLUENCES

Some of the personal factors that will determine your needs and wants include your **culture, age, gender, hobbies** and **attitudes**.

Different cultures and religions have set rules and customs, which in turn produce different needs and wants. For example, most people living in Ireland celebrate Christmas, which creates a need to find Christmas gifts for friends and family in December.

Certain hobbies create specific needs and wants. For example, if you participate in surfing, you will require a board and a wetsuit. You need to have access to this surfing gear and may achieve that by buying, renting or borrowing it. You probably **want** to own the latest and best equipment, but you may not have the resources to buy it.

WORKING WITH OTHERS

- In pairs, discuss how **age** might influence your needs and wants.
- How might **gender** influence your needs and wants?
- How might **attitudes** influence your needs and wants?

2. SOCIAL INFLUENCES

Your family and friends probably have a strong effect on your needs and wants. You may also be influenced by trends in fashion, or perhaps you strive to look like a famous star, which then contributes to your needs and wants in terms of clothes and hairstyle.

The internet, social media, television and music can influence what people think of as normal, and change how we act, what we like, and what we need and want.

The needs of the 21st century are very different from those of the 20th century.

9

Peer pressure

People who are your own age (e.g. your fellow students) are called your peers. Sometimes your peers will try to influence how you act or what you do. This is called **peer pressure**. Peers can also influence your needs and wants.

3. ECONOMIC INFLUENCES

The state of the economy affects people's wants and needs. If your family has a low income or is committed to paying back a large mortgage (long-term loan on a home), financial resources will be scarce.

When a country's economy is healthy, it may encourage people to borrow money to buy items that they cannot afford. This happened in Ireland at the start of the 21st century. When Ireland went from a boom economy to a bust economy, people became more prudent (careful) and conscious of spending.

4. ENVIRONMENTAL INFLUENCES

We need to look after our planet so that future generations can also enjoy it.

Some people are really **environmentally friendly**, building sustainable houses, using solar energy panels, recycling waste, conserving water, etc.

Some people are particularly concerned about the way we treat animals and as a result choose not to eat animal products and not to buy fur or leather accessories.

5. PSYCHOLOGICAL INFLUENCES

Psychological (emotional) factors can affect your needs and wants. For example, you may decide to buy something just to make yourself feel better, or to thank someone for their support.

Marketing companies use these psychological influences to alter our needs and wants. Advertising, the persuasive powers of a salesperson or the clever location of a product can result in **impulse buying** (unplanned spending). It is important to plan your spending in order to avoid these traps.

Time to think

1. What are your social influences?
2. How might holidays affect your needs and wants?
3. Can you recall a time when your peers influenced you and it cost money? Where did you get the money from? Did it cost more than planned? How did you get the extra money? Did you have to pay it back? Was it difficult/challenging?

Time to think

In what ways are you environmentally friendly? Explain why you make these choices.

PERSONAL RESOURCES 1.1

6. GOVERNMENT INFLUENCES

Even the government has an effect on what you buy. A government decision to increase value-added tax (VAT) will make products/services more expensive and as a result you may buy less, whereas a decrease in VAT may lead you to spend more. The introduction of a tax on plastic bags in 2002 strongly encouraged shoppers to invest in reusable shopping bags.

Time to think

1. List six areas that might influence your needs and wants. Give an example for each area.
2. Which do you think might be the strongest influence? Explain why.
3. Which has the least influence? Explain why.

CAREFUL SPENDING

Careful spenders plan what they are going to spend their money on. They know how much money they have and how much they can afford to spend on a particular item. They do not spend any more than they can afford, even if the product or service is something they need.

When it comes to taking action to meet your needs and wants, you should aim to be a careful spender. A **careful spender** is not necessarily a **mean spender**, but he or she is definitely a **smart spender.**

WORKING WITH OTHERS

- In pairs, decide which actions are mean, which are smart and which are extravagant.
  Insert **M**, **S** or **E** as appropriate.

Mean = Selfish M / Smart = Clever S / Extravagant E	
Saving a little every week	
Comparing prices of mobile phones and call rates	
Bringing a packed lunch to school	
Going to a fast-food outlet every day	
Buying in a second-hand shop	

Mean = Selfish M / Smart = Clever S / Extravagant E	
Buying designer labels	
Spending all your pocket money	
Buying bottled water	
Buying the most up-to-date soccer gear	
Making your own fruit smoothie	

- Are you a careful spender? Give examples of when you were or were not careful with your spending.

11

PLANNING FOR THE FUTURE

What are your goals? What do you hope to achieve over the course of your life? Once you have worked out what your **goals** are, you can start **planning** for your financial future.

A useful starting point is to work out what you are worth **now**, in money terms. To do this you need to know your **assets** (things you own) and your **liabilities** (debts that you owe) and the relationship between the two.

> **Assets** are items of value that you own (e.g. mobile phone, bicycle).

Assets give us pleasure, but they can also earn an income. For instance, if you own and can play a guitar, which is an asset, you may also be able to earn some money playing your guitar, busking or providing guitar lessons.

> When you owe money to another person or to a company, you are in debt. The **debt** is the amount that you owe.

If your friend agrees to sell you his old PlayStation for €75 and you can pay him only €25 for now, then you will owe him €50. The €50 is the debt that you owe your friend, and he would be unwise to give you anything else until you pay him what you owe him.

The more money you owe other people, the more debt you have. When you are older you may well **borrow** large sums of money to buy a car or a home. Most people borrow money from a bank for such major purchases. Banks charge **interest** on the money they lend, which means that borrowers must pay back more than the amount they borrowed.

Businesses also encounter debt, as do governments.

WEALTH VERSUS INCOME

When you work out what you are worth **now**, in money terms, you are really working out your wealth.

> **Wealth** is what you own (assets) minus what you owe (debts). It is the money you have in the bank and the assets you own *after* the bills have been paid.
>
> **Income** is money that you receive (e.g. your wage/salary, benefits). It is the money that you have before the bills are paid.

> It is important to live within your means and also to save for a rainy day.

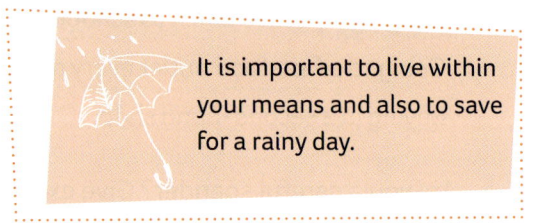

PERSONAL RESOURCES 1.1

It is possible to earn a high income (lots of money) and still end up with no wealth. For example, if you earned €150,000 last year and spent €160,000, you would have debt of €10,000 and no wealth. In fact you have **negative wealth** of €10,000.

Also, you can earn a low income and still have some wealth. For example, if you earned €25,000 last year and saved €100 a month, your wealth will be €1,200 (€100 x 12 months) – plus any interest paid on your savings.

CHECKING IN...

1. Give an example of careful spending.
2. Give an example of an asset and a debt.
3. Explain the difference between wealth and income.

SUSTAINABILITY

Sustainability is a theme across the three strands of your course. It is about looking after the world we live in, for now and for the future generations. We must act in a sustainable way in all areas of our lives; at home, in our community, in business and in our hobbies.

Do you ever consider the impact on the environment when you buy goods and services? You might think about issues such as pollution and the use of precious non-renewable resources.

Consider the environmental impact of the following:

- **Farming** uses poisonous sprays to fertilise crops.
- **Transporting** food to supermarkets uses non-renewable resources, which release carbon dioxide into the atmosphere and contribute to climate change.
- **Pollution** of rivers with plastics.
- **Wildlife** in a city can be disrupted by the noise and lights.

FARMING

DELIVERIES

POLLUTED RIVER

CITY FOX

1.1 BE BUSINESS: PERSONAL FINANCE

- **Factory production** can use up lots of water and energy.
- **Waste** has an impact on the environment. Dumping old electrical items is good for the manufacturers, but the environment loses out.
- **Cutting turf** will use up this natural resource if over-harvesting continues.
- **Logging** is the cutting down of forests. This destroys natural habitats and our source of oxygen.
- **Fuel burning** creates carbon dioxide and therefore causes climate change.

> It is important to remember that our needs and wants have an effect not only on us, but on our society and even on our planet.

MEAT FACTORY
DUMP
CUTTING TURF
LOGGING
WOOD FIRE

1. BUYING A MOBILE PHONE

Is a mobile phone a need or a want?

How often do you replace your mobile phone?

What do you do with your old phone? Once a mobile phone is thrown away and goes into a landfill site, it has the potential to damage our environment and the future of our planet.

How do you pay for your new phone? Where do you source your finance?

Survey your class to see how often they change mobile phones. Display the results in a graph (make sure it is accurate and clearly labelled).

Be Aware

PERSONAL RESOURCES 1.1

2. BUYING CHEAP CLOTHES

Clothes are a need, but sometimes clothes can become a want. Explain why.

Where were your clothes produced? Did you know that already or did you have to check the labels?

Have you heard of sweat shops? Describe or find out what one might look like.

How do you pay for new clothes? Where do you source your finance?

If you were about to buy a flattering pair of trousers and you heard about the terrible conditions of the workers who made those trousers, might you change your mind about buying them? Give reasons for your answer.

It is important to be aware of the effects of our actions and to make informed decisions. That does not necessarily mean that you should refuse to buy cheap clothes. You may have no other choice, given your own limited income. Or you may believe that the sweat shop is a rare source of income for workers in very poor economies and it would be better to support them.

WORKING WITH OTHERS

- You have received €30 for your birthday. You need to buy some new clothes for a school trip, but have just read on social media that your favourite shop imports all its cheap clothes from a supplier who uses sweat shops. What will you do? Work with a partner to come up with two possible choices. Discuss their likely outcomes on people, profits (businesses) and the planet. Set out those impacts in a table.

Choice 1	Positive impact	Negative impact

Choice 2	Positive impact	Negative impact

- Share your choices with others. You may change your decision after listening to their thoughts. It is important that you are open to, and able to reflect upon, new information. You can make use of the decision tree template on p. 546.

15

CASE STUDY: THE PROBLEM WITH BOTTLED WATER

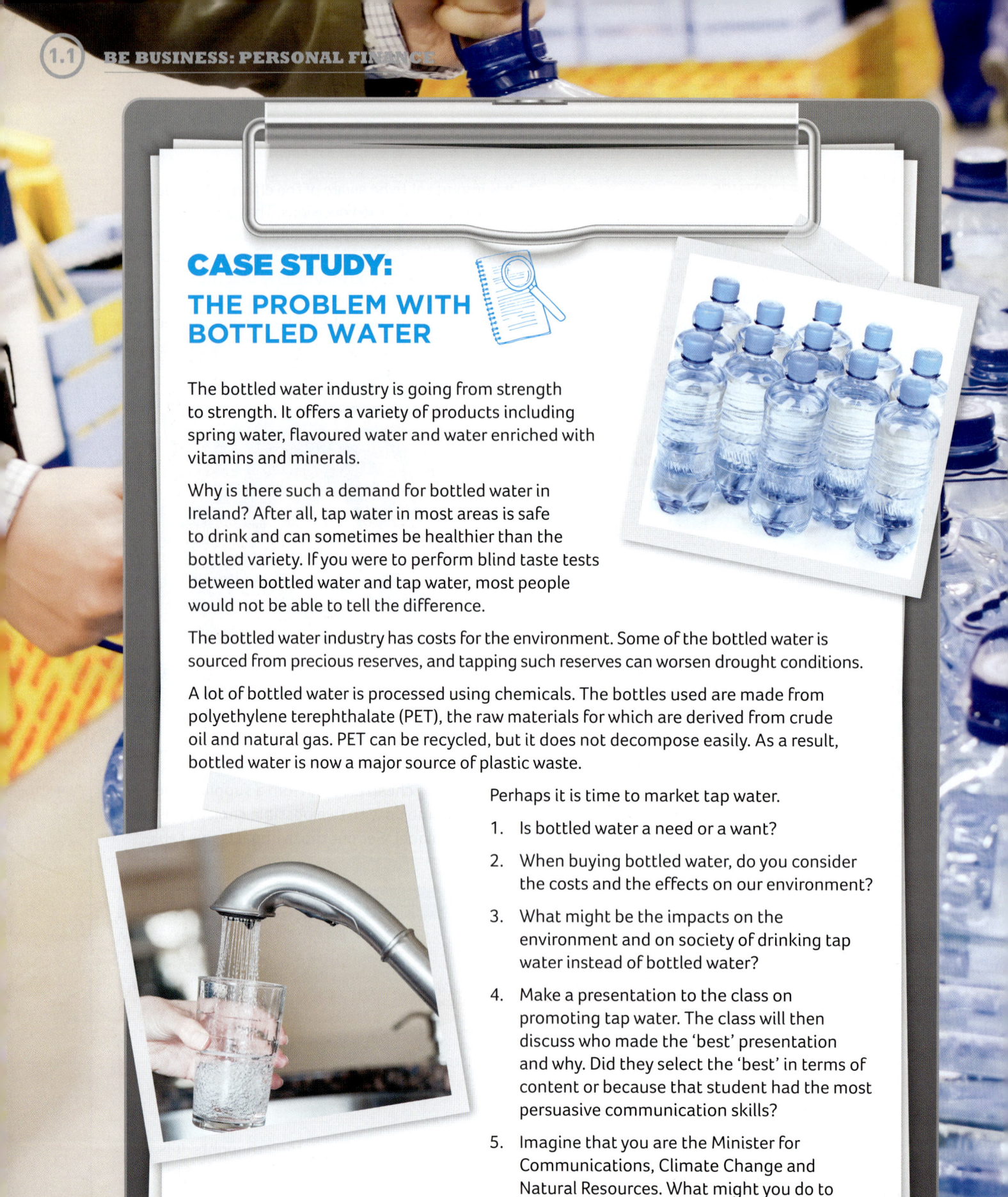

The bottled water industry is going from strength to strength. It offers a variety of products including spring water, flavoured water and water enriched with vitamins and minerals.

Why is there such a demand for bottled water in Ireland? After all, tap water in most areas is safe to drink and can sometimes be healthier than the bottled variety. If you were to perform blind taste tests between bottled water and tap water, most people would not be able to tell the difference.

The bottled water industry has costs for the environment. Some of the bottled water is sourced from precious reserves, and tapping such reserves can worsen drought conditions.

A lot of bottled water is processed using chemicals. The bottles used are made from polyethylene terephthalate (PET), the raw materials for which are derived from crude oil and natural gas. PET can be recycled, but it does not decompose easily. As a result, bottled water is now a major source of plastic waste.

Perhaps it is time to market tap water.

1. Is bottled water a need or a want?
2. When buying bottled water, do you consider the costs and the effects on our environment?
3. What might be the impacts on the environment and on society of drinking tap water instead of bottled water?
4. Make a presentation to the class on promoting tap water. The class will then discuss who made the 'best' presentation and why. Did they select the 'best' in terms of content or because that student had the most persuasive communication skills?
5. Imagine that you are the Minister for Communications, Climate Change and Natural Resources. What might you do to reduce our consumption of bottled water?

PERSONAL RESOURCES 1.1

WORKING WITH OTHERS

- Thinking in terms of the planet, decide whether the following are needs or wants.

NEED ☐ WANT ☐ Clean water

NEED ☐ WANT ☐ A holiday

NEED ☐ WANT ☐ Opportunities to play

NEED ☐ WANT ☐ Spare money to spend on treats

NEED ☐ WANT ☐ The right to practise a religion

NEED ☐ WANT ☐ Education

NEED ☐ WANT ☐ A mobile phone

NEED ☐ WANT ☐ Fast food

NEED ☐ WANT ☐ Decent shelter

NEED ☐ WANT ☐ A laptop

NEED ☐ WANT ☐ Clean air

OUR RESPONSIBILITIES

We need to be aware of the planet's limited resources and act responsibly to preserve them. Take, for example, our right to unpolluted waters. It is our responsibility to neither waste nor pollute water.

Time to think

Name another right and describe our responsibility to protect it.

CHECKING IN...

1. Give an example of how your needs and wants might impact negatively on society.
2. What is sustainability? Give an example of a sustainable consumer choice.
3. Why should we seek to protect the planet's resources?

1.1 BE BUSINESS: PERSONAL FINANCE

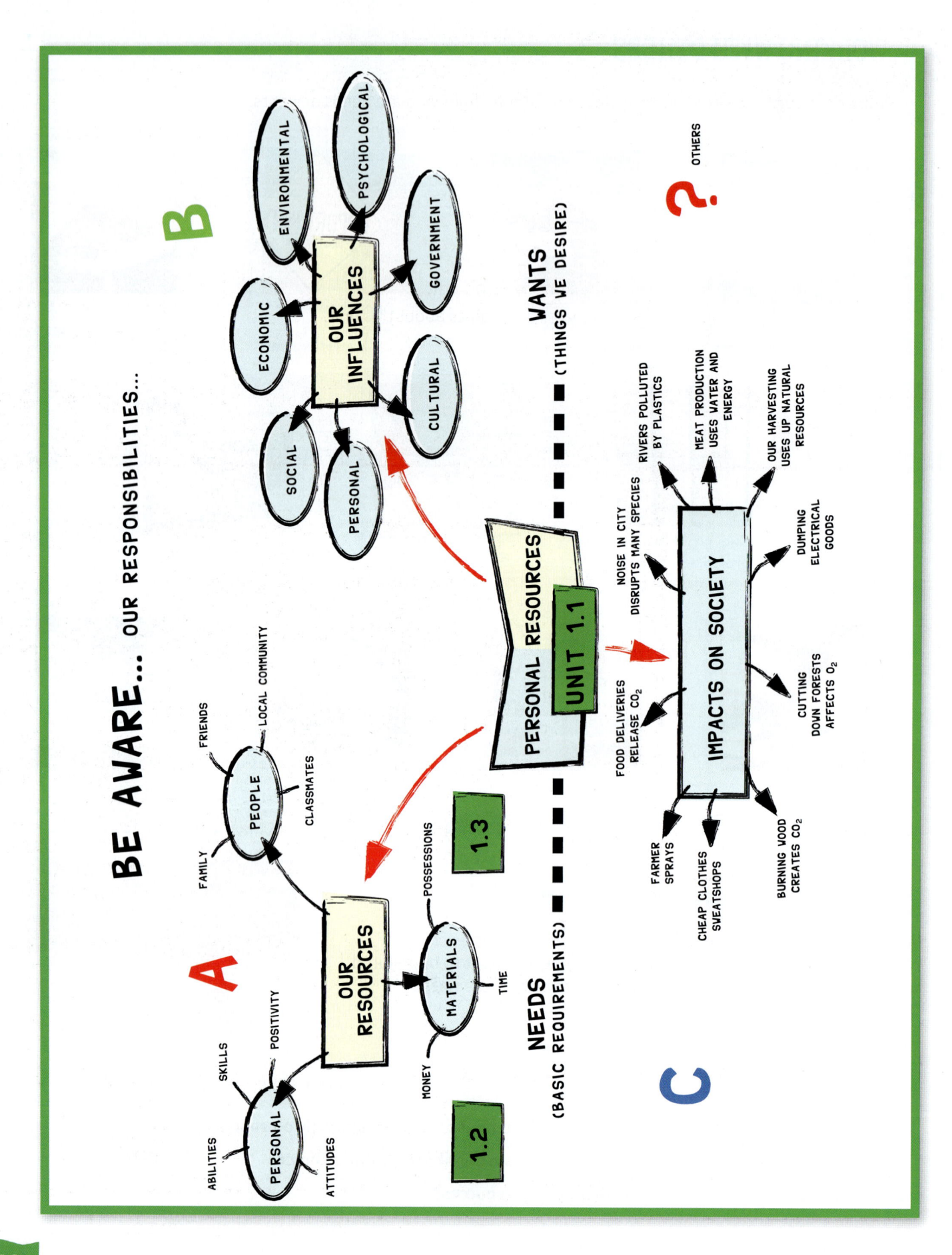

BE AWARE... OUR RESPONSIBILITIES...

A — OUR RESOURCES

PEOPLE: FAMILY, FRIENDS, LOCAL COMMUNITY, CLASSMATES

PERSONAL: ABILITIES, SKILLS, POSITIVITY, ATTITUDES

MATERIALS: MONEY, TIME, POSSESSIONS

1.2 *1.3*

B — OUR INFLUENCES

ENVIRONMENTAL, PSYCHOLOGICAL, GOVERNMENT, CULTURAL, PERSONAL, SOCIAL, ECONOMIC

PERSONAL RESOURCES — UNIT 1.1

NEEDS (BASIC REQUIREMENTS)

WANTS (THINGS WE DESIRE)

C — IMPACTS ON SOCIETY

- NOISE IN CITY DISRUPTS MANY SPECIES
- RIVERS POLLUTED BY PLASTICS
- MEAT PRODUCTION USES WATER AND ENERGY
- OUR HARVESTING USES UP NATURAL RESOURCES
- DUMPING ELECTRICAL GOODS
- CUTTING DOWN FORESTS AFFECTS O_2
- BURNING WOOD CREATES CO_2
- CHEAP CLOTHES SWEATSHOPS
- FARMER SPRAYS
- FOOD DELIVERIES RELEASE CO_2

? OTHERS

PERSONAL RESOURCES 1.1

Be Prepared: My Support Sheets

Completing the activities here will help you to reflect on and reinforce your learning before you move on to the next unit.

- Write down the **key terms** in this unit and make sure you understand them. See if they match the ones at the back of the book.
- List the key **concepts/themes** in this unit.
- List the **three most interesting points** about this unit.

Invent a quiz: Jot down three questions on needs and wants. Choose one of the three questions and write your answer in detail.

Finance in Action Idea!

Using the title 'My Resources and My Influences', either:

1. Create a poster or 'wall' on Padlet (www.padlet.com)

or

2. Write a report

Padlet is a free, online 'virtual wall' tool where users can express thoughts on topics of their choice. It's like a piece of paper, but on the Web.

Success criteria:
- A clear title
- Three resources and three influences
- Clear visuals
- No mistakes in grammar, punctuation or spelling

Success criteria:
- Title and introduction
- Clear purpose and focus
- Three resources and three influences
- No mistakes in grammar, punctuation or spelling
- Conclusion – summarise main points

QUESTION TIME

1. List ten resources that you have.
2. Which of these resources are the most important. Why?
3. Describe what is meant by 'influences'.
4. Have you ever experienced peer pressure to buy something? Explain.
5. How might you plan for the future?
6. What are the differences between assets and wealth?
7. How might you be a careful spender?

1.1 BE BUSINESS: PERSONAL FINANCE

EVALUATE MY LEARNING: DAR

Describe
- Did I/we meet my/our learning intentions?
- What went well? What are my/our strengths?

Assess
- How did I/we work with others?
- Were there challenges?

Recommend
- What skills and learning might I apply to new situations?
- How might I improve?

Evaluation should be ongoing. Initially evaluate yourself, then working with others, your class, and, where appropriate, the visitor to the classroom.

Do your **Key Check** in the workbook for this unit and then mark your learning position on the following rating scale:

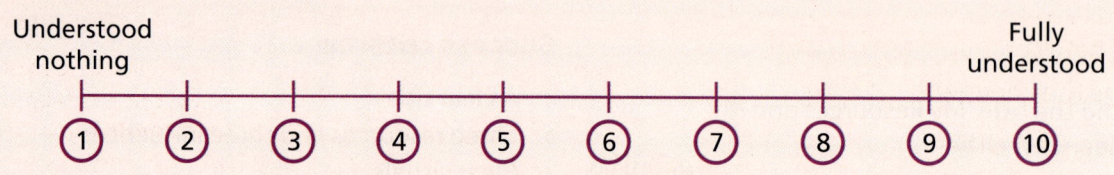

Understood nothing — 1 2 3 4 5 6 7 8 9 10 — Fully understood

How can you move up the rating scale? What can you **say, make, write** and **do** to illustrate your learning?

CBA 1 Business in Action:
Will I use this unit for my topic for **Economics in Action** or **Finance in Action**?

You need to be preparing for your CBAs
- Exceptional
- Above expectations
- In line with expectations
- Yet to meet expectations

Stop and think

Do I have any questions or concerns?

What are the mistakes or errors I made in this unit?

1.2 PERSONAL INCOME AND EXPENDITURE

Identify and classify sources of income and expenditure, compare options available to best manage financial resources, evaluating the risks associated with each option and making informed and responsible judgements.

Learning Intentions

At the end of this unit I will:

- Know about income and expenditure
- Understand opportunity cost, false economy and gross wages
- Understand the need to manage income and expenditure and live within our means
- Be able to explain the difference between regular and irregular income, and between a wage and a salary
- Value the importance of money

Making the links with other LOs:

- 1.1 Personal resources
- 1.3 Personal financial life cycle
- 1.11 Wage slip and personal tax liability
- 1.12 Budgeting
- 1.13 Income, expenditure and bank statements
- 3.1 Scarcity and choice
- 3.2 Circular flow of income

Are there other LOs?

INCOME

Income is money and/or something of value that you receive. It may be earned, e.g. through paid employment, or unearned, e.g. from a state benefit.

Key Concepts

- ✓ Income and expenditure
- ✓ Opportunity cost
- ✓ Impulse buying
- ✓ False economies
- ✓ Living within your means

Wonderful Worthwhile Websites

www.makingcents.ie
www.consumerhelp.ie
www.mabs.ie
www.aib.ie
www.mymoneysense.com
www.bankofireland.com

'3Ts' = Think, Turn, Talk

- What does the word 'income' mean to you?
- List as many different sources of income as you can.
- What does the word 'expenditure' mean to you?
- List as many different types of expenditure as you can.

21

1.2 BE BUSINESS: PERSONAL FINANCE

The income of **individuals** is **limited**, and we do not always have enough income to buy **all** the things we would like to buy. The income of students is particularly limited and you need to be aware of your income to manage your finances.

Household income will depend on **who lives in the house**. There may be just one source of income or a range of different incomes in the one household.

You need to **manage** your income, **record** your income and decide how best to **use** your income.

SOURCES OF INCOME

The source of any income that you receive will depend on your circumstances at the time. Are you in primary, post-primary or third-level education? Are you employed or unemployed? Are you self-employed and running your own business? Have you retired from employment? Are you entitled to any state benefits?

Students

WORKING WITH OTHERS

- Survey your classmates on their main sources of income and complete the table below.
- Use the total number of students in the class to calculate the percentage for each category.

Student Income – Post-primary

	Numbers	%
A Pocket money		
B Part-time work		
C Babysitting		
D Other income		
Total no. of students		

Success criteria:
- Appropriate title
- Clear labels
- Accurate presentation of the data

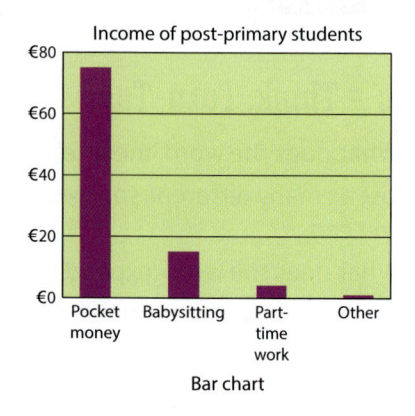

- What is the main source of income among your classmates?
- Present your answers using a bar chart or a graph.

Income of post-primary students (Bar chart)

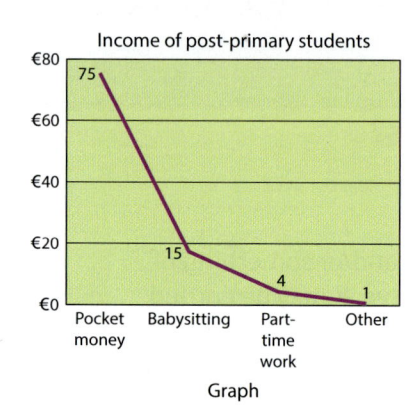

Income of post-primary students (Graph): Pocket money 75, Babysitting 15, Part-time work 4, Other 1

PERSONAL INCOME AND EXPENDITURE 1.2

Third-level students
Third-level students often take on part-time jobs to supplement their income. Here are some other sources:

- Student grant, scholarship
- Maintenance money from parents
- Part-time work
- Grinds to post-primary students
- Lessons to pass on skills (e.g. piano)
- Establishing a business
- Other

People of Working Age
People who have completed their full-time education usually try to find income through work.
- If they are successful in finding **employment**, they will receive either a **salary** (monthly payment) or a **wage** (usually a weekly payment) from their employer.
- If they opt to become **self-employed** and run their own business, their income will come from the **profit** made by that business.
- **Unemployed people** who are available to work but are unable to find a job will receive **jobseeker's benefits** (paid from state funds).

Some people receive additional income from the state. For example, a person with a child will receive **child benefit**; a person with a disability will receive **disability benefits**.

Retired People
Any person who has retired from work, having reached a certain age, will receive a **pension**. They may receive either a **state pension** (paid from state funds) or a **private pension** (that they contributed to when they were working) or **both**.

23

Other Forms of Income

Income is not always in the form of a money payment. It can also be in the form of **benefits** (something of value that saves you money).

Examples of benefits (sometimes known as benefits-in-kind) include:

- A retired person has the benefit of **free travel**.
- An unemployed person can avail of **free medical care**.
- A student can avail of discounts in stores, on public transport, etc. with a **student discount card**.
- Employees may receive **perks** such as a company car, a mobile phone, work clothes or private health insurance.

Time to think

Name some benefits that do not come in the form of money.

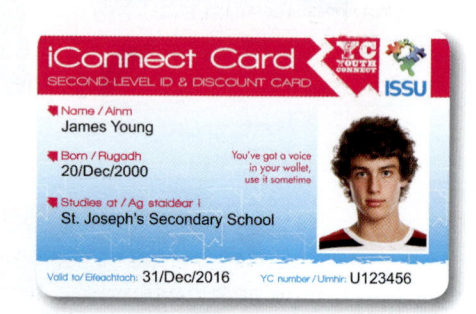

REGULAR AND IRREGULAR INCOME

Income is money you receive and/or a benefit-in-kind. We also classify income into regular and irregular income:

Regular Income

It is certain that you will receive this income and it is usually paid at agreed intervals such as every Thursday or the last Friday of the month.

Examples of regular income include:

- A **wage/salary**, which is paid every week/fortnight/month
- **Child benefit**, which is paid every four weeks to the parent/guardian of each child under the age of sixteen
- **Jobseeker's allowance**, which is paid each week to people who are unable to find work
- **Pensions** from the state and/or a private pension fund are paid weekly/monthly to retired people.

Irregular Income

It is not certain that you will receive this income as there may be, for example, conditions to be met before it is paid, or it just may not happen. It is important not to rely on irregular income to pay fixed expenses.

Examples of irregular income include:

- A **tax refund** from the government, which will be received only by someone who paid more tax than they needed to
- Rent for a room in your house through **Airbnb**, which will be received only if and when anyone takes up the offer
- An **inheritance** (in the form of assets or money), which will be received only following the death of a relative or friend.

EMPLOYEE INCOME

An **employee** is a person who works for an employer (person who hires them) in return for a wage/salary.

A **wage** is paid per hours worked or per product made, and a salary is fixed regardless of time worked.

Time rate means payment for the time worked (e.g. per hour, per day). It is important to keep track of time with a clock in/clock out machine or by signing in and out of work.

PERSONAL INCOME AND EXPENDITURE 1.2

Overtime is when you work additional hours and get paid extra per hour.

A **commission** on sales is an incentive to ensure the salesperson sells more. The more you sell, the more commission you receive. A hairdresser may earn a basic salary for hairdressing, plus commission for selling the salon's products such as GHDs, gift packs, shampoo and conditioners.

Occasionally a business will provide an employee with a **bonus**. This is extra income and is usually awarded for reaching a sales target or meeting a tight deadline.

Some businesses give employees a percentage of the company's profit. This is known as **profit sharing**. Bonuses and profit-sharing schemes motivate employees to work harder.

Bonuses and profit-sharing schemes motivate employees to achieve targets/deadlines.

WORKING WITH OTHERS

- Discuss the types of income listed in the table. Insert a tick ✓ in the correct column to show which is a regular and which is an irregular source of income.

Type of income	Regular	Irregular
Salary	☐	☐
Interest from fixed bank account	☐	☐
Money from selling your bicycle	☐	☐
Bonus	☐	☐
Cash gift from colleagues	☐	☐
Sales commission	☐	☐
Work expenses	☐	☐
Lottery win	☐	☐

- Compare and contrast regular and irregular income using a Venn diagram. List similarities in the overlapping centre and differences in the outer circles.

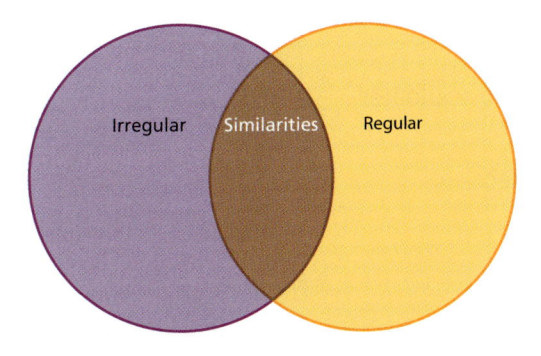

A Venn diagram is a great visual stimulus when answering a compare and contrast question.

1.2 BE BUSINESS: PERSONAL FINANCE

CHECKING IN...

1. List three sources of income in the form of money.
2. List three sources of income in the form of benefits.
3. Explain the difference between regular and irregular income. Give examples of each.

EXAMPLE: WAGE CALCULATIONS

1. Adam works 30 hours a week and is paid €20 per hour (time rate):

   Wages = 30 hours x €20 = €600 per week

2. Amy works 40 hours a week at €20 per hour. Any time over 40 hours is **overtime** and she gets paid double time (€20 x 2) for overtime. This week she worked 50 hours:

   Basic wage = 40 hours x €20 = €800

   Overtime (50 hours – 40 hours = 10 hours)

   10 hours x €20 x 2 (double time) = €400

   Gross pay = €1200

   If overtime was paid at a rate of time and a half (€20 x 1.5), what would Amy's gross pay be?

3. Alan receives a basic wage of €200 per week and is also paid 10% commission on his sales. His sales this week amounted to €1,500:

   Basic wage = €200

   Commission (€1,500 (sales) x 10%) = €150

   Gross pay = €350

4. Alison receives a salary of €400 per week and worked 50 hours:

   Salary = €400

   With a **salary**, the rate is the same regardless of the number of hours worked.

   If Alison's employer announced a 5% increase in salaries, what would her new salary be?

   What would her salary be if her employer announced a 2% decrease in salaries?

Time to think

Which method of wages/salary would you prefer? Why?

PERSONAL INCOME AND EXPENDITURE 1.2

Be Numerate

Wage calculations:

1. Breda works 35 hours a week and is paid €15 per hour. Calculate her weekly wage:

   Wages = _____ hours x _____ rate = _____

   Breda is paid a _____ _____.

2. Ben works 36 hours a week at €18 per hour. Any time over 36 hours is overtime, which is paid at a rate of time and a half. This week he worked 45 hours. Calculate his wage:

   Basic wage = _____ hours x _____ rate = _____

   Overtime = _____ hours x _____ rate = _____

   Gross pay = _____ wage + _____ overtime = _____

   If overtime was double time, what would Ben have been paid for the extra hours he worked?

   Overtime = _____ hours x _____ rate = _____

3. Barbara receives a basic wage of €350 plus 15% commission on sales. She made sales of €2,000 this week. Calculate her wage:

   Basic wage = _____

   Commission = _____ sales x _____ rate = _____

   Gross pay = _____ wage + _____ commission = _____

4. Barry receives a salary of €400 and worked 50 hours. How much was he paid?

   Salary = _____

5. Belinda works 42 hours a week at €22 per hour. Any time over 42 hours is overtime and she gets paid double time for overtime. This week she worked 45 hours. Calculate her wage:

   Basic wage = _____ hours x _____ rate = _____

   Overtime = _____ hours x _____ rate = _____

   Gross pay = _____ wage + _____ overtime = _____

   If overtime was time and a half, what would Belinda have been paid for the extra hours she worked?

   Overtime = _____ hours x _____ rate = _____

6. Brendan receives a basic wage of €600 plus 10% commission on sales. His sales this week totalled €1,500. Calculate his wage:

   Basic wage = _____

   Commission = _____ sales x _____ rate = _____

   Gross pay = _____ wage + _____ commission = _____

Time to think

Using your knowledge of wages/salaries, create three more examples and show your calculations.

Top Tip!

Excel and Google Sheets are great resources to help with calculations.

27

1.2 BE BUSINESS: PERSONAL FINANCE

RECORDING INCOME

You need to know your income. Keeping records will help you to **plan** and **manage** income. You can keep records of your weekly, monthly and/or yearly income. The table shows a simple record of income for three weeks.

Income	Week 1 €	Week 2 €	Week 3 €	Total €
Wages	500	500	500	1,500
Child benefit	140	140	140	420
Interest from bank account			40	40
Total income	**640**	**640**	**680**	**1,960**

CHECKING IN...
1. Explain the difference between a wage and a salary.
2. Give three examples of ways employers can use extra payments to motivate employees to work harder.
3. Why might you keep records of your income?

EXPENDITURE

Expenditure is the amount of money you **spend** during a particular time. Spending should be planned carefully.

TIPS ON PLANNING EXPENDITURE

1 Always **live within your means** – even wealthy people can end up bankrupt!

2 Save on a regular basis – it is smart to put money aside for a rainy day.

3 Prioritise your bills – pay for the things you need first and clear any other debt as soon as you can.

4 Know the timing of bills. When is the next bill due to be paid, and the one after that? Can you pay bills in instalments?

5 Pay into a **pension fund** as early as possible – it may seem crazy to ask you to think about your pension at such a young age, but if you contribute to a pension from the first day you start work, you will receive the maximum benefit.

TYPES OF EXPENDITURE

Expenditure (spending) may be **fixed**, **irregular** or **discretionary**.

1. Fixed Expenditure

Fixed expenditure is money spent at the **same time** each week, each month and/or each year (annually). The **amount is usually fixed** and does not, for example, depend on usage.

Examples: mortgage, rent, loan repayment, TV licence fee

PERSONAL INCOME AND EXPENDITURE 1.2

2. Irregular Expenditure

With irregular expenditure, the bill may or may not be paid at regular intervals, but the **amount paid out varies**. The more you use, the more you pay.

Examples: petrol, phone bill, groceries, school supplies

3. Discretionary Expenditure

Discretionary expenditure is money spent on things you can live without (**luxuries**). You should buy these items only if you have money left over after all the bills are paid. The **amount varies**.

Examples: Sky TV, designer clothes, holidays, take-away meals. See capital and current expenditure on p. 34.

Time to think

A pension is the income you receive when you retire. What is the current retirement age in Ireland?

Do you think it will be the same age when you come to retire? Give reasons for your answer.

WORKING WITH OTHERS

- Discuss the types of spending listed in the table. Insert a tick ✓ in the correct column to show whether the expenditure is fixed, irregular or discretionary.

Type of expenditure	Fixed	Irregular	Discretionary
Rent	☐	☐	☐
Bus fare	☐	☐	☐
Groceries	☐	☐	☐
Taxes	☐	☐	☐
Holidays	☐	☐	☐
Landline phone bill	☐	☐	☐

Type of expenditure	Fixed	Irregular	Discretionary
Mobile phone contract	☐	☐	☐
Magazine subscription	☐	☐	☐
Diesel for a car	☐	☐	☐
Insurance premium	☐	☐	☐
New car	☐	☐	☐
Birthday gift	☐	☐	☐
Private health insurance	☐	☐	☐
Motor tax	☐	☐	☐

- Compare and contrast fixed and irregular expenditure using a Venn diagram. List similarities in the overlapping centre and differences in the outer circles.

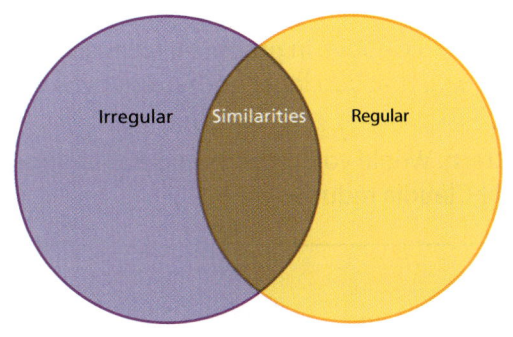

Irregular | Similarities | Regular

1.2 BE BUSINESS: PERSONAL FINANCE

RECORDING EXPENDITURE

It is important to know how you spend your money. Keeping records of your weekly, monthly and/or yearly expenditure will help you to keep track of what proportion of your income is spent on specific items.

Expenditure calculations:

Claudia's income for the month is €1,400, and she spends the following percentages of her income on the items listed in the table. Calculate the amount of income that she spends on each item.

Items	Percentage	Amount
Clothes and make-up	40%	
Entertainment	10%	
Savings	10%	
Charity donations	5%	
Membership of sports club	25%	
Other	10%	
Total	**100%**	**€1,400**

This table is an example of how you could record your expenditure.

WORKING WITH OTHERS

- Present the information from the table above in graphical form using a bar chart. The title should be 'Claudia's Expenditure'. Make sure that you label both axes. It is a good idea to use graph paper to ensure accuracy.
- Discuss Claudia's spending pattern. Would you recommend any changes? What area of expenditure might Claudia reduce?

MANAGING INCOME AND EXPENDITURE

It is really important to **monitor** (keep track of) your income and expenditure each month. That means knowing how much money is coming in and how much is going out.

You need to be careful and plan your activities so that you **live within your means**. If you spend more than you have, you will end up in **debt**. If you save some money as often as you can, then you will have those **savings** to fall back on when you need extra money.

You should also decide which of your expenditures you must **prioritise**. For example, if you are running low on money at the end of a month, paying your rent is much more important than buying tickets for a concert. It is all about priorities: having somewhere to live is a **need**, whereas a concert is a **want**. Needs must come first.

DECISIONS ON SPENDING

The more information you have about your income and expenditure, the easier it will be to make decisions on how best to manage your finances.

Priorities

If your income is limited, you must plan carefully how you will spend it. You must first make sure that you have adequate income for:

1. **Fixed** expenditure
2. **Irregular** expenditure

And then, and only if you do have money left over, you can afford:

3. **Discretionary** expenditure.

A **deficit** occurs when expenditure (spending) is greater than income.

If you think you will encounter a **deficit**, what might you do?

The first step would be to stop or at least reduce discretionary expenditure, which may be enough to solve the problem. If not, you will need to consider other expenditures as well to see if you can reduce them and live within your means.

1.2 BE BUSINESS: PERSONAL FINANCE

OPPORTUNITY COST

When you make a financial decision to do without an item due to your limited or scarce resources, then the item not selected is called the **opportunity cost**. It is the opportunity you have forgone.

Let's say you are planning a night out and have €10 to spend. You can either buy a ticket to see the latest movie at the cinema **or** you can go out for a pizza and a soft drink. If you choose the cinema ticket, then:

Opportunity cost = pizza and a soft drink

Financial cost = €10

Have you ever had to make a similar choice between two items? The choice you sacrificed was an opportunity cost.

> Later in the strand you will learn how to create a budget to help you to plan and understand your finances.

IMPULSE BUYING

Impulse buying is unplanned buying. It is buying on the spur of the moment, without thinking or planning.

Have you ever bought something in a rush and regretted it later? If so, you are guilty of impulse buying and should consider how to avoid making the same mistake again.

A good idea is to have a shopping list and to stick to it. Another suggestion if you ever find yourself under pressure to buy from a shop assistant is to just say 'I will have to think about this.' It's all about managing yourself.

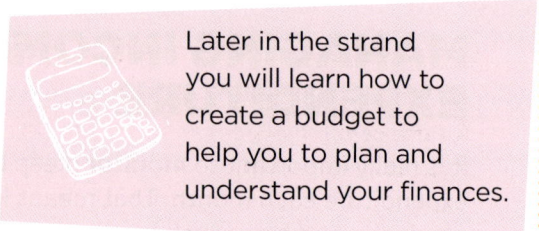

Time to think

Faced with the following choices, which would you decide to buy? What would be the opportunity cost and the financial cost of each decision?

(a) Spend €349.99 on an Xbox or save the €349.99 in a Post Office account.
   Choice: _____
   Opportunity cost: _____
   Financial cost: _____

(b) Spend €20 on phone credit or buy a new personalised phone cover.
   Choice: _____
   Opportunity cost: _____
   Financial cost: _____

(c) Buy a €75 ticket to watch Real Madrid play or purchase new clothes.
   Choice: _____
   Opportunity cost: _____
   Financial cost: _____

PERSONAL INCOME AND EXPENDITURE 1.2

FALSE ECONOMY

A **false economy** is an action that seemed as though it would save money, but in the long term it resulted in money being wasted rather than saved.

If you are at the supermarket and see an offer of '2 bags of carrots for the price of 1', you may be tempted to buy the carrots because they are cheap. You buy them even though you do not need carrots and you did not go to the shop to buy carrots. Then a week later you find yourself throwing out the carrots because they have started to go off. That was a false economy.

Say the offer was for '2 bars of chocolate for the price of 1' and even though you had not intended to buy chocolate, you bought the bars and ate them while watching TV later that night. That was another false economy because you ended up buying something you did not need – an unhealthy food – and then eating too much of it.

Other examples of false economies include cheap household appliances that do not last and have to be replaced sooner than expected – think of the effect on the environment too! Or buying a cheap school bag for €10 that falls apart after three months, whereas a €35 quality school bag would have lasted for five years.

WORKING WITH OTHERS

- Have you ever bought something on impulse and regretted it? How might you avoid making that mistake again?
- Have you ever bought cheap products? What happened? Would you buy them again?

BUYING BATTERIES

Most batteries contain cadmium, lead, mercury, copper, zinc, manganese, lithium and/or potassium. These substances are **hazardous** to our environment and also to our health. When batteries are disposed of in landfills, these harmful materials soak into the soil and water, and can release toxins into the air.

WHAT CAN YOU DO?

- You should always **recycle** batteries.
- You should consider using **rechargeable** batteries.
- We should want to ensure that our planet is clean, green and healthy.

YOU NEED TO MAKE INFORMED DECISIONS

This will happen when you:

- Are aware of your income and your spending habits
- Plan for your income and spending appropriately
- Become aware of wealth and debt
- Understand financial costs as well as opportunities forgone.

33

1.2 BE BUSINESS: PERSONAL FINANCE

CAPITAL AND CURRENT EXPENDITURE

Capital expenditure is money spent on durable items that will last a long time (e.g. a car, a house, a hospital).

Most types of buyer purchase items that are expected to last for years (long term). For example:

- As an **individual/student**, you will have capital expenditure, e.g. a laptop.
- **Households** have capital expenditure, e.g. a bed.
- **Businesses** have capital expenditure, e.g. machinery.
- **Governments** have capital expenditure, e.g. roads.

Current expenditure is spending on day-to-day items that will last for a limited period only (e.g. food, phone charges, medicines).

Again, most types of buyer purchase items for immediate use (short term). For example:

- As an **individual/student**, you will have current expenditure, e.g. mobile phone credit.
- **Households** have current expenditure, e.g. electricity.
- **Businesses** have current expenditure, e.g. rent.
- **Governments** have current expenditure, e.g. wages.

Preparing a **budget** is a good way to decide your planned income and expenditure. Later in this strand you will learn how to create a budget and how to keep a cash book. (In the meantime you might like to take a quick look at a budget, see Unit 1.12, now that you have studied the important terms.)

CHECKING IN...

1. Explain each of the following important terms. Give one example of each.
   - Capital expenditure
   - Fixed expenditure
   - Impulse buying
   - Current expenditure
   - Discretionary expenditure
   - False economy
   - Opportunity cost
   - Regular income
   - Irregular expenditure
   - Irregular income

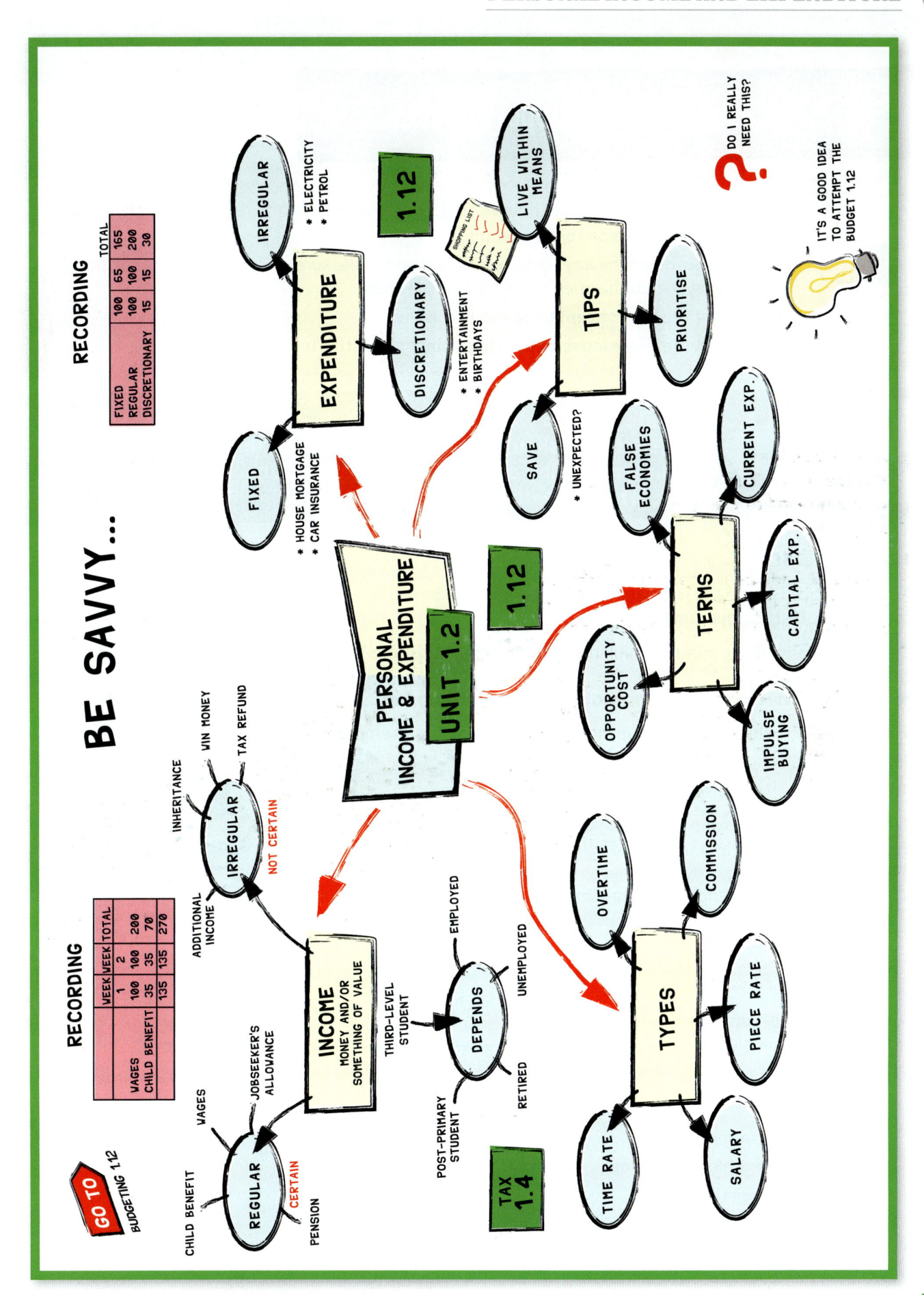

PERSONAL INCOME AND EXPENDITURE 1.2

BE SAVVY...

RECORDING

	WEEK 1	WEEK 2	TOTAL
WAGES	100	100	200
CHILD BENEFIT	35	35	70
	135	135	270

GO TO BUDGETING 1.12

INCOME — MONEY AND/OR SOMETHING OF VALUE

- REGULAR (CERTAIN)
  - CHILD BENEFIT
  - WAGES
  - JOBSEEKER'S ALLOWANCE
  - PENSION
- IRREGULAR (NOT CERTAIN)
  - ADDITIONAL INCOME
  - INHERITANCE
  - WIN MONEY
  - TAX REFUND
- DEPENDS
  - THIRD-LEVEL STUDENT
  - EMPLOYED
  - UNEMPLOYED
  - RETIRED
  - POST-PRIMARY STUDENT

TAX 1.4

TYPES
- OVERTIME
- COMMISSION
- PIECE RATE
- SALARY
- TIME RATE

PERSONAL INCOME & EXPENDITURE — UNIT 1.2

1.12

EXPENDITURE
- IRREGULAR
  - ELECTRICITY
  - PETROL
- DISCRETIONARY
  - ENTERTAINMENT
  - BIRTHDAYS
- FIXED
  - HOUSE MORTGAGE
  - CAR INSURANCE

RECORDING

			TOTAL
FIXED	100	65	165
REGULAR	100	100	200
DISCRETIONARY	15	15	30

TIPS
- LIVE WITHIN MEANS
- PRIORITISE
- SAVE (UNEXPECTED?)
- FALSE ECONOMIES

TERMS
- CURRENT EXP.
- CAPITAL EXP.
- IMPULSE BUYING
- OPPORTUNITY COST

DO I REALLY NEED THIS?

IT'S A GOOD IDEA TO ATTEMPT THE BUDGET 1.12

35

1.2 BE BUSINESS: PERSONAL FINANCE

Be Prepared: My Support Sheets

Completing the activities here will help you to reflect on and reinforce your learning before you move on to the next unit.

- Write down the **key terms** in this unit and make sure you understand them. See if they match the ones at the back of the book.
- List the key **concepts/themes** in this unit.
- List the **three most interesting points** about this unit.

Create a video

Create a group video presentation on opportunity cost. The presentation should last between one and three minutes. Plan your video using a storyboard template. Check out animoto.com. Ask for peer feedback at the end.

THE SIZZLING SEAT

A chair is placed facing the class and a student is given a character.
For example: **Be the government**.

Class groups spend five minutes thinking up challenging questions to ask the character.
For example: **Why does the government not build more houses?**

Students ask the character their questions and the character attempts to answer them.

Afterwards the class consider the following questions:

1. What did you learn from this exercise?
2. What did you find fascinating and helpful?
3. Would you challenge anything that the character said? Give reasons.
4. Has this exercise changed your opinion? Give reasons.

Finance in Action Idea!

Create a blog post on income and expenditure in your life.

Success criteria:
- Know your target readers
- Be yourself; a blog is personal
- Include images
- Include three different points of information

Top Tip!

These skills are really important for your Finance in Action and your individual presentation.

PERSONAL INCOME AND EXPENDITURE 1.2

QUESTION TIME

1. Explain the terms 'income' and 'expenditure'.
2. Why should you plan your expenditure?
3. Compare and contrast regular and discretionary expenditure.
4. Explain what a false economy is and give an example.
5. Create a summary of this unit using the fishbone template on p. 546.

Stop and think

Do I have any questions or concerns? What are the mistakes or errors I made in this unit?

EVALUATE MY LEARNING: DAR

Describe
- Did I/we meet my/our learning intentions?
- What went well? What are my/our strengths?

Assess
- How did I/we work with others?
- Were there challenges?

Recommend
- How might I improve?
- What skills and learning might I apply to new situations?

Do your **Key Check** in the workbook for this unit and then mark your learning position on the following rating scale:

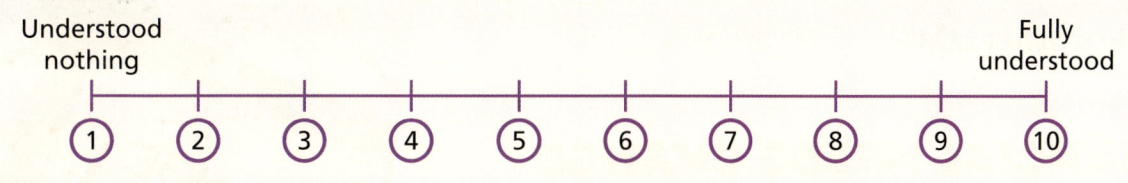

Understood nothing — 1 2 3 4 5 6 7 8 9 10 — Fully understood

How can you move up the rating scale? What can you **say, make, write** and **do** to illustrate your learning?

CBA 1 Business in Action:
Will I use this unit for my topic for **Enterprise in Action /Finance in Action**? ☐

You need to be preparing for your CBAs

- Exceptional
- Above expectations
- In line with expectations
- Yet to meet expectations

37

1.3 PERSONAL FINANCIAL LIFE CYCLE

Construct a personal financial life cycle to identify financial needs at different life stages.

Learning Intentions

At the end of this unit I will:

- Know the different financial needs at different life stages
- Understand where the finance will come from at different life stages
- Be able to create a personal financial life cycle plan
- Know the value of a personal financial life cycle plan

Key Concepts

- ✓ Financial needs
- ✓ Savings and pensions
- ✓ Income, expenditure, choices and goals
- ✓ Personal financial life cycle

Making the links with other LOs:

- 1.1 Personal resources
- 1.2 Personal income and expenditure
- 1.5 Personal saving and borrowing
- 1.6 Personal insurance
- 3.1 Scarcity and choice
- 3.2 Circular flow of income

Wonderful Worthwhile Websites

www.mymoneysense.com
www.careersportal.ie

Are there other LOs?

FINANCIAL NEEDS CHANGE

'3Ts' = Think, Turn, Talk

- What are your goals?
- Might your goals change during your lifetime? Why?
- What impact might these changes have on your finances?

SETTING GOALS

It is important that you **write** your goals down. Research shows that people who write down their goals are more successful and more likely to achieve them.

You need to be able to achieve your goals, and that will be easier if your goals are SMART.

Be SMART with goals:

Specific – What? Why? Where? How? Who? Use precise language to describe the goal.

Measurable – You must be able to confirm that the goal has been achieved.

Attainable – It must be possible to achieve the goal with the resources available to you.

Relevant – You should aim for something that is worth achieving.

Time-bound – Set a specific time frame for achieving the goal. This may be short (1 year), medium (1–5 years) or long term (5 or more years) as appropriate.

Businesses and governments need to apply SMART goals too. Many goals require cash in order to be achieved, which means they require sound financial planning.

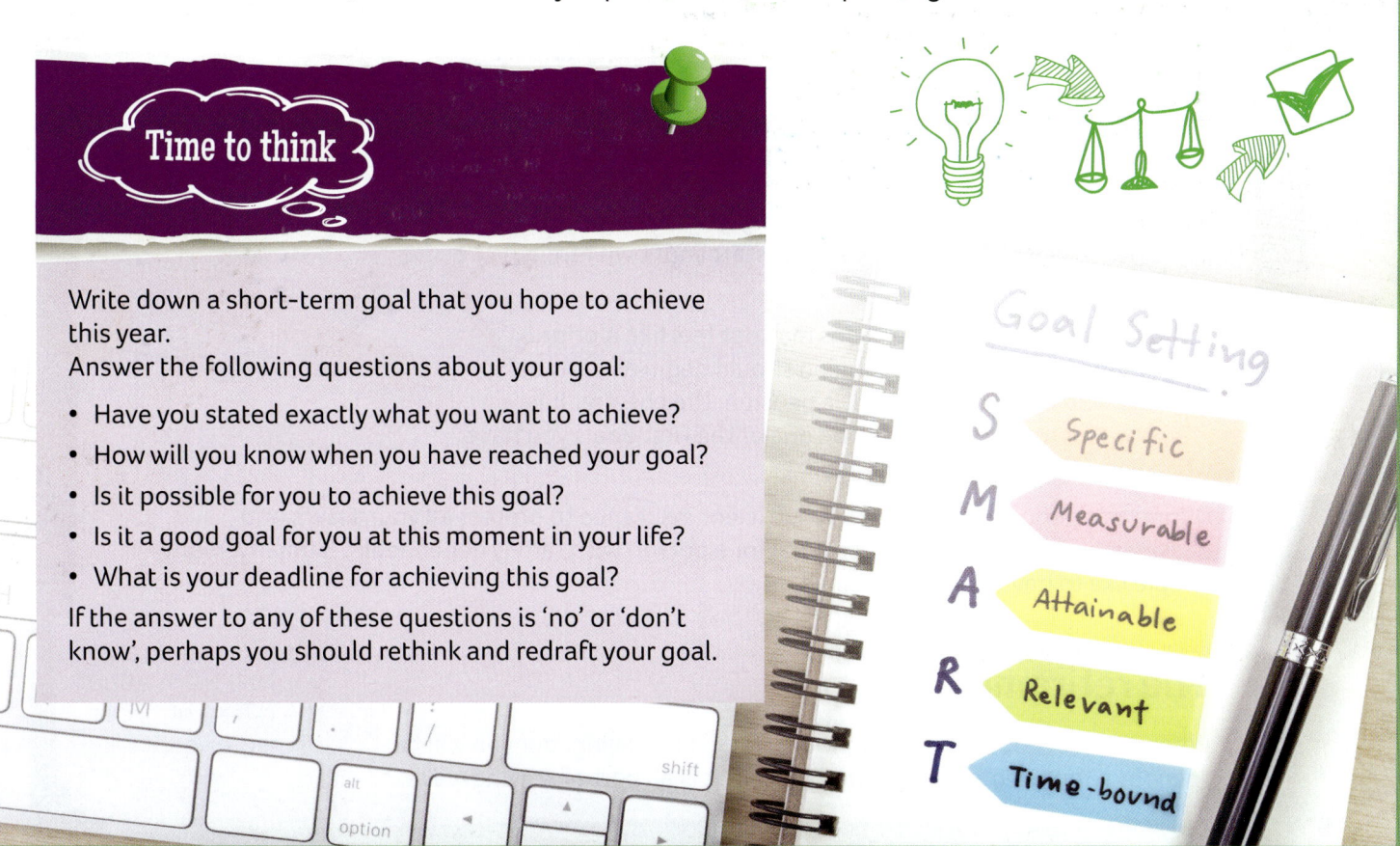

Time to think

Write down a short-term goal that you hope to achieve this year.
Answer the following questions about your goal:

- Have you stated exactly what you want to achieve?
- How will you know when you have reached your goal?
- Is it possible for you to achieve this goal?
- Is it a good goal for you at this moment in your life?
- What is your deadline for achieving this goal?

If the answer to any of these questions is 'no' or 'don't know', perhaps you should rethink and redraft your goal.

CASE STUDY: YOUR FINANCIAL LIFE CYCLE

The majority of financial changes in your life will occur as a result of you moving through the various **life stages**: birth, infancy, starting school, being a student, your first job, building your life, acquiring your possessions, paying into a pension, retirement. It is all about **managing yourself**.

The first 18 years…

Your early and teenage years will generally be non-income making: you are in school and financially dependent on your parents/guardians for support. It is only after your education is complete that your financial life cycle will fully commence. Nevertheless, even in your school years you may have to plan how to finance a holiday or your debs.

Building up your wealth

After you complete third-level education or an apprenticeship, you will start to build up wealth. During your working life you will earn an income and you will have a number of major expenditures (e.g. your first car, an apartment/house). Eventually you may start your own family, which will take priority.

Although retirement and pensions may not feel like a priority, they should be. Retirement planning should begin as early as possible. The earlier you pay into a pension, the cheaper it is. Preparing for retirement should be one of the first goals you have when you commence your first job.

During this period you will also buy sufficient insurance to protect all your assets and possessions. Life insurance is essential for a person with family dependents. Similarly, many people like to have health insurance.

The retirement years…

When you reach retirement, you will no longer be saving, but you will be spending. You need to be prepared for this. It is all part of staying well.

> Later in the strand you will learn about the different types of insurance.

PERSONAL FINANCIAL LIFE CYCLE 1.3

WHAT IS A PERSONAL FINANCIAL LIFE CYCLE PLAN?

A **personal financial life cycle plan** presents your needs and wants at each stage of your life and matches them with sources of finance. The plan can be a chart, a table, a mind map or any other form that works for you. It may be handwritten on paper or prepared electronically.

It is a good idea to **draw up your life plan** … and then to revisit, edit and even delete and rewrite it at regular intervals. You can also create a soft copy (see www.padlet.com). It is good to be creative when managing information and yourself! Your plan needs to be flexible. Unplanned events such as a job loss or the death of a spouse may dramatically affect your goals. Personal financial planning is always an ongoing process.

MY PERSONAL FINANCIAL LIFE CYCLE
MY LIFE CYCLE PATH
DATE:

- Further Training/Studies
- College
- Careers in
- DETOUR
- Post Primary in
- Primary School in
- Born

SIGNED:

PERSONAL FINANCIAL LIFE CYCLE

START

- BORN:
- PRIMARY SCHOOL:

POST-PRIMARY
* SCHOOL
* LIKES / INTERESTS
* EXTRA ACTIVITIES

WILL YOU VOLUNTEER?
SET UP A MINI-COMPANY?
INVOLVED IN SPORTS?

FURTHER EDUCATION
THIRD LEVEL
* WHERE?
* COURSES?

APPRENTICESHIP
* OTHER?

€ ?
FINANCE

WORK PART-TIME?
GAP YEAR
FINANCE?
WHERE?

PERSONAL FINANCIAL LIFE CYCLE PLAN

PERHAPS ESTABLISH A…

FOR-PROFIT ORGANISATION OR NOT-FOR-PROFIT ORGANISATION

EMPLOYMENT
* IDEAL JOB
* WAGES
* INTERESTS
* TRAVEL
* POSSESSIONS

- LOANS
- MORTGAGES
- SAVINGS

CHANGE CAREERS?

VOLUNTEER?
- CONSUMER
- EMPLOYER / EMPLOYEE

RETIREMENT
* AGE?
* WHERE?
* INTERESTS/HOBBIES?
* FINANCES?

WWW.CAREERSPORTAL.IE

BE SUSTAINABLE?

BE ETHICAL…

41

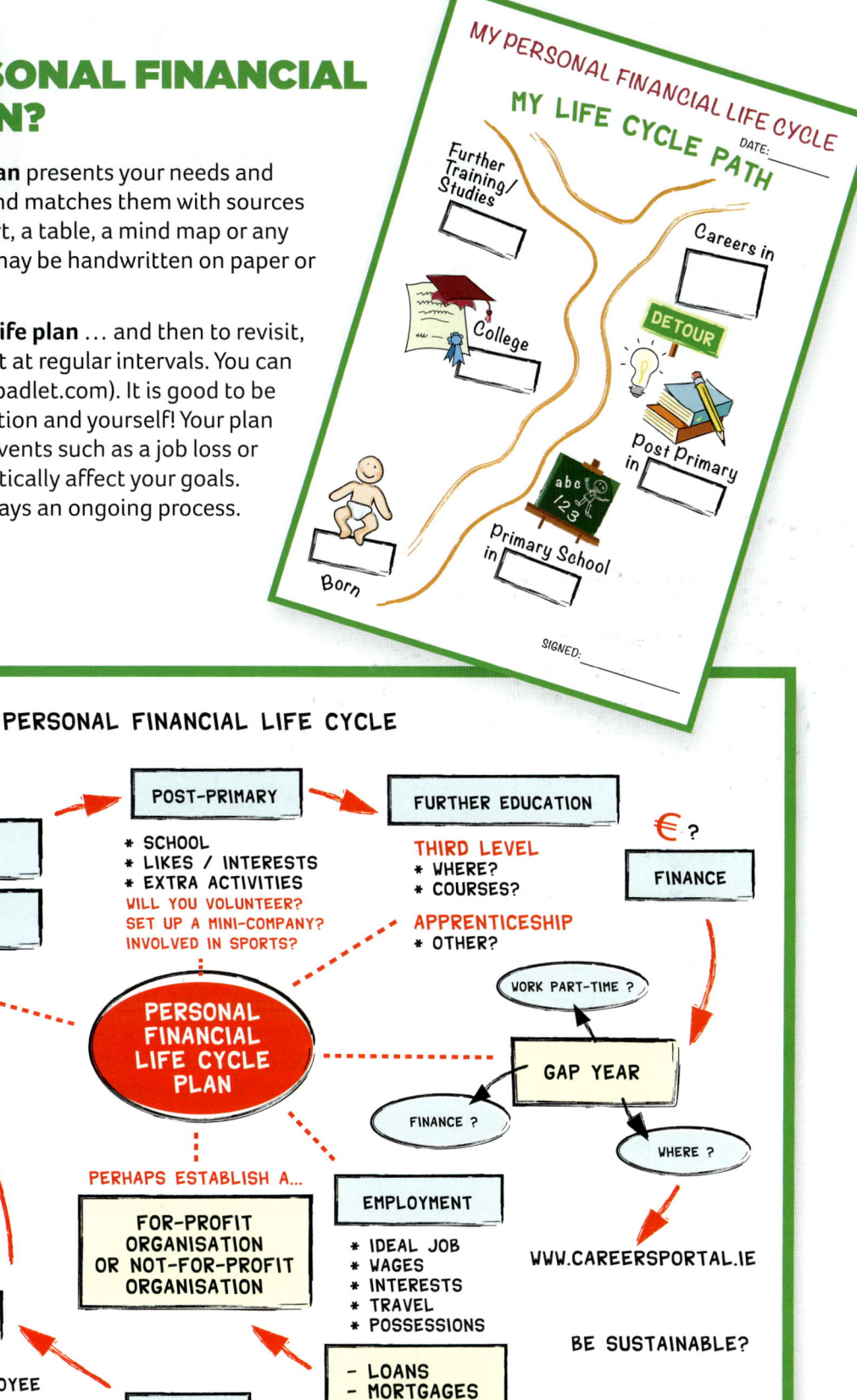

1.3 BE BUSINESS: PERSONAL FINANCE

CREATE A PERSONAL FINANCIAL LIFE CYCLE PLAN

Divide your personal financial life cycle plan into **five broad, but important, stages**:

1. **Dependence stage** – you are dependent on parents or guardians.
2. **Independence stage** – you can finance yourself.
3. **Emerging stage** – you can also finance others, e.g. your family.
4. **Pre-retirement stage** – you are building up your finances again.
5. **Retirement stage** – you are spending your finances.

1. Dependence Stage

Summary: Age 0 to 18 years: baby, toddler, child, primary school, teenager, post-primary school, maybe third-level student. You live at home, events/expenses are paid for by your parents/guardians, you may work part time.

Needs and wants: Food, clothes, transport, mobile phone, books, entertainment, holidays, fees.

Sources of finance: Parents/guardian, child benefit. You may earn income through part-time work. Your debs/school trip are two events that you might need to plan for.

2. Independence Stage

Summary: You may go to college and start work (part time or full time). You may do an apprenticeship or another form of training. You will probably leave home.

Needs and wants: Rent, electricity, oil, gas, bin charges, water charges, TV licence, broadband, phone, cable/satellite TV, transport and, of course, food, clothes and entertainment. You may learn to drive (theory test, lessons, driving test) and buy, run and maintain a car. You may take out insurance (property, disability, health, liability, travel, etc.). You may be paying off debt (perhaps a college or family loan). You may wish to explore the world on holidays or extended periods of travel, or even to live and work overseas.

Sources of finance: Wage/salary, scholarships, jobseeker's allowance, borrowings.

Loans

There may be times when you need a loan, i.e. borrowing money from the bank or another financial institution. It is important to ensure that you receive the best deal by comparing the Annual Percentage Rates (APRs) on offer. The APR is the true rate of interest.

Time to think

Elaborate on what happens at each stage:

List your **needs** (what you need to survive) and your **wants** (things that you would like to have) for each of the stages.

Note where you might receive the income or finance to pay for what you need and want at the various stages.

Be decisive! You will find ideas and suggestions for each stage in the text.

3. Emerging Stage

Summary: Working and encountering life experiences such as love, marriage, children, community work.

Needs and wants: As above. You may also change from renting to buying a home – a deposit of 10% of the cost of the property is required to get a first mortgage (a long-term loan borrowed to buy a house), and then you must cover all the extra costs: legal fees, surveys, stamp duty, insurance, furniture, etc. You may get married, which can be expensive. You may become a parent and the cost of a child is approximately €10,000 a year.

Sources of finance: Wage/salary, jobseeker's allowance, borrowings. You might also be enterprising to raise money: rent out a room or another property, perhaps start your own business.

Enterprise

If you decide to become an entrepreneur (a person who starts their own business) be sure to get all the advice you can. Good planning is the key to a successful new business. Contact your Local Enterprise Office (LEO) for advice on setting up a business, and your local bank about your business plan. Find out if your business is eligible for finance and any start-up grants.

4. Pre-retirement Stage

Summary: Your children have grown up and moved on, giving you greater freedom. You continue to source income and save, travel, spend time with family and build wealth.

Needs and wants: These will depend on your circumstances, e.g. health, family commitments. For example, you might want to give financial help to members of your family.

Sources of finance: Wage/salary, jobseeker's allowance, income from savings and investments.

Changing Job/Career

As your goals change, you may decide you want to change your job/career and do something completely different at work. This may mean going for a promotion, returning to college, upgrading your skills, learning something new and/or moving to a different part of the country/world.

You need to plan for such changes and decide how you can best achieve your new goal. It is worth taking time to work out what it is that you can offer (experience, attributes and skills) before applying for a new job. You also need to be clear about how much you need/want to earn. If returning to college, work out how you will survive financially.

1.3 BE BUSINESS: PERSONAL FINANCE

5. Retirement Stage

Summary: You have retired from work and are enjoying doing what you like to do.

Needs and wants: As above – these will depend on your circumstances, e.g. health, family commitments. You may want to travel a lot or to help out your family financially.

Sources of finance: Involves the transition from earning to spending. Private pension, state pension, savings and investments.

WORKING WITH OTHERS

Working in groups, complete a Personal Financial Plan for a fictitious student. Each group should take a stage and fill in their part of the table.

Stage	Define stage	What are your needs and wants?	How will you finance this stage?
1			
2			
3			
4			
5			

CHECKING IN...

1. What is a personal financial life cycle plan?
2. What are the five main stages in a personal financial life cycle plan?
3. Why might you revisit your personal financial life cycle plan at regular intervals?

Time to think

Are you ready to create your own plan? Prepare a visual for how it might look and then start writing. You will then develop your plan as you study different concepts in this book.

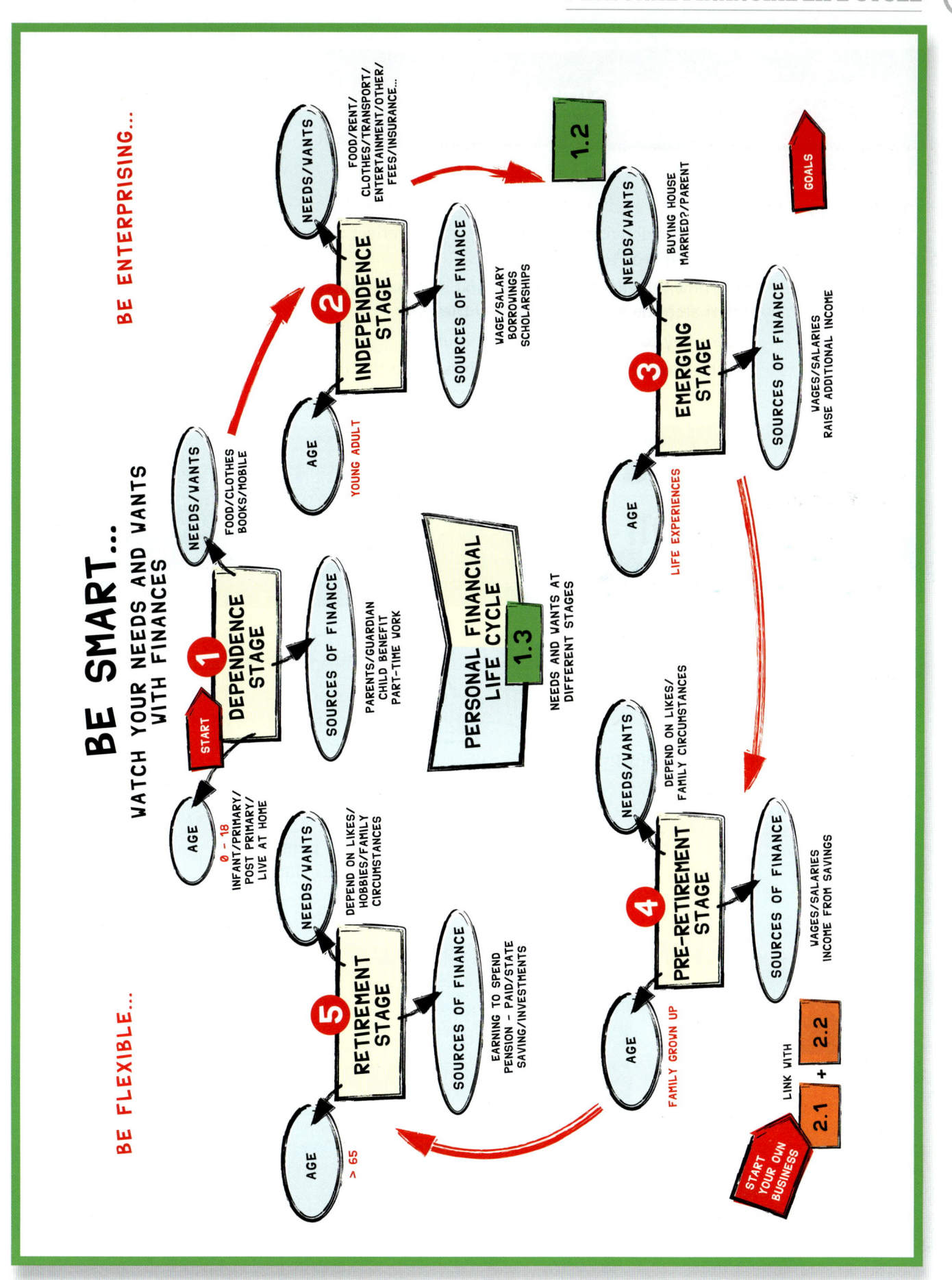

PERSONAL FINANCIAL LIFE CYCLE 1.3

BE SMART...
WATCH YOUR NEEDS AND WANTS WITH FINANCES

BE ENTERPRISING...

BE FLEXIBLE...

PERSONAL FINANCIAL LIFE CYCLE 1.3 — NEEDS AND WANTS AT DIFFERENT STAGES

1. DEPENDENCE STAGE (START)
- AGE: 0 – 18, INFANT/PRIMARY/POST PRIMARY/LIVE AT HOME
- NEEDS/WANTS: FOOD/CLOTHES/BOOKS/MOBILE
- SOURCES OF FINANCE: PARENTS/GUARDIAN, CHILD BENEFIT, PART-TIME WORK

2. INDEPENDENCE STAGE
- AGE: YOUNG ADULT
- NEEDS/WANTS: FOOD/RENT/CLOTHES/TRANSPORT/ENTERTAINMENT/OTHER/FEES/INSURANCE
- SOURCES OF FINANCE: WAGE/SALARY, BORROWINGS, SCHOLARSHIPS
- (link to 1.2)

3. EMERGING STAGE
- AGE: LIFE EXPERIENCES
- NEEDS/WANTS: BUYING HOUSE, MARRIED?/PARENT
- SOURCES OF FINANCE: WAGES/SALARIES, RAISE ADDITIONAL INCOME
- GOALS

4. PRE-RETIREMENT STAGE
- AGE: FAMILY GROWN UP
- NEEDS/WANTS: DEPEND ON LIKES/FAMILY CIRCUMSTANCES
- SOURCES OF FINANCE: WAGES/SALARIES, INCOME FROM SAVINGS

5. RETIREMENT STAGE
- AGE: > 65
- NEEDS/WANTS: DEPEND ON LIKES/HOBBIES/FAMILY CIRCUMSTANCES
- SOURCES OF FINANCE: EARNING TO SPEND, PENSION – PAID/STATE, SAVING/INVESTMENTS

LINK WITH 2.1 + 2.2 — START YOUR OWN BUSINESS

45

1.3 BE BUSINESS: PERSONAL FINANCE

Be Prepared: My Support Sheets

Completing the activities here will help you to reflect on and reinforce your learning before you move on to the next unit.

- Write down the **key terms** in this unit and make sure you understand them. See if they match the ones at the back of the book.
- List the key **concepts/themes** in this unit.
- List the **three most interesting points** about this unit.

Make a presentation

Make an individual presentation on the personal financial life cycle. The presentation should last between one and three minutes. The best presentations are well researched, provide evidence to support claims, display an interest in the topic and use variety, creativity and superb communication skills to hold the audience's attention.

Finance in Action Idea!

In pairs, create a poster explaining personal financial life cycle plans.

Success criteria:

- Clear and informative title
- Five different points of information
- Use of visual material; accurate graphs
- Accurate spelling, clear and consistent text

Conduct a class vote to select the **best personal life cycle**. Why was it the best? The visuals? The use of IT? The content? Or something else?

Do a role play

In groups of four, prepare a personal financial life cycle plan. Each member of the group plays one of four roles:

- Post-primary student
- Third-level student
- Full-time employee
- Pensioner

State your needs and wants and explain how you will finance them.

PERSONAL FINANCIAL LIFE CYCLE **1.3**

QUESTION TIME

1. Imagine you are a third-level student. Describe your income and expenditure.
2. Research some careers in business. Which business roles appeal most to you?
3. Document what might be the costs of a school trip and/or your school debs.
4. Create a summary of this unit using the fishbone template on p. 546.

EVALUATE MY LEARNING: DAR

Describe
- Did I/we meet my/our learning intentions?
- What went well? What are my/our strengths?

Assess
- How did I/we work with others?
- Were there challenges?

Recommend
- How might I improve?
- What skills and learning might I apply to new situations?

Do your **Key Check** in the workbook for this unit and then mark your learning position on the following rating scale:

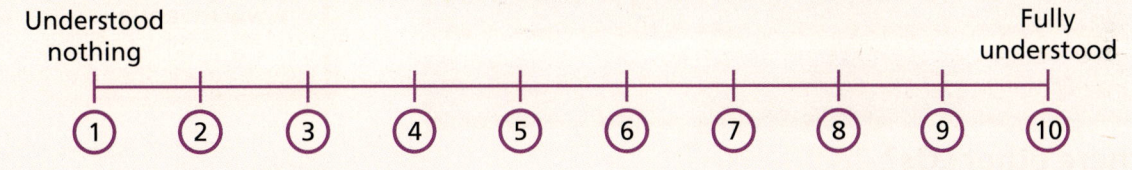

Understood nothing — 1 2 3 4 5 6 7 8 9 10 — Fully understood

How can you move up the rating scale? What can you **say, make, write** and **do** to illustrate your learning?

CBA 1 Business in Action:
Will I use this unit for my topic for **Finance in Action**? ☐

CBA 2 Presentation:
Will I use this unit for my topic for my **Presentation**? ☐

You need to be preparing for your CBAs
- ○ Exceptional
- ○ Above expectations
- ○ In line with expectations
- ○ Yet to meet expectations

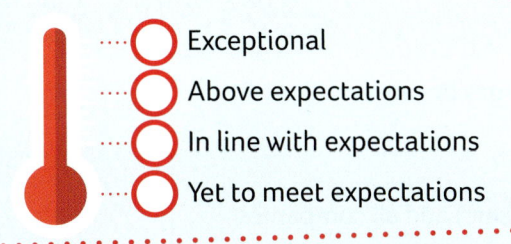

Stop and think

Do I have any questions or concerns?

What are the mistakes or errors I made in this unit?

1.4 KEY PERSONAL TAXES

Explain key personal taxes and charges and suggest the occasions when and why they might arise.

Learning Intentions

At the end of this unit I will:
- Be able to explain what taxation is
- Be able to explain gross pay, deductions and net pay
- Understand taxation terms
- Understand why taxes are imposed
- Value the importance of taxation

Making the links with other LOs:

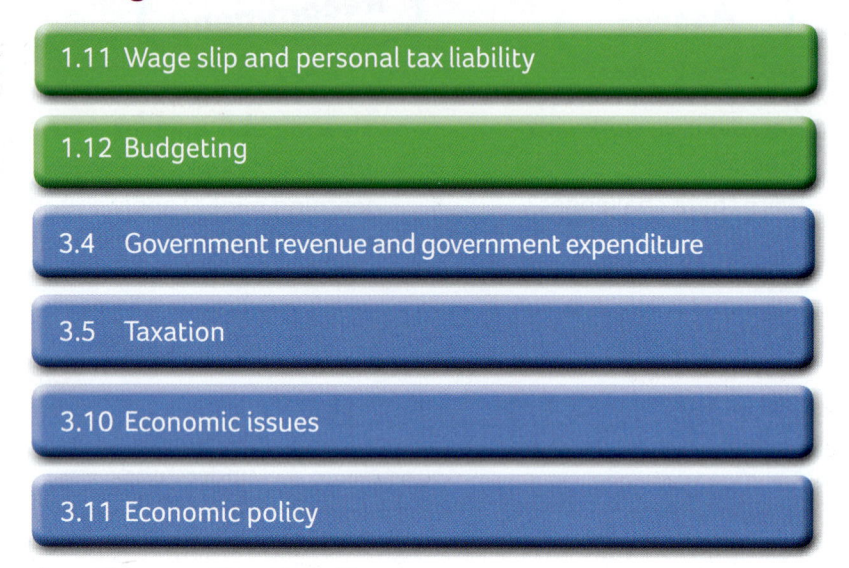

- 1.11 Wage slip and personal tax liability
- 1.12 Budgeting
- 3.4 Government revenue and government expenditure
- 3.5 Taxation
- 3.10 Economic issues
- 3.11 Economic policy

Key Concepts
- ✓ Taxation
- ✓ Income tax
- ✓ Pay As You Earn (PAYE)
- ✓ Pay Related Social Insurance (PRSI)
- ✓ Universal Social Charge (USC)
- ✓ Tax rates

Wonderful Worthwhile Websites
www.revenue.ie

Are there other LOs?

> **'3Ts' = Think, Turn, Talk**
> - Write down the first thing that comes into your head when you think of tax.
> - Discuss what you have written with your partner.
> - Together, try to come up with the reasons for tax.

WHY HAVE PERSONAL TAXES AND CHARGES?

Taxation is the taxes and charges collected by the state to pay for things that we all share and need as a country.

You need to know about personal taxes and charges because:
- They affect everyone's quality of life.
- The law states that we have to pay them.
- They are paid by individuals, employees (workers) and all companies.
- They provide income for the state, and we all need the resources that our government spends its income on.

KEY PERSONAL TAXES 1.4

RESOURCES FUNDED BY THE GOVERNMENT

These resources include:

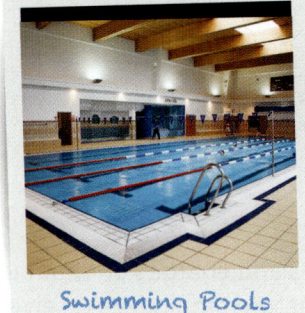

- Infrastructure
- Roads
- Parks
- Schools
- Hospitals
- Reservoirs
- Sewage Systems
- Playgrounds
- Libraries
- Swimming Pools

Did you know?
The government is the largest employer in Ireland.

The government must also finance the **cost of running these resources**. For example, heating and lighting them and the wages paid to doctors, nurses, soldiers, gardaí, teachers, etc.

The government makes and enforces laws and regulations to protect children, consumers (buyers of products/services), employees (workers), employers (those who employ workers), entrepreneurs (people who start a business), etc.

Time to think

What might Ireland be like if the government could no longer provide these services?

Who would deal with emergencies and keep your community safe?

How would you get an education?

Where would you go if you were sick or injured?

Who would ensure that your food and your water are safe?

1.4 BE BUSINESS: PERSONAL FINANCE

The government has a really important job in running our country and providing the services we need. The taxes/charges that we pay provide us with many benefits every hour of every day, seven days a week, 365 days a year.

You'll see more on how the government spends money in Unit 3.4 and on the reasons for taxation in Unit 3.5.

If the government increases taxes or introduces new taxes and charges, it will receive more money and be able to improve services.

If the government decreases taxes or gets rid of a tax or charge, it will have less money to spend and will have to reduce services (cutbacks).

You should always pay your taxes and understand their importance from **ethical**, **values** and **moral** perspectives.

Top Tip!

The government may decide to make tax changes when it prepares its **National Budget**. For all up-to-date tax rates check out www.revenue.ie.

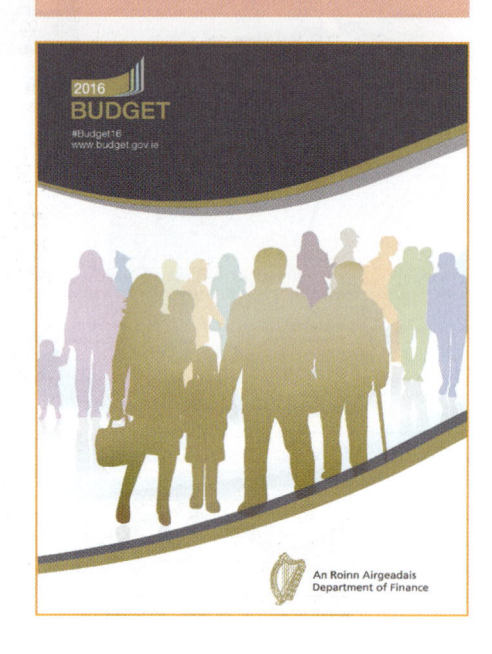

REVENUE COMMISSIONERS

The state body responsible for collecting taxes in Ireland is known as the Office of the Revenue Commissioners (often called Revenue for short). Revenue collects tax on behalf of the government.

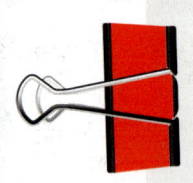

CHECKING IN...

1. What is taxation?
2. Who pays taxes and charges?
3. Name three services provided by tax income.

TAXES ON INCOME

Most people who are earning an income will pay taxes and charges on that income. In the majority of cases, these taxes and charges are deducted (taken away) before employees receive their wage/salary. The employer collects the tax on behalf of the government.

Note the difference between work and employment: **work** is anything you do that requires effort; **employment** is work for which you are paid.

WORKING WITH OTHERS

Take part in a class discussion or debate on the following questions: Should you pay tax on your pocket money? Should any money you receive from babysitting be taxed? If you start up a mini-company in school, should any profits you make be taxed? What might be the advantages of working and paying taxes?

Taxes on income are calculated on **gross pay**, which is the total money you earned before any deductions have been made.

Gross pay = Basic pay + overtime + commission + bonus

Net pay is your take-home pay after any deductions have been made.

Net pay = Gross pay − deductions

KEY PERSONAL TAXES 1.4

Be Numerate

Calculate gross pay for each of the following:

1. 35 hours @ €15.50 per hour
2. 37 hours @ €10.25 per hour
3. 35 hours @ €17 per hour
4. 35 hours @ €10.50 per hour and a bonus of €100
5. 39 hours @ €15 per hour and 6 hours overtime at double time
6. 37 hours @ €18 per hour and 5 hours at time and a half
7. 39 hours @ €15 per hour but worked 42 hours and overtime is paid at double time
8. 38 hours @ €12.50 per hour and received a commission of 10% on sales of €5,000
9. 36 hours @ €15.50 per hour and received a commission of 2% on sales of €12,000
10. 37 hours @ €13.50 per hour and profit sharing of 1% of profits of €39,590

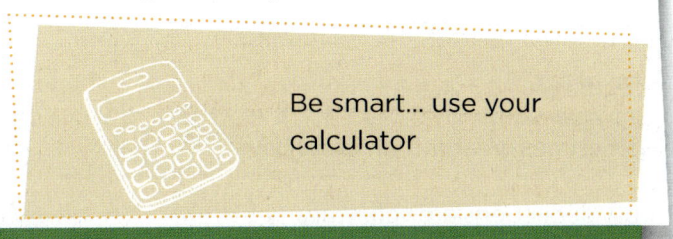

Be smart... use your calculator

DEDUCTIONS

The system for taxing the income of employees is known as PAYE or Pay As You Earn. It means that any taxes and charges you must pay to the state are deducted from your wage/salary (gross pay) before you are paid (net pay).

Statutory deductions are items that are **compulsory** (you must pay them) and that are taken away from your gross pay and given to the government.

There are three main types of statutory deduction:

- **Income tax (PAYE)** is paid on the amount a person earns; it is a percentage of gross income
- **PRSI (Pay Related Social Insurance)** is given to the Department of Social Protection and used to pay social welfare benefits such as Jobseeker's Benefit and state pensions
- **USC (Universal Social Charge)** is another tax on income.

See pp. 53–6 for more on these deductions.

Non-statutory deductions are items that are **voluntary** (you choose to pay them) and that you agree can be deducted from your gross pay.

Examples include payments to:

- **Pension scheme** – you may choose to pay into a private scheme to provide you with a pension income when you retire from employment.
- **Trade union subscriptions** – this is a voluntary fee you pay to a union. A union is an organisation that aims to help, support and protect workers.
- **Health insurance** – you may choose to pay into a private scheme such as VHI (Voluntary Health Insurance) or Aviva, to cover you for healthcare.

1.4 BE BUSINESS: PERSONAL FINANCE

WORKING WITH OTHERS

Place a tick ✓ to indicate if the following statements are True or False:

	True	False
Lotto winnings are regular income	☐	☐
Net pay is take-home pay	☐	☐
PAYE = Pay As You Earn	☐	☐
Voluntary deductions are payable by law	☐	☐
Overtime is additional hours worked over the agreed working week	☐	☐
UCH is a non-statutory deduction	☐	☐
PAYE is a form of tax	☐	☐
Net pay is sometimes greater than gross pay	☐	☐
Non-statutory deductions are voluntary	☐	☐
USC = Universal Social Charge	☐	☐
Statutory deductions are payable by law	☐	☐
Health insurance is a statutory deduction	☐	☐
Union fees are non-statutory deductions	☐	☐
Gross pay is greater than net pay	☐	☐
A bonus can be added to basic pay	☐	☐
Tax is normally expressed as a percentage	☐	☐
PRSI = Pay Related Social Insurance	☐	☐

CALCULATING TAX

It is essential to understand how tax is calculated so that you can work out how much tax will be deducted from your earnings.

In this section you will carry out some income and tax calculations. Later in the strand you will prepare a wage slip.

KEY PERSONAL TAXES 1.4

TAX RATES

Tax is always charged as a **percentage (%)**. Different rates may apply to different levels or **bands** of income. The percentage rates of tax may change each year. The main rates for a single person in **2016** are set out below.

Income Tax (PAYE)

Income tax is charged at 20% on the first €33,800 earned – this is called the **standard rate** of tax. Anything earned above €33,800 is taxed at 40% – this is called the **higher rate** of tax.

	Standard rate (2016)	Higher rate (2016)	Standard rate (20__)	Higher rate (20__)	Standard rate (20__)	Higher rate (20__)
Single person	20% First €33,800	40% Remainder				

Tax credits decrease the tax you pay. Everyone receives a personal tax credit (€1,650) and an employee tax credit (€1,650) which amounts to €3,300. This means that if you do not earn more than €16,500 you won't pay any tax.

Time to think

When recording tax rates, always date your information. Check the rates after each year's national budget.

EXAMPLE 1: ANNE O'BRIEN'S PAYE

Anne O'Brien has started a new job working for MCB Promotions. She commences with a salary of €16,500. What is the tax rate for Anne and how much income tax is to be paid each year?

Answer: Tax rate = 20%

20% of €16,500 = €3,300

Less Tax Credits €3,300

Tax to pay: NIL

53

1.4 BE BUSINESS: PERSONAL FINANCE

Be Numerate

The following individuals each have a tax credit of €3,300 per year. In each case, what tax rate applies and how much income tax needs to be paid?

1. Anthony earns €18,000
2. Breda earns €20,000
3. Conor earns €33,800

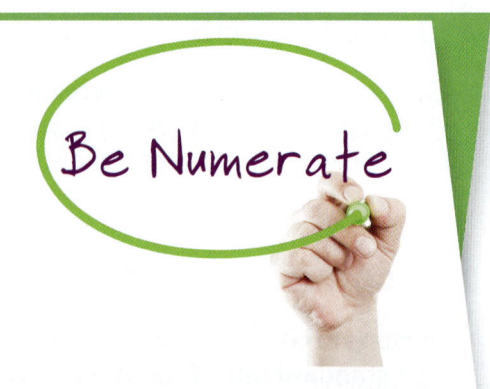

EXAMPLE 2: ANNE O'BRIEN'S PAYE

MCB are delighted with Anne's performance. The HR (Human Resources) manager, who deals with employment and pay, has offered Anne a permanent position with a salary of €40,000. What income tax rate will apply to Anne now and what amount of tax will she have to pay per year (given that she has a tax credit of €3,300 a year)?

Answer:

Income = €40,000	€
First 33,800 @ 20%	6,760
Remainder @ 40% (€40,000 – 33,800) = €6,200 @ 40%	2,480
Total PAYE	9,240
Less Tax Credit	3,300
Income tax	5,940

Be Numerate

The following individuals each have a tax credit of €3,300 per year. In each case, what tax rate applies and how much income tax needs to be paid?

1. Donal earns €38,000
2. Agata earns €50,000
3. Fiachra earns €53,800

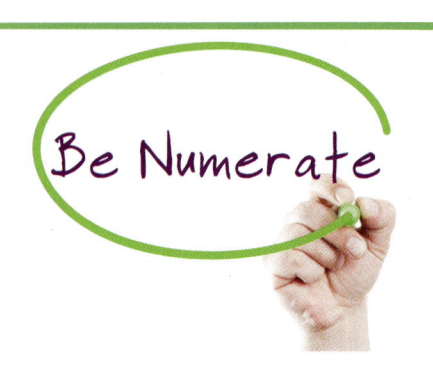

KEY PERSONAL TAXES   1.4

Pay Related Social Insurance (PRSI)

PRSI is charged at a rate of 4% of gross income. People who are between the ages of 16 and 66 have to pay PRSI.

EXAMPLE 3: HANNAH BURNS' PRSI

Hannah Burns has an annual gross income of €20,000. PRSI is 4%. Calculate Hannah's PRSI.

Answer:

PRSI = 4% of €20,000 = €8,000

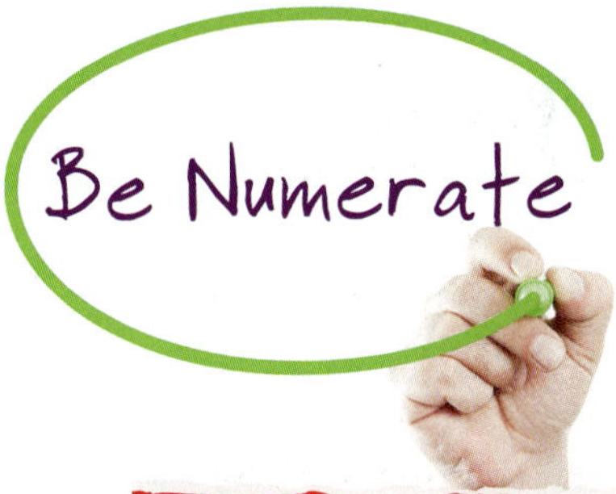

James Leahy has an annual gross salary of €30,000. PRSI is 4%. Calculate James's PRSI:

What is his monthly gross income and monthly PRSI?

What is his weekly gross income and weekly PRSI?

Be Numerate

Top Tip

These calculations may seem challenging, but your calculator will help!

Universal Social Charge (USC)

The percentage of USC you pay increases as your income increases. If you earn less than €13,000 in a year you will not pay USC.

Gross income €	USC rate %	Amount of USC to pay if you earn the full amount	
Up to €12,012	1%	€120.12	i.e. 1% of the first €12,012 earned
€12,012.01 to €18,668	3%	€199.68	i.e. 3% of the next €6,655.99 earned
€18,668.01 to €70,044	5.5%	€2,825.68	i.e. 5.5% of the next €51,375.99 earned
€70,044.01 and above	8%	Depends on how much more you earn	

These rates may change.

1.4 BE BUSINESS: PERSONAL FINANCE

EXAMPLE 4: PAT LYNCH'S USC

Pat Lynch works for Woodcrafts Ltd, a company designing Irish wooden furniture for the corporate market. His annual gross income is €40,000. Calculate the amount of USC that Pat must pay.

Answer:

Gross income €	USC rate %	Amount of USC to pay if you earn the full amount
First €12,012	1%	€120.12
Next €6,655.99	3%	€199.68
Remainder €21,332.01	5.5%	€1,173.26 (i.e. 5.5% €40,000 – €18,667.99)
Total USC		€1,493.06

Calculate the annual and monthly rate of USC for the following:

1. Katie earns a gross income of €13,000
2. Leona earns a gross income of €22,000
3. Martin earns a gross income of €33,000

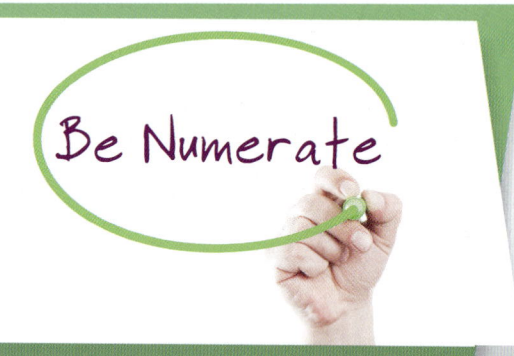

Be Numerate

TAX ON SAVINGS

Another form of income can be the interest earned on savings, which may also be taxed. The tax that applies is called **DIRT** (**D**eposit **I**nterest **R**etention **T**ax). The rate of DIRT in 2016 was 41%.

LEARN MORE ABOUT TAX

TAX CREDITS

As you saw earlier, **tax credits** reduce the amount of tax you have to pay. Every person who works gets a **personal tax credit**. In 2016 this was €1,650 for a single person.

Your personal circumstances will determine whether you are entitled to other tax credits. For example, tax credits are available for home carers and for one-parent families.

After your tax is calculated, the tax credit is deducted and this reduces the amount of tax that you have to pay. So a tax credit of €2,000 will reduce the total amount of tax you pay by €2,000.

Tax Credit Certificate

When you are working, your employer must deduct tax from your pay under the PAYE system. To make sure that your tax is properly dealt with from the start and that your employer deducts the right amount of tax from your pay, you should do two things:

1. Give your employer your **personal public service (PPS)** number. This is a unique reference number that helps you access social welfare benefits, public services and information in Ireland. Your employer will then tell the tax office that you have started work.

2. Apply for a **Tax Credit Certificate**. This shows the rate of tax that applies to your income and the tax credits that reduce the tax you have to pay. The tax office will also send a summary of this certificate to your employer so that they can deduct the correct amount of tax before paying you your net pay.

If your employer has not received this information from Revenue, you will be taxed on a temporary basis with an **emergency tax**. You can avoid emergency tax by registering the details of your new job with Revenue.

TAX ALLOWANCES

Tax allowances can also reduce the amount of tax you have to pay. Unlike tax credits, tax allowances are subtracted from your gross pay **before** it is taxed. This means that if you earn enough to pay the higher rate of income tax, the amount of tax you have to pay will be reduced by a greater amount.

If, for example, you have a tax allowance of €200 and the highest rate of tax you pay is 20%, then your tax will be reduced by €40 (€200 x 20%). However, if the highest rate of tax you pay is 40%, then the amount of your income that is taxed at 40% is reduced by €200 and so your tax reduction is €80 (€200 x 40%). This is known as tax allowance at the **marginal rate**.

Examples of tax allowances are those paid for having a guide dog or making pension contributions.

> **Top Tip**
>
> Tax rates will change depending on government decisions. It is really important in your third year of this course to be aware of different rates, new taxes and even taxes that might be abolished. It is all about managing information and thinking.

1.4 BE BUSINESS: PERSONAL FINANCE

OTHER TAXES

There are many taxes and you will come across some of them in this Business Studies course. Here are a few examples:

- Companies have to pay **corporation tax**, which is a tax on their profits.
- When we buy goods and services we are often paying VAT (value-added tax).
- There are also **customs duties**, which are a tax on imported goods (goods brought into Ireland from abroad). An **excise duty** is a tax on some home-produced goods.
- Owners of property must pay **property tax**. The rate of property tax you pay depends on the value of the property.

WORKING WITH OTHERS

In small groups, discuss and research each of the headings in the table. Agree suitable definitions. Be sure to have the latest information and rates.

Income tax	Gross pay
Define: Rate %:	Define:
Tax credits	**Statutory deductions**
Define:	Define:
Tax rates	**Non-statutory deductions**
Define:	Define:
Tax allowances	**Other taxes**
Define:	Examples:

KEY PERSONAL TAXES 1.4

EXAMPLE 5: MAX REYNOLDS' TAX CALCULATIONS

This table shows the annual tax calculations for Max Reynolds. It may look a little daunting at first, but the explanation below will help you to understand it.

Take your time and go through it carefully. When you come to working out other examples for yourself, you will be given the figures and rates and you will have a calculator (if needed) to do the addition, subtraction and percentages. The vital part to understand now, therefore, is how to do the calculations.

Max Reynolds			
Gross Pay:			€32,000
Deductions:			
PAYE (20% of 32,000)	6,400		
Less Tax Credits (3,600)	− 3,600		
Net PAYE		2,800	
PRSI (4% of 32,000)		1,280	
USC (3% of 32,000)		960	
Total Deductions			€5,040
Net Pay:			€26,960

Explanation
- The first column lists the main headings (gross pay − deductions = net pay) and breaks down the various deductions from Max's wage.
- The fourth column lists the key figures (gross pay − total deductions = net pay).
- The extra columns in the middle give space to show the tax calculations.
- Max's gross pay for the year was €32,000.
- Max pays PAYE at a rate of 20% on his gross pay. The calculation is €32,000 x 20/100 = €6,400.
- Max is entitled to tax credits of €3,600. A tax credit is subtracted from tax. The calculation is €6,400 − €3,600 = €2,800. So Max's tax credits reduce the amount of tax he has to pay to €2,800.
- Max also has to pay PRSI, which is 4% of gross pay. The calculation is €32,000 x 4/100 = €1,280.
- Max also has to pay USC, which is 3% of gross pay. The calculation is €32,000 x 3/100 = €960.
- The deductions are then added together to give the total deductions to be taken from Max's gross pay. The calculation is €2,800 + €1,280 + €960 = €5,040.
- It is now possible to work out Max's total take-home pay for the year:

Gross pay	− Deductions	= Net pay
€32,000	€5,040	€26,960

1.4 BE BUSINESS: PERSONAL FINANCE

Calculate Ronaldo Gomez's **net pay**:
- Gross pay for the year is €47,000
- PAYE is 20%, PRSI 4%, USC 3%. Tax credit is €3,600.

Be Numerate

WORKING WITH OTHERS

- Jamelia Storey is considering setting up a landscape business called Go Green Fingers. Jamelia will be self-employed and she will employ one landscaper, Joe Scrap. Discuss the pros and cons of being self-employed (working for yourself). Agree on two good points and two not so good points about being self-employed.
- Jamelia estimates that the total annual expenses (costs) of her new business will be €120,000. What will the average monthly expenses of the business be? How much money would Jamelia have to make in sales each month to receive an average monthly profit of €4,500?
- Jamelia employs one landscaper, Joe Scraps, to work in Go Green Fingers. Joe's normal working week is 39 hours. His basic wage is €10 an hour. Overtime is paid at double time. This week he worked 48 hours. What will his gross pay be for this week?
- Joe pays income tax at 20% and PRSI at 8%. His annual (yearly) tax credit is €2,000. (Remember to divide by 52 to calculate the weekly amount.) He contributes €2 per week to a trade union and contributes €25 a week to an investment fund. Work out his deductions and net pay for this week.
- Joe is paid on a time rate basis. State and explain one other method of determining gross wages.

CHECKING IN...

1. Explain the difference between work and employment.
2. State three statutory deductions and three non-statutory deductions that may be taken from an employee's wages.
3. Explain the main difference between a tax credit and a tax allowance.

KEY PERSONAL TAXES 1.4

WAGE SLIPS

EXAMPLE 6: RONAN MURRAY'S WAGE SLIP

Look closely at this wage slip for an employee called Ronan Murray and then take your time to read the explanation below carefully.

Name	Period	Gross Pay			Deductions					Net Pay
	(Week 1)	Basic	Overtime	Total	PAYE	PRSI	USC	Savings	VHI	
Ronan Murray	01/01/2016–07/01/2016	€600	€100	€700	€100	€20	€20	€50	€10	€500

Explanation

- The **white section** of this wage slip states the employee's name and the period covered by the wage slip. This is the wage slip of Ronan Murray and it covers his income for the week from 1 January 2016 to 7 January 2016. The tax year starts on 1 January so Week 1 is the first week in January.
- The **blue section** deals with Ronan's gross pay. This week he has earned €700 (a basic pay of €600 plus an overtime payment of €100). Overtime is additional hours to the normal working week and it is usually paid at a higher rate.
- The **yellow section** deals with deductions from Ronan's pay. You will see that this includes statutory deductions (taxes you have to pay by law) for PAYE €100, PRSI €20 and USC €20. It also includes non-statutory deductions (optional items that you choose to pay for) for savings €50 and VHI (private health insurance) €10. Ronan's total deductions are €200.
- The **green section** states Ronan's net pay. The calculation for net pay is gross pay minus total deductions. This week Ronan will take home €500. That's €700 (gross pay) less €200 (total deductions).

Gross pay €700	– Deductions €200	= Net pay €500

PREPARE A SIMPLE WAGE SLIP

Copy and complete the wage slip below using the following information:

The wage slip is for Mary Madden, Week 8, 22 to 28 February.

Mary worked 38 hours at €15 per hour and 4 hours overtime paid at time and a half.

Mary's deductions are: PAYE €75, PRSI €35, USC €10; union fees €8.10 and VHI €19.

Be Numerate

Name	Period	Gross Pay			Deductions					Net Pay
		Basic	Overtime	Total	PAYE	PRSI	USC	Union	VHI	

What was Mary's gross pay?   What were her total deductions?

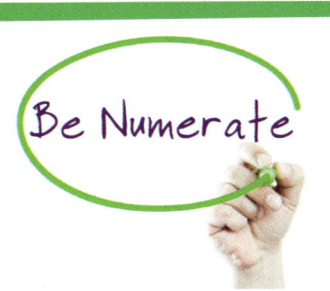

1.4 BE BUSINESS: PERSONAL FINANCE

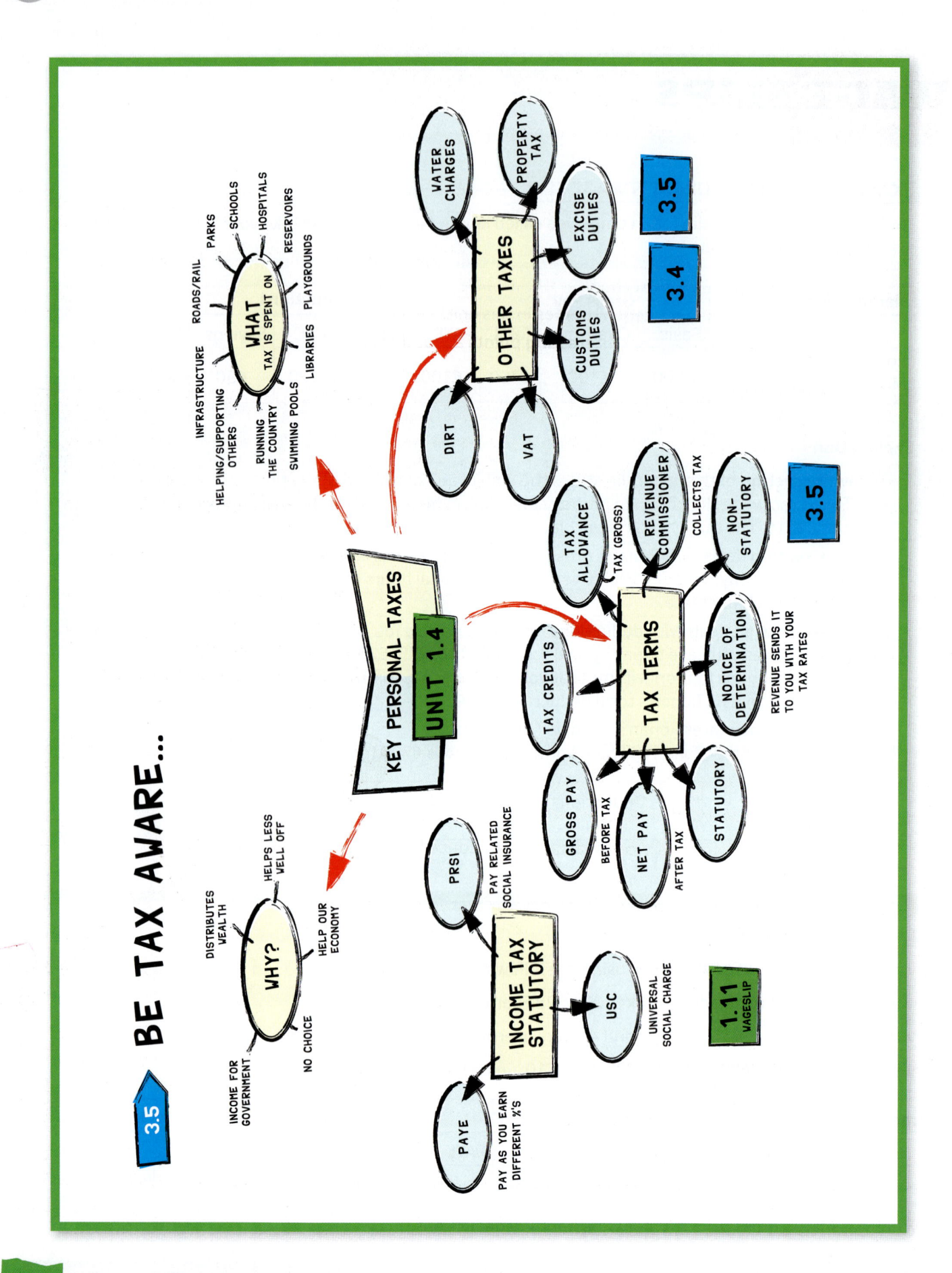

BE TAX AWARE...

KEY PERSONAL TAXES — UNIT 1.4

WHY?
- INCOME FOR GOVERNMENT
- DISTRIBUTES WEALTH
- HELPS LESS WELL OFF
- HELP OUR ECONOMY
- NO CHOICE

WHAT TAX IS SPENT ON
- INFRASTRUCTURE
- ROADS/RAIL
- PARKS
- SCHOOLS
- HOSPITALS
- RESERVOIRS
- PLAYGROUNDS
- LIBRARIES
- SWIMMING POOLS
- RUNNING THE COUNTRY
- HELPING/SUPPORTING OTHERS

OTHER TAXES
- WATER CHARGES
- PROPERTY TAX
- EXCISE DUTIES
- CUSTOMS DUTIES
- VAT
- DIRT

TAX TERMS
- TAX ALLOWANCE (TAX GROSS)
- REVENUE COMMISSIONER — COLLECTS TAX
- NON-STATUTORY
- NOTICE OF DETERMINATION — REVENUE SENDS IT TO YOU WITH YOUR TAX RATES
- STATUTORY
- NET PAY — AFTER TAX
- GROSS PAY — BEFORE TAX
- TAX CREDITS

INCOME TAX STATUTORY
- PRSI — PAY RELATED SOCIAL INSURANCE
- USC — UNIVERSAL SOCIAL CHARGE
- PAYE — PAY AS YOU EARN DIFFERENT %'S

1.11 WAGESLIP

3.4 3.5

KEY PERSONAL TAXES 1.4

Be Prepared: My Support Sheets

Completing the activities here will help you to reflect on and reinforce your learning before you move on to the next unit.
- Write down the **key terms** in this unit and make sure you understand them. See if they match the ones at the back of the book.
- List the key **concepts/themes** in this unit.
- List the **three most interesting points** about this unit.

Have a debate

Class Debate: Why does the government have to take money (taxes) from people? Have a class debate on the proposal that 'The government should get a job and work and pay tax like everyone else.' For guidelines on how to debate, see Unit 1.9, p. 130.

Finance in Action Idea!

Be the Minister for Finance and write a report on personal taxes.

Success criteria:
- Title and introduction
- Clear purpose and focus
- Five points of information
- Conclusion - summarise main points
- Visual(s) to support information

QUESTION TIME

1. Write a short paragraph on income tax.
2. What might happen to services if taxation was reduced? What might happen to services if taxation was increased?
3. Be the government: can you think of a new tax that you might introduce? If the country's health services needed additional income, what might you do?
4. Define the following: PAYE, PRSI and USC.
5. Why, do you think, did the government introduce property tax? Source the current rates at www.revenue.ie and calculate the property tax for houses worth €200,000, €300,000 and €400,000.
6. Do you think tax is fair? Why/why not?
7. What might Ireland be like if we had no taxes?

1.4 BE BUSINESS: PERSONAL FINANCE

EVALUATE MY LEARNING: DAR

Evaluation should be ongoing. Initially evaluate yourself, then working with others, your class, and where appropriate the visitor to the classroom.

Describe
- Did I/we meet my/our learning intentions?
- What went well? What are my/our strengths?

Assess
- How did I/we work with others?
- Were there challenges?
- How might I improve?

Recommend
- What skills and learning might I apply to new situations?

Do your **Key Check** in the workbook for this unit and then mark your learning position on the following rating scale:

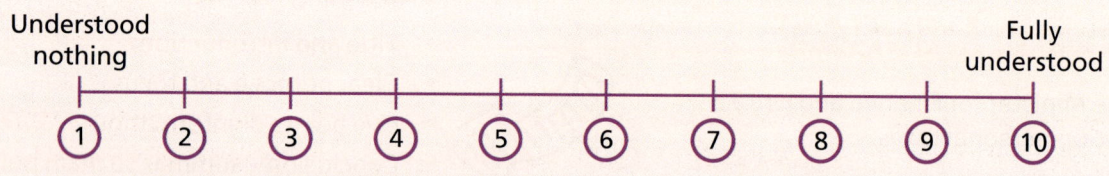

Understood nothing — 1 2 3 4 5 6 7 8 9 10 — Fully understood

How can you move up the rating scale? What can you **say, make, write** and **do** to illustrate your learning?

CBA 1 Business in Action:
Will I use this unit for my topic for **Finance in Action**? ☐

You need to be preparing for your CBAs
- ○ Exceptional
- ○ Above expectations
- ○ In line with expectations
- ○ Yet to meet expectations

Stop and think

Do I have any questions or concerns?

What are the mistakes or errors I made in this unit?

1.5 PERSONAL SAVING AND BORROWING

Identify reasons for saving and borrowing money, relate the reasons to determining appropriate sources of finance with respect to their purpose, costs and risks.

Learning Intentions

At the end of this unit I will:

- Know about and understand savings, including pensions
- Know about and understand borrowing, including mortgages
- Understand the importance of the cost of borrowing
- Value saving and preparing for the future
- Be able to calculate interest on savings, pensions and borrowings

Making the links with other LOs:

- 1.3 Personal financial life cycle
- 1.11 Wage slip and personal tax liability
- 3.2 Circular flow of income

Are there other LOs?

'3Ts' = Think, Turn, Talk

- What is saving? Do you have any savings?
- What is borrowing? Have you ever borrowed money?
- What might be the pros and cons of saving and of borrowing?
- Why do people save money?

Key Concepts

- ✓ Savings
- ✓ Borrowing
- ✓ Mortgages
- ✓ Pensions

Wonderful Worthwhile Websites

www.mortgages.ie
www.mymoneysense.ie
www.bankofireland.ie
www.creditunion.ie

You are never too young to think about savings and investments. Start saving today, not tomorrow.

FINANCIAL INDEPENDENCE

'If I were a rich man, yubba dibba dibba dibba dibba dibba dum'

Google the lyrics of this well-known song and you will read what one character would do if he had the money. You may have quite different ideas and goals! But there is no doubt that financial independence (knowing you have money saved for when you need it) will give you greater **freedom** when it comes to making **choices** in your life.

Financial independence might mean being able to take a holiday whenever you want to, starting your own business, helping family/ friends when they need it, taking on a job with less pay. And although it may seem alien to you at this stage of your life, preparing for a financially healthy retirement means that you can retire when you want to!

1.5 BE BUSINESS: PERSONAL FINANCE

SAVING

Saving means holding on to and not spending your money. Saving should be done on a **regular basis**. You should begin the **habit** of saving money regularly now if you have not started already.

Work out what you are saving for (e.g. emergencies/unforeseen events, education, car, retirement) and then look for the best financial institution (e.g. bank, building society, credit union, post office) to save your money in. You have many options and you want the one that gives the best return (in the form of **interest** paid) on your money.

When you have some spare money (perhaps birthday gifts), it is a good idea to lodge it safely in your savings account as soon as you can.

> You may need to dip into your savings from time to time, but you will build them up again. It takes a bit of work, but it is a habit worth getting into.

Top Tip!

If you would like to own your own home one day, you will need to get saving. Most mortgages (house loans) require a percentage of the value of the house as a **deposit** (down payment).

CASE STUDY:

JOSHUA AND ERICA'S REASONS FOR SAVING

Joshua is 16 years old. He and his mother are regular savers. They have different plans for their savings, but both of them get top marks for thinking of the future.

Joshua saves €20 every month. His reasons for saving are:

- Future purchases for me such as a new mobile phone.
- Unforeseen events – maybe my favourite band will come to Ireland and I can get a ticket for the gig.
- Education – I'll need some extra cash for the school tour next year.
- Income for the future… who knows what might happen?

Joshua's mum, Erica, saves €500 every month. Her reasons for saving are:

- Future purchases for the family such as a new washing machine. I'll save now and buy one in the sales.
- Unforeseen events – maybe one of us will get sick and there will be unexpected medical bills.
- Education – the children always need uniforms, books, fees, etc.
- Income for the future . . . who knows what might happen?

Being prepared in case the unexpected happens is an excellent reason for saving. As Joshua and Erica said: Who knows what might happen?

PERSONAL SAVING AND BORROWING 1.5

REASONS FOR SAVING

There are many reasons for saving.

- To buy something in the future, e.g. a new laptop.
- To earn additional income though interest on savings.
- To have a deposit to buy a house.
- For a future event, like a world trip or a ski holiday.
- For unforeseen events such as emergencies.

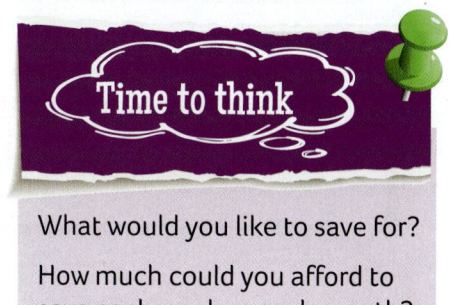

Time to think

What would you like to save for?

How much could you afford to save each week or each month?

FACTORS TO CONSIDER WHEN SAVING

Safety: Is your money safe? Most people save with a financial institution (bank, building society, An Post or a credit union – see pp. 77–78). These bodies offer a **guarantee** to protect savers.

Income: How much **interest** (income) will I earn?

Taxation: How much **DIRT** (deposit interest retention tax) – tax on interest earned on savings – will I pay? Some state savings accounts offer no tax on interest.

Convenience: Can I **withdraw** money whenever I want or is there a delay? Some savings accounts require you to give notice before withdrawing cash, or limit the number of withdrawals you can make in a year.

Internet Access: Are my savings easy to access online or offline?

Top Tip!

Shop around for the best value and always do your research.

INTEREST ON SAVINGS

When stating the rate of interest, most financial institutions give the **CAR** (**C**ompound **A**nnual **R**ate). This means that the interest on your savings is added each year to the principal (the amount of money you saved). However, in the second year that figure will be your original principal plus the interest you earned in the first year.

EXAMPLE 1: ROZ'S LOAN USING CAR

Roz saves €1,000 in her local bank in 2017 at an interest rate of 10%. At the end of the year she will earn €100 in interest:

€1,000 (principal) at 10% (interest) = 1,000 x 10/100 = €100

The total money in the savings account will then be €1,100 (€1,000 + €100).

At the end of 2018 she will earn €110 in interest:

€1,100 (new principal including 2017 interest) at 10% (interest) = 1,100 x 10/100 = €110

EXAMPLE 2: ROZ'S DIRT ON SAVINGS

Roz has to pay DIRT – tax on interest on savings – of 41%. In 2017 she earned €100 in interest, which means that she must pay €41 in tax:

€100 (interest) at 41% (DIRT) = 100 x 41/100 = €41

This means that Roz earned €59 in interest after tax in 2017 (€100 – €41 = €59)

1.5 BE BUSINESS: PERSONAL FINANCE

Be Numerate

1. Look at Roz's CAR example above and calculate the new principal and interest for 2019 and for 2020.
2. Calculate her DIRT interest after tax for 2018, 2019 and 2020.

CHECKING IN...

1. Give three reasons for getting into the savings habit.
2. Explain how CAR (compound annual rate) interest works.
3. What is the name of the tax paid on savings?

INVESTMENTS

Investing means putting your money/savings into a product or scheme that should make a **profit** (income). There are many types of investment available, from stocks and shares to bonds or even buying property.

Having **shares** in a company means that you will have a share of the profits that company makes. The shares in successful and well-established companies tend to be a lot more expensive than those in new or struggling businesses.

Investments offer the **opportunity** to make more money for you than savings; however, they also carry a greater **risk**: at worst, you could lose all the money you have invested. We saw this with shares and property when Ireland went from being a boom economy to a bust economy.

Time to think

If you were investing in shares, what type of company would you choose to invest in?

Check out the share price of Google. Would you invest in it at that price?

PENSIONS

When you are working you pay into a fund (similar to a savings account) to provide for your retirement (when you will receive an income known as a pension). The state offers a pension of approximately **€230 a week**; however, if you plan on travelling and enjoying your retirement you will need additional finance/money. To get that, you need to pay into a **pension plan**.

People are living longer. You may well live to be 100 years old. If that's the case, you are going to need a very good pension plan.

PERSONAL SAVING AND BORROWING 1.5

According to the National Pension Initiative, retired people need on average half of the gross salary they earned at work. So if your gross salary is €80,000, you will require a pension of €40,000.

The younger you start paying into a pension fund the cheaper it is. The following example highlights the differences:

To have a pension of €40,000:

- Start contributing at **25 years of age** and your pension contribution will be **€238** a month
- Start contributing at **35 years of age** and your pension contribution will be **€432** a month
- Start contributing at **45 years of age** and your pension contribution will be **€864** a month.

The important message is if you do not **start paying into a pension at a young age** you will pay a much higher price when you are older.

Also, when you contribute to a pension, the money is invested in a fund and earns interest. In addition, you are entitled to claim tax relief on your contributions. So that's two more benefits of paying into a pension: receive greater returns and reduce your tax payments.

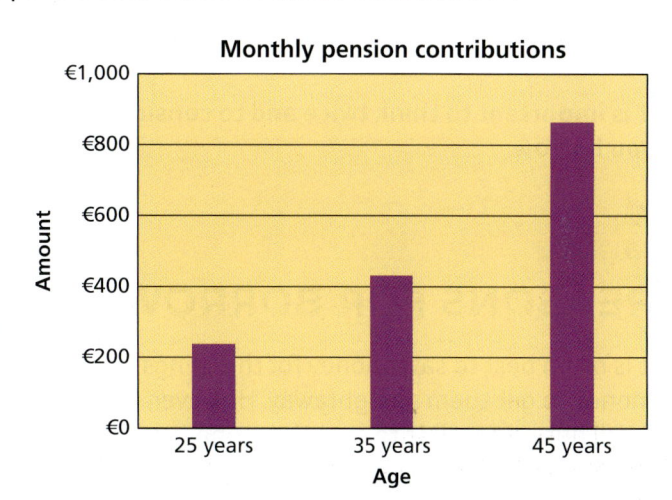

WORKING WITH OTHERS

- Discuss why it is sensible to start paying into a pension as soon as you start work.
- The population is getting older. People are living longer and fewer babies are being born in the West. At the moment there are six working people for every one retired person in Ireland. Within forty years, this may have reduced to just two working people for every one retired person in Ireland. What are the likely effects of these changes?

CHECKING IN...

1. What is a pension?
2. Why should you start paying into a pension fund at an early age?
3. How might a pension fit into your personal financial life cycle plan?

Top Tip!

The best financial advice is to go to a broker that you trust and shop around for a deal.

BORROWING

In Business Studies **borrowing** means receiving money (a **loan**) from a financial institution that you must pay back with **interest**.

There will be other conditions:

- You must be 18 years of age or older.
- You must be creditworthy and have a good track record of paying back other loans and of being a regular saver.
- You must have a regular income.
- You may have to offer some form of collateral – property or other assets, which the lender can take if you fail to repay the loan.

It is important to think twice and to consider other options before you borrow.

REASONS FOR BORROWING

It is often best to save money for the things we want rather than borrowing money to get them straightaway. However, there are some situations when it will not be possible to save the money you need in advance. For example:

- College fees: education is an investment in your future and you may not be able to pay college fees in advance. However, your qualifications will help you get a better-paid job and pay back the loan.
- Major purchases such as a house might take a lifetime to save for and you need somewhere to live. It often makes more sense to be paying back a mortgage to live in your house rather than paying rent.

It is all about managing information and thinking.

Time to think

You would really like to learn to play the violin. You have seen a beautiful violin in the local music shop, but it is very expensive. You cannot afford to buy it and to pay for lessons to learn how to play the violin. Should you get a loan? What other options might be open to you?

TYPES OF BORROWING

Financial institutions offer numerous financial services to potential borrowers. For example: debit cards, credit cards, overdrafts, loans, mortgages.

Debit and Credit Cards

These come in various forms:

- When you use a **debit card** to make a purchase, the money is paid out instantly from your bank account. With chip and PIN you insert your card in the reader and enter your PIN to authorise the deduction. With contactless payments, you can make purchases at home and abroad by just tapping your card on the reader.

- When you use a **credit card** to make a purchase, you will be billed for the money at the end of the credit period (usually one month). If you do not pay the bill on time, you will be charged interest.

- Government **stamp duty** applies to all debit and credit cards. In 2016 the rates were €2.50 to €5.00 for a debit card and €30 for a credit card.

- **Student credit cards** are specifically designed to suit people living on a tight budget. They offer a low credit limit (perhaps €400) to students in their first or second year of full-time study and an increased rate (up to €850) for those in third year or above.

- **Affinity cards** are the same as credit cards, but in addition the bank makes a donation to an agreed organisation (often a college or charity).

Top Tip

If you have to use a **credit card** (buy and pay later, with a cost) ensure that you pay off the full amount within the month. It could cost you twice as much if you don't as interest rates on credit cards are quite high. Saving money should mean that you are always able to pay off your credit card bill on time.

Overdrafts

Cash flow (having sufficient ready cash) is a concern for individuals, households, businesses and even governments. One way to reduce the worry is to have an overdraft facility with your bank. It allows you to withdraw more money than you have in your bank account.

You will need a current account with the bank and you need to have reached an agreement on the **limit** of the overdraft **before** you withdraw the money. Banks offer an online system for application.

An overdraft is similar to a loan. You will pay interest on the extra money that you withdraw. You pay interest only on what you use. If you agree an overdraft of €1,000 with the bank, but withdraw only €600, then you just pay interest on the €600.

As you must repay your overdraft at the end of the year, it is a short-term source of finance (money). An overdraft is the most common source of short-term finance.

Loans

A loan is a fixed amount of money that you borrow and agree to repay with interest. Usually the loan will be for a fixed period of time. Once your loan is approved, the money is paid directly into your current account.

You must shop around to find the most competitive rate. Some banks will offer incentives to attract your business. Some may offer to let you defer (delay) your first three monthly repayments. However, if you defer the first three monthly repayments you will end up paying more in interest than if you had paid them as normal.

When comparing interest rates you should always look at the **APR** (annual percentage rate). The APR takes into account the repayments and therefore is the true rate of interest.

> ### EXAMPLE 3: COST OF CREDIT
> Martha decides to borrow €7,000 to buy a second-hand car. She arranges a loan with her bank. She agrees to repay the loan and interest over five years (60 monthly payments). The rate of interest is 11.5% APR and her repayment each month will be €151.85.
>
> Martha's total repayments will be: €151.85 x 60 (months) = €9,111
>
> The total cost of the credit is: €9,111 (repayments) − €7,000 (loan) = €2,111

Mortgages

A mortgage is a **long-term loan** used to buy a house. Mortgages are typically for **20 to 30 years**. They are provided by financial institutions.

You will need to be able to pay a **deposit** (money paid up front for the property) – normally 20% of the value, but 10% for people buying their first home – before the institution will agree to the mortgage.

Top Tip!

Most banks offer online calculators to work out repayments. Excel is also a good resource for making calculations.

PERSONAL SAVING AND BORROWING 1.5

You use the house (or the deeds of the house) as collateral for the loan. A **collateral** offers security to the lender, in case of non-payment. This means that if you do not pay back the mortgage, the lender could take the house.

The cost of the mortgage is known as **interest**. You can opt for a **fixed rate of interest** (the rate does not change over the period of the mortgage) or a **variable rate of interest** (the rate will increase or decrease to reflect the state of the economy and other rates in the market).

EXAMPLE 4: COST OF CREDIT

Ava and Kirsty want to buy their first house at a cost of €220,000. They have saved up the deposit of €22,000 (10% of the value of the house). They need a mortgage to cover the remaining €198,000.

They arrange a fixed-rate mortgage with a bank. They agree to repay the mortgage over thirty years (360 monthly payments). The rate of interest is 4.5% and their repayment each month will be €1,003.24.

The total repayments will be:
€1,003.24 x 360 = €361,166.40

The total cost of the credit is:
€361,166.40 – €198,000 = €163,166.40

WORKING WITH OTHERS

- The above is just the repayments for the mortgage: Ava and Kirsty will have other expenses for day-to-day living and for setting up a new home. What might they be?
- Working together, estimate how much money you might need every year for: household goods (furniture and appliances), food, transport, light and heat, insurance, clothes, phone, TV, broadband, entertainment, holidays, miscellaneous items (and anything else you wish to include). Present the information in a graph.

Success criteria:
- Title for graph: short, relevant and creative
- Labels: clear and easy to understand
- Accuracy; spelling correctly

1.5 BE BUSINESS: PERSONAL FINANCE

Be Numerate

The table shows the repayments on a €200,000 mortgage for a 10-year term, a 20-year term and a 30-year term. Calculate the amount you would repay for each of these terms.

Term	Mortgage amount = €200,000	Number of months to repay
10 years	€1,977.72 repayment per month	10 years = 120 months
20 years	€1,159.92 repayment per month	20 years = 240 months
30 years	€898.09 repayment per month	30 years = 360 months

10 years = €1,977.72 × 120 = _____

20 years = €1,159.92 × 240 = _____

30 years = €898.09 × 360 = _____

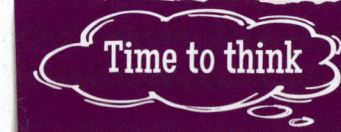

Time to think

Be the banker who is providing the mortgage. What sort of person would you prefer to lend money to? What characteristics would you look out for? Why might you not provide a mortgage to an applicant (the person who has applied for a mortgage)?

If you were refused a mortgage, what changes might you make to be successful next time you apply?

Qualifying for a Mortgage

When deciding whether to offer you a mortgage, financial institutions tend to be cautious and will consider the following questions:

- Are you in **safe and secure employment** and with good salary prospects? Do you have a permanent contract of employment? How long have you been employed there? Do you have relevant skills and qualifications for today's job market?
- Are you a **regular saver**? A good savings record suggests prudent (wise) spending habits and financial management.
- Can you **afford** the repayments?
- Have you **a good credit history**? Do you clear your credit card bills every month? Have you missed any payments on previous loans? Have you any personal debt?
- Are you making a **wise investment**? Is the price of the house good value? Is it in a location where it may be hard to resell the house if you need to?

It is vital to consider the above questions yourself as well. What would you do if you lost your job? What if interest rates increased by 3% – could you still afford the repayments? What other expenses do you have? Have you considered the legal and stamp duty costs involved in buying a house?

If you (or the mortgage providers) decide that you cannot afford a particular mortgage, then you need to either look for a lower mortgage or make a **plan** to save/earn more money so that you can afford it in the future. Or maybe the future is renting/leasing.

PERSONAL SAVING AND BORROWING 1.5

WORKING WITH OTHERS

- It is really important to shop around for the best value that you can afford. Most financial institutions have websites that show their latest mortgage interest rates. Check these out and discuss the range of rates on offer.
- House prices are affected by the state of the economy. In an economic boom they go up and in a bust they drop. What problems might this create for people with mortgages?
- At the moment, a mortgage cannot be for more than 3.5 times your gross income. So if your gross income is €40,000, the maximum mortgage you can get is €140,000 (€40,000 x 3.5). Do you agree or disagree with this limit? Give reasons for your answer.

SHORT-TERM, MEDIUM-TERM AND LONG-TERM FINANCE

Short-term finance is needed to cover the day-to-day running of the household. It will be paid back in a short period of time, usually within one year, making it less risky for the lenders. Examples include **overdrafts** and **credit card** purchases.

Medium-term finance is needed to cover major purchases that cannot be repaid in the short term (e.g. a car or college fees). These loans are usually paid back in three to five years. **Hire purchase** or **leasing** is where monthly payments are made for use of equipment such as a car. Leased equipment is rented and not owned by the person. Hired equipment is owned after the final payment.

Long-term finance is needed to cover major purchases that cannot be repaid in the short or medium term. An example is a **mortgage** for a house.

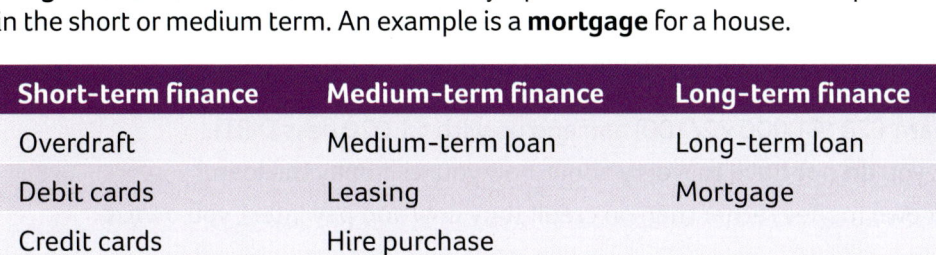

Short-term finance	Medium-term finance	Long-term finance
Overdraft	Medium-term loan	Long-term loan
Debit cards	Leasing	Mortgage
Credit cards	Hire purchase	

You would not take out a loan to buy a concert ticket. In the same way, it would not be possible to buy a car using your credit card. It's important to match the source of finance with the use.

Paying rent while waiting for wages to come into your account	Overdraft
Purchasing clothes for the winter	Debit card
Buying tickets for a concert	Credit card
Paying for college fees	Medium-term loan
New car	Leasing
New TV or computer	Hire purchase
Building an extension to a house	Long-term loan
Buying a house	Mortgage

1.5 BE BUSINESS: PERSONAL FINANCE

CHECKING IN...

1. Give three reasons why you might borrow money.
2. Name the sources of finance for each reason and state why you chose each source.
3. What do you need to consider before applying for a mortgage?

SAVING VERSUS BORROWING

There will be occasions in your life when you must decide whether it is best to:

- Save for something and buy it later, or
- Borrow money to buy it now, but pay interest on the loan.

You need to **research** both options carefully before you make your decision.

WHY SAVE TO BUY?

If possible, it is **better to save** to buy something rather than borrowing:

- Borrowing is not free – there is a **cost**. You usually **pay interest** when you borrow money. So if you borrow €1,000 for a year and the APR is 10%, the cost of the loan is €100 (€1,000 x 10/100) and you end up paying back €1,100.
- Saving money is **free** and can provide an income as you may also **earn interest**. So if you save €1,000 in a savings account that pays 2% interest for one year, you will earn €20 (€1,000 x 2/100) and end up with €1,020 (less DIRT).
- If you save rather than borrow, you **do not have to worry** about how you will repay the loan.
- If you buy something with your own money rather than on credit (buy now and pay later), you **own it outright straightaway**.

WHY BORROW TO BUY?

There are situations when it may be **necessary** to borrow. For example:

- You cannot wait to save because you **need something immediately**. Perhaps your car has broken down and you need to either repair it or buy a new one because there is no alternative form of transport available.
- You want to **take advantage of a special offer**. Perhaps there is a bargain washing machine in the January sales and buying it at this significantly reduced price means that the savings outweigh the cost of borrowing the money to buy it.
- You are investing in something that will benefit you in the future and this opportunity has to be paid for now (e.g. college fees).
- The cost is really expensive and it would take too long to save for. Most people have to borrow (take out a mortgage) to buy their own house.

MAKING THE DECISION

When deciding whether to borrow, ask yourself the following questions:

- How **quickly** do you need the money? If you can afford to wait and save, then saving is likely to be the best option.
- What is the **best option** for borrowing? You need to find out what types of loan might be suitable and how much these cost. Be savvy and shop around for the best deal.
- Will you be **able to borrow**? Financial institutions are careful about who they lend to. Will you meet their criteria? If you want a mortgage, you will need a deposit.
- If you want to buy a new car, you may need to have a down payment in order to get a car loan at a reasonable interest rate. Rather than buying a new car you could look at buying a demonstration model or perhaps a second-hand car.
- Is it worth the **risk** of borrowing? There are risks involved with borrowing money: what will happen if your circumstances change and you cannot make the repayments? If you want the cash for a luxury purchase (say, to be able to fly business rather than economy class to New York), it is really not worth the risk.

If you decide to borrow, you will need to assess the different types of finance using the following criteria:

- **Amount of money required.** If it is a small amount, you won't avail of a mortgage. Likewise you would not use an overdraft to buy a house.
- **How soon the money is required.** The longer you spend researching and applying for a loan, the better (cheaper) the deal you are likely to find. When you need to access the money very quickly, you have to take what is easily available, which may not be a good deal.
- **Cost of credit.** You need to find a loan at a reasonable rate of interest that you can afford.
- **Length of time for finance.** You need to decide how long you need to borrow the money for. Remember that it is cheaper to pay back a loan over one year than over five years, providing you can afford to do so.
- In extreme circumstances you may be tempted to borrow from a money lender, but the interest is very, very high.

PLACES TO SAVE AND BORROW

There is a lot of choice for the consumer in terms of places to save and borrow money. It's important to understand what each of the financial enterprises has to offer, and what they do best for the consumer. Here we will look at An Post, banks, building societies and credit unions.

AN POST

An Post is a major financial enterprise offering a range of services; everything from postal to retail. At your local post office you can buy stamps, pay your TV licence, and organise insurance.

Saving at An Post means you are not liable for DIRT. There are numerous saving schemes including savings bonds, national instalment savings and Prize Bonds.

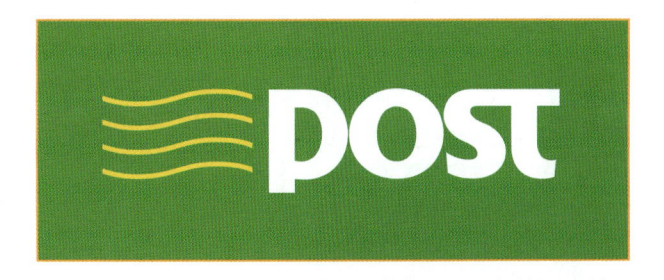

BANKS

Banks are financial institutions/businesses where the product is money. Banks have a huge range of types of customer; from students and families to businesses and the government. Banks offer numerous services and like any other business their objective is to make money/a profit. They provide money at a cost (interest) and take money (deposits) and give interest. Banks lend money at a higher rate of interest than they pay on savings. This is how they make a profit.

Remember, while they pay interest on savings, this interest on savings is income and is liable for Deposit Interest Retention Tax (DIRT).

Most people and most businesses have at least one bank account. The most common accounts are savings and current accounts.

- ✓ A savings or **deposit account** allows you to lodge money and leave it in the account until the money is needed again. Banks usually offer interest on savings accounts. Interest is always given as a percentage, and is a motivational factor to save.
- ✓ A **current account** is used primarily to take money out of an account in order to pay bills and expenses. There are various ways of paying bills: laser cards, smart cards, online banking and cash (from ATMs). In addition, you can apply for an **overdraft**. Telephone and internet banking means that banking is now 24/7/365.

BUILDING SOCIETIES

Building societies provide many banking services, for example saving accounts, ATMs, credit cards, investments and insurance. However, they are predominantly associated with lending for the purpose of buying a home. This kind of long-term loan is called a **mortgage**. There are usually numerous branches which have longer opening hours than banks.

CREDIT UNIONS

Credit unions are **non-profit-making** co-operatives. They encourage members to save on a regular basis and lend at a competitive (inexpensive) rate. They have flexible opening hours, and are located in most towns around the country. Some of their employees are volunteers, to help reduce costs. Savings in a credit union are not liable for DIRT.

> In Business Studies you will constantly reflect on where you will source finance. The same applies to households, businesses and even the government.

PERSONAL SAVING AND BORROWING 1.5

WORKING WITH OTHERS

Interest rates and costs vary and it is important to keep up to date with the latest offers. In pairs, check out the current options available for savers. Present your information in a table (see below).

Savings: Best rates		
Institution	**Account type**	**Rate of return**
AIB		
Bank of Ireland		
Ulster Bank		
An Post		
Rabobank		
Other		

Which savings product might you recommend? Give reasons for your choice.

In pairs, check out the current options available for standard credit card users. Present your information in a table (see below).

Credit cards: Best rates		
Institution	**Card type**	**APR**
AIB		
Bank of Ireland		
Ulster Bank		
Permanent TSB		
Tesco		
Other		

Which credit card might you recommend? Give reasons for your choice.

In pairs, check out the current options available for borrowers of €10,000 over three years. Present your information in a table (see below).

Loans (€10,000 over 3 years): Best rates		
Institution	**APR**	**Monthly repayment**
AIB		
Bank of Ireland		
KBC		
Permanent TSB		
Ulster Bank		
Other		

Which institution do you recommend? Give reasons for your choice.

Please turn over →

1.5 BE BUSINESS: PERSONAL FINANCE

WORKING WITH OTHERS CONTD

In pairs, check out the current options available for a mortgage of €200,000 over twenty years, on a house worth €250,000. Present your information in a table (see below).

Mortgages (€200,000 over 20 years): Best rates		
Institution	APR	Monthly repayment
AIB		
Bank of Ireland		
KBC		
Permanent TSB		
Ulster Bank		
Other		

Which mortgage might you recommend? Give reasons for your choice.

Be an Historian

- What happened to the banks in 1920? (Hint: the Great Depression)
- When Ireland went bust in 2006, the banks guaranteed our deposits. Can you find out what that means? What was the 'Greek crisis'?
- An economics student might have some interesting views on these questions.

CHECKING IN...

1. Give an example of a time when you would decide to save rather than borrow. Give reasons for your choice.
2. Give an example of a time when you would decide to borrow rather than save. Give reasons for your choice.

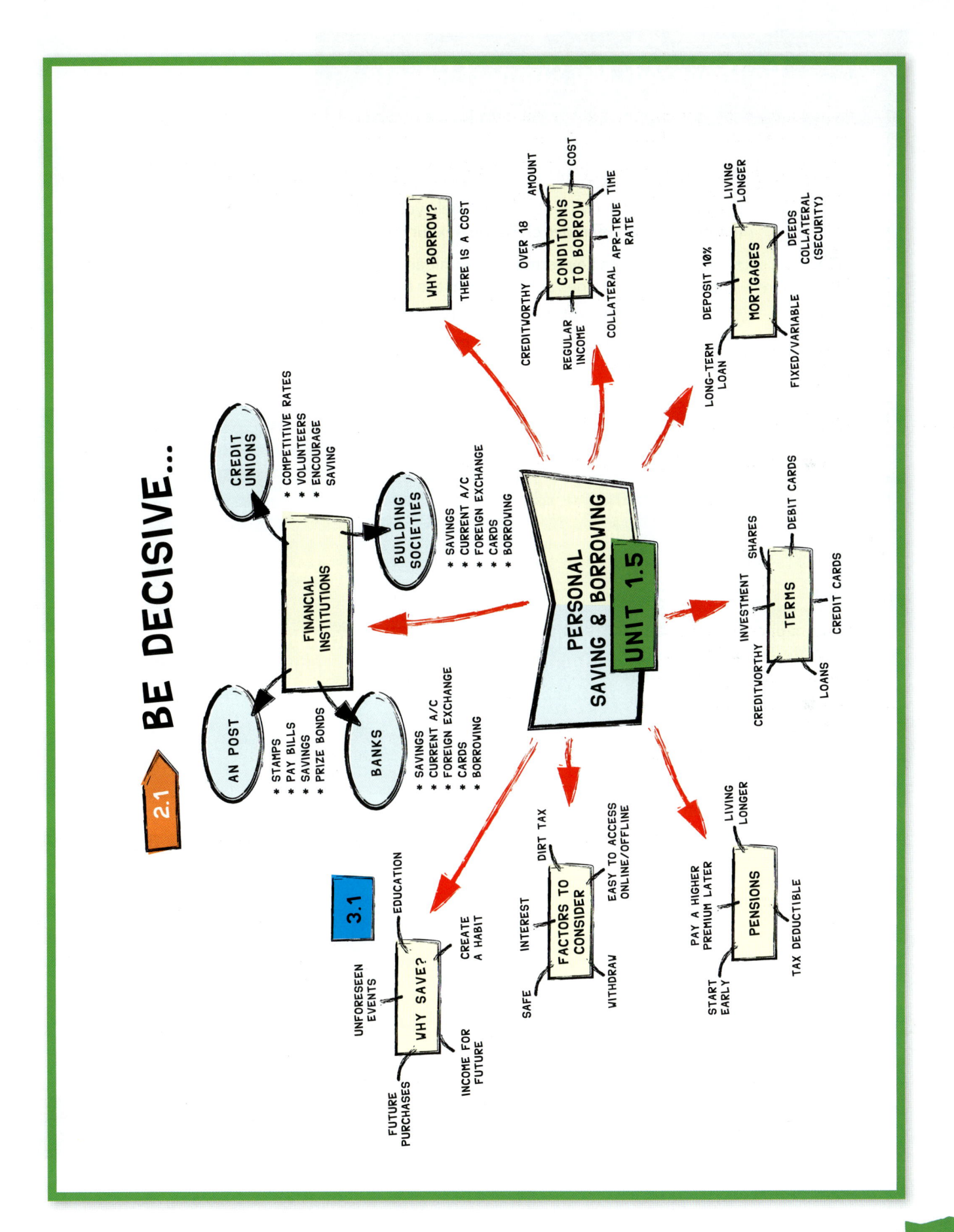

PERSONAL SAVING AND BORROWING — 1.5

BE DECISIVE...

2.1

PERSONAL SAVING & BORROWING — UNIT 1.5

FINANCIAL INSTITUTIONS

- **CREDIT UNIONS**
  - COMPETITIVE RATES
  - VOLUNTEERS
  - ENCOURAGE SAVING

- **BUILDING SOCIETIES**
  - SAVINGS
  - CURRENT A/C
  - FOREIGN EXCHANGE
  - CARDS
  - BORROWING

- **AN POST**
  - STAMPS
  - PAY BILLS
  - SAVINGS
  - PRIZE BONDS

- **BANKS**
  - SAVINGS
  - CURRENT A/C
  - FOREIGN EXCHANGE
  - CARDS
  - BORROWING

WHY BORROW?
- THERE IS A COST

CONDITIONS TO BORROW
- CREDITWORTHY
- OVER 18
- AMOUNT
- COST
- REGULAR INCOME
- COLLATERAL
- APR-TRUE RATE
- TIME

MORTGAGES
- LONG-TERM LOAN
- DEPOSIT 10%
- LIVING LONGER
- DEEDS COLLATERAL (SECURITY)
- FIXED/VARIABLE

TERMS
- CREDITWORTHY
- INVESTMENT
- SHARES
- DEBIT CARDS
- CREDIT CARDS
- LOANS

PENSIONS
- LIVING LONGER
- PAY A HIGHER PREMIUM LATER
- START EARLY
- TAX DEDUCTIBLE

FACTORS TO CONSIDER
- SAFE
- INTEREST
- DIRT TAX
- EASY TO ACCESS ONLINE/OFFLINE
- WITHDRAW

3.1

WHY SAVE?
- UNFORESEEN EVENTS
- EDUCATION
- CREATE A HABIT
- FUTURE PURCHASES
- INCOME FOR FUTURE

81

Be Prepared: My Support Sheets

Completing the activities below will help you to reflect on and reinforce your learning before you move on to the next unit.

- Write down the **key terms** in this unit and make sure you understand them. See if they match the ones at the back of the book.
- List the key **concepts/themes** in this unit.
- List the **three most interesting points** about this unit.

Use placemats

In groups of four, sit around a table with a 'placemat' (see below) in the middle of the table. Each person has a letter, A, B, C and D, and writes in their letter's space all they know about being financially independent. Then write in the 'consensus' space all that you agree on.

Use a Cube Creator (from www.readwritethink.org) to create a cube demonstrating your learning from this unit.

Make a cube

The interactive Cube Creator is an online tool for summarising information. You can save a draft cube to revise later.

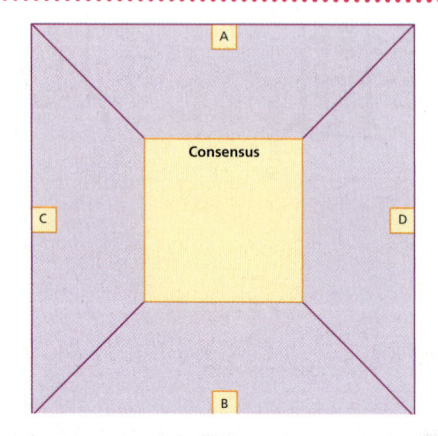

PERSONAL SAVING AND BORROWING 1.5

QUESTION TIME

1. Name four sources of finance.
2. Explain 'saving' and 'borrowing'.
3. When might you borrow rather than save?
4. Mortgages are a waste of time. Explain why you agree/disagree.
5. Create a summary of this unit using the fishbone template on p. 546.

Stop and think

Do I have any questions or concerns?

What mistakes have I made in this unit?

EVALUATE MY LEARNING: DAR

Describe
- Did I/we meet my/our learning intentions?
- What went well? What are my/our strengths?

Assess
- How did I/we work with others?
- Were there challenges?

Recommend
- How might I improve?
- What skills and learning might I apply to new situations?

Do your **Key Check** in the workbook for this unit and then mark your learning position on the following rating scale:

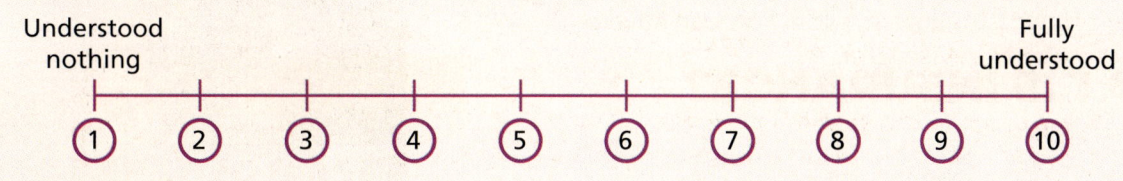

Understood nothing ① ② ③ ④ ⑤ ⑥ ⑦ ⑧ ⑨ ⑩ Fully understood

How can you move up the rating scale? What can you **say, make, write** and **do** to illustrate your learning?

CBA 1 Business in Action:

Will I use this unit for my topic for **Enterprise in Action** and **Finance in Action**?

You need to be preparing for your CBAs

○ Exceptional
○ Above expectations
○ In line with expectations
○ Yet to meet expectations

83

1.6 PERSONAL INSURANCE

Identify appropriate types of insurance for particular personal needs and consider costs, benefits and risks.

Learning Intentions

At the end of this unit I will:
- Know about insurance
- Understand the different types of insurance
- Value the importance of insurance
- Be able to calculate premiums and compensation

Making the links with other LOs:

- 1.3 Personal financial life cycle
- 1.11 Wage slip and personal tax liability

Are there other LOs?

"3Ts" = Think, Turn, Talk
- What is insurance?
- What types of insurance are there?
- Do you think buying insurance is a good idea?

Key Concepts
- ✓ Insurance costs
- ✓ Insurance benefits
- ✓ Insurance risks

Wonderful Worthwhile Websites
www.axa.ie
www.fbd.ie
www.aviva.ie

WHAT IS INSURANCE?

Life has many **risks** – anything from your bicycle being stolen, to your house burning down, to illness preventing you from earning a living. **Unforeseen events**, such as theft, accidents, floods, fire, illness, disability, dismissal or even death, usually involve **significant financial costs**, for example to replace stolen property. Whatever the risk, there is an insurance available to reduce the financial loss to you should these events happen.

> **Insurance** is a way of protecting yourself from the costs that may arise from damage to your property or your health. It is a way of transferring risk.

PERSONAL INSURANCE 1.6

Your home and other belongings cost money to buy. We call them **assets** because they are something of money value. If your assets are damaged, destroyed or stolen, you may not be able to afford to repair or replace them. If you pay a fee (a small proportion of the price of the asset) to insure them, then an insurance company agrees to pay the costs of such losses or accidents. This fee is known as a **premium**.

When you take out an **insurance policy**, you must first fill out a **proposal form.** You must fill in the form honestly or you may not be covered by insurance. **Honesty** is an important principle of insurance. In taking out a policy, you agree to pay specified premiums to an **insurance company**. These premiums create a pool of money that guarantees that you will be compensated for losses caused by occurrences such as fire, accident, illness or death.

Insurance companies decide what the risk is on a particular policy and then charge the appropriate premium. You can pay for the premium monthly or annually (yearly).

You should **shop around** when buying or renewing an insurance policy to make sure you get the best value for your money.

You may either use an **insurance broker**, who will source an insurance company for you at a fee, or speak to the insurance companies direct. However, you can only insure something if you benefit financially from having it and suffer financially if you lose it. You can't insure your neighbour's house! This is also an underpinning rule/principle of insurance.

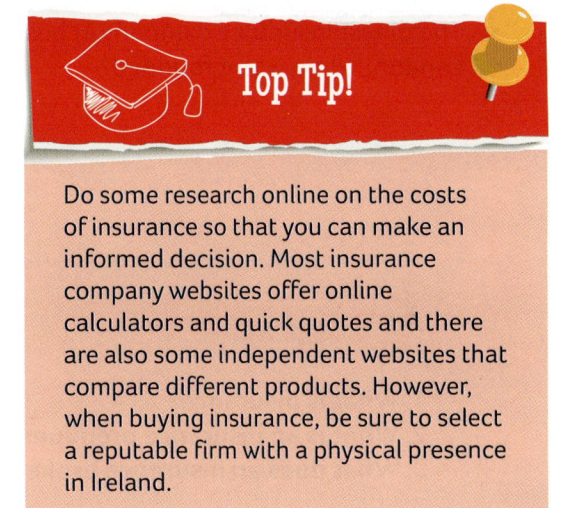

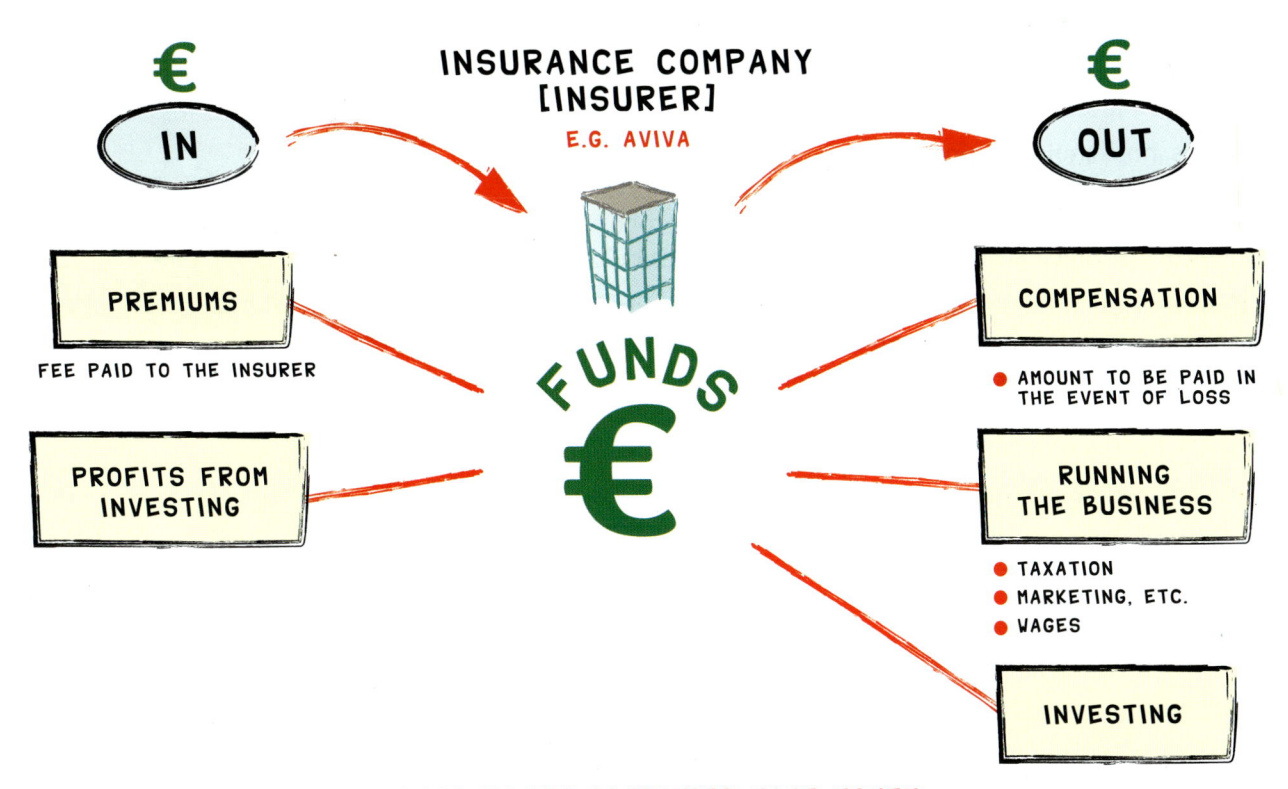

Top Tip!

Do some research online on the costs of insurance so that you can make an informed decision. Most insurance company websites offer online calculators and quick quotes and there are also some independent websites that compare different products. However, when buying insurance, be sure to select a reputable firm with a physical presence in Ireland.

INSURANCE COMPANY [INSURER]
E.G. AVIVA

IN → **FUNDS €** → **OUT**

- **PREMIUMS** — FEE PAID TO THE INSURER
- **PROFITS FROM INVESTING**

- **COMPENSATION**
  - AMOUNT TO BE PAID IN THE EVENT OF LOSS
- **RUNNING THE BUSINESS**
  - TAXATION
  - MARKETING, ETC.
  - WAGES
- **INVESTING**

HOW INSURANCE COMPANIES MAKE MONEY

1.6 BE BUSINESS: PERSONAL FINANCE

Be an Historian

- There is some evidence that insurance started in Babylonian times (18th century BC). What can you find out about it?
- Insurance contracts were invented during medieval times and were mainly used for marine insurance. Suggest why marine insurance may have been needed at that time.
- Property insurance was invented in London in the late 17th century. Which devastating event of 1666 may have been responsible for its introduction?
- The oldest insurance company in business today is Lloyd's of London. When was it founded?

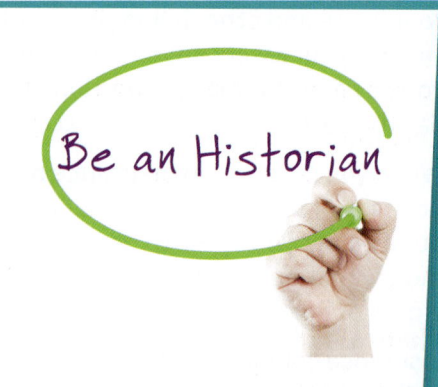

CHECKING IN...

1. What is insurance?
2. What is an insurance premium?
3. What does an insurance broker do?

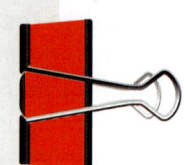

TYPES OF INSURANCE

Individuals, households, businesses, organisations and the government all need insurance. It is an expense that has to be included in budgets and other financial plans. We will focus here on the types of insurance needed by individuals and households.

The **Competition and Consumer Protection Commission (CCPC)** publishes a range of guides that explain how different types of insurance work. The CCPC is an agency that helps consumers. It has also completed numerous surveys and comparisons of insurance premiums in order to recommend the best value.

Of course different individuals and households have different risks and needs and will have different insurances. There are lots available, including:

1. Motor Insurance
2. Home Insurance
3. Health Insurance
4. Life Assurance.

1. MOTOR CAR INSURANCE

Motor car insurance is compulsory by law.

Car insurance may be the first type of insurance that you will need. The cost of insuring a car has increased over recent years and younger drivers have been hardest hit by the higher costs.

Types of Motor Car Insurance

There are three main types of car insurance:

1. **Comprehensive** car insurance is the most common and the most expensive car insurance. It covers you for loss, theft or damage to your vehicle. It also covers you for accidental damage to another vehicle or to property. Without this cover, you will be responsible for paying for the damage to your own car and to others if you cause an accident.
2. **Third party** car insurance is a cheaper option. It covers you for damage to another person's vehicle or property, but not for damage to your own car.
3. Another type of car insurance, known as **'third party, fire and theft'**, covers the risk of your car being destroyed by fire or being stolen.

Setting the Premium

The factors that insurance companies use to determine what premium will be charged for car insurance include: age, occupation, address, type of car, driving experience and qualifications, and any previous claims.

You cannot really change these factors, except perhaps for the **type of car** you drive or hope to drive. When buying a car, remember that insurance costs are more expensive on high-performance engines.

You have a responsibility to tell the **truth** when you apply for insurance. If you leave out important information when applying for insurance, it could result in non-payment by the insurance company when you make a claim.

Some insurance companies offer discounts to young drivers who have completed **advanced driving skills courses** as well as those drivers who have signed up for or taken a minimum of ten **driving lessons** from a registered driving instructor.

If you have held an insurance policy before and not made any claims on it, you may be entitled to a **no claims bonus**, which is a discount on your premium. The size of the reduction increases the longer you drive without needing to make a claim.

Be sure to question your insurer (insurance company) about any discounts that you may be eligible for when taking out insurance.

Often a policy includes an **excess**, which is the portion of a claim you have to pay yourself.

If your policy has an excess of €200, and you need to claim for damages worth €250, then you will pay the first €200 yourself and the insurance company will pay the balance of €50.

You cannot claim for losses that are less than the excess. So if your policy has an excess of €200 and you have damages worth €150, you will have to pay the full amount (€150) yourself and the insurance company will pay nothing.

CHECKING IN...

1. Why do people take out car insurance?
2. Describe two different types of car insurance.
3. Name three factors that car insurance companies consider when setting premiums.

Questions to Ask about Car Insurance

- What type and level of cover best meets your needs? Should you go third party; third party, fire and theft; or fully comprehensive?
- How many quotes do you need to get?
- Do you want to use a broker? What extra services does the broker provide, such as help with making claims? What fee does the broker charge?
- Could you get a lower quote by dealing directly with the insurance company or buying online?
- What **loadings** (extra charges to cover extra risk) are the insurance company applying in your case? Are you paying more because of your car, occupation or where you live? Can you reduce any of those loadings?

- Do you qualify for any discounts?
- Can you decrease your premium if you choose a larger excess?
- What is included in the policy and what is excluded? Remember, the policy offering the lowest premium may not always be the best value for money.

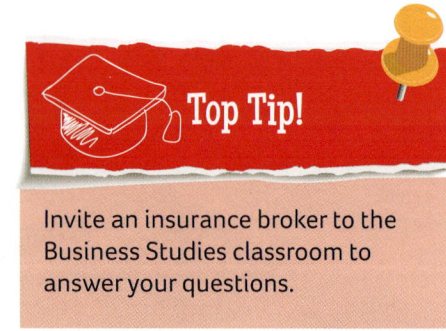

Top Tip!

Invite an insurance broker to the Business Studies classroom to answer your questions.

Do not forget to **bargain**. If you receive a good quote from one company, it is usually worthwhile to see if another is prepared to match or better that quote in order to get or keep your business.

However, price is not the only factor to consider when deciding on taking out insurance. The most important factor is the need to be **looked after sufficiently** when you run into problems. It is, after all, the reason why people take out insurance in the first place.

If your car is damaged, your house is broken into or you require hospital care, you need to know that your insurance company will step in and help you. Those who provide cheap insurance are less likely to provide you with all the cover you need when things go wrong.

Rising Premiums

Premiums are increasing because **insurance companies are losing money** on car insurance. There are many reasons for this. The increase in traffic is a major factor because it leads to more accidents and hence to more claims. In addition, Ireland has a high level of road deaths and injuries, which result in large injury claims.

Another factor is legal expenses – the services of barristers and solicitors do not come cheap. The **Injuries Board** is a government body that assesses claims for compensation from anyone who has been in an accident and suffered an injury. It was set up to reduce the costs and time involved in settling such **personal injury claims**. However, many accident victims opt to pursue their claim through a solicitor instead, which in turn increases the legal costs involved.

Premiums are particularly high for **young drivers**. Young drivers in Ireland are generally classed as all those under the age of 25 years.

A young driver is about three times more likely to crash than an older driver. One in five young drivers will be involved in a road traffic accident during the first year of insurance. Young drivers are also more likely to cause injury to their passengers. As a result, the cost of car insurance for young drivers is considerably higher than that for more experienced or older drivers.

1.6 BE BUSINESS: PERSONAL FINANCE

WORKING WITH OTHERS

- In pairs, check out the current options available for car insurance. Select two insurance companies and research their policies and premiums. Present your information in tabular format (see below).

Contact details	Company 1	Company 2
Name of insurance company		
Contact number/email		
Contact name		

Quotes – Premium	Company 1	Company 2
Third party	€	€
Third party, fire and theft	€	€
Fully comprehensive	€	€
Policy excess	€	€
Date		

Benefits offered (tick where appropriate)	Company 1	Company 2
Breakdown/recovery service		
Driver personal accident emergency service		
EU/international cover		
Legal costs		
Medical expenses		
No claims discount		
Open driving		
New car replacement/hire car limit		
Replacement lock cover and fire brigade charge		
Windscreen cover		
24-hour emergency service		
Other benefits		

- Which insurance policy do you recommend? Give reasons for your choice.

PERSONAL INSURANCE 1.6

CHECKING IN...
1. What is meant by the term 'loadings' in insurance?
2. What is meant by the term 'excess' in insurance policies?
3. Why might premiums be higher for younger drivers?

2. HOME INSURANCE

Home insurance is not a requirement by law. However, insuring your home protects it against the risk of fire or other accidents and damage. Also, home insurance is required by your lender when you have a mortgage (and you will have to take out **mortgage protection insurance** in case you cannot meet your repayments).

What's Covered?

Policies vary, but in general home insurance will cover the **cost of rebuilding** your home (based on a survey or valuation report) in the event of a disaster. It will also include **contents insurance** to cover harm to or loss of your belongings. In addition some **third party** cover will be included in case you damage someone else's belongings in the house you are living in.

What's Not Covered?

Again, policies vary, but in general home insurance does not cover damage caused by acts of terrorism; by storms, flooding or subsidence if your home is in an area where this is likely to happen; or wear and tear in the structure or the inside of your home (e.g. water damage caused by a leaking shower).

As with all types of insurance, you will not be covered for any claim that is less than the **excess** on your policy.

Valuations

You should insure your home for the amount it would cost to rebuild it, which is called the **reinstatement value**. This is different from the market value of your home, which is the price you would get if you sold it.

It is really important that you do not insure your house and contents for too much or too little. If your home is insured for **too little**, your policy might not pay out enough for the full cost of repairing or rebuilding it if it is damaged or destroyed. If it is insured for **too much**, your premium will be higher than necessary, but you will not receive any extra benefit if you do claim, as you are only covered for the **actual cost** of rebuilding or replacing contents.

Time to think
What type of questions will the insurer ask you if you want to take out home insurance?

What should you ask the insurer when taking out home insurance?

Top Tip
Check out the website of the Society of Chartered Surveyors Ireland (www.scsi.ie) for advice on the cost of rebuilding a house.

1.6 BE BUSINESS: PERSONAL FINANCE

Many home insurance policies contain a feature known as **average clause**. This formula is used to calculate the payments due on a claim. It takes into account the relationship between the insurance coverage and the actual replacement cost. So if you have under-insured your property that will mean a reduced payment on the claim.

$$\text{Average clause formula} = \frac{\text{Amount insured}}{\text{Market value}} \times \text{loss}$$

If the contents of your home are worth €20,000 and you insure them for €10,000, you are **under-insured** by 50%. If your contents are damaged, destroyed or stolen, the most you will get from your insurance company is 50% of the total damage.

If the contents of your home are worth €20,000 and you insure them for €30,000, then you are **over-insured** by 50%. If your contents are damaged, destroyed or stolen, the most you will get from your insurance company is the **actual cost** of €20,000 as you are not allowed to make a profit on an insurance policy. This is another important principle of insurance; you cannot benefit financially from insurance.

EXAMPLE 1: CALCULATING COMPENSATION

Eve's house is valued at €300,000. However, so that she would pay a lower premium, she insured it for €150,000 (i.e. half or 50% of its real value). A fire broke out in the house and caused €50,000 worth of damage. How much compensation will Eve receive?

The average clause formula is: $\dfrac{\text{Amount insured}}{\text{Market value}} \times \text{loss}$

In Eve's case the calculation will be: $\dfrac{€150,000}{€300,000} \times €50,000 = €25,000$

Eve insured her house for half its value, therefore she will receive just half the compensation she claimed.

What compensation would Eve receive if she had insured the house for:

a. €100,000?

b. €200,000?

c. €300,000?

d. €400,000?

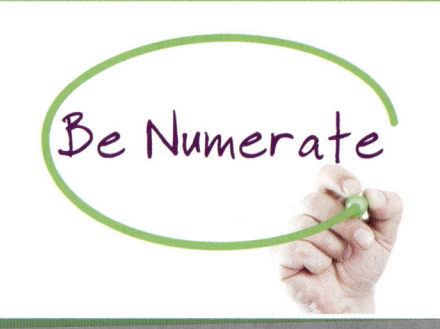

Be Numerate

PERSONAL INSURANCE 1.6

Discounts

Depending on the insurance company, you may get a discount if you have not made any previous claims. Insurance companies may also reward behaviours that reduce risk. For example, if the house has an alarm (especially a monitored one), security locks fitted on doors and windows, sensor lights outside, a guard dog and is located in a neighbourhood watch area, you may be rewarded for the reduced risk of burglary.

Time to think

As an individual, you need to look at your behaviour to decide if you could reduce the risks of an unexpected disaster, and thereby lower the cost of your premium. **For example:**

What risks could drivers avoid?

How could you reduce the risk of a fire in your home?

EXAMPLE 2: CALCULATING PREMIUMS

Stephen's house is valued at €350,000 and the contents are valued at €100,000. He has installed a monitored security alarm. His local insurance company offers house insurance on the following basis:

- €10 per €10,000 for the house
- €5 per €10,000 for contents
- 10% reduction for an alarm.

Calculate the cost of Stephen's house insurance premium:

House €10 x 35 =	€350
Contents €5 x 10 =	€50
	€400
Less 10%	€40
Premium	**€360**

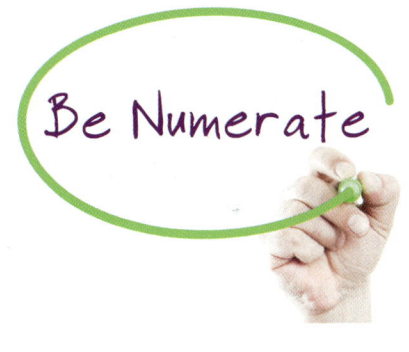

Be Numerate

1. What would the premium be if the house is valued at €280,000, the contents are valued at €70,000 and there is a monitored security alarm?

2. What would the premium be if the house is valued at €780,000, the contents are valued at €170,000 and there is no security alarm?

CHECKING IN...

1. Why do people take out home insurance?
2. What are the three main areas covered by home insurance?
3. Name three areas that are not usually covered by home insurance.
4. Why is it essential to be accurate when valuing your home and its contents for insurance purposes?

3. HEALTH INSURANCE

Your health is extremely precious. If you become sick and need expensive medical treatment, who will pay for it? If you become sick and are unable to work, who will pay the bills? Health insurance is the solution to your problem.

There are many types of health-related policies. For example:

1. **Medical insurance**, which covers private hospital and other medical bills
2. **Critical illness insurance**, which provides a lump sum (once-off payment) if you suffer from certain illnesses such as cancer
3. **Income protection insurance**, which pays a certain percentage of your income on an ongoing basis if you suffer from certain illnesses and are unable to work
4. **Disability insurance**, which pays out a lump sum for permanent disablement through sickness or accident
5. **Mortgage protection insurance**, which covers your mortgage repayments if you cannot work.

4. LIFE ASSURANCE

A life insurance (or assurance) policy provides financial protection for your dependants if you die. This is usually in the form of a lump sum. Life insurance policies are important if you have a partner or children who depend on you to provide for them. This is different from all other types of insurance because we are all going to die at some point!

There are different types of life assurance. For example:

1. **Term life assurance**, which covers you for a fixed number of years (e.g. the length of your mortgage)
2. **Whole of life assurance**, which covers you for the whole of your life until you die.

Term life is the most common form of life insurance and is cheaper than whole of life insurance.

Read the small print! All policies that cover your health or life may have exclusions. They may not cover certain illnesses or illnesses that were diagnosed before you took out the policy.

It is all very technical and even confusing; however, a **broker** can explain these insurances to you and help you to lodge any claim you may have.

5. TRAVEL INSURANCE

It is a really good idea to buy travel insurance for overseas holidays. Travel insurance will cover your belongings against loss or theft, additional costs if your flights are cancelled and, most important, medical treatment if you have an accident or become ill abroad. Medical bills can be really costly in other countries and taking out travel insurance is a necessity . . . just in case!

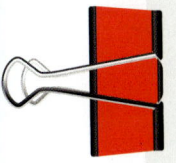

CHECKING IN...
1. Give three examples of health-related insurance.
2. Why might people take out life insurance?
3. Why is travel insurance a good idea?

WORKING WITH OTHERS
- Source an insurance application form and attempt to fill it out.
- Can it be filled in online?
- Are there any challenging questions?

Top Tip

Think about the major financial risks in your life. Choose insurance that lessens those risks.

INSURANCE CLAIMS

Working through this unit you have come across rules/principles that underpin (strengthen) insurance. Although a consumer may not ask the insurance company about the principles/rules of insurance, it is important that anyone taking out insurance is aware of them. If you do not follow the rules, you may not be insured.

1. **Insurable Interest:** you can't insure an item unless you benefit (financially) from its existence and suffer (financially) from its loss. For example, Barry O'Higgins can take out insurance on his own new Audi. Barry cannot take out insurance on his neighbour Will Donnelly's car, as damages to Will's car would not financially affect Barry.
2. **Indemnity:** you can never be left financially better off following an insurance claim. Brendan Waldron bought a new camper van with FBD insurance. The van was worth €30,000. He insured it for €50,000. The van was completely destroyed in a fire; however, Brendan will only receive €30,000.
3. **Utmost good faith:** you must always tell the truth. When filling out her proposal form for car insurance, Susan Ormond did not disclose that she had nine penalty points. She crashed her car and the insurance company would not pay her claim for €1,000. Whether or not you have penalty points is a material fact (important fact) that you must include when filling out the proposal form.

Remember, you can only insure an item with one insurance company.

MAKING A CLAIM

Here are the steps to follow when you need to make a claim:

1. **Check your full policy to see whether you are covered.** You may be covered under more than one policy – for example, if your money is stolen while you are on holiday, you may be covered by an all-risks household policy (an optional extra you can buy to extend the insurance cover on your belongings to outside the home) and also by your travel insurance – but you cannot claim under more than one policy for any loss, so carefully consider which policy to claim against. Also **check any excess**. Remember, you can't benefit financially from insurance.

95

2. Call, email or go online to contact your **insurer or broker** as soon as possible. Give details of the claim and **request a claim form** or whatever form they accept.
3. **Complete** the form **honestly** and submit it as soon as possible.
4. For larger claims, such as a buildings claim, you may want to **hire an assessor**, who will work on your behalf to get you the money that your policy entitles you to claim. The assessor will often negotiate with your insurance company to settle your claim. The assessor's fees are not covered by your policy, so you will have to pay for this service yourself.

WORKING WITH OTHERS

- In pairs, invent an insurance claim 'situation' (perhaps you have been involved in an accident or your house has been flooded or your holiday has been cancelled – be creative).
- Source a claim form from an insurance company and fill it in for your 'situation'.

COMPENSATION

If you are fully insured and you make a claim to the insurer (insurance company), you are entitled to the full amount. If you are over-insured, you will receive only the actual value. If you are under-insured, you will receive only a proportion of the loss, known as average clause (see above).

COMPLAINTS

If you are unhappy with your insurance company, it is best to try to resolve the conflict with the insurance company direct. All companies will have clearly set-out complaints procedures.

The **Financial Services Ombudsman** deals with complaints and disputes between policyholders and insurance companies when the company's complaints procedure fails to resolve the problem. The Ombudsman's decision is binding, but if you are still unhappy with the outcome you may appeal to the High Court.

CHECKING IN...

1. Why is it important to have adequate insurance?
2. Why might insurance costs increase?
3. Are insurance premiums income or expenditure?
4. Describe the steps involved in making an insurance claim.

WORKING WITH OTHERS

Refer back to the 'situation' you made a claim for above. Imagine that the insurance company is refusing to pay out on your claim. Write a letter of complaint.

PERSONAL INSURANCE 1.6

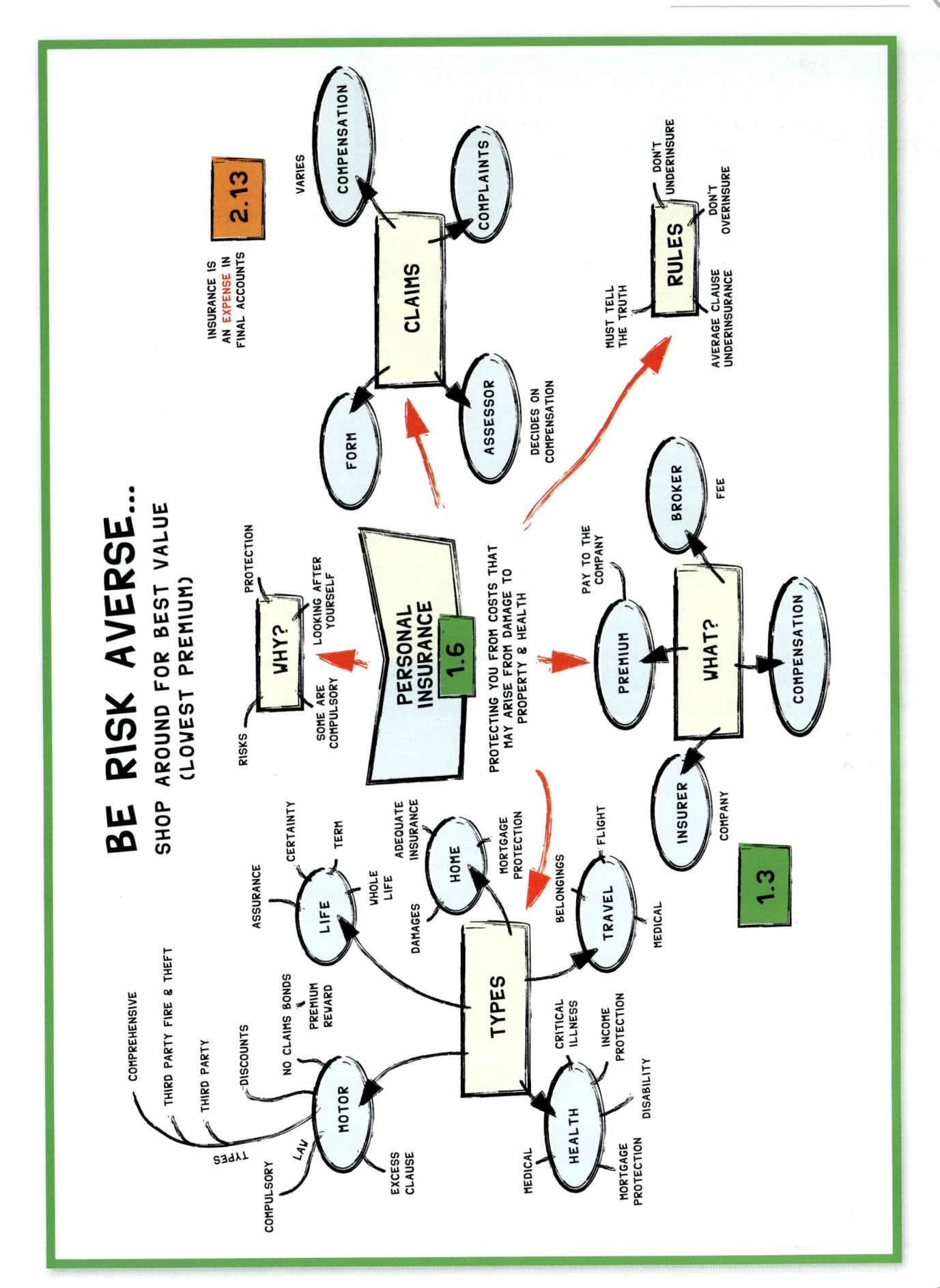

BE RISK AVERSE...
SHOP AROUND FOR BEST VALUE (LOWEST PREMIUM)

2.13 — INSURANCE IS AN **EXPENSE** IN FINAL ACCOUNTS

PERSONAL INSURANCE 1.6 — PROTECTING YOU FROM COSTS THAT MAY ARISE FROM DAMAGE TO PROPERTY & HEALTH

CLAIMS
- COMPENSATION — VARIES
- COMPLAINTS
- ASSESSOR — DECIDES ON COMPENSATION
- FORM

RULES
- DON'T UNDERINSURE
- DON'T OVERINSURE
- AVERAGE CLAUSE UNDERINSURANCE
- MUST TELL THE TRUTH

WHY?
- PROTECTION
- LOOKING AFTER YOURSELF
- SOME ARE COMPULSORY
- RISKS

WHAT?
- PREMIUM — PAY TO THE COMPANY
- BROKER — FEE
- COMPENSATION
- INSURER — COMPANY

1.3

TYPES
- LIFE
  - ASSURANCE
  - CERTAINTY
  - TERM
  - WHOLE LIFE
  - DAMAGES
- HOME
  - ADEQUATE INSURANCE
  - MORTGAGE PROTECTION
  - BELONGINGS
- TRAVEL
  - FLIGHT
  - MEDICAL
- HEALTH
  - CRITICAL ILLNESS
  - INCOME PROTECTION
  - DISABILITY
  - MORTGAGE PROTECTION
  - MEDICAL
- MOTOR
  - EXCESS CLAUSE
  - LAW
  - COMPULSORY
  - TYPES
    - THIRD PARTY
    - THIRD PARTY FIRE & THEFT
    - COMPREHENSIVE
  - DISCOUNTS
    - NO CLAIMS BONUS
    - PREMIUM REWARD

97

1.6 BE BUSINESS: PERSONAL FINANCE

Be Prepared: My Support Sheets

Completing the activities below will help you to reflect on and reinforce your learning before you move on to the next unit.

- Write down the **key terms** in this unit and make sure you understand them. See if they match the ones at the back of the book.
- List the key **concepts/themes** in this unit.
- List the **three most interesting points** about this unit.

Invent a quiz

Jot down three questions on insurance. Choose one of the three questions and write your answer in detail.

Make an individual presentation entitled 'Why be truthful when taking out insurance?'. The presentation should last between one and three minutes. The best presentations are well researched, provide evidence to support claims, display an interest in business and use variety, creativity and superb communication skills to hold the audience's attention.

Make a presentation

QUESTION TIME

1. 'Insurance is a waste of money.' Explain why you agree/disagree with this statement.
2. Describe the two main types of life insurance.
3. What questions should you ask and what research should you do before you buy insurance?
4. Explain why it is a bad idea to under-estimate or over-estimate the value of an item you wish to insure.
5. Apply the fishbone template (see p. 546) to this unit to create your summary.
6. Source an application form for car insurance or design your own.
7. Copy and fill in the star template with five different types of insurance.

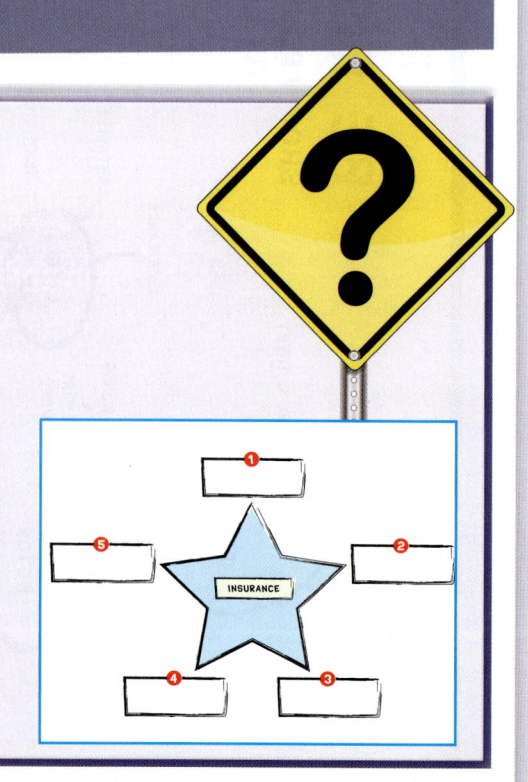

EVALUATE MY LEARNING: DAR

Describe
- Did I/we meet my/our learning intentions?
- What went well? What are my/our strengths?

Assess
- How did I/we work with others?
- Were there challenges?

Recommend
- How might I improve?
- What skills and learning might I apply to new situations?

Do your **Key Check** in the workbook for this unit and then mark your learning position on the following rating scale:

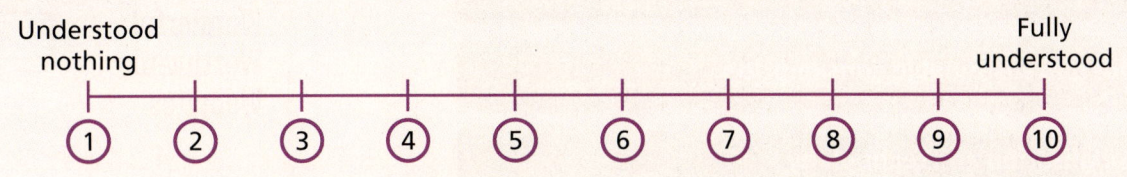

Understood nothing — 1 2 3 4 5 6 7 8 9 10 — Fully understood

How can you move up the rating scale? What can you **say, make, write** and **do** to illustrate your learning?

Stop and think

Do I have any questions or concerns?

What are the mistakes or errors I made in this unit?

1.7 RIGHTS AND RESPONSIBILITIES OF CONSUMERS

Distinguish between and appreciate your rights and responsibilities as a consumer.

Learning Intentions

At the end of this unit I will:
- Know what an informed consumer is
- Know my rights as a consumer
- Know my responsibilities as a consumer
- Value consumer responsibilities

Key Concepts
- ✓ Consumer
- ✓ Rights and responsibilities

Making the links with other LOs:

- 1.8 Services, consumer agencies, financial institutions
- 1.9 Ethics and sustainable consumption
- 1.10 Globalisation and technology
- 2.8 Marketing mix

Are there other LOs?

Wonderful Worthwhile Websites
www.ethicalconsumer.org
www.citizensinformation.ie
www.consumerhelp.ie

CONSUMER CHOICE

A **consumer** is a person who buys goods and services.

'3Ts' = Think, Turn, Talk
- What rights do you have when you buy a product or a service?
- Have you ever been badly treated by a business? Did you complain?
- What responsibilities do you have when you buy a product or a service?

Everyone is a **consumer** and we all buy goods and services from a range of sellers. Some people are **impulse buyers** while others spend a lot of time planning and researching different brands and shopping for the best deal.

As a consumer, you must make **choices** as to how best to use **your limited resources**. Everyone has to make such decisions: the government, businesses, your parents and your friends. The 'best deal', however, is not just about price.

Whenever you buy something, you need to **be aware of the impact** your purchase may have on the earth's scarce resources and on the environment. You need to be aware of your **rights** and your **responsibilities**.

RIGHTS AND RESPONSIBILITIES OF CONSUMERS 1.7

WORKING WITH OTHERS

Buying a mobile phone

Imagine you are buying your first mobile phone. Below is a list of six strategies or different ways of going about buying a mobile phone. They are not listed in any particular order. In pairs, discuss each strategy and rank them in the order in which you would use them (1 being your first choice and 6 your last choice).

A. Discuss phone costs with your parents and talk about the contribution they are going to make, if any.

B. Talk to friends who already have mobiles about different price plans and get their recommendations.

C. Visit stores and talk to sales staff so that you can compare the different networks.

D. Read contracts and get to know the details of different price plans so that you can work out your priorities.

E. Investigate the key differences between pre-paid phones and contracts for one or two years.

F. Do an internet search for independent advice and fact sheets from consumer organisations who compile surveys online.

DO YOU CONSUME TOO MUCH?

About 16% of the world's population is responsible for 80% of consumer spending. In Ireland we are guilty of excessive spending. We are not satisfied with meeting only our basic needs. We want more.

A number of our wants are created by advertisers. Advertisers use clever techniques to create a want. As a result, we are constantly trying to improve our lifestyles to follow the latest fashion or to mimic the rich and famous. This creates a demand for larger homes and luxury products, a constant 'trading up' to more expensive brands.

Such behaviour has high costs. For example, increasing credit card debt, which brings its own worries and challenges. People are working harder and for longer hours in order to pay for their excessive wants.

And don't forget the environmental costs of using up scarce and non-renewable resources.

Time to think

What techniques do advertisers use to encourage you to buy?

What are your responsibilities if you own a mobile phone? Could you upgrade less often?

CONSUMER RIGHTS

Rights are **legal entitlements**. As a consumer you are entitled to:

1. Goods that are of **merchantable quality**. The item must be of reasonable quality, safe to use and work properly, taking **price** and **use** into consideration. If you purchase a Dyson vacuum cleaner and use it to vacuum hot ashes and it breaks, you have used it beyond its merchantable quality and cannot expect any redress (compensation).
2. Goods that are **fit for purpose**. The item must do what it is supposed to do, for example a washing machine should wash clothes and a smartphone should allow you to make and receive calls.
3. Goods that **conform to (match) the sample shown**. If you are shown and order the most up-to-date iPhone, then that is what you must receive.
4. Goods that are the **same as described**. If the outside of the box says that there is 500g of rice inside, then that is what you should find when you open the box.
5. **Food labels that** state unit price, best-before date and ingredients. Ingredients must be listed in descending order, for example if yogurt contains mostly goat's milk and a small amount of sodium, then goat's milk will appear before sodium in the list of ingredients.
6. Services that are **supplied by skilled and qualified service providers**. You can expect that those offering you services are capable of doing the job, for example a gas installer must have the necessary qualifications to offer that service and a mechanic must be able to service your car.
7. Services that are provided using **proper care and attention**. If you go to your hairdresser for a cut, you can expect it to be done properly and carefully.
8. Services that use **materials/parts that are of merchantable quality**. The hairdresser in the example above must use a scissors that is of merchantable quality.
9. Financial products that state **interest rates – loans must show the APR** (annual percentage rate), which is the true rate of interest. This makes it easier to compare like with like when deciding to borrow.
10. Your contract is with the seller (whoever you bought the goods from).

BUYING GIFT VOUCHERS

There are different types of gift voucher depending on who issues them, including those that can be used in:

- A specific shop, e.g. Mattie's Butcher, Bagenalstown, Co. Carlow
- A specific chain of shops, e.g. Eason, Dunnes Stores
- A wide range of different traders, e.g. One4all vouchers.

Gift vouchers can be a very convenient present, but there may be drawbacks and some risk to them as well. For example, you do not have the right to get change when you use a gift voucher unless the voucher's terms specifically state that change will be given.

When you buy or receive a gift voucher or gift card always **check the terms and conditions**, including the expiry date. You can minimise the risk by buying vouchers that can be used at more than one outlet or chain.

Use your vouchers as quickly as possible. Expiry dates vary widely. Some shops give you just three months to redeem your voucher, so a gift voucher you received at Christmas and left in the bottom drawer will be no use by Easter.

RECYCLING ELECTRICAL EQUIPMENT

If you buy electrical goods, the shop or manufacturer must collect your old equipment when they deliver the new goods to replace them. The replacement must be for a similar piece of equipment, for example a washing machine for a washing machine, but not a washing machine for a fruit blender.

FAULTY GOODS

If a product is faulty, you have a legal right to a **repair**, a **replacement** or a **full refund**. Therefore it is an 'offence' for shops to put up notices that say: 'credit notes only given' or 'goods not exchanged'. You may agree to a credit note or an exchange, but you do not have to. When a shop accepts that you have a valid complaint, you can refuse a credit note and insist on a refund or ask that the goods be replaced. See p.112 for the steps you should take if you've bought faulty goods.

SALE ITEMS

Goods you buy in a sale or at a reduced price are treated no differently by the law from goods sold at any other time. So sale goods must be of **'merchantable quality'**, **'fit for purpose'** and **'as described'**.

However, if the goods are marked **'imperfect'** or **'shop soiled'**, then you are being informed that they are not of the usual quality.

DEPOSITS

A seller may ask you to pay a deposit (part payment in advance) when you order or reserve goods and services. You should really **avoid** deposits if possible, especially cash deposits. The business may be entitled to hold on to your deposit if you change your mind. Also the seller may go out of business.

SALE OF GOODS AND SUPPLY OF SERVICES ACT 1980

CONSUMER PROTECTION ACT 2007

COMPETITION AND CONSUMER PROTECTION ACT 2014

> A product cannot be described as 'reduced' unless it was previously and openly available at the original price for a reasonable period.

> The law protects you whether you pay for goods by cash, by credit card, by paying rent, or even by hire purchase (paying in instalments).

1.7 BE BUSINESS: PERSONAL FINANCE

CHECKING IN...
1. Name three rights that apply when a consumer buys goods.
2. Name three rights that apply when a consumer buys services.
3. What information should be on food labels?

YOUR RIGHTS ONLINE

Buying online can be a quick and easy way to shop, but there are risks. To **protect yourself**:

1. Research the website before you buy.
2. Make sure the payment method is secure – credit card companies have secure options.
3. Look for reviews from others who have bought from the website.
4. Check that there is a postal address and phone number for the business.
5. Ensure you are not on a public computer or wireless connection.
6. Try to purchase from EU-based sites so that you are protected by EU laws and consumer rights.

> Contracts for goods and services bought online can be cancelled without penalty within fourteen days. This is known as the cooling-off period.

@ONLINE SHOPPING

SECOND-HAND GOODS

You have the same consumer rights if you buy a second-hand product from a business as you have when buying new products.

If you buy something second hand through a private sale, however, your rights are very limited. You have no comeback so the term *caveat emptor* – let the buyer beware (see below) – applies.

KNOW YOUR CONSUMER LAW

Consumers have a significant body of rights and it is important that you are aware of these rights. Read existing and new laws to keep up to date.

Laws change on a regular basis. They are updated in response to changing consumer patterns and new challenges that emerge. You need to monitor such changes.

A **contract** is a legally binding agreement, and this is what a seller and buyer enter into when buying and selling goods. The sales contract is between the seller and the buyer (you). Your **receipt** is proof of this contract.

104

RIGHTS AND RESPONSIBILITIES OF CONSUMERS — 1.7

GIFTS

If you pass on the product to another party as a gift, that person does not have a contract with the seller and does not have the usual buyer's rights. However, some shops offer a **gift receipt** that does not state the price, which allows the buyer to pass on a proof of purchase with the gift.

GUARANTEES AND WARRANTIES

A **guarantee** is a legal promise from the manufacturer to offer a refund or repair or replacement if the product you purchased is faulty.

A **warranty** is an additional promise to repair or replace a faulty product. It is offered by the seller (usually for a fee) and lasts longer than a guarantee.

Guarantees and warranties are legally binding.

If you have bought faulty goods, the **seller** (e.g. shop), not the manufacturer, must sort out your complaint. But you may have extra protection if the manufacturer or supplier has provided a written guarantee that it will cover repairs or replacements.

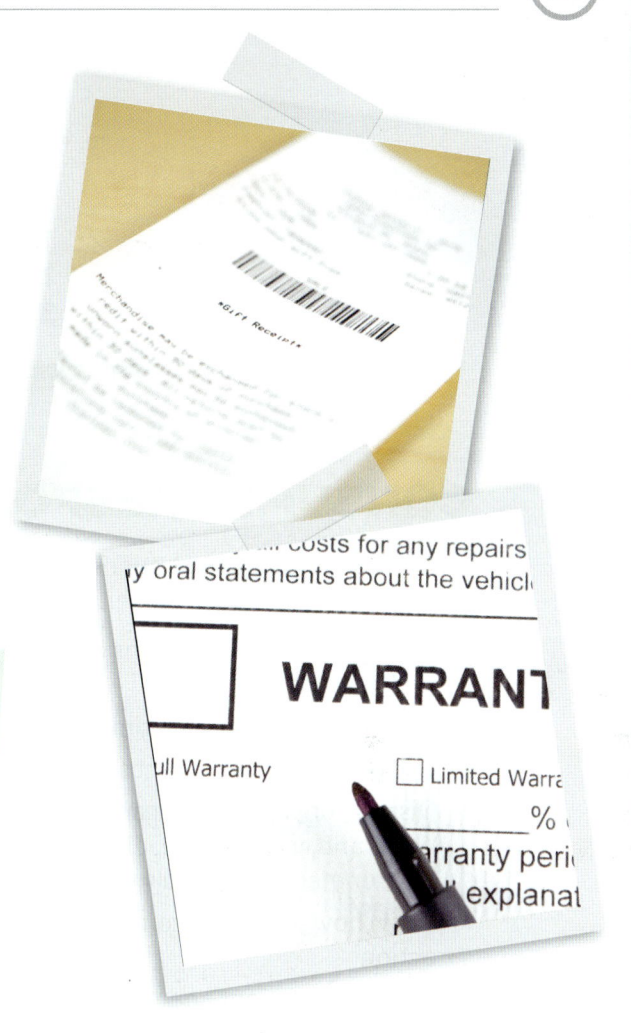

CAVEAT EMPTOR – LET THE BUYER BEWARE

The legal concept of *caveat emptor* – let the buyer beware – requires that buyers take responsibility for the condition of the goods/services that they purchase. You should shop around and ask questions before buying any product or service. You should also read any terms and conditions and ask for explanations if there is something you do not understand. This research will help you to get the best value for money.

LABELLING

Under EU law, some products such as **electrical appliances and furniture** should carry labels showing that they meet EU **safety standards**.

Clothing, footwear and furniture must also have labels showing what textiles and certain other materials they are made of.

Food products must by law have a wide variety of information on their labels or packaging. This includes the name and address of the manufacturer or seller, the ingredients used and the product's use-by or best-before date.

Every product that is offered for sale must have its price displayed. When goods are sold by weight, volume or measure, shops must display the unit price on or near the item. Examples of unit prices are: price per litre, price per kilo and price per metre.

1.7 BE BUSINESS: PERSONAL FINANCE

CHECKING IN...

1. What is a 'cooling-off period'?
2. Explain the differences between a guarantee and a warranty.
3. Explain the concept of *caveat emptor*.

CONSUMER RESPONSIBILITIES

We sometimes talk about our rights and forget about our responsibilities. As a consumer, it is your responsibility to:

- Be aware of sale conditions and of the after-sales service and guarantees
- Pay the agreed price on time
- Use the goods as instructed and for the purpose intended
- Dispose of packaging in an environmentally friendly way – and, if applicable, dispose of the product in an environmentally friendly way when you are finished with it
- Know how to make a complaint and how to take appropriate action
- Know the relevant agencies to contact when your rights are not adhered to.

BEING AN INFORMED CONSUMER

You can be an informed consumer by:

- Creating and keeping to a budget
- Shopping around for best value and not making impulse purchases
- Knowing your rights under consumer law
- Knowing what agencies to contact
- Being aware of your responsibilities
- Keeping receipts and guarantees.

Time to think

Are you an informed consumer? Explain your answer.

What issues might an ethical consumer be concerned about?

BEING AN ETHICAL CONSUMER

You can be a responsible and an ethical consumer by thinking globally and acting locally. Know the effects of consumption on society, the environment and individual life quality around the world.

Consumers are becoming more ethical. They know more about the origins and policies of providers of goods and services and this influences their decisions when buying. As a result, both buyers and sellers are making positive changes.

Numerous shops now include a wide range of **fair trade, organic** and **free range** products on their shelves and are careful to ensure detailed labelling of all products, including relevant ethical standards.

Consumers are anxious about **fair work standards** and **effects on our environment**.

Consumers are becoming more **health conscious**. We are what we eat and research indicates that certain foods and processing methods can lead to serious illnesses such as heart disease, obesity, cancer and respiratory problems.

CHECKING IN...

1. Name three consumer responsibilities.
2. Give an example of a way that sellers can be more ethical.
3. Give an example of a way that consumers can be more ethical.

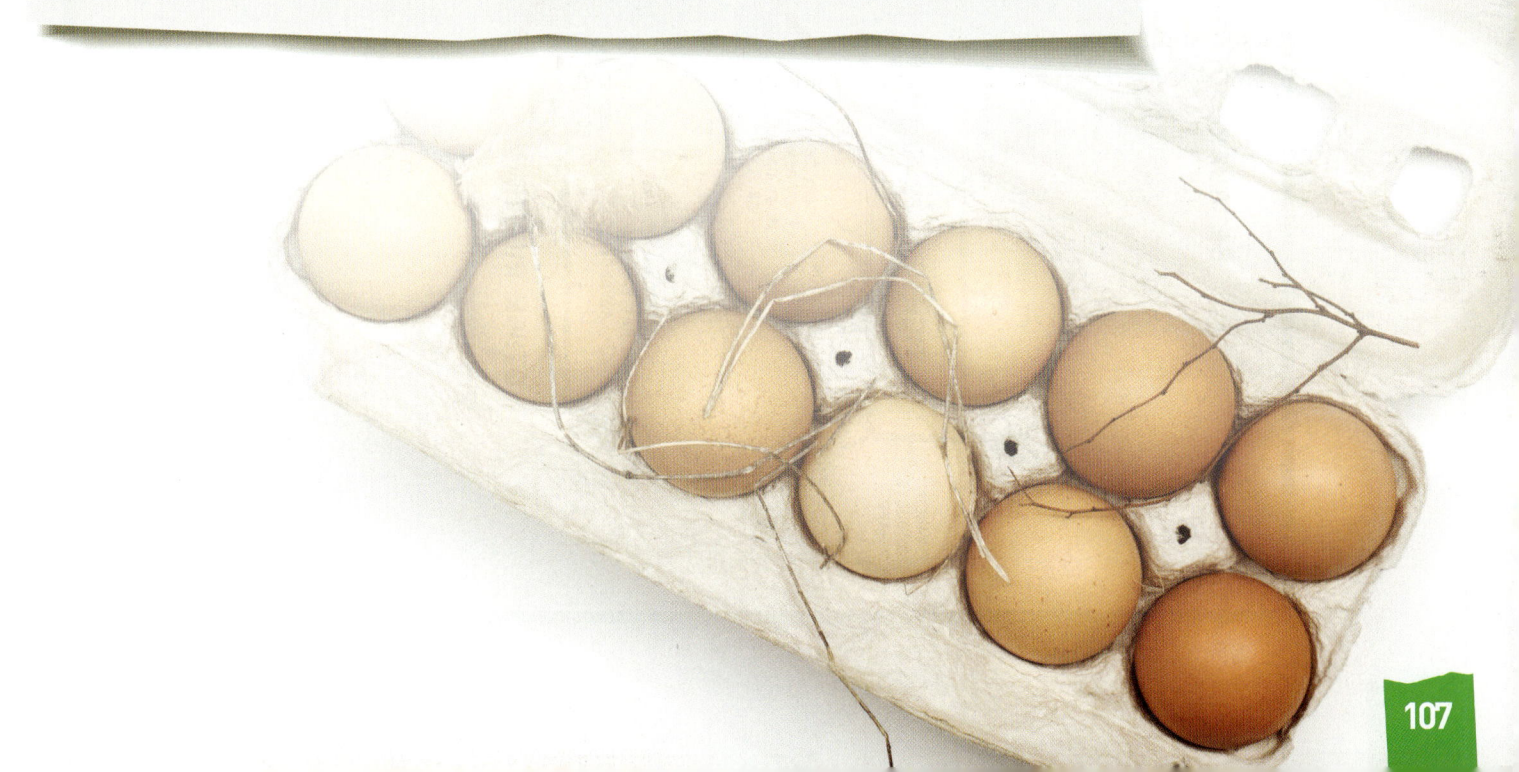

1.7 BE BUSINESS: PERSONAL FINANCE

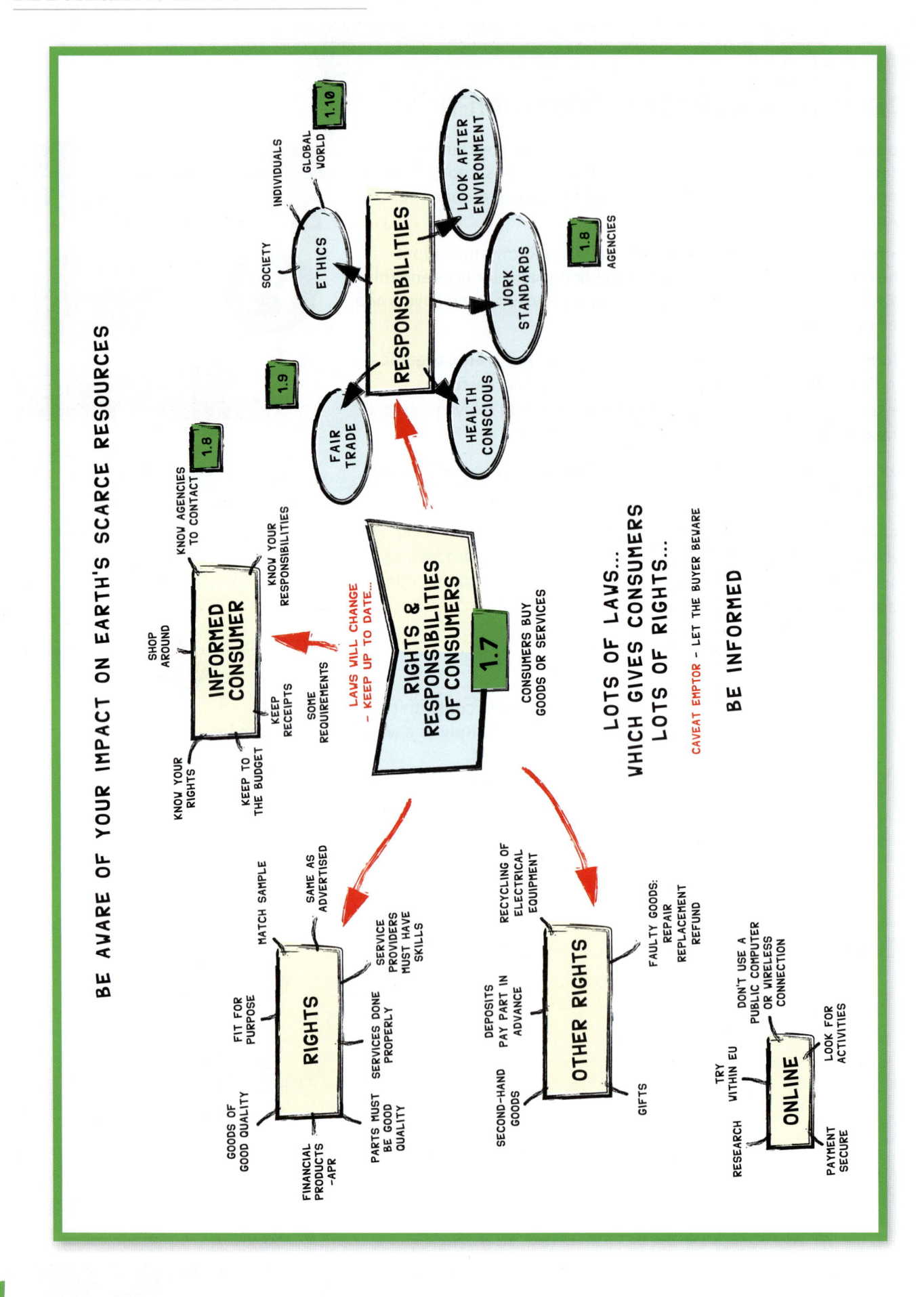

BE AWARE OF YOUR IMPACT ON EARTH'S SCARCE RESOURCES

RIGHTS & RESPONSIBILITIES OF CONSUMERS — 1.7

CONSUMERS BUY GOODS OR SERVICES

LAWS WILL CHANGE – KEEP UP TO DATE...

LOTS OF LAWS... WHICH GIVES CONSUMERS LOTS OF RIGHTS...

CAVEAT EMPTOR – LET THE BUYER BEWARE

BE INFORMED

RESPONSIBILITIES
- ETHICS
  - SOCIETY
  - INDIVIDUALS
  - GLOBAL WORLD (1.10)
- LOOK AFTER ENVIRONMENT
- WORK STANDARDS (1.8 AGENCIES)
- HEALTH CONSCIOUS
- FAIR TRADE (1.9)

INFORMED CONSUMER
- KNOW AGENCIES TO CONTACT (1.8)
- KNOW YOUR RESPONSIBILITIES
- SOME REQUIREMENTS
- KEEP RECEIPTS
- SHOP AROUND
- KEEP TO THE BUDGET
- KNOW YOUR RIGHTS

RIGHTS
- FIT FOR PURPOSE
- MATCH SAMPLE
- SAME AS ADVERTISED
- SERVICE PROVIDERS MUST HAVE SKILLS
- SERVICES DONE PROPERLY
- PARTS MUST BE GOOD QUALITY
- FINANCIAL PRODUCTS – APR
- GOODS OF GOOD QUALITY

OTHER RIGHTS
- DEPOSITS PAY PART IN ADVANCE
- RECYCLING OF ELECTRICAL EQUIPMENT
- FAULTY GOODS: REPAIR REPLACEMENT REFUND
- GIFTS
- SECOND-HAND GOODS

ONLINE
- TRY RESEARCH WITHIN EU
- DON'T USE A PUBLIC COMPUTER OR WIRELESS CONNECTION
- LOOK FOR ACTIVITIES
- PAYMENT SECURE

108

RIGHTS AND RESPONSIBILITIES OF CONSUMERS | 1.7

Be Prepared: My Support Sheets

Completing the activities below will help you to reflect on and reinforce your learning before you move on to the next unit.

- Write down the **key terms** in this unit and make sure you understand them. See if they match the ones at the back of the book.
- List the key **concepts/themes** in this unit.
- List the **three most interesting points** about this unit.

Make a presentation

Make a group presentation on the rights and responsibilities of consumers. The presentation should last between one and three minutes. The best presentations are well researched, provide evidence to support claims, display an interest in the topic and use variety, creativity and superb communication skills to hold the audience's attention. Look at Unit 1.9 when you are doing your research.
You might like to create a Padlet notice board (www.padlet.com) and include it in your presentation.

Padlet is a free, online 'virtual wall' tool where users can express thoughts on topics of their choice. It's like a piece of paper, but on the Web.

THE SIZZLING SEAT

A chair is placed facing the class and a student is given a character.

For example: **Be the informed consumer**.

Class groups spend five minutes thinking up challenging questions to ask the character.

Students ask the character their questions and the character attempts to answer them.

Afterwards the class consider the following questions:

1. What did you learn from this exercise?
2. What did you find fascinating and helpful?
3. Would you challenge anything that the character said? Give reasons.
4. Has this exercise changed your opinion? Give reasons.

1.7 BE BUSINESS: PERSONAL FINANCE

QUESTION TIME

1. Explain the rights of a consumer.
2. What advice would you give to a consumer who is about to make a purchase online?
3. Have you rights when you buy products in sales?
4. Explain the responsibilities of a consumer.
5. Create a summary of this unit using the fishbone template on p. 546.

Stop and think

Do I have any questions or concerns?

What are the mistakes or errors I made in this unit?

EVALUATE MY LEARNING: DAR

Describe
- Did I/we meet my/our learning intentions?
- What went well? What are my/our strengths?

Assess
- How did I/we work with others?
- Were there challenges?

Recommend
- How might I improve?
- What skills and learning might I apply to new situations?

Do your **Key Check** in the workbook for this unit and then mark your learning position on the following rating scale:

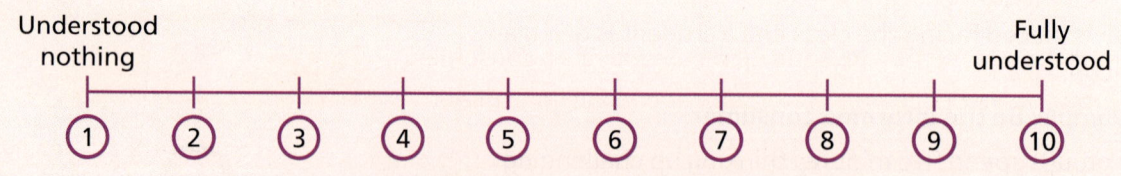

Understood nothing 1 2 3 4 5 6 7 8 9 10 Fully understood

How can you move up the rating scale? What can you **say, make, write** and **do** to illustrate your learning?

CBA 2 Presentation:
Will I use this unit for my topic for **Enterprise in Action and Finance in Action**?

You need to be preparing for your CBAs

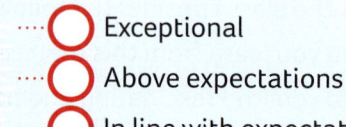

- Exceptional
- Above expectations
- In line with expectations
- Yet to meet expectations

1.8 SERVICES, CONSUMER AGENCIES, FINANCIAL INSTITUTIONS

Compare the services provided by consumer agencies and financial institutions to assist and support customers.

Learning Intentions

At the end of this unit I will:

- Be able to explain what consumerism is
- Be able to list the various consumer agencies in Ireland and understand what they do
- Value rights of and supports for consumers

Key Concepts

- ✓ Consumerism
- ✓ Consumer agencies
- ✓ Financial institutions

Making the links with other LOs:

- 1.5 Personal saving and borrowing
- 1.7 Rights and responsibilities of consumers
- 1.9 Ethics and sustainable consumption
- 1.10 Globalisation and technology

Wonderful Worthwhile Websites

www.ccpc.ie
www.ethicalconsumer.org
www.citizensinformation.ie

Are there other LOs?

'3Ts' = Think, Turn, Talk

- In what ways might you stand up for yourself as a consumer?
- Do you know of any organisations that protect consumers?
- Why might consumers need protection?

Consumerism involves protecting consumers and promoting their interests.

CONSUMER COMPLAINTS

If you are dissatisfied with any product or service you buy, you should let the seller know. If you do not inform the business, it will not rectify the problem and other consumers may suffer as well. If you are not satisfied with the response, it is your right to make a formal complaint.

1.8 BE BUSINESS: PERSONAL FINANCE

WORKING WITH OTHERS

- All class members should complete this brief questionnaire:

	Yes	No
Do you know how to complain if goods are faulty?	☐	☐
Are you confident enough to make a complaint?	☐	☐

- Collate the results. Calculate the percentages answering Yes and No for each question.
- Create some bar charts or other suitable graphical diagrams to present the results.

KNOW HOW TO COMPLAIN

If, as a consumer, you come across a problem with a product/service, you can use your rights to fix the problem. It is therefore important to be aware of these rights.

The following are the eight steps in making a complaint.

Step 1	Know your rights	There are certain times when you can't complain, e.g. if you change your mind or misused a product/service.
Step 2	Know your documents	Gather all **related documents** (adverts, contracts, photographs, emails, etc.) Remember you will need proof of purchase – a receipt or a bank statement.
Step 3	Know your time	**Act quickly!** If you keep using the faulty good, it shows that you are probably accepting it and that can weaken your case. Some services state that you must make a complaint within a certain time period, e.g. with some package holidays you must make a complaint within 28 days after you return from the holiday.
Step 4	Know who to contact	Contact the **person in charge**. Give them the opportunity to put things right.
Step 5	Informal complaint	It might be a good idea to phone first or have a **face-to-face** discussion. Remember: Be polite and calm, explain your problem, state your rights, tell them what you want (a refund, repair or replacement).
Step 6	Formal complaint	If your problem continues, you may decide to make your complaint more formal by writing a letter or email. Remember the advice in Step 5.
Step 7	Know how to seek help	If you are still unsatisfied, contact **external agencies**. The CCPC and Citizens Information can give advice on where to go, for example: • The Advertising Standards Authority for Ireland (ASAI) – complaints about an advertisement • Trade associations – complaints about a type of business, e.g. Magazines Ireland is the trade association of magazine publishers • Ombudsman – complaints about certain public bodies, e.g. government departments and the HSE • Financial Services Ombudsman – complaints about financial institutions and insurance companies.
Step 8	Know when you can take legal action	In some cases you may be able to take **legal action**. In that case you need to contact a solicitor. In the Small Claims court (see p. 116) you can make claims up to €2,000.

In most cases the person/organisation will want to ensure that complaints are dealt with efficiently and if they have provided inferior goods or services, they will follow with apologies and usually try to exceed expectations if possible.

SERVICES, CONSUMER AGENCIES, FINANCIAL INSTITUTIONS — 1.8

Financial Services Ombudsman

CASE STUDY: MAKING A COMPLAINT ABOUT A FINANCIAL INSTITUTION

Step 1: Identify the problem and gather all necessary documentation for evidence.

Step 2: Try to sort out your complaint with the financial institution directly. Talk calmly to the contact person, explaining your problem and stating clearly the solution you want (e.g. an explanation, an apology or compensation). Many problems can be sorted out quickly.

Step 3: If the problem remains unresolved, complain formally by putting the complaint in writing to the financial institution. Include your account, policy or reference number in the letter or email. State all relevant facts, dates and names. Again, be as clear as you can about the solution you want. Attach copies of any relevant documents – always keep the original documents for yourself.

Step 4: If you are not happy with the response/outcome, you can take your complaint to an external agency such as the **Financial Services Ombudsman (FSO)**.

The FSO tries to resolve complaints using informal methods, including mediation (negotiation), by telephone and through meetings. If this approach does not resolve the dispute, both parties can have their complaint independently judged. A legally binding finding will be made, and you may receive compensation for any loss you have suffered. If you are unhappy with the finding, you can appeal to the High Court.

If you would prefer to take a case to court rather than refer it to an ombudsman scheme, you are free to do so, but only if you have not referred it to an ombudsman scheme already. Similarly, if you have already taken a case to court, you cannot refer your complaint to an ombudsman scheme later.

LETTER OF COMPLAINT

A letter of complaint is a **formal letter** and it should display your address, the date, the name and address of the person or organisation that you are making the complaint to, and (perhaps) a brief title summarising the contents, at the top of the page.

If you know the name of the owner or manager of the business, use that to open the letter (e.g. Dear Ms Jordan); otherwise use the general Dear Sir/Madam.

Use clear and concise language to state the facts of your complaint:

1. The date when you made the purchase
2. Description of the product/service purchased (e.g. name, serial number, price)
3. Description of the problem (e.g. not working properly because . . ., not completed properly because . . .)
4. Any previous attempts to resolve the problem (e.g. spoke to sales assistant who . . .).

State that you are attaching a copy of your receipt (do not send the original receipt) and any other information you wish to enclose (e.g. a photograph).

State the solution you want – a repair, a replacement or a refund – and request a response within, say, ten working days. If you are happy to be contacted by phone or email, then include your number/address.

Finish with 'Yours sincerely' if you are writing to a named person or 'Yours faithfully' if you are writing to an unnamed person.

WORKING WITH OTHERS

- In pairs, invent a complaint claim 'situation' (perhaps the hairdresser dyed your hair black instead of red or the volume does not work on your new television).
- Individually, write a letter of complaint for your 'situation'.
- Compare and contrast the two letters.

Sample Letter of Complaint

High Street
Letterkenny
Co. Donegal
3 April 2019

Sales Manager
Electric Ireland Ltd
Ring Road
Donegal
Re: Faulty Laptop

Dear Sir/Madam

My name is Margaret Togher. I am a first-year Business Studies student in St Philomena's Secondary School.

I wish to lodge a complaint regarding a laptop (model: QWE123), which I bought for €450 from your shop on 1 April 2019.

The laptop has not worked for me. It fails to store information and deletes all data when I shut it down. The product is faulty.

I am asking you to replace my laptop with one that works properly. I need this problem to be resolved immediately as I have commenced first year and need my laptop for my ePortfolio and to conduct research for all my subjects.

Please find enclosed a copy of the receipt as evidence of my purchase.

Yours faithfully

Margaret Togher

Margaret Togher

CONSUMER REDRESS – PUTTING THINGS RIGHT

Consumer redress means ensuring that you (the consumer) are compensated for a problem with something you have purchased. To make sure that you do not lose out, you are entitled to seek one of the following solutions:

1. Repair
2. Replacement
3. Refund

CHECKING IN...

1. Explain what is meant by the term 'consumerism'.
2. Describe the steps involved in making a complaint to a financial institution.
3. What forms of consumer redress are you entitled to seek?

CONSUMER AGENCIES

There are a number of consumer agencies and institutions that assist and provide services to customers.

WORKING WITH OTHERS

In pairs, see how many consumer agencies and institutions you can list.

COMPETITION AND CONSUMER PROTECTION COMMISSION (CCPC)

The CCPC is the government body responsible for **enforcing consumer protection and competition law** in Ireland. These laws may apply to Ireland alone or to the EU as a whole. For example, the CCPC ensures that product safety standards are being complied with through the EU's **General Product Safety Directive** and other regulations.

It **safeguards the interests of consumers** and seeks to make the marketplace work better for consumers. It represents the views of consumers locally, nationally and internationally.

It provides personal finance **information and education** to consumers through its helpline and website, and by conducting public awareness campaigns and working on financial education programmes for schools and workplaces.

It also works to ensure that markets are competitive and plays a role in **making Ireland a better place in which to do business**.

Top Tip!

As it has an educational brief, you should email the CCPC for advice if you have any questions from a consumer's perspective.

ADVERTISING STANDARDS AUTHORITY FOR IRELAND (ASAI)

The ASAI was set up by the advertising industry to ensure that all commercial advertisements are **legal, decent, honest and truthful**.

It protects consumers by monitoring advertisements in newspapers and magazines, on posters and moving screens, in brochures and messages sent by post, email or text, on television or radio, and online. It deals with complaints from the general public about adverts or other forms of marketing and promotion.

SMALL CLAIMS COURT

The Small Claims service is part of the District Court. It provides a cheap, fast and easy way for consumers to resolve complaints without resorting to a solicitor. A judge listens to both sides and issues a decision. The maximum compensation is **€2,000**.

Consumer claims can be made for faulty goods, bad workmanship, minor damage to your property or the non-return of a rent deposit. Businesses can make claims against other businesses.

Claims cannot be made for debts, personal injuries or breach of leasing or hire purchase agreements.

If you are not satisfied with the decision of the Small Claims Court, you can appeal your case to the Circuit Court. Careful consideration should be given to this decision. Why did your case fail? How likely are you to succeed in another court?

Both the claimant (the consumer making the complaint) and the respondent (the seller being complained about) must be living or based in Ireland. If either party lives or is based in another EU member state, then they must avail of the **European Small Claims Procedure**.

OMBUDSMAN

> An **ombudsman** hears and investigates complaints made by private individuals against government bodies or officials.

The **Office of the Ombudsman** was established to investigate complaints against government departments, the Health Service Executive (HSE), publicly funded third-level education bodies and local authorities. It can now investigate complaints against over 180 public bodies. It provides an independent, impartial and free service.

There is also a **Financial Services Ombudsman**, dealing with financial institutions, including insurance companies; and an **Ombudsman for Children**, which promotes the rights and welfare of children and young people up to 18 years old.

SERVICES, CONSUMER AGENCIES, FINANCIAL INSTITUTIONS 1.8

TRADE ASSOCIATIONS

> A **trade association** is an organisation that represents all the businesses that sell a particular type of product or service.

Most trade associations have developed a **code of conduct** that their members agree to follow. When a dissatisfied customer is not happy with a purchase they have the option of making a complaint to the relevant trade association.

Here are two examples of Irish trade associations:

Irish Health Trade Association (IHTA)

The IHTA represents the interests of manufacturers, importers and distributors of specialist health products in Ireland. These include vitamin and mineral supplements, herbal preparations, homeopathic products, flower remedies, natural body care products and health foods. These products are typically stocked in health/health food stores and also increasingly in community pharmacies nationwide.

Irish Travel Agents Association (ITAA)

The ITAA represents travel agents and tour operators. It also offers consumer advice on holidays, air travel and information from the Department of Foreign Affairs.

CHECKING IN...
1. Describe the role of the CCPC.
2. What is an ombudsman?
3. What is a trade association?

1.8 BE BUSINESS: PERSONAL FINANCE

BE INFORMED...

UNIT 1.8 – SERVICES, CONSUMER AGENCIES, FINANCIAL INSTITUTIONS

COMPETITION & CONSUMER PROTECTION COMMISSION
CCPC
- Enforces consumer protection & competition law in Ireland.
- Also compliance with EU laws.
- Makes Ireland a better place to do business

ADVERTISING STANDARDS AUTHORITY OF IRELAND
ASAI
Advertisements must be
- Legal
- Decent
- Honest
- Truthful

TRADE ASSOCIATION
Organisation that represents all the businesses that sell a particular type of product/service
E.g. **ITAA** represents travel agents and tour operators

SMALL CLAIMS COURT
Part of the district court. Cheap, fast. Deals with complaints. Max compensation €2000

OMBUDSMAN
Complaints – government departments

ALSO **FINANCIAL SERVICES OMBUDSMAN**
Complaints against financial institutions, insurance companies

CONSUMER COMPLAINTS
IF DISSATISFIED INFORM

CONSUMER REDRESS
- Repair
- Replacement
- Refund

SIX STEPS
1. Identify problem
2. Proof of purchase (receipt)
3. Contact provider
4. Complain – letter/email
5. Not satisfied, contact **EXTERNAL ORGANISATION**
6. If still unsatisfied take **LEGAL** action

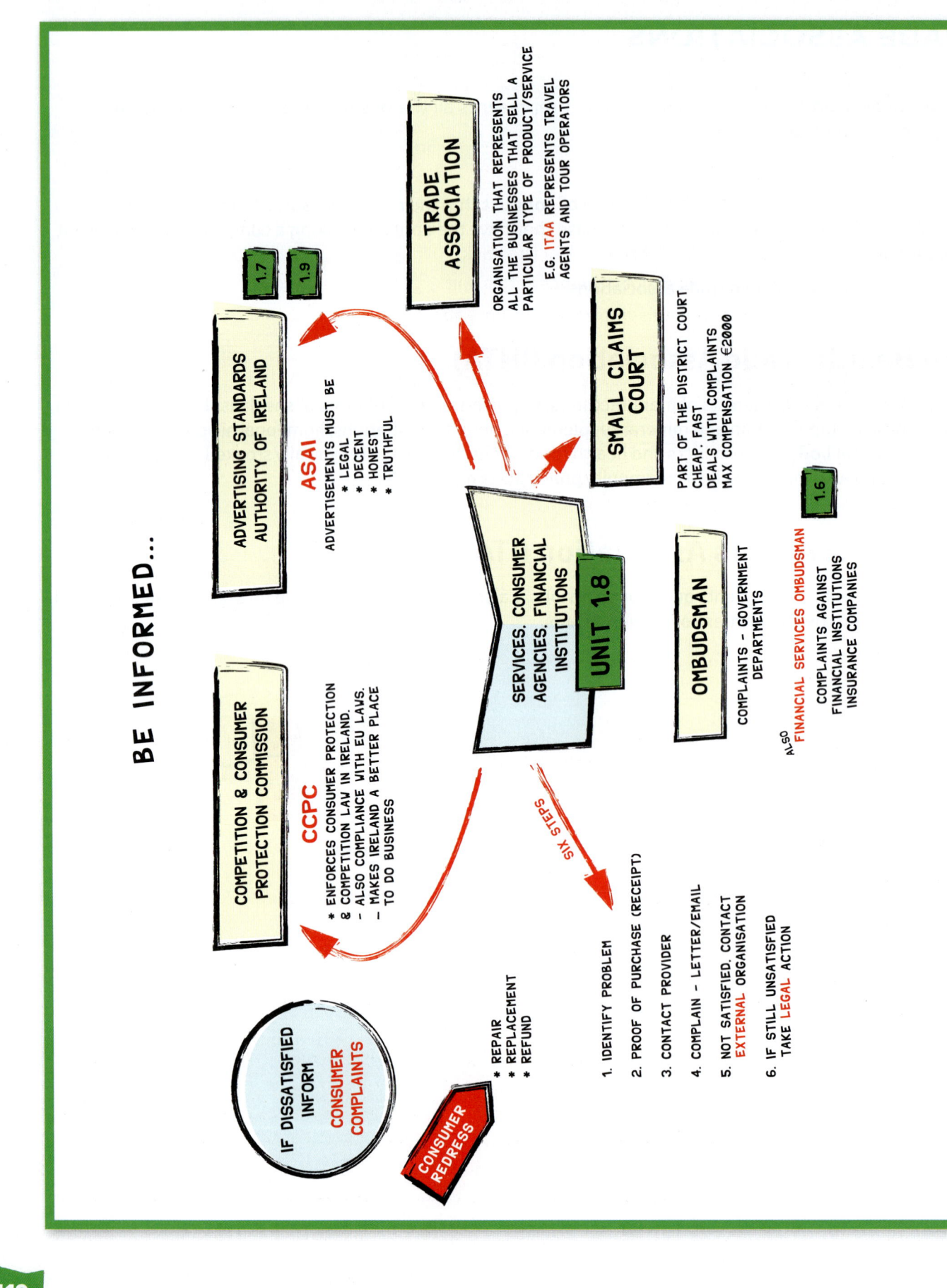

118

SERVICES, CONSUMER AGENCIES, FINANCIAL INSTITUTIONS 1.8

Be Prepared: My Support Sheets

Completing the activities below will help you to reflect on and reinforce your learning before you move on to the next unit.

- Write down the **key terms** in this unit and make sure you understand them. See if they match the ones at the back of the book.
- List the key **concepts/themes** in this unit.
- List the **three most interesting points** about this unit.

Invent a quiz

Jot down three questions on insurance. Choose one of the three questions and write your answer in detail.

Success criteria:
- Title and introduction
- Clear purpose and focus
- Three rights and three responsibilities
- Conclusion – summarise main points
- Information from a variety of sources

Finance in Action Idea!

Write a short report on My Rights and Responsibilities as a Consumer.

QUESTION TIME

1. What important points should a letter of complaint contain?
2. What information will you need when making a complaint?
3. Name an agency that can help you with a consumer problem. Explain how they would help.
4. Write an article to show your understanding of your legal rights as a consumer.
5. Source or name an advertisement that you feel is not honest. What should you do? Who should you contact?
6. If you have a complaint about a financial institution, who might you contact and what should you do?
7. The CCPC protects consumers and ensures that Ireland is a better country to trade. Go to www.ccpc.ie and write a brief report to the European Union (EU) on what the CCPC does.

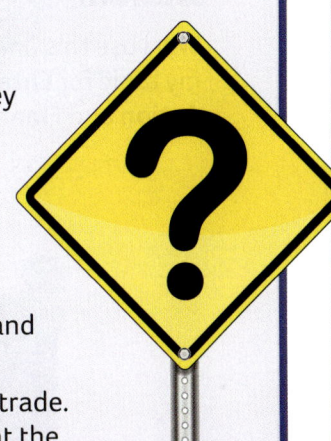

1.8 BE BUSINESS: PERSONAL FINANCE

EVALUATE MY LEARNING: DAR

Evaluation should be ongoing. Initially evaluate yourself, then working with others, your class, and where appropriate the visitor to the classroom.

Describe
- Did I/we meet my/our learning intentions?
- What went well? What are my/our strengths?

Assess
- How did I/we work with others?
- Were there challenges?

Recommend
- How might I improve?
- What skills and learning might I apply to new situations?

Do your **Key Check** in the workbook for this unit and then mark your learning position on the following rating scale:

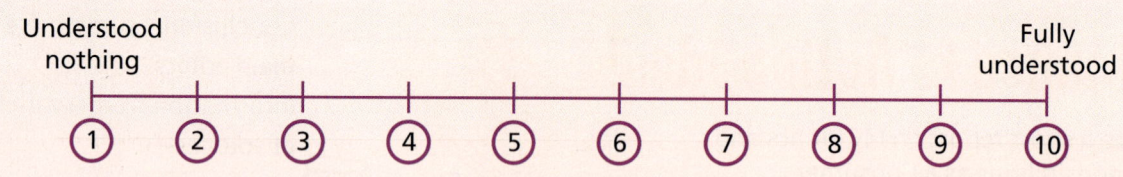

Understood nothing 1 2 3 4 5 6 7 8 9 10 Fully understood

How can you move up the rating scale? What can you **say, make, write** and **do** to illustrate your learning?

CBA 1 Business in Action:
Will I use this unit for my topic for **Enterprise in Action** and **Finance in Action**?

You need to be preparing for your CBAs
- Exceptional
- Above expectations
- In line with expectations
- Yet to meet expectations

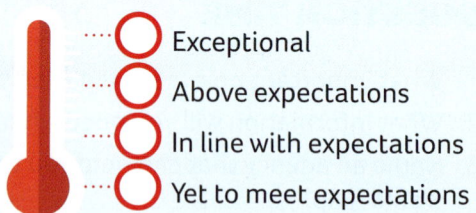

Stop and think
Do I have any questions or concerns?
What are the mistakes or errors I made in this unit?

1.9 ETHICS AND SUSTAINABLE CONSUMPTION

Debate the ethical and sustainability issues that arise from your consumption of goods and services and evaluate how you can contribute to sustainable development through consumer behaviour.

Learning Intentions

At the end of this unit I will:
- Know about ethical issues
- Know about sustainable development and sustainability issues
- Be able to contribute to sustainable development when consuming
- Be able to debate ethical and sustainable issues
- Value our planet

Making the Links with other LOs:

- 1.7 Rights and responsibilities of consumers
- 1.8 Services, consumer agencies, financial institutions
- 2.5 Organisations' positive and negative impacts on communities
- 3.7 Globalisation of trade
- 3.8 European Union: benefits and challenges

Key Concepts

✓ Ethics
✓ Sustainability
✓ Debating

Wonderful Worthwhile Websites

www.ethicalconsumer.org
www.carbonfootprint.com

Are there other LOs?

> **"3Ts" = Think, Turn, Talk**
> - What does it mean to be an ethical consumer? Give examples of ethical consumption.
> - What does it mean to be sustainable? Give examples of sustainable consumption.
> - Why should consumers consider ethical and sustainability issues?

IMPACT OF CONSUMPTION

As an individual, you should know and understand the impact of what you consume on your area, the environment and the planet. For example, you should be aware where the items you buy have come from or where they were manufactured. Businesses and governments also need to understand the impacts of their consumption.

CASE STUDY:
BEN AND JERRY'S
A global company that cares

Ben & Jerry's is a multinational company that produces a wide range of very popular ice creams. The company aims to make a profit from making great ice cream; but Ben & Jerry's wants to do more than that. They have another purpose which they say is:

'To use our company in innovative ways to make the world a better place.'

How do they do that?

- It is part of the company's purpose that all **stakeholders** (suppliers, employees, farmers, customers, etc.) **share in the success** of the company. For example, farmers are given a good price for their harvest, investors get a good return on investment and employees are offered a variety of career opportunities.

- They are always looking for opportunities to **improve the quality of life** locally, nationally and internationally. Some Ben & Jerry's employees are given the funding and time to participate in programmes to improve local communities where they work.

- The company uses all **natural ingredients**. They try and minimise any chemicals used and support local farmers in this. The main source of raw materials is milk, and the Caring Dairy™ programme helps each farmer to use methods that are good for the **environment**. In exchange for participating, Caring Dairy™ farmers get a little extra for their effort.

- They also try to reduce their environmental impact on the **planet** in four areas: water, solid waste, energy, and CO_2 emissions.

- **Fairtrade** is a global movement to make sure small farmers in developing countries can compete in the global economy. When you buy Fairtrade products, you can be sure that the farmers received a fair price for their harvest and use environmentally friendly farming practices. Ben & Jerry's source Fairtrade certified ingredients for all their products.

1. Have you ever bought Ben & Jerry's ice cream? Would the above case study influence your decision to buy their ice cream?

2. How does Ben & Jerry's support people, profit and the planet?

ETHICS AND SUSTAINABLE CONSUMPTION 1.9

ETHICS

Being ethical means taking the right course of action.

Ethics is really about **moral principles**; it is a system that defines **right and wrong** and provides a guiding philosophy for every decision you make.

Over time you will develop your ethics, attitudes, morals, values and beliefs as an individual, as a student in the school, as a citizen in the local community, as a consumer, as an employee/employer/entrepreneur, etc.

> Be ethical: think ethically and act ethically.
>
> Ethics is about rights and wrongs.

BUSINESS ETHICS

Acting ethically takes into account **all** factors when conducting business. Everything from production, all the processes, behaviour with customers, along with the impact on local communities and on the environment. It is about **doing the right thing in everything the company does**. It is all about integrity (honesty, morality), excellence and understanding all stakeholders (interested parties).

If a business is to be ethical it should also be sustainable. There are laws and regulations to encourage businesses (and others) to adopt ethical and sustainable practices. For example, anti-pollution laws place strict limits on levels of CO_2 emissions.

CHECKING IN...

1. Explain what is meant by the term 'ethics'.
2. What is an ethical consumer?
3. What is an ethical business?

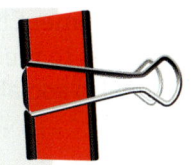

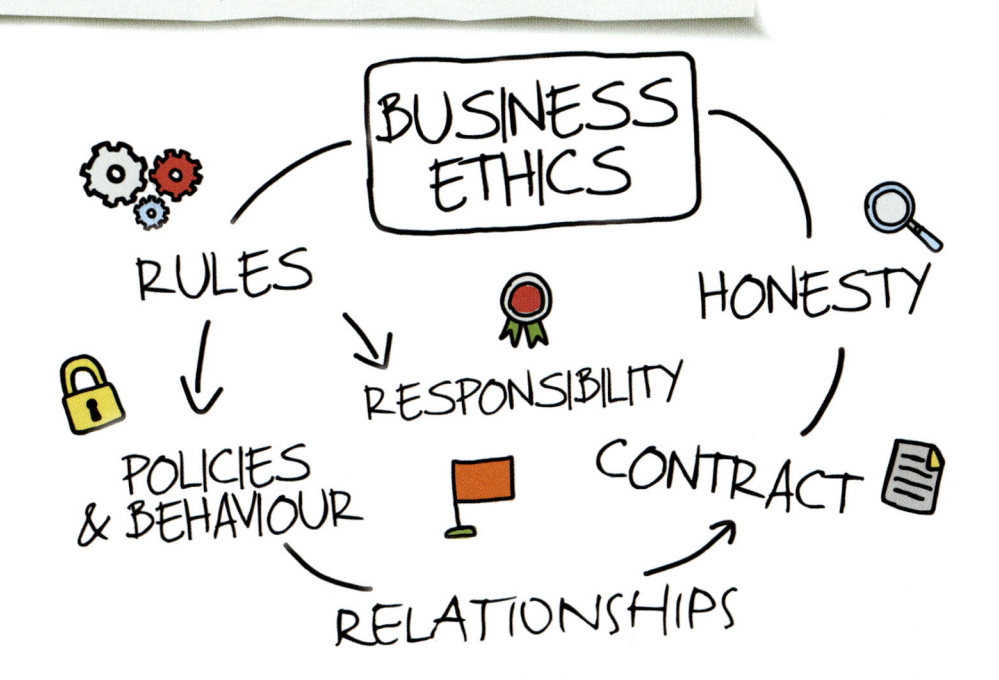

123

1.9 BE BUSINESS: PERSONAL FINANCE

SUSTAINABILITY

Being sustainable means having a balanced approach to economic activity by taking the environment into consideration.

The issue of sustainability must be looked at from the perspectives of individuals, consumers, businesses, governments, large groupings such as the EU, and the planet. Most countries have a national strategy for sustainable development.

We need to satisfy present world energy requirements without compromising the ability of future generations to satisfy their needs. It is all about **respecting the environment** we live in and preventing the depletion (using up) of natural resources.

We need to **reduce the production of waste and reduce the world's energy consumption**. We must look for better ways and, most important, environmentally friendly ways of doing business, while at the same time being economically efficient.

> The EU has determined a strategy to facilitate more sustainable development.

SUSTAINABLE DEVELOPMENT

Sustainable development allows the planet's resources to be protected for future generations and natural assets to be shared.

Everyone should have **access to water, education, health, employment**, and we need to win the fight against hunger and malnutrition.

Another aim of this type of development is to **improve quality of life**, which involves easier access to medical care, social services, culture, and therefore also social wellbeing.

Challenges to Sustainable Development

The challenges include:

- **Population growth** – in **2100** the world's population is expected to be over **11 billion**.
- The planet's **limited energy resources**, especially since individual consumption has been increasing considerably as the less developed countries try to catch up with the others.
- **Global warming** – the overall temperature on earth is rising due to the greenhouse effect of increased levels of CO_2 and other pollutants. Global warming is the result of human activity and it carries risks of shortages due to the disruption of supplies of fresh water (resulting in drought) and fertile soil (resulting in famine). This means that the future development of all species living on earth, including human beings, is under threat.
- Other evidence of climate change: the global **sea level** rose about 17 cm in the twentieth century. The rate in the first decade or so of the twenty-first century is nearly double that of the entire last century.

> Scientists agree: global warming is caused by humans.

ETHICS AND SUSTAINABLE CONSUMPTION 1.9

SUSTAINABLE ENERGY

We need to develop low-cost sustainable energy. It is a moral responsibility for all: you, your family, your local community, organisations and governments.

Extracting and burning fossil fuels (e.g. coal, oil, petrol) for human activities such as electricity generation and transportation, releases CO_2 into the air. Every government needs to plan to **reduce greenhouse gas emissions**. Extensive research and development is the key. Provision and promotion of public transport is also vital.

Everyone else can make an impact on sustainable development by choosing to use **renewable energy sources**, whether partly or exclusively.

Sustainable energy is abundantly provided by the sun, the wind, the earth's heat, waterfalls, tides and the growth of plants. It creates little or no waste or polluting emissions. By using these sustainable sources, we preserve the planet's fossil resources, such as natural gas and petroleum, the reserves of which are naturally limited and will inevitably be exhausted.

In France 75% of energy produced is by **nuclear power**, which has zero carbon energy. However, nuclear power has risks. When there is an accident at a nuclear power station, the consequences can be devastating – see what you can find out about the disaster in Chernobyl. There is also the issue of hazardous waste, although the volume of waste produced is small. Germany hopes to close all its nuclear power plants by 2020 in favour of sustainable energy that is not so risky.

On a smaller scale, you can **buy less.** That way, you can make a difference. Every step counts. It is a shared responsibility and it really is down to every individual.

Floating tidal stream turbine

As consumers we have rights, but just as important are our responsibilities.

We need to be green, think green and act green . . .

It is fundamental not just for the next generation, but for now.

Time to think

Which sources of sustainable energy might be most suited to Ireland? Give reasons for your answer.

How might the government encourage you to use more sustainable forms of energy? Consider incentives such as grants and recycling facilities as well as deterrents such as increased taxes and prices.

What steps could you take to reduce your household's use of non-sustainable energy? Consider your use of transport, sources of electricity, types of heating, holiday destinations, waste disposal habits.

Think before you consume!

1.9 BE BUSINESS: PERSONAL FINANCE

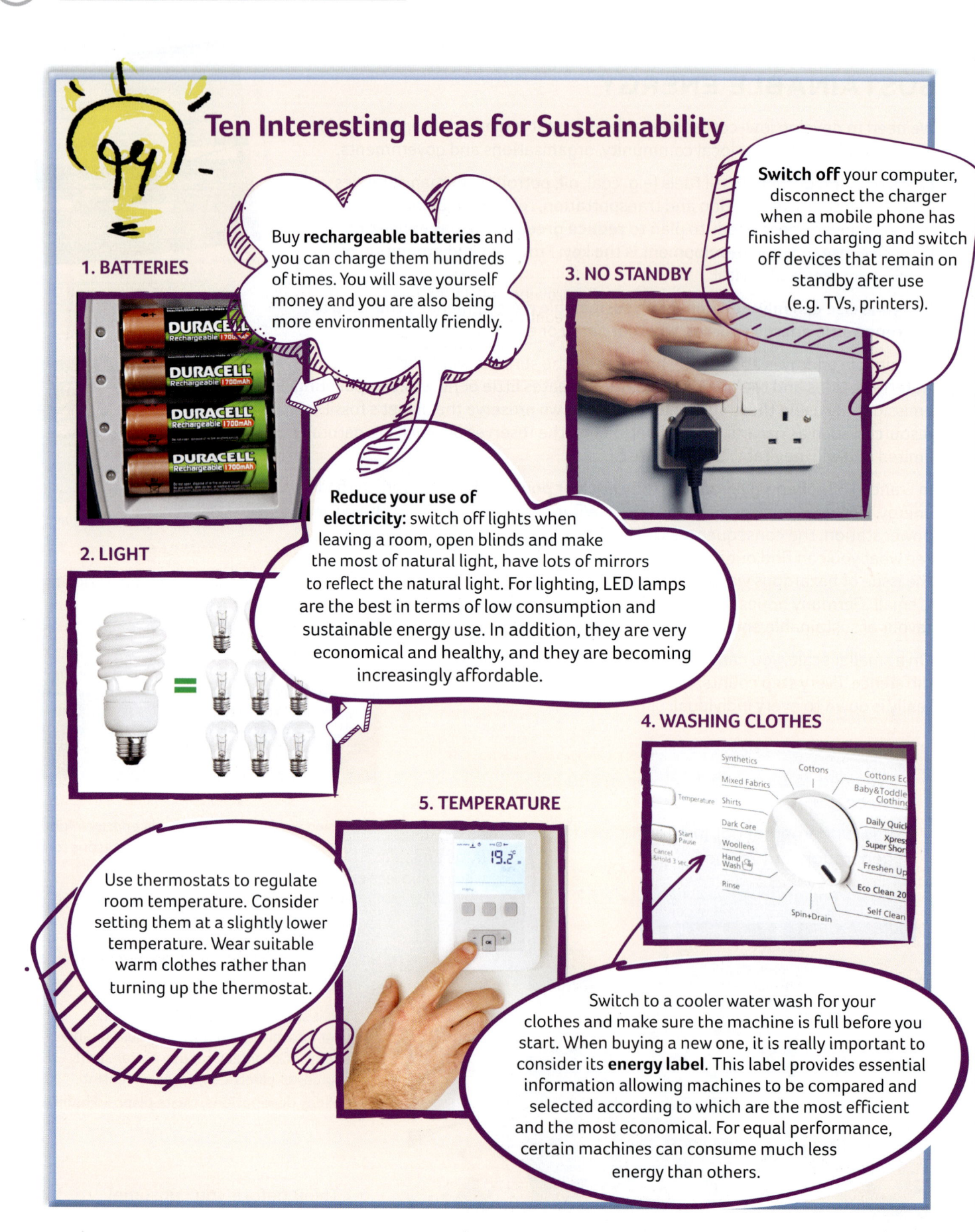

Ten Interesting Ideas for Sustainability

1. BATTERIES

Buy **rechargeable batteries** and you can charge them hundreds of times. You will save yourself money and you are also being more environmentally friendly.

3. NO STANDBY

Switch off your computer, disconnect the charger when a mobile phone has finished charging and switch off devices that remain on standby after use (e.g. TVs, printers).

2. LIGHT

Reduce your use of electricity: switch off lights when leaving a room, open blinds and make the most of natural light, have lots of mirrors to reflect the natural light. For lighting, LED lamps are the best in terms of low consumption and sustainable energy use. In addition, they are very economical and healthy, and they are becoming increasingly affordable.

4. WASHING CLOTHES

5. TEMPERATURE

Use thermostats to regulate room temperature. Consider setting them at a slightly lower temperature. Wear suitable warm clothes rather than turning up the thermostat.

Switch to a cooler water wash for your clothes and make sure the machine is full before you start. When buying a new one, it is really important to consider its **energy label**. This label provides essential information allowing machines to be compared and selected according to which are the most efficient and the most economical. For equal performance, certain machines can consume much less energy than others.

ETHICS AND SUSTAINABLE CONSUMPTION 1.9

Ten Interesting Ideas for Sustainability

6. MEAT

Livestock contribute to greenhouse gas production. Could you eat less meat? Why not try a fish Friday or meatless Monday? Try growing and eating more vegetables and fruits.

7. COMPOSTING

You might start composting kitchen and garden waste: start small with a simple composting bin.

8. RECYCLING

Try to decrease waste. Use less in the first place and then reuse if possible, or recycle. We have become a throwaway culture and we need to change this (e.g. avoid unnecessary packaging, reuse shopping bags).

9. INSULATION

The more insulated a house is (attic and walls) the warmer it will be, and less energy will be required to heat it.

10. NUCLEAR POWER

Nuclear power generates much debate and the issue is complex. Learn about it and form your own opinion on the pros and cons of nuclear energy.

Always dispose of goods in a sustainable way.

1.9 BE BUSINESS: PERSONAL FINANCE

WORKING WITH OTHERS

- Household appliances (microwave ovens, washing machines, tumble dryers, etc.) are all extremely convenient and useful, but they consume a large amount of energy. In pairs, research the energy efficiency of ten household appliances.
- Log on to www.carbonfootprint.com and calculate your carbon footprint. Any surprises?
- What might you and your classmates do to improve your carbon footprint? How can you be more sustainable? As a class, can you come up with 100 ideas? The examples above may inspire you. Be creative!
- Many businesses have been successful by placing importance on the environment. Can you think of or find some examples?

Mobile Phones and Sustainability

Any scientists in the room?

Scarce resources are mined from the earth for use in nearly all consumer electronics. In the case of mobile phones, these include rare metals such as yttrium and scandium, as well as copper, gold, palladium, platinum, aluminium and magnesium. Extracting these resources creates pollution and waste.

The outside of a mobile phone is made from polycarbonate, a manufactured material that has a high impact resistance, relatively good temperature resistance and surface flexibility.

Toxic materials such as lead, cadmium, mercury and polyvinyl chlorides (PVCs) are also common in some mobile phones. These materials pose a risk to the environment if a mobile phone is disposed of in landfill.

How often do you buy/replace a phone?

Do you think about the impact of your decision on the environment? Its **environmental costs**?

Think Globally and Act Locally

Sustainability is not just an idea. **Action** is needed to create a sustainable culture, sustainable structures and sustainable strategic thinking.

Everyone has a role in this: individuals, households, communities, organisations (for-profit and not-for-profit) and governments.

ETHICS AND SUSTAINABLE CONSUMPTION   1.9

CASE STUDY: THINKING AND ACTING GLOBALLY

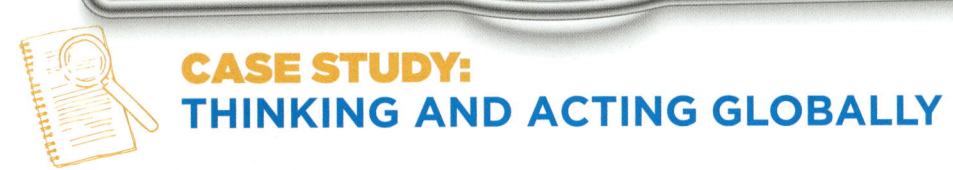

Katie might purchase food in her local supermarket in Ennis, Co. Clare, but some of it has had a long journey to get there. Her shopping bags hold oranges from Israel, tea from Kenya, jam from Monaghan, cereals and nuts grown in America but packed in Ireland, Fair Trade coffee from Brazil, etc.

Katie's family car is German, a Volkswagen, but it was assembled in England at a factory where many of the employees are Indian immigrants. This factory buys parts for its cars from a variety of different countries within and outside the European Union (EU).

When Katie visits McDonald's in Limerick to order a 'Big Mac', it looks and tastes exactly the same as the 'Big Mac' in McDonald's in Hong Kong.

Katie travelled to Dublin by bus to participate in the Student Enterprise Awards. She really enjoyed the event and even got to taste Ciara's cupcakes, which were made in Carlow with cocoa imported from Cameroon.

Interestingly, the Bus Éireann bus was manufactured in northern Spain, but the passenger seats came from southern Italy and they were fitted in Dublin, Ireland.

When Katie watches television, she often learns about events on the other side of the world minutes after they have happened. She watches the same serials and soaps that many teenagers watch globally. She sees the same advertisements tempting her to buy products.

The jeans Katie wears were made in Hungary, under contract for a high street chain of shops. Most of her shirts and tops were made in China, again under contract for a particular seller, although the labels rarely contain the name of the country of origin.

The washing instructions on the labels of Katie's clothes, the barcodes on the goods her family buys, the road signs she passes in the car are all regulated by agreements made at EU level.

Sometimes Katie's mum, Theresa, talks to her about the importance of the environment and of **sustainable development**. Theresa was not happy with Volkswagen and the scandal the company was involved in about carbon dioxide (CO_2) emissions. However, Katie is not really interested in or aware of the impacts on the environment.

1. Are you aware of where the products you use come from?
2. Create your own case study about where your products/services originate. The title should be:
   My Case Study: I may be local, but I act globally in my daily life.

129

1.9 BE BUSINESS: PERSONAL FINANCE

CHECKING IN...
1. Explain what is meant by the term 'sustainability'.
2. Describe three challenges to sustainable development.
3. Name four forms of sustainable energy.

ETHICS AND SUSTAINABILITY DEBATE

It is important to think about the ethical and sustainability issues that arise from your consumption of goods and services. A great way to do this is to take part in a class debate on the topic. Preparing for the debate will help you to form opinions on sustainable development. Listening to the views of others will help you to develop and refine your attitudes and values and perhaps reach a decision to adjust your consumer behaviour. It is all about managing information and thinking.

Debate motion: **It is pointless for me to think about ethical and sustainability issues when I go shopping.**

Top Tip

Debating is a superb way to develop your public speaking and communication (including listening) skills.

DEBATING TIPS

1. Research Stage

Preparing for the debate means you must research the topic thoroughly. Do not rely on hearsay. Source actual **evidence** and ensure your **data** is correct. This will help you to back up your statements during the debate.

Remember that there are other **search engines** besides www.google.ie. Check out www.scoilnet.ie, duckduckgo.com, www.instagrok.com, www.visuwords.com, www.kidrex.org.

Make notes for **both sides of the argument**. Even though you will be arguing either for or against the motion, it is important to have considered the points that the opposing speakers will make as well. Summarise these notes into a pro (for) and con (against) list for the topic.

2. Writing Stage

It will take several attempts to write your debate speech. Start with a rough draft and then you can edit it to sharpen up your arguments and stick to the time limit.

Your speech should have a clear structure:

- **State your name** and why you are speaking.
- **Address your audience**, e.g. 'Chairperson, members of the proposition/opposition, ladies and gentlemen'.
- **Introduce the topic** clearly and concisely, ensuring the audience know which side of the debate you are on.
- Make approximately **four key points** to support your argument – sub-divide points and provide examples, statistics and other evidence.
- End with a **strong conclusion** that summarises your key points.
- **Thank the audience** for their attention.

Use techniques that grab and hold the audience's attention. For example:

- **Ask a direct question** to get them thinking.
- Bring in **real world events** that they can relate to.
- Use **confident, persuasive language**: 'I firmly believe . . .'
- Use language to reveal the **structure of your argument**: 'My first point is . . . second . . . furthermore . . . . finally . . . to conclude . . .'
- **Be persuasive** by appealing to the emotions, sense of values and ethics of the audience.
- Refer to any **visual stimulus** that you intend to provide (e.g. a graph, a photograph or even a prop).
- Reach a definite and **memorable conclusion** – perhaps an apt quotation.
- Always **be literate**: ensure that the spelling, grammar and punctuation are correct in your speech, especially if writing for assessment purposes.

Top Tip

You need to be able to debate your opinions for all three strands. Why not practise by debating the various learning outcomes as you encounter them during this Business Studies course?

3. Rehearsal Stage

Practice makes perfect. Practising your speech is an opportunity to perfect your timing and your delivery:

- Your debate speech should be **carefully timed** so that you can deliver all the points – speaking clearly and naturally – in the time allowed
- Know how to use any **props** or equipment to display graphs, photographs, etc.
- Is your **body language** convincing? Assume that the audience disagrees with you so that you really have to persuade them – be confident and they are more likely to believe you.

  Good luck!

1.9 BE BUSINESS: PERSONAL FINANCE

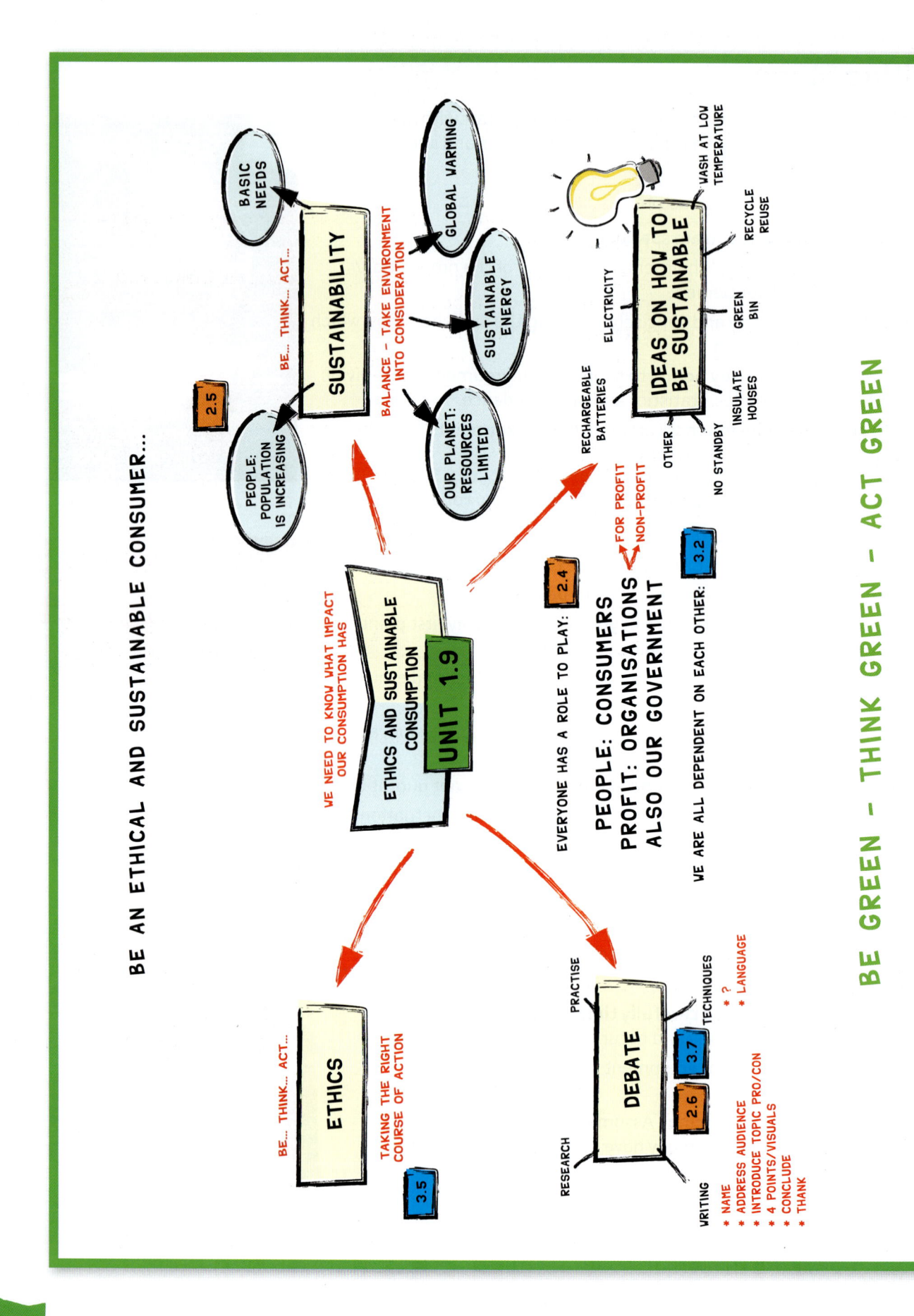

BE AN ETHICAL AND SUSTAINABLE CONSUMER...

SUSTAINABILITY
BE... THINK... ACT...
- BASIC NEEDS
- GLOBAL WARMING
- SUSTAINABLE ENERGY
- OUR PLANET: RESOURCES LIMITED
- PEOPLE: POPULATION IS INCREASING

BALANCE – TAKE ENVIRONMENT INTO CONSIDERATION

2.5

IDEAS ON HOW TO BE SUSTAINABLE
- WASH AT LOW TEMPERATURE
- RECYCLE REUSE
- ELECTRICITY
- GREEN BIN
- INSULATE HOUSES
- NO STANDBY
- OTHER
- RECHARGEABLE BATTERIES

ETHICS AND SUSTAINABLE CONSUMPTION — UNIT 1.9

WE NEED TO KNOW WHAT IMPACT OUR CONSUMPTION HAS

EVERYONE HAS A ROLE TO PLAY:
PEOPLE: CONSUMERS
PROFIT: ORGANISATIONS — FOR PROFIT / NON-PROFIT
ALSO OUR GOVERNMENT

WE ARE ALL DEPENDENT ON EACH OTHER:

2.4   *3.2*

ETHICS
BE... THINK... ACT...
TAKING THE RIGHT COURSE OF ACTION

3.5

DEBATE
- PRACTISE
- RESEARCH
- TECHNIQUES
  - ?
  - LANGUAGE
- WRITING
  * NAME
  * ADDRESS AUDIENCE
  * INTRODUCE TOPIC PRO/CON
  * 4 POINTS/VISUALS
  * CONCLUDE
  * THANK

2.6   *3.7*

BE GREEN – THINK GREEN – ACT GREEN

ETHICS AND SUSTAINABLE CONSUMPTION 1.9

Be Prepared: My Support Sheets

Completing the activities below will help you to reflect on and reinforce your learning before you move on to the next unit.

- Write down the **key terms** in this unit and make sure you understand them. See if they match the ones at the back of the book.
- List the key **concepts/themes** in this unit.
- List the **three most interesting points** about this unit.

Make a group presentation on ethics and sustainability. The presentation should last between one and three minutes. The best presentations are well researched, provide evidence to support claims, display an interest in the topic and use variety including IT, creativity and superb communication skills to hold the audience's attention.

Make a presentation

THE SIZZLING SEAT

A chair is placed facing the class and a student is given a character.

For example: **Be the Minister for Communications, Climate Change and Natural Resources.**

Class groups spend five minutes thinking up challenging questions to ask the character.

For example: **Why does the government not invest in sustainable energy such as solar power?**

Students ask the character their questions and the character attempts to answer them.

Afterwards the class consider the following questions:

1. What did you learn from this exercise?
2. What did you find fascinating and helpful?

1.9 BE BUSINESS: PERSONAL FINANCE

QUESTION TIME

1. Have you ever thought about the effects on the environment when you purchased a product/service? What kind of concerns did you have?
2. Does over-consumption affect the environment? How?
3. Explain sustainable development.
4. We all have a role to play in ensuring sustainability. What might the government do to continue and improve sustainability?
5. How could you become a more sustainable consumer?

EVALUATE MY LEARNING: DAR

Describe
- Did I/we meet my/our learning intentions?
- What went well? What are my/our strengths?

Assess
- How did I/we work with others?
- Were there challenges?

Recommend
- How might I improve?
- What skills and learning might I apply to new situations?

Stop and think

Do I have any questions or concerns?

What are the mistakes or errors I made in this unit?

Do your **Key Check** in the workbook for this unit and then mark your learning position on the following rating scale:

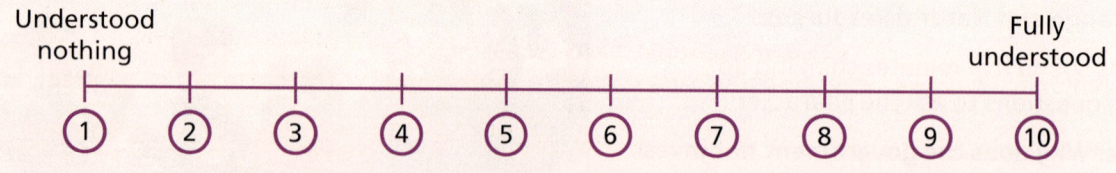

Understood nothing 1 2 3 4 5 6 7 8 9 10 Fully understood

How can you move up the rating scale? What can you **say, make, write** and **do** to illustrate your learning?

CBA 2 Presentation:
Will I use this unit for my topic for my **Presentation**?

You need to be preparing for your CBAs

- Exceptional
- Above expectations
- In line with expectations
- Yet to meet expectations

134

1.10 GLOBALISATION AND TECHNOLOGY

Discuss and evaluate how globalisation and developments in technology impact on consumer choice and behaviour.

Learning Intentions

At the end of this unit I will:

- Know about globalisation
- Be able to list the advantages and disadvantages of globalisation
- Know about technology
- Be able to explain how globalisation and technology impact on consumer choice and behaviour
- Know what globalisation means from the perspectives of people, profit and our planet

Making the links with other LOs:

- 1.7 Rights and responsibilities of consumers
- 1.8 Services, consumer agencies, financial institutions
- 1.9 Ethics and sustainable consumption
- 2.6 Digital technology: benefits and costs
- 3.7 Globalisation of trade
- 3.8 European Union: benefits and challenges

Are there other LOs?

Key Concepts

✓ Globalisation
✓ Technology
✓ Consumerism

Wonderful Worthwhile Websites

www.irishtechnews.net
www.economicsonline.co.uk

'3Ts' = Think, Turn, Talk

- Name as many global brands and businesses as you can.
- What might be the pros and cons of global businesses?
- What role might technology play in globalisation?

GLOBALISATION

Globalisation is the process of turning the world into one massive global marketplace.

Globalisation has occurred because of international trade and improvements in transport and communications. Most people travel and want to use products or services that they encounter around the world. Technology has developed to allow people to communicate and order goods worldwide.

135

1.10 BE BUSINESS: PERSONAL FINANCE

There are many global businesses and brands: Amazon, Apple, Coca-Cola, Disney, Google, Ikea, Intel, Kellogg's, Lego, L'Oréal, Microsoft, Nike, Samsung, Toyota, Visa…

These companies are exceptionally large. They have established manufacturing plants and shops in more than one country and are known as **multinationals** or **transnational companies (TNCs)**.

WORKING WITH OTHERS

- In pairs, list as many multinationals as you can that have located in Ireland.
- Discuss why these companies have opened offices, factories or shops in Ireland. What has attracted them to Ireland?

WHY HAVE SO MANY MULTINATIONALS LOCATED IN IRELAND?

Some of the factors that motivate companies to set up in Ireland include:

1. Low **corporation tax** (the tax paid on company profits)
2. **English-speaking** population and a highly educated and skilled workforce
3. Established **member of the EU**
4. Reasonably good **infrastructure** (e.g. roads, ports, air routes, power supplies, telephone and broadband).

PROS AND CONS OF GLOBALISATION

Globalisation can be both good and bad. Why? Let's view it through the lens of people, profit (i.e. business) and planet:

GLOBALISATION	PROS	CONS
People	• Greater employment opportunities • Greater variety of goods and services	• Excessive choice • Inferior goods • Challenges of consumer protection
Profit	• More competitive prices due to economies of scale • Access to bigger markets, as the world becomes one large market • Lower tax	• May obstruct the development of less developed countries. • Smaller companies may not be able to compete with larger global companies
Planet	• Improved standards of living • Longer lives through science and research	• Countries become increasingly dependent on other countries • Environmental damage • Spread of infectious disease

GLOBALISATION AND THE CONSUMER

At first glance, globalisation should be good for consumers as it will bring greater choice and cheaper products. However, there are many challenges that are of concern to consumers, such as the exploitation of **cheap labour**, the production of **genetically modified (GM) foods** and the **destruction of rainforests**. There can be conflict between what is good economically and what is good for the environment and for society.

There is a range of views on globalisation and it is important for you to be informed about the issues and to form your own opinions.

Time to think

1. Can you think of other pros and cons of globalisation?
2. Do you think globalisation is better for people or for businesses?
3. Do you think globalisation is better for developed countries or developing countries?

Pros and Cons for the Consumer

PROS	CONS
• More choice	• Exploitation of employees
• Lower prices	• GM foods
• Often better quality	• Environmental damage
• More variety of options	• Service can be impersonal

CHECKING IN...

1. Explain what is meant by the term 'globalisation'.
2. Give three reasons why multinationals locate in Ireland.
3. Name four ways in which globalisation affects consumers.

TECHNOLOGY

Technology is the machinery and other devices that have been developed by scientists and engineers to carry out a task, solve a problem, make life easier for human beings, etc. Technology is truly amazing. It has been developing rapidly in recent years and is continuing to change as you are reading this book.

We are surrounded by technology all day, every day. From the alarm clock that wakes you up to the light you switch off before going to bed, it plays a vital role. It can entertain or distract you, it can help you to study or work and it can save your life.

In this section, we will focus on information and communications technology (ICT), which involves using computers, phones and other electronic devices to **transmit information**.

ICT is used for storing, protecting, processing, securing, transferring and retrieving information. It has transformed education: the ways we source and present information.

1.10 BE BUSINESS: PERSONAL FINANCE

> **WORKING WITH OTHERS**
> - In pairs, discuss the ways in which you might use ICT as a consumer.
> - Compare and contrast online shopping with shopping in a town centre.

Technology has made products smaller, faster and suited to meet individual needs. You can have apps to help you with keeping fit and ensuring you stay well. It has also made the world feel like a smaller place. If you have relations or friends living abroad, you can interact with them via Skype and see where they live.

Top Tip

Keep track of and document all the technology that you encounter and use during your Junior Cycle studies. Some technologies and software may be specific to a particular subject.

TECHNOLOGY AND THE CONSUMER

ICT provides today's consumers and potential consumers with powers that our ancestors would never have even contemplated. You have **access to any amount of information**, which of course is interactive and instantaneous across the globe. In fact, you probably have **information overload** and need to be able to process and manage it to make informed decisions. You can research online, order online, pay online and give your personal feedback online.

Traditional businesses such as shops and hotels now provide information about their products and services through their own **websites** and via social networks. In addition, a new world of businesses that operate only online has given consumers another option for purchasing goods.

ICT can help you be a **more informed consumer**. If you need to buy something, you can do your research before you set foot out of the door. Say you want to buy a new iron. You can look at all the irons available and compare their features, read reviews about them, etc. Once you pick the iron you want, you can them compare various shops and find the most competitive price.

Once upon a time, people would visit travel agents and read brochures to decide where to go on holiday. Today, you can do all your research and bookings online and even view a video of your destination. You can **compare prices** on trivago.ie, look at customer reviews on TripAdvisor and view important areas on Google apps.

GLOBALISATION AND TECHNOLOGY 1.10

Social media offers a whole new network to acquire information about products and services. Not only can consumers buy, they can also **influence other consumers** – even people they have never met and are never likely to meet. Reading reviews can affect consumers buying behaviour and now they have a public forum to voice their opinions.

Websites, blogs, Twitter, Instagram, YouTube, Facebook and Myspace are all popular among consumers. These platforms allow people to communicate, share ideas and opinions about a product, and express what they like or dislike worldwide.

Pros and Cons for the Consumer

PROS	CONS
• Access to information	• Information overload
• More informed choices	• Too many options
• Share information with others	• Hard to verify information
• Online shopping anywhere	• Too easy to purchase online without thinking

TECHNOLOGY AND BUSINESS

Technology is revolutionising the way companies do business. Functions such as decision making, customer service, marketing and human resource management are being **transformed** with the use of technology.

In addition, **research** can now be done directly, including qualitative research such as in-depth surveys, to improve sales and consumer loyalty.

Businesses need to stay up to date with (or ahead of) the changes. They need to make sure that all their information is available to consumers and to continue to build a relationship with their customers. They need to seize the opportunity to engage and interact with potential consumers via **social media**. Businesses also make use of social media for traditional marketing practices such as advertising.

See **Unit 2.6** for more on how digital technology affects organisations.

Time to think

1. What might be the advantages and disadvantages of online shopping?
2. What are the implications of online shopping for traditional shops?
3. Should businesses see ICT as a threat or an opportunity?
4. Will there be a need for libraries and information centres in the future?

CHECKING IN...

1. Explain what is meant by the term 'ICT'.
2. Name three ways in which ICT affects consumers.
3. Name three ways in which ICT affects businesses.

1.10 BE BUSINESS: PERSONAL FINANCE

BE AWARE OF GLOBALISATION & TECHNOLOGY

UNIT 1.10 – GLOBALISATION & TECHNOLOGY

GLOBAL BUSINESSES: APPLE – IKEA – GOOGLE

TECHNOLOGY
* BUSINESSES NEED TO BE AWARE OF WHAT CONSUMERS ARE USING… PLATFORMS

TECHNOLOGY GIVES POWER TO CONSUMERS

INFORMATION OVERLOAD!
* RESEARCH ONLINE
* BUY ONLINE
* GIVE ADVICE ONLINE
* INFLUENCE OTHER CONSUMERS

(2.6)

GLOBALISATION

PEOPLE
- EMPLOYMENT
- VARIETY OF GOODS
- **BUT**
- EXCESSIVE CHOICE
- INFERIOR GOODS

PLANET
* IMPROVE STANDARDS
* CAN DO RESEARCH
* **BUT**
* COUNTRIES DEPENDENT
* ENVIRONMENT DAMAGE
* DISEASES – SPREAD

PROFIT
* ECONOMIES OF SCALE – SELL CHEAPER
* LOW TAX
* **BUT**
* LESS DEVELOPED COUNTRIES
* **AND**
* SMALLER COMPANIES CAN'T COMPETE

TURNING THE WORLD INTO ONE MARKET – INTERCONNECTIONS

(3.7)

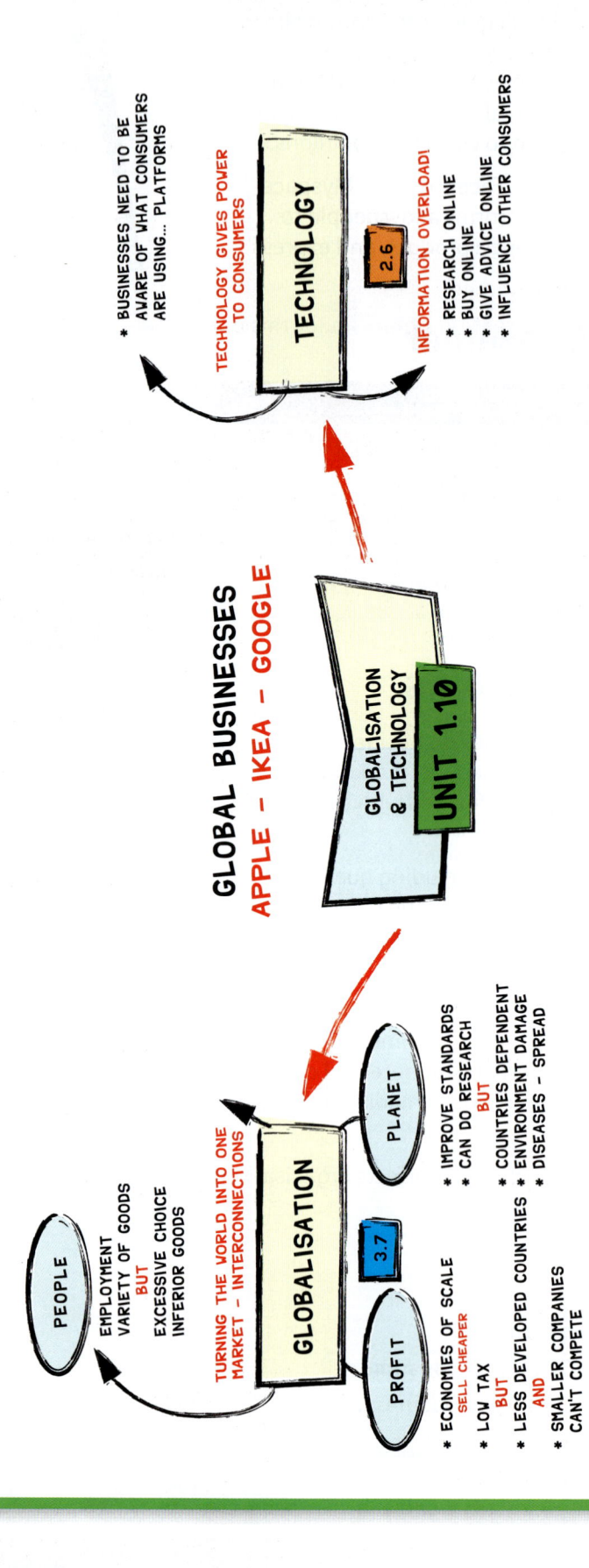

TECHNOLOGY IS FANTASTIC FOR COMPARING GOODS & SERVICES

* MORTGAGE/LOANS
* HOLIDAYS – PRICES – FOOD – FLIGHT – TICKETS – MATCHES
* BOOKING YOUR TRAIN SEAT!

CBA 1 : ENTERPRISE IN ACTION

CBA 2 : PRESENTATION

140

Be Prepared: My Support Sheets

Completing the activities below will help you to reflect on and reinforce your learning before you move on to the next unit.

- Write down the **key terms** in this unit and make sure you understand them. See if they match the ones at the back of the book.
- List the key **concepts/themes** in this unit.
- List the **three most interesting points** about this unit.

Make a presentation

Make an individual presentation on globalisation and technology. The presentation should last between one and three minutes. The best presentations are well researched, provide evidence to support claims, display an interest in the topic and use variety (maybe some IT), creativity and superb communication skills to hold the audience's attention.

Presentation Idea!

Create a presentation on 'The Impact of Technology on Consumerism'. Perhaps use a free video creation tool like Animoto (www.animoto.com) to develop a short digital video that includes music, photos, video clips and text.

Success criteria:
- Clear structure
- Relevant content
- Use vocabulary from this unit
- Include visuals to explain

QUESTION TIME

1. Name a multinational located in Ireland. Why might large multinationals locate in Ireland? How do they benefit the community?
2. Define globalisation and discuss the benefits and concerns about globalisation. Are there more benefits than concerns?
3. Have you ever used technology as a consumer? Was it useful? How does technology benefit consumers? In your opinion, has technology created a demand for different products?
4. How can technology benefit a business?
5. You have decided to go to the next Olympics. List all the ways technology could help you in planning the trip, making the trip and evaluating the trip.
6. Make a list of websites that would help you:
   - book cheap flights
   - find the best value hotels
   - compare the prices of smartphones
   - find specialist sports gear.
7. How can technology influence consumers' decisions?

EVALUATE MY LEARNING: DAR

Describe
- Did I/we meet my/our learning intentions?
- What went well? What are my/our strengths?

Assess
- How did I/we work with others?
- Were there challenges?

Recommend
- How might I improve?
- What skills and learning might I apply to new situations?

Do your **Key Check** in the workbook for this unit and then mark your learning position on the following rating scale:

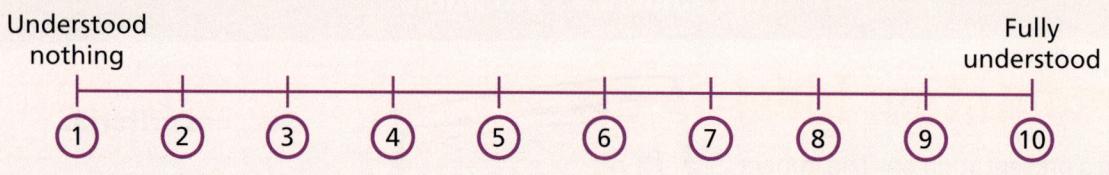

Understood nothing — 1 2 3 4 5 6 7 8 9 10 — Fully understood

How can you move up the rating scale? What can you **say, make, write** and **do** to illustrate your learning?

CBA 1 Business in Action:
Will I use this unit for my topic for **Enterprise in Action and Finance in Action?**

CBA 2 Presentation:
Will I use this unit for my topic for my **Presentation?**

You need to be preparing for your CBAs
- Exceptional
- Above expectations
- In line with expectations
- Yet to meet expectations

Stop and think

Do I have any questions or concerns?

What are the mistakes or errors I made in this unit?

Top Tip!

These skills are really important for your Finance in Action and your individual presentation.

1.11 WAGE SLIP AND PERSONAL TAX LIABILITY

Interpret a wage slip and calculate personal tax liability arising from employment.

Learning Intentions

At the end of this unit I will:
- Know about wages and taxation
- Understand wage slips
- Be able to create and calculate a wage slip

Making the links with other LOs:

- 1.2 Personal income and expenditure
- 1.4 Key personal taxes
- 1.6 Personal insurance
- 3.4 Government revenue and government expenditure
- 3.5 Taxation
- 3.10 Economic issues

Are there other LOs?

Key Concepts
- ✓ Wages
- ✓ Taxation
- ✓ Deductions

Wonderful Worthwhile Websites

www.revenue.ie/en/personal/index.html

www.citizensinformation.ie

"3Ts" = Think, Turn, Talk

- What is a wage slip?
- What would you expect to see on a wage slip?
- What should you do with your wage slip?

WAGE SLIPS

Employees receive payment in return for work. When a business has employees (people employed to work in the business), one of the main functions is to pay employees either weekly or monthly. This process includes calculations and deductions for PAYE, PRSI and USC (see p. 51). In addition, all employees have a legal right to a wage slip (also known as a pay slip).

> A **wage slip** is a statement from your employer showing your gross pay (before deductions), all deductions made and your net pay (after deductions).

1.11 BE BUSINESS: PERSONAL FINANCE

Technology plays a part in wage calculations as most employers use software packages to calculate pay and deductions and to print wage slips.

Your wage slip can be provided to you either in electronic format or in hard copy. As well as gross pay, deductions and net pay, it will state general information on the employer, employee and period of work covered. It may also show the total earned in the year to date.

INFORMATION ON A WAGE SLIP

Name of the employer	Organisation/owner name
Date	The date the wage slip was issued (and the payment was made)
Name of the employee	Person being paid
Personal Public Service (PPS) number	A unique identifier issued by the state for use in any transactions with public bodies (e.g. Revenue Commissioners). It comprises seven numbers and one or two letters.
The week number	The tax year begins on 1st January, so Week 1 is 1st to 7th January
Basic wage	Normal payment
Overtime	Additional payment for hours worked beyond the normal hours
Gross wages	Basic wage plus overtime
Statutory deductions	Compulsory payments – you have no choice
PAYE	Income tax: Pay As You Earn
PRSI	Pay Related Social Insurance
USC	Universal Social Charge
Non-statutory deductions	Voluntary payments – you don't have to pay
Pension	Payment to a fund to receive an income (pension) when you retire
Health insurance	Payment to a private health insurer such as Aviva or VHI
Total deductions	Statutory deductions plus non-statutory deductions
Net wages	Gross wages less total deductions

Gross Pay

Gross pay is your **total pay**. A number of factors will influence your gross pay. For example, you may be employed on a part-time, full-time or contract basis. You may work fixed or flexible hours.

You may be paid by your time, known as **time rate**, which means that your employer must keep track of time worked using a clock in and clock out system.

Or you may be paid for each unit of a product made, known as **piece rate**, to encourage you to work harder, which means that your employer must have a system in place to monitor the units produced.

You may also work overtime, which is usually paid at a higher rate than your normal working rate – often one and a half times or double the normal rate – as an incentive to you to work longer hours.

If you work in sales, you may work on a **commission system**, where you receive a percentage of the sales you make. Usually you will receive a small basic pay, with the majority of your pay being based on your sales. This is a way of motivating employees to sell more.

Gross pay is your basic pay, plus any overtime earnings and in some cases commissions or bonuses.

Deductions

Revisit **Unit 1.4** for a refresher on personal taxation.

Your wage slip will show **statutory deductions** (taxes and charges that must be paid by law) such as PAYE, PRSI and USC, and **non-statutory deductions** (voluntary contributions) such as pension contributions, health insurance fees and union subscriptions.

Total deductions is statutory deductions plus non-statutory deductions.

Net Pay

Revisit **Unit 1.2** for a refresher on pay calculations.

Net pay is your **take-home pay**. It is the amount of money that has been given to you in your pay packet/cheque or that has been transferred to your current account.

Net pay is your gross pay less all deductions.

EXAMPLE 1: WAGE SLIP FOR SIMON HARRIS

The following sample wage slip is for an employee called Simon Harris. Simon's gross pay is €1,000 (basic pay but no overtime or commission). His deductions add up to €450 and include statutory deductions for PAYE, PRSI and USC as well as a non-statutory deduction for a pension contribution. Simon's net pay is €550 or €1,000 (gross pay) less €450 (total deductions). Study the following wage slip carefully and note the information provided.

Employee No. 6666	Employee Name Simon Harris	Date 1/1/2019	Pay Period Week 1
PPS No: 1234567H		PRSI Class	
Earnings	Amount	Deductions	Amount
Basic wage Overtime	1,000.00 300.00	PAYE PRSI USC Pension	320.00 60.00 20.00 50.00
Gross Pay	€1,300.00	Total Deductions	450.00
		Net Pay	€850.00

This sample can be used as a template when you are creating a wage slip in the exercise below.

1.11 BE BUSINESS: PERSONAL FINANCE

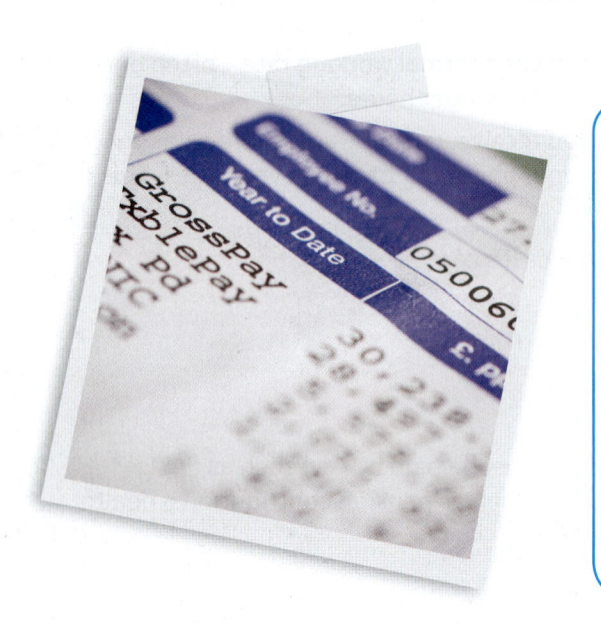

WORKING WITH OTHERS

Create a wage slip (perhaps use Excel or Google Sheets) containing the following headings:

- Employer
- Employee
- Date
- PPS Number
- Week Number
- Gross Pay
- Less Deductions
- Statutory Deductions
- PAYE
- PRSI
- USC
- Non-statutory Deductions
- Pension
- Union
- Health Insurance
- Total Deductions
- Net Pay

CHECKING IN...

1. Explain what is meant by the term 'wage slip'.
2. Name five things you would expect to see on your wage slip.
3. Explain what is meant by the term 'piece rate'.

PAYMENT OF WAGES ACT 1991

All employers must comply with the Payment of Wages Act 1991, which covers methods of payment, making deductions and issuing wage slips.

Employers need to understand:

- How to pay salaries/wages
- The type of wage slip to issue, and the information it should contain
- What taxes should be deducted and the various rates
- The payment processes that need to be in place
- How to avoid unnecessary disputes/rows.

Employees sometimes ask their employer to deduct union fees, insurance contributions, etc. This helps employees to live within their means, as such fees/contributions are paid before they receive their net pay. Employers need to have systems in place to facilitate such deductions and payments.

Most employers today arrange to have wages/salaries transferred from the business's bank account directly into the bank account of the employee using a system called **Paypath**. This is a really quick method for the employee, who can access the money immediately through an **ATM** (automated teller machine). It saves time and is usually error free. However, there is a fee charged by financial institutions (e.g. the bank) for this service.

WAGE SLIP AND PERSONAL TAX LIABILITY 1.11

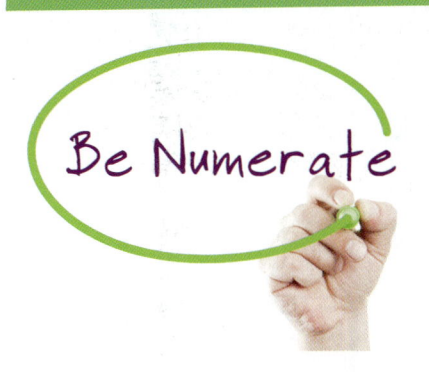

Be Numerate

1. Esther works for Prepared Vegetables selling and delivering prepared vegetables to shops and hotels in Navan. She is paid a basic wage of €180 per week plus a 5% commission on weekly sales in excess of €2,000. Her sales last week were €9,400. Calculate Esther's gross pay for the week.

2. Esther was offered overtime and declined. Why might Esther decline overtime?

3. Esther is considering becoming self-employed and starting her own business, Picture Perfect. Explain, with an example, how being self-employed differs from employment. Outline two good points and two not so good points of being self-employed.

4. Esther will have to recruit one employee. She appoints Kelly Fitzsimmons. Outline three responsibilities of Kelly, as an employee.

5. Esther estimates that the total annual expenses of Picture Perfect will be €160,000. Calculate the average monthly sales required if she is to make an average monthly profit of €4,000.

CHECKING IN...

1. What legislation covers the issuing of wage slips?
2. Name five things that your employer needs to know when preparing your wage slip.
3. Explain what is meant by the term 'Paypath'.

BE BUSINESS: PERSONAL FINANCE

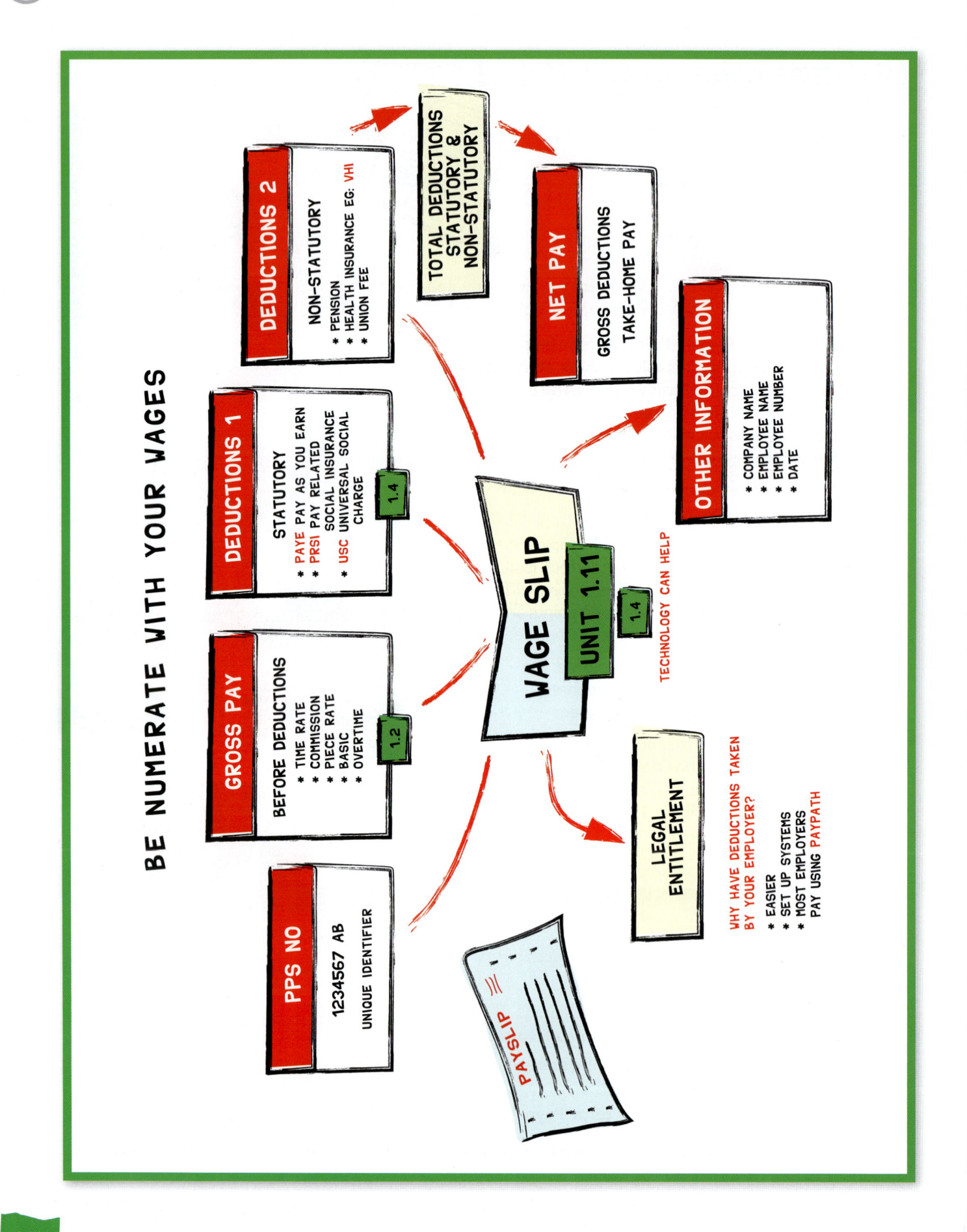

BE NUMERATE WITH YOUR WAGES

PPS NO
1234567 AB
UNIQUE IDENTIFIER

GROSS PAY
BEFORE DEDUCTIONS
* TIME RATE
* COMMISSION
* PIECE RATE
* BASIC
* OVERTIME
(1.2)

DEDUCTIONS 1
STATUTORY
* PAYE PAY AS YOU EARN
* PRSI PAY RELATED SOCIAL INSURANCE
* USC UNIVERSAL SOCIAL CHARGE
(1.4)

DEDUCTIONS 2
NON-STATUTORY
* PENSION
* HEALTH INSURANCE EG: VHI
* UNION FEE

TOTAL DEDUCTIONS STATUTORY & NON-STATUTORY

NET PAY
GROSS DEDUCTIONS
TAKE-HOME PAY

OTHER INFORMATION
* COMPANY NAME
* EMPLOYEE NAME
* EMPLOYEE NUMBER
* DATE

WAGE SLIP
UNIT 1.11
(1.4)
TECHNOLOGY CAN HELP

LEGAL ENTITLEMENT

WHY HAVE DEDUCTIONS TAKEN BY YOUR EMPLOYER?
* EASIER
* SET UP SYSTEMS
* MOST EMPLOYERS PAY USING PAYPATH

PAYSLIP

Be Prepared: My Support Sheets

Completing the activities below will help you to reflect on and reinforce your learning before you move on to the next unit.

- Write down the **key terms** in this unit and make sure you understand them. See if they match the ones at the back of the book.
- List the key **concepts/themes** in this unit.
- List the **three most interesting points** about this unit.

Make a poster

In pairs, create a poster explaining wage slips. Conduct a class vote to select the best poster.

QUESTION TIME

1. Explain and draft a wage slip.
2. Discuss the advantages of Paypath.
3. Compare and contrast gross pay and net pay.
4. Discuss the types and purpose of pay deductions under the headings 'statutory' and 'non-statutory'.
5. Interpret and deconstruct a sample completed wage slip of your choice.
6. Create a summary of this unit using the fishbone template on p. 546.
7. Copy and fill in the star template with important points on wage slips.

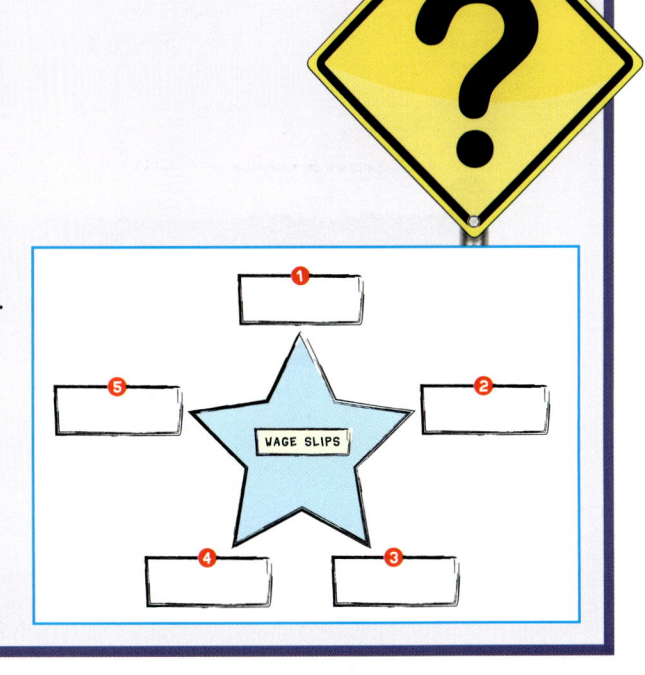

1.11 BE BUSINESS: PERSONAL FINANCE

EVALUATE MY LEARNING: DAR

Describe
- Did I/we meet my/our learning intentions?
- What went well? What are my/our strengths?

Assess
- How did I/we work with others?
- Were there challenges?

Recommend
- How might I improve?
- What skills and learning might I apply to new situations?

Do your **Key Check** in the workbook for this unit and then mark your learning position on the following rating scale:

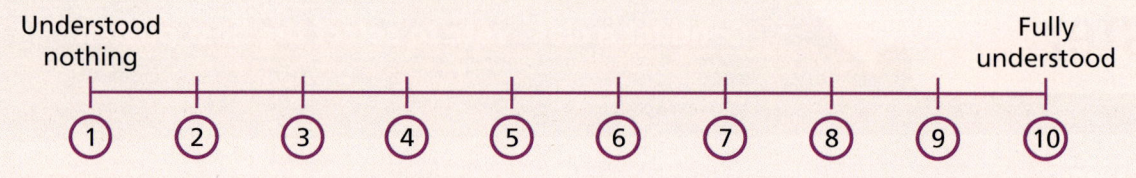

Understood nothing — 1 2 3 4 5 6 7 8 9 10 — Fully understood

How can you move up the rating scale? What can you **say, make, write** and **do** to illustrate your learning?

Stop and think

Do I have any questions or concerns?

What are the mistakes or errors I made in this unit?

1.12 BUDGETING

Prepare and analyse a budget, determine the financial position, recommend appropriate action and present the analysis in tabular and graphic formats.

Learning Intentions

At the end of this unit I will:
- Be able to budget
- Understand income and expenditure for an individual or a household
- Understand and evaluate a surplus and a deficit
- Value financial planning and budgeting

Making the links with other LOs:

- 1.2 Personal income and expenditure
- 1.13 Income, expenditure and bank statements
- 2.11 Cash budget
- 3.4 Government revenue and government expenditure

Are there other LOs?

Key Concepts

- ✓ Income and expenditure
- ✓ Budgets
- ✓ Surpluses and deficits
- ✓ Revised budgets
- ✓ Visual communications

Wonderful Worthwhile Websites

www.makingcents.ie
www.consumerhelp.ie
www.mabs.ie
www.personal.aib.ie
www.mymoneysense.com
www.bankofireland.com

FINANCIAL PLANNING: BUDGETING

Many of us claim to be smart with our finances. However, it can be a complex area. Taking time to understand the options available to you and working out your budget are important habits to develop.

You have already studied income and expenditure in **Unit 1.12**, which are the bases for the preparation of a budget.

Budgeting is not just about calculations. Once a budget has been prepared, you need to be able to determine **financial position** (whether there is extra money or debt) and **recommend appropriate action**.

1.12 BE BUSINESS: PERSONAL FINANCE

WHAT IS A BUDGET?

A budget is a statement of estimated (likely) income and expenses for a period of time.

A budget is an essential and helpful tool that you can use throughout your life. It is important for you as an individual, for your family as part of household planning, as well as for businesses and governments.

A budget will help you to monitor and **control spending**. Drafting a budget may sound boring, but it is really the only way to take control of your money. It is all about **making decisions**, **being prepared**, looking after yourself and your loved ones and even your retirement!

WHY BUDGET?

Budgeting will ensure that you have sufficient money to pay your bills as they occur. In other words, it will help you to be aware of your income and expenditure and to **live within your means**.

Budgeting is knowledge. For example, it highlights months when you will have a lot of expenditure and when you will need to delay discretionary spending or use other methods such as borrowing to pay essential bills.

Discretionary spending for an individual is spending on things that they want to buy rather than on things they need.

Budgeting is an important basis for good financial management, for managing information and for managing yourself.

Preparing a Budget

We will examine the five steps for preparing a household budget later on, but first have a look at the following **simple personal budget** for a student for **one month**.

Top Tip!

Budgeting is easy using Excel. Or you may prefer to try special budgeting websites or apps such as the Credit Union's 'My BudgetBuddy'.

152

BUDGETING 1.12

EXAMPLE 1: HUGH'S SIMPLE PERSONAL BUDGET FOR ONE MONTH

Hugh, a sixth-year student, has decided to prepare a budget for January because he has over-spent on Christmas gifts and is short of money.

He has pocket money and works part time, but he needs to make changes so that he can spend more time studying. He would love to study music and eventually set up his own business in the music industry.

Hugh has €10 cash at the beginning of the month.

He has the following planned income this month:

- Pocket money from his parents of €50
- Part-time work at the local shop for €60
- He gives guitar lessons for €70

He has the following planned **expenditure** (spending) this month:

- He gives his parents €10 for a savings fund
- Food will cost €60
- Guitar costs will be €20
- He will use phone credit of €20
- He will spend €30 on entertainment
- He will buy a birthday gift for €20

Here is how that information is placed in a budget. Study it carefully and then answer the questions below.

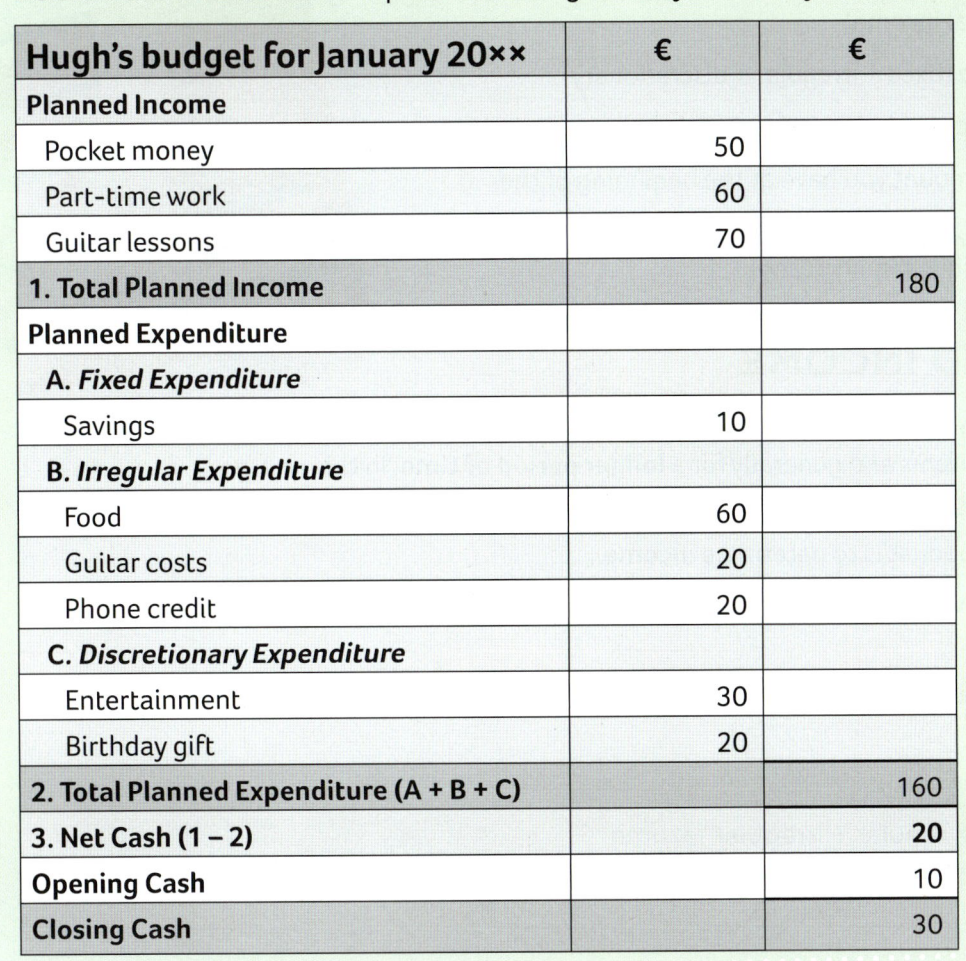

Hugh's budget for January 20××	€	€
Planned Income		
Pocket money	50	
Part-time work	60	
Guitar lessons	70	
1. Total Planned Income		180
Planned Expenditure		
A. *Fixed Expenditure*		
Savings	10	
B. *Irregular Expenditure*		
Food	60	
Guitar costs	20	
Phone credit	20	
C. *Discretionary Expenditure*		
Entertainment	30	
Birthday gift	20	
2. Total Planned Expenditure (A + B + C)		160
3. Net Cash (1 − 2)		**20**
Opening Cash		10
Closing Cash		30

153

1.12 BE BUSINESS: PERSONAL FINANCE

CHECKING IN...

1. What is Hugh's opening cash for February?
2. Did Hugh live within his means in January?
3. What expense might Hugh reduce?
4. Hugh's parents invest the €10 he saves each month in a fund for him to use later. Why might Hugh's parents do this?
5. What changes would Hugh need to make if he were to give up his part-time work while he studies for his exams?
6. Present Hugh's budget graphically. Include a title and labels and make sure that the data is accurate.
7. Create your own personal budget for next month, using a template similar to Hugh's.

Always record information precisely, units under units, aligning your figures carefully:

28,456
1,356
224
20
30,056

CREATING A HOUSEHOLD BUDGET

When preparing a budget you need to work out:

Step 1. Planned income (total income)

Step 2. Planned expenditure (fixed + irregular + discretionary)

Step 3. Net cash (planned income - planned expenditure)

Step 4. Opening cash (the amount you have at the beginning of the month)

Step 5. Closing cash (net cash + opening cash)

STEP 1: PLANNED INCOME

When creating a budget for a **household**, the basic concepts shown in Hugh's budget apply, but with more items and generally for a **longer period of time**. In this unit we will prepare a household budget for Mr and Mrs Smith for three months.

The first step in preparing a budget is to determine **income**.

Regular income is received every week or every month (e.g. wage, salary, jobseeker's benefits, student grant and pension).

Irregular income is only received now and again (e.g. a bonus, overtime, bingo winnings, local GAA lottery win and Prize Bond win).

> **Total planned income** = regular + irregular income

154

BUDGETING 1.12

EXAMPLE 2: SMITHS' PLANNED INCOME FOR THREE MONTHS

The Smith family have the following **regular income**:

- Mr Smith earns a salary of €2,150 per month.
- Mrs Smith earns a salary of €660 per month.
- The Smiths receive child benefit of €140 per month.

They also have some **irregular income**:

- In February, the couple will receive additional income of €6,800.

They have recorded their planned income as follows:

	Jan €	Feb €	March €	Total €
Planned Income				
Mr Smith wage	2,150	2,150	3,150	7,450
Mrs Smith wage	660	660	660	1,980
Child benefit	140	140	140	420
Other		6,800		6,800
1. Total Planned Income	2,950	9,750	3,950	16,650

If you add up all the incomes down (total of each row) and then all the incomes across (total of each column), both should add up to the same figure, in this case €16,650.

CHECKING IN...

1. How much did Mr Smith earn in wages for the three months?
2. How much income did the Smiths receive in February? Break this down into regular and irregular income.
3. How much regular income did the Smiths receive for the three months?
4. How much irregular income did the Smiths receive for the three months?
5. The Smiths received additional income of €6,800 in February. What might that be?

WORKING WITH OTHERS

Copy and complete the following table to show your understanding of income.

Person	Regular income	Irregular income	Picture/photo
Post-primary student			
Employed			
Unemployed			
Retired			

STEP 2: PLANNED EXPENDITURE

The second step in preparing a budget is to determine your expenditure.

Fixed expenditure is predictable every week or every month (e.g. rent, bus fares).

Irregular expenditure varies with usage (e.g. electricity bill).

Discretionary expenditure is for items such as holidays or gifts.

Discretionary spending should be planned for only after you have budgeted for fixed and irregular expenditure.

Total expenditure = fixed expenditure + irregular expenditure + discretionary expenditure

EXAMPLE 3: SMITHS' FIXED EXPENDITURE FOR THREE MONTHS

The Smiths have the following expected **fixed expenditure** for the next three months:

- Mortgage repayments to Bank of Ireland (BOI) will be €800 per month in January and February and €864 in March.
- Loan repayments to AIB will be €400 in January and €3,500 in February.
- Car insurance will be €65 in January and €35 per month in February and March.

They have recorded their planned fixed expenditure as follows:

	Jan €	Feb €	March €	Total €
A. Fixed Expenditure				
BOI mortgage	800	800	864	2,464
AIB loan	400	3,500		3,900
Car insurance	65	35	35	135
Subtotal	**1,265**	**4,335**	**899**	**6,499**

If you add up all the incomes down (total of each row) and then all the incomes across (total of each column), both should add up to the same figure, in this case €6,499.

CHECKING IN...

1. How much do the Smiths spend on car insurance for the three months?
2. How much fixed expenditure do the Smiths have in January?
3. Why might the Smiths' mortgage repayments have to increase in March?
4. What do the varying repayments on the AIB loan suggest to you?
5. Why might the Smiths' car insurance be less expensive after January?

Top Tip!

Even though some expenses are priced **annually** (yearly), such as car insurance, you can opt to set up a direct debit to pay them in monthly instalments.

BUDGETING 1.12

EXAMPLE 4: SMITHS' IRREGULAR EXPENDITURE FOR THREE MONTHS

The Smiths have the following expected **irregular expenditure** (on bills that depend on usage) for the next three months:

- The expected household costs are €660 per month.
- Car running costs will be €150 in January and €70 per month for February and March.
- Light and heat will cost €245 in January and €190 in March.
- Mobile phone costs will be €50 per month except in March, when costs will be €140.

They have recorded their planned irregular expenditure as follows:

	Jan €	Feb €	March €	Total €
B. Irregular Expenditure				
Household costs	660	660	660	1,980
Car running costs	150	70	70	290
Light and heat	245		190	435
Mobile phone	50	50	140	240
Subtotal	**1,105**	**780**	**1,060**	**2,945**

If you add up all the incomes down (total of each row) and then all the incomes across (total of each column), both should add up to the same figure, in this case €2,945.

CHECKING IN...

1. How much do the Smiths spend on running their car for the three months?
2. How much irregular expenditure do the Smiths have in March?
3. Suggest how the Smiths manage to keep household costs the same for three months.
4. Why might there be no light and heat costs in February? Why is light and heat less expensive in March than it is in January?
5. Why might the cost of running the Smiths' car be more expensive in January?
6. Why might the Smiths' mobile phone costs be more in March?

157

1.12 BE BUSINESS: PERSONAL FINANCE

EXAMPLE 5: SMITHS' DISCRETIONARY EXPENDITURE FOR THREE MONTHS

The Smiths have the following expected **discretionary expenditure** for the next three months:

- They plan to spend €100 per month on entertainment.
- They are budgeting for gifts of €300 in January and €250 in March.
- They are not going to plan any holidays from January to March.

They have recorded their planned discretionary expenditure as follows:

	Jan €	Feb €	March €	Total €
C. Discretionary Expenditure				
Entertainment	100	100	100	300
Gifts	300		250	550
Holiday				0
Subtotal	400	100	350	850

If you add up all the incomes down (total of each row) and then all the incomes across (total of each column), both should add up to the same figure, in this case €850.

EXAMPLE 6: SMITHS' TOTAL PLANNED EXPENDITURE FOR THREE MONTHS

Total expenditure = fixed + regular + discretionary

	Jan €	Feb €	March €	Total €
A. *Fixed Expenditure Subtotal*	1,265	4,335	899	6,499
B. *Irregular Expenditure Subtotal*	1,105	780	1,060	2,945
C. *Discretionary Expenditure Subtotal*	400	100	350	850
2. Total Planned Expenditure (A + B + C)	2,770	5,215	2,309	10,294

CHECKING IN...

1. How much do the Smiths spend on gifts over the three months?
2. How much discretionary expenditure do the Smiths have in March?
3. What is the Smiths' total planned expenditure for the three months?

STEP 3: NET CASH

Net cash is the difference between your total planned income and your total planned expenditure.

Net cash = total planned income − total planned expenditure.

Putting all their planned income and expenditure together, the Smiths have recorded their net cash as follows:

	Jan €	Feb €	March €	Total €
Planned Income				
Mr Smith wage	2,150	2,150	3,150	7,450
Mrs Smith wage	660	660	660	1,980
Child benefit	140	140	140	420
Other		6,800		6,800
1. Total Planned Income	**2,950**	**9,750**	**3,950**	**16,650**
Planned Expenditure				
A. Fixed Expenditure				
BOI mortgage	800	800	864	2,464
AIB loan	400	3,500		3,900
Car insurance	65	35	35	135
Subtotal	**1,265**	**4,335**	**899**	**6,499**
B. Irregular Expenditure				
Household costs	660	660	660	1,980
Car running costs	150	70	70	290
Light and heat	245		190	435
Mobile phone	50	50	140	240
Subtotal	**1,105**	**780**	**1,060**	**2,945**
C. Discretionary Expenditure				
Entertainment	100	100	100	300
Gifts	300		250	550
Holiday				0
Subtotal	**400**	**100**	**350**	**850**
2. Total Planned Expenditure (A + B + C)	**2,770**	**5,215**	**2,309**	**10,294**
Net cash (1 − 2)	**180**	**4,535**	**1,641**	**6,356**

STEP 4: OPENING CASH

Opening cash = the money that you expect to have at the beginning of the month.

The Smiths have €500 at the beginning of January. Opening cash is placed beneath net cash in the account.

NOTE: The opening cash figure (number) in the **Total** column is always the same as the opening cash figure in the **first month** of the budget.

	Jan €	Feb €	March €	Total €
Net cash	180	4,535	1,641	6,356
Opening cash	500	680	5,215	500

NOTE: The reason the net cash + opening cash from March is not placed in the opening cash Total column is because of closing cash… see below.

STEP 5: CLOSING CASH

Closing cash is the money that you expect to have at the end of the month. Your closing cash for January becomes your opening cash for February. Your closing cash in February will be the opening cash for March.

Closing cash = net cash + opening cash

Here the closing cash in January is €680, and that will be the opening cash in February.

	Jan €	Feb €	March €	Total €
Net cash	180	4,535	1,641	6,356
Opening cash	500	680	5,215	500
Closing cash	680	5,215	6,856	6,856

Have you worked out that the closing cash in the Total is now going to be the opening cash for the next period?

The above shows a surplus of €6,856

If it was a negative – a deficit – you would insert brackets (€6,856)

Now we join up all the different extracts and create a budget for the three months.

THE COMPLETE HOUSEHOLD BUDGET

EXAMPLE 6: THE SMITHS' HOUSEHOLD BUDGET FOR THREE MONTHS

The Smiths' household budget for Jan to Mar 20××	Jan €	Feb €	March €	Total €
Planned Income				
Mr Smith wage	2,150	2,150	3,150	7,450
Mrs Smith wage	660	660	660	1,980
Child benefit	140	140	140	420
Other		6,800		6,800
1. Total Planned Income	**2,950**	**9,750**	**3,950**	**16,650**
Planned Expenditure				
A. *Fixed Expenditure*				
BOI mortgage	800	800	864	2,464
AIB loan	400	3,500		3,900
Car insurance	65	35	35	135
Subtotal	1,265	4,335	899	6,499
B. *Irregular Expenditure*				
Household costs	660	660	660	1,980
Car running costs	150	70	70	290
Light and heat	245		190	435
Mobile phone	50	50	140	240
Subtotal	1,105	780	1,060	2,945
C. *Discretionary Expenditure*				
Entertainment	100	100	100	300
Gifts	300		250	550
Holiday				0
Subtotal	400	100	350	850
2. Total Planned Expenditure (A + B + C)	**2,770**	**5,215**	**2,309**	**10,294**
Net cash (1 − 2)	180	4,535	1,641	6,356
Opening cash	500	680	5,215	500
Closing cash	680	5,215	6,856	6,856

Summary for Creating a Budget

1 Draft a list of your **planned income**. Remember, you have regular income and irregular income.

2 Draft a list of your **planned expenditure**. Remember, you have fixed expenditure, irregular expenditure and discretionary expenditure. However, plan for discretionary spending only when all other bills have been paid.

3 Subtract total expenditure from total income to calculate **net cash**.

4 Add **opening cash** to **net cash** to calculate **closing cash**.

5 The closing cash of the first month becomes the opening cash of the second month, and so on.

6 Remember that the opening cash in the first month will also be the opening cash in the Total column.

CHECKING IN...

Using the Smiths' budget above as an example, create a household budget for the Browne family based on the following information:

The Brownes are preparing a budget for April to June 20××. Here is their information:

Planned Income

Regular
- Mr Browne earns a salary of €2,000 per month.
- Mrs Browne earns a salary of €1,200 per month.
- The Brownes receive child benefit of €140 per month.

Irregular
- Interest on savings will be €500 in June.

Planned Expenditure

Fixed
- Mortgage repayments to Bank of Ireland (BOI) €800 per month.
- Loan repayments to AIB €400 per month.
- Car insurance €60 in April and €80 per month in May and June.

Irregular
- The expected household costs are €600 per month.
- Car running costs will be €70 per month.
- Light and heat will cost €200 in April and €100 in June.
- Mobile phone costs will be €50 per month.

Discretionary
- They plan to spend €200 per month on entertainment.
- They are budgeting for gifts of €300 in April and €50 in May.
- They don't plan on taking holidays from April to June.

ANALYSING THE BUDGET

Budgeting is an invaluable tool to help you manage your money. It can help ensure that you have enough money for the things you need and the things that are important to you.

It is important to remember that a budget has to be analysed, changed, improved and revised on a regular basis because income and/or expenses may change.

When analysing a budget you either have a budget deficit or a budget surplus.

BUDGET DEFICIT

If your budget highlights a potential shortfall or deficit (i.e. **planned income is less than planned expenditure**), what might you do?

1. Take on **extra work** (e.g. overtime or a second job).
2. Raise **additional income** (e.g. rent out a room or sell off some of your possessions).
3. Arrange to pay off bills in **instalments**, e.g. monthly, rather than a single annual (yearly) payment.
4. **Shop around** for cheaper alternatives to your current suppliers; check out comparison websites.
5. **Reduce certain bills and leave out discretionary spending** as it is not a necessity.
6. Perhaps you could **make gifts** rather than buying them.
7. **Borrow** more money (in extreme circumstances only), looking for the lowest cost credit, and only borrowing what you can afford to pay back.

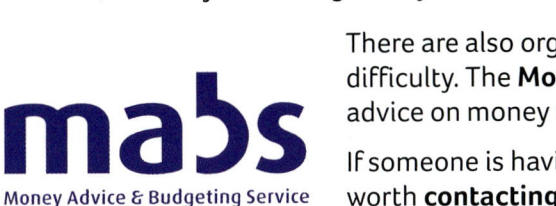

There are also organisations that can help someone in financial difficulty. The **Money Advice and Budgeting Service (MABS)** gives advice on money matters.

If someone is having a problem paying back a loan, it's always worth **contacting the financial institution** that they borrowed from to discuss options, such as paying back over a longer period.

WORKING WITH OTHERS

In pairs, research some tips on escaping money troubles. Create a poster/presentation on the 'Top Ten Tips for Managing Finance'. Ensure that your research is accurate and name your sources.

BUDGET SURPLUS

If your budget identifies months with a potential surplus (i.e. **planned income is greater than planned expenditure**), what might you do?

1. Buy **necessities** that you had done without previously.
2. **Invest** your surplus to try to earn more income.
3. **Save** the surplus in case of unexpected events and expenses.

Be prudent with your money and keep budgeting to ensure that your relationship with money is healthy and happy!

REVISED BUDGET

When there are changes in the financial situation that are not planned, it is a good idea to revise your budget.

What changes might happen?

Positive changes: Income increases/expenditure decreases

Negative changes: Income decreases/expenditure increases

Positive Changes in your Financial Position

Sometimes your financial circumstances improve and your budget must be adjusted. There are a variety of reasons why this might happen:

- There could be an **increase in wages**, for example through a promotion or a rise.
- A **bonus** or extra commission/overtime might be received.
- There may be a Lotto **win**, **gift** or **inheritance** (when someone leaves you something in their will when they die).
- The children's allowance/jobseeker's allowance/social welfare **payment could be increased**.
- Income **taxation could decrease** (PAYE, PRSI or USC).
- There may be a **decrease in expenditure** on insurance, food, etc.
- There may be a **decrease in interest** on a loan, overdraft or mortgage.

Negative Changes in your Financial Position

- There could be a **decrease in wages**, for example through a change of job.
- A **redundancy** (losing your job) could happen and there are no wages for a time.
- There may be **pay cuts** or a reduction in working hours.
- The children's allowance/jobseeker's allowance/social welfare **payment could be decreased**.
- Income **taxation could increase** (PAYE, PRSI or USC).
- There may be an **increase in expenditure** on insurance, food, etc.
- There may be an **increase in interest** on a loan, overdraft or mortgage.

In all these circumstances it's important to implement the changes and revise your budget.

CHECKING IN...

1. What change in circumstances might lead to an increase in income?
2. What changes in circumstances might lead to a decrease in income?
3. What changes might you make to improve your circumstances?

BUDGETING 1.12

REVISING THE SMITHS' BUDGET

The **Smith** household have decided to revise their budget.

After preparing the budget from January to March, the following changes occurred in their financial situation.

1. Mr Smith's salary was offered a new job, with a global IT company, starting in January with a salary of €48,000 annually after tax.

2. Mrs Smith got a promotion and was offered a new salary of €3,000 a month.

3. Mrs Smith thought it was a good idea to buy a new Qashqai car. The car costs €35,000. After trading in her own car she needed a €15,000 loan and decided to secure one from AIB. The repayment on this loan will be €500 a month over 5 years.

4. Insurance has remained the same, however car running costs will now be €300 in total per month.

5. Entertainment will increase by €100 a month.

6. The Smiths decided to go on a family holiday. They will go to New York for St Patrick's Day, which will cost €2,000.

7. All other figures remain the same.

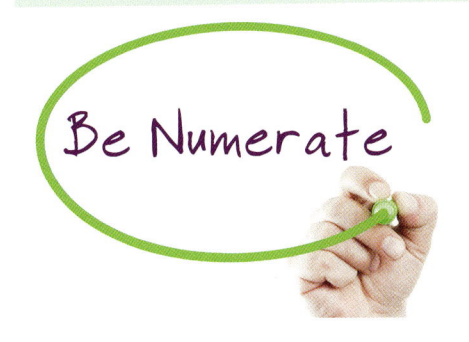

Be Numerate

Some calculations are needed before creating the revised budget. Make sure you understand these before you go any further:

- Mr Smith's salary is €48,000 after tax **annually** = yearly. €48,000/12 = €4,000 per month (up from €2,150)
- Mrs Smith's wages change to €3,000 per month (up from €660)
- AIB loan is €500 per month plus the €400 in Jan (so €900) and €3,500 in February (so €4,000)
- Car running costs are €300 per month (up from €150 in Jan and €70 in February and March)
- Entertainment will increase by €100 (up from €100) = €200 a month
- Family holiday will cost €2,000 in March.

Always have paper to do your rough work and be really careful with calculations.

BE BUSINESS: PERSONAL FINANCE

BUDGETED AND ACTUAL FIGURES

The grey part of the table below shows the Smiths' original budget; the green shows the revised budget. Changed figures are given in orange.

The Smiths' household budget for Jan to Mar 20××, Budgeted versus Actual

	Budgeted Jan €	Budgeted Feb €	Budgeted March €	Budgeted Total €	Revised Jan €	Revised Feb €	Revised March €	Revised Total €
Mr Smith wage	2,150	2,150	3,150	7,450	4,000	4,000	4,000	12,000
Mrs Smith wage	660	660	660	1,980	3,000	3,000	3,000	9,000
Child benefit	140	140	140	420	140	140	140	420
Other		6,800		6,800		6,800		6,800
Total Planned Income	2,950	9,750	3,950	16,650	7,140	13,940	7,140	28,220
Planned Expenditure								
Fixed Expenditure								
BOI mortgage	800	800	864	2,464	800	800	864	2,464
AIB loan	400	3,500		3,900	900	4,000	500	5,400
Car insurance	65	35	35	135	65	35	35	135
Subtotal Fixed	1,265	4,335	899	6,499	1,765	4,835	1,399	7,999
Irregular Expenditure								
Household costs	660	660	660	1,980	660	660	660	1,980
Car running costs	150	70	70	290	300	300	300	900
Light and heat	245		190	435	245		190	435
Mobile phone	50	50	140	240	50	50	140	240
Subtotal Irregular	1,105	780	1,060	2,945	1,255	1,010	1,290	3,555
Discretionary Expenditure								
Entertainment	100	100	100	300	200	200	200	600
Gifts	300		250	550	300		250	550
Holiday				0			2,000	2,000
Subtotal Discretionary	400	100	350	850	500	200	2,450	3,150
Total Planned Expenditure	2,770	5,215	2,309	10,294	3,520	6,045	5,139	14,704
Net cash	180	4,535	1,641	6,356	3,620	7,895	2,001	13,516
Opening cash	500	680	5,215	500	500	4,120	12,015	500
Closing cash	680	5,215	6,856	6,856	4,120	12,015	14,016	14,016

It is a useful exercise to compare your **budget** with your **actual income and expenditure** for the same period. Did you receive or spend more or less than you had planned for? You should be able to account for any differences. The knowledge gained will help you to prepare future budgets.

COMPARISON STATEMENT

When comparing budgeted versus actual you can use a comparison statement, where there is a 'difference' column.

EXAMPLE 7: RYAN HOUSEHOLD COMPARISON STATEMENT

Ryan Household Income Jan to Dec 20××, Budgeted versus Actual			
	Budget	Actual	Difference
	Jan–Dec	Jan–Dec	Use ( ) for a minus figure
	€	€	€
Salaries and wages	50,000	30,000	20,000
Child benefit	1,400	1,400	–
Interest on AIB deposit accounts	540	240	(300)

To get the difference, subtract actual figures from budgeted figures. In this example there is a plus figure, a figure that remains the same and a negative figure:

- €20,000 = plus
- \- = no change
- (300) = minus… to show a minus you always insert brackets around the figure.

BUDGET FOR HOUSEHOLDS: CLIMB THE LADDER

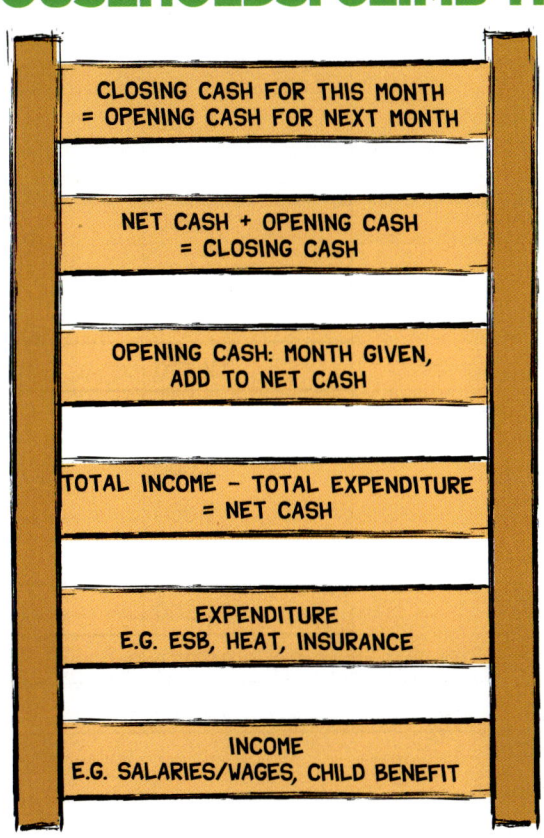

Ladder rungs (bottom to top):
- INCOME E.G. SALARIES/WAGES, CHILD BENEFIT
- EXPENDITURE E.G. ESB, HEAT, INSURANCE
- TOTAL INCOME – TOTAL EXPENDITURE = NET CASH
- OPENING CASH: MONTH GIVEN, ADD TO NET CASH
- NET CASH + OPENING CASH = CLOSING CASH
- CLOSING CASH FOR THIS MONTH = OPENING CASH FOR NEXT MONTH

1.12 BE BUSINESS: PERSONAL FINANCE

CHECKING IN...

1. In pairs, complete the difference column for the Ryan Household Budget Comparison Statement

Ryan Household Budget			
	Budget Jan-Dec €	Actual Jan-Dec €	Difference Use brackets for a minus figure €
Planned Income			
Salaries and wages	52,000	38,480	
Child benefit	3,600	3,900	
Interest on AIB deposit account	540	280	
Local GAA lotto win		4,200	
1. Total Income	56,140	46,860	
Planned Expenditure			
Fixed			
EBS mortgage	10,200	10,605	
Car insurance	670	460	
House insurance	580	551	
A. Subtotal Fixed	11,450	11,616	
Irregular			
Household running costs	8,880	9,990	
Car maintenance	1,640	1,340	
Clothes	1,900	1,750	
Light and heat	3,100	3,782	
Health insurance	1,600	1,808	
B. Subtotal Irregular	17,120	18,670	
Discretionary			
Entertainment	3,000	2,250	
Gifts	1,000	1,300	
Holidays	7,500	4,900	
C. Subtotal Discretionary	11,500	8,450	
2. Total Expenditure (A + B + C)	40,070	38,736	
Net Cash (1 – 2)	16,070	8,124	

BUDGETING 1.12

CHECKING IN...

2. Now view the Carter Budget that shows Budgeted, Actual and Difference. You are required, from your knowledge of budgeting, to suggest a reason for any difference that has occurred.

Carter Household Budget			
	Budget €	Actual €	Difference €
Planned Income			
Salaries and wages	21,000	21,840	840
Child benefit	720	880	160
Interest on savings	250	180	(70)
Other	0	400	400
1. Total Income	**21,970**	**23,300**	**1,330**
Planned Expenditure			
Fixed			
EBS mortgage	4,080	4,230	150
Car insurance	560	476	(84)
House insurance	235	325	90
A. Subtotal Fixed	**11,450**	**11,616**	
Irregular			
Household costs	7,800	8,385	585
Car costs	1,550	1,925	375
Clothing and footwear	2,000	1,700	(300)
Light and heat	1,600	1,504	(96)
Doctor's fees	400	2,900	2,500
B. Subtotal Irregular	**17,120**	**18,670**	
Discretionary			
Holidays	1,560	1,410	(150)
Gifts	300	490	190
Entertainment	1,800	0	(1,800)
C. Subtotal Discretionary	**3,660**	**1,900**	**(1,760)**
2. Total Expenditure (A + B + C)	**21,885**	**23,345**	**1,460**
Net Cash (1 – 2)	85	(45)	(130)
Opening Cash	1,400	1,400	
Closing Cash	1,485	1,355	

PRESENTING DATA GRAPHICALLY

When analysing budgets, it can be helpful to present the data in a graph or a chart. You may decide to draw it yourself or use Excel or Google Sheets to create it. Always add a useful title and clear labels.

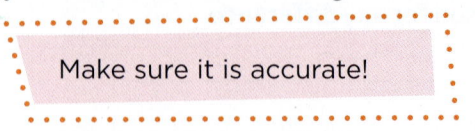

> Make sure it is accurate!

Look back at Hugh's simple personal budget on p. 153. There are many ways to show this information in graphical format. Each format presents the information in a way that allows you to see it from a different perspective.

BAR CHART

A bar graph (also called bar chart) is a graphical display of data using bars of different heights.

We can use bar graphs to show the relative sizes of things and so they are useful when you need to do comparisons.

We can see at a glance that Hugh spends most on his irregular spending and least on his fixed spending. His discretionary spending is half his irregular.

LINE GRAPH

A line graph is a graph that shows information that is connected in some way (such as change over time).

Graphs are a good way to assess trends. The line graph for Hugh's spending below would be more useful if we had more than one month. It would be ideal to show total expenditure the first month, second month and so on and show a trend; whether it is increasing or decreasing.

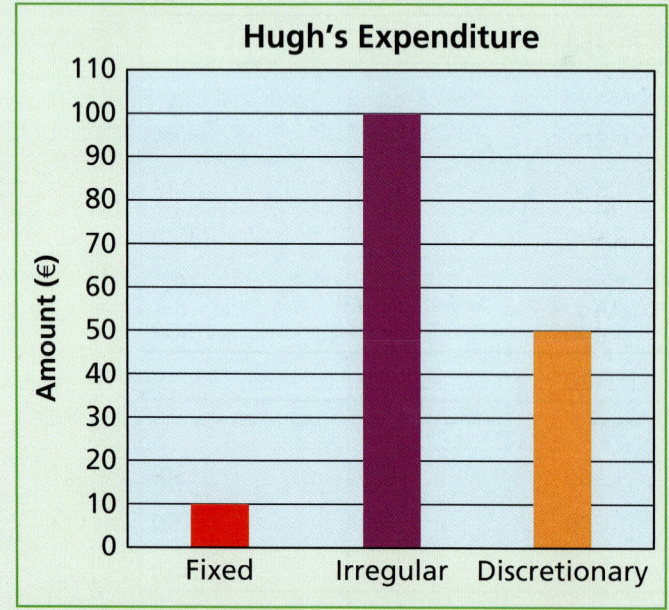

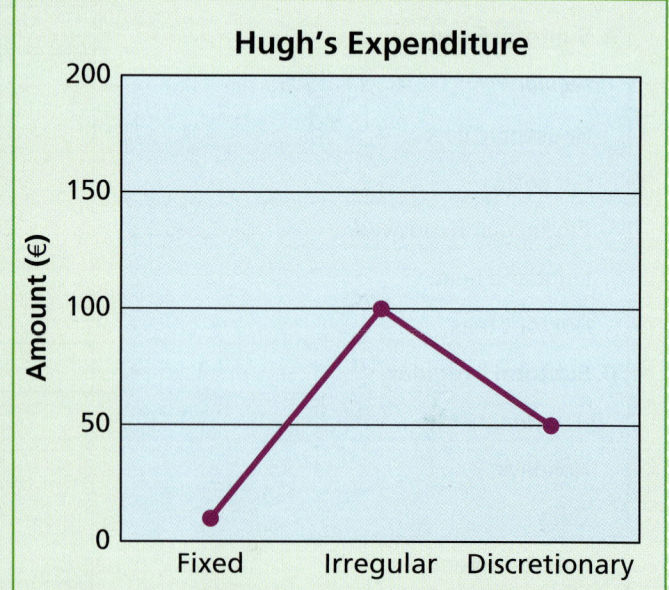

Bar charts can also be presented with horizontal bars.

BUDGETING 1.12

PIE CHART

A pie chart is used to show percentages of a whole.

EXAMPLE: CREATING A PIE CHART

Hugh's total planned expenditure is €160. To find out the percentage of his total expenditure he spend on the various items you would calculate as follows:

€160 = 100%

Fixed expenditure = €10

$$\frac{10}{160} \times \frac{100}{1} = 6.25\%$$

Irregular expenditure = €100

$$\frac{100}{160} \times \frac{100}{1} = 62.5\%$$

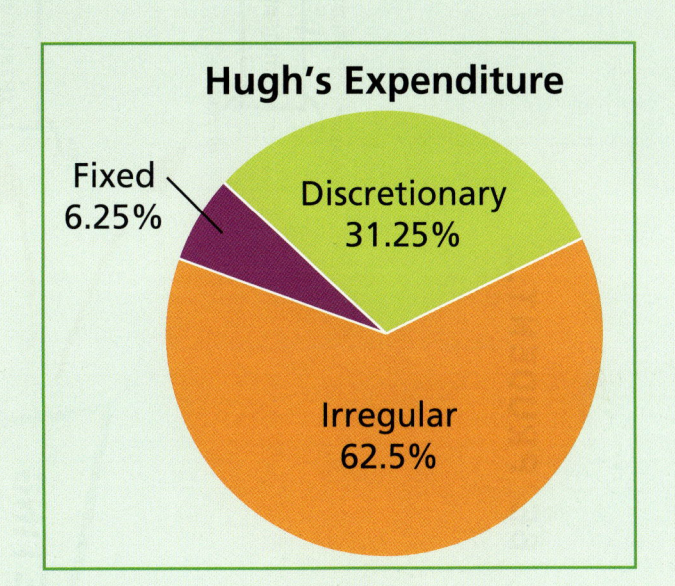

Discretionary expenditure = €50

$$\frac{50}{160} \times \frac{100}{1} = 31.25\%$$

Hugh's Expenditure

- Fixed 6.25%
- Discretionary 31.25%
- Irregular 62.5%

Success criteria:
- Label/title
- Draw to scale
- Label the x-axis and y-axis for charts and graphs
- You may decide to create charts/graphs online

CHECKING IN...

1. Create a bar chart for the Smiths income for January, February and March.

2. Create a line graph showing the Smiths closing cash for January, February and March.

3. Create a pie chart for the Smiths total expenditure for three months, showing Fixed, Irregular and Discretionary.

171

1.12 BE BUSINESS: PERSONAL FINANCE

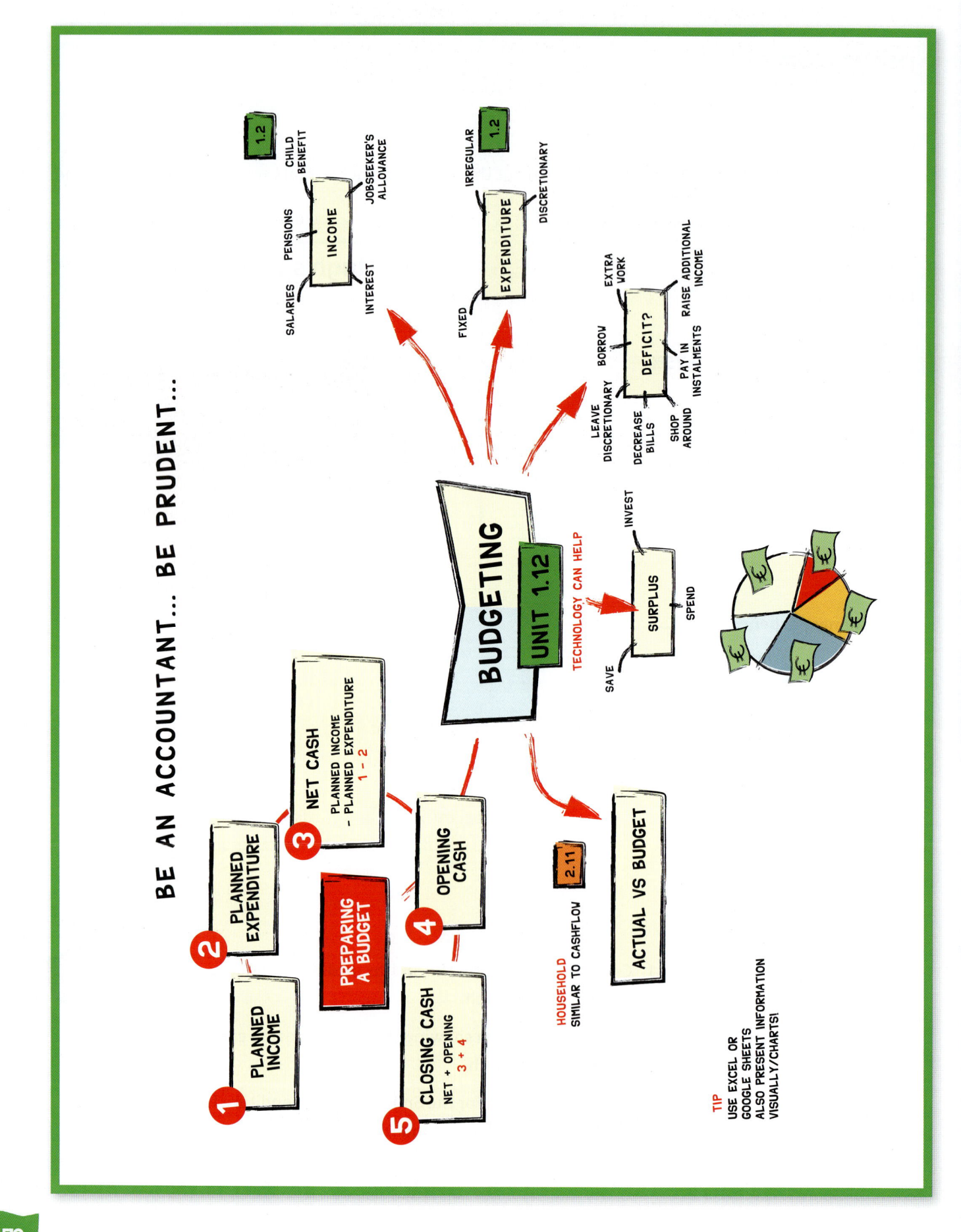

BE AN ACCOUNTANT... BE PRUDENT...

BUDGETING — UNIT 1.12

INCOME (1.2)
- SALARIES
- PENSIONS
- CHILD BENEFIT
- JOBSEEKER'S ALLOWANCE
- INTEREST

EXPENDITURE (1.2)
- FIXED
- IRREGULAR
- DISCRETIONARY

DEFICIT?
- LEAVE DISCRETIONARY
- DECREASE BILLS
- SHOP AROUND
- BORROW
- PAY IN INSTALMENTS
- EXTRA WORK
- RAISE ADDITIONAL INCOME

SURPLUS
- SAVE
- SPEND
- INVEST

TECHNOLOGY CAN HELP

ACTUAL VS BUDGET

HOUSEHOLD — SIMILAR TO CASHFLOW (2.11)

PREPARING A BUDGET

1. **PLANNED INCOME**
2. **PLANNED EXPENDITURE**
3. **NET CASH** — PLANNED INCOME − PLANNED EXPENDITURE (1 − 2)
4. **OPENING CASH**
5. **CLOSING CASH** — NET + OPENING (3 + 4)

TIP
USE EXCEL OR GOOGLE SHEETS
ALSO PRESENT INFORMATION VISUALLY/CHARTS!

172

BUDGETING 1.12

Be Prepared: My Support Sheets

Completing the activities below will help you to reflect on and reinforce your learning before you move on to the next unit.
- Write down the **key terms** in this unit and make sure you understand them. See if they match the ones at the back of the book.
- List the key **concepts/themes** in this unit.
- List the **three most interesting points** about this unit.

Make a poster

Prepare a poster on 'The Importance of Budgeting'.

Stop and think

Do I have any questions or concerns?

What are the mistakes or errors I made in this unit?

EVALUATE MY LEARNING: DAR

Describe
- Did I/we meet my/our learning intentions?
- What went well? What are my/our strengths?

Assess
- How did I/we work with others?
- Were there challenges?

Recommend
- How might I improve?
- What skills and learning might I apply to new situations?

Do your **Key Check** in the workbook for this unit and then mark your learning position on the following rating scale:

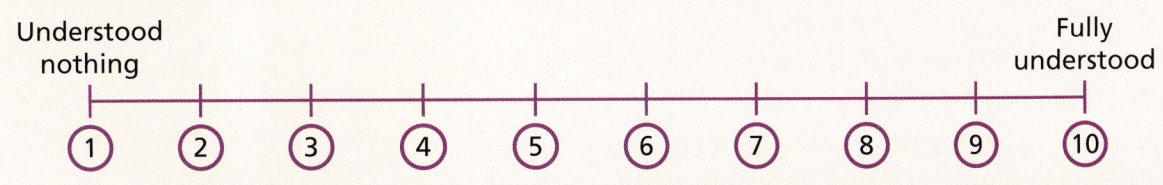

Understood nothing ① ② ③ ④ ⑤ ⑥ ⑦ ⑧ ⑨ ⑩ Fully understood

How can you move up the rating scale? What can you **say**, **make**, **write** and **do** to illustrate your learning?

173

1.13 INCOME, EXPENDITURE AND BANK STATEMENTS

Monitor and calculate income and expenditure data, determine the financial position, recommend appropriate action and present the analysis in tabular and graphic formats.

Learning Intentions

At the end of this unit I will:

- Know about recording income and expenditure in a cash account
- Be able to prepare an analysed cash book
- Understand financial position
- Be able to present information graphically
- Understand bank statements
- Value accounts for individuals and households
- Value financial planning and budgeting

Key Concepts

- ✓ Income and expenditure
- ✓ Cash and bank transactions
- ✓ Tabular and graphic forms
- ✓ Bank statements

Making the Links with other LOs:

- 1.2 Personal income and expenditure
- 2.12 Cash book, ledger and trial balance
- 2.13 Final accounts

'3Ts' = Think, Turn, Talk

- Why should you keep good financial records?
- What is a cash book?
- What should you do with your bank statements?

Are there other LOs?

KEEPING RECORDS

We need to keep a record of what money we receive and what we spend so that we know how much is left over. It can be time-consuming to have to source this information by trawling through wage slips, bills and receipts. It can also be challenging as some bills will be paid online and you may not have printed off a paper record.

A good idea is to create and maintain a cash account, which means that you will always have the information you need on your financial position at your fingertips.

CASH ACCOUNT

A cash account is a way of monitoring your cash income and cash expenditure. You need to keep track of your cash and the only way is to record what happens. We refer to this recording as **keeping accounts**. The cash account can be viewed as the simple building block of an accounting system.

In the previous unit you were budgeting for income and expenditure. In this unit you will be recording the **actual income and expenditure**: the cash that came in and the cash that went out.

If the cash coming in is equal to the cash going out, your accounts will be **balanced**. But if the cash coming in is greater than the cash going out, you will have **surplus** cash that you can save/invest. This will be the same for households, businesses and the government.

PREPARING A CASH ACCOUNT

It is important to learn how to **keep a simple cash account**. Everyone is capable of doing this.

A cash account can be **manual** (i.e. in a book) or **electronic** (e.g. Google Sheets, Excel). Find a system that is easy for you to use and easy for you to understand. However, it is recommended that you start off by recording your accounts manually so that you get a clear understanding of the process before you move on to a software package.

You will study the recording of financial information and accounts in all three strands of this Business Studies course.

Rules for a Cash Account

Cash Account	
Left	**Right**
Cash in	Cash out
Receive	Give
Plus	Minus
Debit side	Credit side

The key principle is:

Left = cash in

Right = cash out

Then you enter the **balance** (difference) on the smallest side.

1.13 BE BUSINESS: PERSONAL FINANCE

IT IS IMPORTANT TO HAVE RULES SO THAT EVERYONE CAN UNDERSTAND

1. Record the date of transactions in order of time, e.g. 1 January, 2 January, 3 January ...
2. Record receipts (who money is coming from) and payments (who money is being paid to).
3. Record the cash amount being paid in (left side) or taken out (right side). Keep the account neat, lining up units under units.

Here is a template for a cash account. It should be divided into six columns, three for the left/debit side and three for the right/credit side.

Cash Account January 20××					
Debit – Cash in – Left			**Right – Cash out – Credit**		
Date	Details (Receipts)	Total cash	Date	Details (Payments)	Total cash
①	②	③	①	②	③
01 Jan	Wages	200	02 Jan	Ticketmaster	40
[Actual date the money was received]	[Where the money was received from]	[Amount of money (euro)]	[Actual date the money was paid out]	[Where the money was spent]	[Amount of money (euro)]

Left = Love it! = **Debit** = Delightful 😃

Right = Rubbish! = **Credit** = Cruel 😒

EXAMPLE 1: CIARA'S CASH ACCOUNT

Let's try a simple example to understand the cash account concept.

Ciara is a post-primary student running her own mini-company, Ciara's Cupcakes. It is essential that she keeps a record of all the business's cash transactions (i.e. anything she buys with cash or sells for cash). All Ciara's business transactions are in cash.

She maintains a cash account to record all these transactions. They are entered into the cash account in chronological order (i.e. in order of time): 1 January, 10 January, 12 January, etc.

Ciara has the following cash transactions. Decide whether each one is cash in or cash out.

Transaction	Which side?
01 Jan Bank loan €1,000	Cash in / Cash out
02 Jan Purchased goods for cash €500	Cash in / Cash out
07 Jan Cash sale €300	Cash in / Cash out
08 Jan Paid wages €200	Cash in / Cash out

Here is Ciara's cash account filled in:

Cash Account					
Debit - Cash in - Left			**Right - Cash out - Credit**		
Date 20××	Details	Total €	Date 20××	Details	Total €
01 Jan	Bank loan	1,000	02 Jan	Purchased goods	500
07 Jan	Sales	300	08 Jan	Paid wages	200

Balancing a Simple Cash Account

The cash account is balanced at the end of a given period, say one month.

1. To do that you must first calculate the **total of the debit side** of the cash account at the end of the month (€1,000 + €300 = €1,300).
2. Then calculate the **total of the credit side** (€500 + €200 = €700) – but don't write it in yet!

Cash Account					
Debit - Cash in - Left			**Right - Cash out - Credit**		
Date 20××	Details	Total €	Date 20××	Details	Total €
01 Jan	Bank loan	1,000	02 Jan	Purchased goods	500
07 Jan	Sales	300	08 Jan	Paid wages	200
		1,300			

€700

Since cash payments cannot be more than the cash receipts, **the debit side total is always greater than the credit side**.

3. Next you must **make the totals the same** (and so balance the cash account).
   a. Calculate the **difference** between the two totals (€1,300 – €700 = €600).
   b. Insert the difference on the credit side on the last day of the period as '**balance carried down**' or '**balance c/d**' from the left side to the right side. This means that the totals are now the same on both sides.

Cash Account

Debit - Cash in - Left			Right - Cash out - Credit		
Date 20××	Details	Total €	Date 20××	Details	Total €
01 Jan	Bank loan	1,000	02 Jan	Purchased goods	500
07 Jan	Sales	300	08 Jan	Paid wages	200
			08 Jan	Balance c/d	600
		1,300			1,300

This balance shows the amount of cash in hand at the beginning of the next period. In other words, it shows your **financial position**. The balance is the amount required to make the smallest side add up to the larger total.

In the next period, this balance is entered on the debit side of the cash book as '**balance brought down**' or '**balance b/d**' from the last period. This will be the starting position for the next period's transactions.

Cash Account

Debit - Cash in - Left			Right - Cash out - Credit		
Date 20××	Details	Total €	Date 20××	Details	Total €
01 Jan	Bank loan	1,000	02 Jan	Purchased goods	500
07 Jan	Sales	300	08 Jan	Paid wages	200
			08 Jan	Balance c/d	600
		1,300			1,300
09 Jan	Balance b/d	600			

Both totals are always the same. The difference on the smallest side is the amount of cash you have left. Ciara has €600.

CHECKING IN...

1. Explain what is meant by the term 'cash account'. State why you might keep a cash account.
2. What might happen if Ciara did not have sales of €300? Recalculate for sales of €100.
3. Present the above information for Ciara graphically in the form of a pie chart, a bar chart and a line graph (see pp. 170–171).

ANALYSED CASH BOOK

Once you are comfortable preparing a simple cash account, you are ready to move on to a more comprehensive cash account called the analysed cash book.

Analysing means breaking something down into parts. Analysing a cash account means dividing the recorded information into different categories to learn more about how cash was received and spent. An analysed cash book is very similar to a cash account but it has additional columns.

The analysed cash book is used to record all money received and all money paid out. It can be created and used by an individual, a household or an organisation (for-profit and not-for-profit).

PREPARING AN ANALYSED CASH BOOK

You still follow the simple rules of the cash account when preparing an analysed cash book. However, you will include additional columns to describe money in and money out. For example, you might have the following **extra analysis columns**:

1. **Car expenses column**, with all expenses related to the car: diesel costs, repairs, new tyres
2. **Household costs column:** food, cleaning, house insurance
3. **School expenses column:** uniform, school books, school transport
4. **Other column:** once-off items or those that do not suit your chosen columns.

This means that (apart from the opening balance) all transactions are entered **twice**:

1. **Once in the Total column**
2. **Once in a suitable analysis column**

For example, diesel would be entered in:

1. Total column
2. Car expenses column

At the end you add up each column, but you balance only the Total columns.

EXAMPLE 2: SIMPSONS' ANALYSED CASH BOOK

Let's try a simple example to understand the analysed cash book concept.

The Simpsons are going to prepare an analysed cash book for their household. They will use the following headings:

Debit side: Total; Wages; Child benefit; Other

Credit side: Total; Grocery; Car; House; Other

They record the following transactions:

1.13 BE BUSINESS: PERSONAL FINANCE

Date: 20xx	Transaction	Amount €	Cash in / cash out?	Side total	Analysed column
1 Jan	Balance	500	in	debit	–
2 Jan	Diesel	20	out	credit	Car
3 Jan	Groceries	90	out	credit	Grocery
4 Jan	Eir	75	out	credit	House
5 Jan	Wages	890	in	debit	Wages
6 Jan	Gas	45	out	credit	House
10 Jan	Groceries	89	out	credit	Grocery
18 Jan	Diesel	30	out	credit	Car
19 Jan	Diesel	30	out	credit	Car
20 Jan	Mortgage	800	out	credit	House
22 Jan	Groceries	90	out	credit	Grocery
23 Jan	Child benefit	100	in	debit	Child benefit
29 Jan	Car service	95	out	credit	Car
29 Jan	Gifts	100	out	credit	Other

Look closely at the Simpsons' analysed cash book with these transations on the next page. Do you agree that it is easier to **analyse** than a simple cash account?

INCOME, EXPENDITURE AND BANK STATEMENTS 1.13

Simpsons' Analysed Cash Book

Debit Side +

Date	Details	Total Cash €	Wages €	Child benefit €	Other €
20xx					
1/1	Balance	500			
5/1	Wages	890	890		
23/1	Child benefit	100		100	
		1,490	890	100	
1/2	Balance b/d	26			

Credit Side −

Date	Details	Total Cash €	Grocery €	Car €	House €	Other €
2/1	Diesel	20		20		
3/1	Groceries	90	90			
4/1	Eir	75			75	
6/1	Gas	45			45	
10/1	Groceries	89	89			
18/1	Diesel	30		30		
19/1	Diesel	30		30		
20/1	Mortgage	800				
22/1	Groceries	90	90			
29/1	Car service	95		95		
29/1	Gifts	100				100
30/1	Balance c/d	26				
		1,490	269	175	120	100

See analysis on the next page.

181

1.13 BE BUSINESS: PERSONAL FINANCE

Analysis

1. The Simpsons had an opening cash balance of €500; however, their closing cash is just €26. This is not so good. What might happen next month?
2. Should the Simpsons have spent €100 on gifts? Are they living within their means?
3. What might the Simpsons do to improve their cash position? Could they earn extra money, shop around for cheaper bills?
4. If they had no opening cash of €500, what would be their new balance? Be savvy and make sure you can explain all the numbers.

> Be savvy and make sure you can explain all the numbers.

This analysed cash book assumes that all the transactions are cash. However, most people have bank accounts and their wages/salaries are paid into their bank account. They also pay their bills using credit cards and direct debits. How can you show this in an analysed cash book?

PREPARING AN ANALYSED CASH BOOK: BOTH CASH AND BANK

In reality, households use cash for minor purchases only – even parking can be paid for by text or online now. To reflect this in your analysed cash book, you need to add in a column for 'Bank' so that you now have a **Total cash** column and a **Total bank** column.

The analysed cash book for bank transactions can have an opening balance on the debit side (money in the bank) or credit side (owe money to the bank). Remember, the analysed cash book for cash transactions could only have the balance on the debit side as when dealing with cash you can only spend what you have. With a bank you have the option to have an **overdraft**, where you can overdraw on your account for a period of time.

Contra entries

Contra entries are special entries for when you **transfer money**.

When you **withdraw** cash from the bank, you are:

| Receiving cash | **Debit Cash** |
| Reducing bank | **Credit Bank** |

When you **lodge** cash into the bank, you are:

| Receiving cash | **Debit Bank** |
| Taking cash | **Credit Cash** |

182

INCOME, EXPENDITURE AND BANK STATEMENTS 1.13

EXAMPLE 3: COWELLS' ANALYSED CASH BOOK

Here's an example for the Cowell household to see how this works.

First, read through the Cowells' list of transactions below and mark if they are in or out and so debit or credit.

Transactions for Cowell Household		In/Out	Debit/Credit
1 Jan	opening cash balance €100		
1 Jan	opening bank balance €120		
2 Jan	received wages €850 by Paypath		
3 Jan	lodged cash in bank €100		
4 Jan	paid for groceries €50 cash		
9 Jan	paid for books €150 by debit card		
11 Jan	received child benefit in cash €120		
16 Jan	paid for electricity €145 by credit card		
17 Jan	paid for diesel €30 cash		
19 Jan	paid for heating €440 by debit card		

Top Tip!

When attempting a question, always check each transaction carefully.

Is it money in? Is it money out?

Money in = Debit.

Money out = Credit.

Solution

Look closely at the Cowells' analysed cash book with these transactions on the next page. Can you see how the 'Bank' column works in practice? Note that the opening balance is on the debit side for cash and for bank. The Cowells obviously have money in the bank.

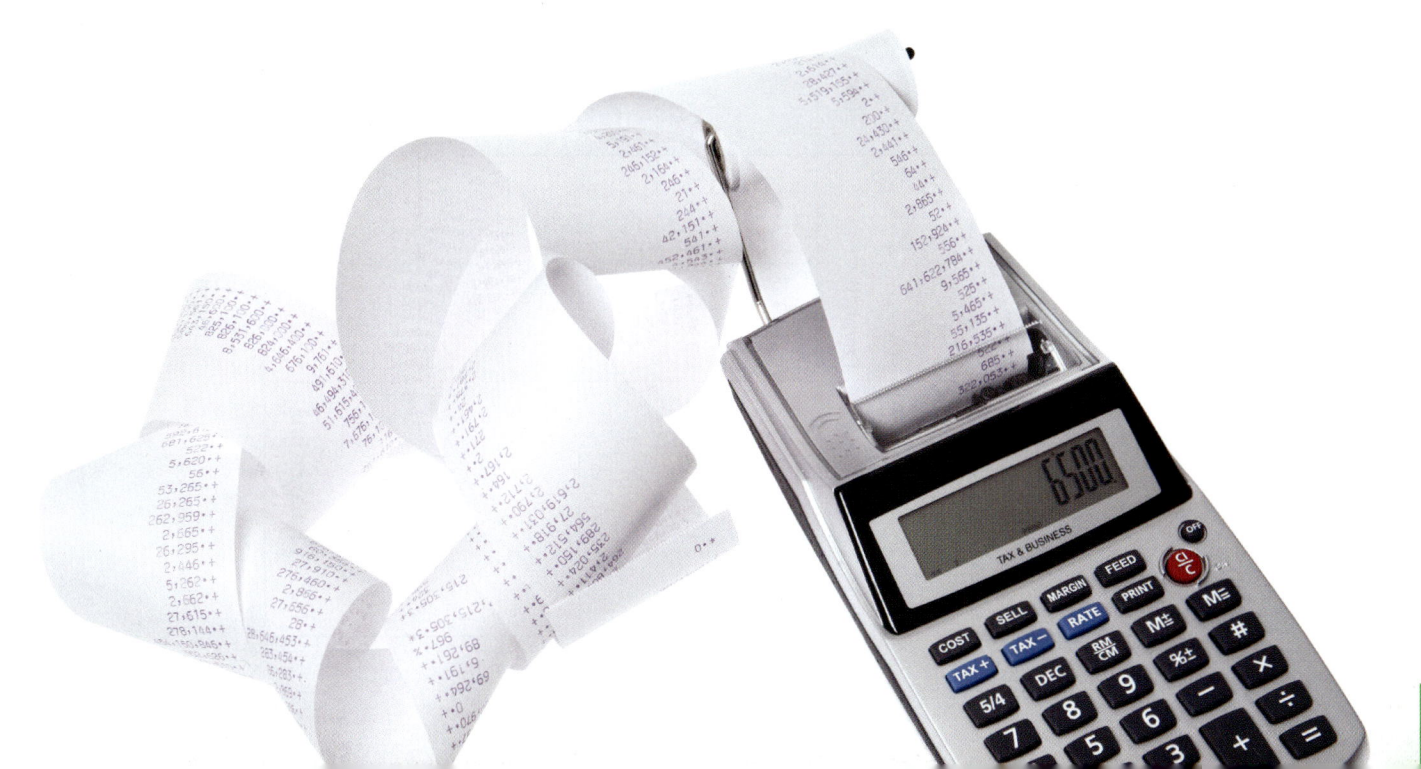

1.13 BE BUSINESS: PERSONAL FINANCE

Cowell's Analysed Cash Book

Debit

Date	Details	Method	Total cash €	Total bank €	Analysis Columns Wages €	Analysis Columns Child benefit €
20xx						
1/1	Balance b/d		100	120		
2/1	Wages	Paypath		890	850	
3/1	Bank	Cash	100			
11/1	Child Benefit	Cash	120			120
			320	970	850	120
1/2	Balance b/d		240	135		

Credit

Date	Details	Method	Total cash €	Total bank €	Analysis Columns Light & heat €	Analysis Columns School €	Analysis Columns Other €
20xx							
3/1	Cash	Cash		100			
6/1	Groceries	Cash	50				50
9/1	School books	Visa debit		150		150	
16/1	Electricity	Credit card		145	145		
17/1	Diesel	Cash	30				30
19/1	Central heating	Visa debit		440	440		
21/1	Balance c/d		240	135			
			320	970	585	150	80

Remember to **balance** the Total columns for Cash and Bank, and just total all the other columns.

INCOME, EXPENDITURE AND BANK STATEMENTS 1.13

More on Contra Entries

Let's look more closely at some contra entries (transferring cash into the bank account or withdrawing money from the bank to keep as cash). Be really careful with the Cash and Bank columns.

In the example there was a transaction as follows:

3 Jan Lodged cash in bank €100

If you withdraw **€100 from your bank account** so that you have **€100 cash in your wallet**, the transaction affects **both sides of the cash book**:

- Your cash balance has increased ↑ so you **debit** the **Total cash** column (and write 'bank' in the details)
- Your bank balance has decreased ↓ so you **credit** the **Total bank** column (and write 'cash' in the details to explain where it went).

Taking these transactions from the above cash book on their own, they look as follows:

Cowells' Analysed Cash Book													
Debit								Credit				
Date 20xx	Details	Method	Total cash €	Total bank €	Wages €	Child benefit €	Date 20xx	Details	Method	Total cash €	Total bank €	Light & heat €	School €	Other €
3/1	Bank	Cash	100				3/1	Cash	Cash		100			

If you had instead lodged €100 in your bank account, the transaction would look like this:

Cowells' Analysed Cash Book													
Debit								Credit				
Date 20xx	Details	Method	Total cash €	Total bank €	Wages €	Child benefit €	Date 20xx	Details	Method	Total cash €	Total bank €	Light & heat €	School €	Other €
3/1	Bank	Cash		100			3/1	Cash	Cash	100				

Your bank balance has increased ↑ so you **debit** the **Total bank column** (and write 'cash' in the details).

Your cash balance has decreased ↓ so you **credit** the **Total cash column** (and write 'bank' in the details).

1.13 BE BUSINESS: PERSONAL FINANCE

CHECKING IN...

1. Explain what is meant by the term 'analysed cash book'.
2. What advantages does an analysed cash book have over a cash account?
3. Explain what is meant by the term 'contra entry'. Give an example to show how it works in practice.

BANK STATEMENTS

Financial institutions keep records of all bank transactions. They display the records of each customer in a document known as a bank statement. Examine the sample bank statement below.

SAMPLE BANK STATEMENT

Current Account
Bank Statement with BASTI Bank
Branch 51 06 01

Mr Liam Mc Laughlin *(Customer)*
Main Street
Kerrykeel
Co. Donegal

Statement No. 99
Account No. 8899887
Date of Statement: 29 April 2020
Page: 32

IBAN: IE25 IBK 9312 3412 3450 87 (BIC: BKIE2D)
Authorised Limit at Date of Statement €500

*The account balance is shown after each transaction. This is known as **continuous balance**.*

C/T = Credit Transfer +

Date	Details	Debit €	Credit €	Balance €
01 APRIL	Balance forward			100.00
02 APRIL	Lodgement C/T		700.00	800.00
03 APRIL	AXA insurance DD	50.00		750.00
07 APRIL	ATM Grafton Street	200.00		550.00
15 APRIL	BOI loan DD	250.00		300.00
20 APRIL	Bank charges	17.50		282.50

DD = Direct debit -
Amount in bank account

See an explanation of these transactions on the next page.

INCOME, EXPENDITURE AND BANK STATEMENTS 1.13

Liam Mc Laughlin has a bank account with BASTI Bank. Remember, the debit is a minus and the credit is a plus.

01 April Liam had €100 in his bank account. If the statement said (€100) he would have a minus figure, so probably an overdraft.

02 April Liam's mum lodged €700 directly into his account by credit transfer (C/T) from her account. This increases his bank balance and he now has €800 in the bank.

03 April Liam paid AXA insurance €50 directly from his account by direct debit (DD) and he now has €750 in the bank.

07 April Liam was in Dublin and withdrew €200 cash from the ATM in Grafton Street, and he now has a balance of €550.

15 April Liam transferred money to Bank of Ireland by DD. This is for a loan repayment of €250, and he now has a balance of €300.

20 April The bank added charges of €17.50 for DD, C/T and ATM transactions, and he now has €282.50 in the bank.

WORKING WITH OTHERS

- In pairs, discuss the statement above. Does it all make sense to you? Is there anything you do not understand?
- What is a direct debit? What is a credit transfer?
- How much money does Liam have in his account?
- Create your own bank statement with at least five transactions.

Time to think

Imagine you are a bank. A customer lodges money into his or her bank account. Explain why you record it on the credit side (see statement for Luke Lavelle on the next page).

Find out the meaning of the term 'liability'. Is a lodgement a liability from the bank's perspective?

PREPARING A BANK STATEMENT

The bank prepares the bank statement in six steps:

1. State the opening balance in the bank account.
2. Show all payments out of the bank account.
3. Show all lodgements in to the bank account.
4. Show any banking charges: the bank charges fees for standing orders, credit transfers, etc.
5. Show any interest received and interest paid.
6. State the closing balance in the bank account. Sometimes this differs from the customer's own records due to money being lodged or withdrawn after the statement was prepared. The opening and/or closing balance may show that the account is overdrawn.

1.13 BE BUSINESS: PERSONAL FINANCE

WORKING WITH OTHERS

- Luke Lavelle received the following bank statement on 2 June 2020. In pairs, explain all the transactions on this bank statement, in the order they occur.

Bank Statement
Ulster Bank
Claremorris, Co. Mayo

Luke Lavelle
Main Street
Claremorris
Co. Mayo

Branch Code:
91-09-19
Account No:
145362
Date: 31 May 2020

Date	Details	Debit €	Credit €	Balance €
1 May 2020	Balance forward			679
4 May 2020	Electricity DD	174		505
18 May 2020	Wages: Paypath		2,450	2,955
19 May 2020	DD – Insurance	750		2,205
22 May 2020	ATM – Claremorris	400		1,805
28 May 2020	Lodgement		200	2,005
28 May 2020	Bank charges	105		1,900

- Luke is thinking about buying a second-hand car and borrowing from the bank. Compare and contrast an overdraft with a bank loan.
- What information might the bank require from Luke before granting a loan?
- If the bank refuses a loan, what other options might Luke have?

CHECKING IN...

1. What is the purpose of a bank statement?
2. Name three items that are included on a bank statement.
3. Why does a bank credit a lodgement?

INCOME, EXPENDITURE AND BANK STATEMENTS — 1.13

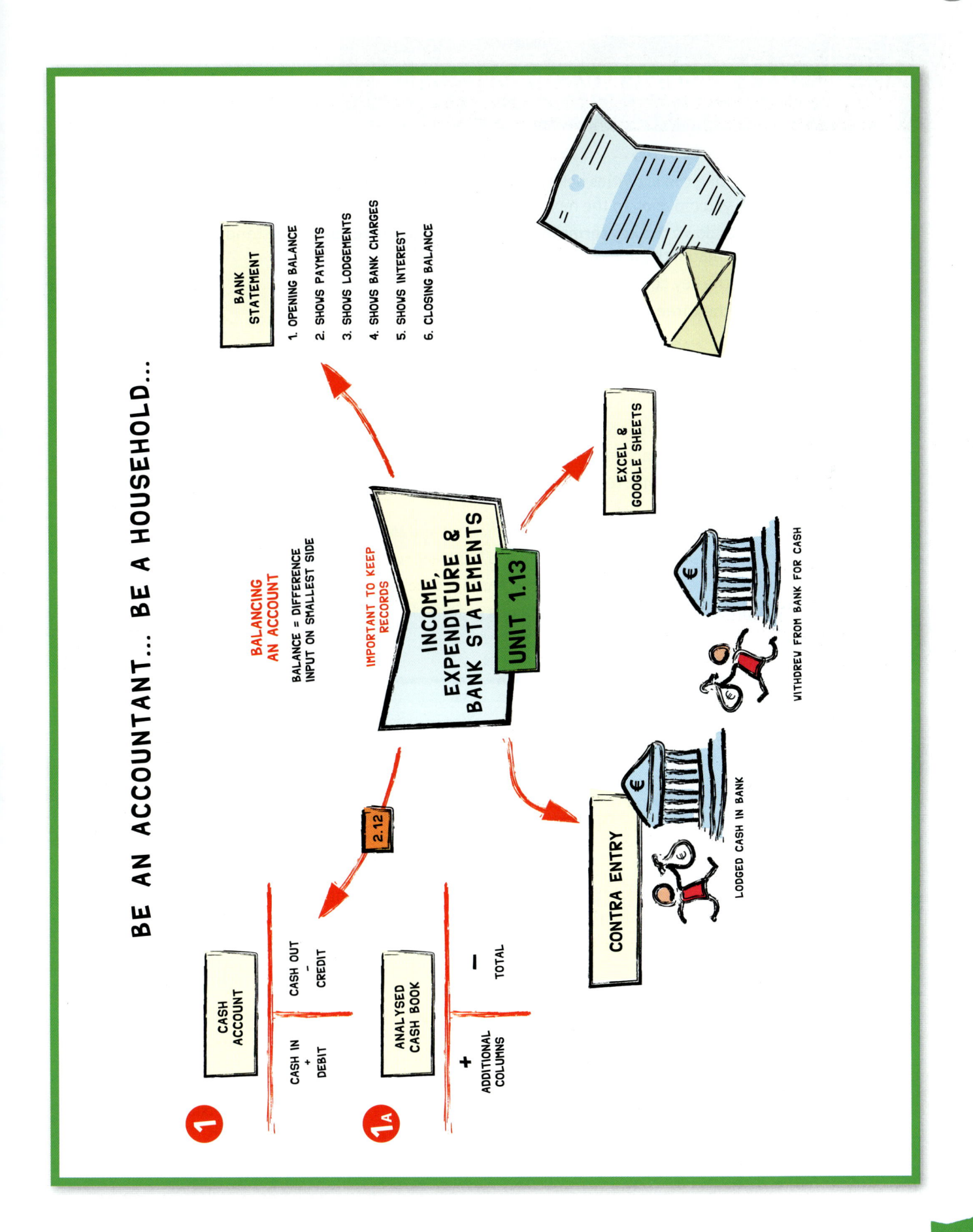

BE AN ACCOUNTANT... BE A HOUSEHOLD...

INCOME, EXPENDITURE & BANK STATEMENTS — UNIT 1.13

IMPORTANT TO KEEP RECORDS

BALANCING AN ACCOUNT
BALANCE = DIFFERENCE
INPUT ON SMALLEST SIDE

BANK STATEMENT
1. OPENING BALANCE
2. SHOWS PAYMENTS
3. SHOWS LODGEMENTS
4. SHOWS BANK CHARGES
5. SHOWS INTEREST
6. CLOSING BALANCE

EXCEL & GOOGLE SHEETS

CONTRA ENTRY
- WITHDREW FROM BANK FOR CASH
- LODGED CASH IN BANK

① CASH ACCOUNT
- CASH IN + DEBIT
- CASH OUT − CREDIT

(2.12)

①A ANALYSED CASH BOOK
- + ADDITIONAL COLUMNS
- − TOTAL

189

1.13 BE BUSINESS: PERSONAL FINANCE

Be Prepared: My Support Sheets

Completing the activities below will help you to reflect on and reinforce your learning before you move on to the next unit.

- Write down the **key terms** in this unit and make sure you understand them. See if they match the ones at the back of the book.
- List the key **concepts/themes** in this unit.
- List the **three most interesting points** about this unit.

QUESTION TIME

1. What are the advantages of recording financial information in a cash account?
2. Explain the rules of the cash account.
3. What does the opening balance tell us and what does the closing balance tell us?
4. Explain what we mean by 'analysed'. Why might income and expenditure be divided into smaller parts?
5. Why might you have a separate cash account and bank account in an analysed cash book?
6. How can a household reduce expenses and increase income?
7. Why might you present accounts information in a graph? How can technology help you create accounts?
8. Source a bank statement and explain the contents.

EVALUATE MY LEARNING: DAR

Describe
- Did I/we meet my/our learning intentions?
- What went well? What are my/our strengths?

Assess
- How did I/we work with others?
- Were there challenges?

Recommend
- How might I improve?
- What skills and learning might I apply to new situations?

Stop and think
Do I have any questions or concerns?
What are the mistakes or errors I made in this unit?

Do your **Key Check** in the workbook for this unit and then mark your learning position on the rating scale.

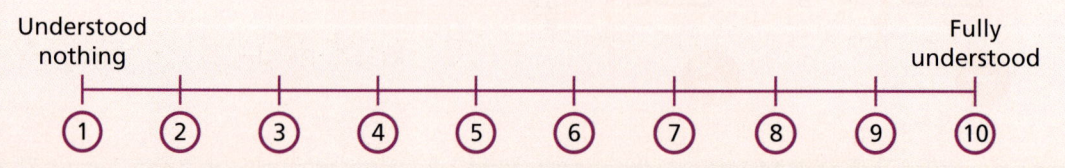

Understood nothing — 1 2 3 4 5 6 7 8 9 10 — Fully understood

How can you move up the rating scale? What can you **say**, **make**, **write** and **do** to illustrate your learning?

② ENTERPRISE

Enterprise encourages you to identify opportunities and turn them into practical and targeted activities within business and wider society through the development and application of their understanding, skills and values. In this strand you will learn about being enterprising, the functions of an organisation and the business environment.

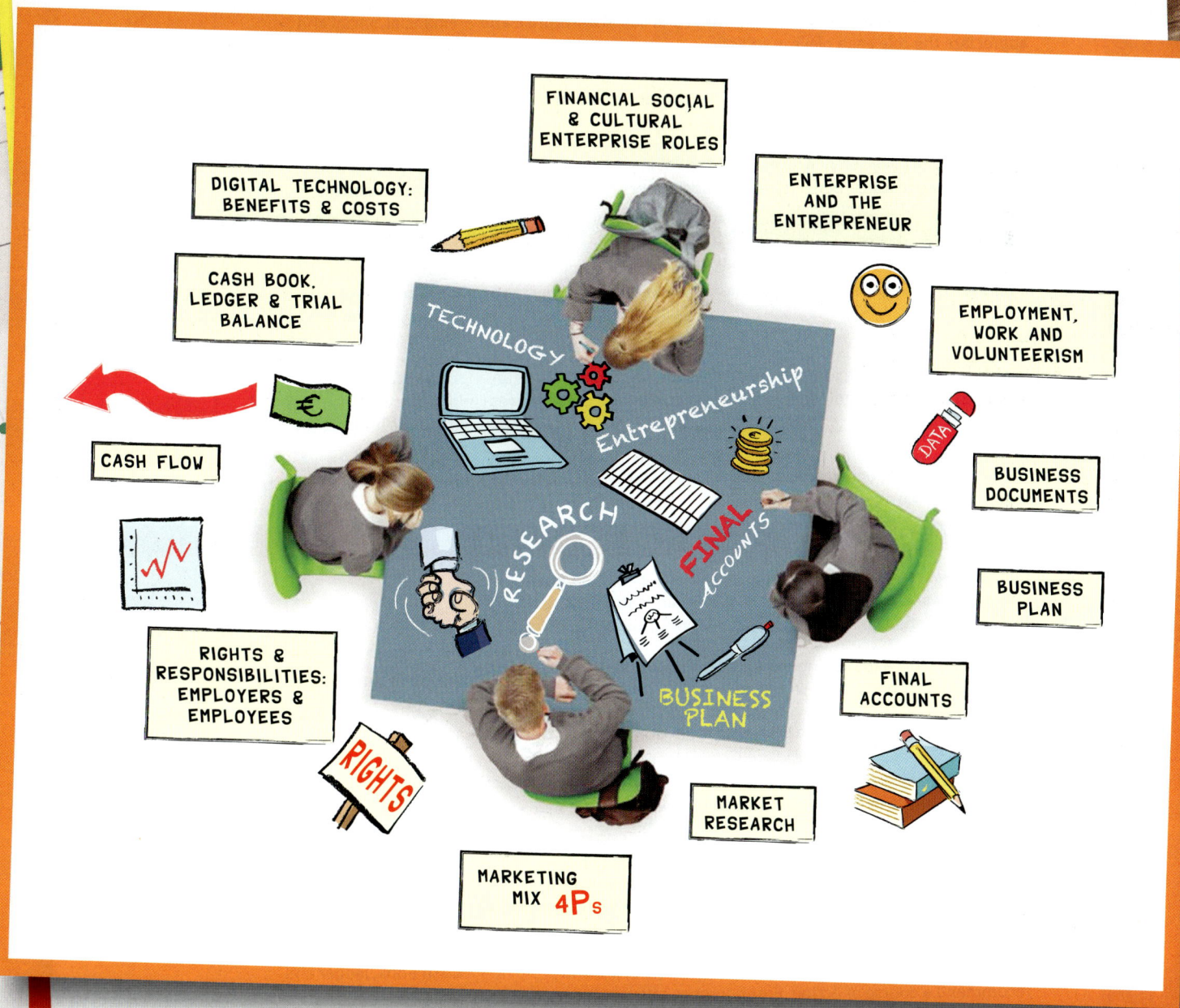

- FINANCIAL SOCIAL & CULTURAL ENTERPRISE ROLES
- ENTERPRISE AND THE ENTREPRENEUR
- DIGITAL TECHNOLOGY: BENEFITS & COSTS
- EMPLOYMENT, WORK AND VOLUNTEERISM
- CASH BOOK, LEDGER & TRIAL BALANCE
- BUSINESS DOCUMENTS
- CASH FLOW
- BUSINESS PLAN
- RIGHTS & RESPONSIBILITIES: EMPLOYERS & EMPLOYEES
- FINAL ACCOUNTS
- MARKET RESEARCH
- MARKETING MIX 4Ps

STRAND 2 LEARNING OUTCOMES (LOs):

Engaging with enterprise you should be able to: ✓

OUTCOME	UNIT	DONE	REVISED	GOT IT
MANGING MY RESOURCES				
2.1 Identify different types of financial, cultural and social enterprise and appreciate the role each plays in society	Financial, social and cultural enterprise roles	☐	☐	☐
2.2 Describe the skills and characteristics of being enterprising and appreciate the role of an entrepreneur in an organisation, in society and in the economy	Enterprise and the entrepreneur	☐	☐	☐
2.3 Differentiate between employment, work and volunteerism, identifying and describing features, benefits, rewards and careers in each	Employment, work and volunteerism	☐	☐	☐
EXPLORING BUSINESS				
2.4 Distinguish between the rights and responsibilities of employer and employee from legal, social, environmental and ethical perspectives	Rights and responsibilities: employers and employees	☐	☐	☐
2.5 Investigate the positive and negative impacts on a community of an organisation from economic, social and environmental perspectives	Organisations' positive and negative impacts on communities	☐	☐	☐
2.6 Discuss the impact of technologies on an organisation, debating the associated rewards and costs	Digital technology: benefits and costs	☐	☐	☐
USING SKILLS FOR BUSINESS				
2.7 Conduct market research in order to investigate an entrepreneurial opportunity and analyse, interpret and communicate the research findings using relevant terminology and representations	Market research	☐	☐	☐
2.8 Devise and apply a marketing mix in order to promote a new or existing product or service	Marketing mix	☐	☐	☐
2.9 Develop a simple business plan for a new or existing product or service	Business plan	☐	☐	☐
2.10 Complete and interpret key business documents that an organisation uses to manage its transactions for accountability purposes	Key business documents	☐	☐	☐
2.11 Assess the importance of planning an organisation's cash flow, propose suitable sources of finance to manage expenditure and prepare a cash flow budget	Cash flow	☐	☐	☐
2.12 Prepare a cash account to monitor income received and payments made by an organisation, evaluate its financial position and recommend a course of action. Post figures to relevant ledgers and extract a trial balance	Cash book, ledger and trial balance	☐	☐	☐
2.13 Prepare final accounts to assess the financial performance of an organisation at the end of a trading period, analyse and evaluate its financial position and recommend a course of action	Final accounts	☐	☐	☐

INTRODUCTION

Society and the economy need enterprise and enterprising people to maintain and grow success. You will be the next generation of Irish entrepreneurs (business people) and hopefully you will be enterprising citizens in all areas of life. As students, you will begin thinking about your future studies and career. This exciting Business Studies course will expose you to entrepreneurship.

ENTERPRISE VS ENTREPRENEURSHIP

It's important to recognise that enterprise and entrepreneurship are not the same thing. Entrepreneurship can be a result of being enterprising.

Being enterprising doesn't just relate to the ability to make money. Enterprise is when an individual (or a group of people) takes the initiative to start something new. For example, learning a new skill, organising a fundraising event for a GAA club or starting a charity.

Entrepreneurship is a particular type of enterprise; it involves taking the risk of organising all the resources necessary to provide a product or service while trying to make a profit. For example, developing new products or expansion into new markets.

Enterprise is an attitude and a set of skills, highly valued by employers, which will enable a person to seize opportunities, be creative and develop problem-solving skills.

Entrepreneurship is using that creativity to look for opportunities while also having a willingness to take risks to create new businesses that make a profit.

2 BE BUSINESS: ENTERPRISE

Look at the images of entrepreneurs on this page. Do you know what they do?

Tony Ryan

Ramona Nicholas

Arianna Huffington

John Collison

Time to think

Do you think you have been enterprising in your life so far?

Have you ever wanted to do something new but didn't – what stopped you?

Top Tip!

You will encounter numerous key words in this Strand. Document the key words/concepts in your folder. Use the **Business Studies key terms glossary** at the back of this book.

When you come across a new word, **listen** to the word, say the word, **write** it down and **apply** it.

OVER TO YOU

Enterprise is a key skill in the Junior Cycle framework: being creative, implementing ideas and taking action. Teaching enterprise cannot just be in a classroom. If you want to learn to drive a car, you need to sit directly in the driver's seat. Similarly, to get a full experience of enterprise, you need to get into board rooms, design labs, construction sites, trading floors and shop floors, so you can see the full picture.

In Business Studies, and in this strand in particular, you will have an opportunity to be enterprising and to engage in entrepreneurial activities. As you study this strand, continually evaluate and articulate the skills that you are developing and these skills will help you now and into the future.

ENTERPRISE 2

Enterprise: 5 Ways of Thinking

- Think locally
- Think nationally
- Think European
- Think sustainability (being environmentally friendly)
- Think globally (our world, our planet)

WORKING WITH OTHERS

Can you share a story about a local enterprising person? Jot down the main points into your copy/folder.

Accountant
Hairdresser
Baker
Shopkeeper
Dentist
Painter
Farmer
Doctor
Plumber
Student & yes!

Think about mini-companies (see www.studententerprise.ie)

✓ Are there businesses that have closed down in your local area?
✓ Is there a need for a particular enterprise in your local area, e.g. a bakery?
✓ Divide local enterprises into profit and non-profit enterprises.

195

IDEA GENERATION

Entrepreneurship is exciting, challenging and worthwhile. Entrepreneurs need to have many qualities. It's all about developing the best possible product or service and at the same time making a profit.

All successful entrepreneurs are good at generating new ideas and 'thinking outside the box'. **Idea generation** (coming up with ideas) is a skill that can be learned by anyone; all you need is the ability to see things differently. It's about **creative thinking**, and not being afraid to break the rules when coming up with ideas.

A really popular technique for idea generation is **brainstorming.** This is when a group of people write down as many new ideas as possible – no matter how unbelievable/ridiculous they are – about a product, service or plan. They then discuss the ideas, rejecting some of them, and eventually prioritise the best idea. You could use the decision tree (p. 546) too!

CREATIVITY

When we are allowed to do anything we can, we are most likely to return to whatever we previously found worked; in other words, we are creatures of habit.

When we do this we are not being creative. So we need to be more open to **new ideas** and different ways of doing things. We need to think bigger … think smaller … think backwards … think faster!

Think **Bigger** – TVs. What's the largest screen available?

Think **Smaller** – Smart cars

Think **Backwards** – Prevention … eating healthily and keeping fit to prevent ill health

Think **Faster** – Smartphones

Introducing **limitations** can be a good way to inspire **creativity**. When you can't do something the way you've always done it, you have to be creative to succeed.

WORKING WITH OTHERS

You have been asked to come up with some creative ways to raise money for a local charity. Think of three original ideas. (You can't choose to hold a flag day or a raffle!) When everyone has put their ideas forward, the class can vote on the best idea.

Business in Action/Presentation Idea

Pursue the idea and raise money for a worthy cause!

Top Tip!

Set up an **ideas box**, an **ideas file/portfolio** or an **ideas notebook**. Document the ideas you come across. Always date ideas and revisit them regularly. Why not have a **best ideas competition**?

Ideas!

The students in the case study below started by brainstorming potential business ideas for a 'mini-company' in their classroom … and look where it got them!

CASE STUDY:
SQUEAZY: COLLABORATING BUSINESS WITH SCIENCE CONCEPTS

Three budding entrepreneurs from Leitrim established Squeazy. Matthew Hewston, Fergus Munday and Luke Sheridan from St Clare's Comprehensive School, Manorhamilton, Co. Leitrim were awarded first prize in the senior category at the County and City Enterprise Boards' 11th Annual Student Enterprise Awards National Finals in Croke Park.

The Squeazy is an innovative game, aimed at mainly primary school children. The game consists of two characters called Drip and Drop – in a liquid-filled bottle. The game is based on the science of pressure and water. Using the concept of Cartesian divers, the aim of the game is to squeeze the bottle to try to catch Drop (with a hook) and Drip (with a loop).

Be Creative

1. Mousetrap design

Could you design the best mousetrap ever?

What might persuade people to buy your mousetrap?

- ✓ Cost
- ✓ Attractiveness
- ✓ Not recognisable, so visitors will not realise that it's a mousetrap
- ✓ Sustainability
- ✓ Made in Ireland

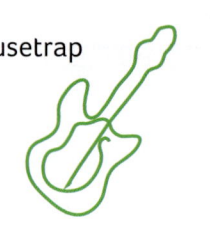

2. Paperclip challenge

First try this task by yourself. How many uses can you think of for a paperclip?
You have **2 minutes** to complete this task.

Now try the task working with others. Did you find more ideas working with others?

3. Ideal toothbrush

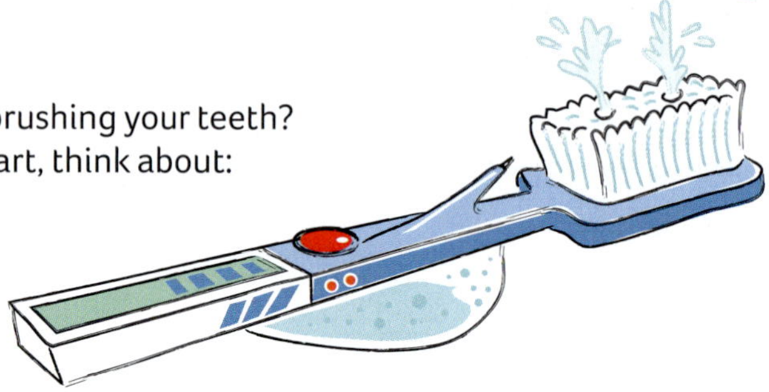

What could make life easier for you when brushing your teeth?
Design the ideal toothbrush. Before you start, think about:

- ✓ Pre-cleaning
- ✓ Cleaning
- ✓ Post-cleaning

You have **5 minutes** to complete the following.

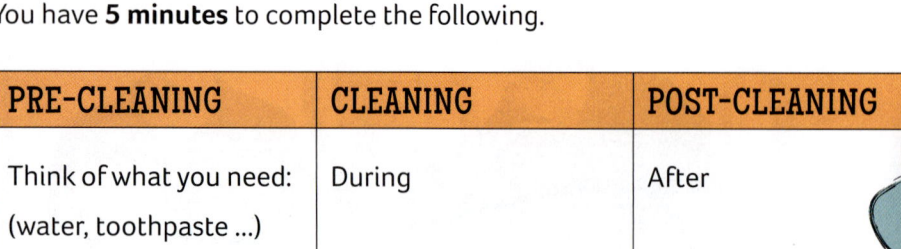

PRE-CLEANING	CLEANING	POST-CLEANING
Think of what you need: (water, toothpaste …)	During	After

Now draw your design and describe your ideal toothbrush with all its features in your copy/folder.

Success criteria:
- What might the best toothbrush look like?
- Give your toothbrush a short, relevant and creative **name**
- It must be **functional**
- It must have **five** distinctive features
- Techniques used

Wonderful Worthwhile Website

Visit blogs.solidworks.com/solidworksblog/ to learn how to create a toothbrush.

Fun Fact

Lego are in the process of changing their product to become more environmentally friendly.

4. Lego task

Do you have any Lego at home? Perhaps you can borrow some from a brother or sister.

Design and build an iPhone holder made from Lego.

Success criteria:
- What makes a good iPhone holder?
- What might the best iPhone holder look like?
- Give your iPhone holder a short, relevant and creative **name**
- Use three **colours** – give a rationale about your colours
- Make the **design** different/unusual
- It must be **functional**: an iPhone must fit in the holder and be easy to remove
- Use sport, fashion or music as a **theme**

5. Paper task

Design and build the **tallest paper tower** you can using only A3 paper and a pair of scissors!

Success criteria:
- What might the tallest paper tower look like?
- Choose a suitable name with a sustainability theme
- Make the tallest paper tower possible
- Make sure that it will stand up
- Techniques used

Top Tip!

Perhaps a DCG student could design a 3D product for you, using **Solidworks** CAD software? Perhaps an art student can help.

Are there other products you could design?

Why not present your ideas to your classmates and have a vote on the best design?

BE ENTERPRISING

IN YOUR SCHOOL

There are many ways of being enterprising in your school.

- **Set up a mini-company:** Start a mini-enterprise to provide a service or manufacture a product and then market and sell the product/service. *H*ave you come across any good ideas for mini-companies in your school?
- **Organise a school event:** You might like to organise an enterprise event that will help improve the environment. The **Green Flag** is a really good example (www.greenschoolsireland.org).
- **Hold fundraising activities:** Raising funds for the school or local charities is a superb school activity. For example, some schools organise **Strictly Come Dancing** events to fundraise for their school.
- **Ask an entrepreneur to visit the classroom:** Inviting a local business person, entrepreneur or enterprising person to speak to your class can give you a real business perspective. Investigate business stories in your local newspaper. Do you know any entrepreneurs/enterprising people in your area?
- **Have a field visit to an enterprise:** Contact your Local Enterprise Offices to arrange such a visit. See how a business really works. Can you think of other enterprising events that have occurred in your school?

> **Wonderful Worthwhile Websites** 
>
> See some ideas from students who have participated in the student enterprise awards (www.studententerprise.ie).

Business in Action/Presentation Idea

Run an enterprising activity for charity.

IN YOUR LOCAL COMMUNITY

- ✓ Get involved in the TidyTowns committee.
- ✓ Participate in Charity work, e.g. old folks' drop-in centre.
- ✓ Fundraise for local clubs, e.g. a sponsored run for your local football club.
- ✓ Get involved in local politics.

IN YOUR HOME

- ✓ Work from home.
- ✓ Have a car boot sale to sell off unwanted possessions.
- ✓ Rent out rooms for Airbnb.
- ✓ Avoid housework!

> Enterprise is not a sprint, it's a marathon.

ENTERPRISE 2

Do you have the **E** (enterprise) **Factor**? Copy the following questions into your copy and answer them truthfully by placing a ✓ in the appropriate box.

Are you entrepreneurial?	Yes ☐	No ☐
Would you consider becoming an entrepreneur?	Yes ☐	No ☐
Are entrepreneurs born?	Yes ☐	No ☐
Can you learn to be an entrepreneur?	Yes ☐	No ☐
Would you consider setting up your own business in the future?	Yes ☐	No ☐

Business in Action/Presentation Idea

Invite an entrepreneur to the classroom. You could visit or Google some local and national business leaders in business, contact someone you've seen on the RTÉ programme *Dragons' Den*, invite an entrepreneur from a voluntary (non-profit) organisation, or an enterprising Transition Year student who runs their own business/mini-company.

Top Tip!

Don't forget, you can use other search engines too, e.g. DuckDuckGo (https://duckduckgo.com), or InstaGrok (www.instagrok.com).

Being enterprising means making things happen in a world where demand for products/services is constantly changing. In order to do that you need to **develop an entrepreneurial mind-set**.

If you ask anyone to name an entrepreneur, there's a good chance they will come up with Richard Branson (Virgin), Steve Jobs (Apple) or Mark Zuckerberg (Facebook). Remember, all these people started with an idea. We need to celebrate *all* entrepreneurs, from our local shop owner to those very successful, internationally recognised entrepreneurs.

All entrepreneurs, local or global, play a vital role in society and it's important for you to see how the enterprise route can be a successful one. The more you see **role models** (good examples) of entrepreneurs who are successful in creating jobs and wealth, the more likely you are to feel that this is the route for you. You can never be too young to see the possibility of a career as an entrepreneur. This Business Studies course will provide you with excellent opportunities to explore what it means to be an entrepreneur.

Top Tip!

If you don't have a business idea yourself, why not Google one (search for 'business ideas')? It's much easier to come up with ideas when you have technology at your fingertips – the world's your oyster.

We should not be afraid to take measured risks by being creative and innovative in all aspects of our lives.

201

2.1 FINANCIAL, SOCIAL AND CULTURAL ENTERPRISE ROLES

Identify different types of financial, cultural and social enterprise and appreciate the role each plays in society.

Learning Intentions

At the end of this unit I will:
- Know what it takes to be enterprising
- Understand financial, cultural and social enterprises
- Understand the role of these enterprises in society
- Develop enterprise skills

Key Concepts
- ✓ Entrepreneurship
- ✓ Different types of enterprise
- ✓ Idea generation

Making the links with other LOs:

- 2.2 Enterprise and the entrepreneur
- 2.5 Organisations' positive and negative impacts on communities
- 3.2 Circular flow of income

Wonderful Worthwhile Websites
www.thinkbusiness.ie
www.khanacademy.org
www.studententerprise.ie

Are there other LOs?

'3Ts' = Think, Turn, Talk
- What do you think is meant by 'financial enterprise', 'cultural enterprise' and 'social enterprise'?
- What kind of organisation is not interested in making a profit?

WHAT IS AN ORGANISATION?

Organisations can be divided into 'for-profit' and 'not-for profit'.

An **organisation** is a group of people deliberately organised to achieve an overall, common goal or set of goals. Business organisations can range in size from one person to tens of thousands.

FOR-PROFIT ORGANISATIONS

The main aim of a 'for-profit' organisation is to provide goods and/or services whilst making a profit.

Examples include banks, building societies, insurance companies, hairdressers, restaurants, fast-food outlets, laundries, grocery shops, butchers and garages. Most are commonly known as businesses or enterprises. They can be owned by an individual, known as a sole trader, or a group of individuals, known as a company.

NOT-FOR-PROFIT ORGANISATIONS

Not-for-profit organisations do not earn profits for the owners. All of the money earned by or donated to a not-for-profit organisation is used in pursuing the organisation's objectives. Typically these are sports clubs, hospitals, schools, churches, political organisations, volunteer organisations, museums and charities (e.g. GOAL or Trócaire).

Time to think

Would you like to work for a 'non-profit' organisation? Why?

FORMS OF BUSINESS

A business is a type of organisation that they can be set up in different ways. The main types for discussion here are:

- ✓ Sole traders
- ✓ Private limited companies
- ✓ Cooperatives

State-sponsored bodies will be covered in Unit 3.2.

SOLE TRADER

A sole trader is someone who sets up a business **on their own**. They may sell **goods**, for example a butcher, baker, florist or newsagent, or provide a **service**, for example a beautician, painter, taxi driver or cleaner.

The sole trader provides or raises the capital (money) to start the business. They make all the decisions and are personally liable (responsible) for all legal actions and debts. Their **liability is unlimited**; which means that if the business fails, they can lose their private property and even the family home.

203

The **profits**, however, that the sole trader makes belongs solely to the individual.

If using a name other than their own name (e.g. Molly Walker) the sole trader must register the business name (e.g. Beauty4U) with the Registrar of Business Names.

In addition a **licence** is needed to sell certain goods/services like prescription goods and alcohol.

PRIVATE LIMITED COMPANY

A private limited company can be owned by 1–149 **shareholders** (investors). They provide the capital to start the business. The capital of a company is divided into equal parts or **shares**. In return for their risk, they receive a **dividend** (payment), which is interest on their shares. The amount they receive depends on how many shares they own.

The great advantage is that shareholders enjoy the privilege of **limited liability**. This means that they only lose the amount of money they invested in the company if the business fails. Compare this with Molly Walker, a sole trader, who can lose her personal possessions if her business closes.

Private limited companies have to register with the Register of Companies. They must have a registered office and the company name will now have the words Ltd (Limited) or Teo (Teoranta) at the end (e.g. Walkers Snack Foods Ltd). They receive a certificate of incorporation which allows them to trade.

Public limited companies trade on the stock exchange. They have the words Plc after their name, for example Glanbia Plc.

CO-OPERATIVES

A co-operative is an organisation which is owned by a group of people (e.g. farmers) who produce and distribute goods and services. The co-operative exists to benefit the owners. There are many types of co-operative such as housing (Galway Co-operative Housing Development Society Ltd.), financial (Drogheda Credit Union Limited), and agricultural (Western Farming Co-Op Ltd).

There must be a minimum of 7 members to create a co-operative. Members enjoy the benefits of limited liability, similar to the private limited company. The co-operative's name must include the word 'Society' and/or Ltd (Limited) or Teo (Teoranta). Certain documentation must be forwarded to the Registrar of Friendly Societies.

FINANCIAL, SOCIAL AND CULTURAL ENTERPRISE ROLES 2.1

THE TRANSFORMATION PROCESS

An organisation needs resources in order to function. These resources are **inputs**, referred to as 'factors of production' – land, labour, capital and enterprise. These resources are turned into **outputs** – products and services that customers are willing to pay for.

> The process of converting inputs into outputs is known as the **transformation process**.

It doesn't matter whether the organisation is a for-profit company, a not-for-profit organisation (charities, hospitals, etc.) or a government agency; all organisations must try to have the best quality transformation process to add value and therefore meet customer needs.

Where the inputs are raw materials, it is relatively easy to identify the transformation involved, as when milk is transformed into cheese and butter. Where the inputs are information or people, the nature of the transformation may be less obvious. For example a hospital transforms ill patients (the input) into healthy patients (the output).

Labour

Land

ADDING VALUE

If the value of what customers pay for the outputs is more than the cost of the inputs, the business can be said to have added value. So the transformation process is about adding value. Added value is the difference between the cost of inputs involved in making a product or service and the price received for them.

Capital

Enterprise

Be numerate

Num Num is a sustainable company that sells protein snacks for health-conscious customers.

Costs to make 10,000 units:

Raw materials	€ 6,000
Labour	€ 8,500
Other costs	€ 2,500
TOTAL	**€17,000**

Sales 10,000 units sold for €4 each   €40,000

Added Value = €40,000 – €17,000 = €23,000

PRIMARY, SECONDARY AND TERTIARY SECTORS

There are **three** main types of industry in which firms operate. These **sectors** form a chain of production which provides customers with finished goods or services.

1. **Primary production:** this involves acquiring **raw materials**. For example, metals and coal have to be mined, oil drilled from the ground, rubber tapped from trees, foodstuffs farmed and fish trawled.
2. **Secondary production:** this is the **manufacturing and assembly** process. It involves converting raw materials into components, for example, making plastics from oil. It also involves assembling the product, e.g. building houses, bridges and roads.
3. **Tertiary production:** this refers to the **commercial services** that support the production and distribution process, e.g. insurance, transport, advertising, warehousing and other services such as teaching and health care.
4. **Quaternary sector:** this provides information services, such as computing and ICT (information and communication technologies). This is sometimes categorised under the tertiary sector.

See more on inputs, or factors of production, in **Unit 3.2**.

WORKING WITH OTHERS

Identify the main resources (inputs), the type of transformation process and the main outputs (goods or services) in each of the following operations. Copy and fill in the table.

Inputs	Type of transformation	Outputs
Making bread		
Assembling cars		
Online banking		
Charity donations		
Running a soup kitchen		

CHECKING IN...

1. Give three examples of for-profit organisations in your area.
2. What is the purpose of a not-for-profit organisation?
3. Name three forms of business and the main differences between them.
4. What are the advantages of being your own boss?
5. Explain what is meant by adding value, inputs and outputs.

FINANCIAL, SOCIAL AND CULTURAL ENTERPRISE ROLES 2.1

TYPES OF ENTERPRISE

Enterprises come in many forms. When discussing their role in society, it can be useful to categorise them as follows:

1. Financial enterprises
2. Social enterprises
3. Cultural enterprises

FINANCIAL ENTERPRISES

The forms of business outlined earlier in this unit are financial enterprises, as they generate profit (money) through the sale of goods or services.

Financial enterprise can also refer to an organisation that provides finance (money) and/or financial services, such as An Post, Banks, Building Societies and Credit Unions

`Unit 1.5`.

Some of our state enterprises provide finance, such as Enterprise Ireland.

Financial enterprises also play an important role in society by offering finance and support to other organisations, from community-based projects to start-up businesses generating employment.

Social finance (to improve the community) is an innovative finance tool. Providers offer repayable loans at an affordable rate.

- Clann Credo: a social investment fund that provides loans to community organisations, charities and social enterprises.
- UCIT (Ulster Community Investment Trust) Ireland: providers of flexible finance for community enterprises throughout Ireland.
- LEDP (Limerick Enterprise Development Park): specialists in community development and micro-enterprises in the Limerick region.

2.1 BE BUSINESS: ENTERPRISE

WORKING WITH OTHERS

Divide the class into groups. Each group should investigate one type of financial enterprise in detail. Copy and use the learning sheet below.

MY FINANCIAL ENTERPRISE LEARNING SHEET

Date -/-/-	Enterprise in Action	Revisit in third year to document any major changes

Name of financial organisation	[picture/logo]

Aims of organisation

Website

List services	Rate of interest on loans?
	Rate of interest on deposit accounts
	APR for borrowing (annual percentage rate – the true cost of borrowing)
	Is interest liable for DIRT tax?

How do you contribute to society, our local community and impact on our world/planet?

Reflections

Have you learned any new information?

Do you need to investigate this organisation further?

What skills have you developed?

CULTURAL ENTERPRISES

A cultural enterprise is one that is set up to promote the arts.

Promoting **cultural entrepreneurship** is so important for our world. Cultural enterprises showcase beauty, skills and talent, while having the potential for making profit and creating jobs. Cultural tourism is a growth area both nationally and globally.

- **Fáilte Ireland** is the semi-state body that promotes tourism. Ireland is steeped in culture and our unique history and rugged landscape offer enormous potential for tourism. One recent initiative from Fáilte Ireland was the promotion of the **Wild Atlantic Way**, a long-distance touring route stretching along the Atlantic coast from Donegal to west Cork. The aim was to develop a route that would achieve greater visibility for the west coast of Ireland, especially in overseas tourist markets.

- In 1994 Moya Doherty and John McColgan were given the task of producing a show for the interval of the **Eurovision Song contest**. They assembled Michael Flatley, Jean Butler, the Anúna choir and many traditional Irish dancers to perform an original new Irish dance with music composed by Bill Whelan. The show was named **Riverdance**. The now world-famous stage show is another successful Irish cultural initiative.

- The Gaelic Athletic Association or Cumann Lúthchleas Gael, better known as the **GAA**, is a 32-county sporting and cultural organisation. It is Ireland's largest sporting organisation and a superb example of an amateur sporting association with a worldwide presence. With over 2,300 clubs, the GAA is volunteer-led and community-based, promoting Gaelic games such as hurling, camogie, football and handball. The association's headquarters are at Croke Park in Dublin. The stadium has a capacity of 82,300 and hosts the highest-profile events in the Irish sporting calendar.

These cultural enterprises benefit society through creating employment and attracting tourists and other spin-off businesses.

> **WORKING WITH OTHERS**
>
> What might our lives be like without the GAA?

'3Ts'
- Compile a list of other examples of cultural enterprise. What role do they play in society?

SOCIAL ENTERPRISES

A social enterprise tackles social, economic and environmental issues and supports vulnerable people in our community.

We are extremely lucky in Ireland to have an organisation called Social Entrepreneurs Ireland. It supports, through funding and mentoring, budding entrepreneurs who have ideas about ways to make Ireland a better place.

Go to www.socialentrepreneurs.ie to find out what what organisations they have supported.

There are many Irish enterprises working to ensure a better life for all and to improve our local communities.

In your school perhaps you could support an organisation that you or your school has a link with. You might be able to volunteer, fundraise, or even raise awareness.

An interesting example of social entrepreneurship awareness is the **Young Social Innovator (YSI)**. This gives young people the opportunity to collaborate on innovative social projects. You can address **social issues** that affect you and your community. This is a win/win situation: you benefit from giving something back to your community. With a creative and caring attitude you can help your local community and in doing so make your world a better place. You also have an opportunity to showcase your project at an YSI national event. Areas that have been addressed in YSI include mental health, bullying, homelessness and immigration.

FINANCIAL, SOCIAL AND CULTURAL ENTERPRISE ROLES 2.1

WORKING WITH OTHERS

- Identify as many voluntary organisations in your area as you can.
- What might life be like without our social entrepreneurs?

After reading this unit, you should be becoming more aware of entrepreneurship and enterprise and how it is all about a '**can do' attitude**. This thinking can be applied to **all aspects of our lives**; in school, at home, in your local community, as a future employer/employee, as a business person, a social entrepreneur and as a citizen of the country.

BUMBLEance is an ambulance service specifically designed for children

Wonderful Worthwhile Websites

www.gaa.ie
www.youngsocialinnovators.ie
www.socialentrepreneurs.ie

CHECKING IN...

1. Name three types of financial enterprise and say how each provides a service.
2. Name three cultural enterprises and explain the role each plays in society.
3. Name one social enterprise and say how it makes a difference in your school, home or community.

Be a Researcher

Has your school participated in the YSI? What project did it submit?

Investigate YSI and source some interesting projects.

211

2.1 BE BUSINESS: ENTERPRISE

CHECKING IN...

1. Which of the following do you agree or disagree with? Place a tick ✓ in the appropriate box.

	Agree	Disagree
Enterprise is all about making a profit	☐	☐
A deposit account can earn interest	☐	☐
Banks provide a higher rate of interest than the interest charged on borrowings	☐	☐
Credit unions are an example of a financial enterprise	☐	☐
Mini-companies are examples of enterprise in schools	☐	☐
A 'can do' attitude is what enterprise is all about	☐	☐
Trocáire is an example of a financial enterprise	☐	☐

2. Copy the following table into your copy and match the terms with the correct statement.

1	2	3	4	5	6

1	Turning opportunities and ideas into value for others	A	Brainstorming
2	A popular technique for idea generation	B	Creativity
3	Open to new ideas and different ways of doing things.	C	Product screening
4	Selecting the most promising ideas	D	Entrepreneurship
5	An Post is an example of this type of enterprise	E	Young Social Innovator (YSI)
6	A social entrepreneurship organisation	F	Financial enterprises

3. 'Entrepreneurship can be taught.' Do you agree/disagree? Give reasons for your answer.

4. Create a fishbone summary of this unit using the template on p. 546.

5. Create a wordle for this unit with www.wordle.net. (This is an IT tool that creates 'word clouds' from the information you enter.)

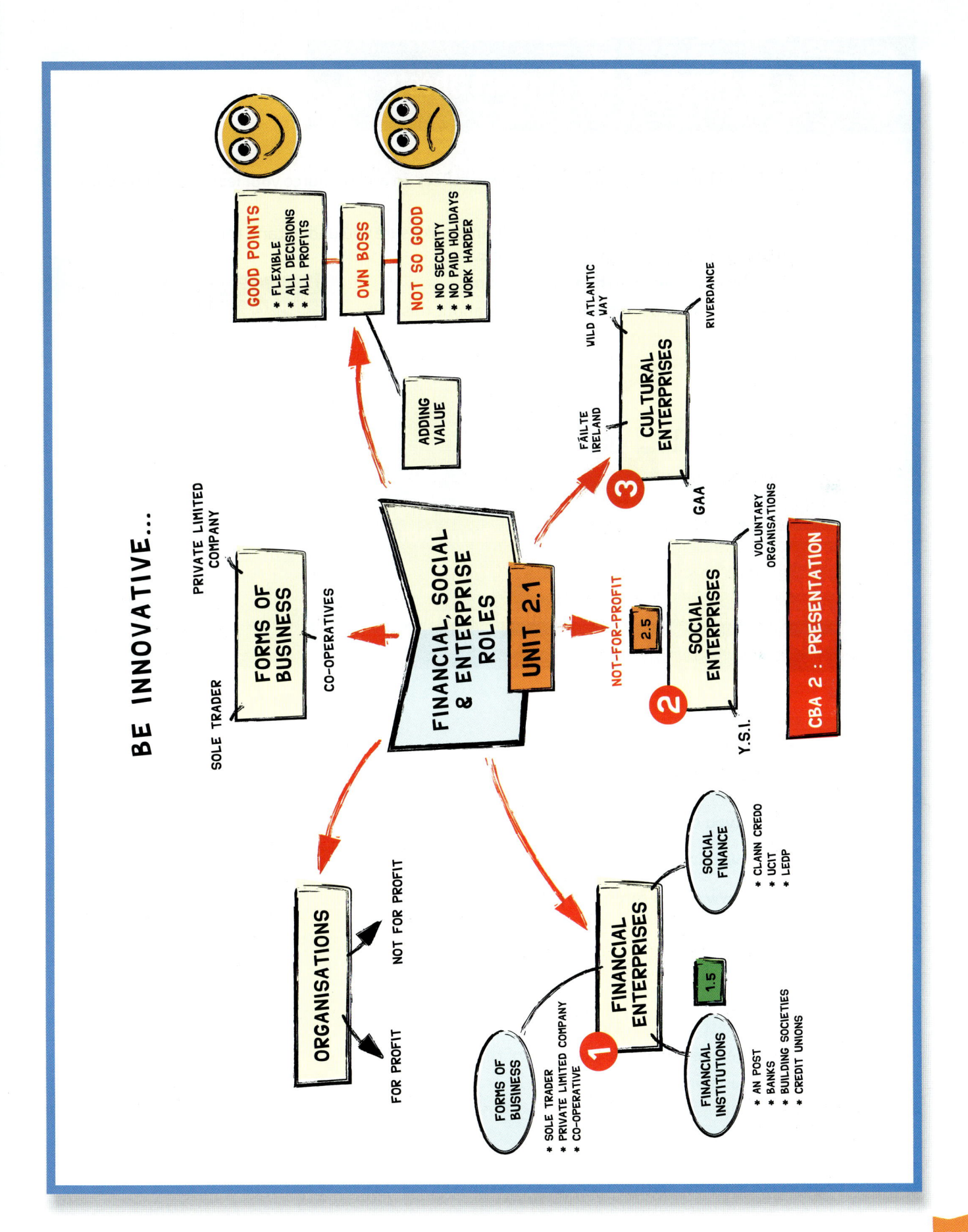

FINANCIAL, SOCIAL AND CULTURAL ENTERPRISE ROLES 2.1

BE INNOVATIVE...

FINANCIAL, SOCIAL & ENTERPRISE ROLES — UNIT 2.1

FORMS OF BUSINESS
- SOLE TRADER
- PRIVATE LIMITED COMPANY
- CO-OPERATIVES

ADDING VALUE

GOOD POINTS
* FLEXIBLE
* ALL DECISIONS
* ALL PROFITS

OWN BOSS

NOT SO GOOD
* NO SECURITY
* NO PAID HOLIDAYS
* WORK HARDER

ORGANISATIONS
- FOR PROFIT
- NOT FOR PROFIT

③ CULTURAL ENTERPRISES
- WILD ATLANTIC WAY
- RIVERDANCE
- FÁILTE IRELAND
- GAA

② SOCIAL ENTERPRISES
- NOT-FOR-PROFIT (2.5)
- VOLUNTARY ORGANISATIONS
- Y.S.I.

CBA 2 : PRESENTATION

① FINANCIAL ENTERPRISES (1.5)

FORMS OF BUSINESS
* SOLE TRADER
* PRIVATE LIMITED COMPANY
* CO-OPERATIVE

FINANCIAL INSTITUTIONS
* AN POST
* BANKS
* BUILDING SOCIETIES
* CREDIT UNIONS

SOCIAL FINANCE
* CLANN CREDO
* UCIT
* LEDP

213

Be Prepared: My Support Sheets

Completing the activities here will help you reflect on and reinforce your learning before you move on to the next unit.
- Write down the **key terms** in this unit and make sure you understand them. See if they match the ones at the back of the book.
- List the key **concepts/themes** in this unit.
- List the **three most interesting** points about this unit.

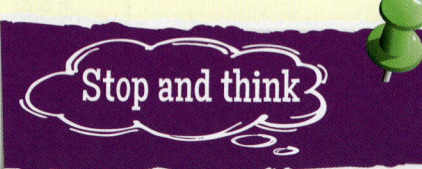

Stop and think

Do I have any questions or concerns?

What are the mistakes or errors I have made in this unit?

Make a presentation

Working by yourself, in pairs or in a team of three or four, plan a perfect presentation. Work with others and present individually (one to three minutes each). Choose one of the following:
- A field visit to a local enterprise
- An investigation of a local business enterprise
- An investigation of a financial enterprise

Presentation Idea!

You have been commissioned to present the newest smart card. It may be the newest existing smart card or you can create your own. Present this project in one of the following formats:

1. A presentation (you could use, eg. www.prezi.com)
2. A video (eg. www.animoto.com)
3. A podcast (eg. www.sourceforge.net/projects/audacity)

Success criteria:
- What might the best smart card look like?
- A clear title: remember to include the name of the card!
- Clear visual material
- Key features
- The impact on our planet

FINANCIAL, SOCIAL AND CULTURAL ENTERPRISE ROLES | 2.1

QUESTION TIME

1. Explain enterprise in your school, home and local community.
2. Illustrate inputs, outputs and added value.
3. Define financial enterprise, cultural enterprise and social enterprise.
4. Compare financial, cultural and social entrepreneurship.
5. List the services provided by banks and explain one in detail.
6. Evaluate how social enterprises can contribute to society.
7. Name a voluntary organisation that you are familiar with and discuss its contribution to our society.

EVALUATE MY LEARNING: DAR

Describe
- Did I/we meet my/our learning intentions?
- What went well? What are my/our strengths?

Assess
- How did I/we work with others?
- Were there challenges?
- How might I improve?

Recommend
- What skills and learning might I apply to new situations?

Do your **Key Check** in the workbook for this unit and then mark your learning position on the following rating scale:

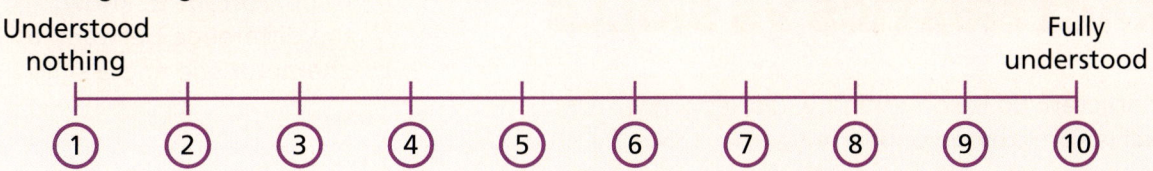

Understood nothing — 1 2 3 4 5 6 7 8 9 10 — Fully understood

How can you move up the rating scale? What can you **say**, **make**, **write** and **do** to illustrate your learning?

CBA 2 Presentation:
Will I use this unit for my topic for my **Presentation**?

You need to be preparing for your CBAs

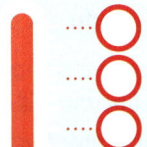

- Exceptional
- Above expectations
- In line with expectations
- Yet to meet expectations

215

2.2 ENTERPRISE AND THE ENTREPRENEUR

Describe the skills and characteristics of being enterprising and appreciate the role of an entrepreneur in an organisation, in society and in the economy.

Learning Intentions

At the end of this unit I will:
- Know about the characteristics and skills of entrepreneurs
- Understand and appreciate the role of the entrepreneur
- Value the skills of the entrepreneur

Making the links with other LOs:

- 2.1 Financial, social and cultural enterprise roles
- 2.3 Employment, work and volunteerism
- 2.4 Rights and responsibilities: employers and employees
- 3.6 Positive and negative economic growth and sustainability

Are there other LOs?

Key Concepts
- ✓ Skills and characteristics; profiling an entrepreneur
- ✓ Role of the entrepreneur in an organisation, in society and in the economy

Wonderful Worthwhile Websites

www.thinkbusiness.ie
www.khanacademy.org
www.foroige.ie
www.studententerprise.ie
www.businesseducation.ie

CHARACTERISTICS VS SKILLS

> A characteristic is something you are born with.
> A skill is something you learn.
> You can work on both characteristics and skills. Both can be improved!

It's important to know the difference between a characteristic and a skill.

A characteristic is something you are born with; it is part of you and your personality and it may change as you get older.

A skill is something you learn to do over a period of time. In school, at home and as you progress through life you will learn many skills. You will learn many skills during your Junior Cycle studies.

ENTERPRISE AND THE ENTREPRENEUR 2.2

'3Ts'

Why do you think self-help books are so successful?

Hint: you can learn skills like communication.

ENTERPRISING CHARACTERISTICS

Enterprising people have certain characteristics and skills that make them who they are.

The following are some characteristics that enterprising people display in their activities.

- **Innovative/creative** – able to come up with new ideas
- **Hard-working** - willing to work hard to achieve goals
- **Risk-taking** - prepared to do things that might not work out, but willing to try
- **Decisive** - not afraid to make a decision and stick to it
- **Self-confident** – self-belief, positive and secure in yourself and your abilities
- **Determined** – wanting to do something and ensuring that no one will stop you
- **Committed** – willing to put energy into things
- **Adaptable** – flexible, able to change to fit a situation

INNOVATIVE • HARD-WORKING • RISK-TAKING • DECISIVE
SELF-CONFIDENT • DETERMINED • COMMITTED • ADAPTABLE

Be Literate

Can you explain each of the eight 'characteristic' words above?

WORKING WITH OTHERS

Working in small groups, decide what you think are the three most important enterprising characteristics? How did you agree on these three?

2.2 BE BUSINESS: ENTERPRISE

ENTERPRISING SKILLS OF AN ENTREPRENEUR

- **Planning and goal setting** – organised, able to sequence what needs to be done
- **Decision-making** – able to choose one action over another
- **Communication** – successful at conveying information
- **Delegation** – able to give work to others
- **Motivation** – enthusiasm for doing something
- **Leadership** – having a clear vision
- **Time management** – good control over the way you use your time
- **Networking** – able to build good relationships with people for mutual benefit

PLANNING AND GOAL SETTING | DECISION-MAKING | COMMUNICATION | DELEGATION

MOTIVATION | LEADERSHIP | TIME MANAGEMENT | NETWORKING

Be Literate
Can you explain each of the eight 'skills' above?

WORKING WITH OTHERS
Working in small groups, decide what you think are the three most important enterprise skills. How did you agree on these three?

Business in Action/Presentation Idea!
Your Business Studies class could compile a list of well-known Irish entrepreneurs or entrepreneurs working in your area. Create profiles of the entrepreneurs. Include their business details, contact details, email, websites and any other relevant information. Perhaps you could contact some of the entrepreneurs and see if they would be willing to be interviewed or to answer some questions. Record your profiles and keep a copy in your copy/portfolio.

ENTERPRISE AND THE ENTREPRENEUR 2.2

WORKING WITH OTHERS

Working in small groups, create a profile of an Irish entrepreneur. Copy and use the questionnaire below in your research.

Profile of an Irish Entrepreneur

1. Personal details   Name: Location: Email: Facebook: Twitter: LinkedIn:
2. The enterprise   Describe in detail what the business does. What are its unique selling points? Does it sell in Europe? Globally?
3. Characteristics and skills   What, do you think, are the characteristics and skills required to be an entrepreneur?
4. What challenges did the entrepreneur encounter?
5. Describe the success the entrepreneur achieved.
6. How does technology benefit the organisation/business.
7. What role does the entrepreneur play in the organisation/business?
8. What role does the entrepreneur play in the local community and society?
9. How does the organisation/business ensure sustainable development?
10. Does the organisation/business trade internationally and what are the challenges of this?

2.2 BE BUSINESS: ENTERPRISE

CHECKING IN...

1. How do you think the entrepreneur in the profile has demonstrated enterprise?
2. What did you learn from the profile?

ENTREPRENEURS

Entrepreneurs are a certain kind of enterprising person. They are interested in starting businesses and making profit. They have the desire for success, the endurance (stamina) to achieve it and the belief that their challenges can become strengths.

Entrepreneurs are the risk-takers, who use their own money (or borrowed money) to invest in a business or an idea. Without them, individual firms would not exist and businesses would be run by the state or government. Almost all businesses were started by entrepreneurs, for example Apple, Coca-Cola, Google, IBM, Microsoft, Supermac's, Tayto and even your local Supervalu.

THE ROLE OF THE ENTREPRENEUR IN THE ORGANISATION

The success of any business is due to many factors. However, the entrepreneur can play a key role. The entrepreneur may have degrees, experience, business knowledge, technological know-how, but it is **the personality of the entrepreneur** that is key.

Within the organisations that they create, entrepreneurs are the driving force and inspiration for those around them. Their enthusiasm, persistence and confidence can encourage those around them to work harder and try to succeed.

Entrepreneurs often want their organisations to grow and become bigger and better, and their skills and characteristics often make that a reality.

Not every entrepreneur wants to start their own enterprise. Some entrepreneurs are willing to apply their entrepreneurial characteristics and skills within an organisation. This is known as **intrapreneurship**, and it plays an important role in all kinds of organisations.

Being an entrepreneur is the same wherever you are in the world. Entrepreneurship is like a global (world) language. Entrepreneurs in **Hong Kong** have to come up with an idea, write business plans, manage cash and make a profit just like entrepreneurs in **Ireland**.

Time to think

'Entrepreneurs are born, not made.' Do you agree with this statement? Why/why not?

Time to think

How could you be enterprising in school, at home and in your local community?

How could you be enterprising as part of the Junior Cycle Business Studies course?

THE ROLE OF THE ENTREPRENEUR IN SOCIETY

It's not only the entrepreneur who benefits when a new business is established. Society also benefits.

- **New jobs** are important to society.
- Businesses in **associated industries**, such as cafés, hotels and financial services, benefit.
- Infrastructure development organisations and property companies benefit when a new business is created.
- Entrepreneurs can change the way we live and work. Successful innovations and new ideas can **improve our standard of living**.
- Entrepreneurs often contribute to **local charities**.

Our country's **economy grows**. More income for employees and more income (through taxation) for our government brings many benefits.

From the highly qualified programmer to the scientist or local butcher, the entrepreneur brings benefits to a broad spectrum of our economy.

CREATING SOCIAL CHANGE

By supplying **new** goods and services, entrepreneurs break away from tradition and reduce dependence on outdated systems and technologies. This change results in an improved quality and standard of living; for example Steve Jobs, who founded Apple, introduced the first tablet device to the market.

Some enterprises work to make people's lives better, even thought they make a profit. The pharmaceutical (medicines) industry is an excellent example of this. Can you think of others? An entrepreneur who invents an app to help us count our calories, or to monitor our fitness, improves our standard of living. Can you name other apps that help improve our lives? Perhaps a homework app!

COMMUNITY DEVELOPMENT

Entrepreneurs often develop **non-profit** entrepreneurial projects and invest in **community projects**. Some famous entrepreneurs, such as Bill Gates, have used their money to finance causes from education to public health.

Bono, from U2, funds Music Generation. **Music Generation** is Ireland's national music education programme, which aims to transform the lives of children and young people through access to high-quality performance music education. Check out their website, www.musicgeneration.ie

> Not-for-profit organisations are about helping people rather than making a profit. These organisations need enterprising individuals to drive them and make them a success. Local clubs and societies, charities and local services (e.g. meals on wheels) provide a valuable contribution to society and would not exist without the people who run them voluntarily.

2.2 BE BUSINESS: ENTERPRISE

A Franchise

Some entrepreneurs choose to establish a franchise rather than try a brand new idea. A **franchise** is a licence agreement that allows the franchisee (the person starting the business) to sell the goods/services of the franchisor (an existing business).

Buying a **franchise** is one option for someone looking to start their own business.

Being part of a franchise allows you to follow established procedures that have proven to be successful. In return, you agree to follow the rules of the franchise and to pay a **fee**.

Examples of franchises include McDonald's, KFC, Eddie Rocket's, Pizza Hut, Starbucks and Centra.

WORKING WITH OTHERS

Do you think a franchise is a good idea? What franchise would you like to be part of?

The Zip Yard was voted franchise of the year in Ireland 2015/2016. It is a clothing alterations boutique that can restyle, remodel, refit, renew, retrend and repair your clothes. It was established after extensive market research which found a gap in the market – body shapes don't always conform to standard sizes. In addition, people don't have the time to alter garments; and if they need an expensive item altered, they want to make sure that it is done properly. The Zip Yard began in Ireland and now has branches in Britain.

ENTREPRENEURS CREATE ENTREPRENEURS

Entrepreneurs can create something called the **multiplier effect**. This is when growth in one area of the economy causes growth in other related areas. New business opportunities are created and new entrepreneurs are given more choices in terms of what business to get into.

For example, Steve Jobs and his partners created Apple computers in their garage and made computers a household item. They used technology that some big companies didn't see the value of. Think of all the other businesses that now benefit from Apple creations and technology.

Entrepreneurial companies usually grow quickly and are responsible for much of the job creation in an economy. For a business to succeed it must be profitable. These profits are invested in new businesses or spent, and both of these activities help our economy.

ENTERPRISE AND THE ENTREPRENEUR   2.2

CHECKING IN...

1. Which of the following do you agree or disagree with? Place a tick ✓ in the appropriate box.

	Agree	Disagree
Entrepreneurs impact on our world	☐	☐
Entrepreneurs are risk-takers	☐	☐
A diploma or degree is really important for an entrepreneur	☐	☐
A skill is something you are born with	☐	☐
Skills are more important than characteristics	☐	☐
Communication is a skill	☐	☐

2. Copy the following table into your copy and match the terms with the correct statement.

1	2	3	4

1 Being innovative
2 Innate characteristics of entrepreneur
3 Being decisive
4 An example of a franchise

A Skill
B Born with
C McDonald's
D Entrepreneurship

3. Copy the Venn diagram below into your copy and use it to compare and contrast skills and characteristics.

Skills — Similarities — Characteristics

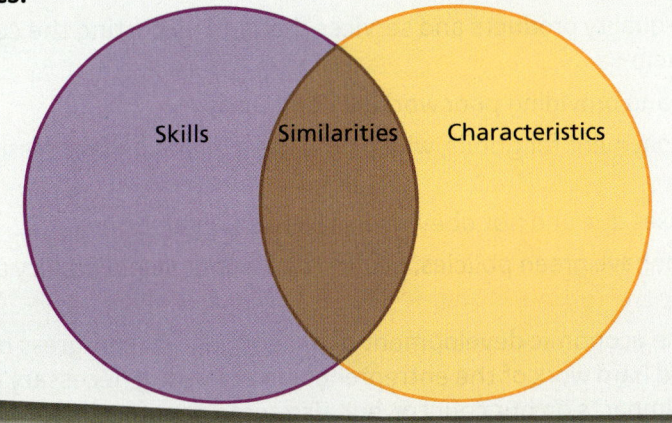

The **Venn diagram** is a great visual stimulus to structure an answer for compare and contrast. Common elements can be seen where the circles intersect or cross. Contrasting elements can be seen in the outer circles.

THE ENTREPRENEUR AND OUR ECONOMY

Entrepreneurs contribute to improving our economy.

When people are in employment they spend money in local businesses, such as clothing, car expenses, house expenses, cafés and restaurants. Each of these activities helps local businesses grow. The existence of a new company can encourage others to open businesses in the same area, which in turn creates new job creation.

This idea of private ownership of businesses is known as **capitalism**. Capitalism is part of an economic system in which trade, industries, and the means of production are owned **privately** and operated for **profit**. (The opposite of capitalism is when businesses are controlled by the state.)

The profits created by enterprise play an important role in in the growth of the **national income**. The entrepreneur's investment will help **economic progress**. It also contributes to our country's **gross domestic product** (GDP).

The **GDP** of a country is calculated based on the total number of products and services produced in a country. The more products and services produced, the higher the GDP. It indicates the **economic prosperity** (wealth) of a country.

When Ireland's GDP increases we have growth in our country **Unit 3.9**.

Entrepreneurship and the Economic Development of our Country

- Creates jobs and employment
- Distributes wealth, and ensures lots of benefits
- Improves the standard of living
- Increases our exports, when we sell to other countries
- Creates revenue/income for our Government

UNETHICAL PRACTICES

Some entrepreneurs and businesses have negative impacts through unethical practices.

The following are five possible areas of **bad practice** that affect:

- **Customers:** providing inferior-quality products and services that end up costing the customer more because they have to replace them
- **Employees:** paying low wages and providing poor working conditions
- **Suppliers of goods:** delaying payment for goods, which puts the supplier under pressure as they also have bills to pay
- **Government:** not paying all taxes due and not obeying all laws and regulations
- **Planet:** some enterprises do not have green policies, do not think about sustainability and are not environmentally friendly

The entrepreneur is essential for the economic development of our country. The progress of a country depends upon the skills, talents and hard work of the entrepreneur in delivering necessary goods and services. Entrepreneurs have many positive impacts on our country, but also some negative impacts.

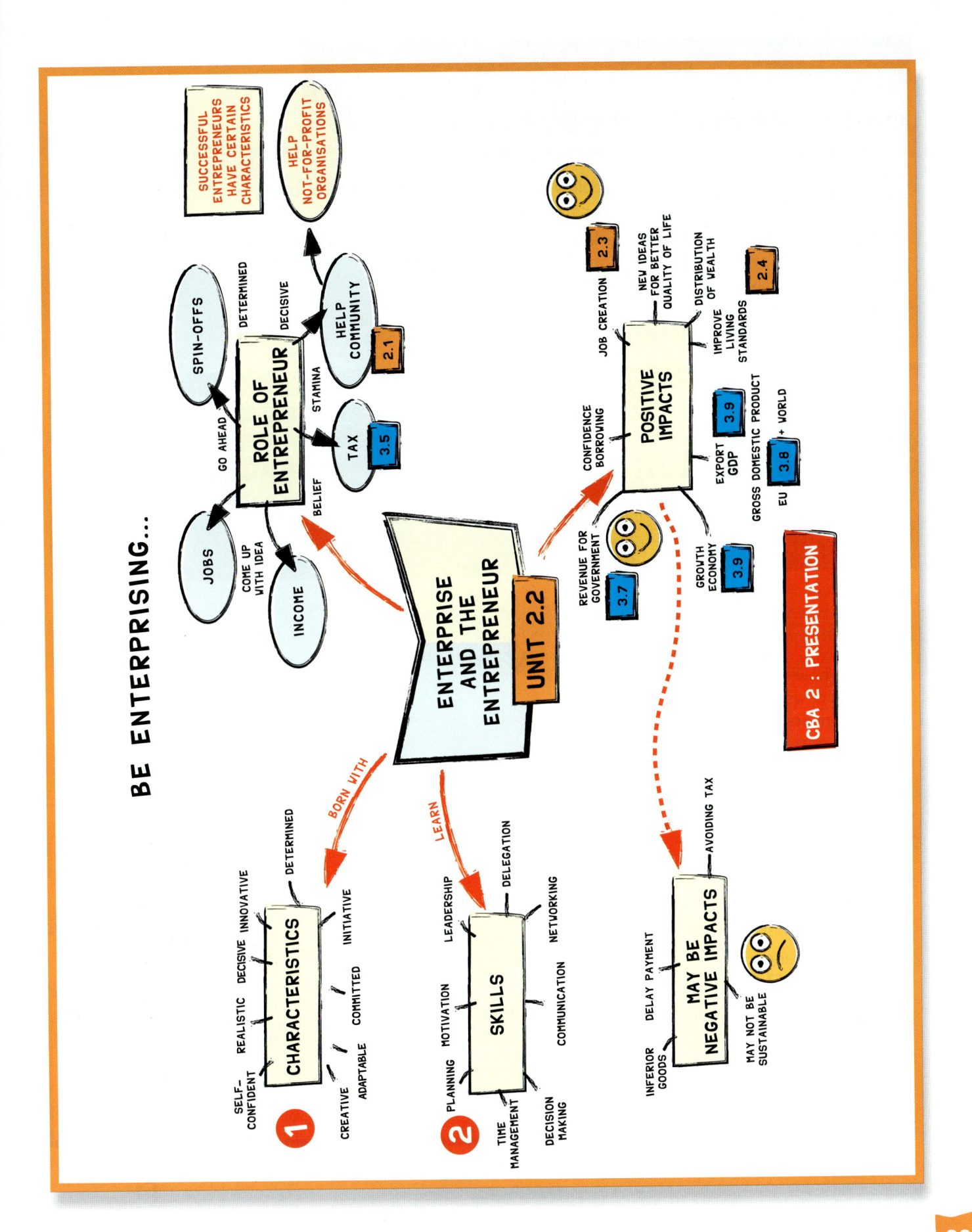

ENTERPRISE AND THE ENTREPRENEUR 2.2

BE ENTERPRISING...

ENTERPRISE AND THE ENTREPRENEUR — UNIT 2.2

ROLE OF ENTREPRENEUR
- SPIN-OFFS
- JOBS
- INCOME (COME UP WITH IDEA)
- GO AHEAD
- DETERMINED
- DECISIVE
- STAMINA
- BELIEF
- HELP COMMUNITY (2.1)
- TAX (3.5)

SUCCESSFUL ENTREPRENEURS HAVE CERTAIN CHARACTERISTICS

HELP NOT-FOR-PROFIT ORGANISATIONS

① CHARACTERISTICS (BORN WITH)
- SELF-CONFIDENT
- REALISTIC
- DECISIVE
- INNOVATIVE
- DETERMINED
- CREATIVE
- ADAPTABLE
- COMMITTED
- INITIATIVE

② SKILLS (LEARN)
- LEADERSHIP
- DELEGATION
- NETWORKING
- COMMUNICATION
- DECISION MAKING
- TIME MANAGEMENT
- PLANNING
- MOTIVATION

POSITIVE IMPACTS
- JOB CREATION
- NEW IDEAS FOR BETTER QUALITY OF LIFE
- DISTRIBUTION OF WEALTH (2.4)
- IMPROVE LIVING STANDARDS
- EXPORT (3.9)
- GROSS DOMESTIC PRODUCT
- EU + WORLD (3.8)
- GROWTH ECONOMY (3.9)
- REVENUE FOR GOVERNMENT (3.7)
- CONFIDENCE BORROWING
- (2.3)

MAY BE NEGATIVE IMPACTS
- AVOIDING TAX
- DELAY PAYMENT
- MAY NOT BE SUSTAINABLE
- INFERIOR GOODS

CBA 2 : PRESENTATION

225

2.2 BE BUSINESS: ENTERPRISE

Be Prepared: My Support Sheets

Completing the activities below will help you reflect on and reinforce your learning before you move on to the next unit.

- Write down the **key terms** in this unit and make sure you understand them. See if they match the ones at the back of the book.
- List the **key concepts/themes** in this unit.
- List the **three most interesting points** about this unit.

Make a presentation

Work with others to plan a presentation and then present individually (one to three minutes). Use resources such as www.animoto.com. Choose one of the following:

- Leaders in Irish business
- The impact of an entrepreneurial organisation on its locality

Enterprise in Action Idea!

Create a newspaper article for your local business newspaper on the theme: 'What do entrepreneurs bring to society?' When you have finished, present your article to your group.

Success criteria:

- An eye-catching title
- A relevant photograph or image
- Two positive points and two negative points

QUESTION TIME

Working in pairs, discuss and then document your answers.

1. Explain characteristics and skills.
2. 'Entrepreneurs are born, not made.' Do you agree or disagree with this statement?
3. Evaluate the role of the entrepreneur in an organisation.
4. List the most important characteristics that an entrepreneur should possess.
5. Evaluate how entrepreneurs contribute to society.
6. Apply the fishbone template (p. 546) to create a summary of the entrepreneur's role.

EVALUATE MY LEARNING: DAR

Describe
- Did I/we meet my/our learning intentions?
- What went well? What are my/our strengths?

Assess
- How did I/we work with others?
- Were there challenges?

Recommend
- How might I improve?
- What skills and learning might I apply to new situations?

Do your **Key Check** in the workbook for this unit and then mark your learning position on the following rating scale:

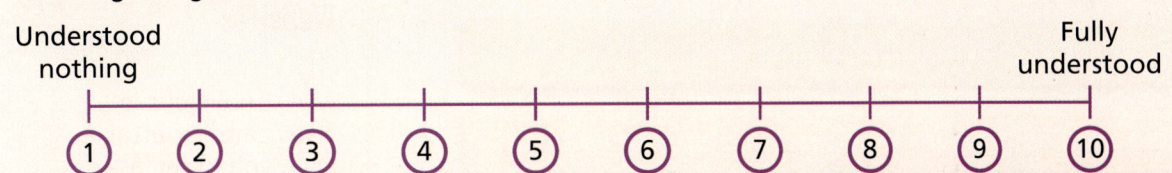

Understood nothing — 1 2 3 4 5 6 7 8 9 10 — Fully understood

How can you move up the rating scale? What can you **say**, **make**, **write** and **do** to illustrate your learning?

CBA 2 Presentation:
Will I use this unit for my topic for my **Presentation**?

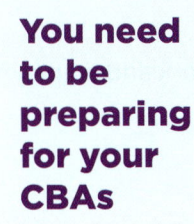

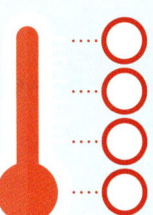

You need to be preparing for your CBAs

- Exceptional
- Above expectations
- In line with expectations
- Yet to meet expectations

Stop and think

Do I have any questions or concerns?
What are the mistakes or errors I made in this unit?

2.3 EMPLOYMENT, WORK AND VOLUNTEERISM

Differentiate between employment, work and volunteerism, identifying and describing features, benefits, rewards and careers in each.

Learning Intentions

At the end of this unit I will:

- Know about and understand work
- Understand volunteering
- Be able to value work, employment and volunteering
- Understand the skills required for employment, work and volunteering

Making the links with other LOs:

2.1 Financial, social and cultural enterprise roles

2.4 Rights and responsibilities: employers and employees

3.6 Positive and negative economic growth and sustainability

Are there other LOs?

Key Concepts

- ✓ Work
- ✓ Volunteering
- ✓ Employment

Wonderful Worthwhile Websites

www.publicjobs.ie
www.careersportal.ie
www.volunteer.ie
www.irishaid.ie
www.vso.ie

3Ts

- What do you think is the difference between work and employment?
- Is the government an employer?
- Is your school an employer? Explain.

WORK AND EMPLOYMENT

Work is generally defined as a **job**, which requires effort. You don't necessarily receive payment for work.

Employment is work undertaken for payment.

Work: Chef Donal Skehan cooks a barbecue for family and friends.

Employment: He cooks for an RTÉ programme and receives payment for cooking.

EMPLOYMENT, WORK AND VOLUNTEERISM 2.3

Work: A bodhrán maker in the Aran Islands makes bodhráns for a friend.

Employment: A local company pays the same bodhrán maker to make a batch for distributing around the world.

Work: Remy coaches the local under-11 soccer team with no payment.

Employment: Derek manages a Premier League football team and receives a large salary.

An **employer** hires the employee and pays them a wage or salary in return for their effort.

Employees provide work in return for a wage or salary.

A **wage** is usually paid weekly and is based on the number of hours worked.

A **salary** is usually paid monthly and is the same every month, however many hours are worked.

The **unemployed** are people who are willing to work but are unable to find suitable work.

The **labour force** is all the people who are available to work.

Which of the following do you consider to be work and which are employment?

1. Schoolwork
2. Housework
3. Voluntary work
4. Training schemes work
5. Job sharing
6. Flexitime
7. Full-time work
8. Part-time work
9. Temporary work
10. Self-employment

Housework

Voluntary Work

Self-employment

Schoolwork

The company in the case study below include the slogan 'Think Global, Act Local' in their sales campaign. This forward way of thinking seems to have worked well for them!

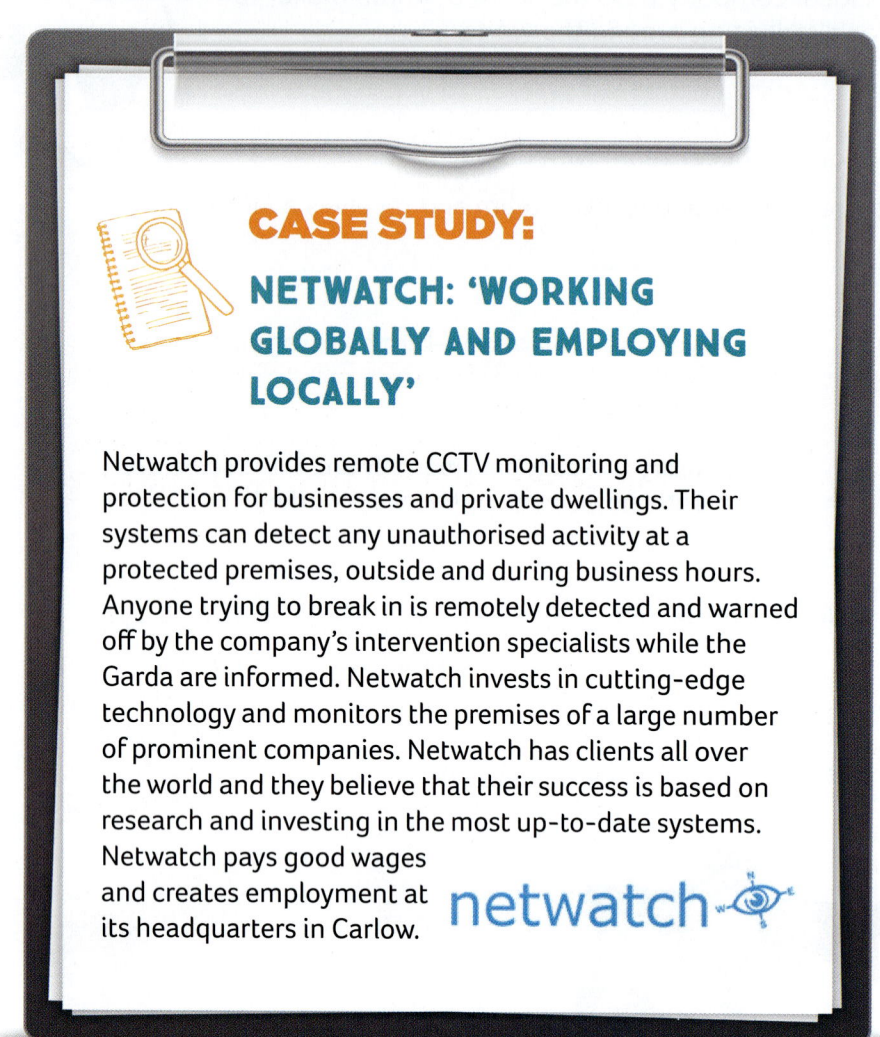

CASE STUDY:

NETWATCH: 'WORKING GLOBALLY AND EMPLOYING LOCALLY'

Netwatch provides remote CCTV monitoring and protection for businesses and private dwellings. Their systems can detect any unauthorised activity at a protected premises, outside and during business hours. Anyone trying to break in is remotely detected and warned off by the company's intervention specialists while the Garda are informed. Netwatch invests in cutting-edge technology and monitors the premises of a large number of prominent companies. Netwatch has clients all over the world and they believe that their success is based on research and investing in the most up-to-date systems. Netwatch pays good wages and creates employment at its headquarters in Carlow.

Top Tip!

You will need numerous skills over your lifetime. Developing your skills helps you to live up to your fullest potential. Remember, practice makes perfect.

Time to think

The Business Studies course will provide you with numerous opportunities to develop important skills. Top skills that will make you more employable include:

- Communication skills
- Teamwork skills
- Creative skills
- IT skills
- Motivational skills

Do you have any of these skills? Can you name the skills you do have? Are there skills you can improve on?

EMPLOYMENT RIGHTS

As an employee you have certain basic **employment rights** (see Unit 2.4). One of these rights is a written statement of terms and conditions of employment: this is called a **contract of employment**.

A contract of employment covers the following terms and conditions:

- A written statement of pay or wage slip (information on income and deductions)
- A minimum wage, which the government decides on
- A maximum working week
- Unpaid breaks during working hours
- Annual leave from work
- A minimum amount of notice before termination (ending) of employment

EMPLOYMENT, WORK AND VOLUNTEERISM 2.3

HUMAN RESOURCES

It is important that there are **good relationships between employers and employees**. This relationship is known as **industrial relations**. If there is a good relationship between employers and employees, people will be content and motivated. This leads to increased productivity, greater sales and more profits. When there are good industrial relations there is less chance of **industrial action**, for example **strikes**.

A **strike** occurs when employees refuse to work as a form of protest, usually about working conditions, such as low pay.

Trade Unions

Many workers are members of a **trade union**. Trade unions are **organisations** that are set up to **protect workers**. The Association of Secondary Teachers in Ireland (ASTI) and the Teachers' Union of Ireland (TUI) are examples of teachers' trade unions. The employee pays a **fee** to the union. In return the union can **negotiate** with employers for better terms and conditions of work – holidays, hours of work, etc. Unions also represent employees when there are disputes. Trade unions provide strength in numbers as together employees are more powerful than they are as individuals.

Shop Steward

The shop steward is elected by employees as the union representative. Shop stewards recruit new members, collect fees and keep the employees informed on any updates. They can also negotiate with management on behalf of an employee.

Communication is an important feature of industrial relations. A trade union and an employer can work through many procedures to ensure that a dispute is resolved before industrial action is taken.

Be a Researcher

Source reports of a recent dispute from a newspaper or news online.

- What was the dispute about?
- Name the parties involved: the employer(s) and the union(s).
- How many days were lost in the dispute?
- Was the dispute resolved? If so, how?
- What might you have done to resolve the dispute?
- What was your source of information?

Did You Know?

ISSU (Irish Second-Level Students' Union) is a union for post-primary students.

231

EMPLOYMENT LEGISLATION

Employment legislation is in place to ensure that people are treated fairly and that employers don't discriminate against employees. Employment legislation ensures that employees are not unfairly dismissed. The employer must comply with health and safety legislation and deal with conflict and disputes in a fair manner.

The following are **five** important pieces of legislation that protect young employees:

1. **Young Persons Act 1996:** ensures that young people are not exploited in employment and sets out their rights, in terms of times, breaks and working during school term.
2. **Employment Equality Act 1998/2004:** ensures there is no discrimination when recruiting on the basis of gender, marital status, family status, sexual orientation, religious belief, age, disability, race and membership of the travelling community.
3. **Unfair Dismissals Act 1977:** allows for employees who have been dismissed under certain conditions to bring a claim against the employer.
4. **Health and Safety Act 2005:** states the obligations and responsibilities for health and safety at work.
5. **Industrial Relations Act 1990:** promotes improved industrial relations by outlining procedures for conducting and settling industrial disputes.

There are also many pieces of legislation that cover the role of the **employer**. As Ireland is a member of the European Union (EU), employers must also comply with EU legislation.

Be a Researcher

Source information on the Acts listed above.

Research laws that may affect you as a worker.

Wonderful Worthwhile Websites

www.youth-connect.ie

BENEFITS AND REWARDS OF EMPLOYMENT

Being employed gives you **financial freedom** and **independence**.

- You will earn a wage/salary (income) that you can spend as you want. You can buy necessities and the occasional luxury. An income gives you the opportunity to save, as outlined in Strand 1: Personal Finance. You have money to pay for **important protections**, for example life assurance, health insurance, holiday insurance and dental insurance. When you are employed you are entitled to holidays, some sick leave and parental leave, and you can acquire **retirement benefits**.
- As employment promises a salary or wage at regular intervals, you will feel **financially secure**.
- Being employed may give you the opportunity to borrow to **purchase a home**, to save for a rainy day and to plan for your retirement by participating in a pension scheme.
- Employment also gives you the opportunity to increase your **knowledge** and **skills**, either for self-improvement or to make you more employable in the future.

BEING UNEMPLOYED

People can become unemployed for various reasons, for example seasonal work or a business closing down. Unemployment in an economy occurs when there are people who are willing and able to work but don't have a job. For example, if a person recently lost their job and is looking for work, they are known as unemployed.

If you are unemployed you may qualify for a payment from the government knows as **Jobseeker's Benefit** (JB).

If you are unemployed you should always be improving your skills to make you more employable. One way to do that is to choose to volunteer in your local community.

> Find a job you love and you will never have to work a day!

Wonderful Worthwhile Websites

The following websites will give you some ideas of career options.
www.careersportal.ie
www.jobs.ie

CHECKING IN...

1. Explain, using examples, the difference between work and employment.
2. Discuss the features of employment.
3. Is it good to be employed? Why?
4. Name three laws that protect employees.

VOLUNTEERING

Volunteering means doing something, without payment, that will benefit other people, society or the environment.

Volunteering is a meaningful activity for all ages – teenagers, adults and retirees. Research has shown that there are many **positive rewards** in helping others.

BENEFITS AND REWARDS OF VOLUNTEERING

The work of a volunteer often goes unrewarded. The volunteer's time is given freely and with no expectation of payment. Volunteering has many **benefits** and **rewards**.

- We volunteer because we want to feel good, we want to help others, and we want to see the impact we can make. But volunteering has more to give than just the **feel-good factor**.
- When applying for employment, adding your volunteer experience to your **curriculum vitae (CV)** can help you to stand out. Listing

Time to think

Do you know anyone who volunteers? What would you say about them?

Have you ever had an opportunity to volunteer? How did it make you feel?

2.3 BE BUSINESS: ENTERPRISE

voluntary experience shows your initiative and commitment and allows you to list the skills you have gained or developed through volunteering. An employer might be impressed by your voluntary activities, especially if they are relevant to the job you are applying for. Volunteering can **positively impact your career** by providing opportunities that might not otherwise be immediately available to you.

- Being involved in voluntary organisations outside school or work gives you a chance to give your time and skills to help others. Helping others is often a **satisfying experience**, which comes with an opportunity to meet new people while growing as an individual. No matter what area you choose to volunteer in, you have a chance to leave a lasting impact in your local community.
- Volunteering allows you to **develop new skills** and to transfer your existing skills into new roles.
- As a volunteer, you have the opportunity to make **connections** that might not otherwise be available to you. Volunteering gives you the chance to make friends and to connect with other like-minded individuals.

Did You Know?

Actress Angelina Jolie gives her time to help those in need. As a Special Envoy for the United Nations High Commissioner for Refugees (UNHCR) she travels around the world highlighting the plight of refugees. She also works to promote other causes such as women's rights, education and conservation.

Many celebrities work to make a difference. Can you make a difference?

BEING A VOLUNTEER

The key to being a successful volunteer is to find a cause you truly **believe in**. When you enjoy what you are doing it will become a rewarding experience.

When working as a volunteer:

- Be respectful
- Be reliable
- Be professional
- Be confident
- Be ethical
- Be the best

Time to think

How would you feel about working for nothing?

WORK, EMPLOYMENT AND VOLUNTEERISM

	Work	**Employment**	**Volunteerism**
Features	No payment No employer No security No contract	Payment Employer/employee Laws in place to protect Contract of employment	No payment No employer No security No contract
Benefits and rewards	Personal satisfaction for getting things done Apply/improve knowledge and skills Thanks from relatives/friends Health benefits of being active	Getting paid for work done Apply/improve knowledge and skills Appreciation from employer and colleagues Easier to find work when already working	Feeling good about helping others/society Apply/improve knowledge and skills Appreciation from those you help Making connections that can help in life and career
Careers	Any kind of work that you do, whether paid or unpaid, allows you to improve your skills and knowledge and enhances your chances of employment or promotion.		

CHECKING IN…

1. Explain, using examples, the difference between employment and volunteering.
2. What are the rewards and benefits of volunteering?
3. Name three ways in which volunteering can help you in your career.

2.3 BE BUSINESS: ENTERPRISE

BE CAREER FOCUSED...

UNIT 2.3 — EMPLOYMENT, WORK AND VOLUNTEERISM

WORK EXPERIENCE MAY BE AVAILABLE IN EMPLOYMENT & VOLUNTEERING

EMPLOYMENT

- **TYPES**: LOTS OF TYPES, LOTS OF JOBS + SECTORS
- **KNOWLEDGE, SKILLS, VALUES**
- **PAID** = YES
- **FEATURES**: GET PAID FOR WORK DONE
- **ALWAYS OPPORTUNITIES** – CAREER
- **CONTRACT**:
  * WAGES
  * MINIMUM WAGE
  * LEAVE
  * RIGHTS

LAWS (IRISH / EU)

* YOUNG PERSONS ACT
* EMPLOYMENT EQUALITY
* UNFAIR DISMISSALS
* HEALTH & SAFETY
* INDUSTRIAL RELATIONS

WORK

- **TYPES**: SCHOOLWORK, HOMEWORK, WORK EXPERIENCE (OTHER TYPES PAID)
- **NON-CONTRACTUAL**
- **PAID** = NO
- **FEATURES**: JOBS THAT REQUIRE EFFORT
- **CAREER MAY HELP**
- **KNOWLEDGE, SKILLS, VALUES**

VOLUNTEERING

- **IMPROVES JOB PROSPECTS, CAREER**
- **NON-CONTRACTUAL**
- **KNOWLEDGE, SKILLS, VALUES**
- **PAID** = NO
- **FEATURES**: DOING SOMETHING THAT WILL BENEFIT OTHERS
- **TYPES**:
  * LOCAL
  * NATIONAL
  * GLOBAL / INTERNATIONAL

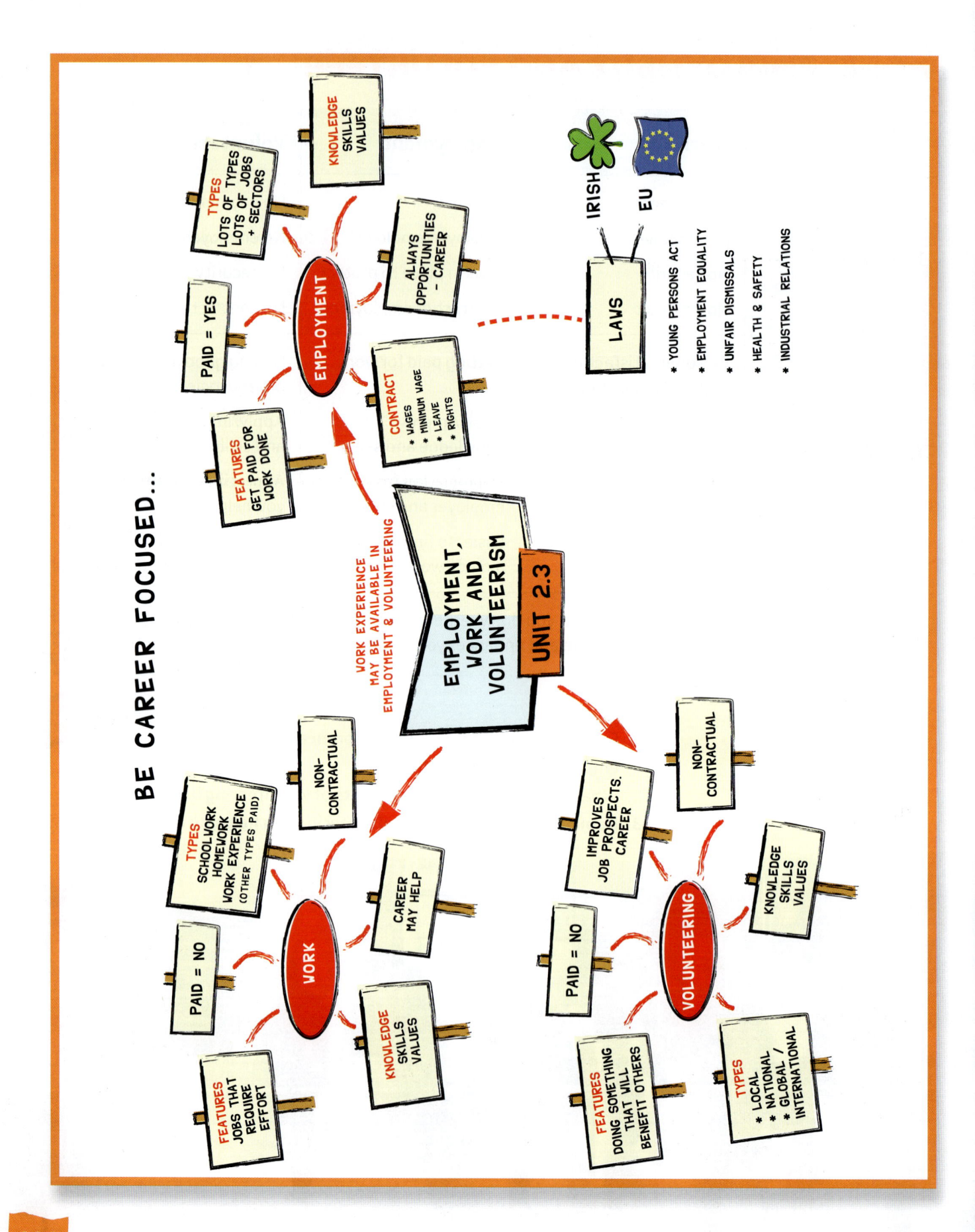

236

EMPLOYMENT, WORK AND VOLUNTEERISM | 2.3

Be Prepared: My Support Sheets

Completing the activities here will help you to reflect on and reinforce your learning before you move on to the next unit.

- Write down the **key terms** in this unit and make sure you understand them. See if they match the ones at the back of the book.
- List the key **concepts/themes** in this unit.
- List the **three most interesting points** in this unit.

Do a role play

Do a role play. In pairs, role play being a volunteer, highlighting the benefits of volunteering. Take turns being a volunteer and the person the volunteer is helping.

Stop and think

Do I have any questions or concerns?

What are the mistakes or errors I made in this unit?

Volunteering in Action Idea!

Create a poster explaining volunteering

Volunteering...

Success criteria:
- An appropriate title
- A visual
- Key points of information
- Clear and consistent lettering

QUESTION TIME

1. Explain work and its benefits.
2. Define employment.
3. What are the disadvantages of being unemployed?
4. List the reasons why industrial disputes occur. How might a dispute be resolved?
5. List the benefits of being employed.
6. Evaluate the benefits of volunteering.
7. What job might suit you? Why?

EVALUATE MY LEARNING: DAR

Describe
- Did I/we meet my/our learning intentions?
- What went well? What are my/our strengths?

Assess
- How did I/we work with others?
- Were there challenges?

Recommend
- How might I improve?
- What skills and learning might I apply to new situations?

Do your **Key Check** in the workbook for this unit and then mark your learning position on the following rating scale:

Understood nothing ① ② ③ ④ ⑤ ⑥ ⑦ ⑧ ⑨ ⑩ Fully understood

How can you move up the rating scale? What can you **say**, **make**, **write** and **do** to illustrate your learning?

CBA 2 Presentation:
Will I use this unit for my topic for my **Presentation**?

You need to be preparing for your CBAs
- Exceptional
- Above expectations
- In line with expectations
- Yet to meet expectations

2.4 RIGHTS AND RESPONSIBILITIES: EMPLOYERS AND EMPLOYEES

Distinguish between the rights and responsibilities of employer and employee from legal, social, environmental and ethical perspectives.

Learning Intentions

At the end of this unit I will:
- Know about rights and responsibilities
- Understand rights and responsibilities from different perspectives

Making the links with other LOs:

2.2 Enterprise and the entrepreneur

3.4 Government revenue and government expenditure

Are there other LOs?

Key Concepts

- ✓ Rights, ethics, values, responsibilities
- ✓ Corporate and social responsibilities

Wonderful Worthwhile Websites

www.citizensinformation.ie
www.youthconnect.ie

Business in Action/Presentation Idea!

Invite a speaker from Citizens Information or Youth Connect to speak to your Business Studies class.

RIGHTS AND RESPONSIBILITIES

Rights are what every human being is entitled to, no matter who they are or what part of the world they are from.

Some rights are for people to live in a fair and just society. Other rights include the right to food, clothing, education and freedom of speech.

It is important to be aware that with rights come responsibilities.

A **responsibility** is something that you have a duty to do. It is something that affects not only our lives but the lives of others.

Be a Researcher

Investigate the Universal Declaration of Human Rights. This declaration was drawn up by the United Nations in 1948 and it was a milestone in human rights. Find out what it says, how it came about and which countries have signed up to it.

Some of our responsibilities include following the rules at home, at school and in the community.

Students, individuals, employers, employees, consumers, investors, for-profit and not-for-profit organisations and our government all have rights and responsibilities.

The relationship between the employer and employee can be understood better if the rights and responsibilities of each are examined. To fully understand rights and responsibilities you need to look at them from a variety of perspectives (viewpoints).

- **Legal perspective** refers to laws – these include Irish and European laws
- **Social perspective** refers to our family background, our community and our culture
- **Environmental perspective** refers to our effect on the planet
- **Ethical perspective** refers to what is morally right or wrong

While in this unit we are concentrating on employers' and employees' rights and responsibilities, you too as students have rights and responsibilities. For example, in Ireland you have a right to an education and to be treated fairly with no discrimination regardless of gender, nationality, income, disability or background. Students have responsibilities too, for example to be punctual, to treat everyone with respect and dignity and to respect the property of the school and the local community.

> **Time to think**
>
> 'Students should be part of the decision-making process in schools.' Write reasons for and reasons against this motion.

1. Legal Perspective

From a **legal perspective,** employees and employers have to follow laws (Unit 2.3). There are laws governing the wage an employee receives. It is a legal right for an employee to receive a wage slip. There are health and safety regulations that have to be adhered to in the workplace. Everyone in the workplace has the right to be treated alike, with respect and dignity. People can't be discriminated against when being employed or promoted. Even dismissals from employment need to be fair.

2. Social Perspective

We are all unique, important and special in this world. We start learning about rights with our family, friends, school and in our community. We learn skills like using manners, taking our turn, sharing, being truthful and honest. We continue to add to these skills and learn more about the responsibilities that go with our rights. We learn that some things that humans do are not acceptable because we are not considering the rights of others. Things like **bullying, violence, destroying others' property, and stealing** do not respect the rights of others.

> **Be a Researcher**
>
> Find out what the minimum wage is in Ireland today.
>
> What might happen if the minimum wage were increased?
>
> Would it affect the government's budget?

An organisation has a social responsibility towards its employees. People want to work for organisations that are socially responsible; that pay decent wages and offer good working conditions. In turn, being a socially responsible employer makes it easier to recruit and keep workers as people want to work for you.

Consumers also want to know that an organisation behaves in a responsible way. For example, the Body Shop is very successful because of its stance on human and animal rights.

3. Environmental Perspective

Humans are responsible for many changes that have happened in our world. Many of these changes have had negative impacts on plants, animals and even people. We all have a responsibility to learn the skills of sharing our planet with other living things. We also have a responsibility to make our world a cleaner and safer place for all to live.

If we want to have rights, then we have to act in a responsible way, so that everyone and everything on our earth benefits.

We should try to:

- 'Reduce, Reuse, Recycle'
- Use **green energy** such as wind energy, solar energy, sea energy
- **Reduce carbon emissions**
- **Reduce pollution**

Caring for the environment and acting in a sustainable way are themes across all three strands of this course.

4. Ethical Perspective

Ethics are the moral principles that govern a person's behaviour.

Ethics refers to **principles, morals, values and standards**. Just because something is **legal** does not necessarily mean that it is **ethical**. Something might be unethical but legal. As individuals, we often look out for our own interests without considering others. If we are to be ethical, we must consider the rights of all human beings, not just our own rights. We must also obey the law. An organisation may do something that it is convinced is legal and will be protected by law; however, it may not be ethical.

Culture also impacts on ethics. What is acceptable in one culture may not be acceptable in others. The ethics of one culture and the way people in that culture behave is neither better nor worse than the ethics of another culture.

The following table shows some examples of rights and responsibilities of employers and employees from the different perspectives.

Employees' Rights	
Legal	To receive the minimum wage, a copy of a wage slip, with tax (PAYE, PRSI, USC) deducted from pay
Social	To be treated fairly and not be subjected to bullying
Environmental	To work in a safe environment
Ethical	To not to be discriminated against
Employees' Responsibilities	
Legal	To do an honest and fair day's work to the best of their ability
Social	To respect others, regardless of gender, culture, income or disability, and to report any concerns
Environmental	To respect the property of the employer and if possible take the environment/sustainability into consideration
Ethical	To be trustworthy and behave ethically
Employers' Rights	
Legal	To expect that employees have been honest with them about their experience and qualifications to do the work
Social	To expect employees to do their best while at work
Environmental	To expect employees to respect their workplace and keep it clean
Ethical	To be treated with respect by employees and report employees involved in any wrongdoing
Employers' Responsibilities	
Legal	To obey all employment laws, e.g. employment equality, and to pay the minimum wage and deduct taxes
Social	To allow employees to join a trade union and be open to negotiations to deal with any industrial relations issues
Environmental	To ensure that their operations don't have a negative impact on the local environment and community
Ethical	To provide a safe and ethical workplace and conditions for employees

RIGHTS AND RESPONSIBILITIES: EMPLOYERS AND EMPLOYEES 2.4

EMPLOYEES

RIGHTS
* FAIR WAGE/EQUAL PAY AND PAY SLIP
* SAFE AND HEALTHY WORKPLACE
* HOLIDAYS AND LEAVE
* TO BE TREATED FAIRLY

RESPONSIBILITIES
* HONEST AND TRUSTWORTHY
* FAIR DAY'S WORK
* RESPECT PROPERTY OF EMPLOYER
* PUNCTUAL

EMPLOYERS

RIGHTS
* HIRE SUITABLE STAFF
* DISMISS EMPLOYEES
  - PROVIDED IT IS DONE FAIRLY
* THE RIGHT TO RUN A BUSINESS

RESPONSIBILITIES
* PAY A FAIR WAGE
* ADHERE TO ALL TAX REGULATIONS
* MAINTAIN SAFE AND HEALTHY WORKING CONDITIONS
* OBEY ALL LAWS

WORKING WITH OTHERS

Working in pairs or small groups, discuss the above rights and responsibilities of an employee. We are often very aware of our rights, but we must not forget our responsibilities and obligations. Can you come up with some more rights and responsibilities?

CHECKING IN...

1. Explain rights and responsibilities.
2. Explain ethical responsibilities.
3. Compare social responsibilities with environmental responsibilities.
4. Rewrite the table on p. 242 giving specific rights and responsibilities of a supermarket (as employer) and a checkout assistant (as employee).

DECISION-MAKING

When making decisions enterprises should go through a process to ensure they are making the best choices.

They should:

1. Know all the **details**.
2. Find out all the **options**.
3. Ask the following **questions** for each option: Is it **legal**? Is it **ethical**? Does it **benefit all**?
4. Follow the **legal** and **most ethical** option.

Our government can use this process when it makes decisions and so can we, as individuals.

Corporate social responsibility (CSR) is an idea that enterprises should include social and environmental concerns in their day-to-day operations on a voluntary basis (see Ben & Jerry's Case Study p.122).

243

2.4 BE BUSINESS: ENTERPRISE

When an enterprise acts in a socially responsible way, it can often increase its profits, along with improving its image. However, being socially responsible can be costly, which in turn can reduce profits for the business.

Two companies that have shown a degree of CSR are Häagen-Dazs and Ulster Bank Group

Häagen-Dazs

Honeybees are vanishing at an alarming rate. Bees play a vital role in pollinating a lot of the foods we eat, including some of the ingredients of ice creams and sorbets. The ice cream company Häagen-Dazs creates awareness and donates funding to research the bees' problems.

Ulster Bank Group

The Ulster Bank Group developed MoneySense for Schools in collaboration with teachers and financial experts. It is a financial education resource with over 40 hours of interactive lessons delivered online. The idea was to help future customers of the bank become more financially literate.

CHECKING IN...

1. Which of the following do you agree or disagree with? Place a tick ✓ in the appropriate box.

	Agree	Disagree
Ethics is all about honest principles, morals, values and standards	☐	☐
CSR looks at the ethics of a business	☐	☐
Equal pay is a responsibility of an employee	☐	☐
Employers do not have social responsibilities	☐	☐
Reducing waste is an environmental responsibility	☐	☐
When something is legal it is also ethical	☐	☐

2. Copy the Venn diagram into your copy and use it to compare and contrast the rights of the employee and the employer.

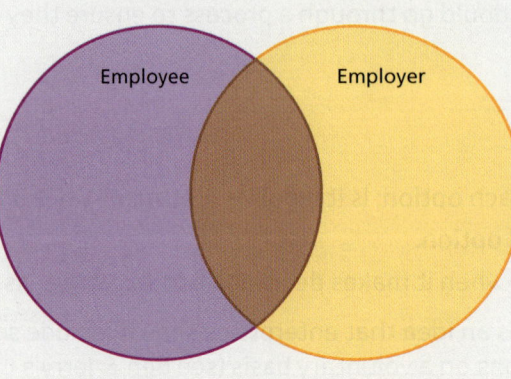

(Venn diagram: Employee | Employer)

Time to think

'When an enterprise acts in a socially responsible way it can increase its profits.'
Do you agree with this statement? Give reasons for your answer.

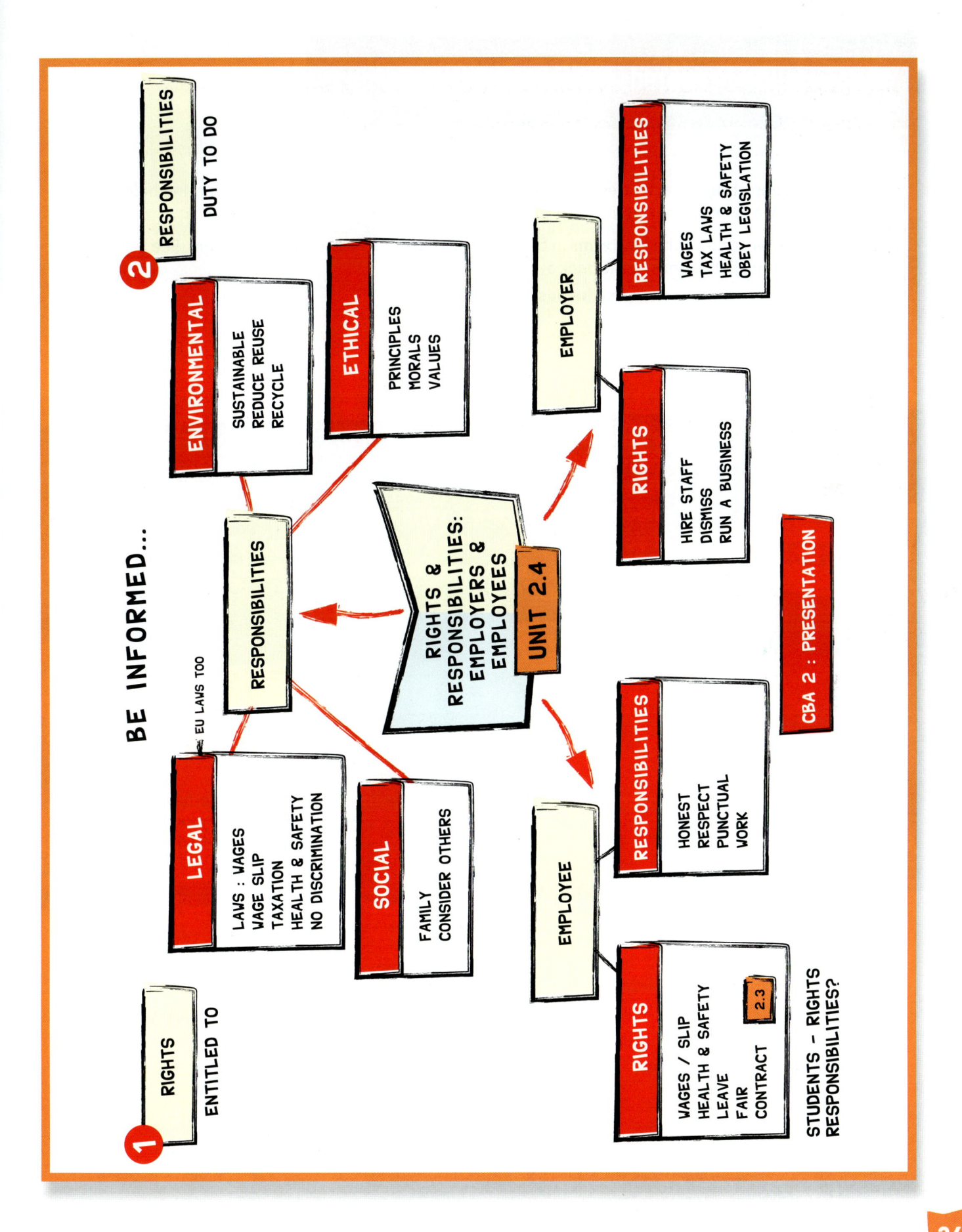

RIGHTS AND RESPONSIBILITIES: EMPLOYERS AND EMPLOYEES 2.4

BE INFORMED...

1 RIGHTS — ENTITLED TO

2 RESPONSIBILITIES — DUTY TO DO

RIGHTS & RESPONSIBILITIES: EMPLOYERS & EMPLOYEES — UNIT 2.4

RESPONSIBILITIES

- **LEGAL**
  - LAWS : WAGES
  - WAGE SLIP
  - TAXATION
  - HEALTH & SAFETY
  - NO DISCRIMINATION
  - (EU LAWS TOO)

- **SOCIAL**
  - FAMILY
  - CONSIDER OTHERS

- **ENVIRONMENTAL**
  - SUSTAINABLE
  - REDUCE REUSE RECYCLE

- **ETHICAL**
  - PRINCIPLES
  - MORALS
  - VALUES

EMPLOYER

RESPONSIBILITIES
- WAGES
- TAX LAWS
- HEALTH & SAFETY
- OBEY LEGISLATION

RIGHTS
- HIRE STAFF
- DISMISS
- RUN A BUSINESS

EMPLOYEE

RESPONSIBILITIES
- HONEST
- RESPECT
- PUNCTUAL
- WORK

RIGHTS
- WAGES / SLIP
- HEALTH & SAFETY
- LEAVE
- FAIR CONTRACT (2.3)

CBA 2 : PRESENTATION

STUDENTS – RIGHTS RESPONSIBILITIES?

245

2.4 BE BUSINESS: ENTERPRISE

Be Prepared: My Support Sheets

Completing the activities here will help you reflect on and reinforce your learning before you move on to the next unit.

- Write down the **key terms** in this unit and make sure you understand them. See if they match the ones at the back of the book.
- List the key **concepts/themes** in this unit.

Use placemats

Working together in groups of four (A, B, C and D) and using the placemat template:

- Individually write down all employees' **rights**.
- Collectively write down a consensus in the middle.
- Collectively prioritise the three most important employees' rights.
- Now complete the task again, this time for employees' responsibilities.

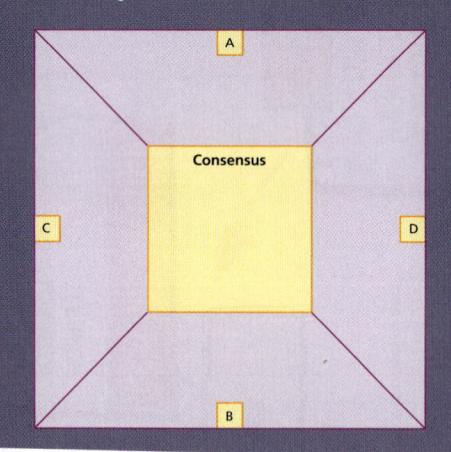

Top Tip!

Working with others is really important for your Enterprise in Action and individually for your Presentation.

Enterprise in Action Idea!

Create a presentation on legal, social, environmental and ethical rights.

Success criteria:
- A clear title
- Appropriate visuals
- Presentation and communication skills
- Relevant IT skills

RIGHTS AND RESPONSIBILITIES: EMPLOYERS AND EMPLOYEES   2.4

QUESTION TIME

1. Explain the rights and responsibilities of an employee.
2. Explain the rights and responsibilities of an employer.
3. Compare social, ethical and environmental responsibilities.
4. Evaluate the importance of ethics from an employee perspective.
5. Create a fishbone summary of this unit using the template on p. 546.

EVALUATE MY LEARNING: DAR

Describe
- Did I/we meet my/our learning intentions?
- What went well? What are my/our strengths?

Assess
- How did I/we work with others?
- Were there challenges?

Recommend
- How might I improve?
- What skills and learning might I apply to new situations?

Do your **Key Check** in the workbook for this unit and then mark your learning position on the following rating scale:

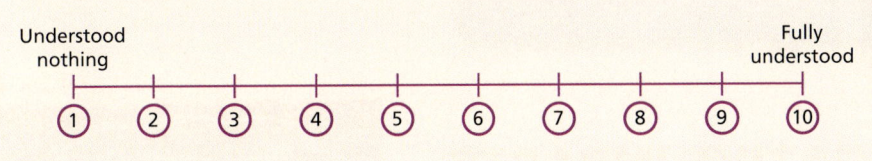

Understood nothing ① ② ③ ④ ⑤ ⑥ ⑦ ⑧ ⑨ ⑩ Fully understood

How can you move up the rating scale? What can you **say**, **make**, **write** and **do** to illustrate your learning?

Stop and think

Do I have any questions or concerns?

What are the mistakes or errors I made in this unit?

CBA 2 Presentation:
Will I use this unit for my topic for my **Presentation**?

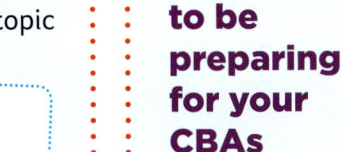

You need to be preparing for your CBAs

○ Exceptional
○ Above expectations
○ In line with expectations
○ Yet to meet expectations

2.5 ORGANISATIONS' POSITIVE AND NEGATIVE IMPACTS ON COMMUNITIES

Investigate the positive and negative impacts on a community of an organisation from economic, social and environmental perspectives.

Learning Intentions

At the end of this unit I will:
- Know about and understand the positive impacts that an organisation has on a community
- Know about and understand the negative impacts that an organisation has on a community
- Value organisations in my community

Making the links with other LOs:

- 1.9 Ethics and sustainable consumption
- 2.1 Financial, social and cultural enterprise roles
- 3.6 Positive and negative economic growth and sustainability
- 3.7 Globalisation of trade

Are there other LOs?

Key Concepts

- ✓ Positive and negative impacts
- ✓ Community
- ✓ Sustainability

Wonderful Worthwhile Websites

www.lauralynn.ie
www.tidytowns.ie
www.gaa.ie

POSITIVE AND NEGATIVE IMPACTS

An impact is an effect or influence that you can have on someone or something. An impact can be positive or negative.

All organisations have positive and negative impacts on society.

Positive impact: a good influence or effect

Negative impact: an unfavourable influence or effect.

To fully understand the impact an organisation can make, it's useful to look at it from different perspectives (viewpoints): economic, social and environmental.

Time to think

What might be the impact on the local community if the rock band U2 played two concerts at Croke Park on the Saturday and Sunday of the June bank holiday weekend?

IMPACTS OF AN ORGANISATION ON A COMMUNITY

It's not only for-profit business organisations that impact on a community. Not-for-profit organisations – voluntary, social and community – can impact on communities too.

The impact of an organisation is easy to see, but it can be challenging to measure.

1. ECONOMIC PERSPECTIVE

The economic perspective looks at the impacts that result from the flow of money into and out of a community.

Monetary Impact	
Positive Impacts	**Negative Impacts**
Extra **income** that results from an increase in **employment** means people have the option to **spend** or **save**, which can boost local enterprises (e.g. local credit union).	Pressure can be put on local services; often the infrastructure is not good enough and **local government** finances can be stretched.
An organisation needs support from local service organisations, for example the hospitality industry. These organisations then see their **business increase**.	An increased demand for housing can cause a **shortage of housing**. Property and rental **prices may increase,** placing a financial burden on the local community.
Successful enterprises can result in **spin-off businesses** that emerge to support its operation (e.g. local farmer provides wool to wool factory).	The **cost of living** can rise as more people enter the community and demand for goods and services increases (e.g. prices and insurance premiums rise).

EXAMPLE: SILICON DOCKS

Silicon Docks is a name given to the area around Grand Canal Dock in Dublin. It is where the Dublin offices of Google, Facebook and Twitter are located. These big companies have attracted other smaller service businesses to the area, for example new cafés and restaurants.

2. SOCIAL PERSPECTIVE

The social perspective looks at how the activities of an organisation can affect those living in the community.

Many companies have social aims as part of their business plans. They do things that directly benefit society, for example sponsoring a local sports team.

2.5 Be Business: Enterprise

Impact on Members of a Community	
Positive	**Negative**
An organisation can **sponsor** local events, perhaps for schools or social enterprises.	Some smaller local businesses may not be able to compete and may **close down**.
Voluntary enterprises can often **benefit individuals**, for example ALONE helps older people in need. Community enterprises can benefit everyone in the community, for example the annual TidyTowns committee.	The influx of more people to an area can sometimes result in **anti-social behaviour**, which can result in, for example, older people feeling threatened.
The operations of some organisations can lead to **improved infrastructure** – such as paths, lighting, schools and parking – which helps improve **living standards**.	More traffic in an area can bring **traffic jams** and delays to members of the community.
Positivity from employment and an improvement in living standards can improve **wellbeing** and create **pride** in a community.	If an organisation is not treating employees well or is not acting ethically this can lead to **resentment** and anger in the community.

EXAMPLE: THE GAA

Local community organisations face many challenges, including a lack of finance and volunteers. The GAA is a great example of a strong community organisation. It is Ireland's largest sporting organisation with over 2,000 clubs throughout the country, each run by a team of volunteers.

EXAMPLE: LAURALYNN

LauraLynn is a not-for-profit organisation that provides hospice care to children with life-limiting conditions and support to their families, allowing parents to be 'Mum and Dad' rather than full-time carers.

The needs of the child and family are at the heart of everything they do, and care is provided where families prefer: at their hospice or in the family home, or in hospital if required. Children from birth to age 18 can be referred for their care from anywhere in Ireland.

Care is provided free to families because of the generosity of fundraising efforts and donations from individuals, schools, communities and businesses.

Time to think

TidyTowns is an organisation that strives to improve the environment and build community relations. Can you name any other community organisations? What positive and negative impact do they make on the community?

ORGANISATIONS' POSITIVE AND NEGATIVE IMPACTS ON COMMUNITIES 2.5

3. ENVIRONMENTAL IMPACT

The environmental perspective sees things as they relate to a community's air, water, land, wildlife, etc.

Understanding the effects organisations have on society and the environment is vital to achieving sustainability. The underlying idea behind sustainability is that we must act responsibly about the products we produce and consume in order to be able to support the billions of people on this planet for ever.

Impact on Air, Water, Wildlife and Farmland	
Positive Impacts 😃	Negative Impacts 😟
Energy-efficient buildings (e.g. good insulation) and work practices (e.g. recycling) can have a positive impact on a locality and **set** a good example.	Many organisations create **environmental problems** through industrial waste and water, noise and air pollution.
If employment is available in a locality then people don't have far to travel to work. Less **fuel usage** means less carbon dioxide released into the atmosphere.	The need for more housing as organisations grow can **put** pressure on local government to use land that would otherwise be there for **conservation**.
By using equipment such as rainwater tanks, solar heating panels and solar hot water systems, organisations can **reduce their reliance on natural resources**.	Pressure on **local services** such as sewerage and water can mean **quality control** is difficult.

Business in Action/Presentation Idea!

A local business provides many opportunities. It generates employment and many other businesses benefit indirectly. Research a local business and discuss the impact it has on the community. Does the business employ students during the summer? Would there be an opportunity for a work placement or work experience scheme with the company?

CHECKING IN...

Name one positive and one negative impact the following organisations might have in a local community.

- Crèche
- Post-primary school
- Post office
- IT business
- Garden centre
- Library
- Local soccer club
- Citizens Information Centre
- Charity shop: Barnardos Ireland
- Bank

251

2.5 BE BUSINESS: ENTERPRISE

Be a Researcher

Choose a not-for-profit organisation and investigate how it impacts on the community in which it operates. The learning outcomes in the Business Studies Specification will help you with the questions you need to ask.

EXAMPLE: ELECTRIC CARS

When we think of Amsterdam we think of canals, coffee shops and cycling. There are around 400 km of cycle paths in the city, ensuring a bike-friendly and environmentally clean city.

Amsterdam also has e-cars. The city promotes sustainable transport through an electric car system known as Amsterdam Electric. When the scheme was introduced by the government (an organisation), those using electric vehicles were offered free access to charging points and free parking too. Today, e-drivers are automatically placed at the head of parking space waiting lists (it can take a year or more to get a parking permit in Amsterdam!).

WORKING WITH OTHERS

Imagine you are a member of the council in Amsterdam. Discuss the possible impact on the city of introducing e-cars.

ORGANISATIONS' POSITIVE AND NEGATIVE IMPACTS ON COMMUNITIES — 2.5

CASE STUDY:
IMPACT OF VISUAL ON THE TOWN OF RATHLOWAN

A new arts centre, called 'Visual: Centre for Entrepreneurship, Arts and Theatre' will be opened in a town called Rathlowan. The town has a population of 20,000 and the centre will cost €3 million. The centre is funded by a local entrepreneur and a grant from the Arts Council. The centre will employ ten people full time and up to twenty on a part-time basis, including the local security company.

The centre will be located beside the church just off a residential estate. It will have a coffee shop and some space for local artists to rent. Exhibitions will be held in the summer and the organisers hope to run an adventure week, when the centre can be used for activities.

A film club will be run over the winter months and a concert will be held on the first Saturday of every month. On Sunday afternoons there will be a rotation of jazz, traditional and country and western groups.

Local artists will have an opportunity to exhibit their work and 10 per cent of proceeds will go towards the local TidyTowns organisation. Art classes will be available every Saturday morning.

The centre will also link with the four post-primary schools and offer discounts for events and will ensure to run events that are linked to Leaving Certificate Art and Music curricula. They will also offer talks to students, in particular transition year students.

The centre itself will be sustainable, with energy-efficient solar panels, and wind energy will be used to generate electricity.

Many for-profit organisations welcome the centre as they hope to benefit economically from increased business.

However, a local group is concerned as the majority of people in the area are elderly and this centre could impact negatively on their lives. They worry about noise levels, insufficient parking and the extra burden on the very limited infrastructure in the area. They are also concerned about litter and noise.

2.5 BE BUSINESS: ENTERPRISE

WORKING WITH OTHERS

Working in pairs or small groups, discuss the positive and negative impacts of 'Visual: Centre for Entrepreneurship, Arts and Theatre' on Rathlowan. Copy and use the template below to list the impacts. Initially list the positive and negative impacts and then categorise them into Economic, Social and Environmental.

Economic Perspective	
Positive Impacts	**Negative Impacts**

Social Perspective	
Positive Impacts	**Negative Impacts**

Environmental Perspective	
Positive Impacts	**Negative Impacts**

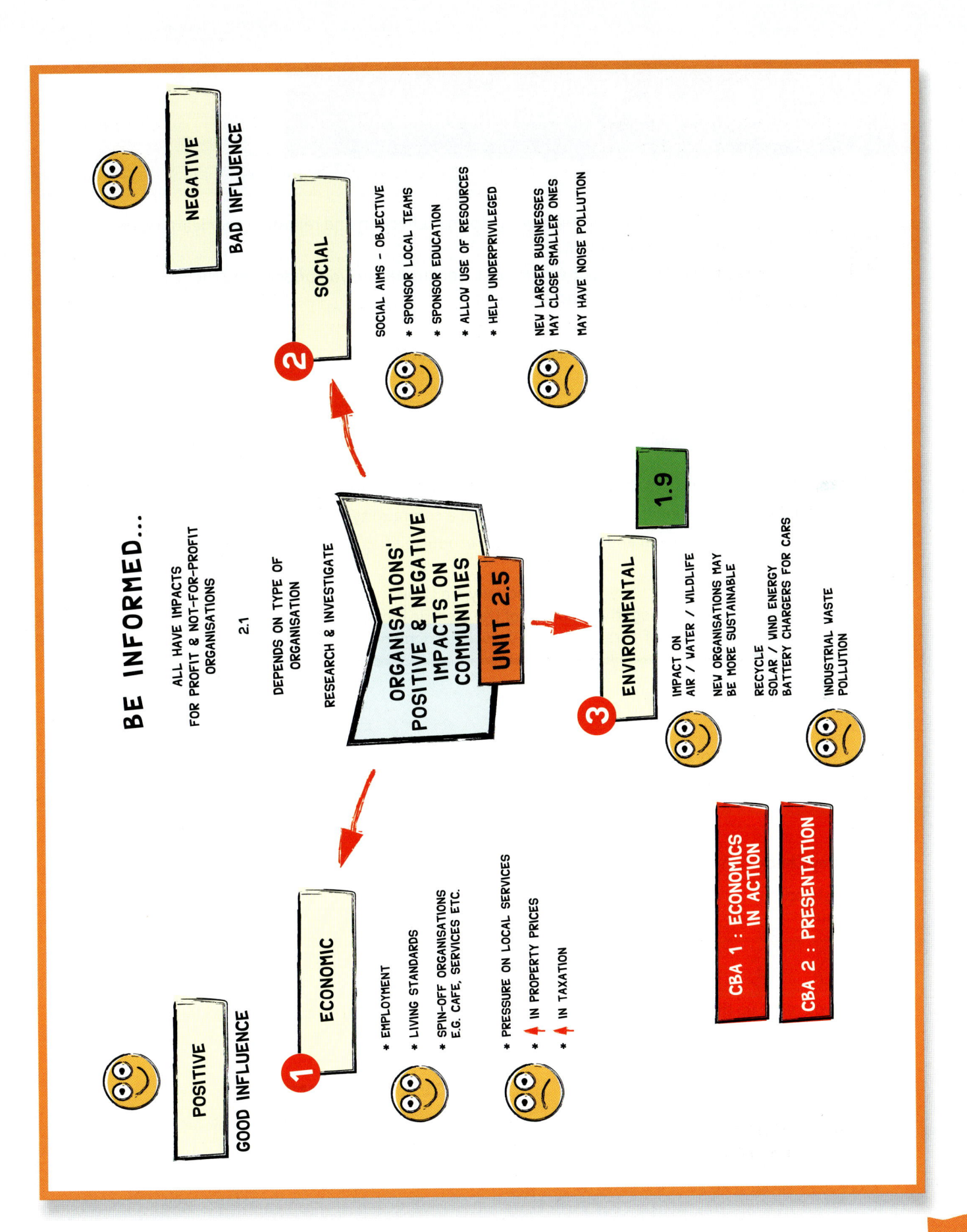

ORGANISATIONS' POSITIVE AND NEGATIVE IMPACTS ON COMMUNITIES (2.5)

BE INFORMED...

- ALL HAVE IMPACTS FOR PROFIT & NOT-FOR-PROFIT ORGANISATIONS (2.1)
- DEPENDS ON TYPE OF ORGANISATION
- RESEARCH & INVESTIGATE

ORGANISATIONS' POSITIVE & NEGATIVE IMPACTS ON COMMUNITIES — UNIT 2.5

POSITIVE — GOOD INFLUENCE

1. ECONOMIC
- EMPLOYMENT
- LIVING STANDARDS
- SPIN-OFF ORGANISATIONS E.G. CAFE, SERVICES ETC.
- PRESSURE ON LOCAL SERVICES
- ↑ IN PROPERTY PRICES
- ↑ IN TAXATION

NEGATIVE — BAD INFLUENCE

2. SOCIAL
- SOCIAL AIMS – OBJECTIVE
- SPONSOR LOCAL TEAMS
- SPONSOR EDUCATION
- ALLOW USE OF RESOURCES
- HELP UNDERPRIVILEGED
- NEW LARGER BUSINESSES MAY CLOSE SMALLER ONES
- MAY HAVE NOISE POLLUTION

3. ENVIRONMENTAL (1.9)
- IMPACT ON AIR / WATER / WILDLIFE
- NEW ORGANISATIONS MAY BE MORE SUSTAINABLE
- RECYCLE SOLAR / WIND ENERGY BATTERY CHARGERS FOR CARS
- INDUSTRIAL WASTE POLLUTION

CBA 1 : ECONOMICS IN ACTION

CBA 2 : PRESENTATION

255

2.5 BE BUSINESS: ENTERPRISE

Be Prepared: My Support Sheets

Completing the activities below will help you reflect on and reinforce your learning before you move on to the next unit.
- Write down the **key terms** in this unit and make sure you understand them. See if they match the ones at the back of the book.
- List the key **concepts/themes** in this unit.
- List the **three most interesting points** about this unit.

QUESTION TIME

1. Explain the negative impacts of an organisation on a community.
2. Explain the positive impacts of an organisation on a community.
3. Compare the social, ethical and environmental responsibilities of an organisation.
4. The Electric Picnic is held every year in Stradbally, Co Laois. Discuss the positive and negative impacts of the Electric Picnic on the small community of Stradbally. See www.electricpicnic.ie.

Success criteria:
- Use an appropriate title
- Include a visual/graphic
- Carry out research and evaluate the research
- Conclude with how an organisation might improve its impact

Economics in Action Idea!

Working together, draft a report on the positive and negative impacts of an organisation on a community.

Do your **Key Check** in the workbook for this unit and then mark your learning position on the following rating scale:

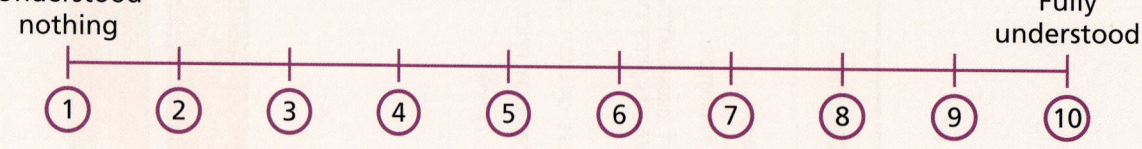

Understood nothing ①—②—③—④—⑤—⑥—⑦—⑧—⑨—⑩ Fully understood

How can you move up the rating scale? What can you **say**, **make**, **write** and **do** to illustrate your learning?

CBA 1 Business in Action:
Will I avail of this unit for my topic for **Economics in Action**?

CBA 2 Presentation:
Will I avail of this unit for my topic for my **Presentation**?

2.6 DIGITAL TECHNOLOGY: BENEFITS AND COSTS

Discuss the impact of technologies on an organisation, debating the associated rewards and costs.

Learning Intentions

At the end of this unit I will:
- Know about the impacts of technology on organisations
- Understand these impacts
- Be able to evaluate the costs and rewards of technology
- Apply debating skills

Making the links with other LOs:

1.10 Globalisation and technology

3.7 Globalisation of trade

Are there other LOs?

Key Concepts

- ✓ Digital technology
- ✓ Costs and rewards
- ✓ Debating

Wonderful Worthwhile Website

www.irishtechnews.net

DIGITAL TECHNOLOGY

Technology is an integral part of our lives. Everyone uses technology to some extent, whether it be booking a holiday online or making new scientific discoveries.

Technology is about how technical knowledge and skills are applied to all aspects of our lives.

The term **digital technologies** is used to describe the use of digital tools and resources to find, analyse, create, communicate, view, share and use information in a digital context.

ICT (information and communications technology) refers to the use of technology to send, receive, gather, store, analyse, distribute and communicate information.

Information can be used to solve problems and make decisions so that people and organisations can meet their goals. We are living in an age when information and our ability to manage it have become extremely important.

When using digital technology, it is vital for individuals and organisations to be responsible, safe and ethical. Digital technology allows information to be shared very fast and easily. Take care how you manage yourself and how you manage your information.

Top Tip!

Technology offers many opportunities to work on your Junior Cycle skills. You can use technology while you work with others, as you complete communications tasks, to test and improve your numeracy and literacy skills. It's also an ideal platform to develop creativity.

2.6 BE BUSINESS: ENTERPRISE

> **WORKING WITH OTHERS**
> - List the different technologies that you have used so far today.
> - What might life be like without your smartphone, emails or social media?
> - Without technology, how might you arrange to meet with your friend?

What might life be like without technology?

An interesting way to advertise your availability!

ORGANISATIONS AND TECHNOLOGY

Modern technologies have changed the way organisations work. Organisations use a variety of digital technologies to help them make decisions and do things more quickly.

- Most organisations use **devices** in their everyday work – desktop computers, laptops, tablets and smartphones – to allow them to make **use** of other technologies.
- When members of an organisation need to **communicate** with each other and share information, the devices are usually set up on a **network**. This allows for private and secure exchange of information within the organisation.
- In order to **store** and maintain data or information, devices are usually connected to an organisation's **server**. This is a powerful computer in a central location.
- In the past, information was stored on disks, memory keys and computer hard drives. Over the last number of years many individuals and organisations have moved their storage of data and information to 'the cloud'. **Cloud computing** is a general term for the delivery of services over the internet. Organisations can purchase space and other services and do their business online.
- Many organisations use **information systems** to gather, produce and analyse the information they need to solve problems. These include accounting, payroll, data entry, project management and customer service systems. The use of information within organisations is not new, but computer technology has enabled accurate and current information to be created with ease.

DIGITAL TECHNOLOGY: BENEFITS AND COSTS 2.6

Drone technology is being used by Dublin Fire Brigade to gather crucial operational intelligence on fires and other emergency situations.

What else might drones be used for in the future?

DIGITAL TOOLS FOR ORGANISATIONS

All organisations, no matter what size, can use **digital tools** to their advantage. The technology world is constantly changing. Some apps that are popular now might not be popular in a short time. Look at the list below: are these all in use as you read this? If not, can you replace them with more popular ones?

1. Application programs (e.g. Microsoft Office, Google Docs)
2. Video conferencing/voice call (e.g. Google Hangout, Facetime, Skype)
3. Websites (organisation's own, www.revenue.ie)
4. Email (e.g. Microsoft Outlook, Gmail)
5. Text messaging (e.g. phone providers or WhatsApp/Viber)
6. Social media (e.g. blogs, Facebook, Twitter, Instagram, YouTube, Pinterest, LinkedIn, Snapchat)
7. Online banking (e.g. Bank of Ireland Banking 365, PayPal)
8. Instant messaging (you can chat via text or online in real time)
9. Elearning (e.g. learning done using a device, often online)
10. Apps for mobile devices (e.g. Google and social media programs)

Did You Know?
The term 'app' comes from 'application', which is a shorter form of 'application program'. An application program is software designed to perform a specific function for the user. Apps are used on mobile devices.

Time to think
How can technology benefit you in your Business Studies course?

What might the classroom of the future look like? Will robots replace teachers?

Using Digital Tools

Paula Joyce, is one of the co-founders of Gourmet Foods, a food outlet that provides excellent goods with a friendly professional service. They have a number of restaurants and specialise in healthy eating.

The following are the top ten examples of how Gourmet Foods uses technology.

1. **Application programs:** Paula uses Microsoft Word for **typing** documents and PowerPoint for creating and giving **presentations**.

    She also uses Excel for **calculations** with spreadsheets. Spreadsheets contain rows and columns, where you can add formulae to do various calculations. She finds spreadsheets an invaluable tool for doing **accounts** such as Cash Budget (planned cash in and planned cash out, Income Statement profit/loss for the year) and Statement of Financial Position (list of assets and liabilities at a particular date).

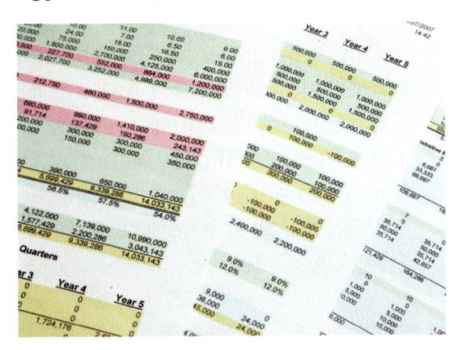

Paula realises the importance of **financial planning** and also uses spreadsheets to work out break-even (where a company is making neither a profit nor a loss) and look at 'what if' scenarios: 'What if the business reduced the price of their food by 10% and added a free gift costing €1?' This in turn helps the company decide if it should go ahead with a change in pricing.

2. **Video conferencing/voice call:** Paula uses Google Hangout to **chat** with her partner, who is in the south of France testing new food ideas.

3. **Websites:** The Gourmet Foods website gives potential customers lots of **information** about the company 24/7, 365 days of the year. It was inexpensive to set up and it generates revenue by allowing other companies related to their business to advertise in banners on the site. Paula has recently given the website a make-over and now customers can give **feedback** and **order online**.

   The website also allows Gourmet Foods to reach new economic markets. Rather than just selling in the local market, her business can now reach regional, national, EU and global markets.

   Paula can do her **VAT and tax returns** using the Revenue online service www.ros.ie.

4. **Emailing:** Gourmet Foods sends emails to its customers, attaching their invoice (bill). Email speeds up the **sending of business documents** and reduces administration costs.

   Technology allows the company to store large lists of customer email addresses and target them directly through **email marketing**.

   It also affords employees the opportunity to **work remotely**. Paula can stay in touch with the business when visiting the restaurants or working abroad.

5. **Text messaging:** Via text messaging, Paula was able to inform her staff, at short notice, that she would be hosting a breakfast meeting at 7 a.m. in the meeting room.

6. **Social media:** Paula has created a new **blog** (this is a regularly updated website or web page) on wellbeing and healthy eating to show customers that she is an expert in the area.

   She has set up a new **Twitter** account (@gourfoods) to make links with customers and other contacts in the world of healthy eating. She also links to people and organisations that show an interest in sustainability.

   The Gourmet Foods **Facebook** page lets customers and potential customers find out more about the business. Customers can post a review of a business, they can message the business if they want to make contact and they can post recommendations and feedback. Facebook data can be analysed to see how effective posts are and how many 'likes' the page receives.

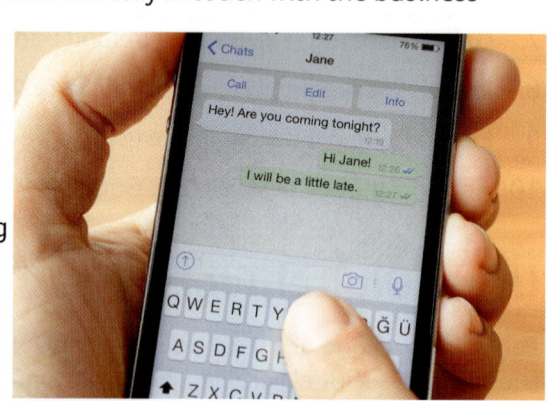

7. **Online banking:** Paula avails of **online banking**, which she finds extremely convenient and a real time saver.

    Paula uses PayPath to pay her employees' **wages** directly into their bank accounts.

    She also uses PayPal to take **payments** safely online and to keep a record of payments.

8. **Instant messaging:** Gourmet Foods customers can ask an agent a question online and chat with them in real time to get an answer.

9. **Elearning:** Paula has decided that she needs to do a course to improve how she gives presentations. As she doesn't want to take time off work to attend a course, she's decided to do an online course that she can work through in her own time.

10. **Apps:** Paula uses a health app to keep all her health and fitness information in one place. She loves this app as it helps her to achieve a good work–life balance.

As you can see from the Gourmet Foods example, digital technologies have a massive impact on organisations. They provide superb tools for planning, decision-making, co-ordination and communications. It is essential that organisations remain adaptable and open to new technologies to succeed into the future.

CHECKING IN...

1. Discuss the impact of digital technologies on the Gourmet Foods business.
2. Can you think of how technology might be having a negative impact on the organisation or its employees?
3. List the ways that technology is used in an organisation you know, e.g. a local club or voluntary organisation.

Time to think

At the time of writing this book, quite a number of the global technology companies have branches located in Ireland, including Google, Apple, Intel, PayPal, Facebook, Airbnb and Amazon. Why might technology companies locate in Ireland?

Ireland is a member of the EU. Do you think that helps?

COSTS

There is no doubt that technology can improve performance in an organisation, but there are also costs associated with the introduction of new technologies: financial, social and environmental.

FINANCIAL

The following are **financial costs (time, resources and money)** to a business of using technology:

1. **Capital costs** of purchasing new technology. Money also needs to be budgeted for the ongoing maintenance of technology, and there are costs involved in insuring technology.
2. **Keeping up to date** and sourcing new technology. For example, anti-virus packages must be kept up to date, broadband may need to be upgraded and social media needs to be constantly updated.

3. **Training** employees in the use of new technologies.
4. **Loss of revenue** if technology doesn't work or there is a problem with the internet. When data is lost, it is expensive to **retrieve information**.
5. If video conferencing internationally, you may have to **pay staff extra** to work at irregular hours.

SOCIAL

The following are **social costs** (people and communities) to a business of using technology:

1. Having mobile devices means that it can be difficult for employees to **'switch off'** from work, which affects their work–life balance.
2. Employees can have email **overload**, when they spend more time answering mails than getting their work done.
3. Communicating digitally can mean there is **less interaction** with colleagues, which can affect the social aspect of working.
4. Automated systems can mean there are **fewer jobs** available.
5. As technology is constantly being updated, employees may need to be trained regularly, which can be an **added stress** in their working lives.

ENVIRONMENTAL

The constant replacing and upgrading of technology can affect an organisation's status as environmentally friendly.

Did You Know?
The United Nations (UN) has calculated that producing the average computer and monitor requires 240 kg of fossil fuels, 21 kg of chemicals and 1,360 kg of water.

REWARDS

Technology can also have a very positive impact on an organisation, bringing financial, social and environmental rewards.

FINANCIAL

The following are **financial rewards (time, resources and money)** to a business of using technology:

1. Technology provides fantastic tools for **communicating instantly**, both internally (within the organisation) and externally (outside the organisation).
2. Tasks can be achieved much **more quickly** with technology, which allows time for other areas of the business.
3. **Information** generated with technology can be **more accurate** and give the organisation a better basis for decision making.
4. It can be **cost effective** to do certain things **online**: for example researching, banking and marketing.
5. Organisations can reach a **worldwide audience** more easily using technology.

SOCIAL

The following are **social rewards (people and communities)** to a business of using technology:

1. Working remotely can allow people to spend **more time at home** with family. It can also **reduce travel time** for employees.
2. Application programs can make **mundane tasks easy and quick**, e.g. using Excel for accounts.
3. Learning new skills can make employees feel more **confident about using technology** in their lives in general.
4. Using technology can improve how a person does their work, which in turn can give them more **satisfaction in their role**.

ENVIRONMENTAL

Keeping files digitally and sending bills and other documents digitally means less paper and fuel are used, which helps organisations be more sustainable.

COST-BENEFIT ANALYSIS

A cost-benefit analysis is where you list the **costs** and the **benefits** associated with an investment and then decide if is it worthwhile.

EXAMPLE:

EIREGRIDS Ltd wants to move its administrative operations online. The following is an example of what might be included in a cost-benefit analysis.

Cost-Benefit Analysis	
Costs	Benefits/rewards
1. Updating computers	1. Savings in time
2. Training	2. Savings in postage/administration/travel
3. Ensure back-up data	3. Bills/invoices sent faster
4. Antivirus – worry about hacking	4. Use to contact customers and potential customers about promotions
5. May have to have redundancies: pay lump sum if you're letting employees go	5. Savings in labour/workers

An associated financial cost would be put against each item before a decision is made to proceed.

CHECKING IN...

1. List five costs to an organisation of using technology.
2. List five rewards to an organisation of using technology.
3. Why is a cost-benefit analysis a useful exercise?

2.6 BE BUSINESS: ENTERPRISE

BE TECHNOLOGY AWARE...
TECHNOLOGY BENEFITS ALL ORGANISATIONS FOR-PROFIT & NOT-FOR-PROFIT

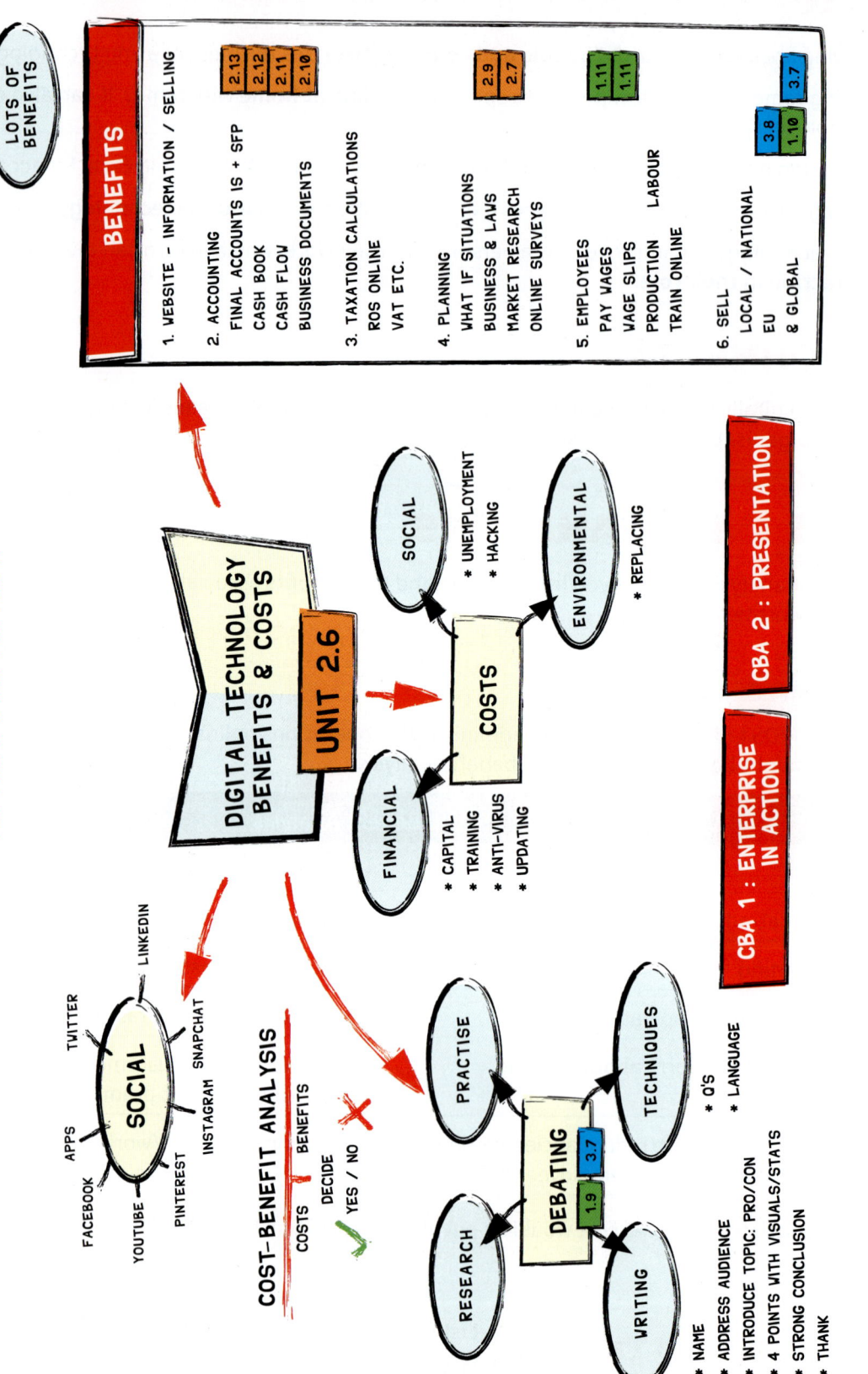

LOTS OF BENEFITS

BENEFITS
1. WEBSITE – INFORMATION / SELLING
2. ACCOUNTING
   - FINAL ACCOUNTS IS + SFP
   - CASH BOOK
   - CASH FLOW
   - BUSINESS DOCUMENTS
3. TAXATION CALCULATIONS
   - ROS ONLINE
   - VAT ETC.
4. PLANNING
   - WHAT IF SITUATIONS
   - BUSINESS & LAWS
   - MARKET RESEARCH
   - ONLINE SURVEYS
5. EMPLOYEES
   - PAY WAGES
   - WAGE SLIPS
   - PRODUCTION LABOUR
   - TRAIN ONLINE
6. SELL
   - LOCAL / NATIONAL
   - EU
   - & GLOBAL

UNIT 2.6 — DIGITAL TECHNOLOGY BENEFITS & COSTS

COSTS

- SOCIAL
  * UNEMPLOYMENT
  * HACKING
- ENVIRONMENTAL
  * REPLACING
- FINANCIAL
  * CAPITAL
  * TRAINING
  * ANTI-VIRUS
  * UPDATING

SOCIAL
- FACEBOOK
- YOUTUBE
- PINTEREST
- APPS
- INSTAGRAM
- TWITTER
- SNAPCHAT
- LINKEDIN

COST-BENEFIT ANALYSIS
COSTS BENEFITS
DECIDE
YES / NO

DEBATING
- PRACTISE
- TECHNIQUES
  * Q'S
  * LANGUAGE
- RESEARCH
- WRITING

* NAME
* ADDRESS AUDIENCE
* INTRODUCE TOPIC: PRO/CON
* 4 POINTS WITH VISUALS/STATS
* STRONG CONCLUSION
* THANK

CBA 1 : ENTERPRISE IN ACTION

CBA 2 : PRESENTATION

DIGITAL TECHNOLOGY: BENEFITS AND COSTS | 2.6

Be Prepared: My Support Sheets

Completing the activities below will help you reflect on and reinforce your learning before you move on to the next unit.

- Write down the **key terms** in this unit and make sure you understand them. See if they match the ones at the back of the book.
- List the key **concepts/themes** in this unit.
- List the **three most interesting points** about this unit.

Have a debate

Have a debate on the impact of technology on organisations.

a. Do your research, prepare for the debate thoroughly. (See p. 130 for debating tips.)
b. Ensure your data is correct.
c. Working in pairs, write a **pro** (for) and a **con** (against) list for the impact of technologies on organisations. Ensure you have four key points for each side.
d. Use a visual stimulus, for example a graph, a photograph or even a prop.

You could also have a **walking debate**. As you put forward your points, the students who agree move to one side of the classroom and the students who disagree move to the other side of the classroom. Any student can be asked why they agree or disagree with the motion.

QUESTION TIME

1. Explain the negative and positive impacts of technology on an organisation.
2. What might the future paperless office look like?
3. Using a Venn diagram, compare the costs and the rewards of technology for an organisation.
4. Technology allows you the opportunity to work remotely. Discuss the benefits.
5. 'Technology opens up a global market.' Discuss this statement.
6. State the benefits of technology for the following:
   - Employees
   - Management
   - Administration
   - Manufacturing
   - Finance

2.6 BE BUSINESS: ENTERPRISE

Presentation Idea!

Create a presentation on the rewards and costs of technology.

Success criteria:
- A clear title
- At least three rewards and three costs
- Some visuals
- Use technology to create the presentation

EVALUATE MY LEARNING: DAR

Describe
- Did I/we meet our learning intentions?
- What went well? What are my/our strengths?

Assess
- How did I/we work with others?
- Were there challenges?

Recommend
- How might I improve?
- What skills and learning might I apply to new situations?

Do your **Key Check** in the workbook for this unit and then mark your learning position on the following rating scale:

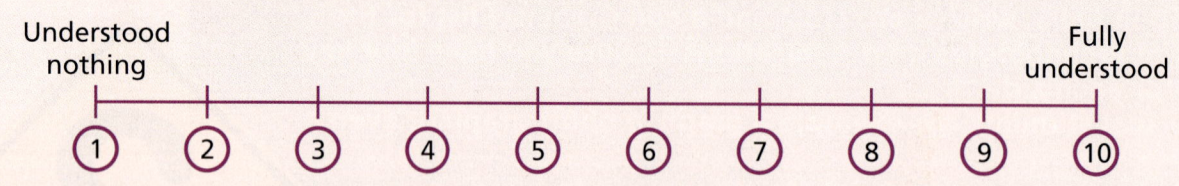

Understood nothing 1 — 2 — 3 — 4 — 5 — 6 — 7 — 8 — 9 — 10 Fully understood

How can you move up the rating scale? What can you **say**, **make**, **write** and **do** to illustrate your learning?

CBA 1 Business in Action:
Will I avail of this unit for my topic for my **Enterprise in Action**?

CBA 2 Presentation:
Will I avail of this unit for my topic for my **Presentation**?

You need to be preparing for your CBAs
- Exceptional
- Above expectations
- In line with expectations
- Yet to meet expectations

Stop and think

Do I have any questions or concerns?

What are the mistakes or errors I made in this unit?

2.7 MARKET RESEARCH

Conduct market research in order to investigate an entrepreneurial opportunity and analyse, interpret and communicate the research findings using relevant terminology and representations.

Learning Intentions

At the end of this unit I will:

- Know about market research
- Understand the different types of market research
- Be able to analyse and interpret research findings
- Know how to compile and administer a questionnaire
- Be able to communicate research findings

Making the links with other LOs:

- 1.10 Globalisation and technology
- 3.7 Globalisation of trade

Are there other LOs?

RESEARCH

Research is all about looking for information on a specific topic or challenge in order to gather facts and knowledge.

You have probably done some research before buying a particular product, maybe when you bought a smartphone or some sports gear. Your parents may have researched online to choose the most suitable holiday or car for the family, or to get the best value mortgage or loan.

You and your parents are **consumers**, and businesses and other organisations are interested in what you like, what you want to buy and how much you are prepared to spend. The key to any successful organisation is understanding the **customer's wants and needs** in the context of the product or service being provided.

To understand a customer's wants and needs an organisation should do some market research.

Key Concepts

- ✓ Market research
- ✓ Surveys
- ✓ Questionnaires

Wonderful Worthwhile Websites

www.thinkbusiness.ie
www.studententerprise.ie
www.cso.ie

Time to think

Have you ever carried out research on something you were thinking of buying? Where did you get your information? How did you know the source was reliable?

Did You Know?

The government also carries out research. The **census** is a form of research for the government.

2.7 BE BUSINESS: ENTERPRISE

WORKING WITH OTHERS

'Giving any resources to an untested business idea is a formula for disaster. Exact and trustworthy information is needed in order for the business to be successful.'

Working in pairs or small groups, discuss the above statement. Do you agree or disagree? Why?

MARKET RESEARCH

Market research is gathering and analysing information related to a product or service to enable an organisation to make informed and up-to-date decisions.

Be Literate

Market segmentation involves dividing consumers into different categories based on socio-economic groups (groups with different amounts of money to spend), religion, geographic location, age, gender, etc.

A **target market** is a particular group of consumers at which a product is aimed. For example, a business making nappies will have a target market of new parents.

A **niche market** is a small, specific, specialised market. For example, a company that makes dog food might target owners of a specific breed of dog.

WORKING WITH OTHERS

Working in pairs, name five markets and subdivide each into three smaller markets (for example, the teenage market could be subdivided into male/female, sports fans, music enthusiasts …).

WHY CARRY OUT MARKET RESEARCH?

An organisation uses the results of market research to decide if an idea or product is worth pursuing. Once this has been decided, good market research will give the organisation valuable information about potential customers. The organisation can then make informed decisions about products and services.

The following table shows the areas that an organisation needs to understand following market research.

Area	Need to know	Example: Less Stress More Success revision books
The market	How many people could or might want to buy the product?	Gill Education needs to know how many students there are to purchase their Less Stress More Success revision series.
The consumer	What are the likes, dislikes, needs and wants of the potential buyer?	The company will need to find out what students want from a revision book and what they like and dislike about revision books.
Available spending	What price would potential buyers be prepared to pay?	The Less Stress More Success series will have to be pitched at a price appropriate for the market and comparable with the competitors.
Appropriate media	Where would be the best place to advertise?	If money is to be spend on advertising, then the marketing team must understand what students watch/listen to in the media (e.g. radio, TV, newspapers, magazines and social media).
Distribution channels	Where should the product be sold?	Should the books be sold online, in bookshops, in schools or somewhere else?
Competitors	What competitive advantage do they have?	In order to make their product better, the company needs to understand why other similar products might be doing well or badly.
Risks	Are there any risks with the project?	Market research should also identify any risks associated with a project, e.g. is there upcoming curriculum change that means the revision books would be out of date quickly?

TYPES OF MARKET RESEARCH

Market research can be done at a desk (desk research) or by going out into the marketplace to talk to and observe people (field research).

Desk Research

Desk research is also known as **secondary research** because it involves working with information that is already available. Sources may include:

- Social media
- Magazines
- Trade journals
- Reports
- Newspapers
- Central Statistics Office (CSO)
- Government agencies

The information is usually **free**, but it can take time to trawl through it to find what is needed. The information can be quite **general**, but it can give you what you need in order to plan your more focused field research.

Online Research

Online research is one of the most accessible forms of research for a business. The arrival of the **internet** presented organisations with a wealth of additional resources to use in conducting free or minimal-cost market research. Online tools can gather market information with the help of a few mouse clicks; you can check out competitors, their prices, discounts, etc.

Blogs are another great tool as they are constantly updated and are a great way to gauge customers' opinions about new ideas, products and services.

Online surveys and **interviews** are an inexpensive way to do market research to find out if an idea or a product will appeal to customers.

Field Research

Field research is also known as **primary research** because it involves gathering information at the source. It involves going out into the marketplace and interviewing or observing potential customers. There are many ways to conduct field research, which include:

1. Surveys/questionnaires/interviews
2. Direct observation
3. Product testing/consumer panels

1. Surveys/Questionnaires/Interviews

A **survey** is a process for gathering and examining data from a sample of people. A sample is a smaller, manageable version of a larger group.

A wide **variety of data collection methods** can be used when conducting a survey, for example observation, a printed questionnaire, over the telephone, by mail, in person, or via the web.

When researching opinion, questionnaires and/or interviews are useful methods.

MARKET RESEARCH 2.7

A **questionnaire** is a list of questions developed to extract certain information from the respondent (person who answers the questions).

A questionnaire must be **carefully planned** and designed so that the required information is gathered. Before designing a questionnaire, consideration needs to be given to **what has to be found out** and **what questions** are likely to give this information.

See later in this unit for tips on compiling your own questionnaire.

An **interview** is a conversation where questions are asked and answers are given.

Wonderful Worthwhile Websites

Google Forms (www.google.com/forms) or SurveyMonkey (www.surveymonkey.com) can help when it comes to analysing information and dealing with large quantities of data.

In market research face-to-face interviews allow you to get complete attention from your respondents and remove distractions. You can conduct face-to-face interviews with select consumers in their homes, by stopping people on the street or targeting people at an event. Being with the person allows you to ask follow-up questions on the spot.

With **telephone interviews** you can reach many more people in the time it would take to arrange face-to-face appointments or stop people at an event.

2. Direct Observation

Direct observation involves watching consumers, without them knowing, to see how they behave.

For example, a mystery shopper would observe people in a shop, see what they're interested in and what they buy, or a mystery restaurant-goer would see how people react to the food in a restaurant. They would then report on their observations.

3. Product Testing/Consumer Panels

A business might give out free samples of a new chocolate bar to test consumers' reactions. The number of people should be large enough to give a good idea if the bar would be popular. Feedback from product testing can be taken into account and the product may be improved before it is launched.

Product testing involves asking potential consumers to try out a product.

A **consumer panel** is a group of consumers who report on products they have used so that the companies can improve them or use what the panel says about them in advertising.

271

2.7 BE BUSINESS: ENTERPRISE

CHECKING IN...
1. Why do organisations carry out market research?
2. List three kinds of desk research and why you might use them.
3. List three kinds of field research and give one example of each in practice.

CASE STUDY:

Ben White is an entrepreneur willing to take a risk and open a new state-of-the-art garden centre in Naas. He is also planning to grow Christmas trees and offer an innovative service called 'Picka3'. This is where children can visit and watch their Christmas tree grow and are given a certificate to say it's theirs when they collect it at Christmas.

The following table outlines how he is researching his entrepreneurial opportunity.

Business: GreenGo Garden Centre	Information required	Why?	How?
Ben White is going to open **a new garden centre**, GreenGo, on the outskirts of Naas.	Number of consumers.	To find out the potential market.	1. Check Central Statistics Office for population figures. 2. Research how many centres are already in Naas. 3. Contact the National Roads Authority for the number of cars passing through the area.
Ben has **segmented his market** into garden products, food, seasonal gifts and 'Picka3'.	Ben needs to understand his target markets.	To ensure he has the right products and services to meet their needs.	1. Conduct a survey. 2. Review garden magazines, note the adverts. What's selling? 3. Research online. 4. Become a member of the International Garden Centre Association (IGCA).
Ben has located the land on which he hopes to grow **Christmas trees**.	How long does it take to grow Christmas trees?	To determine if he has the time and resources to wait for them to grow.	1. Do a survey. 2. Get advice from Coillte; a state-sponsored body. 3. Ask other tree growers in Ireland, and find out if there are any tree growers' societies.

MARKET RESEARCH 2.7

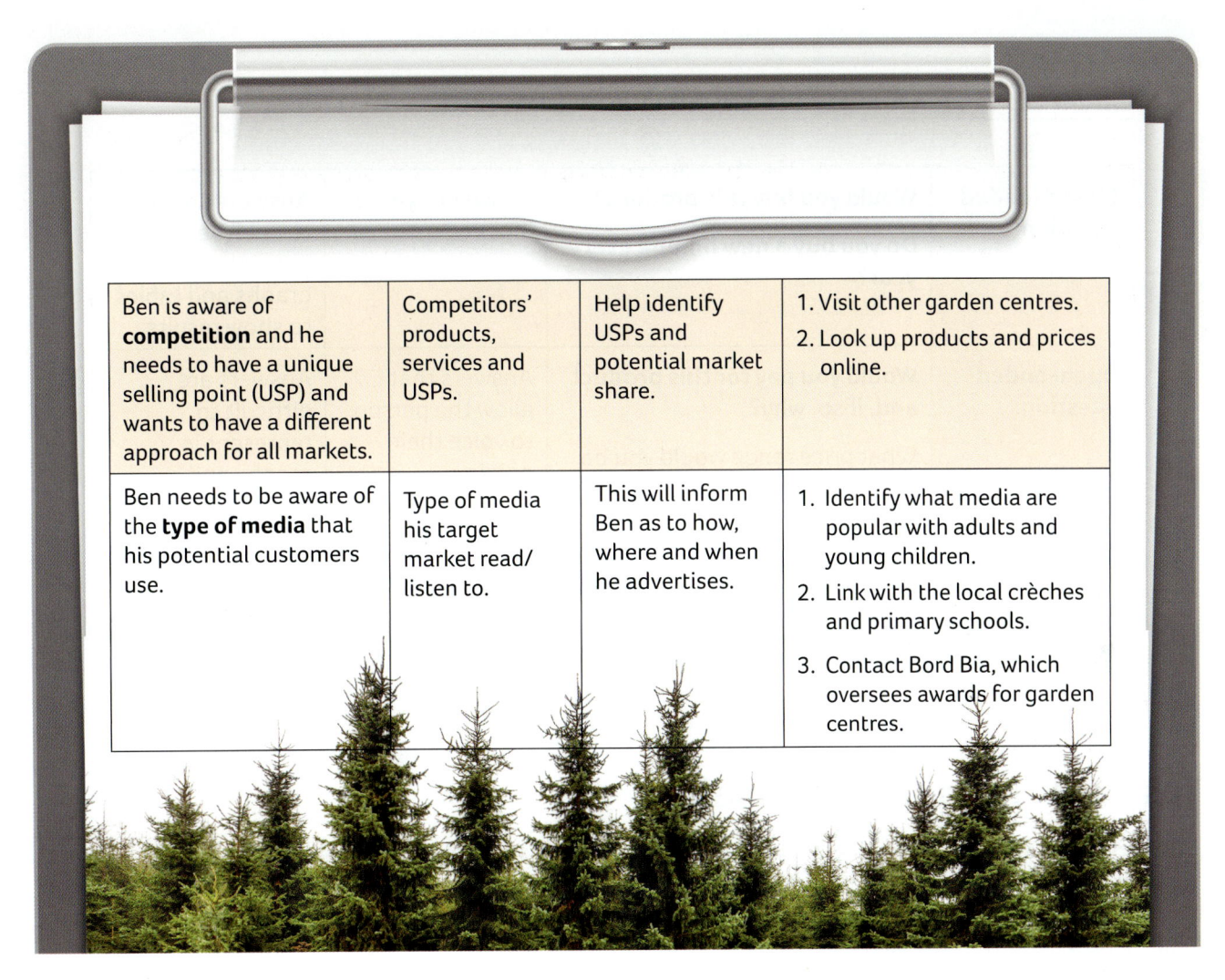

Ben is aware of **competition** and he needs to have a unique selling point (USP) and wants to have a different approach for all markets.	Competitors' products, services and USPs.	Help identify USPs and potential market share.	1. Visit other garden centres. 2. Look up products and prices online.
Ben needs to be aware of the **type of media** that his potential customers use.	Type of media his target market read/listen to.	This will inform Ben as to how, where and when he advertises.	1. Identify what media are popular with adults and young children. 2. Link with the local crèches and primary schools. 3. Contact Bord Bia, which oversees awards for garden centres.

OVER TO YOU

In Junior Cycle you may need to conduct your own research. Before you conduct your own research there are three important questions to consider:

1. **What** are you going to research?
2. **Why** are you going to research it?
3. **How** are you going to research it?

One of the easiest methods of research is the questionnaire.

WRITING A QUESTIONNAIRE

Before compiling a questionnaire, make sure you have answered the first two questions above. Only ask questions that are needed. If you don't need to know the gender of the respondent, i.e. male/female, then don't ask. Questions used in a questionnaire can be **open-ended** or **closed-ended**.

Time to think

Is there information already available about what you need to know?

273

2.7 BE BUSINESS: ENTERPRISE

EXAMPLE: OPEN AND CLOSED-ENDED QUESTIONS

Closed-ended question:	Would you buy this product? Do you buy a new iPhone every year?	Answer is 'yes' or 'no'.	Answers are easy to analyse and present using graphs and tables to show results.
Open-ended question:	Would you pay for this product and, if so, why? What price range would you be willing to pay?	Answers that allow the person to voice their opinion.	Answers are difficult to represent in graphs and charts as they are a collection of opinions.

When you need to know *how many* people have a certain opinion, closed-ended questions are useful. When you want to know more detail about *what people feel or think*, open-ended are suitable.

Tips on Writing Questionnaires

1. **Be Brief:** Limit yourself to ten questions, which should take someone five minutes to answer. If surveys are much longer, people will abandon them and the next time you send them a survey it will be deleted. A great idea for online questionnaires is to have a status bar at the top of each question page so that respondents know how close they are to the end. It keeps them motivated to complete the questions.

2. **Be Realistic:** Avoid too many open-ended questions that require lengthy answers. Closed-ended questions can be answered by a click on a button or a tick – **yes/no**.

3. **Be Persistent:** If you are asking customers to do a survey it is acceptable to send an invitation or a reminder once or twice.

4. **Be Patient:** Questionnaires take time to design and to administer. When the results are in, it also takes time to interpret them.

WORKING WITH OTHERS

'Social media is creating an environment that gives lots of feedback, both positive and negative'. Working in pairs or small groups, discuss this statement.

Business in Action Idea!

Enterprise in Action: Copy and use the questionnaire below. Work with a partner and then your Business Studies class. Collate your results. Use graphics to display your results.

Ciara's Cupcakes Ltd

Please tick (✓) the appropriate box

1. Are you

    Male ☐   Female ☐

2. Which age group are you in?

    (a) 12–18 ☐   (b) 19–22 ☐   (c) 22–29 ☐   (d) Other ☐

3. Would you buy cupcakes?

    Yes ☐   No ☐

4. Which type of cupcake would you be interested in purchasing?

    Plain ☐   Healthy option ☐   Personalised ☐   Other ☐

    Please specify _____

5. How much are you willing to pay for a cupcake?

    €1 ☐   €1–2 ☐   More than €2 ☐

    Please specify

6. Any other comments. _____

Thank you for taking time to complete our questionnaire.

CHECKING IN...

1. What type of questions are used in the above questionnaire?
2. How would you distribute the questionnaire?
3. How would you evaluate your findings?

2.7 BE BUSINESS: ENTERPRISE

REPORTING ON MARKET RESEARCH

Ben White contacted the Local Enterprise Office (LEO) for advice on his new idea, Picka3, which would be operated from GreenGo Garden Centre. They asked him to compile a short report on his research findings on Picka3.

Top Tip!

This could be an Enterprise in Action report.

Title: Report on market research for Picka3, an entrepreneurial opportunity

Executive summary

GreenGo Garden Centre will offer many products and services. One of the unique services it hopes to offer is Picka3, an additional service for those purchasing Christmas trees from the garden centre.

Following desk and field research, I discovered that this idea was indeed unique to the Irish market and there was a strong demand for it. The price point and costs mean a substantial profit can be made in year 1 and onwards.

Introduction

GreenGo will be a garden centre with a difference… **Picka3**.

This is a service whereby children can choose a growing Christmas tree at the centre, give it a name and visit it or view it online as it grows. They then collect it during Christmas week, along with a certificate of ownership. GreenGo will also offer the sustainable service of recycling the tree after Christmas.

I undertook both desk and field research to ensure there was a potential market and that it was worth the risk. I also needed to know when and where to advertise and what my price point should be. I had to ensure Picka3 was the USP for the garden centre that I needed.

Research

Desk research: I researched online at various websites including www.christmastreesireland.com, www.bordbia.com and www.intgardencentre.org. I watched YouTube clips on picking Christmas trees and other related videos.

Field research: I visited local garden centres and other places where trees are sold. I compiled a questionnaire for children and contacted the local primary schools. With the permission and assistance of teachers and parents, and using a colouring competition as an added incentive to complete them, I received 700 student responses. I also sent questionnaires to the parents' councils.

Analysis of research

Desk research helped me to understand how this kind of business is being run in other places. I determined that €60 was a good price to charge. I also concluded that I needed to advertise on the local, rather than a national, radio station, and that I should put print ads in the local newspaper to let people know about the service. There is no comparable service in Ireland.

Field research showed that that 80% of students questioned loved the idea of picking and visiting/viewing their own growing tree. Price was not a factor for the student, but parents agreed with a price of €60 per tree. Location was suitable; just off the N7 is a really busy junction with lots of cars passing daily.

Conclusions
- I estimate that with the potential market I can sell 10,000 trees in Year 1, rising to 100,000 in Year 3.
- I can sell at a price of €60 a tree.
- I can keep costs to €50 a tree.
- This will provide a profit of €100,000 in Year 1 (see calculations in Appendix 1).

Recommendations
- It will be important to expand and keep up to date on children's preferences around purchasing Christmas trees.
- Promotion and advertising will play a key part in achieving targets of 100,000 trees in Year 3.
- Money will need to be reinvested back into the business to achieve targets.

Appendix 1
Costings: Profit and Sales

	€	€
Selling price per tree		60.00
Cost per tree/unit		
Tree	30.00	
Insurance	1.00	
Advertising	1.00	
Extras	8.00	
Labour	10.00	
Total cost per tree		50.00
Profit per tree		10.00

Sales of 10,000 trees in Year 1 = 10,000 x 10 = €100,000 profit

Sales of 100,000 in Year 3 = 100,000 trees x 10 = €1,000,000 profit

[Costs will remain the same as there will be benefits from producing in large numbers.]

Signed: *Ben White*   **Dated:** 1/7/20XX

WORKING WITH OTHERS
In groups, compile an imaginary report on researching an entrepreneurial opportunity. Use the template above. When you have completed the report answer the following questions:
- What was my role and what were my responsibilities?
- How did I contribute to the research?
- How did I contribute to writing the report?
- How did we work as a team? Were there any challenges?

2.7 BE BUSINESS: ENTERPRISE

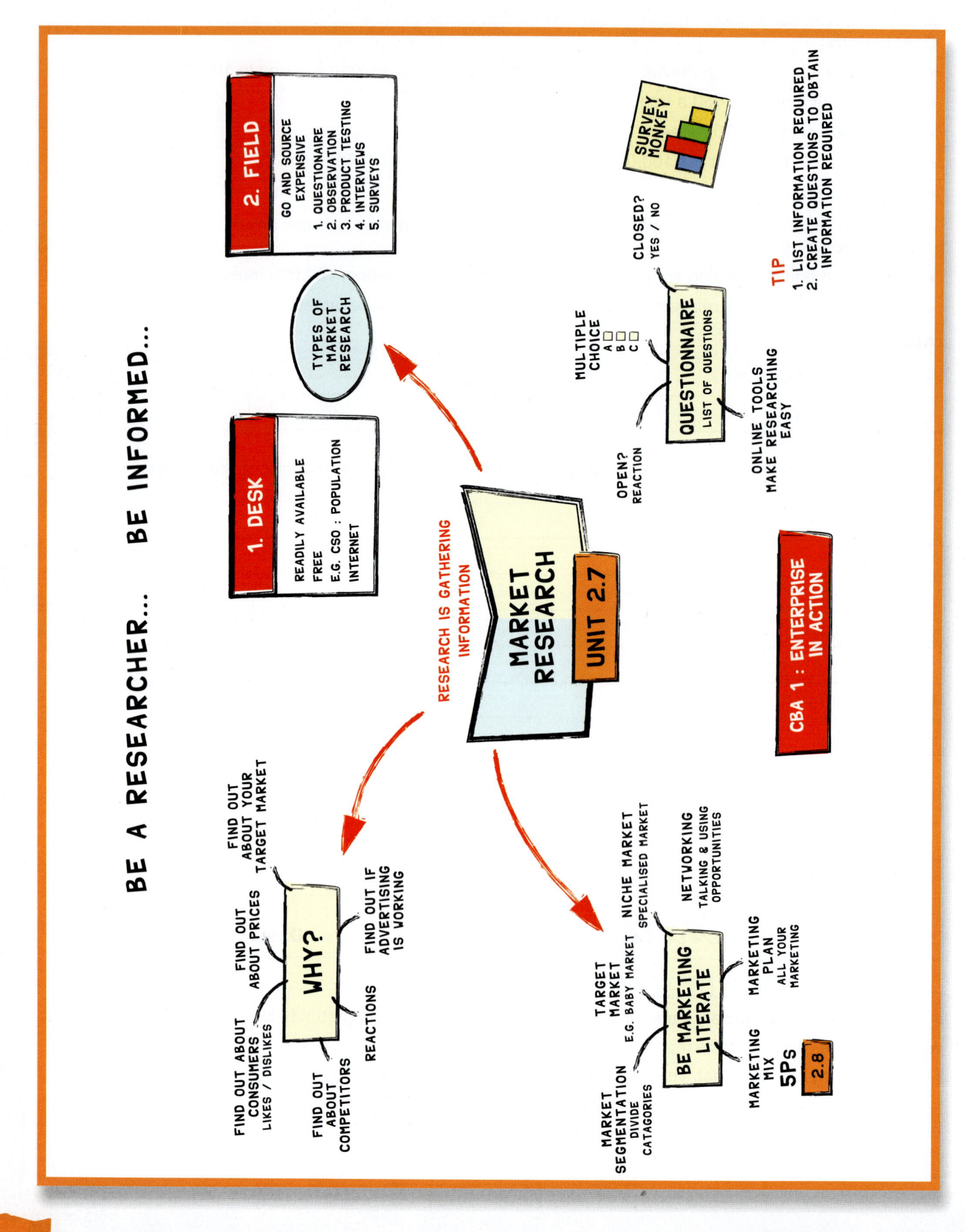

BE A RESEARCHER... BE INFORMED...

MARKET RESEARCH — UNIT 2.7

Research is gathering information

1. DESK
- READILY AVAILABLE
- FREE
- E.G. CSO : POPULATION
- INTERNET

2. FIELD
- GO AND SOURCE
- EXPENSIVE
1. QUESTIONNAIRE
2. OBSERVATION
3. PRODUCT TESTING
4. INTERVIEWS
5. SURVEYS

TYPES OF MARKET RESEARCH

QUESTIONNAIRE — LIST OF QUESTIONS
- MULTIPLE CHOICE (A / B / C)
- CLOSED? YES / NO
- OPEN? REACTION
- ONLINE TOOLS MAKE RESEARCHING EASY

SURVEY MONKEY

TIP
1. LIST INFORMATION REQUIRED
2. CREATE QUESTIONS TO OBTAIN INFORMATION REQUIRED

WHY?
- FIND OUT ABOUT CONSUMERS — LIKES / DISLIKES
- FIND OUT ABOUT PRICES
- FIND OUT ABOUT YOUR TARGET MARKET
- FIND OUT IF ADVERTISING IS WORKING
- FIND OUT ABOUT COMPETITORS — REACTIONS

BE MARKETING LITERATE
- MARKET SEGMENTATION — DIVIDE CATAGORIES
- TARGET MARKET — E.G. BABY MARKET
- NICHE MARKET — SPECIALISED MARKET
- NETWORKING — TALKING & USING OPPORTUNITIES
- MARKETING PLAN — ALL YOUR MARKETING
- MARKETING MIX — 5Ps (2.8)

CBA 1 : ENTERPRISE IN ACTION

Be Prepared: My Support Sheets

Completing the activities below will help you reflect on and reinforce your learning before you move on to the next unit.

- Write down the **key terms** in this unit and make sure you understand them. See if they match the ones at the back of the book.
- List the key **concepts/themes** in this unit.
- List the **three most interesting ideas** in this unit.

Invent a quiz

Working by yourself, in pairs or in a team of three or four, write a quiz based on this unit. Pick one of your quiz questions and give your own answer in detail.

Make a presentation

Make a presentation. Make an individual presentation entitled 'Choosing not to use social media for research'. The presentation should last three minutes. Remember, the best presentations are well researched, provide evidence to support claims, display an interest in business and use variety, creativity and superb communication skills to hold the audience's attention.

Business in Action/Presentation Idea!

Carry out market research for a new or existing product using a questionnaire. You could use an online research tool such as SurveyMonkey, which makes it easy to analyse your results and also has a feature that creates visuals at the touch of a button!
Complete the following steps.

1. Decide on your reason for carrying out the research. What are you trying to find out?
2. Design and compile a questionnaire.
3. **Test** the questionnaire. Ask three students to complete your questionnaire. What were the changes you needed to make? What did you learn?
3. **Edit** the questionnaire and implement any changes. Ensure that the questionnaire is **error-free**, with correct grammar, spelling and punctuation.

Success criteria:
- Clear and suitable title
- At least eight questions
- Include at least one open-ended question and one closed-ended question
- Use IT if possible

2.7 BE BUSINESS: ENTERPRISE

4. **Distribute** the questionnaire to a minimum of 20 participants.
5. **Collate** (gather) your results and then **analyse** them.
6. **Present** your findings in a report.

Success criteria:
- Clear and suitable title
- Introduction: why the research was carried out
- Details of research: how the research was carried out
- Show your findings: use a diagram/cartoon
- Make conclusions and recommendations (what you would advise doing next)
- Appendix: additional information, e.g. how many people completed the questionnaireresearch.

QUESTION TIME

1. Why might it be important to research the number of customers in your market?
2. Why might it be important to understand what the competition offers?
3. Explain target market and give examples of target markets in your school.
4. What might be the most important things to remember when conducting market research?
5. Are there personal questions that should be avoided when conducting research?
6. Battery & Salt, a seafood company has decided to establish a business without conducting market research. Write a short paragraph on why they should conduct market research.
7. Decide on an idea/product/service and conduct some market research on its viability. Write a short report on your research and findings.

EVALUATE MY LEARNING: DAR

Describe
- Did I/we meet our learning intentions?
- What went well? What are my/our strengths?

Assess
- How did I/we work with others?
- Were there challenges?

Recommend
- How might I improve?
- What skills and learning might I apply to new situations?

MARKET RESEARCH | 2.7

Do your **Key Check** in the workbook for this unit and then mark your learning position on the following rating scale:

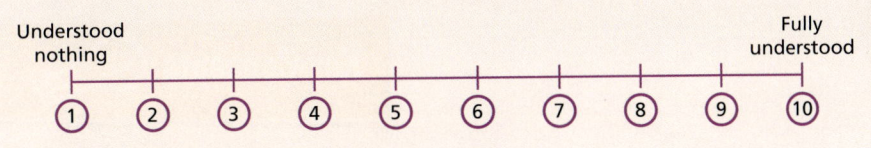

Understood nothing ①②③④⑤⑥⑦⑧⑨⑩ Fully understood

How can you move up the rating scale? What can you **say**, **make**, **write** and **do** to illustrate your learning?

Stop and think

Do I have any questions or concerns?
What are the mistakes or errors I made in this unit?

CBA 1 Business in Action:

Will I use this unit for my topic for **Enterprise in Action** and my **Finance in Action**?

You need to be preparing for your CBAs

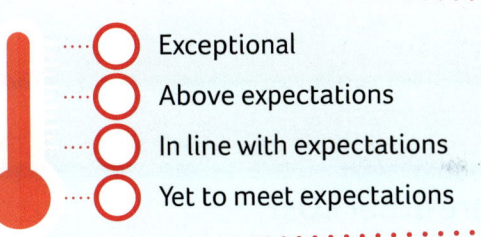

○ Exceptional
○ Above expectations
○ In line with expectations
○ Yet to meet expectations

281

2.8 MARKETING MIX

Devise and apply a marketing mix in order to promote a new or existing product or service.

Learning Intentions

At the end of this unit I will:

- Understand the concept of marketing
- Know how to explain the marketing mix and advertising
- Value and be able to apply the marketing mix

Making the links with other LOs:

- 2.7 Market research
- 2.9 Business plan

Are there other LOs?

Key Concepts

✓ Marketing mix
✓ Advertising

Wonderful Worthwhile Websites

www.thinkbusiness.ie
www.khanacademy.org
www.studententerprise.ie

MARKETING

Today's business world is **highly competitive**, with thousands of businesses trying to attract the same customers with similar products and services. **Highlighting a very small difference could make a product more attractive and increase sales.**

Marketing involves identifying what the customer wants and promoting and selling the product/service so that the company makes a profit.

Marketing is central to any business plan. There is an **80/20 idea** in business that says that 80 per cent of sales come from about 20 per cent of customers. In reality the percentages vary, but it highlights the need of businesses to recognise where their profits come from and to **target** those **important customers** and find the best way to communicate with them.

THE MARKETING MIX

The marketing mix refers to the actions or tactics that a company uses promote its brand or product/service in the market. A typical marketing mix is made up of what is known as the **4Ps**:

1. **P**roduct
2. **P**rice
3. **P**lace
4. **P**romotion

Time to think

Think of what made you buy your mobile phone. Was it the features of the phone, the price, how the sales rep convinced you or perhaps a special offer like a free gift?

The marketing mix is about having the right **product (or service),** at the right **price**, in the right **place,** and with the right **promotion** in order to sell it and make a profit. Each P in the marketing mix is like an ingredient and it is important to have all the ingredients working together.

MARKETING MIX 2.8

> **Did You Know?**
> The idea of the 4Ps was introduced in the 1960s. In recent years, people have extended the mix to include other Ps like packaging and personnel.

PRODUCT

The product is the item/service for sale.

- **Research** to ensure you provide a product/service that is needed and wanted by customers. There must be a demand for your product/service Unit 3.3.
- What is the **unique selling point (USP)**? It is important to stand out from your competition.
- Develop a **brand image**, e.g. Apple, BMW, Domino's Pizza, and Tayto.
- Have **suitable packaging** with any **labelling** required by law. Packaging should **protect** the product but also make it eye-catching.
- Consider **safety** issues.
- Is the product a new invention? Does it need a **patent**? (A patent protects the business legally and will not allow others to copy the product).
- Understand where the product/service is in its **product life cycle**. Very few products will last for ever as they go through a process known as the product life cycle: introduction, growth, maturity and decline.

PRICE

Price is the value placed on a product, and usually that means the price a consumer is prepared to pay.

- Choose the most **suitable price** for the intended market.
- **Cover costs** (how much it takes to make) and have a profit margin. Some organisations have a high margin and sell in small numbers (e.g. a jewellery shop), while others have a small profit margin and sell many products (e.g. a supermarket like Dunnes Stores).
- **Profit margin** will depend on the organisation. A for-profit organisation needs to make a profit, but in a not-for-profit organisation profit is not the main aim.
- You must take **competitors'** prices into consideration, as customers will always compare and may go for the cheaper price.
- Price will also depend on your **target market**, for example if your target market is students, you may charge a low price.
- If it is **a new product**, you may decide to enter the market at a cheaper price to encourage sales, or you may start with an expensive price to create a superior image.
- You may charge **different prices**, for example discounts for pensioners and students, sales or special offers.

283

PLACE

Place refers to the point of sale. Identify your market and choose the most appropriate way to distribute your product, known as the **channel of distribution**.

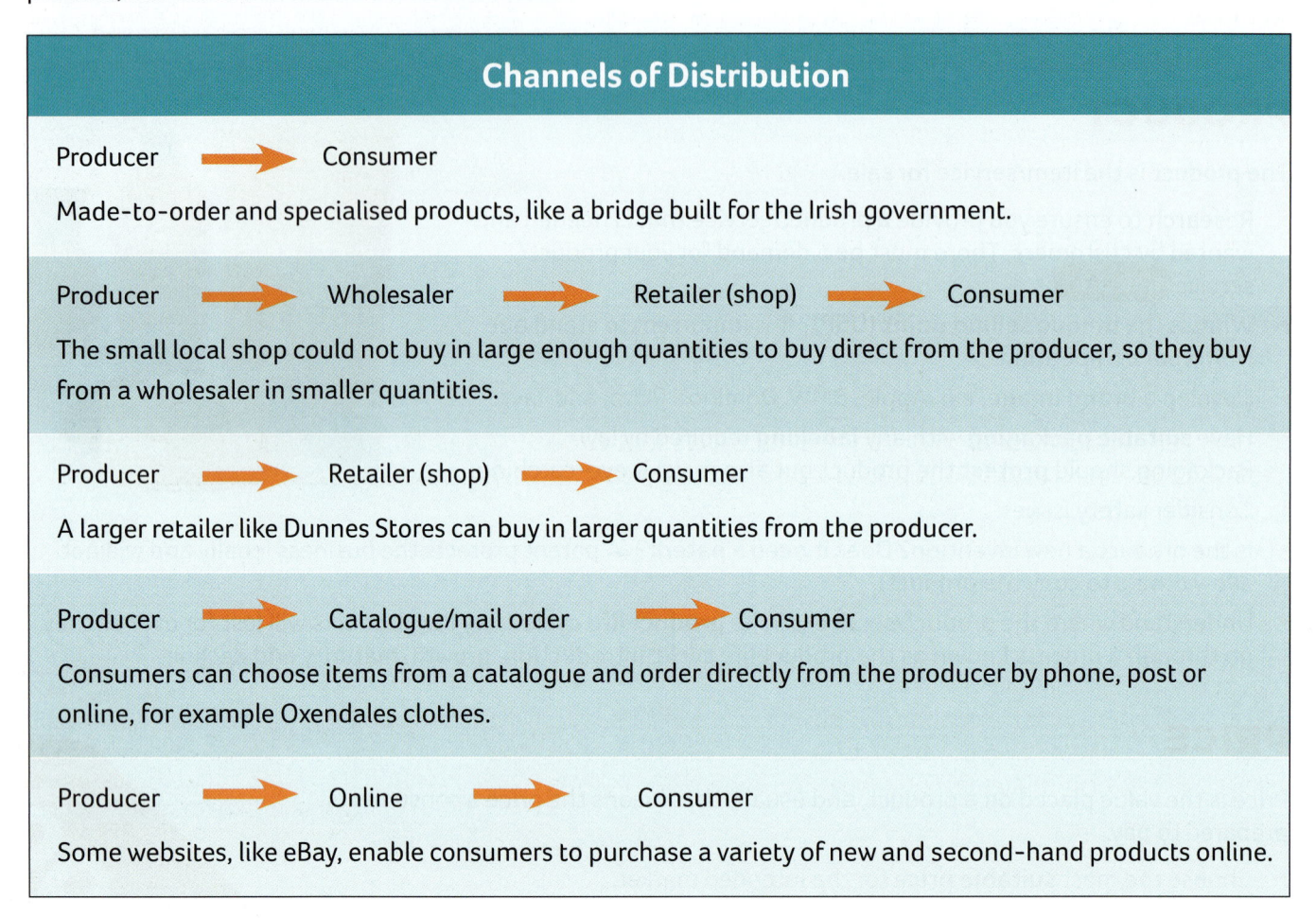

Channels of Distribution

Producer → Consumer

Made-to-order and specialised products, like a bridge built for the Irish government.

Producer → Wholesaler → Retailer (shop) → Consumer

The small local shop could not buy in large enough quantities to buy direct from the producer, so they buy from a wholesaler in smaller quantities.

Producer → Retailer (shop) → Consumer

A larger retailer like Dunnes Stores can buy in larger quantities from the producer.

Producer → Catalogue/mail order → Consumer

Consumers can choose items from a catalogue and order directly from the producer by phone, post or online, for example Oxendales clothes.

Producer → Online → Consumer

Some websites, like eBay, enable consumers to purchase a variety of new and second-hand products online.

While online shopping is increasing, there is still a demand for physical stores, as can be seen from the record-breaking crowds shopping at Dundrum centre, Kildare Village and other shopping centres.

Time to think

Have you ever bought online? Were you happy with the product/service?

Will all retailers move to an online platform in the future?

Why might more and more advertising be moving to an online/digital platform?

PROMOTION

Promotion is all about getting the attention of the customer so they know about the product/service. You must choose the most appropriate promotion to publicise your product/service.

- **Sales promotion** is a way of using **special offers** to encourage customers to buy a product/service. Methods include supplying free gifts, offering three for the price of two, encouraging loyalty cards and giving an extra amount free.
- **Personal selling** is done either face to face or through telemarketing. It's important to have persuasive salespeople. If an organisation was introducing a new computer system, they would require sales representatives (sales reps) to demonstrate the key features and benefits of the product/service.
- **Public relations (PR)** is about communicating with the media and creating a **positive public image** for the organisation/brand. Public relations activities help the public to understand the company and its products, and they often put the organisation in a good light, for example the fast food chain Supermac's sponsors the Galway hurling team. **Celebrity endorsement** is when a business uses a famous person's image to get consumers to know and have confidence in a product, for example Taylor Swift for Diet Coke.
- **Advertising** is about sending messages to the consumer to make them want to buy the product/service. You can see advertisements in newspapers and magazines, on billboards, TV and radio and throughout social media and the internet, etc. (More on advertising later in this unit.)

Social media is a fantastic way to market products and services. Facebook, Twitter, Instagram and LinkedIn are now part of our daily lives. These media are incredibly powerful marketing tools. Social media can be used to identify and to market to very specific customer groups for very little cost.

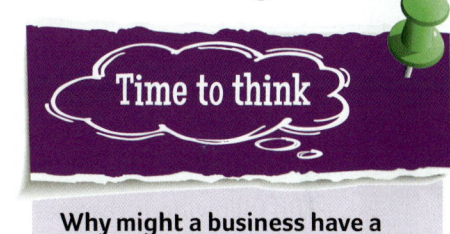

Time to think

Why might a business have a brand name?

1. Product — Product: meeting the customer's needs

2. Price — Price: the cost, ensuring profit while still being acceptable to the customer

3. Place — Place: distributed and available in a location convenient to the customer at the right time

4. Promotion — Promotion: successful advertising and promotion

2.8 BE BUSINESS: ENTERPRISE

CHECKING IN...

1. Name the 4Ps and give an example of each in action.
2. Copy and complete the star to demonstrate the marketing mix.

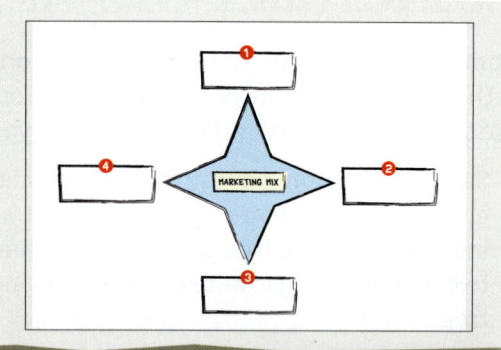

CASE STUDY: THE MARKETING MIX FOR GREENGO

Ben White has established GreenGo, a garden centre with a mixture of garden and seasonal products and services. Ben has come up with an innovative idea, a service called 'Picka3'. He is aware of the importance of the marketing mix, ensuring he has the right product, at the right price, in the right place, and with the right promotion.

The following is the marketing mix for GreenGo's Picka3 service.

Elements	
Product/service	• Picka3 is unique service where children can visit and watch their Christmas tree grow and are given a certificate to say it's theirs when they collect it at Christmas. • Each tree will have a unique identifier (number), and a name can be added if required. The tree can be visited physically and virtually (online) and families can attend the chopping ceremony. • There will be spin-off products including a personalised Christmas story book including the tree and the name of the child. • Target market: infants to 12-year-olds.
Price	• It will cost €60 to purchase a tree. • The price includes the accompanying Picka3 service and the certificate. • Discounts of 10% will be given if you purchase more than three trees. • Spin-off products will vary in price.

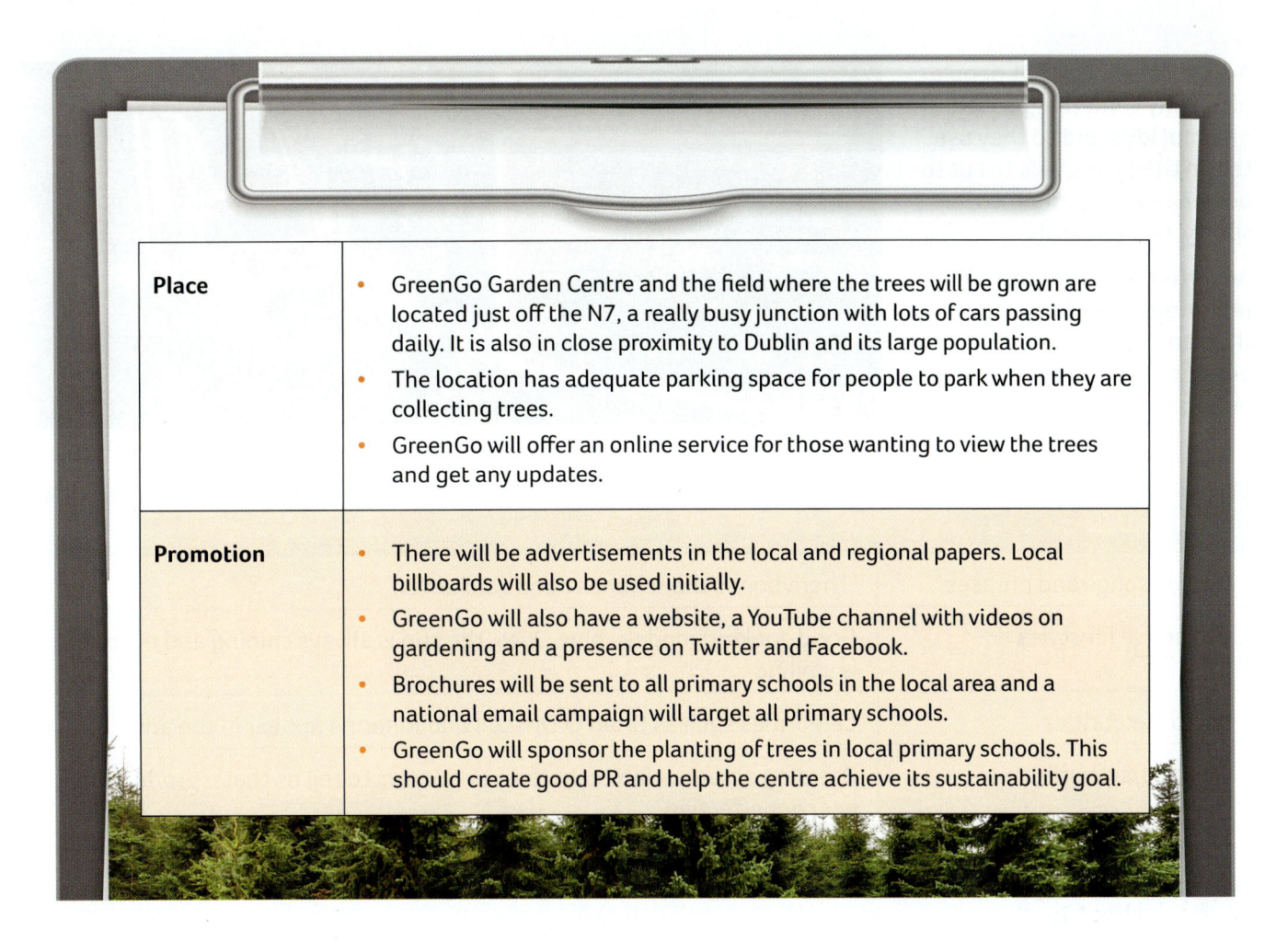

Place	• GreenGo Garden Centre and the field where the trees will be grown are located just off the N7, a really busy junction with lots of cars passing daily. It is also in close proximity to Dublin and its large population. • The location has adequate parking space for people to park when they are collecting trees. • GreenGo will offer an online service for those wanting to view the trees and get any updates.
Promotion	• There will be advertisements in the local and regional papers. Local billboards will also be used initially. • GreenGo will also have a website, a YouTube channel with videos on gardening and a presence on Twitter and Facebook. • Brochures will be sent to all primary schools in the local area and a national email campaign will target all primary schools. • GreenGo will sponsor the planting of trees in local primary schools. This should create good PR and help the centre achieve its sustainability goal.

REVIEWING THE MARKETING MIX

Organisations must continually review the marketing mix to ensure that they remain close to their market. They may need to change prices, adapt promotion and even update products/services.

Ben from GreenGo is already thinking he should offer a delivery service for busy parents who may not have the time to collect the trees. He will research this further to ensure that there is a demand. Ben knows that he must have the right marketing mix to meet his customers' needs while also making a profit.

ADVERTISING

Advertising is the paid promotion of a product or service with the aim of informing and influencing people about the product or service.

Time to think

Have you ever been influenced by an advertisement?

Advertising is expensive and a cost in the business accounts (income statement: shows the profits/losses of a business, Unit 2.12). Some businesses spend millions of euros on advertising, for example Apple, Coca-Cola and McDonald's.

2.8 BE BUSINESS: ENTERPRISE

Advertisers know that people often buy something based on **emotions** and so they use this in theirs ads. Ads tell us to be healthy, be glamorous, be sporty, be beautiful.

Advertisers use interesting **techniques** and **language** in their ads. See if you recognise any of the techniques listed below:

Techniques	
Catchy songs and phrases	'Them bones them bones need calcium …'
Attractive lifestyles	Good-looking models, blue skies, the sun is always shining and everyone is smiling
Use of celebrities	Celebrities such as Brian O'Driscoll and Rihanna appear in the ads
An air of authority	Dressing actors as lab technician or doctors to tell us that a product is 99 per cent effective

Language	
Positive words	100 per cent natural, fresh, homemade, enjoyable, newest, fastest, cleanest, biggest, best
Sense of urgency	Buy now, act immediately, offer ends soon, when it's gone it's gone!
Slogans	A slogan is a catchy phrase that advertisers use to help people remember their product or company: **McDonald's: I'm loving it** Yorkie: It's not for girls Nike: Just do it

Time to think

Can you associate other products with slogans? Why do you think you remember these slogans?

WORKING WITH OTHERS

- Working in pairs or small groups, source an advertisement. Has the advertiser used any of the above techniques?
- Download an ad from YouTube and list the advertising techniques used. Would the ad convince you to buy the product?

Be a Researcher

Find out the cost of a standard full-page advertisement in a national newspaper.

REASONS FOR ADVERTISING

Advertising communicates information about a product or service, with a view to persuading potential customers to buy the product or service.

Reasons for advertising – **AIDA**.

- Advertising attracts **attention**
- It inspires **interest**
- It develops a **desire**
- It achieves **action** – that is, it persuades the customer to purchase the product or service

TYPES OF ADVERTISING

There are three types of advertising:

1. **Informative** provides factual information, for example the price of a smartphone.
2. **Persuasive** aims to convince you that you need this product/service. The George Foreman grill was called the 'Lean, mean, fat-reducing grilling machine!'.
3. **Competitive** shows that a particular brand is better. Two brands are placed side by side to show customers the differences, for example in 2006 Apple launched the 'I'm a Mac, I'm a PC' campaign to portray Apple Mac users as cool and PC users as not so cool.

FORMS OF ADVERTISING

There are many forms of advertising. Companies use whatever way they can to spread the word about their products and services:

- Social media
- Magazines
- Shopping bags
- Television
- Cinema
- Competitions
- Websites
- Newspapers
- Sponsorship
- Radio
- Billboards

2.8 BE BUSINESS: ENTERPRISE

The form of advertising you choose will depend on:
- The media preferences of the **customers**
- The **type** of product/service
- The **budget**
- If there is a need to **demonstrate** the product/service
- If it needs to be advertised **locally or nationally**

PLANNING AN ADVERTISING CAMPAIGN

When planning an advertising promotion, it is important to:
- Have clear **outcomes or intentions**. (What do you hope to achieve?)
- Decide on a **budget**. (Remember, advertising is an expense.)
- Choose an **appropriate form** of advertising.
- Decide whether to use an **advertising agency** or employ someone in your business.

Evaluate the Campaign

After the campaign, **evaluate** to see:
- What worked well?
- What would you do differently?

How can you **evaluate**?

1. Identify the costs involved and see if the campaign was cost-effective.
2. Survey the public.
3. Check whether sales have increased significantly.
4. Ask employees for their opinions.

Time to think

What's your favourite advertisement? Why?

Identify a plus and a minus for each form of advertising listed on the previous page.

Did You Know?

The National Lottery's advertising slogan is 'It could be you!' However, with 47 numbers to choose from, the chances of winning the jackpot are nearly one in 11 million!

CHECKING IN...

1. Name three techniques used by advertisers to get our attention.
2. List the types of advertising and say why an organisation would choose each one.
3. What are the key elements in planning and evaluating an advertising campaign?

Time to think

How might a business advertise globally?

MARKETING MIX 2.8

BE THE BEST BUSINESS WITH THE PERFECT MARKETING MIX...

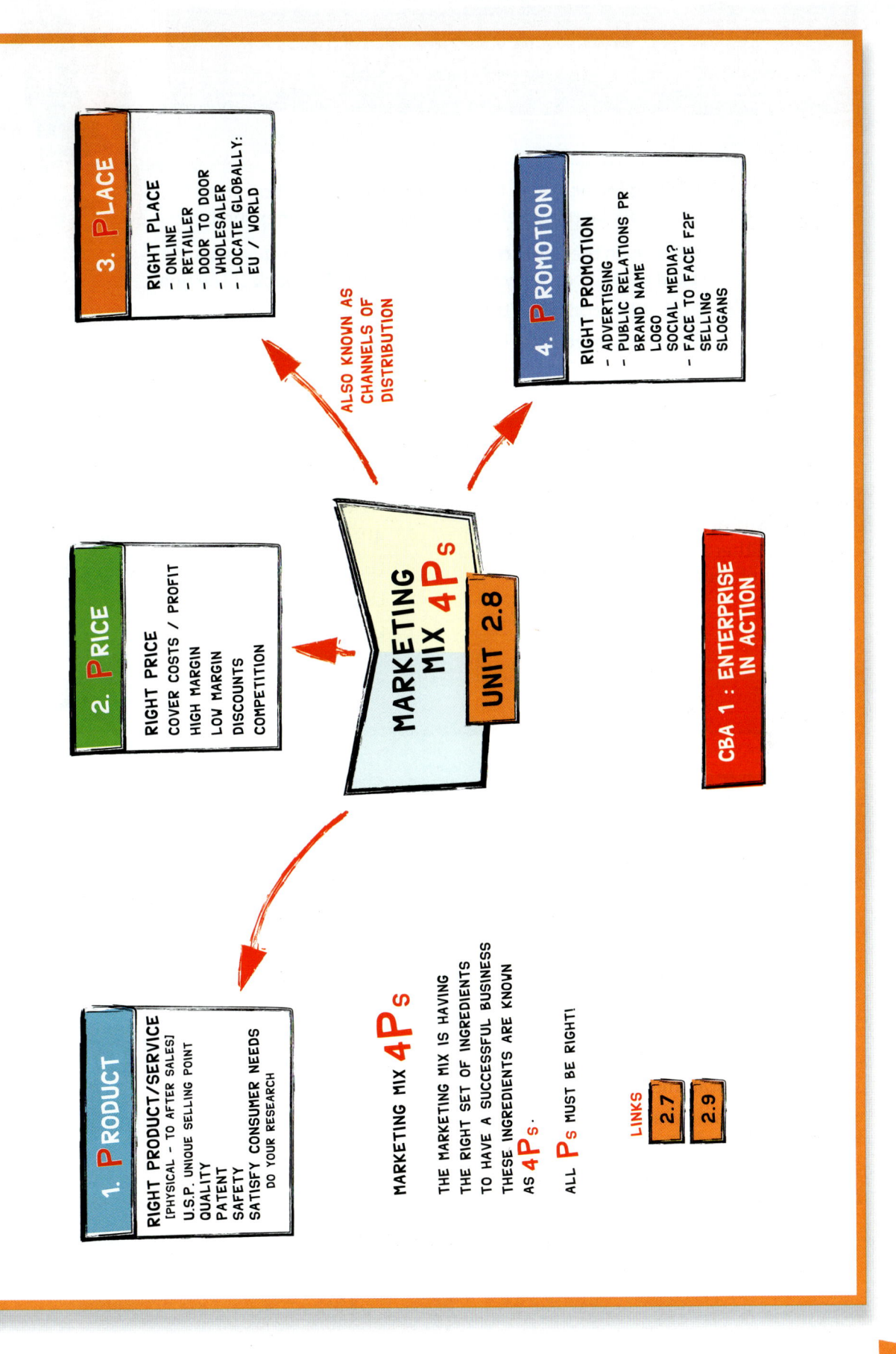

MARKETING MIX 4Ps

UNIT 2.8

1. PRODUCT
RIGHT PRODUCT/SERVICE
(PHYSICAL – TO AFTER SALES)
- U.S.P. UNIQUE SELLING POINT
- QUALITY
- PATENT
- SAFETY
- SATISFY CONSUMER NEEDS
- DO YOUR RESEARCH

2. PRICE
RIGHT PRICE
- COVER COSTS / PROFIT
- HIGH MARGIN
- LOW MARGIN
- DISCOUNTS
- COMPETITION

3. PLACE
RIGHT PLACE
- ONLINE
- RETAILER
- DOOR TO DOOR
- WHOLESALER
- LOCATE GLOBALLY: EU / WORLD

ALSO KNOWN AS CHANNELS OF DISTRIBUTION

4. PROMOTION
RIGHT PROMOTION
- ADVERTISING
- PUBLIC RELATIONS PR
- BRAND NAME
- LOGO
- SOCIAL MEDIA?
- FACE TO FACE F2F
- SELLING
- SLOGANS

CBA 1 : ENTERPRISE IN ACTION

MARKETING MIX 4Ps

THE MARKETING MIX IS HAVING THE RIGHT SET OF INGREDIENTS TO HAVE A SUCCESSFUL BUSINESS THESE INGREDIENTS ARE KNOWN AS **4Ps**.

ALL **Ps** MUST BE RIGHT!

LINKS: 2.7, 2.9

291

2.8 BE BUSINESS: ENTERPRISE

Be Prepared: My Support Sheets

Completing the activities below will help you reflect on and reinforce your learning before you move on to the next unit.

- Write down the **key terms** in this unit and make sure you understand them. See if they match the ones at the back of the book.
- List the key **concepts/themes** in this unit.
- List of the **three most interesting ideas** in this unit.

Business in Action Idea!

Design and apply the marketing mix for either a new or an existing product of your choice.

Success criteria:
- A title
- 4Ps applied
- Understanding of each P and how they are all related
- Use of visuals/photographs/graphics
- Use of technology

QUESTION TIME

1. Explain the marketing mix.
2. Explain sales promotion and personal selling.
3. How might a for-profit organisation improve its image? How might a not-for-profit organisation improve its image?
4. Can you name a product/service that has a USP?
5. Have you ever purchased a product just because of its brand? In your class devise a list of the top five brands used in the last year. Document the results visually.
6. 'You should always set your price low.' Jot down three points for this statement and three points against this statement.
7. 'Advertising is a waste of time'. Write a fifty-word newspaper article on this statement.

Stop and think

Do I have any questions or concerns?

What are the mistakes or errors I made in this unit?

EVALUATE MY LEARNING: DAR

Describe
- Did I/we meet my/our learning intentions?
- What went well? What are my/our strengths?

Assess
- How did I/we work with others?
- Were there challenges?

Recommend
- How might I improve?
- What skills and learning might I apply to new situations?

Do your **Key Check** in the workbook for this unit and then mark your learning position on the following rating scale:

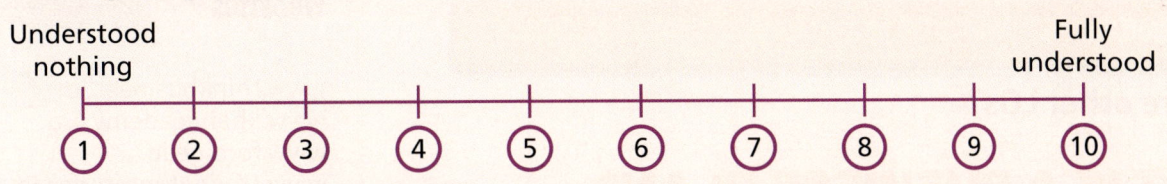

Understood nothing — 1 2 3 4 5 6 7 8 9 10 — Fully understood

How can you move up the rating scale? What can you **say**, **make**, **write** and **do** to illustrate your learning?

CBA 1 Business in Action:
Will I avail of this unit for my topic for my **Enterprise in Action**?

You need to be preparing for your CBAs

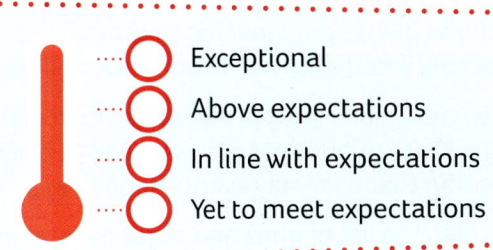

- Exceptional
- Above expectations
- In line with expectations
- Yet to meet expectations

2.9 BUSINESS PLAN

Develop a simple business plan for a new or existing product or service.

Learning Intentions

At the end of this unit I will:
- Know about business plans
- Understand planning
- Value, apply and create a business plan
- Develop the skill of planning

Making the links with other LOs:

2.7 Market research

2.8 Marketing mix

Are there other LOs?

Key Concepts

- ✓ Business plans
- ✓ Finance
- ✓ Marketing
- ✓ SWOT

Wonderful Worthwhile Websites

www.thinkbusiness.ie
www.khanacademy.org
www.foroige.ie
www.studententerprise.ie

WHAT IS A BUSINESS PLAN?

A business plan is a written document that describes in detail how a new business is going to achieve its goals. A business plan will lay out a **written plan** from a marketing, financial and operational viewpoint. Sometimes a business plan is prepared for an established business that is moving in a new direction; it can help the business to decide whether or not to pursue a business idea.

A business plan is like a **road map** which states where the business is now, where it wants to go and how it plans to get there. A business plan should not be considered as a limit on what can be done, but instead as a way of ensuring that everyday events happen in an organised and planned way.

The plan is a list of **aims and objectives**, alongside a budget for the business. It is the framework for the business.

It is important that the plan is **flexible**; it must allow for changes and be able to cope with any unexpected events. The plan should monitor how the business is performing and whether the business is achieving its aims.

It is a form of **control**. Has the business achieved what it set out to achieve? Having a plan enables the business to compare actual outcomes against initial aims.

A plan should be **amended** as often as necessary. This enables the owners/managers to keep the business on track. Research shows that businesses that plan are more likely to make a higher profit.

3Ts
- Do you think a business plan is similar to a personal financial life cycle (see Unit 1.3)?
- Is planning a waste of time?

Planning is important for you too! You need to plan for your Enterprise in Action project!

BUSINESS PLAN 2.9

REASONS FOR PREPARING A PLAN

A business plan:

1. Sets outs the **aims/objectives** and **target market**
2. Shows what **resources** are required to achieve goals
3. Is a **necessary document** when looking for a bank loan, a grant or new investors
4. Provides a SWOT (strengths/weaknesses /opportunities/threats) analysis
5. Is a road map, identifying the **direction** you need to take to achieve the organisation's goals.
6. Is an excellent tool for **reviewing** and **evaluating** and to understand what actions must be taken to achieve the aims/goals

Time to think

Have you ever planned for something? How did you prepare?

STRUCTURE OF A BUSINESS PLAN

Typically a business plan will contain the following elements:

1. **Title**: Business Plan
2. **Name of business**
3. **Table of contents**
4. **Executive summary:** this may include a mission statement that outlines what the business does and its values; summary of the organisation and future plans
5. **Details of product/service:** quality, patents and unique selling point (USP)
6. **Personnel:** owners/management and their expertise, legal structure, form of business (sole trader or company)
7. **Details of production** (only in manufacturing)
8. **Marketing:** market research (desk and field), marketing mix (4Ps)
9. **Finance:**
   a) Final accounts: income statement/statement financial position/cash budget, which shows the cash flow
   b) Sources of finance – how the business will be financed (loans, grants, shares)
10. **Appendices:** other relevant information (leases, legal documents, CVs of key staff, patents/royalties). If producing goods, include production, quality certificates, awards, etc.
11. **Signature** and **date**

Remember to sign and date your business plan.

Time to think

What might a mission statement contain?

Does your school have a mission statement? Source a copy and give your opinion on it.

Source a mission statement from a for-profit company and a not-for-profit organisation. Compare the two and share your findings.

295

2.9 BE BUSINESS: ENTERPRISE

CREATING YOUR BUSINESS PLAN

Put time and effort into creating your business plan as the work at the beginning makes the process itself run more smoothly.

1. The starting point is **what the business actually does**.
2. Do a **SWOT analysis** to assess the current position of the company.
3. Establish **aims**. Where do you want the business to go? Think of all the stakeholders in your business – you, your staff, consumers, the government and the environment.
4. Look at the **market**. How big is the market? What share of the market do you hope to achieve? Look at your competition.
5. Identify **finances**. How much do you need? Where will you source your finance?
6. What **resources** and **assets** do you require? For example, premises, machines, raw materials, etc.

Remember, the business plan shows potential finance providers that the business proposal is viable and that you have the commitment and willpower to succeed.

The plan needs to be easily understood and present the best possible picture of the business.

The cover of the business plan gives the reader an instant impression of the business so it needs to look professional. It should show the business name and logo.

> When you have finished this course you will be able to complete a more detailed plan. It might be a good idea to wait until you have completed final accounts before you finalise your business plan.

SWOT ANALYSIS

When assessing the current position of a business you can use a technique known as a SWOT analysis. This looks at strengths, weaknesses (sometimes known as challenges), opportunities and threats.

Strengths and weaknesses are **internal** – they are inside the business.

Opportunities and threats are **external** – they are inside the business.

- **Strengths:** good internal things about the business, for example the product, knowledge or customer relations.
- **Weaknesses:** internal weaknesses in the business, for example, outdated equipment, lack of expertise or poor location.
- **Opportunities:** good external business factors that the business can use to its advantage, for example a new international market, a competitor leaving the market or a merger.
- **Threats:** external factors that could threaten the business, for example a change in consumer taste, a new competitor in your market or new taxes on your product.

You can use a SWOT analysis to analyse any organisation – a retail business such as Ciara's Cupcakes, a voluntary organisation like St Vincent de Paul, or a financial institution such as a bank.

CASE STUDY:
SWOT ANALYSIS – CIARA'S CUPCAKES

Ciara Carew is a post-primary student who bakes cupcakes in her home and sells them at school. She is preparing a business plan as she wants to expand and needs a loan to do it. Here is her SWOT analysis.

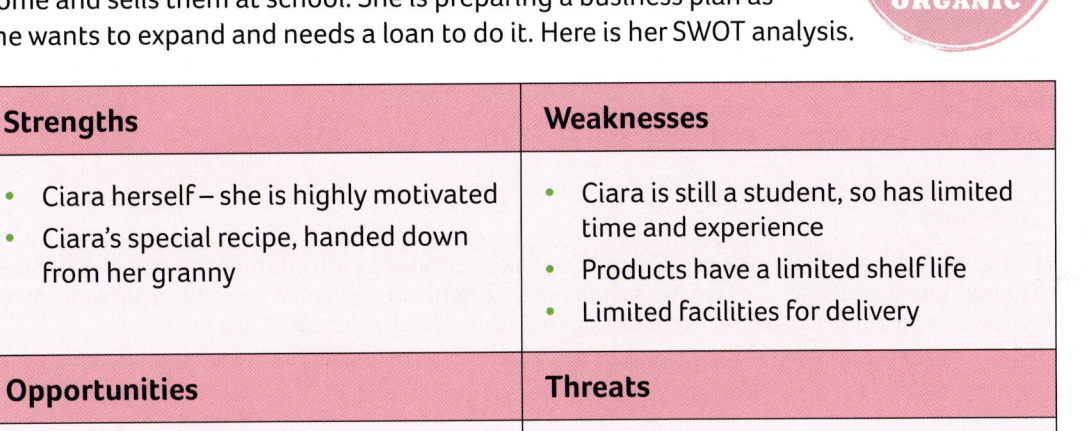

Strengths	Weaknesses
• Ciara herself – she is highly motivated • Ciara's special recipe, handed down from her granny	• Ciara is still a student, so has limited time and experience • Products have a limited shelf life • Limited facilities for delivery
Opportunities	**Threats**
• Demand for cupcakes in local markets and school shops • Weddings and special occasions market	• Competition • Health and safety laws • People's concerns about sugar consumption

WORKING WITH OTHERS

Draft a SWOT analysis for a business of your choice. Use the following headings.
- Strengths – Internal
- Weaknesses – Internal
- Opportunities – External
- Threats – External

CHECKING IN...

1. What do you think are the three most important reasons to create a business plan?
2. What advice would you give to a student when starting a plan?
3. Why is it important to have USPs in a business plan?

Sample Simple Business Plan for Ciara's Cupcakes

One of the strongest inspirations for Ciara was her grandmother, Marian Walsh Senior. Marian was an entrepreneur for many years. During her school holidays, Ciara loved spending time with her granny, who taught her how to bake. The following is Ciara's business plan.

Business Plan for Ciara's Cupcakes

Table of Contents

Page 1 Executive summary
Page 2 Product
Page 3 Personnel
Page 4 Production
Page 5 Marketing
Page 6 Finance
Page 7 Appendices

Executive summary

Ciara Carew is a sole trader and her business, Ciara's Cupcakes, produces affordable tasty cupcakes. She makes the cupcakes in her house and sells them in her school each lunchtime. She also provides a service where she will decorate the cupcakes to match a special occasion, such as a birthday or graduation.

MISSION STATEMENT

To provide organic, tasty, affordable, visually appealing cupcakes that are fresh every day.

After a successful year selling in the school and for special occasions, Ciara has decided to expand and sell in the local market every Saturday in Carlow.

Her parents are supportive of her decision and are willing to finance a loan, interest free, to help her expand. They wanted to see a business plan before giving her the loan.

Product

- Ciara's Cupcakes are made from fresh **organic** ingredients and free-range eggs.
- They have a **variety** of flavours, icings, colours and decorative finishings.
- They are sold at an **affordable** price for her target market.
- She uses a **secret recipe** to make the cupcakes that she was given by her granny; so this is a key USP for the business.
- Another USP is her ability to **individualise** the cupcakes for special occasions.
- She eliminates all waste in a **sustainable** way, utilising her parents' recycling and organic bins.
- She bakes on the morning of sales and this means an early start, but her product is therefore always **fresh**.

Personnel

- Legal structure: **sole trader**
- **Ciara Carew** is highly motivated, hard-working and an excellent baker. She is extremely creative and produces individualised cupcakes for special occasions. When she takes on large orders she can call on her family to help her.

- Ciara was a **national finalist** in the Student Enterprise awards.
- For the expansion, she will employ her brother **Conor**.

Production
- Ciara produces her cupcakes in batches of 24.
- She uses high-quality organic ingredients and maintains strict quality controls.
- She always follows safety regulations, wearing a hair net and sterilising all cooking equipment.

Marketing
- Ciara undertook **market research** at the local market to find out if there was an interest in her idea. She conducted a survey and asked potential customers about the 4Ps (product, price, place and promotion).
- **Product**: the favourite flavours in the survey were lemon and cinnamon.
- **Price**: people were prepared to pay €1 per cupcake. This price was the cost per cupcake plus a 20% profit margin.
- **Place**: the location of her stall would have to be near the other food sellers.
- **Promotion**: Ciara currently advertises in school and on Facebook and Twitter. She is going to place an advert in the local paper to let people know about her new stall at the market. For her first Saturday market she will have a tasting day and she will limit supply.

Finance
The business is profitable at the moment and Ciara has €1,200 in savings from profits.

Income statement:

	Sales/Revenue	€2,500
	Expenses	€700
	Net profit	€1,800

Statement of financial position

a) **Finance required** for expansion: €2,500

b) **Finance available:** €1,800 from profits already made with the business

c) **Investment/loan required:** €700 loan from parents to be repaid over 5 years interest free

d) **Assets:** €1,800 cash, a mixer and a stock of ingredients

Appendices
Appendix I Results of market research surveys

Appendix II Final accounts:
- Income statement
- Statement of financial position
- Cash budget, which shows the cash flow

Signed: *Ciara Carew* (owner)   Dated: 1/4/2019

Note: Ciara had hoped to receive a grant (non-repayable) from her parents rather than a repayable loan.

2.9 BE BUSINESS: ENTERPRISE

BE PREPARED & PLAN...

BUSINESS PLAN — UNIT 2.9

1. TITLE
BUSINESS PLAN FOR _____
ROADMAP

2. EXECUTIVE SUMMARY
SUMMARY OF BUSINESS

3. MISSION STATEMENT
WHAT THE BUSINESS IS ABOUT – VALUE.
INCLUDED IN SUMMARY

4. THE BUSINESS & PEOPLE
PRODUCT/SERVICE/SOLE TRADER/ PARTNERSHIP/COMPANY
PEOPLE CVs – PATENT

5. PRODUCTION *(ONLY IF MANUFACTURING)*
QUALITY
HEALTH & SAFETY
ONCE OFF, BATCH, MASS

6. FINANCE
CAPITAL: MONEY YOU START OFF WITH
1. INCOME STATEMENT — 2.13
2. STATEMENT OF FINANCIAL POSITION — 2.13
3. CASH FLOW FORECASTS — 2.11
   CASH IN – CASH OUT
4. SOURCES OF FINANCE — 2.11
   SHORT MEDIUM LONGTERM
   OVERDRAFT LEASING CAPITAL
   CREDITORS H.P. RETAINED PROFITS

7. MARKETING
MARKET RESEARCH — DESK / FIELD — 2.7
MARKETING MIX 5Ps — 2.8
USP UNIQUE SELLING POINT
TARGET MARKET

CBA 1: ENTERPRISE IN ACTION

8. OTHER RELEVANT INFORMATION
LEASES
LEGAL DOCUMENTS
PATENT: YOUR INVENTION CANNOT BE COPIED
AWARDS

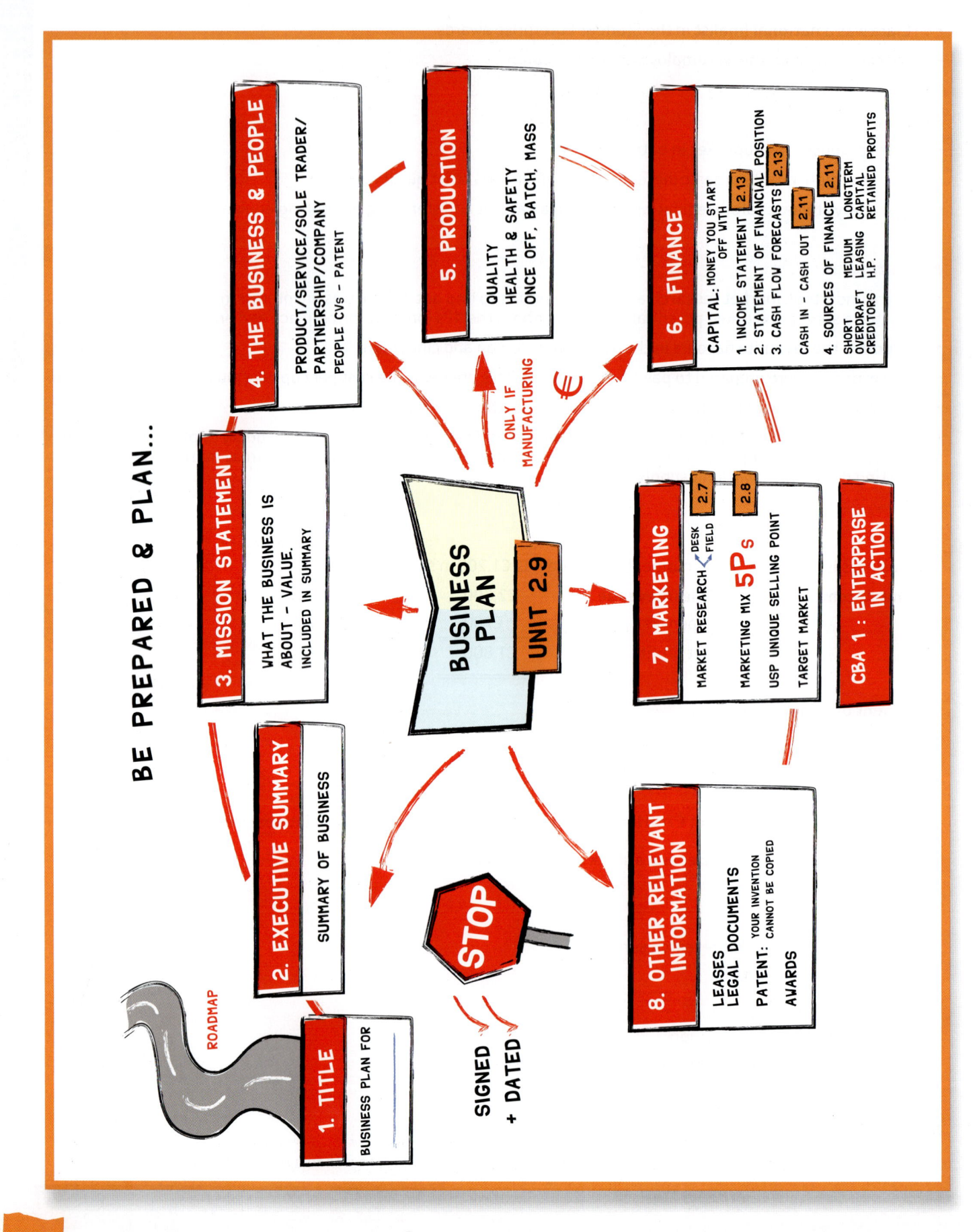

STOP — SIGNED + DATED

Be Prepared: My Support Sheets

Completing the activities below will help you reflect on and reinforce your learning before you move on to the next unit.

- Write down the **key terms** in this unit and make sure you understand them. See if they match the ones at the back of the book.
- List the key **concepts/themes** in this unit.
- Make a list of the **three most interesting ideas** in this unit.

Business in Action Idea!

For your Enterprise in Action, create a business plan for a business of your choice.

Choose from one of the following options:

1. Invent an imaginary for-profit organisation, with a name and a product/service that you are familiar with, and create a business plan similar to the business plan for Ciara's Cupcakes.
2. Write a business plan on a business you are familiar with.
3. Write a paragraph of no more than 50 words on the importance of a business plan...

Success criteria:
- Title – including an innovative business name and logo
- Nine sections as shown in this unit
- Show an understanding of each section
- Use of business terms you have learned in your Business Studies course
- Use of visuals
- Use of technology, if appropriate

Success criteria:
- Title
- At least five points
- Use of visuals

QUESTION TIME

1. Describe something you planned for, perhaps going to a concert or attending a game abroad. What did you do? Did your plan change? If so, describe the changes.

2. Describe a business plan.
3. If an organisation decides not to plan, what might happen?
4. Explain SWOT and devise a SWOT analysis for a product/company of your choice.
5. Why might it be important to identify your strengths, weaknesses, opportunities and threats? Which might you have greater control over? Why?
6. What might be the advantages of creating a plan?
7. Ciara Carew created her plan, but she did not disclose her granny's recipe. Why might Ciara not disclose such important information?

Stop and think

Do I have any questions or concerns?

What are the mistakes or errors I made in this unit?

EVALUATE MY LEARNING: DAR

Describe
- Did I/we meet our learning intentions?
- What went well? What are my/our strengths?

Assess
- How did I/we work with others?
- Were there challenges?

Recommend
- How might I improve?
- What skills and learning might I apply to new situations?

Do your **Key Check** in the workbook for this unit and then mark your learning position on the following rating scale:

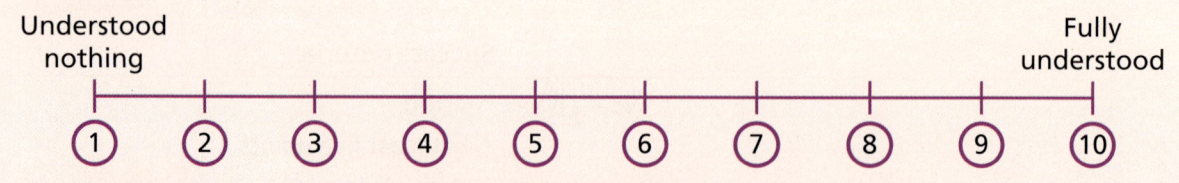

Understood nothing ① ② ③ ④ ⑤ ⑥ ⑦ ⑧ ⑨ ⑩ Fully understood

How can you move up the rating scale? What can you **say**, **make**, **write** and **do** to illustrate your learning?

CBA 1 Business in Action:
Will I avail of this unit for my topic for my **Enterprise in Action**?

You need to be preparing for your CBAs

○ Exceptional
○ Above expectations
○ In line with expectations
○ Yet to meet expectations

2.10 KEY BUSINESS DOCUMENTS

Complete and interpret key business documents that an organisation uses to manage its transactions for accountability purposes.

Learning Intentions

At the end of this unit I will:
- Know about relevant business documents when buying and selling
- Understand about business documents
- Value the importance of recording information

Making the links with other LOs:

- 1.2 Personal income and expenditure
- 2.11 Cash budget
- 2.12 Cash book, ledger and trial balance
- 2.13 Final accounts
- 3.4 Government revenue and government expenditure

Are there other LOs?

> **'3Ts' = Think, Turn, Talk**
>
> If you owned a business, what areas might you need to keep track of? How do you think you would do this?

Key Concepts

- ✓ Letter of enquiry
- ✓ Quotation
- ✓ Order
- ✓ Delivery docket
- ✓ Invoice
- ✓ Credit note
- ✓ Receipt
- ✓ Debit note
- ✓ Statement of account

Wonderful Worthwhile Websites

www.sageone.ie
www.revenue.ie
www.thinkbusiness.ie

INTRODUCTION TO BUSINESS DOCUMENTS

Business documents contain important information that is key to creating an organisation's accounts. The documents are an important paper trail, tracing all transactions (buying and selling of goods and services) from the initial enquiry to the final payment. They provide figures for accounts and also contain information on terms and conditions agreed. Revenue (for tax purposes) and other financial enterprises may need to see them. If there is a dispute over number of goods ordered, quantity, prices, terms or delivery, the owners can check and refer to the specific documents.

2.10 BE BUSINESS: ENTERPRISE

These documents were originally produced on paper but today many organisations use computer programs to record their documents. The most important thing is that they are organised logically and are easy to find, whether by name, document number or even coding (e.g. using codes for customers). For example, if a customer complains about a late delivery, you can check the delivery document. If there is a complaint about price, you can refer to the quotation.

Businesses must complete certain important documents before transferring information to accounts.

Important business documents used and payment when purchasing stock include:

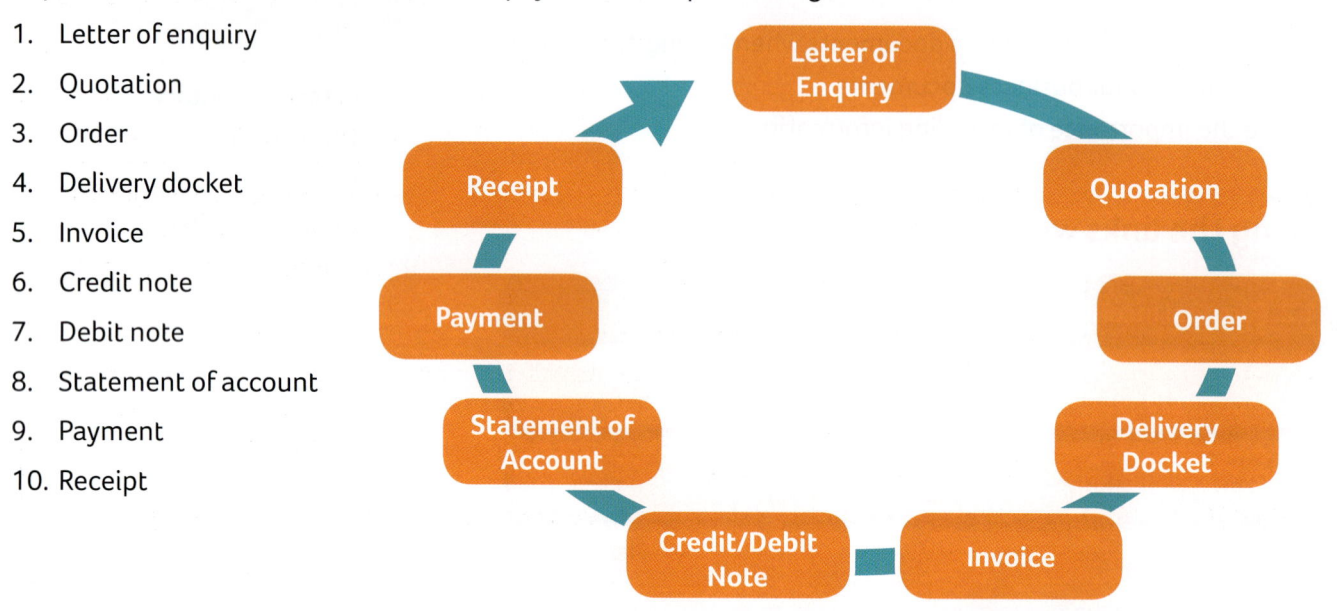

1. Letter of enquiry
2. Quotation
3. Order
4. Delivery docket
5. Invoice
6. Credit note
7. Debit note
8. Statement of account
9. Payment
10. Receipt

The documents are quite similar, so it is important to know the answers to these questions:

1. What is the **name** of the document, e.g. letter of enquiry?
2. **Who sends** the document, e.g. the buyer?
3. **Who receives** the document, e.g. the seller?
4. What important **information** is in the document, e.g. products/price?
5. **What to do** with the document?
6. You should also be able to understand the documents from different **perspectives**: the buyer and the seller.

SUMMARY OF BUSINESS DOCUMENTS

Name of document	Who sends/who receives	Information
Letter/email of enquiry	Buyer → Seller	Buyer of the goods sends this document to the seller to obtain information about goods, e.g. price.

KEY BUSINESS DOCUMENTS 2.10

Name of document	Who sends/who receives	Information
Quotation	Seller → Buyer	Seller sends a quotation in response to the enquiry. This is similar to a price list. The quotation will give prices and terms and conditions. A business will shop around for the best quotation from many suppliers, ensuring that they receive the best deal in relation to price, quality, delivery and terms.
Order	Buyer → Seller	The order is completed by the buyer to place an order for the exact quantity and models required.
Delivery docket	Seller → Buyer	A delivery docket is sent with the goods from the seller. The buyer will sign the delivery docket if everything is in order. A signed delivery docket is proof that the goods were received.
Invoice	Seller → Buyer	An invoice is sent by the seller when the goods have been delivered. It is similar to a bill; it states how much the goods cost in total.
Credit note	Seller → Buyer	A credit note is issued by the seller when goods are returned or overcharged.
Debit note	Seller → Buyer	A debit note is issued by the seller when the seller undercharges the buyer. It tells the buyer how much they owe the seller.
Statement of account	Seller → Buyer	A statement of account is sent at the end of the month by the seller, showing all transactions and the amount due.
Payment	Buyer → Seller	Buyer pays the seller. There are different ways to pay: by debit card, credit card, online credit transfer or with cash.
Receipt	Seller → Buyer	Seller sends a receipt to the buyer as proof of purchase and acknowledgement of payment.

WORKING WITH OTHERS

- Name the documents sent from the buyer to the seller.
- Name the documents sent from the seller to the buyer.
- Which documents might be the most important? Why?

1. LETTER/EMAIL OF ENQUIRY

Buyer of the goods sends this document to the seller.

A letter of enquiry, a phone call or email is sent to several suppliers enquiring about prices and terms. You are enquiring:

- If the goods are **available**.
- What **discounts** are available? When you buy in bulk, the seller will give a percentage (%) discount (money off).
- What are the **terms and conditions**?
- How much **credit** will you receive? You might have to pay in one month or two months. The longer the period of credit, the better. In financial terms, credit is like a **short-term loan**.
- **How long** before you receive the goods? Some suppliers may demand cash with your order **(CWO) or cash on delivery (COD)**.

It is important to shop around and to ensure you get the best value for money when buying stock. Compare the price of the stock and also the terms of trade:

- Who pays for the **delivery**, e.g. when carriage is paid there is no delivery charge.
- **Credit** terms, e.g. two months credit.
- **Discounts** for buying in bulk or for paying your bill promptly, e.g. 10% cash discount if you pay within a week.
- **VAT** rates. Remember, VAT increases the price.

> Remember, a letter of enquiry could be an email, a phone call or a letter.

EXAMPLE 1: LETTER OF ENQUIRY

Surf Sports Club sends a letter of enquiry to Irish Sports Supplies on 1 April 2020.

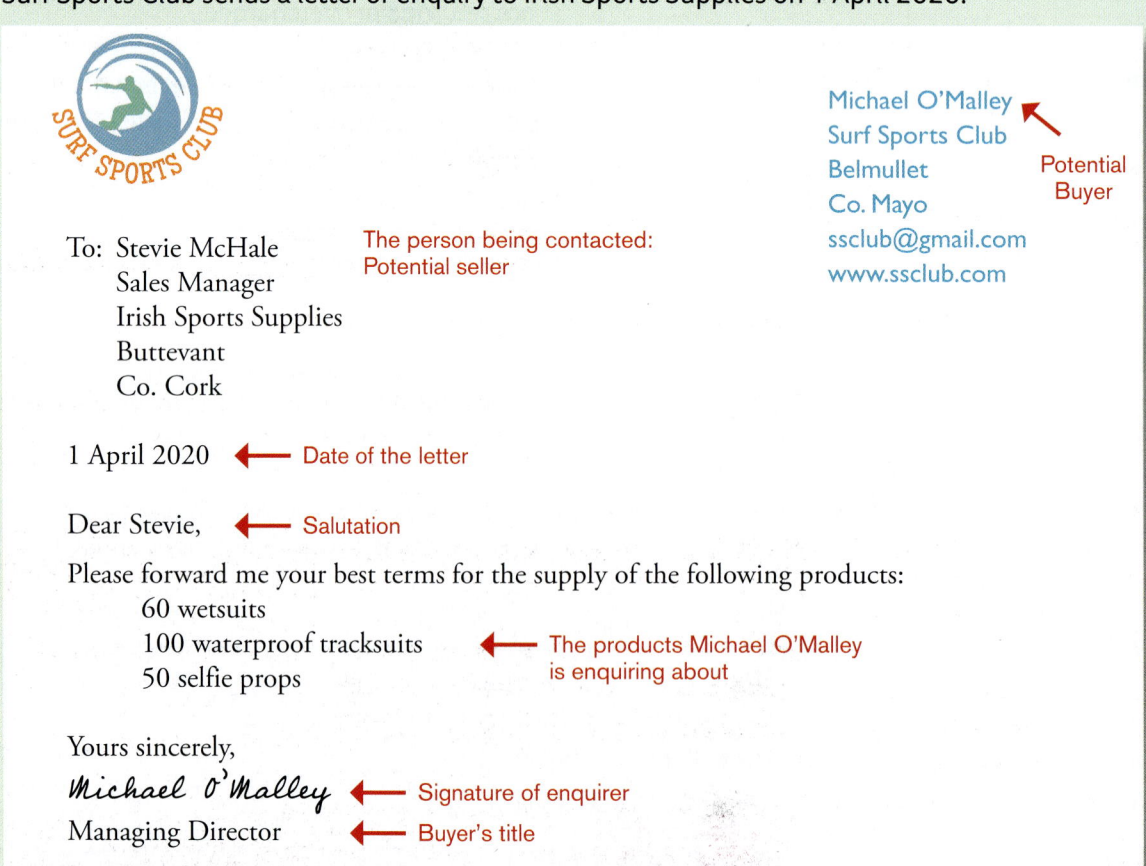

Michael O'Malley
Surf Sports Club
Belmullet
Co. Mayo — *Potential Buyer*
ssclub@gmail.com
www.ssclub.com

To: Stevie McHale
Sales Manager
Irish Sports Supplies
Buttevant
Co. Cork
— *The person being contacted: Potential seller*

1 April 2020 ← *Date of the letter*

Dear Stevie, ← *Salutation*

Please forward me your best terms for the supply of the following products:
 60 wetsuits
 100 waterproof tracksuits ← *The products Michael O'Malley is enquiring about*
 50 selfie props

Yours sincerely,

Michael O'Malley ← *Signature of enquirer*
Managing Director ← *Buyer's title*

Know your Letter of Enquiry

What is the **name** of the document?	Letter of enquiry, just like any formal letter, or it may be by email.
Who sends the document?	Potential buyer: Michael O'Malley from Surf Sports Club
Who receives the document?	Potential seller: Stevie McHale from Irish Sports Supplies
What important **information** is in the document?	Date: need to respond promptly. Contact person: Michael O'Malley. Details of the products that are required
What to do with the document? Be Michael, the **buyer**	Keep a copy of the letter. Check that name and address is correct for Irish Sports Supplies.
Be Stevie, the **seller**	Contact Michael O'Malley, the buyer, immediately, as he may have made enquiries to other organisations. Send a quotation with price and terms included and ensure that you have adequate stock.

CHECKING IN...

Do you understand the letter on the previous page?
1. Who is the potential buyer?
2. Who is the seller?
3. When was the letter sent?
4. What is the enquiry?

2. QUOTATION

Seller of the goods sends this document to the buyer.

The seller will send you a quotation in response to your enquiry. This is similar to a **price list**. The quotation will give prices, rate of VAT, trade discounts and cash discounts along with other terms and conditions, e.g. if carriage is paid.

Organisations will shop around for the best quotation from many suppliers, ensuring that it receives the best deal in terms of price, quality, delivery and terms.

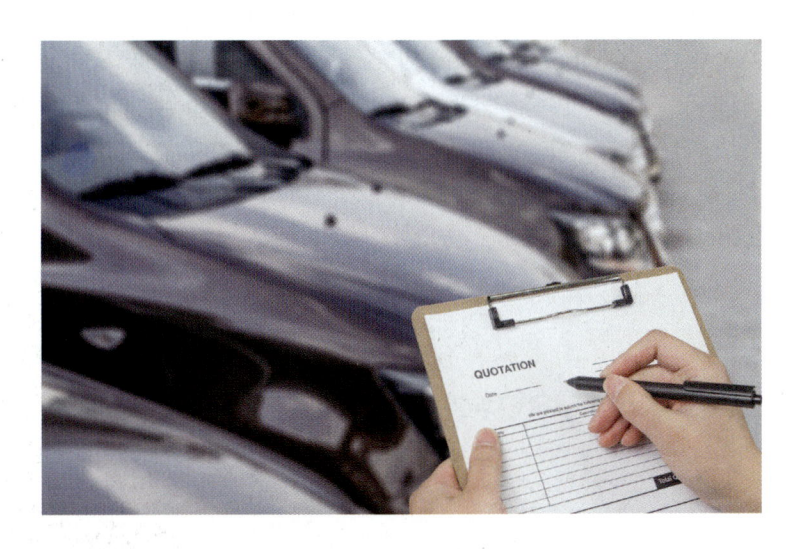

EXAMPLE 2: QUOTATION

Irish Sports Supplies sends the following quotation to Surf Sports club on 15 April 2020.

IRISH SPORTS SUPPLIES

Stevie McHale, Irish Sports Supplies, Buttevant, Co. Cork

Telephone: 021 1616611; VAT Reg. No. IE 771234 ← VAT is a tax

QUOTATION No. 99 ← Title

Michael O'Malley
Surf Sports Club
Belmullet
Co. Mayo

Date: 15/4/2020

Dear Michael ← From Stevie McHale to Michael O'Malley

Thank you for your enquiry of 01 April.

Quantity	Description	Ref	Price each €
60	Wetsuits	AW SG	100
100	Tracksuits	Ref TS	80
50	Selfies prop	Ref S	10

← Details of products

Terms: Carriage paid ← Transport paid
VAT @ 21%
Cash discount 10% if paid within 1 week
Trade discount 20%

Looking forward to doing business with you.

Quotation is valid for 21 days.
Yours sincerely

Stevie McHale ← Potential seller
Sales Manager

Know your Quotation

What is the **name** of the document?	Quotation
Who sends the document?	Potential seller: Stevie McHale from Irish Sports Supplies
Who receives the document?	Potential buyer: Michael O'Malley from Surf Sports Club
What important **information** is in the document?	Price of products (including VAT information). Terms: Carriage and trade and cash discount. Dates: only valid for 21 days so need to respond promptly. Price won't change for 3 weeks. Contact person:
What to do with the document? Be Michael, the **buyer**	• Compare the quotation with the letter of enquiry. • Compare the quotation with other quotations received. • Take prices, discounts and terms into consideration. • Reply within 21 days.
Be Stevie, the **seller**	• Keep a copy of the quotation, as it contains important information. • Perhaps follow with a phone call, an email or even a call from a sales representative.

CHECKING IN...

Do you understand the above quotation?
1. Who is the potential buyer?
2. Who is the seller?
3. When was the quotation sent?
4. What are the prices given?
5. What are the terms?
6. What is the quotation number?

3. ORDER

Buyer of the goods sends this document to the seller.

This document is completed by the buyer to place an order for the exact **quantity** and models required.

2.10 BE BUSINESS: ENTERPRISE

EXAMPLE 3: ORDER

Surf Sports Club sends the following order to Irish Sports Supplies on 28 April 2020.

Buyer → Michael O'Malley
Surf Sports Club
Belmullet
Co. Mayo
ssclub@gmail.com
www.ssclub.com

ORDER No. 77 ← Title and order reference number

Telephone: 086 7612317; VAT Reg. No. IE 5544123

To: Steve McHale ← Seller
Irish Sports Supplies
Buttevant
Co. Cork

Date: 20/4/2020
Quotation No. 99

Quantity	Description	Ref	Price each €
60	Wetsuits	AW SG	100
100	Tracksuits	Ref TS	80
40	Selfies prop	Ref S	10

Exact quantity → (Quantity column)
Description ← Details of order

Goods to be delivered to the above address within 5 days.

Yours sincerely

Margaret Togher

Senior Sales Representative

Know your Order

What is the **name** of the document?	Order (with an order number for reference)
Who sends the document?	Buyer: Michael O'Malley from Surf Sports Club
Who receives the document?	Seller: Stevie McHale from Irish Sports Supplies

What important **information** is in the document?	Details of exact quantity ordered. Michael did not order all the items on the quotation. Date: goods are required to be delivered in five days. Contact person: Margaret Togher has signed the order.
What to do with the document? Be Michael, the **buyer**	• Keep a copy and file the order either manually or electronically. • Ensure you're ordering the correct amount.
Be Stevie, the **seller**	• Check details and file the order either manually or electronically. • Check you have the quantities required in stock. • Send a copy to the accounts department and organise an invoice and delivery docket. • Dispatch the goods and invoice.

> When you sell a product to someone and they can't pay you for it, this is known as a bad debt.

Selling on Credit

The seller must decide whether to sell on credit (pay later). A **credit check** should be done to ensure that the buyer is trustworthy. When selling on credit:

- Look for a reference
- Do a credit check
- Take out insurance

Why might Irish Sports Supplies decide to sell on credit?

- Increases sales and in turn increases profit.
- Competitors offer credit.

CHECKING IN... Do you understand the order on the previous page?
1. Who is the buyer?
2. Who is the seller?
3. When was the order sent?
4. What are the prices given?
5. What are the terms?
6. What is the order number?
7. Who signed the order?
8. What VAT is payable?

4. DELIVERY DOCKET

Buyer of the goods signs this document on receipt of the goods.

Once everything is agreed, the seller will send the goods. When the goods are delivered, the person making the delivery will ask the recipient to sign a **delivery docket**. A signed delivery docket is **proof** that the buyer received the goods.

EXAMPLE 4: DELIVERY DOCKET

Irish Sports Supplies sends the goods along with the following delivery docket to Surf Sports Club on 25 April 2020.

IRISH SPORTS SUPPLIES
Stevie McHale, Irish Sports Supplies, Buttevant, Co. Cork
Telephone: 021 1616611; VAT Reg. No. IE 771234

DELIVERY DOCKET No. 6666 ← Title and reference number

To: Surf Sports Club
Belmullet
Co. Mayo

Date: 25/4/2020
Order No. 77

Quantity	Description ← Details of order	Ref	Price each €
60	Wetsuits	AW SG	100
100	Tracksuits	Ref TS	80
40	Selfies prop	Ref S	10

Goods received:

Lilia May Togher ← Signed by the buyer
On behalf of the Managing Director

Know your Delivery Docket

What is the **name** of the document?	Delivery Docket (with a number for reference)
Who sends the document?	Seller: Stevie McHale from Irish Sports Supplies
Who receives the document?	Buyer: Michael O'Malley from Surf Sports Club

KEY BUSINESS DOCUMENTS 2.10

What important **information** is in the document?	**Date**: needs to be signed by buyer as it is proof of delivery.
What to do with the document? Be Michael, the **buyer**	• Compare the delivery docket with the order to ensure that everything has been delivered. • Check that you are happy with the delivery and sign. Michael got Lilia May to sign as he was not available. • File the delivery docket either manually or electronically.
Be Stevie, the **seller**	• Check that the name and address are correct. • Compare with the order to ensure you are delivering all goods ordered. • File the delivery docket either manually or electronically in case of any disputes.

CHECKING IN...

Do you understand the above delivery docket?
1. Who is the buyer?
2. Who is the seller?
3. When was the delivery docket presented?
4. What are the prices given?
5. What are the terms?
6. What is the order number?
7. Who signed the document?
8. What VAT is payable?

5. INVOICE

Seller of goods sends this document to the buyer.

An invoice is sent by the supplier when the goods have been delivered. An invoice shows a list of products given to a customer along with all the costs. In other words, **an invoice is a bill**.

An invoice is sent to someone because they owe a business money. It is a tool to ask for money that is owed.

An invoice also contains terms. It states when the bill must be paid and details any discounts available.

Invoices come in all sizes and shapes, from a handwritten page to a sophisticated template using software.

Your invoice reflects an image of your business, so it's important to use a professional-looking template.

FINANCIAL RECORD

An invoice is a document that is used for recording financial records.

Invoices are used for VAT, which is a form of taxation by the government. If you are registered for VAT, you are required by law to issue and hold these documents.

2.10 BE BUSINESS: ENTERPRISE

Be the Seller: An invoice is a bill from the seller; from the buyer's viewpoint it is **sales**.

Be the Buyer: An invoice is a bill received by the buyer for goods purchased: from the buyer's viewpoint it is **purchases**.

This may seem confusing, but it is really important to understand the different perspectives or viewpoints of the seller and buyer.

Most businesses have software packages to complete business documents and invoices are processed electronically.

EXAMPLE 5: INVOICE

Irish Sports Supplies sends the following Invoice (bill) to Surf Sports Club on 28 April 2020.

IRISH SPORTS SUPPLIES
Stevie McHale, Irish Sports Supplies, Buttevant, Co. Cork
Telephone: 021 1616611; VAT Reg. No. IE 771234

INVOICE No. 99

To: Surf Sports Club
Belmullet
Co. Mayo

Date: 28/4/2020
Order No. 77

Quantity	Description	Code	Price each €	TOTAL €
60	Wetsuits	AW SG	100	6,000
100	Tracksuits	Ref TS	80	8,000
40	Selfies prop	Ref S	10	400
			Total (Excluding VAT)	14,400.00
	Less Trade discount →		Trade Discount 20%	2,880.00
			Subtotal	11,520.00
Carriage Paid		*Add on VAT →*	VAT 21%	2,419.20
E&OE			Total (Including VAT)	13,939.20

Note: Trade discount decreases the price → minus
VAT increases the price → add

KEY BUSINESS DOCUMENTS 2.10

Know your Invoice

What is the **name** of the document?	Invoice (with a number for reference)
Who sends the document?	Seller: Irish Sports Supplies
Who receives the document?	Buyer: Surf Sports Club
What important **information** is in the document?	Cost of goods including VAT and discounts. E&OE
What to do with the document? Be Michael, the **buyer**	• Check that you actually ordered the goods and check the prices quoted. Check against the order. • Check that you actually received the goods. Check goods against the delivery docket. • Check calculations and totals. • Use the invoice for your records and accounts – Purchases. • Check terms to see if you should avail of cash discounts. • File the invoice either manually or electronically.
Be Stevie, the **seller**	• **Check that the goods on the invoice were actually ordered and delivered.** • **Check that prices and terms on the invoice are the same as in the quotation.** • **Check calculations and totals.** • **Use the invoice for your records and accounts – Sales.** • **Check name and address are correct.** • File the invoice either manually or electronically.

Be aware of what all the initials and terms on the invoice mean.

E&OE = errors and omissions excepted. If the seller makes a mistake with prices, the buyer still pays the correct price.

For example: if the invoice says '40 selfie props @ €1 each = €40' but it should say '40 selfie props @ €10 each = €400'. If the invoice has 'E & OE' on it, the buyer will have to pay €400, not €40 as would be on the invoice.

Trade discount is offered from the seller to the buyer if the buyer is going to sell the goods on. Remember to subtract trade discount from the subtotal and then add on VAT.

315

2.10 BE BUSINESS: ENTERPRISE

CHECKING IN...

Do you understand the above invoice?
1. Who is the buyer?
2. Who is the seller?
3. On what date was it sent?
4. What are the prices given?
5. What is the total price?
6. What are the trade discounts?
7. What are the terms?
8. What is the order number?
9. Who signed the order?
10. What is the VAT number?
11. What VAT is payable?
12. Are the calculations correct?

WORKING WITH OTHERS

Insert a tick ✓ in the box to indicate if each statement is true or false.

	True	False
An invoice is a bill for goods sold on credit.	☐	☐
VAT is a tax paid to our government.	☐	☐
E&OE means that that a firm is bound by mistakes.	☐	☐
Trade discount is subtracted after VAT is added on.	☐	☐
The seller sends the invoice.	☐	☐
Quotations contain the total amount owed.	☐	☐
An invoice is a bill.	☐	☐

6. CREDIT NOTE

Seller of goods sends this document to the buyer.

A credit note is a document that is sent to correct a mistake:

a) If the invoice (bill) is for too much.

b) To compensate the buyer if the goods have been returned.

WHY MIGHT GOODS BE RETURNED?

- If goods are damaged.
- If the buyer receives more than was ordered.
- If the goods are of inferior quality.

If you return goods to a supplier or if a customer returns goods to you for a full or partial credit, a credit note must be issued. You will have to adjust your financial records to take account of the credit note.

EXAMPLE 6: CREDIT NOTE

Surf Sports Club returned 10 of the wetsuits as they were not waterproof. Irish Sports Supplies sends the following credit note to Surf Sports Club on 30 April 2020.

IRISH SPORTS SUPPLIES

Stevie McHale, Irish Sports Supplies, Buttevant, Co. Cork
Telephone: 021 1616611; VAT Reg. No. IE 771234

CREDIT NOTE No. 11

To: Surf Sports Club
Belmullet
Co. Mayo

Date: 30/4/2020
Order No: 77

Quantity	Description	Code	Price each €	TOTAL €
10	Wetsuits (were not waterproof)	AW SG	100	1,000.00
			Total (Excluding VAT)	1,000.00
			Trade Discount 20%	200.00
			Subtotal	800.00
Carriage Paid			VAT 21%	168.00
E&OE			Total (Including VAT)	968.00

Know your Credit Note

What is the **name** of the document?	Credit Note
Who sends the document?	Seller: Irish Sports Supplies

2.10 BE BUSINESS: ENTERPRISE

Who receives the document?	Buyer: Surf Sports Club
What important information is in the document?	Date Refund amount (€632) Reason for return (the wetsuits were faulty).
What to do with the document? Be Michael, the **buyer**	• Check name and address. • Check calculations and total. • File the credit note, either manually or electronically.
Be Stevie, the **seller**	• Check name and address. • Check calculations and total. • File the credit note, either manually or electronically.

CHECKING IN...

Do you understand the above credit note?
1. Who is the buyer?
2. Who is the seller?
3. On what date was it sent?
4. Why was it sent?

7. DEBIT NOTE

A debit note has the same layout as a credit note, but is used when the buyer has been undercharged.

EXAMPLE 7: DEBIT NOTE

If Surf Sports Club has been undercharged for those 10 wetsuits, instead of returning them, they would have received the following Debit Note sent on 30 April 2020 for the amount undercharged.

IRISH SPORTS SUPPLIES

Stevie McHale, Irish Sports Supplies, Buttevant, Co. Cork
Telephone: 021 1616611; VAT Reg. No. IE 771234

DEBIT NOTE No. 13

To: Surf Sports Club
Belmullet
Co. Mayo

Date: 30/4/2020
Order No: 77

Quantity	Description	Code	Price each €	TOTAL €
10	Wetsuits (undercharged)	AW SG	100	1,000.00
		Total (Excluding VAT)		1,000.00
		Trade Discount 20%		200.00
		Subtotal		800.00
Carriage Paid		VAT 21%		168.00
E&OE		Total (Including VAT)		968.00

Know your Debit Note

What is the **name** of the document?	Debit Note
Who sends the document?	Seller: Irish Sports Supplies
Who receives the document?	Buyer: Surf Sports Club

What important information is in the document?	Date Amount undercharged, so owed (€632). Reason for return (undercharged for wetsuits).
What to do with the document? Be Michael, the **buyer**	• Check name and address • Check calculations and total • File the debit note either manually or electronically. Send a copy to accounts.
Be Stevie, the **seller**	• Check name and address. • Check calculations and total. • File the debit note either manually or electronically. Send a copy to accounts.

8. STATEMENT OF ACCOUNT

A statement of account is a business document issued by a seller/supplier to a customer. It lists all of the transactions between the seller and a buyer over a given period, normally a month. The statement of account will include details of invoices, payments received and the total amount payable by the customer.

eStatements are processed electronically. They are more environmentally friendly than paper statements.

Always check calculations in case of errors. Most business documents will note 'E&OE' (errors and omissions excepted) – remember, this means that if the seller makes a mistake the buyer has to pay the correct price.

Before sending the Statement of Account the seller will:

1. Check that all transactions are included.
2. Cross-reference with invoices and credit notes, debit notes and payments.
3. Ensure correct discounts have been applied.
4. Make sure name and address is correct.
5. Check calculations and totals.
6. Ensure the statement is paid within the agreed time.
7. File the statement either manually or electronically.

KEY BUSINESS DOCUMENTS 2.10

EXAMPLE 8: STATEMENT OF ACCOUNT

Irish Sports supplies sends the following Statement of Account to Surf Sports Club on 1 May 2020.

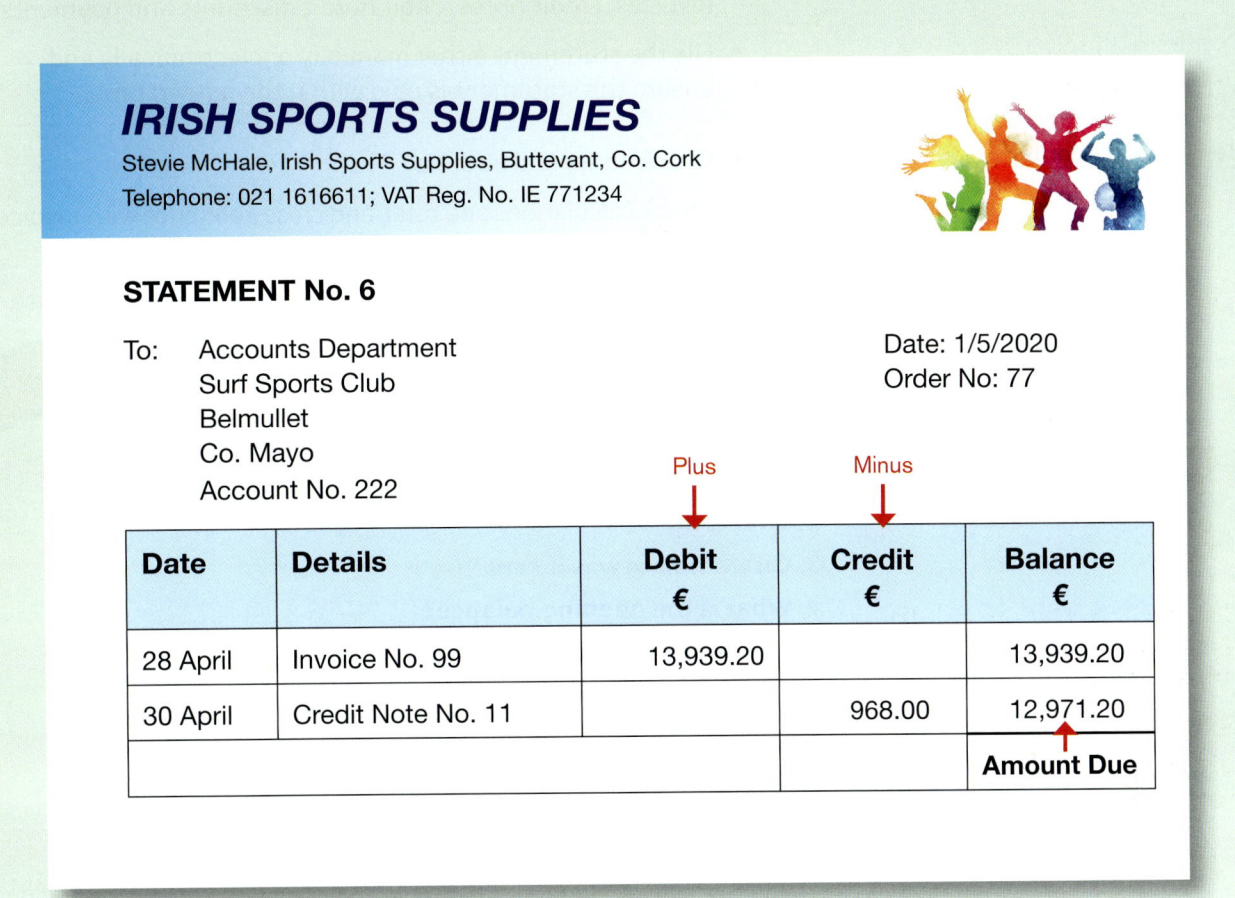

IRISH SPORTS SUPPLIES
Stevie McHale, Irish Sports Supplies, Buttevant, Co. Cork
Telephone: 021 1616611; VAT Reg. No. IE 771234

STATEMENT No. 6

To: Accounts Department
Surf Sports Club
Belmullet
Co. Mayo
Account No. 222

Date: 1/5/2020
Order No: 77

Plus → Debit
Minus → Credit

Date	Details	Debit €	Credit €	Balance €
28 April	Invoice No. 99	13,939.20		13,939.20
30 April	Credit Note No. 11		968.00	12,971.20
				Amount Due

The statement is sent from the seller, stating that €12,971.20 is due.

Know your Statement of Account

What is the **name** of the document?	Statement of Account
Who sends the document?	Seller: Irish Sports Supplies
Who receives the document?	Buyer: Surf Sports Club
What important **information** is in the document?	Date as Cash discount 10% if paid within 1 week (on the quotation).
	The calculations and total shows what you owed at the beginning, amount of invoices (bills) plus any credit/debit notes, payments and amount owed at the end of the month.

2.10 BE BUSINESS: ENTERPRISE

What to do with the document? Be Michael, the **buyer**	• Check name and address. • Check calculations and total and cross-reference with invoices, credit notes, debit notes, discounts and payments. • File the statement either manually or electronically and ensure the statement is paid within the agreed time.
Be Stevie, the **seller**	• Check name and address. • Check calculations and total, and cross-reference with invoices, credit notes, debit notes and payments. • File the statement either manually or electronically. Send a copy to accounts if it wasn't sent to them directly.

CHECKING IN...

Do you understand the above Statement of Account?
1. Who is the buyer?
2. Who is the seller?
3. On what date was it sent?
4. What is the opening balance?
5. How much is owed?
6. Check the calculations.

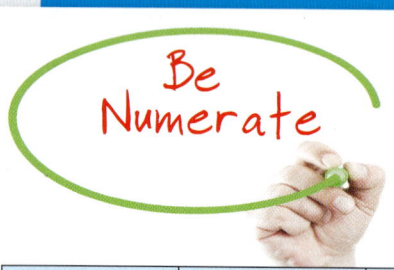

Be Numerate

Complete the balance column in this statement of account.

Details	Debit €	Credit €	Balance €
Invoice	700		
Debit Note	70		
Credit Note		50	
Payment		500	

Think Time

1. If Surf Sports Club had only paid €3,000, what would be the amount due at the end of the month?
2. What is the current VAT rate in Ireland? Find out at www.revenue.ie.
3. Name the different ways Surf Sports Club could pay Irish Sport Supplies.
4. Why might it be important to keep receipts?

9. PAYMENT

Finally, the buyer pays the seller using a Visa debit card, a credit card or by electronic transfer from a bank account.

KEY BUSINESS DOCUMENTS 2.10

Know about Payments

Who sends the payment?	Buyer: Surf Sports Club
Who receives the payment?	Seller: Irish Sports Supplies
What to do with the document? Be Michael, the **buyer**	• Check you are paying the correct amount to the correct account. • Record cash payment on the **credit side** of the **analysed cash book**. 😳
Be Stevie, the **seller**	• Check the payment from the buyer is correct • Check calculations and total. Record cash received on the **debit side** of the **analysed cash book**. 😬 • Send a receipt.

10. RECEIPT

Seller of goods sends this document to the buyer.

The seller issues a receipt to the buyer once payment has been received. The buyer needs to file receipt as this is proof of purchase and the seller should file a copy.

EXAMPLE 9: RECEIPT

Penny White, from Irish Sports Supplies, issued a receipt to Surf Sports Club on 30 June 2020.

IRISH SPORTS SUPPLIES

Stevie McHale, Irish Sports Supplies, Buttevant, Co. Cork
Telephone: 021 1616611; VAT Reg. No. IE 771234

RECEIPT No. 99

To: Michael O'Malley
    Surf Sports Club
    Belmullet
    Co. Mayo
    Account No. 222

Date: 30/6/2020

Received from: Mikey O'Malley, Surf Sports Club, Belmullet, Co Mayo

The sum of:	Twelve thousand, nine hundred and seventy-one euro twenty cent	€12,971.20

With thanks
Signed: *Penny White*
Accounts Department

323

2.10 BE BUSINESS: ENTERPRISE

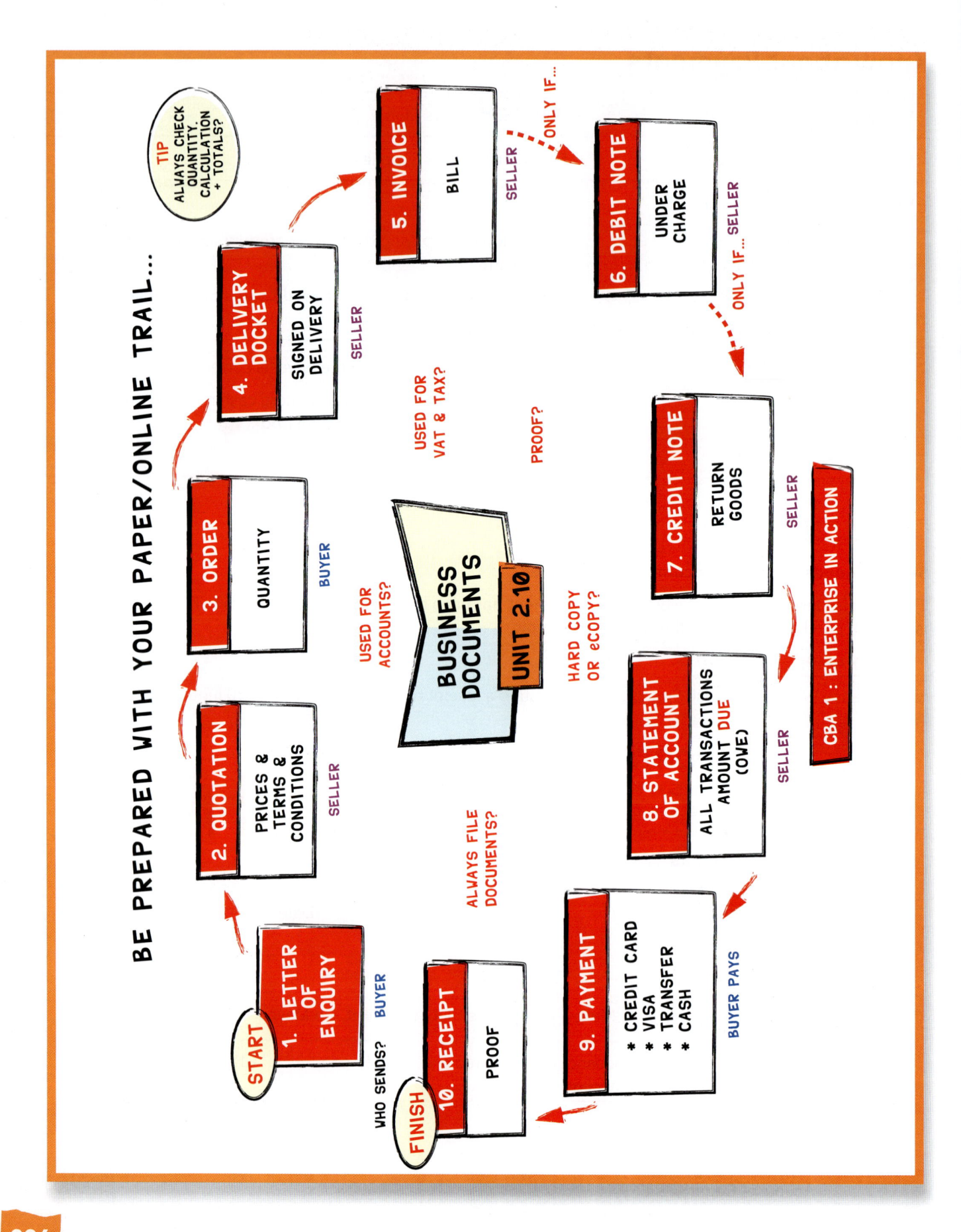

BE PREPARED WITH YOUR PAPER/ONLINE TRAIL...

BUSINESS DOCUMENTS — UNIT 2.10

START
1. **LETTER OF ENQUIRY** — BUYER
   - WHO SENDS?

2. **QUOTATION** — PRICES & TERMS & CONDITIONS — SELLER

3. **ORDER** — QUANTITY — BUYER
   - USED FOR ACCOUNTS?

4. **DELIVERY DOCKET** — SIGNED ON DELIVERY — SELLER
   - TIP: ALWAYS CHECK QUANTITY, CALCULATION + TOTALS?

5. **INVOICE** — BILL — SELLER
   - USED FOR VAT & TAX?

6. **DEBIT NOTE** — UNDER CHARGE — ONLY IF... SELLER

7. **CREDIT NOTE** — RETURN GOODS — SELLER
   - PROOF?
   - CBA 1: ENTERPRISE IN ACTION

8. **STATEMENT OF ACCOUNT** — ALL TRANSACTIONS AMOUNT DUE (OWE) — SELLER
   - HARD COPY OR eCOPY?

9. **PAYMENT**
   - CREDIT CARD
   - VISA
   - TRANSFER
   - CASH
   - BUYER PAYS
   - ALWAYS FILE DOCUMENTS?

10. **RECEIPT** — PROOF
FINISH

324

KEY BUSINESS DOCUMENTS | 2.10

Be Prepared: My Support Sheets

Completing this activity will help you reflect on and reinforce your learning before you move on to the next unit.

- Write down the **key terms** in this unit and make sure you understand them. See if they match the ones at the back of the book.
- List the **key concepts/themes** in this unit.
- List the **three most interesting points** about this topic.

Business in Action Idea!

For your Finance in Action preparation, create your own invoice.

Success criteria:
- Name and address of buyer and seller
- A minimum of three transactions
- Trade discount of 12%
- VAT 21%

Finance in Action Idea!

Write a newspaper article explaining business documents.

Success criteria:
- An eye-catching title
- A relevant photograph or image
- An explanation of each document

QUESTION TIME

1. Explain the importance of business documents.
2. Name the different methods of payment.
3. Source an invoice, either hard copy or electronic, and write about the important pieces of data it contains.
4. What might be the advantages of using electronic documentation?

2.10 BE BUSINESS: ENTERPRISE

5. Copy and complete the table below. Choose the correct word from the list given to complete the four unshaded areas.

   Invoice   Credit Note   Quotation   Payment

	Buyer Sends		Seller Sends
1.	Letter of enquiry	2.	
3.	Order	4.	
5.	Returns	6.	
		7.	Statement
8.		9.	Receipt

EVALUATE MY LEARNING: DAR

Describe
- Did I/we meet my/our learning intentions?
- What went well? What are my/our strengths?

Assess
- How did I/we work with others?
- Were there challenges?

Recommend
- How might I improve?
- What skills and learning might I apply to new situations?

Do your **Key Check** in the workbook for this unit and then mark your learning position on the following rating scale:

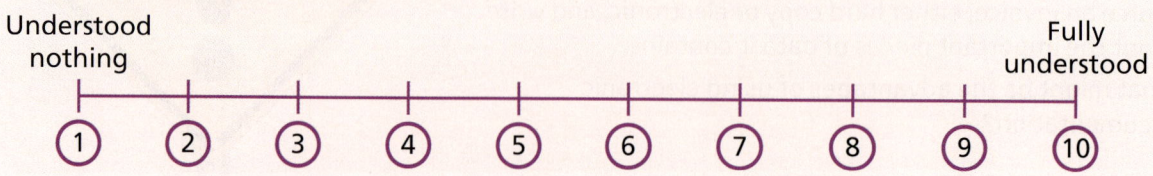

Understood nothing   1 2 3 4 5 6 7 8 9 10   Fully understood

How can you move up the rating scale? What can you **say**, **make**, **write** and **do** to illustrate your learning?

KEY BUSINESS DOCUMENTS 2.10

CBA 1 Business in Action:
Will I use this unit for my topic for my **Finance in Action**?

You need to be preparing for your CBAs

- Exceptional
- Above expectations
- In line with expectations
- Yet to meet expectations

Stop and think

Do I have any questions or concerns?

What are the mistakes or errors I made in this unit?

327

2.11 CASH BUDGET

Assess the importance of planning an organisation's cash flow, propose suitable sources of finance to manage expenditure and prepare a cash flow budget.

Learning Intentions

At the end of this unit I will:

- Understand the importance to an organisation of preparing a cash budget
- Be able to prepare a cash budget
- Be able to apply my bookkeeping skills
- Value sources of finance and how they are used

Key Concepts

- ✓ Cash budget
- ✓ Sources of finance

Making the links with other LOs:

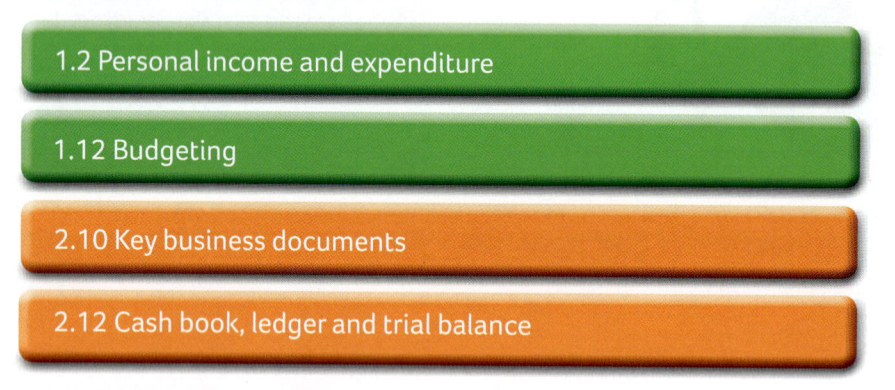

- 1.2 Personal income and expenditure
- 1.12 Budgeting
- 2.10 Key business documents
- 2.12 Cash book, ledger and trial balance

Are there other LOs?

Wonderful Worthwhile Website

www.sageone.ie

RECORD-KEEPING

Every organisation needs to know where it stands **financially** (what money it has). Cash is the lifeblood of any organisation.

The key questions for any organisation are:

1. Are we making a **profit**?
2. How much are we **selling**?
3. What are our **costs**?
4. Do we have sufficient **cash** – enough to **pay bills as they become due**?

These questions can only be answered if the organisation keeps suitable **records** on its finances. The records must be both **correct** and **timely**. There is no point knowing at the end of the year that you are short of cash!

3Ts' = Think, Turn, Talk

Profit does not equal cash. Why might that be?

Profit ≠ Cash

CASH BUDGET 2.11

An organisation's record-keeping allows it to manage:

1. Cash
2. Debtors
3. Stock

1. CASH

An organisation needs cash to pay bills, buy materials and cover delays in payments from suppliers (debtors). It is very important to have enough cash. An organisation may be able to sustain a negative cash flow (when spending is greater than cash coming in) in the short term, but in the long term the organisation won't survive. Having a cash safety net is vital for an organisation. This is known as cash control.

2. DEBTORS

An organisation needs to keep track of its debtors (people we sell goods to on credit – they owe us) and to ensure that it doesn't have bad debts (a debtor that won't pay, perhaps has gone bankrupt). This is known as credit control.

3. STOCK

An organisation must ensure it has sufficient stock. Having too much stock is a waste of cash, as stock can become damaged and out of date. Having too little stock could cause you to lose customers. This is known as stock control. Good stock control is essential.

CASH BUDGET

A cash budget, also called a cash flow budget, is a really important tool in managing an organisation's money. It shows all of the **projected** (planned/likely) **cash coming in** to an organisation and all of the **projected cash going out**. This is usually shown on a **month-by-month** basis.

A cash budget will reveal times when an organisation may need extra cash to cover expenditures. There may be months when the organisation is short of cash and other months when the organisation has a surplus of cash. The organisation may need to arrange a loan (borrow money).

Investors and **banks** are always interested in the cash flow of an organisation.

HOW TO PREPARE A CASH BUDGET

In Units Unit 1.12 **and** Unit 1.13 you saw how individuals/families prepare budgets, in particular a **household budget**, to manage income and expenditure.

Most organisations use a **cash budget template**, either manual, in Google Sheets, Excel or a software package.

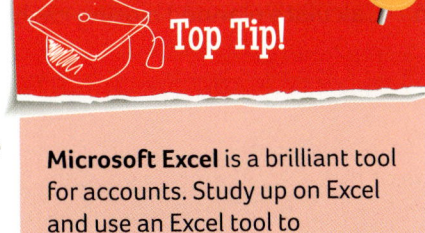

Top Tip!

Microsoft Excel is a brilliant tool for accounts. Study up on Excel and use an Excel tool to understand cash flow.

A cash budget should list all the **incoming** and **outgoing cash items** for **12 months**.

Cash In: Planned/Projected Receipts	Cash Out: Planned/Projected Payments
• Cash sales • Cash received from debtors (we sold on credit, they owe us) • Money invested by owners (extra capital) • Selling off fixed assets • Loans • Grants	• Cash purchases • Cash paid to creditors (we bought on credit and we have to pay them) • Money taken out by the owners (known as **drawings**) • Purchasing fixed assets • Repaying loan and interest • Paying expenses (rent, rates, wages) and taxation

From the list you can see that an organisation does not just deal in cash sales and cash purchases, it can also trade on credit and delayed payments.

A **debtor** is someone we sell goods to on credit. They **owe us** money. The debtor will pay the organisation at a later date. They are **an asset** – something of value.

A **creditor** is someone we buy goods from on credit. We **owe them**. The organisaton will pay them at a later date. They are a **liability** – something that we owe.

Time to think

Why might we sell on credit?
Why might we buy on credit?

SIX STEPS TO CREATING A CASH BUDGET

1. Prepare a skeleton template and insert opening cash
2. Record all receipts/cash in and total receipts
3. Record all payments/cash out and total payments
4. Calculate net cash position
5. Calculate planned opening cash
6. Calculate planned closing cash

CASH BUDGET 2.11

EXAMPLE: WILDSURF CASH BUDGET

WildSurf is a company selling surfboards on the west coast of Kerry. They have actual cash of €400 at the beginning of the year. You are to create their cash budget for three months, January to March.

Step 1: Create a skeleton template and insert opening cash

- Label the template 'Cash Budget for Wildsurf'.
- The number of columns will depend on the number of months that you are preparing the budget for. You will have one column for details, one column for each month and one for total. A cash budget for three months will have five columns; one for 12 months will have 14 columns. WildSurf will have five columns.
- The number of rows will depend on the number of receipts and the number of payments. Leave one for Receipts and Total Receipts and one for Payments and Total Payments. Leave one or two extra rows.
- Insert opening cash and also place it in the total column. The total column is a summary of the previous three months. Wildsurf have opening cash of €400.

Cash Budget for WildSurf

Details	January	February	March	Total January to March
	€	€	€	€
Receipts				
1. Total Receipts				
Payments				
2. Total Payments				
3. Net Cash (1 − 2)				
4. Opening Cash	400			400
5. Closing Cash (3 + 4)				

331

Step 2: Record all receipts/cash in and total receipts

- WildSurf plan to have the following receipts:
  - Sales of €3,000 per month
  - €1,500 in February and €500 in March from investors
  - A grant in February of €600
- Below you can see how the above receipts are placed in the relevant cells. The various receipts for each month are totalled (€9,000, €2,000 and €600) and then the Total January to March column is a summary of the three months (€11,600).

Cash Budget for WildSurf for the three months January to March 20xx				
Details	January	February	March	Total January to March
	€	€	€	€
Receipts				
Sales	3,000	3,000	3,000	9,000
Capital		1,500	500	2,000
Grant		600		600
1. Total Receipts	3,000	5,100	3,500	11,600

Step 3: Record all payments/cash out and total payments

- WildSurf plan to have the following expenditure:
  - Wages of €1,200 per month
  - Paint €1,400 in February and March
  - Administration wages €400 in February and March
  - Business cards €300 in January
  - Posters €100 in March
  - Phone calls €100 in March
  - Travel €100 in February
- Below you can see how the above costs are placed in the relevant cells. The various expenditures for each month are totalled, and then the Total January to March column is a summary of the three months (€7,800).

Cash Budget for WildSurf for the three months January to March 20xx				
Details	January	February	March	Total January to March
	€	€	€	€
Payments				
Labour	1,200	1,200	1,200	3,600
Paint		1,400	1,400	2,800
Admin Wages		400	400	800
Business Cards	300			300
Posters			100	100
Phone Calls			100	100
Travel		100		100
2. Total Payments	1,500	3,100	3,200	7,800

Step 4: Calculate net cash position

Net cash is total receipts minus total payments.

Cash Budget for WildSurf for the three months January to March 20xx				
Details	January	February	March	Total January to March
	€	€	€	€
Receipts				
Sales	3,000	3,000	3,000	9,000
Capital		1,500	500	2,000
Grant		600		600
1. Total Receipts	**3,000**	**5,100**	**3,500**	**11,600**
Payments				
Labour	1,200	1,200	1,200	3,600
Paint		1,400	1,400	2,800
Admin Wages		400	400	800
Business Cards	300			300
Posters			100	100
Phone Calls			100	100
Travel		100		100
2. Total Payments	**1,500**	**3,100**	**3,200**	**7,800**
3. Net Cash (1 – 2)	1,500	2,000	300	3,800

Step 5: Calculate planned opening cash

WildSurf had opening cash of €400 in January. This is added to net cash to give opening cash for February and so on.

Cash Budget for WildSurf for the three months January to March 20xx				
Details	January	February	March	Total January to March
	€	€	€	€
1. Total Receipts	**3,000**	**5,100**	**3,500**	**11,600**
2. Total Payments	**1,500**	**3,100**	**3,200**	**7,800**
3. Net Cash (1 – 2)	1,500	2,000	300	3,800
4. Opening Cash	400	1,900	3,900	400

The opening cash in **Total** is the opening cash of **January** = **€400**.

Step 6: Calculate planned closing cash

To calculate your planned closing cash, you add net cash to opening cash.

Cash Budget for WildSurf for the three months January to March 20xx

Details	January €	February €	March €	Total January to March €
Receipts				
Sales	3,000	3,000	3,000	9,000
Capital		1,500	500	2,000
Grant		600		600
1. Total Receipts	**3,000**	**5,100**	**3,500**	**11,600**
Expenditure				
Labour	1,200	1,200	1,200	3,600
Paint		1,400	1,400	2,800
Admin Wages		400	400	800
Business Cards	300			300
Posters			100	100
Phone Calls			100	100
Travel		100		100
2. Total Payments	**1,500**	**3,100**	**3,200**	**7,800**
3. Net Cash (1 – 2)	1,500	2,000	300	3,800
4. Opening Cash	400	1,900	3,900	400
5. Closing Cash (3 + 4)	1,900	3,900	4,200	4,200

You can see that:

- The opening cash of January is €400
- The closing cash of January is €1,900
- The closing cash of January becomes the opening cash of February
- The opening cash in **Total** is the opening cash **of January €400**

Correct use of a cash budget will ensure that an organisation has the cash when it is needed. An organisation cannot survive without cash. The cash budget makes an organisation think about planned receipts and planned payments. If an organisation does not have sufficient cash to pay bills it will run into financial difficulty.

It's the same concept as budgeting for individuals or households. Even our government has to budget to ensure the smooth running of our country.

Create a Cash Budget

Q-Pulse Ltd is an innovative company that produces medical equipment.

You are required to complete a Cash Budget for the months of June, July, August and September 20xx (see next page – April and May have already been filled in).

In addition, you must complete the total column (remember, the total column will be for April, May, June, July, August and September).

Opening cash in June is €64,200.

When you have completed the budget, answer the questions below the budget template.

Additional information:

- Monthly cash sales will increase by 25% on 1 September (only for September).
- Shareholders will invest €190,000 extra money in shares in the business in July.
- Light and heat: this expense is payable every two months, and in August it will increase by 20%.
- Wages will remain the same, except in August, when an additional bonus of 15% will be paid.
- New machinery costing €80,000 will be purchased in August.
- The loan repayments will end after July.
- Monthly cash purchases will increase by 20% in September.
- Transport costs are expected to increase by 10% in September.

Notes:

- When you come across a figure in brackets, this indicates a minus or negative figure.
- Net cash in April is (106,800). Q-Pulse had €54,000 in April as opening cash and now its closing cash is (52,800). What caused the deficit? It was the purchase of machinery of €120,000. What might Q-Pulse have done instead of paying for the machine?
- In May the net cash is €117,000. The closing cash in April is the opening cash in May (52,800). The closing cash is €64,200.

2.11 BE BUSINESS: ENTERPRISE

Cash Budget of Q-Pulse Ltd for the period April to September 20xx								
Details	April	May	June	July	August	September	Total April to September
	€	€	€	€	€	€	€
Receipts							
Cash Sales	75,000	75,000					
Share Capital							
Grant		100,000					
1. Total Receipts	75,000	175,000					
Expenditure							
Light and heat	3,800						
Wages	24,000	24,000					
Machinery	120,000						
Loan Repayments	5,000	5,000					
Cash Purchases	18,000	18,000					
Transport Costs	11,000	11,000					
2. Total Payments	181,800	58,000					
3. Net Cash (1 – 2)	(106,800)	117,000					
4. Opening Cash	54,000	(52,800)	64,200				
5. Closing cash (3 + 4)	(52,800)	64,200					

Questions:

- Why might a business prepare a cash budget?
- Working together, can you explain each transaction?
- List five tips for preparing a cash budget.
- Can you name an expense that may not appear in the cash budget?
- Create a tweet to show your understanding of a cash budget.
- What advice would you give Q-Pulse?
- If Q-Pulse has a surplus what might they do?
- If Q-Pulse has a deficit what might they do?
- Explain opening cash and closing cash.

FINANCING AN ORGANISATION

You will have already discovered sources of finance for an individual and a household in **Unit 1.5**. When preparing your personal financial life cycle, you have to identify how you will finance (obtain money for) your needs at various stages. So too do organisations (both for-profit and not-for-profit) and the government. There are many ways in which an organisation can find finance. The type of finance an organisation will choose will depend on different features:

1. **Size** of an organisation. If an organisation is large, it will have access to a wide variety of finance options. A smaller organisation may have limited access to sources of finance.
   a. A large organisation could sell **shares**, known as ordinary share capital.
   b. A small organisation could use the owner's **savings** or borrow from family and friends.
2. **Stage** of an organisation. Is it a start-up organisation or a well-established organisation? A start-up will need a lot of investment.
3. **Type** of organisation. Is it a for-profit or a not-for-profit organisation? A not-for-profit may have limited sources of finance and it might be able to avail of fundraising and/or government grants.
4. The type of finance also depends on the **timeframe** – when the money is needed and how long it is needed for.

MATCHING PRINCIPLE

When deciding on a type of finance, it is important to use the matching principle. This means matching the source of finance with the use of finance. There are short-, medium- and long-term sources of finance to choose from.

If a short-term source of finance is used to finance a long-term need, this will put enormous pressure on the organisation.

Short-term finance (0–1 year)

Short-term finance is money used to finance short-term needs. This money needs to be paid back within a year. For an organisation, this kind of finance is used to pay expenses such as wages and salaries, insurance, light and heat and interest and to buy stock (goods to be resold).

Remember, you must finance short-term needs with short-term sources of finance.

Source of Finance	From Whom	Any Costs?	Why is it a Source?
Creditors	Suppliers	No, though it may mean not getting a cash discount.	Use of the goods without paying so could invest the money short-term.
Expenses due	Suppliers of services (e.g. electricity suppliers)	No. However, payment has to be made after a short time or electricity may be cut off and that means a reconnection fee.	Use of the money that would have been spent on the bills to finance needs.

Credit card/Charge card	Financial enterprises	Free, if you pay your bill within agreed time; otherwise really high rates of interest.	Similar to a loan; can withdraw money up to an agreed amount.
Bank overdraft	Bank	Interest is paid on the amount overdrawn for the time it is overdrawn, e.g. account is overdrawn by €1,200 at 8% interest for one month: €1,200 x 8% = €96 /12 = €8	Can withdraw an agreed amount of money, usually from a current account, and interest is charged on overdrawn amount.

CHECKING IN...

1. Ben White from GreenGo needs to paint the wall surrounding his garden centre and forest. He needs to purchase paint costing €500. What short-term source of finance might he use and why?
2. If Ben decides to overdraw his current account by €1,500 for five months and interest is charged at 8%, what interest will he pay? What interest would be pay if he had the overdraft for a full year?
3. Ben has applied to his local bank for a credit card. What advice might you give Ben about using a credit card?
4. What short-term sources of finance might an individual use? Why?

Medium-term finance (1–5 years)

Medium-term finance is money used to finance medium-term needs. This money needs to be paid back within five years. For an organisation, this kind of finance is used to pay for items such as cars, computers and other equipment.

Remember, you must finance medium-term needs with medium-term sources of finance.

Source of Finance	From Whom	Any Costs?	Why is it a Source?
Medium-term loan	Financial enterprises	Interest. The business may also need collateral, which is a form of security in case the loan cannot be repaid.	Provides money to the organisation for a specific need.
Leasing	Leasing companies	Can be costly as it is similar to renting for up to five years. Good for items that date quickly. Asset is never owned.	In paying for the lease you have the use of expensive equipment without having to buy it up front.
Hire purchase	Financial enterprises/HP companies	More expensive than loans and leasing, but eventually the asset is owned.	By paying the repayments you have the use of expensive equipment without having to buy it up front.

CHECKING IN...

1. Ben White from GreenGo needs to buy two new cars for his sales representatives.
2. Why might Ben use a medium-term source of finance to purchase cars? Which medium-term source of finance would you recommend and why? Are any of the medium-term sources free?
3. Which medium-term source of finance might a not-for-profit organisation, e.g. a charity, use? Why?

Long-term finance (more than 5 years)

Long-term finance is money used to finance long-term needs. This money can be paid back over a period longer than five years. For an organisation, this kind of finance is used to pay for items such as buildings, land and very expensive equipment.

Remember, you must finance long-term needs with long-term sources of finance.

Source of Finance	From Whom	Any Costs?	Why is it a Source?
Retained earnings	The business itself.	No, as there is no interest and no repayments.	Retained earnings is the portion of income of a business that is retained to reinvest rather than distributed to shareholders as dividends.
Grants	For example, the government, European Union (EU) or Local Enterprise Office (LEO).	No, but there may be conditions, e.g. you have to employ a certain number of people.	Non-repayable sum of money given to the organisation.
Capital	Depends on type of ownership, e.g. a sole trader might have savings or a business might have investors who become shareholders.	Depends on the type of capital. Dividends on shares is paid to shareholders.	Can be money raised when starting off a business. It is money put into the business.
Long-term loan	Financial enterprises	Yes, interest is charged.	Use of a large amount of money for large capital items, e.g. land.

339

BE BUSINESS: ENTERPRISE

CHECKING IN...

1. Ben White from GreenGo has decided to expand. He is going to form a private limited company, GreenGo Ltd. He has invited members of his family to be shareholders to raise extra capital. He wishes to buy land for expansion, which will cost €100,000, and plant additional trees. Why might Ben use a long-term source of finance to purchase land? Which long-term source of finance would you recommend and why?
2. Which long-term source of finance might a not-for-profit organisation, e.g. a charity, use? Why?
3. Can you list which long-term sources of finance cost money?

FACTORS WHEN DECIDING ON A SOURCE OF FINANCE

Individuals, households, organisations and governments must always select a source of finance that matches their needs. When deciding on what type of finance to source, you need to consider the following factors:

Purpose	Is it for a long-term, medium-term or short-term need?
Amount	What can you afford to pay back? Your options may be limited for large amounts.
Cost	Look at the cheapest source of finance first. Are there any sources that are free?
Control	Getting finance from some sources may mean losing control; there may be conditions attached. If you sell shares in a company, the shareholders will have votes that can lessen your control when making decisions about the organisation.
Security	Some lenders may look for collateral; for example, financial institutions may look for the deeds of the property when offering a mortgage.

CHECKING IN...

1. What factors might decide the source of finance used by an organisation?
2. Should a business use an overdraft to buy an expensive piece of equipment? Explain why.
3. When building an extension to a premises, what source might be used? Why?

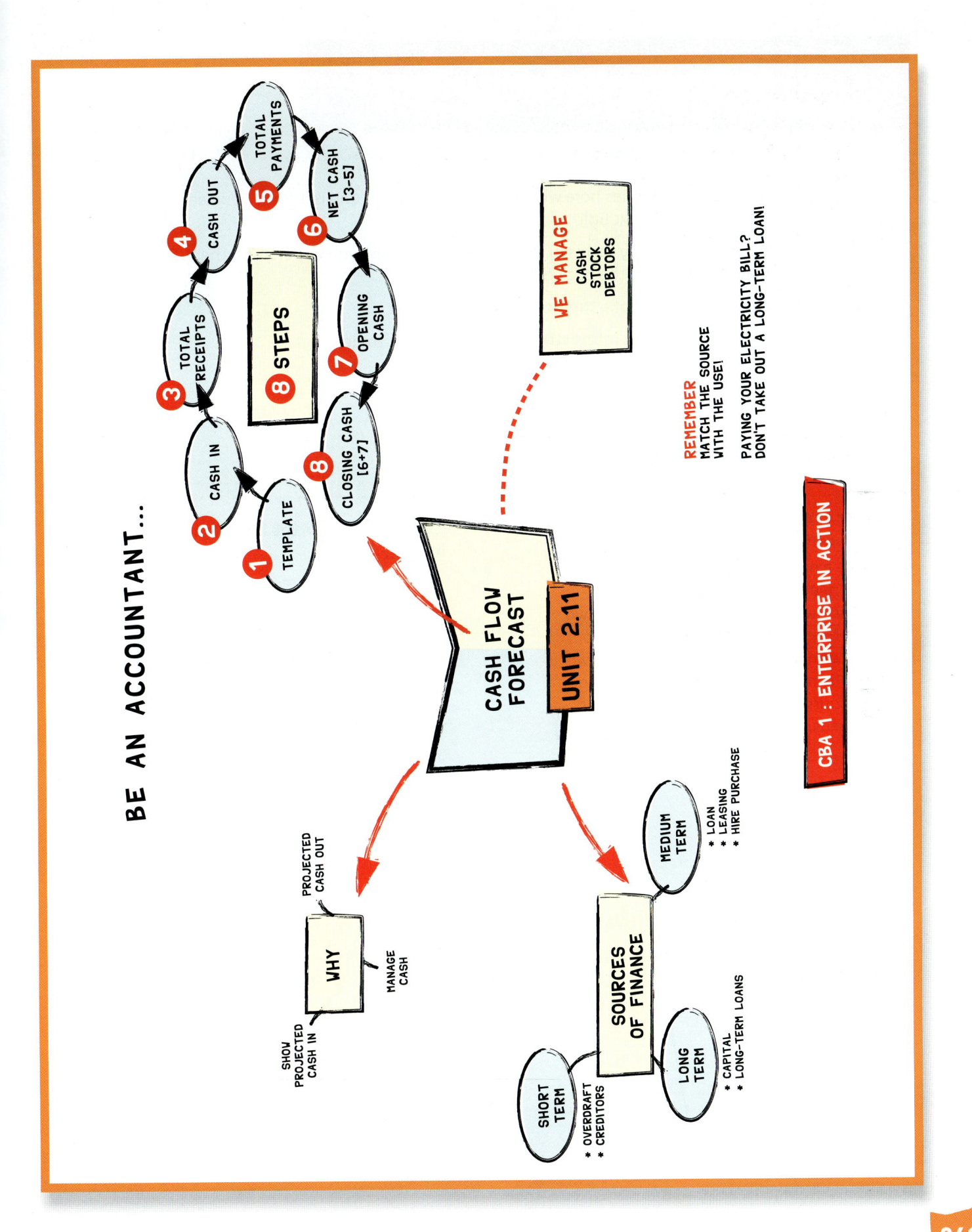

CASH BUDGET 2.11

BE AN ACCOUNTANT...

8 STEPS

1. TEMPLATE
2. CASH IN
3. TOTAL RECEIPTS
4. CASH OUT
5. TOTAL PAYMENTS
6. NET CASH [3−5]
7. OPENING CASH
8. CLOSING CASH [6+7]

CASH FLOW FORECAST — UNIT 2.11

WHY
- SHOW PROJECTED CASH IN
- PROJECTED CASH OUT
- MANAGE CASH

SOURCES OF FINANCE
- SHORT TERM
  * OVERDRAFT
  * CREDITORS
- MEDIUM TERM
  * LOAN
  * LEASING
  * HIRE PURCHASE
- LONG TERM
  * CAPITAL
  * LONG-TERM LOANS

WE MANAGE
- CASH
- STOCK
- DEBTORS

REMEMBER
MATCH THE SOURCE WITH THE USE!
PAYING YOUR ELECTRICITY BILL? DON'T TAKE OUT A LONG-TERM LOAN!

CBA 1 : ENTERPRISE IN ACTION

341

2.11 BE BUSINESS: ENTERPRISE

Be Prepared: My Support Sheets

Completing the activities here will help you to reflect on and reinforce your learning before you move on to the next unit.

- Write down the **key terms** in this unit and make sure you understand them. See if they match the ones at the back of the book.
- List the **key concepts/themes** in this unit.
- List the three **most interesting points** about this topic.

Business in Action Idea!

Create a report on sources of finance for your business.

Create a name for the business, something short, relevant and easy to remember. Describe what the business does. List two short-term, two medium-term and two long-term needs of the business. List two short-term, medium-term and two long-term sources of finance to meet each of the needs.

Success criteria:
- Title and introduction
- Each need is matched with a correct source of finance
- Visual
- Mention any research

Finance in Action Idea!

Create a report on the importance of a cash budget.

Success criteria:
- Title and introduction
- Explanation of cash budget
- Example with accurate calculations
- Importance of a cash budget
- Conclusions and recommendations
- Visual

Top Tip!

This unit is very important for your Finance in Action.

QUESTION TIME

1. Why does an organisation need to know about cash flow?
2. Copy the following table and indicate with a tick ✓ the statements with which you agree.

	Agree	Disagree
Profit equals cash		
Cash budget shows projected cash		
Money received from a debtor is cash into the business		
A loan is a source of finance		
Creditor is not a source of finance		
With hire purchase you never own the asset		
When leasing an asset you will eventually own it		

3. Copy the following table and match the terms with the correct statement.

   1 Interest on loan
   2 Bank overdraft
   3 An expense that won't appear in the cash flow statement
   4 A loan

   A Interest charged at a daily rate
   B Depreciation
   C Liability
   D Expense

1	2	3	4

4. Copy the following table and write the appropriate terms under each of the headings:

   Creditors   Capital   Leasing   Hire purchase   Capital
   Bank overdraft   Grants

Short term	Medium term	Long term

5. Choose three sources of finance and state the advantages of each.
6. Compare leasing with hire purchase.

EVALUATE MY LEARNING: DAR

Describe
- Did I/we meet my/our learning intentions?
- What went well? What are my/our strengths?

Assess
- How did I/we work with others?
- Were there challenges?

Recommend
- How might I improve?
- What skills and learning might I apply to new situations?

Do your **Key Check** in the workbook for this unit and then mark your learning position on the following rating scale:

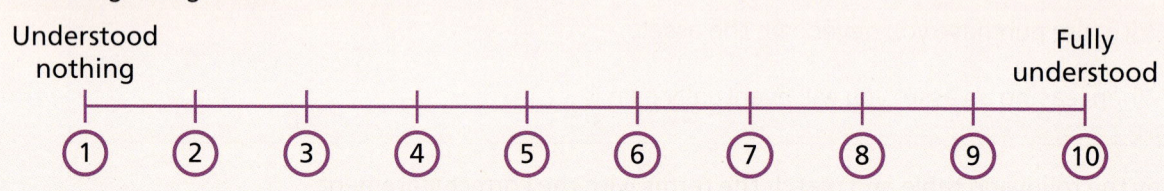

Understood nothing — 1 2 3 4 5 6 7 8 9 10 — Fully understood

How can you move up the rating scale? What can you **say**, **make**, **write** and **do** to illustrate your learning?

CBA 1 Business in Action:
Will I use this unit for my topic for my **Enterprise in Action** and my **Finance in Action**?

You need to be preparing for your CBAs

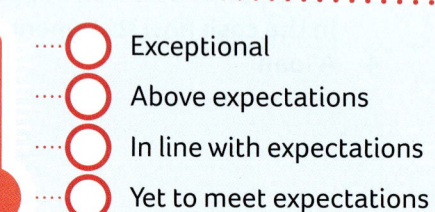

- Exceptional
- Above expectations
- In line with expectations
- Yet to meet expectations

Stop and think

Do I have any questions or concerns? What are the mistakes or errors I made in this unit?

2.12 CASH BOOK, LEDGER AND TRIAL BALANCE

Prepare a cash account to monitor income received and payments made by an organisation, evaluate its financial position and recommend a course of action; post figures to relevant ledgers and extract a trial balance.

Learning Intentions

At the end of this unit I will:

- Know about cash accounts
- Understand balancing an account
- Be able to create a cash account/cash book, analysed cash book and post to the general ledger
- Understand how to extract a trial balance and a list of ledger balances
- Value record-keeping
- Be able to apply bookkeeping skills

Key Concepts

- ✓ Cash book
- ✓ Analysed cash book
- ✓ Ledger
- ✓ Trial balance

Making the links with other LOs:

- 1.2 Personal income and expenditure
- 1.13 Income, expenditure and bank statements
- 2.11 Cash budget
- 2.13 Final accounts

Wonderful Worthwhile Websites

www.sageone.ie
www.revenue.ie

Are there other LOs?

CASH ACCOUNT/CASH BOOK

In Unit **Unit 1.13** you saw how Ciara, of Ciara's Cupcakes, kept a cash account to monitor her cash income and cash expenditure. A cash account is the same for an individual, a household, a for-profit organisation and a not-for-profit organisation.

The cash book works exactly like a cash account, but when the transactions are enormous, the cash book is preferred.

The cash book is also known as the book of original/first entry. It is a record of *all the cash that comes into and goes out of* an organisation on a daily basis.

2.12 BE BUSINESS: ENTERPRISE

Remember that cash in is on the left and cash out is on the right. When we know how much cash there is, we *balance the account.*

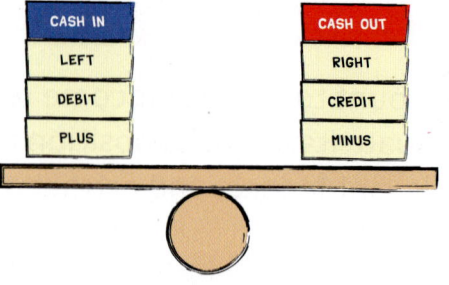

BUSINESS TRANSACTIONS

The types of transaction a for-profit organisation (a business) would include are as follows:

1. Buying goods for cash and credit.
2. Selling goods for cash and credit.
3. Paying expenses such as insurance, rent and advertising.
4. Receiving money from debtors.
5. Paying money to creditors.
6. Receiving money from shareholders.

Transaction is the word we use to describe a transfer from one person or business/organisation to another.

EXAMPLE 1: MINIZONE SIMPLE CASH BOOK

MiniZone is a business that sells miniature guitars for children.

Prepare a simple cash book using the following transactions:

1/6/19   Opening cash at the beginning of the month is €15,000 on the debit side of the account (MiniZone has cash 😊).

7/6/19   MiniZone bought goods for resale (purchases) – so cash decreases so we enter it on the right/credit side of the account (cash out 😟).

15/6/19   MiniZone sold goods (sales) – which increases cash so we enter it on the left/debit side of the account (cash in 😊).

18/6/19   MiniZone paid wages – cash decreases and we enter it on the right/credit side of the account (cash out 😟).

Here is the cash book filled in.

Debit In 😊		Cash Book of MiniZone					Out Credit 😟	
Date	Details	F	€	DATE	Details	F	€
1/6	Balance	b/d	15,000	7/6	Purchases	GL2	4,500
15/6	Sales	GL1	5,000	18/6	Wages	GL3	3,500
				31/6	Balance	c/d	12,000
			20,000				20,000
1/7	Balance	b/d	12,000				

346

CASH BOOK, LEDGER AND TRIAL BALANCE 2.12

Explanation

MiniZone is left with €12,000 at the end of the month. The closing balance is decreasing.

The €12,000 will be the opening cash in the following month, beginning 1/7/19.

You will see an extra column, F, with reference names, GL1, GL2 and GL 3. When figures have been entered into the cash book they are then transferred or 'posted' to other books called ledgers. We'll learn more about these later in this unit.

F stands for Folio and is used to show the reference for where the entry is to be posted (*GL1* stand for General Ledger 1/*GL2* stands for General Ledger 2/*GL3* stands for General Ledger 3).

CHECKING IN...

1. How much cash did MiniZone have at the beginning of June?
2. How much cash did MiniZone have at the end of June?
3. What is happening to the cash? What might MiniZone do?

Copy the template below. Use the following information to fill in a cash book for MiniZone and then balance the account.

Be Numerate

Date	Transaction
1/1/2018	Opening cash €15,000 – always put on the debit side, as opening balance
2/1/2018	Paid wages €1,300
5/1/2018	Cash sales €7,000
9/1/2018	Cash purchases €6,000

Debit In   **Cash Book**   **Out Credit**

Date	Details	F	€	DATE	Details	F	€

Practise simple cash accounts. Start by writing a question with five dates and five transactions. Fill in the figures on the correct side and finish by balancing the account.

Let's look at the recording of financial information.

ANALYSED CASH BOOK FOR A BUSINESS

In **Unit 1.13** you saw how to create an analysed cash book for a household. An analysed cash book is also used to record all money received and all money paid out. However, there are additional columns to describe (or analyse) money in and money out. Here we will look at an analysed cash book for a business.

EXAMPLE 2: MINIZONE ANALYSED CASH BOOK

MiniZone has expanded and has decided to have an analysed cash book.

Prepare the analysed cash book of MiniZone for the month of May 20xx and then balance the account.

You are given the following transactions.

Date	Transactions	Receipt No.	Amount €	What side? Debit/credit
1/5	Paid for materials		8,700	C −
3/5	Received from Will Donnelly, householder	1	900	D +
4/5	Paid for materials		1,300	C −
10/5	Paid for motor van insurance		3,000	C −
12/5	Received from O'Brien Ltd	2	6,000	D +
15/5	Paid wages		2,000	C −
18/5	Received from Cowell School	3	4,700	D +
20/5	Paid petrol bill		210	C −
23/5	Paid advertising bill		1,200	C −
26/5	Received from PDLS Post-Primary School	4	2,800	D +
29/5	Received from Margaret Togher, householder	5	750	D +
30/5	Received from 2 Direction Ltd	6	2,200	D +
31/5	Paid wages		3,500	C −

Use the following money column headings:

Debit (receipts) side: Bank   Householders   Companies   Schools

Credit (payments) side: Bank   Wages   Materials   Motor   Advertising

CASH BOOK, LEDGER AND TRIAL BALANCE 2.12

Analysed Cash Book of MiniZone

Debit (Plus)

Date 2019	Details	Receipt No.	Bank €	House-holders €	Companies €	Schools €
3/5	Will Donnelly	1	900	900		
12/5	O'Brien Ltd	2	6,000		6,000	
18/5	Cowell School	3	4,700			4,700
27/5	PDLS PP	4	2,800			2,800
29/5	Margaret Togher	5	750	750		
30/5	2 Direction Ltd	6	2,200		2,200	
			17,350	1,650	8,200	7,500
31/5	Balance c/d		2,560			
			19,910			

(Minus) Credit

Date 2019	Details	Payment Method	Bank €	Wages €	Material €	Motor €	Advertising €
1/5	Materials		8,700		8,700		
4/5	Materials	Debit card	1,300		1,300		
10/5	Van Insurance	C/T	3,000			3,000	
15/5	Wages	Paypath	2,000	2,000			
20/5	Petrol	Debit card	210			210	
23/5	Advertisement	Debit card	1,200				1,200
31/5	Wages	Debit card	3,500	3,500			
			19,910	5,500	10,000	3,210	1,200
1/6	Balance b/d		2,560*				

You will notice some differences between this analysed cash book and the one in 1.13:

- The **Total** column is now called the **Bank** column. We only have a **bank column** when there are no transactions by cash.
- There is an extra column on the Debit side called **Receipt No.**
- There is an extra column on the Credit side called **Payment Method**.

*Note for later that this balance b/d must be entered in the Trial Balance.

349

2.12 BE BUSINESS: ENTERPRISE

CHECKING IN...

1. Write an explanation for each of the transactions in the analysed cash book for MiniZone.
2. How much cash did MiniZone have in the bank at the beginning of the month?
3. How much cash did MiniZone have in the bank at the end of the month?
4. What is happening with the cash? What might MiniZone do?

Time to think

Is the analysed cash book for a business similar to the analysed cash book for a household in Unit 1.13? What are the differences?

GENERAL LEDGER

A **general ledger** is a company's set of numbered accounts for its accounting records.

The ledger provides a complete record of financial transactions over the life of the company.

A general ledger is used by businesses that use the *double-entry bookkeeping* method, which means that each financial transaction affects at least two general ledger accounts and each entry has a debit and a credit transaction.

EXAMPLE 3: MINIZONE GENERAL LEDGER

Prepare a general ledger for MiniZone.

In the general ledger you open up an account for **every item** in the cash book and number each account. In the case of MiniZone that means Householders account No. 1, Companies account No. 2, Schools account No. 3, Wages account No. 4, Materials account No. 5, Motor account No. 6 and Advertising account No. 7. Account is often written A/C for short.

If it's on the **debit side in the cashbook** it's on the **credit side in the ledger**.

If it's on the **credit side in the cashbook** it's on the **debit side in the ledger**.

To post to the ledger you take the *totals* from the columns and write them in under each heading (account) name.

CASH BOOK, LEDGER AND TRIAL BALANCE   2.12

General Ledger

Debit								Credit
Date	Details	F	Total	Date	Details	F	Total

Householders A/C No. 1

Date	Details	F	Total	Date	Details	F	Total
				1/6	Bank	ACB	1,650

Companies A/C No. 2

Date	Details	F	Total	Date	Details	F	Total
				1/6	Bank	ACB	8,200

Schools A/C No. 3

Date	Details	F	Total	Date	Details	F	Total
				1/6	Bank	ACB	7,500

Wages A/C No. 4

Date	Details	F	Total	Date	Details	F	Total
1/6	Bank	ACB	5,500				

Materials A/C No. 5

Date	Details	F	Total	Date	Details	F	Total
1/6	Bank	ACB	10,000				

Motor A/C No. 6

Date	Details	F	Total	Date	Details	F	Total
1/6	Bank	ACB	3,210				

Advertising A/C No. 7

1/6	Bank	ACB	1,200				

F stands for Folio and is used for cross-reference. It tells us that the information came from the analysed cash book (ACB). We use abbreviations, as it's a narrow column.

TRIAL BALANCE

A **trial balance** is a bookkeeping worksheet in which the balances of all ledgers are compiled into debit and credit columns.

A company prepares a trial balance periodically, usually at the end of every reporting period. Another word for trial is test. The trial balance is to test if the double entry has been carried out properly. Sometimes mistakes are made.

A trial balance is a list of all balances taken from the ledger and the closing balances of the analysed cash book.

No changing sides here, just list everything on the same side as the ledger.

The total of the debit balance should equal the total of the credit balance. These are the balances b/d (brought down).

Where do entries go in the trial balance?

1. Analysed Cash Book	Post to the	Trial Balance
Debit (Closing balance b/d)	→	Debit
Credit (Closing balance b/d)		Credit

2. Ledger	Post to the	Trial Balance
Debit	→	Debit
Credit		Credit

A very simple rule: whatever side the balances b/d are on, they are on the same side in the trial balance.

When the trial balance is totalled, both sides should be equal. If they don't add up, mistakes have been made and it must be fixed by the accountant.

EXAMPLE 4: MINIZONE TRIAL BALANCE

Prepare a trial balance for MiniZone.

Trial Balance of MiniZone as on 1/6/20xx		
	Debit €	**Credit €**
Bank		2,560*
Householders		1,650
Companies		8,200
Schools		7,500
Wages	5,500	
Materials	10,000	
Motor	3,210	
Advertising	1,200	
	19,910	19,910

CASH BOOK, LEDGER AND TRIAL BALANCE 2.12

Both sides of the trial balance are the same (€19,910) so the entries have been done correctly.

*This is the closing balance in the analysed cash book. Don't forget the bank balance when extracting your trial balance. Success Criteria: The trial balance debit and credit balance match.

When you prepare your final accounts in Unit 2.13, you will extract/use the figures from the trial balance.

INCLUDING VAT

You saw in Unit 1.14 that value-added tax (VAT) is a charge on consumer spending. A business must pay VAT on most of the good and services it purchases. If the business is registered for VAT and sells the goods on to someone else, it can claim back VAT.

A. If the VAT the business takes in from sales is more than the VAT it pays out on purchases, then the difference is paid to Revenue.

B. If the VAT the business takes in from sales is less than the VAT it pays out on purchases, then the difference is given back to the business by Revenue.

So you can see that it is important for a business to keep a record of the VAT it pays.

Time to think

Be Revenue: Which situation might Revenue prefer, A or B? Why?

Be MiniZone: Which situation might MiniZone prefer, A or B? Why?

EXAMPLE 5: MINIZONE ANALYSED CASH BOOK WITH VAT

Prepare the analysed cash book of MiniZone for the month of April 20xx and then balance the account.

You are given the following transactions.

Date	Transactions	Amount €	Fill in what side of the ABC? Debit /Credit
10/4	Purchased goods for resale	36,000 + VAT 4,860	
14/4	Sold goods	48,000 + VAT 6,840	
14/4	Paid insurance	3,000	
16/4	Purchased equipment	92,000	
18/4	Received a loan	90,000	
18/4	Purchased goods for resale	46,000 + VAT 6,210	
20/4	Paid for advertising	2,600	
24/4	Sold goods	32,000 + VAT 4,320	

353

Analysed Cash Book of MiniZone

Debit (Plus)

Date 20XX	Details	F	Bank €	Sales €	VAT €	Loan €
14/4	Sales	GL	54,480	48,000	6,480	
18/4	Loan	GL	90,000			90,000
24/4	Sales	GL	36,320	32,000	4,320	
26/4	Balance c/d		9,870			
			190,670	80,000	10,800	90,000

(Minus) Credit

Date 20XX	Details	F	Bank €	Purchases €	VAT €	Ins. €	Equip. €	Ad. €
10/4	Purchases	GL	40,860	36,000	4,860			
14/4	Insurance	GL	3,000			3,000		
16/4	Equipment	GL	92,000				92,000	
18/4	Purchases	GL	52,210	46,000	6,210			
20/4	Advertising	GL	2,600					2,600
			190,670	82,000	11,070	3,000	92,000	2,600
30/4	Balance b/d		9,870					

354

CASH BOOK, LEDGER AND TRIAL BALANCE 2.12

EXAMPLE 6: MINIZONE GENERAL LEDGER WITH VAT

Prepare the general ledger for MiniZone.

General Ledger

Debit							Credit
Date	Details	F	Total	Date	Details	F	Total
	Sales A/C No. 1						
				30/4	Bank	ACB	80,000
Date	Details	F	Total	Date	Details	F	Total
	Purchases A/C No. 2						
30/4	Bank	ACB	82,000				
Date	Details	F	Total	Date	Details	F	Total
	VAT A/C No. 3						
30/4	Purchases	ACB	11,070	30/4	Sales	ACB	10,800
				30/4	Balance c/d		270
			11,070				11,070
30/4	Balance b/d		270				
Date	Details	F	Total	Date	Details	F	Total
	Loan A/C No. 4						
				30/4	Bank	ACB	90,000
Date	Details	F	Total	Date	Details	F	Total
	Insurance A/C No. 5						
30/4	Bank	ACB	3,000				
Date	Details	F	Total	Date	Details	F	Total
	Equipment A/C No. 6						
30/4	Bank	ACB	92,000				
Date	Details	F	Total	Date	Details	F	Total
	Advertising A/C No. 7						
19/5	Bank	ACB	2,600				

Study the VAT account. ACB stands for analysed cash book.

2.12 BE BUSINESS: ENTERPRISE

> **Double Entry**
>
> If it's on the **debit side on the analysed cash book**, it's on the **credit side of the ledger**.
>
> If it's on the **credit side on the analysed cash book**, it's on the **debit side of the ledger**.

EXAMPLE 6: MINIZONE TRIAL BALANCE WITH VAT

Prepare a trial balance for MiniZone for the month of April 20xx.

Trial Balance of Minizone for April 20XX		
	Debit €	Credit €
Sales		80,000
Purchases	82,000	
VAT	270	
Loan		90,000
Insurance	3,000	
Equipment	92,000	
Advertising	2,600	
Bank		9,870*
	179,870	179,870

*This is the closing balance in the analysed cash book. Don't forget the bank balance when extracting your trial balance. Success Criteria: The trial balance debit and credit balance match. 👍

Remember, the analysed cash book is the same or not-for-profit organisations.

CHECKING IN...

1. What side is sales on in the analysed cash book?
2. What side is purchases on in the analysed cash book?
3. What is VAT? How much VAT did MiniZone have on purchases and on sales?
4. Does the business owe VAT to Revenue? Explain your answer.

CASH BOOK, LEDGER AND TRIAL BALANCE 2.12

SUMMARY OF POSTING RULES

Analysed Cash Book (ACB)	
Debit Cash In	Credit Cash Out

Analysed Cash Book (ACB)	Post to the	General Ledger (opposite sides)
Debit in Analysed Cash Book	→	Credit in Ledger
Credit in Analysed Cash Book		Debit in Ledger
Ledger	Post to the	Trial Balance
Debit	→	Debit
Credit		Credit
Analysed Cash Book	Post to the	Trial Balance
Debit (Closing balance b/d)	→	Debit
Credit (Closing balance b/d)		Credit

IMPORTANT PHASES IN RECORD KEEPING

1. The **business documents** you learned about in Unit 2.10 need to be used correctly and filed by an organisation.
2. The **analysed cash book is completed** using these business documents.
3. The entries from the analysed cash book are **posted to the ledger**.
4. Check the accuracy of the analysed cash book and ledger by **preparing a trial balance**.
5. The next phase is preparing final accounts:

   A. Income statement (IS)

   B. Statement of financial position (SFP)

   These will be dealt with in Unit 2.13.

BE AN ACCOUNTANT...

CASH BOOK, LEDGER & TRIAL BALANCE — UNIT 2.12

1. CASH BOOK
- DEBIT + IN
- CREDIT − OUT

ANALYSED CASHBOOK

DATE	DETAILS	F	TOTAL	X	X	DATE	DETAILS	F	TOTAL	X	X
DEBIT +						**CREDIT −**					

* ONLY BALANCE TOTAL COLUMNS
* TOTAL ALL THE ANALYSED COLUMNS

BE REVENUE
ALWAYS KEEP VAT SEPARATE

VAT ON SALES > VAT ON PURCHASE: WE OWE REVENUE
VAT ON SALES > VAT ON PURCHASE: NOTHING
VAT ON SALES < VAT ON PURCHASES: REVENUE OWE US

BALANCING AN ACCOUNT
BALANCE GOES ON THE SMALLER SIDE

2. GENERAL LEDGER
DR IN CASHBOOK = CR IN LEDGER
CR IN CASHBOOK = DR IN LEDGER

3. TRIAL BALANCE
LIST OF LEDGER BALANCES
DR IN LEDGER DR IN TRIAL BALANCE
CR IN LEDGER CR IN TRIAL BALANCE

WE USE THE TRIAL BALANCE TO PREPARE OUR FINAL ACCOUNTS
1. INCOME STATEMENT
2. STATEMENT OF FINANCIAL POSITION

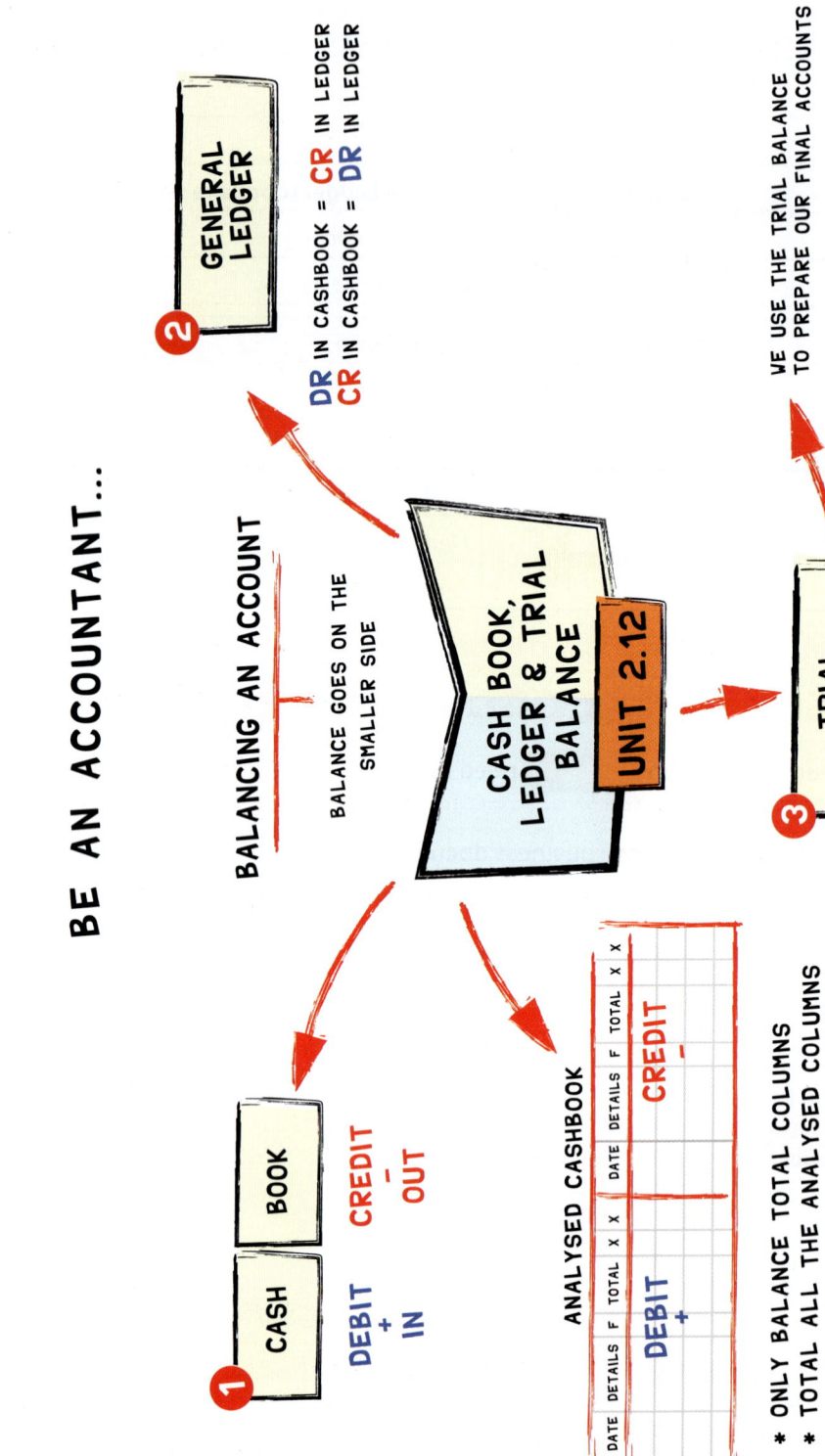

CBA 1: FINANCE IN ACTION

CASH BOOK, LEDGER AND TRIAL BALANCE 2.12

Be Prepared: My Support Sheets

Completing the activities here will help you to reflect on and reinforce your learning before you move on to the next unit.

1. Write down the **key terms** in this unit and make sure you understand them. See if they match the ones at the back of the book.
2. List the key **concepts/themes** in this unit.
3. List the three **most interesting points** about this unit.

EVALUATE MY LEARNING: DAR

Describe
- Did I/we meet my/our learning intentions?
- What went well? What are my/our strengths?

Assess
- How did I/we work with others?
- Were there challenges?

Recommend
- How might I improve?
- What skills and learning might I apply to new situations?

Do your **Key Check** in the workbook for this unit and then mark your learning position on the following rating scale:

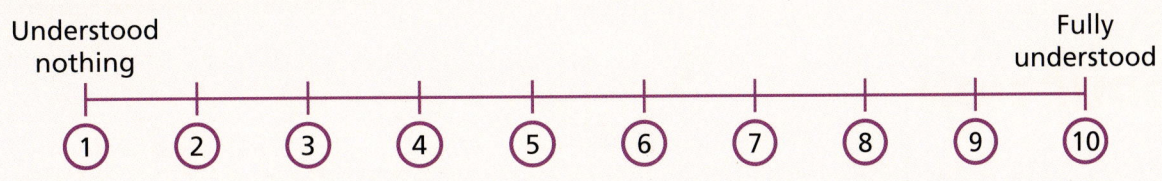

Understood nothing 1 — 2 — 3 — 4 — 5 — 6 — 7 — 8 — 9 — 10 Fully understood

How can you move up the rating scale? What can you **say**, **make**, **write** and **do** to illustrate your learning?

Enterprise in Action Idea!

Create a poster explaining analysed cash book, ledger and trial balance. You may decide to use www.Pictochart.com

QUESTION TIME

1. Explain what the cash book is used for.
2. Explain what the analysed cash book is used for.
3. Explain the reasons for preparing accounts.
4. Write a short report on VAT in the cash book.

2.13 FINAL ACCOUNTS

Prepare final accounts to assess the financial performance of an organisation at the end of a trading period, analyse and evaluate its financial position and recommend a course of action.

Learning Intentions

At the end of this unit I will:

- Be able to prepare an income statement
- Be able to prepare a statement of financial position
- Be able to use ratios to analyse a business
- Understand how to evaluate a business from these accounts
- Value accounting concepts in making business decisions
- Apply previous bookkeeping knowledge and skills to final accounts for a business

Key Concepts

- ✓ Accounts and accounting terms
- ✓ Income statements, statement of financial position, depreciation
- ✓ Assessing/scrutinising a business using ratios – profitability, liquidity and gearing

Linking the Links with other LOs

- 1.13 Income, expenditure and bank statements
- 2.11 Cash budget
- 2.12 Cash book, ledger and trial balance

Are there other LOs?

Wonderful Worthwhile Website

www.sageone.ie

INTRODUCTION

> Excel and Google Sheets make accounting easy! The formulas are inserted, and you enter the figures, press a button and the final accounts are calculated. Use the Be Business Excel resources.

Final accounts show the **profitability** and **financial position** of a business or organisation.

Final accounts are prepared at the **end** of an accounting period, usually a year, for example, 31/12/2019.

The final accounts consist of **two** major accounts:

1. **Income Statement (IS)** – showing the **profit** for the year.
2. **Statement of Financial Position (SFP)** – showing **assets** and **liabilities** at a particular date.

These two accounts show the gross profit, net profit, and distribution of net profit figures of the business or organisation.

Accounts are useful for **all stakeholders**; for management, owners and other interested parties, for example financial institutions, shareholders and customers.

ASSETS AND LIABILITIES

We are going to follow a simple **step-by-step** approach to understanding and simplifying final accounts.

Let's start with some important accounting definitions. Every business has assets and liabilities. Not-for-profit organisations have assets and liabilities too.

> An **asset** is something of money value. A business will use capital to acquire assets.

Remember that capital is the business term for money that you invest in the business. Examples of assets include:

- Motor vehicles
- Premises/buildings
- Equipment
- Cash
- Stock – products the business sells. For example, in a garage stock is cars as the garage sells cars
- Debtors – we sell them goods on credit. They will pay us later, so this is an asset – something of money value

3Ts' = Think, Turn, Talk

Can you list some assets in your Business Studies classroom?
Can you list some assets in your home?
Can you list some assets in a local organisation, e.g. your local hurling club?

A business will also have liabilities.

A **liability** is something a business owes. The business will have to pay it back.

> A **liability** is something a business owes. The business will have to pay it back.

Examples of liabilities include:

- Loan – money borrowed from a financial institution (e.g. a bank) that will have to be paid back with interest.
- Bank overdraft – a short-term source of finance that may be repaid within one year. The business will have to pay interest on an overdraft.
- Creditors – we buy goods on credit. We will pay later, so this is a liability – we owe it.

3Ts' = Think, Turn, Talk

Can you list some liabilities your local shop might have?
Can you list some liabilities your local sports club might have?

2.13 BE BUSINESS: ENTERPRISE

Be Creative

Create a short presentation using presentation software (Prezi, PowerPoint, Google Presentation on Google Drive) explaining the difference between assets and liabilities. Then document your learning by writing a blog post. Now that you have made your presentation, think about how to make your blog post effective and interesting.

Success criteria:
- Title
- Visual
- Each slide in the presentation must have a title, for example 'Assets', followed by a definition and an example
- Good communication skills
- The presentation should not exceed three minutes

KEEPING RECORDS AND ACCOUNTS

We know that to keep track of cash flow and budgets it is essential to keep **records** of all goods bought and sold. A business must also keep records of any other money that it spends or receives.

Find out what accounting software your school uses for its accounts.

Remember the important phases in record-keeping:

1. The **business documents** you learned about in Unit 2.10 need to be used correctly and filed by an organisation.
2. The **analysed cash book is completed** using these business documents.
3. The entries from the analysed cash book are **posted to the ledger**.
4. Check the accuracy of the analysed cash book and ledger by **preparing a trial balance**.
5. The next phase is preparing final accounts:
    a) Income statement and
    b) Statement of financial position

We are going to simplify the accounting process and introduce each account transaction by transaction, step by step. Let's start with the **statement of financial position**.

STATEMENT OF FINANCIAL POSITION

The **statement of financial position** is the account that lists all the **assets** and **liabilities** of a business on a certain date, usually the end of the year.

Let's start a new business called SinCom, an IT service business established by Chris Martin. Imagine you are

Chris Martin and this is your business. All the transactions we are going to look at below are from the **business's perspective**.

Transaction 1: Capital

> 1 September 2019 you **invest** €300,000 in a new business called SinCom and open a bank account with **Bank of Ireland**.

The first transaction is when you start the business by investing €300,000. Money invested in a business is called **capital**. Capital is the money you start a business with. Interestingly, **capital is a liability**.

Why might Capital be a Liability?

The business SinCom owes the owner of the business this money. If Chris Martin closes SinCom, he will want the money he invested back.

The business SinCom now has €300,000 in the Bank of Ireland. **Bank is an asset**.

Why is Money in the Bank an Asset?

An asset is something of money value. SinCom has €300,000 in its bank account.

Now we will see a simple way to record Transaction 1 in a **statement of financial position**.

Statement of Financial Position	
	€
Assets	
Bank	300,000
	300,000
Liabilities	
Capital	300,000
	300,000

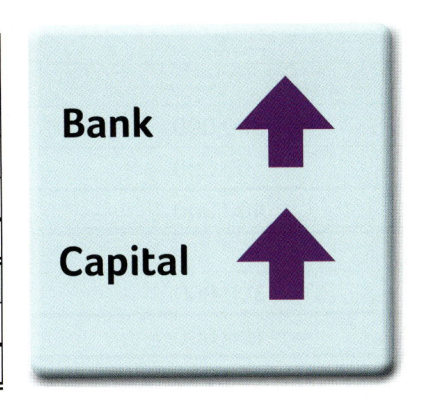

Bank ⬆

Capital ⬆

Time to think

What are the advantages of renting over buying? Think of it from a cash perspective.

In order to run SinCom, you will need to have a **premises**. Remember, you can buy or perhaps rent or lease a premises.

Transaction 2: Buy Premises

You have decided to buy a premises.

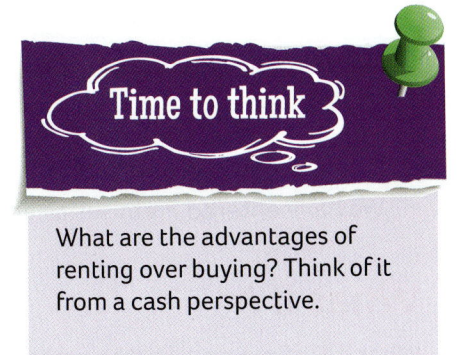

> 10 September 2019 you **buy premises** for €100,000. You pay for the premises with money from SinCom's bank account.

Premises is an asset (something of money value). You paid for the premises by taking money from SinCom's bank account. Bank is an asset. However, the money in the bank has decreased – remember, every transaction affects **two** accounts.

Now we will see a simple way to record Transaction 2 in a **statement of financial position**.

Statement of Financial Position	
	€
Assets	
Bank	200,000
Premises	100,000
	300,000
Liabilities	
Capital	300,000
	300,000

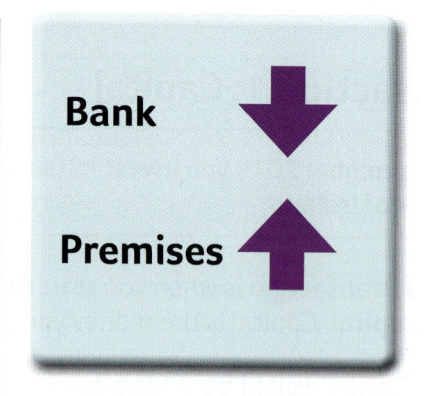

Bank ↓
Premises ↑

Have you noticed that **capital** remains the same?

What if?

What if SinCom had taken out a loan to buy the premises?

Statement of Financial Position	
	€
Assets	
Bank	300,000
Premises	100,000
	400,000
Liabilities	
Capital	300,000
Loan	100,000
	400,000

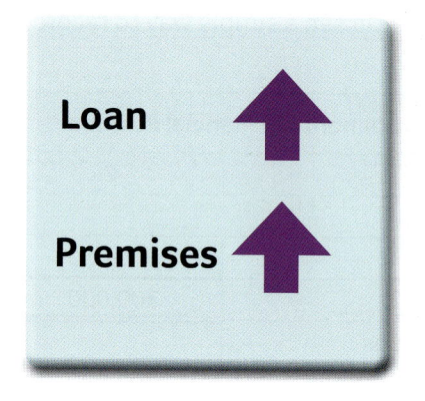

Loan ↑
Premises ↑

- We have entered Loan as a liability. SinCom's liabilities have increased.
- We have entered Premises as an asset. SinCom's assets have increased.

What if?

What if SinCom paid for the premises with €50,000 from the bank and €50,000 from a loan?

- Premises, an asset, increases by €100,000.
- SinCom paid €50,000, therefore the bank, an asset, decreases by €50,000.
- Loan, a liability increases by €50,000.

What else do you require for SinCom? How about a **motor vehicle?** Remember, you can decide to buy or you could rent, hire purchase or lease a motor vehicle instead.

Transaction 3: Buy Vehicle

You have decided to buy a motor vehicle.

> 2 September 2019 you **buy a second-hand car** from Nissan for €30,000. You pay for the car without any loans or mortgages.

SinCom now has a motor vehicle. Motor vehicles is an asset (something of money value). You paid for the motor vehicle by taking money from SinCom's bank account. Bank is an asset. However, the bank has decreased.

Now we will see a simple way to record Transaction 3 in a **statement of financial position**.

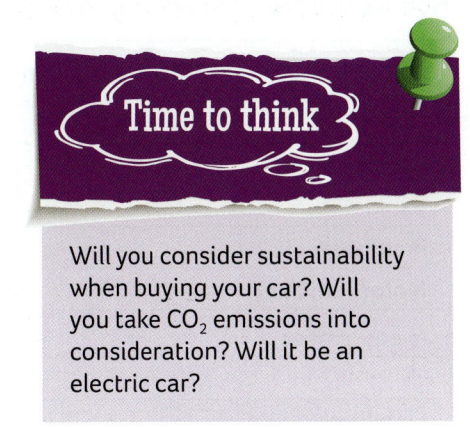

Time to think

Will you consider sustainability when buying your car? Will you take CO_2 emissions into consideration? Will it be an electric car?

Statement of Financial Position	
	€
Assets	
Bank	170,000
Premises	100,000
Motor vehicles	30,000
	300,000
Liabilities	
Capital	300,000
	300,000

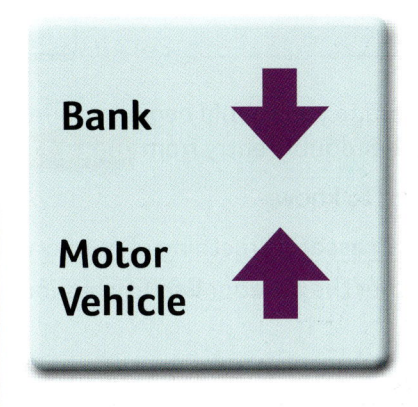

Capital remains the same. SinCom owes you that €300,000.

Bank has decreased as you have bought premises and motor vehicles.

Assets are equal to your liabilities.

WORKING WITH OTHERS

Working in small groups, discuss what might have happened if SinCom had taken out a credit union loan for the motor vehicle.

Transaction 4: Buy IT Equipment

What else does SinCom require? You have decided to buy **an iPad and an iPhone**.

> 2 September 2019 you **buy an iPad and an iPhone** for €900. You pay for these with money from SinCom's bank account.

SinCom now has IT equipment. IT equipment is an asset (something of money value). You paid for the IT equipment by taking money from SinCom's bank account. Bank is an asset. However, the bank has decreased.

2.13 BE BUSINESS: ENTERPRISE

Now we will see a simple way to record Transaction 4 in a **statement of financial position**.

Statement of Financial Position	
	€
Assets	
Bank	169,100
Premises	100,000
Motor vehicles	30,000
IT equipment	900
	300,000
Liabilities	
Capital	300,000
	300,000

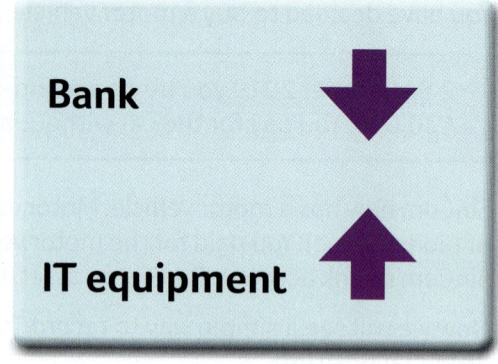

At this stage you should begin to understand that every transaction that happens affects two accounts; remember double entry from **Unit 2.12**?

You need to know:

1. Is it an **asset** (something of money value) or a **liability** (something the business owes)?
2. If either the **asset** or **liability** has increased or decreased.

CHECKING IN...

Create a business. Think of a good name for your business and invent five transactions similar to SinCom's accounts. Begin by investing money in your business. Go through these transactions step by step, as shown in the above examples. Demonstrate how each transaction will impact on the SFP.

Transaction 5: Buy Stock

SinCom now has premises, a motor vehicle and some IT equipment, but it needs goods to sell.

You buy stock at **cost price**, and hope to sell it at a **higher** selling price and make a profit.

> The goods/products that you buy to resell are called **stock**. Stock is an **asset** because it is something of money value.

It is important to shop around and ensure you get the best value for money when buying stock. Remember to compare not just the cost price of the stock, but also terms of trade, who pays for the delivery, credit terms, discounts for buying in bulk or for paying your bill promptly, etc.

> 3 September 2019 you **buy stock** for €20,000. You pay for stock with money from SinCom's bank account.

SinCom now has **stock**. Stock is an asset (something of money value). You paid for the stock by taking money from SinCom's bank account. Bank is an asset. However, the bank has decreased.

Now we will see a simple way to record Transaction 5 in a **statement of financial position**.

Statement of Financial Position	
	€
Assets	
Bank	149,100
Premises	100,000
Motor vehicles	30,000
IT Equipment	900
Stock	20,000
	300,000
Liabilities	
Capital	300,000
	300,000

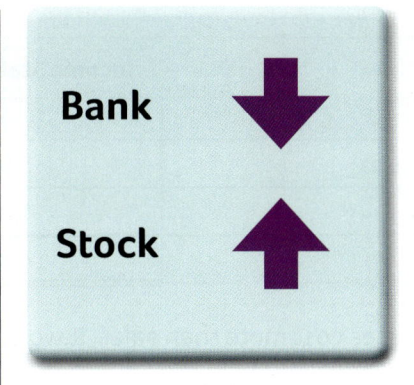

Bank ⬇

Stock ⬆

Before going forward, make sure you understand all the transactions so far. While it is simplifying the statement of financial position, it will give you an understanding of business transactions.

CHECKING IN...

1. Define stock.
2. List three items of appropriate stock for each of the following:

Garage	Farm	National chain of DIY stores
Butcher	Café	National supermarket chain
Baker	Large electrical retailer	

Transaction 6: Make a Profit

SinCom sells computer accessories. Your aim as the owner of SinCom is to buy goods/stock at **cost price** and to sell them at a higher **selling price**. The difference between these two prices is known as **profit**.

> 8 September 2019 SinCom **sells IT accessories** costing €3,000 for €4,800. The money from the sales is lodged to the bank account.

We need to calculate the profit – the difference between the cost price of the goods and the selling price.

€4,800 – €3,000 = €1,800

Sales – Cost of Sales = Profit

2.13 BE BUSINESS: ENTERPRISE

We will now see how this information appears in **account** form. We call this account the **income statement** (this is a very simple IS).

Income Statement of SinCom for year ended 31/12/19			
€	€		€
Purchases	3,000	Sales	4,800
Profit	**1,800**		
	4,800		4,800

If purchases cost more than sales, it would be a gross loss.

How will the sale of these computer accessories and the corresponding profit from the sale affect the **statement of financial position**?

We have already documented the original purchase of the stock. Now we must show what effect the sale of the stock had on the business.

- Decrease in stock – sold stock.
- Increase in money lodged to the bank – from the sales.

SinCom now has a profit. You decide not to withdraw the profit from the business, so it is added to capital. Because we have added the profit to the capital, the business owes us that money back.

CHECKING IN...

1. Use your calculator to calculate the missing figures in the examples below.
   If SinCom purchases stock for €5,000 and sells it for €7,500, the profit is _____.
   If SinCom purchases stock for €6,000 and sells it for €8,500, the profit is _____.
   If SinCom sells stock for €7,500 and the profit is €600, the cost price is _____.
   If SinCom purchases stock for €9,000 and the profit is €2,500, the sale price is _____.
2. Remember, if SinCom sells below cost you will make a loss. Can you identify times when you might have to sell your stock at below cost price?

WORKING WITH OTHERS

Working in pairs or small groups, imagine you have opened a company called Techco. One of Techco's best sellers is a selfie stick.

1. List five transactions carried out by Techco. The first one has been started for you.

   1 January 2020 you invest €200,000 in a new business called _____ and open a bank account with _____ .

2. Demonstrate the effect on the statement of financial position for each of the five transactions.

3. If Techco purchased stock (selfie sticks for reselling) for €6,000 and sold it for €7,500, what is the missing figure below?

Profit	Selling Price/Sales	Cost Price
?	€7,500	€6,000

A new company has opened next door and is selling selfie sticks at 10% cheaper than your selfie stick company. What might you do?

INCOME STATEMENT

Let's look at the **income statement**. We will use a simple example to help us understand the account with just purchases (what we buy) and sales (what we sell).

EXAMPLE 1: GROSS PROFIT

We bought 8 cans of cola for 50c each = €4.00 (bought = purchases)

We sold 8 cans of cola at €1 each = €8.00 (sold = sales)

Sales €8.00 – Cost €4.00 = Profit €4.00

We made a profit of €4, called Gross Profit.

Present this in account format. The name of the account is the **income statement**.

Sales – Purchases = Gross Profit

Income Statement (part)	
	€
Sales	8.00
Purchases	4.00
Gross profit	4.00

EXAMPLE 2: CLOSING STOCK

Using the same information, consider what would happen if we only sold 7 cans. One can would be left over. We know it is stock so we will call it **closing stock** (always value stock at cost).

We bought 8 cans of cola for 50c each = €4.00 (bought = purchases)

We sold 7 cans of cola at €1 each = €7.00 (sold = sales)

One can is left = Closing Stock 1 × 50c = 50c

CLOSING STOCK

The **cost of our sales** is not €4.00, as we have one can left, therefore minus 50c and the cost is €3.50. Take cost of sales from sales (€7.00 – €3.50) and our gross profit is €3.50.

Present this in account format. Note that the extra columns are for subtotals and adding.

Sales – cost of sales = Gross profit

Cost of sales = purchases – closing stock

369

Income Statement (part)		
	€	€
Sales		7.00
Less cost of sales		
Purchases	4.00	
Less closing stock	0.50	
Cost of sales		3.50
Gross profit		3.50

Cost of Sales = opening stock + purchases − closing stock

EXAMPLE 3: OPENING STOCK

Using the same information, consider what would happen if we had 2 cans of Cola at the beginning of the week (**opening stock**). We still bought in 8 cans from our supplier but we only sold 6 cans.

We **purchased** 8 cans to sell = 8 × 50c = €4.00 (remember, we buy at cost)

We had two cans at the beginning = **opening stock** = 2 × 50c = €1.00

We only **sold** 6 cans (sell at selling price) = 6 × €1 = €6.00

We have **closing stock** of 4 cans

(We had 2 cans at the beginning, add 8 cans that we bought = 10 cans, sold 6, so we are left with 4 cans.) Closing stock is 4 × 50c = €2.00

Our **gross profit** = €3.00

Remember, you always value **stock at cost price**.

Present this in account format.

Cost of sales = opening stock + purchases − closing stock

Income Statement (part)		
	€	€
Sales		6.00
Less cost of sales		
Opening stock	1.00	
+ Purchases	4.00	
Cost of goods available for sale	5.00	
− Closing stock	2.00	
Cost of sales		3.00
Gross profit		3.00

Sometimes you may have sales returns. If a customer bought a can of cola and was unhappy with the purchase, he or she could return the can and then your sales would have decreased.

EXAMPLE 4: RETURNS

We **purchased** 8 cans to sell = 8 × 50c = €4.00

We had 2 cans at the beginning = **opening stock** = 2 × 50c = €1.00

We only **sold** 6 cans = 6 × €1.00 = €6.00

An unhappy customer returns one can = sales €6.00 – €1.00 = €5.00

We have **closing stock** of 4 (2 cans at the beginning, add 8 cans that we bought = 10 cans, sold 6, but 1 can was returned, so we are left with 5 cans). Closing stock is 5 × 50c = €2.50

Present this in account format.

Sales – sales returns = true sales

Income Statement (part)		
	€	€
Sales		6.00
Sales returns		1.00
		5.00
Less cost of sales		
Opening stock	1.00	
+ Purchases	4.00	
Cost of goods available for sale	5.00	
– Closing stock	2.50	
Cost of sales		2.50
Gross profit		**2.50**

Something similar can happen with your own purchases. Sometimes you have to return goods you bought from your supplier – the goods may have been damaged or the supplier may have oversupplied; maybe the supplier sent 10 cans of cola instead of 8 cans.

Purchases – purchases returns = true purchases

EXAMPLE 5: INCOME STATEMENT

Here is the full statement with explanations.

Income Statement of SinCom for year ended 31/12/2019	€	€
Sales		6.00
Less **sales returns**		1.00
		5.00
Less **cost of sales**		
Opening stock	1.00	
+ Purchases	4.00	
Cost of goods available for sale	5.00	
− Closing stock	2.50	
Cost of sales		2.50
Gross profit		**2.50**

Sales: 6 cans @ selling price €1.00 = €6.00
Returns: 1 can returned @ selling price €1.00 = €1.00
Sales €6.00 − €1.00 = €5.00
Opening stock: At the beginning of the year, you started off with 2 cans; 2 @ 50c (cost price) = €1.00
Purchased: 8 cans @ 50c (cost price) = €4.00
Cost of goods available for sale: In money terms you have €5 available to sell (10 cans)
Closing stock: However, you have 5 cans left over, value 5 @ 50c (cost price) = €2.50
Cost of sales: So the actual cost of sales = €2.50
Profit = Sales − Cost of Sales = €2.50

Sometimes when buying goods you may have to pay for transport on purchases. This expense is known as **carriage inwards**, or **customs duties** if you are importing from another country.

Both of these expenses will be added to your purchases as they are an added cost for purchases.

Gross profit is not your true profit as you will have **expenses** to run the business and these expenses decrease your profit.

These expenses might include:
- Insurance
- Rent
- Rates
- Wages
- Allowing discounts
- Depreciation – decrease in the value of an asset

These are taken away from gross profit to find your **net profit**.

> Gross profit − expenses = net profit

FINAL ACCOUNTS 2.13

WORKING WITH OTHERS

Working in pairs or small groups, explain the income statement using a method of your choice. Now document your learning from the experience.

Success criteria:
- Understanding the concept of the income statement
- Using initiative to explain it
- Communication skills – clear
- Wow factor!

DEPRECIATION

Depreciation is a term used to describe a reduction in the value of an asset over time, due in particular to **wear and tear**.

If a business buys a car in January, is the car worth the same at the end of the year? The answer is no. The car has higher mileage, wear and tear, and it may have become outdated if there is an updated model on the market. Each of these factors reduces the value of the car.

It is important therefore to 'write off' the expense (decrease in the value of an asset). This expense is called depreciation. There are many different ways to calculate this expense. Normally, depreciation is calculated using a **percentage (%) of the cost of the asset**. Writing off a fixed percentage in depreciation each year is also known as **straight line depreciation**. We will have to record what depreciation does in our business accounts.

Depreciation will be an **expense** in our **income statement** as it reduces profit.

Our assets also **decrease** in value and we will show this in our **statement of financial position**.

EXAMPLE 6: STRAIGHT LINE DEPRECIATION

A business purchased a car for €25,000 on 1/1/2020. Depreciation is 10% and is written off over ten years.

- Depreciation is €25,000 × 10% = €2,500 per year (**income statement**)
- At the end of the year the car (asset) is worth €22,500 (**statement of financial position**)

You will need to enter your up-to-date information into your accounts.

CHECKING IN...

1. What might be the depreciation if you bought the car on 31/6/2020? (Six months' depreciation for 2020.)
2. If one year's depreciation is €2,500, what is 6 months'?
3. Does depreciation affect our cash? Explain.

Time to think

Depreciation won't appear in your cash flow forecast. Why might that be?

373

PREPARING FINAL ACCOUNTS

The **trial balance** (list of ledger balances) is where you will find all the figures to complete your final accounts.

A **statement of financial position** is a snapshot of everything that a business **owns** and everything that a business **owes** at a specific point in time.

What the company owns = **assets**
What the company owes = **liabilities**

Assets	Liabilities
Strengths	Blockages
Owns	Owes
Good for me	Hinder
Build on	Work on

Do you understand everything that has been covered in the chapter so far? Revise all the transactions before proceeding.

We will now look at a full set of **final accounts**: a detailed **income statement** and **statement of financial position**.

Let's start with the **income statement**.

SAMPLE INCOME STATEMENT

Just try to know and understand the accounts initially. Read the labels on this account carefully; they explain key terms and why transactions are placed in specific accounts.

Income Statement of SinCom for year ended 31/12/19		
	€	€
Sales	595,240	
Sales returns	3,000	592,240
Less cost of sales		
Opening stock 1/1/19	20,520	
+ Purchases	371,580	
+ Carriage inwards	24,000	
Cost of goods available for sale	416,100	
Less closing stock	34,560	
Cost of sales		381,540
Gross profit		210,700
Add gains		
Commission receivable		4,340
		215,040
Less expenses		
Rent	5,000	
Wages	13,000	
Phone	5,000	
Advertising	68,620	
Discount allowed	920	
Light and heat	10,000	
Total expenses		102,540
Net profit		112,500
Less dividend		42,000
Profit balance		70,500

Sales is the money value of stock that SinCom sold. Units multiplied by selling price. Some were returned, so you take away returns.

Sales returns are returns inwards. You sold them and they are the value of goods returned back into the business. They could be damaged/faulty goods or you could have sent too many goods by mistake.

Opening stock is the stock at the beginning of the year and is added to purchases (goods you buy for resale).

Purchases is the cost of the goods that you purchased from suppliers.

Carriage inwards is a transport cost on purchases; it is added to purchases as it increases the cost.

Closing stock is the stock left over; it reduces cost of sales. It will also appear in the Statement of Financial Position (we have something of money value at the end of the year).

Gross profit is the difference between sales and the cost of sales. If sales was less than the cost of sales this would be a gross loss.

Gains are received from sources other than part of the normal trading. For example, rent received: you could rent your office. Interest received: from investments or commission received. Also discounts received.

Expenses are the day-to-day running costs of the business.

Discount allowed is an expense.

Net Profit = gross profit less expenses.

Dividend is interest paid to shareholders (these invest money, known as shares) for investing in the business.

SAMPLE STATEMENT OF FINANCIAL POSITION

Now let's see a statement of financial position. Just try to know and understand the statement initially. Read the labels on this statement carefully; they explain key terms.

Statement of Financial Position of SinCom as on 31/12/2019			
	Cost €	Dep €	NBV €
Fixed assets			
Land	500,000	0	500,000
Motor vans	54,000	0	54,000
Total fixed assets	554,000	0	554,000
Current assets			
Closing stock	34,560		
Cash	2,940		
Bank	10,000		
Debtors	20,000	67,500	
Current liabilities			
Creditors	10,000		
Bank overdraft	1,000	11,000	
Working capital			56,500
Total net assets			610,500
Financed by	Authorised	Issued	
Capital	450,000	420,000	
Reserve		70,500	490,500
Long-term liability			
20-year loan			120,000
Capital employed			610,500

Cost: assets cost

Depreciation is an expense. It is the decrease in an asset, usually due to wear and tear.

NBV (net book value) is the cost of assets. We take away depreciation to calculate NBV.

Fixed assets remain relatively unchanged; they are in the business for the long term. There is no depreciation for motor vans in this example. If there was you would decrease the assets.

Current assets are short-term assets that will vary during the year, e.g. stock, as you sell stock.

Debtor is someone we sell to on credit. They owe the business money, so they are a current asset.

Current liabilities are owed by the business and must be paid within a year, e.g. bank overdraft.

Creditor is someone we buy from on credit. We owe them so they are a current liability.

Working capital = current assets less current liabilities

This first total in the top part is fixed assets plus working capital.

Authorised share of capital is the legal or maximum amount of capital the business can issue.

Issued is the actual amount of capital SinCom has issued. Dividends are calculated on issued capital.

20-year loan is a **long-term liability** to be paid back over 5 years. You pay interest on the loan.

Capital employed is the total for the 'Financed by' section.

Total is how the company is financed.

FINAL ACCOUNTS 2.13

PREPARING AN INCOME STATEMENT PART 1

Part 1 is the trading element: sales less cost of sales = gross profit

In this part we find the gross profit.

WORKING WITH OTHERS

Working together in pairs, explain the accounts to each other. One student can explain and the other student check!

Top Tip!

Practise the accounts and make sure you understand each section. Always break the accounts down into achievable chunks. Try using your Google Sheets/Excel resource; it will do the calculations automatically.

EXAMPLE 7: INCOME STATEMENT FOR GROSS PROFIT

We will start with the **gross profit section**.

From the following information prepare the income statement to **gross profit for the year ended 31 December 2020**:

What if the year begins on 1/4/2019? Then it will end on 31/3/2020.

- **Trading period** is one year (always a year)
- **Year begins** 1/1/2020
- **Year ends** 31/12/2020
- Sales €595,240
- Opening stock €20,520
- Sales returns €3,000
- Closing stock €34,560
- Purchases €371,580
- Carriage inwards €24,000

First part of the income statement: find gross profit.

Income Statement for SinCom for year ended 31/12/20		
	€	€
Sales	595,240	
Sales returns	3,000	592,240
Less cost of sales		
Opening stock 1/1/19	20,520	
+ Purchases	371,580	
+ Carriage inwards	24,000	
Cost of goods available for sale	416,100	
Less closing stock	34,560	
Cost of sales		381,540
Gross profit		210,700

See explanation on the next page.

377

Explanation

Did SinCom make a profit or a loss? They made a gross profit.

Always start with **sales**; what we sold our stock for. **Sales returns** means customers must have returned some stock that we sold. Sales is also known as turnover. SinCom had stock at the beginning of the year **(opening stock)** and bought more stock **(purchases)**. We also add **carriage inwards** (cost of transport) to get the **cost of goods available** for sale. However, we did not sell all our stock as we had **closing stock** left over. We take away closing stock to find actual **cost of goods sold**. We deduct this from sales to find our **gross profit**.

PREPARING AN INCOME STATEMENT PART 2

Part 2: gross profit plus gains and less expenses.

Followed by the **net profit section**.

This part records all the expenses and any gains received from non-trading activities. Then we subtract dividend (the interest given to shareholders for investing in the business).

WORKING WITH OTHERS

Working together, turn to your partner and explain each transaction on the income statement on the next page.

EXAMPLE 8: INCOME STATEMENT

Find net profit for year ended 31/12/2019.

- Gross profit €210,700
- Rent €5,000
- Advertising €68,620
- Commission receivable €4,340
- Dividend €42,000
- Light and heat €10,000
- Wages €13,000
- Discount allowed €920
- Phone €5,000

Income Statement for SinCom for year ended 31/12/19		
	€	€
Gross profit		210,700
Add gains		
Commission receivable		4,340
		215,040
Less expenses		
Rent	5,000	
Wages	13,000	
Phone	5,000	
Advertising	68,620	
Discount allowed	920	
Light and heat	10,000	
Total expenses		102,540
Net profit		112,500
Less dividend		42,000
Profit balance		70,500

Explanation

We were given **gross profit** and we add on any gains – income from non-trading – in this case a commission. We then take away **expenses**, the day-to-day running of a business (rent, wages, phone, etc.). When we take expenses from profit, we find our **net profit**. It could be a net loss if expenses are greater than net profit. We paid a dividend (interest) to shareholders which reduces our profit. The **profit balance** figure is what we use in our statement of financial position.

PREPARING A STATEMENT OF FINANCIAL POSITION

EXAMPLE 9: STATEMENT OF FINANCIAL POSITION

Using the information below, prepare a statement of financial position for SinCom.

Land €500,000	Land is an asset (something of money value). It is a **fixed asset**, as it will remain in the business.
Motor vehicles €54,000	Motor vehicles is an asset (something of money value). It is a **fixed asset**, as it will remain in the business.

Creditors €10,000	Creditors is a liability – SinCom bought goods on credit. It is a **current liability** as they have to be repaid within a year.
Closing stock €34,560	Closing stock is an **asset**, something of money value.
Bank overdraft €1,000	Bank overdraft is a liability. It is a **current liability** as it will have to be repaid within a year.
Cash €2,940	Cash is an **asset**.
Bank €10,000	Bank is an **asset**.
Debtors €20,000	Debtors is an **asset**. SinCom sold goods on credit (they owe us), which is an asset.
Long-term loan €120,000	Long-term loan is a **liability**. The business is partly financed by a loan. This is debt capital.
Authorised capital of €450,000 Issued capital €420,000	SinCom has ordinary share capital of €420,000 (issued). It could legally have €450,000 (authorised).

We start with the **fixed assets section**. Fixed assets are items that a business will have for a long time, for example premises.

Statement of Financial Position of SinCom as on 31/12/19			
	€	€	€
Fixed assets	Cost	Dep	NBV
Land	500,000	0	500,000
Motor vehicles	54,000	0	54,000
	554,000	0	554,000

Remember, depreciation would decrease the value of an asset. There was **no** depreciation.

Followed by the **current assets section**. These are items that a business owns for a short term, e.g. one year. Their value changes, for example stock (buy and sell), debtors (if you sell goods on credit you can sell more – debtors pay you).

Current assets			
Closing stock	34,560		
Cash	2,940		
Bank	10,000		
Debtors	20,000	67,500	

Followed by the **current liabilities section**. This is money owed that must be paid within a year, for example, bank overdraft or creditors falling due within a year.

Current liabilities			
Creditors	10,000		
Bank overdraft	1,000	11,000	

> It is important that current assets are greater than current liabilities. We call this **liquidity**. The company must be able to pay its debts as they fall due.

Followed by the **'financed by' section**. This section shows how your business is financed; money from shares, profits reinvested back into the business, long-term loan (borrowed money) or creditors falling due after more than one year.

Financed by	Authorised	Issued	
Capital – ordinary shares	450,000	420,000	
Reserve: profit and loss balance		70,500	
Long-term liability			
20-year 10% loan		120,000	
Capital employed			610,500

Be Numerate

Myona is a music business that creates and supplies apps to improve performance when learning the piano. You are required to prepare final accounts (an **income statement** for the year ending 31 December 2020 and a **statement of financial position** as on that date) for Myona Ltd.

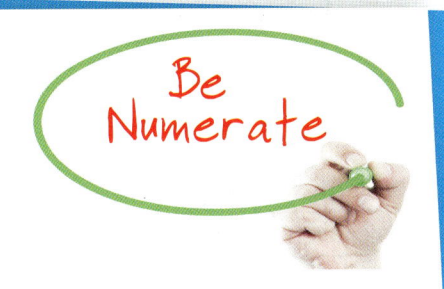

You are given the following information as on 31 December 2020.

- Closing stock €13,500
- Depreciation: machinery 10% and motor vehicles 20%
- The **authorised share capital** is €350,000 – €1 ordinary shares.

Don't forget **depreciation**; it will be an expense in the **income statement**. Depreciation will reduce the value of fixed assets in the **statement of financial position**.

Closing stock goes into the **income statement** and is a current asset in the **statement of financial position**.

Here are the steps to take when preparing to complete final accounts.

1. Draft a **skeleton layout** for income statement and statement of financial position (use the examples in this unit to create your templates).

2.13 BE BUSINESS: ENTERPRISE

2. Label **IS** (income statement) or **SFP** (statement of financial position) beside each entry in the trial balance (this has been done for you below). If you are unsure:

   - Check whether it's an **E**xpense (running costs) (it will go into the IS) or an **A**sset (something of money value) (it will go into the SFP) – **DEBIT**
   - Check whether it's Income/**R**evenue for the business) (it will go into the IS) or a **L**iability (something the business owes) (it will go into the SFP) – **CREDIT**

   Remember: EARL

3. Fill in the items and figures carefully in your skeleton layout.
4. Do all your calculations and totals. Your calculator will help.
5. Extra adjustments at the end of the trial balance will go in **twice**: closing stock and depreciation will be a note after the trial balance. Closing stock will appear in IS and SFP. Depreciation will go into IS and SFP.

The following is the **trial balance** of Myona Ltd on 31 December 2020.

Trial Balance of Myona Ltd as on 31 December 2020	Dr €	Cr €	IS or SFP?
Opening stock	38,500		IS
Purchases and sales	110,000	260,000	IS
Purchases returns		12,000	IS
Import duty	4,500		IS
Telephone	17,000		IS
Insurance	8,000		IS
Light and heat	13,800		IS
Interest receivable		7,500	IS
Machinery	140,000		SFP
Premises	300,000		SFP
Motor vehicles	68,000		SFP
Debtors and creditors	60,000	32,000	SFP
Cash	1,700		SFP
Reserves (profit and loss balance)		40,000	IS
Issued share capital: 350,000 €1 ordinary shares		350,000	SFP
15-year loan		60,000	SFP
	761,500	761,500	

Purchases returns are returns outwards. You bought them and they are the value of goods returned out of the business.

IS or SFP has been filled in above to show where each entry goes. Explain in each case why the item is listed as IS or SFP.

By law a business must keep a set of accounts.

WHO USES THE ACCOUNTS?

Once the final accounts have been prepared, who is interested in them?

Be the manager

Managers are interested in the **performance of a business**. Is performance in line with what was **budgeted**? If not, what changes must be implemented?

Be the investor

Investors are interested in the **profit**, to ensure a good return or a dividend on their shares. They will also compare their return with other businesses' returns.

Be the Revenue Commissioners – government

The Revenue Commissioners are interested in a business's profits to ensure that they are paying corporation tax, VAT and any other relevant taxes.

Be the banks

Banks are interested to see if their loans are safe and if the business will be able to make repayments and pay the interest due. If the business needs additional finance, the accounts will help the banks make a decision.

Be the creditors

Creditors are interested in receiving payments for the goods or services they supplied to the business on credit.

Be the employee

Employees are interested in job security and receiving their wages and benefits.

SCRUTINISING THE BUSINESS

Now that we have completed the final accounts, we need to understand the information. We need a tool that will help us to compare one set of figures against another set. Wouldn't it be helpful to compare this year's figures with last year's figures, or to compare the results from our IT company with figures from similar IT companies? We can use **ratios** to do this.

A ratio is a simple mathematical tool that helps us look at the relationship between numbers. For example, if there is one boy and three girls in a group, the ratio is 3 : 1 – for every one boy there are three girls.

We can analyse the business by examining the final accounts in detail using ratios.

Ratios are great for making comparisons:

- You can compare with past ratios, for example last year's figures and this year's figures.
- You can compare your ratios with other businesses in the same sector.
- You can compare your ratios with different business sectors. This will show trends.
- You can identify strengths or weaknesses of a firm.

We will now look at different types of ratio and the formulas and calculations used for each.

All figures for the various ratios should be taken from the final accounts (income statement and statement of financial position).

1. PROFITABILITY RATIOS

A profitability ratio measures the profitability of a business, which is a way to measure the business's performance. You might compare with last year's percentages (%) or with businesses in similar industries.

Gross profit %/Gross margin

$$\frac{\text{Gross profit}}{\text{Sales}} \times \frac{100}{1} = \underline{\qquad} \%$$

What might a company do if gross profit % is falling? They might try to increase sales and/or reduce cost of sales.

Net profit %/Net margin

$$\frac{\text{Net profit}}{\text{Sales}} \times \frac{100}{1} = \underline{\qquad} \%$$

What might a company do if net profit % is falling? They might try to reduce expenses. How?

Return on capital employed/Return on investment

$$\frac{\text{Net profit}}{\text{Capital employed}} \times \frac{100}{1} = \underline{\qquad} \%$$

Capital employed is the total in the statement of financial position. It is important to receive a good return.

2. LIQUIDITY RATIOS

Liquidity is the ability to pay debts as they fall due.

Liquidity ratios measure a business's ability to pay off its short-term debt. This is done by comparing its current assets to its current liabilities. The figures are found in the statement of financial position.

Current ratio/Working capital ratio

Current assets : Current liabilities

Ideal ratio 2 : 1

What might a company do if it has liquidity problems? It could keep stock levels low and make sure it has money coming from debtors.

Acid test ratio/Quick asset ratio

Current assets − closing stock : Current liabilities

Ideal ratio 1 : 1

The closing stock is taken from assets as it is not realistic that you would use your stock to pay debts. This ratio is a better indication of liquidity (being able to pay debts as they fall due).

Working capital = current assets − current liabilities

3. ACTIVITY/SOLVENCY RATIOS

Solvency is the ability of a company to meet its long-term financial obligations.

Total assets (fixed assets + current assets) are greater than external liabilities.

External liabilities/debt (current liabilities + long-term liabilities) is money owed by the business to people outside (external) the business. In this ratio we don't include shareholders.

Solvency ratios show a business's ability to make payments and pay off its long-term debt. Solvency ratios focus more on the long-term sustainability of a business than on the current liability payments.

A garage selling cars will have a low turnover (it will sell most of its cars once or twice a year), whereas the local supermarket will have a high turnover.

Rate of stock turnover

$$\frac{\text{Cost of sales}}{\text{Average stock}} = \text{X times}$$

4. DIVIDEND POLICY

A dividend is a percentage (%) of profits given by a business to its shareholders. The percentage is decided by the board of directors each year using the company's dividend policy.

Dividend Policy

$$\frac{\text{Dividend policy}}{\text{Issued share capital}} \times \frac{100}{1} = \underline{\quad\quad} \%$$

5. GEARING

Capital is the money a company starts with. Capital can be divided into **debt capital** and **equity capital**.

> **Debt capital** is a long-term source of finance on which interest is paid. It is also known as a **debenture**. Interest is at a fixed rate. An example is a long-term loan.
>
> The company also has shares that it sells. The total shares sold is known as ordinary share capital. This is called **equity capital**.
>
> The relationship between **equity** capital (ordinary shares) and **debt** capital (debentures) is called **gearing**.

A company is **highly geared** if the ratio of debt capital to equity capital is high. This indicates that the business is financed more from borrowings (debentures) than from shareholders' money (equity).

The information necessary to calculate gearing is available in the **statement of financial position**.

Debt : equity ratio

Debt capital : equity capital

EXAMPLE 10: HIGHLY GEARED

A company has a loan (debt capital) of €200,000 at 10% interest, to be repaid in 2020.

It has ordinary share capital (equity capital) of €50,000.

Debt : equity ratio

Debt capital : equity capital   €200,000 : €50,000

                                                                  4 : 1

This business is **highly geared** – its debt capital is four times its equity. It is relying on borrowed money more than money from shareholders.

FINAL ACCOUNTS 2.13

EXAMPLE 11: LOW GEARED

A company has a loan (debt capital) of €100,000 at 15% interest, to be repaid in 2019.

It has ordinary share capital (equity capital) of €500,000.

Debt : equity ratio

Debt capital : equity capital   €100,000 : €500,000

                                 0.20 : 1

This business is **low geared** – its debt capital is 0.20 of its equity. It is relying on shareholders' money more than borrowed money.

So it's good to have less debt capital.

WORKING WITH OTHERS

Be the stakeholders: roleplay a stakeholders' meeting. Each student must take a role. Jot down your learning after the activity.

Top Tip!

Be aware of these ratios if you want to use them for a Finance in Action report.

Business in Action Idea

Compile a report scrutinising SinCom.

Success criteria:
- An appropriate title
- State new information learned
- Take the accounts of the business and apply at least three important ratios
- Explain your answers
- Use visuals

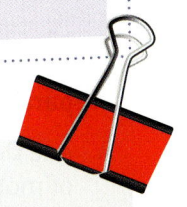

CHECKING IN...

Which of the following do you agree or disagree with? Place a tick ✓ in the appropriate box.

	Agree	Disagree
Long-term loans are known as equity.		
Gearing is the relationship between equity and debt capital.		
Liquidity is fixed assets: current assets.		
Total assets = fixed assets + current assets.		

387

2.13 BE BUSINESS: ENTERPRISE

	Agree	Disagree
Liquid assets = current assets – closing stock.		
A debtor is someone we buy goods on credit from.		
A creditor is someone we sell goods to on credit.		
A debtor is an asset.		
A creditor is a liability.		
Depreciation is an expense.		
A loan is an asset.		
Machinery is a liability.		
Income statement shows your profit.		
Financial statement shows assets and liabilities.		
Accounts don't show all aspects of a business.		
An asset is something of money value.		
Insurance charges can change.		
A liability is something we owe.		
Interest paid on a loan is an expense.		
Money in the bank is an asset.		

WORKING WITH OTHERS

Log on to kahoot.it and use the above information to create a quiz.

Accounting in Practice Questions

Preparing accounts

A. Ace Devices manufactures innovative parts to protect cables of mobile phone chargers. Look at the trial balance and use your knowledge from this unit to answer the questions on the following page.

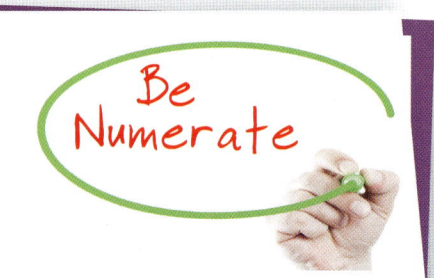

Be Numerate

Trial Balance of Ace Devices on 31 December 2019		
	Dr €	Cr €
Purchases and sales	116,000	283,200
Opening stock 1/1/2019	16,000	
Purchases returns		6,000
Interest	2,500	
Advertising	8,000	
Debtors and creditors	19,000	15,700
Wages	28,000	
Insurance	3,600	
20-year loan		30,000
Motor vehicles	80,000	
Bank overdraft		6,000
Cash	7,800	
Equipment	150,000	
Buildings	330,000	
Issued share capital: 420,000 €1 ordinary shares		420,000
	760,900	760,900

Questions

1. Calculate net purchases.
2. Why might you have purchases returns?
3. What is the legal amount of shares that Ace Devices can have?
4. What's the actual amount of shares that Ace Devices availed of?
5. Explain a debtor. State whether it is an asset or a liability and say why.
6. Explain a creditor. State whether it is an asset or a liability and say why.
7. What is depreciation?
8. Calculate depreciation for motor vehicles and for equipment.
9. Why do businesses advertise?
10. When might wages increase?
11. Explain 20-year loan and state what the cost of a loan is called.
12. Is a loan equity or debt capital? Explain.
13. Are ordinary shares equity or debt capital? Explain.
14. Explain an overdraft.
15. Explain insurance. When can insurance increase?

16. List the current assets and calculate total current assets.
17. List the fixed assets and calculate total fixed assets.
18. List the current liabilities and calculate total current liabilities.
19. What is a trial balance?

B. You are given the following information as on 31 December 2019:
- Closing stock €19,000
- Depreciation: motor vehicles 10% and equipment 12%
- Authorised share capital is 600,000 €1 ordinary shares.

1. From your knowledge of accounts, create an **income statement** for Ace Devices. Copy and use the template below.

2. From your knowledge of accounts, create a **statement of financial position** for Ace Devices. Copy and use the template below.

Income Statement of Ace Devices for year ended			
		€	€
Sales		x	
Sales returns		x	x
Less cost of sales			
Opening Stock 1/1/19		x	
Purchases	x		
Less purchases returns	x		
Net purchases		x	
Cost of goods available for sale		x	
Less closing stock		x	
Cost of sales			x
Gross profit			x
Add gains			
Commission receivable			x
			x
Less expenses			
Total expenses			
Net profit			

Statement of Financial Position of Ace Devices as at			
	Cost €	Dep €	NBV €
Fixed assets			
	x		x
	x		x
	x	x	x
	x		x
Total fixed assets	x	x	x
Current assets			
	x		
	x		
	x		
	x	x	
Current liabilities			
	x		
	x	x	
Working capital			x
Total net assets			x
Financed by	Authorised	Issued	
	x	x	
		x	x
Long-term liability			
			x
Capital employed			x

C. Using information from the statement of financial position, scrutinise the Ace Devices business.

Profitability Ratios for Ace Devices

Gross profit %/Gross margin

$$\frac{\text{Gross profit}}{\text{Sales}} \times \frac{100}{1} = \underline{\hspace{2cm}} \times \frac{100}{1} = \underline{\hspace{1cm}} \%$$

Net profit %/Net margin

$$\frac{\text{Net profit}}{\text{Sales}} \times \frac{100}{1} = \underline{\hspace{2cm}} \times \frac{100}{1} = \underline{\hspace{1cm}} \%$$

Return on capital employed/Return on investment

$$\frac{\text{Net profit}}{\text{Capital employed}} \times \frac{100}{1} = \underline{\hspace{2cm}} \times \frac{100}{1} = \underline{\hspace{1cm}} \%$$

Liquidity Ratios for Ace Devices

Current Ratio/Working Capital Ratio

Current assets : Current liabilities   =   :

Acid Test Ratio/Quick Asset Ratio

(Current assets – closing stock) : Current liabilities   =   :

Discuss Gearing for Ace Devices

Equity : Debt capital   =   :

Accounting in Practice Questions

Comparing a business

iBaubles Ltd provides 3D virtual baubles using Solidworks software. They also personalise baubles. One of their products is a bauble with your favourite place painted on it. When you look at the bauble, you can imagine that you're in your favourite place.

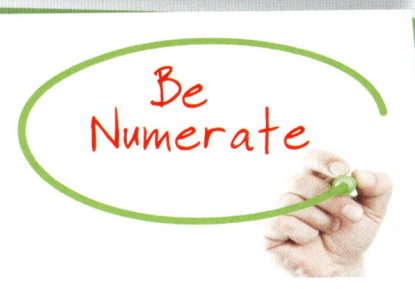

Be Numerate

iBaubles Ltd supplied the following results for the year ending 31 December 2021.

Net profit percentage	12%
Current ratio	3 : 1
Return on capital employed	4%

iBaubles Ltd supplied the following information for the year ending 31 December 2022:

- Net sales €300,000
- Opening stock €40,000
- Closing stock €20,000
- Cost of sales €150,000
- Net profit €45,000
- Current assets (including closing stock) €360,000
- Current liabilities €110,000
- Capital employed €750,000

Questions

1. Using the 2022 information above, calculate the following ratios:
   a) Net profit percentage (margin)
   b) Current ratio
   c) Return on capital employed
2. Compare the performance of 2022 with 2021. You may not require all the figures given. State whether it is an improvement or a disimprovement.
3. Present the above information in a report.

SUMMARY OF ACCOUNTS

Accounts cover performance over a period of time. **Income statement** is based on the **past**.

1. INCOME STATEMENT

The **income statement** is a picture of the business income versus the business expenses. It shows the profit. **Net profit** is the actual profit made by the business when expenses have been deducted from the gross profit. If expenses are greater than the gross profit, the business would make a **net loss**.

- What income did we earn?
- What expenses did we incur?
- Did we make a **profit or loss?**

(Profit = Income is greater than expenses)

(Loss = Income is less than expenses)

2. STATEMENT OF FINANCIAL POSITION

The statement of financial position is a **list of assets and liabilities**. It is based on the present, for example it is 'as at 31 December 2020', if that is the date your financial year ends.

It is a **financial snapshot** of your business on that date. It shows what the business **owns** and what it **owes**.

3. CASH FLOW/BUDGET

Cash flow shows liquidity.

- How much cash do we have?
- How much cash do we pay out?
- Do we have access to cash in case of shortfalls? You need to pay bills as they fall due. Otherwise you're in trouble!

PROBLEMS WITH ACCOUNTS

Accounts have their limitations – they can't solve all business problems.

- Accounts are based on **past** figures. They don't anticipate changes in the economy, such as Ireland's change from 'boom to bust'. You will study economic indicators in Unit 3.9 in Strand 3, in particular inflation (rising prices) which can affect your analysis of accounts.
- Accounts don't show if there are any industrial relations problems in the business.
- Figures in the accounts may not be the correct value. Accounting figures can be overestimated or underestimated.

2.13 BE BUSINESS: ENTERPRISE

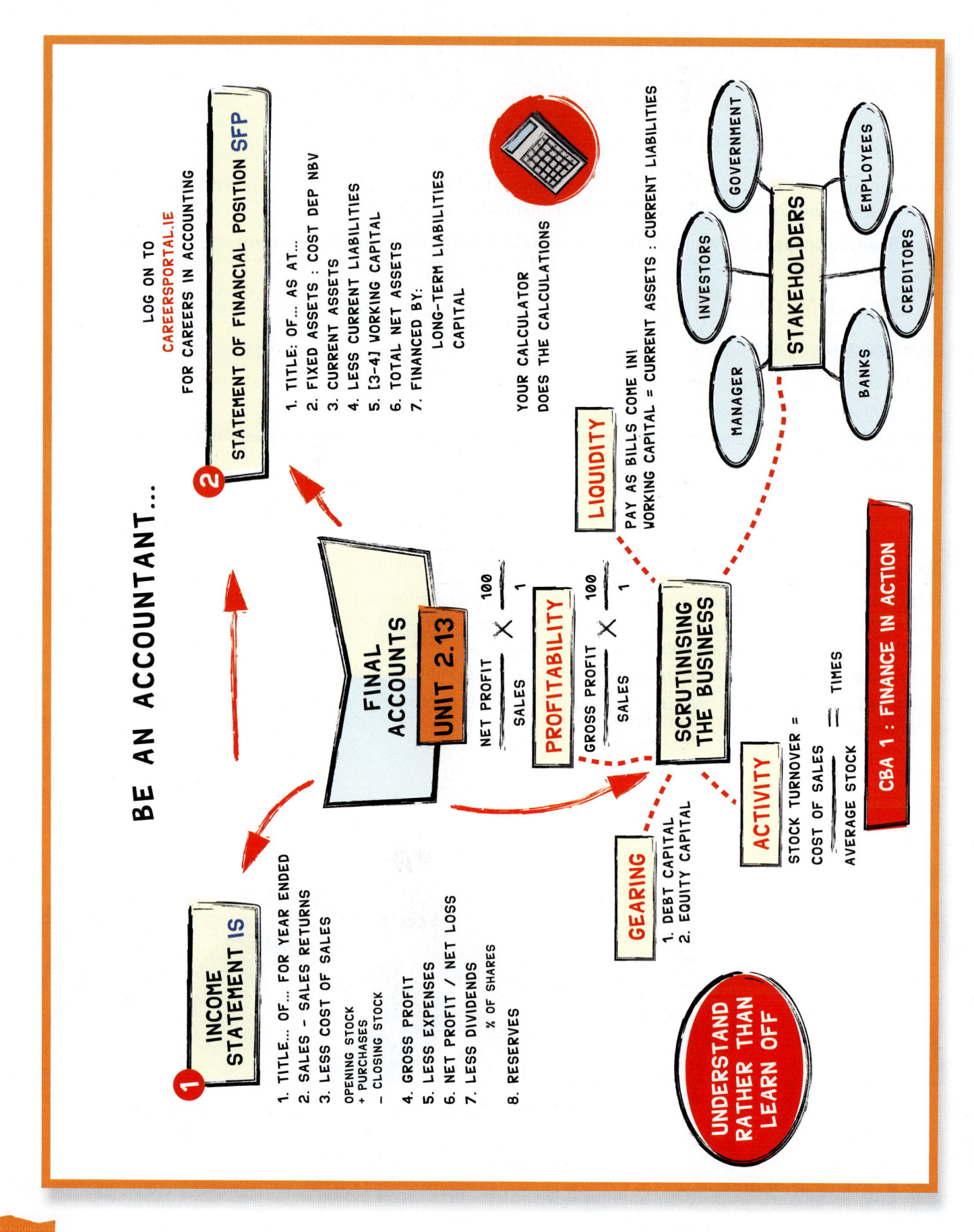

BE AN ACCOUNTANT...

LOG ON TO
CAREERSPORTAL.IE
FOR CAREERS IN ACCOUNTING

② STATEMENT OF FINANCIAL POSITION SFP

1. TITLE: OF... AS AT...
2. FIXED ASSETS : COST DEP NBV
3. CURRENT ASSETS
4. LESS CURRENT LIABILITIES
5. [3-4] WORKING CAPITAL
6. TOTAL NET ASSETS
7. FINANCED BY:
   LONG-TERM LIABILITIES
   CAPITAL

YOUR CALCULATOR DOES THE CALCULATIONS

STAKEHOLDERS
- GOVERNMENT
- EMPLOYEES
- CREDITORS
- BANKS
- MANAGER
- INVESTORS

FINAL ACCOUNTS — UNIT 2.13

PROFITABILITY
$$\frac{\text{NET PROFIT}}{\text{SALES}} \times \frac{100}{1}$$
$$\frac{\text{GROSS PROFIT}}{\text{SALES}} \times \frac{100}{1}$$

LIQUIDITY
PAY AS BILLS COME IN!
WORKING CAPITAL = CURRENT ASSETS : CURRENT LIABILITIES

SCRUTINISING THE BUSINESS

GEARING
1. DEBT CAPITAL
2. EQUITY CAPITAL

ACTIVITY
STOCK TURNOVER = $\frac{\text{COST OF SALES}}{\text{AVERAGE STOCK}}$ = TIMES

CBA 1 : FINANCE IN ACTION

① INCOME STATEMENT IS

1. TITLE... OF... FOR YEAR ENDED
2. SALES – SALES RETURNS
3. LESS COST OF SALES
   OPENING STOCK
   + PURCHASES
   – CLOSING STOCK
4. GROSS PROFIT
5. LESS EXPENSES
6. NET PROFIT / NET LOSS
7. LESS DIVIDENDS
   % OF SHARES
8. RESERVES

UNDERSTAND RATHER THAN LEARN OFF

394

Be Prepared: My Support Sheets

Completing the activities here will help you to reflect on and reinforce your learning before you move on to the next unit.

- Write down the **key terms** in this unit and make sure you understand them. See if they match the ones at the back of the book.
- List the key **concepts/themes** in this unit.
- List the three **most interesting points** about this unit.

Enterprise in Action Idea!

Create a noticeboard for assets and another for liabilities. You could us the online noticeboard creation tool Padlet (www.padlet.com). A feature of this tool is that you can insert weblinks to the different headings you use.

Success criteria:
- Title
- Examples and explanations
- Include relevant visuals (and links if using Padlet)
- If using Padlet, link to a relevant YouTube clip

Business in Action Idea!

Create two tweets using the Twitter template at the back of the book, one on assets and a second on liabilities.

Success criteria:
- Title and explanation
- Include an attachment
- Write in a personal way – Twitter is about person-to-person communication
- Readability – make it easy to read
- Retweetability – people should want to share it

QUESTION TIME

1. Explain income statement.
2. Explain financial statement.
3. Explain the reasons for preparing accounts.
4. Compare an income statement with a statement of financial position.

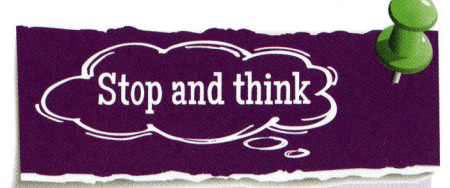

Stop and think

Do I have any questions or concerns?

What are the mistakes or errors I made in this unit?

5. Compare assets and liabilities.
6. Compare and contrast expenses and income.
7. Write a short report on final accounts.

EVALUATE MY LEARNING: DAR

Describe
- Did I/we meet my/our learning intentions?
- What went well? What are my/our strengths?

Assess
- How did I/we work with others?
- Were there challenges?

Recommend
- How might I improve?
- What skills and learning might I apply to new situations?

Do your **Key Check** in the workbook for this unit and then mark your learning position on the following rating scale:

Understood nothing — 1 2 3 4 5 6 7 8 9 10 — Fully understood

How can you move up the rating scale? What can you **say**, **make**, **write** and **do** to illustrate your learning?

CBA 1 Business in Action (Group Activity):
Will I use this unit for my topic for **Finance in Action**?

You need to be preparing for your CBAs

- Exceptional
- Above expectations
- In line with expectations
- Yet to meet expectations

③ OUR ECONOMY

In this strand you will study the dynamic relationship between the local, national and international economic situation. You will improve your ability to identify and understand basic economic concepts as they relate to personal finance, enterprise and the Irish economy. You will learn about the demand and supply of goods and services, the role of the government in managing the economy, and about economic issues such as trade, employment and Ireland's membership of the European Union (EU).

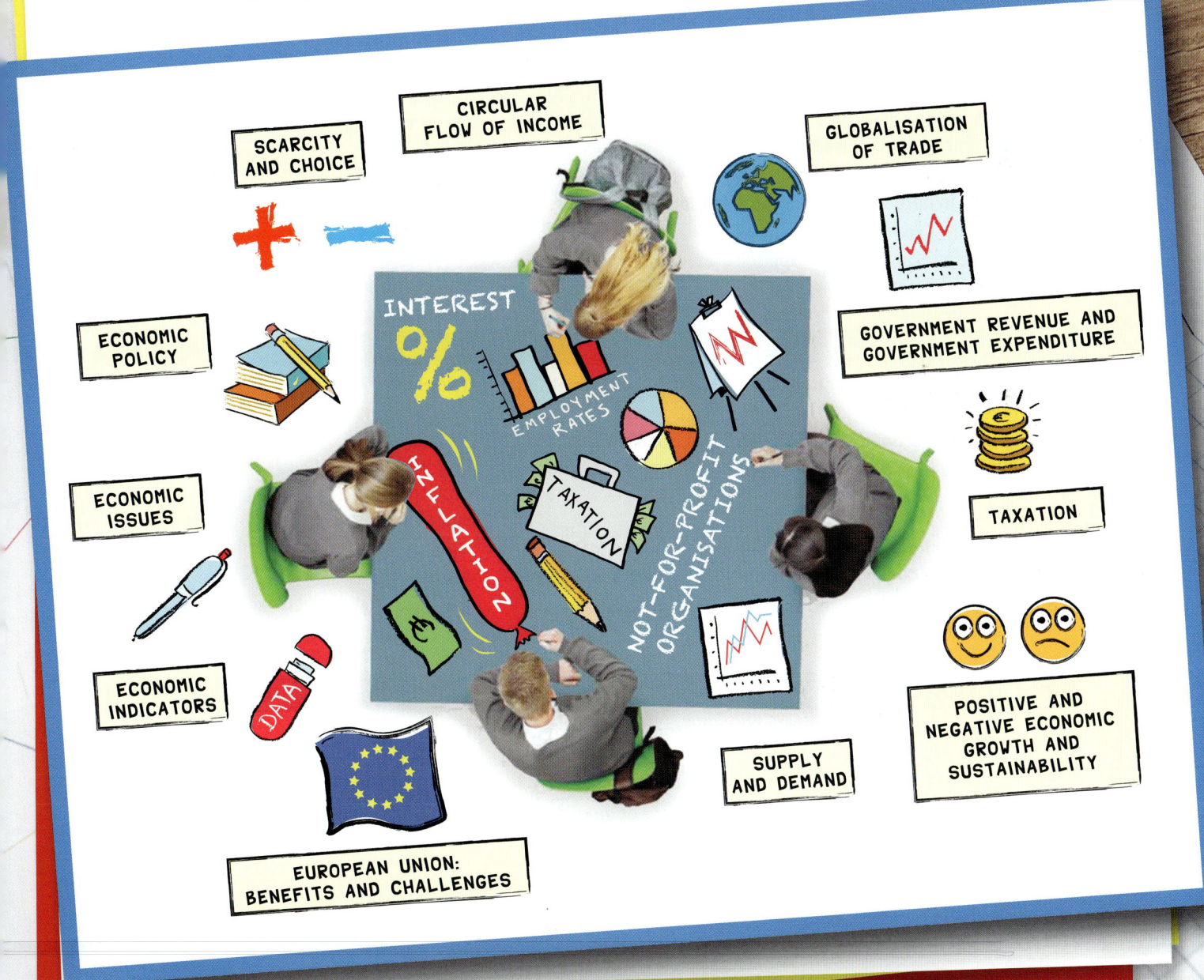

- SCARCITY AND CHOICE
- CIRCULAR FLOW OF INCOME
- GLOBALISATION OF TRADE
- ECONOMIC POLICY
- GOVERNMENT REVENUE AND GOVERNMENT EXPENDITURE
- ECONOMIC ISSUES
- TAXATION
- ECONOMIC INDICATORS
- POSITIVE AND NEGATIVE ECONOMIC GROWTH AND SUSTAINABILITY
- SUPPLY AND DEMAND
- EUROPEAN UNION: BENEFITS AND CHALLENGES

STRAND 3 LEARNING OUTCOMES

Engaging with economics you should be able to: ✓

OUTCOME	UNIT
MANGING MY RESOURCES	
3.1 Explain how scarcity of economic resources results in individuals having to make choices; predict possible consequences of these choices	Scarcity and choice
3.2 Explain how individuals, organisations (profit and not-for-profit) and the government work together to distribute economic resources used to produce goods and services	Circular flow of income
3.3 Evaluate how changes in the supply and demand of goods and services in different markets can affect prices	Supply and demand
3.4 Differentiate between different sources of government revenue and government expenditure	Government revenue and government expenditure
EXPLORING BUSINESS	
3.5 Examine the purpose of taxation from a financial, social, legal and ethical perspective	Taxation
3.6 Explain how economic growth can impact positively and negatively on society and the environment and justify the promotion of sustainable development	Positive and negative economic growth and sustainability
3.7 Debate the implications of globalisation of trade, including the benefits and challenges of international trade	Globalisation of trade
3.8 Discuss the economic and social benefits and challenges of Ireland's membership of the EU	European Union: benefits and challenges
USING SKILLS FOR BUSINESS	
3.9 Explain the relevance of economic indicators such as inflation, employment rates, interest rates, economic growth, national income and national debt for individuals and the economy	Economic indicators
3.10 Use knowledge and information from a range of media sources to discuss current economic issues and present an informed view	Economic issues
3.11 Evaluate the benefits and costs of a government economic policy and assess who enjoys the benefits and who bears the costs	Economic policy

INTRODUCTION

Most of you are already familiar with our economy. When you listen to the radio, tweet, Instagram, share and like on Facebook, watch TV or listen to your family and friends talk about everyday topics you are more than likely listening to information about our economy. Prices increasing, unemployment, employment, savings, water charges, taxation, household charges, government and population – all of these topics are what make up the subject of economics.

WHAT IS ECONOMICS ABOUT?

Economics is the study of the production, consumption and transfer of wealth.

Here are some of the questions that economics tries to answer:

1. How do people decide what to buy?
2. How do producers decide what to produce?
3. Why do prices increase?
4. Why might €10 that we have now be worth less in ten years' time?
5. What causes unemployment?
6. Why does the government take money from us?
7. What does the government spend money on?
8. Why does our country trade with other countries? Why is it a member of the EU?
9. Why are some countries wealthier than others?
10. Why do governments make certain decisions?

BE AN ECONOMIST

An economist carries out research, collects and examines data (information), monitors economic developments and comes up with forecasts (guesses).

An economist's research might focus on topics such as oil costs, inflation (rising prices), interest rates (cost of borrowing), farm prices, exports, imports, employment and population.

In Business Studies you have an opportunity to be an **economist**. You will learn about the economy that we live in and will have an opportunity to do some research too. You can work with others collaboratively to prepare for **Economics in Action**, and you will also have to reflect on your individual contribution. The following chapters contain templates and questions that will help you with your research.

There may also be an area that you have a particular interest in and would like to create a presentation on.

Remember, always evaluate and articulate the skills that you have developed.

Enjoy economics!

Time to think

1. Can you name an economist?
2. Would you like a career in economics?
3. Do you know anyone studying economics?
4. Perhaps after studying this unit you may be interested!

Top Tip!

You will encounter numerous key words in this Business Studies course. Document the key words/concepts in your folder. Use the **Business Studies key word dictionary**.

When you come across a new word, **listen** to the word, **say** the word, **write** it down and **apply** it.

Susan Hayes

David McWilliams

3.1 SCARCITY AND CHOICE

3.1 Explain how scarcity of economic resources results in individuals having to make choices; predict possible consequences of these choices.

Learning Intentions

At the end of this unit I will:
- Know and understand about limited economic resources
- Know and understand scarcity
- Be able to discuss choices we have to make
- Value opportunity cost and possible consequences

Making the links with other LOs:

- 1.1 Personal resources
- 1.2 Personal income and expenditure
- 1.3 Personal financial life cycle
- 3.2 Circular flow of income
- 3.10 Economic issues
- 3.11 Economic policy

Are there other LOs?

Key Concepts

- ✓ Scarcity
- ✓ Choice
- ✓ Opportunity cost

Wonderful Worthwhile Websites

www.businesseducation.ie
www.tutor2u.net/economics
www.finfacts.ie
www.cso.ie
www.centralbank.ie
www.revenue.ie

INTRODUCTION

> **Economics** is the study of how individuals, households, for-profit organisations, not-for-profit organisations and our government choose how to use finite resources to try to satisfy their **needs** and **wants**. A **need** is essential or very important rather than just desirable, e.g. food and water. A **want** is something that you wish for, e.g. an iPad.

Our wants are continuously changing. You might already have forgotten about something that you desperately wanted last Christmas! People's wants generally far exceed their limited resources; we only have a certain income to spend.

It is important to remember too that some resources are non-renewable. A non-renewable resource is also called a finite resource. This is a resource that cannot be replaced when it is used up, e.g. coal.

While part of economics can be explained through formulas, graphs and statistics, the fundamental (important) principles of economics are really all about human behaviour. Economics is about individuals, households, organisations (for-profit and not-for-profit) and government.

RATIONAL AND IRRATIONAL BEHAVIOUR

Economic principles assume **rational behaviour**, but humans often act **irrationally**. Even our government can act irrationally!

RATIONAL BEHAVIOUR

Rational behaviour is a decision-making process people use to make choices that result in them achieving satisfaction.

We assume that people would prefer to:
- be **better off** rather than **worse off**
- have **more of** rather than **less of**

For example, a person is more likely to buy an item at a lower price than a higher one, or to buy items on sale if they believe it to be better value.

IRRATIONAL BEHAVIOUR

Irrational behaviour is the opposite of this. People can behave irrationally when they are lazy when making choices, or are overly influenced by other people.

If the price of ice cream dropped tomorrow, some people might rush out and buy lots of ice cream and store it. Others might assume the ice cream is inferior in quality and not buy it at all.

> **'3Ts' = Think, Turn, Talk**
>
> Have you ever acted irrationally when you bought a product? Explain your decision-making process.
>
> Economics is easier to understand when you understand how human behaviour is tied in with financial (money) decisions. Economics is a social science – a science that studies aspects of human behaviour.
>
> You are familiar with different **needs** and **wants** from Unit 1.1 (Personal Resources) and you have also learned about the importance of budgeting and making planned and informed financial decisions.
>
> We can't have everything we want. Why? Because we have **limited resources**.

SCARCITY

We always want more than we can have. This concept in economics is known as **scarcity**. Scarcity requires us as individuals to make **choices**. We have to **allocate** our resources because our resources won't be adequate to meet unlimited wants. Economics studies how people use **scarce** resources in order to satisfy **unlimited needs and wants**.

Scarcity can be very powerful. Scarcity can force us to:

- make hard choices
- go without a product or service
- pay extra for a product or service
- look elsewhere for the things we want

Scarcity also forces businesses and the government to make choices; to do without, to pay extra and to look elsewhere.

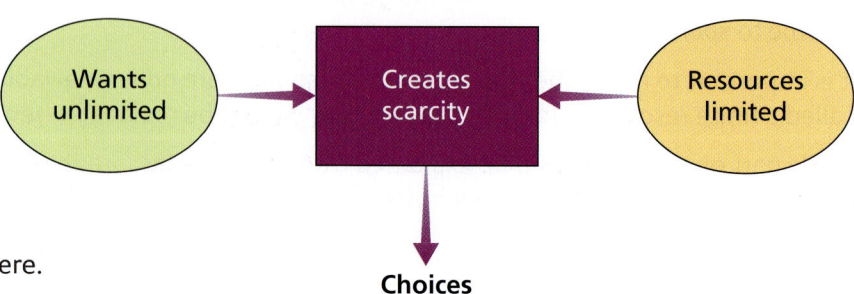

MAKING CHOICES

Individuals have to make choices. So do organisations (for-profit and not-for-profit) and governments.

Businesses (for-profit organisations) have **limited resources.** A business must make choices regarding:

- the **type** of goods and services to produce
- the **quantity** that should be made
- the **price** to charge

The government has **limited resources** and lots of needs to fill. It raises income through **taxation** and **borrowing** to provide vital services such as health, education, social welfare, defence, infrastructure (roads, communication), etc.

For the individual, organisations (for-profit and not-for-profit) and government, managing **limited resources** is a constant challenge.

Choices have to be made about to how best to use those limited resources.

You are constantly making choices. Should you spend your savings on a drone or use the money to attend Irish college to improve your Irish and hopefully your education and your future career?

It's not just a matter of choosing one over the other. What are the implications of each option? Perhaps the drone will give you hours of benefit. You may use it for photography. If you attend Irish college, your Irish may not necessarily improve. Perhaps you don't need Irish for your particular choice of career.

- **A family/household** may choose to cut out luxuries and forgo buying a new car. However, there may be implications, such as the cost of repairing the old car and meeting NCT requirements.
- **A business** (for-profit organisation) might have to cut back on expenses, for example wages, and may even let some employees go. This might result in strike action and all the costs associated with this.
- **A voluntary** (not-for-profit) organisation might have to limit its services rather than doing all the things it wants to.
- **A government** may have to cut spending on health, which will lead to busier emergency departments, longer waiting lists for procedures, unhappy staff and unhappy patients. But if the government decides to increase taxation to pay for the hospitals, will people be happy to pay the extra tax?

It's challenging to keep everyone happy and to do what is in the best interest of all. Decisions and choices have to be made.

Time to think

Can you think of other choices that a business might make, perhaps to do with finance or its employees? With a limited budget and finances, a business will try to produce as cheaply as possible, ensuring it covers all its costs as well as making a profit.

Scarcity = needs and wants > resources

Time to think

Have you ever discovered that something you want isn't available? Think about this in relation to the concept of scarcity. What choice did you make?

When a problem arises, we have to make choices.

3.1 BE BUSINESS: OUR ECONOMY

WORKING WITH OTHERS

Working in pairs or small groups, predict the possible consequences of the choices detailed below. Remember that all choices have consequences.

1. **BE ME**

   Predict what might happen if you spend all your allowance on clothes at the start of the week and there is a disco on Saturday night.

2. **BE A BUSINESS**

   Predict what might happen if a business spends all its cash on decorating its premises and putting up a new sign. At the end of the week, they have no money to pay suppliers.

3. **BE A NOT-FOR-PROFIT ORGANISATION**

   Predict what might happen if a not-for-profit organisation spends all its cash on promoting a fundraising event. They will have no money to provide refreshments at the event.

4. **BE THE GOVERNMENT**

   What if the government spends millions on upgrading our roads and there is a need for money to be spent on hospital care?

OPPORTUNITY COST

The question of choice leads us to another economic concept known as **opportunity cost**.

> **Opportunity cost** is the benefit or value of something that must be given up to acquire or achieve something else.

Every choice has an associated opportunity cost.

When we go shopping, we constantly have to make choices, but by choosing one thing we are not choosing something else.

> By buying one product, another product is forgone. Therefore, scarcity creates a need for decisions and compromises to be made.

Along with financial costs and opportunity costs, there are also **environmental costs**. A lot of our **resources** are **limited**. Our country has limited amounts of land and natural resources. Our government has to make **choices** that benefit our society as a whole.

CALCULATING FINANCIAL COST AND OPPORTUNITY COST

EXAMPLE 1: OPPORTUNITY COST

Joe has €50 to spend. He is trying to decide whether to buy a soccer jersey or to buy some computer games. If Joe buys the soccer jersey, the cost to him (apart from the financial cost of €50) is the computer games that he cannot now buy. This is known as the **opportunity cost** because he has given up the opportunity to buy his second choice. The **financial cost is €50**.

The Individual – Joe	
Financial cost	€50
Opportunity cost	Cost of the next best alternative (computer games)

Time to think

Can you think of an example of an opportunity cost in your own experience? What was the product or service? What was the financial cost? What was the cost of the next best alternative?

EXAMPLE 2: OPPORTUNITY COST

If Sharp Shoes Ltd chooses to spend an additional €200,000 on updating its technology, the opportunity cost may be to forgo the introduction of bonuses for employees.

The Business – Sharp Shoes Ltd	
Financial cost	€200,000
Opportunity cost	Cost of the next best alternative (bonuses for employees)

EXAMPLE 3: OPPORTUNITY COST

If the government chooses to spend €60 million on hospitals it may have to forgo the opportunity of spending money on education, for example iPads for all Business Studies classrooms.

The Government	
Financial cost	€60 million
Opportunity cost	Cost of the next best alternative (iPads for Business Studies classrooms)

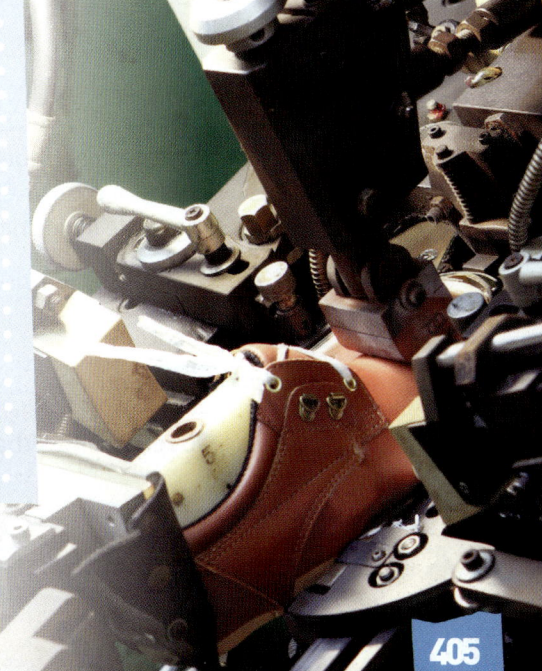

SCENARIO 1

Katie has €350 to spend. She is trying to decide whether to buy an Xbox for €349.99 or to buy a beauty set. Katie is a beauty blogger and hopes to start her own beauty business. She spends €349.99 on the beauty set. Copy and fill in the following table in your copy.

The Individual – Katie	
Financial cost	
Opportunity cost	

Be the Individual: What advice might you give Katie? Why?

SCENARIO 2

Bake is a business making luxury biscuits. The business is trying to decide whether to spend an additional €5,000 on updating their marketing software or to give their employees a bonus of €500 each. They decide to give their 10 employees a bonus of €500. Copy and fill in the following table in your copy.

The Business – Bake	
Financial cost	
Opportunity cost	

Be the Business: What choice might you have made and why?

SCENARIO 3

Our government must choose between spending €50 million on upgrading roads or on increasing nurses' wages at a cost of €50 million. The government decides to upgrade roads. Copy and fill in the following table in your copy.

The Government	
Financial cost	
Opportunity cost	

Be the Government: What choice would you make? Why?

SCARCITY AND CHOICE 3.1

CHECKING IN...

1. Write an explanation of opportunity cost in your own words.
2. Create your own examples of opportunity cost for an individual (based on you and a real-life experience), a family, a business and our government. What might be the effect of your examples on our planet?
3. Which of the following are needs and which are wants? Copy the table below into your copy and place a √ in the appropriate box.

	Need	Want
Food		
Water		
iPad		
Clothes		
Ronaldo football jersey		
iPhone		

4. Copy the grid below and match each term (A–D) with the correct statement (1–4).

1	Forgo one item for another item	A	Rational behaviour
2	When the supply of a product is in short supply	B	Opportunity cost
3	Rather be better off than worse off	C	Limited resources
4	Restricted in what we can buy	D	Scarcity

1	2	3	4

5. Darcy has €1,000. He can pay to go on the school tour to Disneyland Paris, or purchase a new Apple computer. He decides to purchase the computer.
    a. What is the financial cost to Darcy?
    b. What is the opportunity cost?
    c. What choice might you have made?
       What about your Business Studies class? What choice would they make?
    d. What are the effects of Darcy's choice on our planet?

WORKING WITH OTHERS

OIL CRISIS

Your grandparents probably remember the oil crisis in the 1970s when there was an oil shortage. Oil was scarce, people wanted to buy oil, but only a limited amount was available.

This is a good example of scarcity: wants are more than what is available. The supply of oil was low. The demand was greater than the supply so the oil was scarce.

- What choices might you make if there was an oil crisis tomorrow?
- Can you think of any other crisis scenario?

3.1 BE BUSINESS: OUR ECONOMY

CASE STUDY: AN EXTREME EXAMPLE OF SCARCITY

The 1845 Famine in Ireland was only 160 years ago.

A famine is an extreme example of scarcity. In a famine, a country or group of people suffers extreme hunger, even starvation. In Ireland in 1845, the potato crop developed a fungus called Phytophthora, which caused the potatoes to rot very quickly. Potatoes were a major part of the Irish diet, and they were eaten at every meal. When this extreme scarcity happened, farmers lost their income, could not pay their rent and were evicted by landlords. People starved – at least one million died. People emigrated to the USA, England and Australia. They travelled by sea in ships known as 'coffin ships'. The ships were overcrowded and there were many infectious diseases, such as typhus. The population of Ireland dropped by 25%.

CASE STUDY: ONE DECISION: MANY RESULTS/CHOICES

1. **BE THE GOVERNMENT**
   The government introduces **penalty points** along with **fines**. **Capital costs** include the introduction of speed cameras, speed vans, etc. These are a long-term cost. In the short term the government receives **income** from the fines.

2. **BE SOCIETY**
   The introduction of penalty points reduces speed, drivers concentrate and there are fewer accidents and injuries. As a result there is a decrease in the number of insurance claims.

3. **BE INSURANCE COMPANIES**
   Insurance companies will increase premiums if drivers go over a certain number of points; premiums might increase by up to 300%. Insurance companies will benefit financially, with greater profits.

4. **BE THE INDIVIDUAL**
   The individual has to make **choices**: become more conscious of the rules of the road, speeding and using a mobile phone while driving. If the individual acquires penalty points, there will be the cost of a fine and his or her insurance premiums will increase.

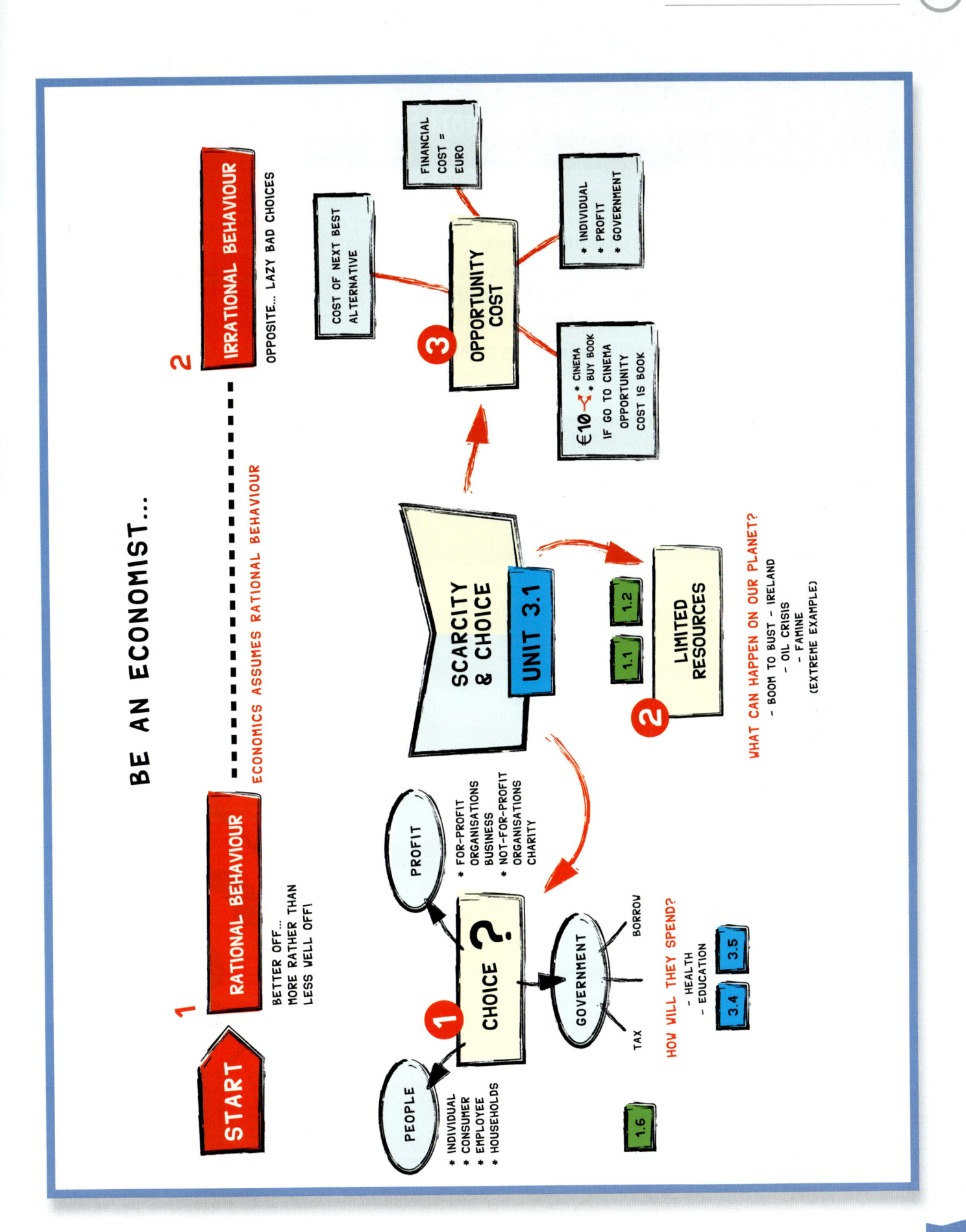

SCARCITY AND CHOICE 3.1

BE AN ECONOMIST...

START

1 RATIONAL BEHAVIOUR
BETTER OFF...
MORE RATHER THAN LESS WELL OFF!

ECONOMICS ASSUMES RATIONAL BEHAVIOUR

2 IRRATIONAL BEHAVIOUR
OPPOSITE... LAZY BAD CHOICES

SCARCITY & CHOICE — UNIT 3.1

1 CHOICE ?
- PROFIT
  * FOR-PROFIT ORGANISATIONS BUSINESS
  * NOT-FOR-PROFIT ORGANISATIONS CHARITY
- PEOPLE
  * INDIVIDUAL
  * CONSUMER
  * EMPLOYEE
  * HOUSEHOLDS
- GOVERNMENT
  - TAX
  - BORROW

HOW WILL THEY SPEND?
- HEALTH
- EDUCATION

(3.4) (3.5)

(1.6)

2 LIMITED RESOURCES

(1.1) (1.2)

WHAT CAN HAPPEN ON OUR PLANET?
- BOOM TO BUST - IRELAND
- OIL CRISIS
- FAMINE (EXTREME EXAMPLE)

3 OPPORTUNITY COST
- FINANCIAL COST = EURO
- COST OF NEXT BEST ALTERNATIVE
- * INDIVIDUAL
  * PROFIT
  * GOVERNMENT
- €10 * CINEMA
       * BUY BOOK
  IF GO TO CINEMA OPPORTUNITY COST IS BOOK

409

Be Prepared: My Support Sheets

Completing the activities here will help you to reflect on and reinforce your learning before you move on to the next unit.
- Write down the **key terms** in this unit and make sure you understand them. See if they match the ones at the back of the book.
- List the **key concepts/themes** in this unit.
- List the **three most interesting points** about this topic.

Write a quiz

Write a quiz based on this unit. Write three questions that relate to the scarcity of economic resources. Pick one of your quiz questions and give your own answer in detail.

Economics in Action Idea!

Write or create a project on 'Scarcity and Choice'. You could use a digital tool to create the project such as Padlet (www.padlet.com) or PowerPoint. Animoto (www.animoto.com) is an online video creation tool if you want to add video.

Success criteria:
- A clear title
- Clear explanation of the concepts
- Visual stimulus

QUESTION TIME

1. Explain limited resources.
2. Discuss opportunity cost and create an example.
3. Explain scarcity and give an example.
4. What is economics?
5. Only individuals have to make choices because of limited resources. Discuss.
6. What might happen at a time of scarcity? Provide an example.

SCARCITY AND CHOICE 3.1

EVALUATE MY LEARNING: DAR

Describe
- Did I/we meet my/our learning intentions?
- What went well? What are my/our strengths?

Assess
- How did I/we work with others?
- Were there challenges?

Recommend
- How might I improve?
- What skills and learning might I apply to new situations?

Do your **Key Check** in the workbook for this unit and then mark your learning position on the following rating scale:

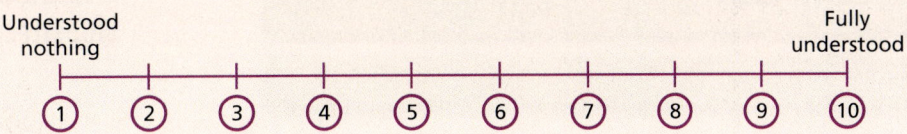

Understood nothing — 1 2 3 4 5 6 7 8 9 10 — Fully understood

How can you move up the rating scale? What can you **say**, **make**, **write** and **do** to illustrate your learning?

CBA 1 Business in Action:
Will I use this unit for my topic for my **Economics in Action** and **Finance in Action**?

CBA 2 Presentation:
Will I use this unit for my topic for my **Presentation**?

You need to be preparing for your CBAs
- Exceptional
- Above expectations
- In line with expectations
- Yet to meet expectations

Stop and think
Do I have any questions or concerns?
What are the mistakes or errors I made in this unit?

3.2 CIRCULAR FLOW OF INCOME

Explain how individuals, organisations (for-profit and not-for-profit) and the government work together to distribute economic resources used to produce goods and services.

Learning Intentions

At the end of this unit I will:
- Be able to explain how an economy works
- Know about factors of production

Making the links with other LOs:

- 1.2 Personal income and expenditure
- 1.3 Personal financial life cycle
- 1.4 Key personal taxes

Are there other LOs?

Most of the Learning Outcomes are directly and indirectly linked to this unit.

Key Concepts

- ✓ Flow of income
- ✓ Factors of production
- ✓ Free economy, centrally planned economy and mixed economy
- ✓ Semi-state bodies and privatisation

Wonderful Worthwhile Websites

www.businesseducation.ie
www.economicsonline.co.uk
www.tutor2u.net/economics

CIRCULAR FLOW OF INCOME

The circular flow of income shows how money flows through our economy.

We are going to take a step-by-step, simple approach to explain how an economy works. We are assuming two groups, namely **households** and **firms** (businesses). The two groups, households and firms, are connected and interact with each other. We will look at how **income flows** from one to another.

An **economy** is a system of organisations involved in the production and distribution of goods and services.

FLOW OF INCOME 1

The household supplies an economic resource (**labour**) to firms.

Firms provide wages (**income**) to the workers in the household. This is an economic resource.

Household: receives income for working.

Business: wages is an expense (it reduces profit).

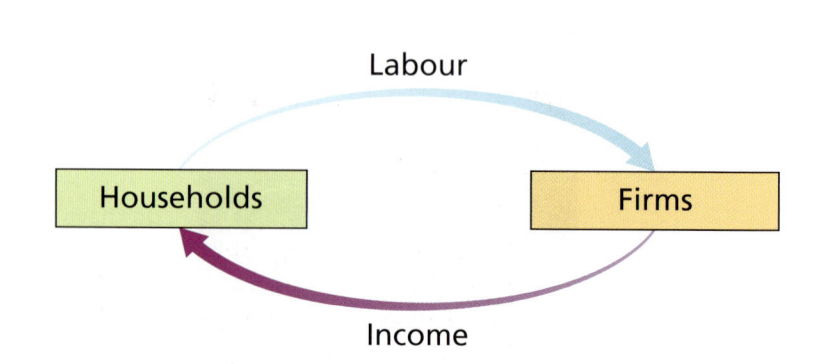

FLOW OF INCOME 2

The household **buys** goods and services from the firm.

The firm supplies the household with goods and services (**sales**).

In this flow we assume all income is spent.

Household: purchases goods – this will cost the household money.

Business: sells goods – the business receives money.

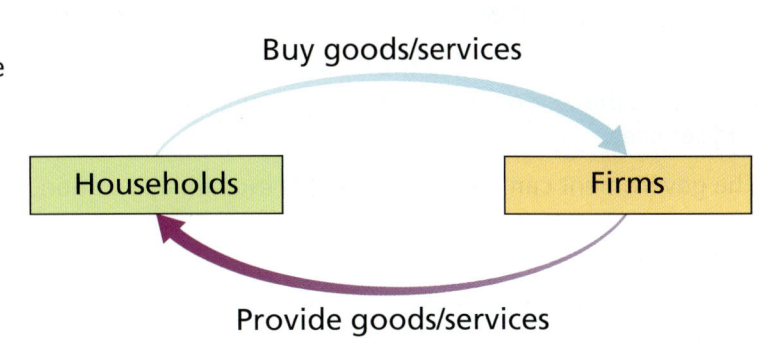

FLOW OF INCOME 3

Let's say the household's wages are greater than spending. We are introducing **savings** and **banks**. The household may receive interest on savings.

The firm can **borrow from banks** for investments and loans and pay interest.

Household: saves and earns interest (income on savings).

Bank: pays interest to the household, so it's a cost. However, the bank now has money to lend to businesses and charge them interest. This is how banks make a profit. They charge a higher rate of interest to borrowers (in this example the business) than they pay for depositing money (in this example the household). Banks are like any other businesses; they need to make a profit.

Business: borrows from the banks, pays interest, therefore it's an expense. However, the business can use the money to invest, expand and make more profits.

FLOW OF INCOME 4

Perhaps the household has another **scarce resource – land**. The household can provide this to the business. The business in return pays **rent** to the household.

Household: receives income.

Business: pays rent.

> **Economic resources** are the human (people) and non-human (e.g. land, financial resources and technology) resources used in producing goods or providing services. They are also known as the factors of production.

> Remember, **natural resources** won't last for ever and many can't be replaced. Oil is **non-renewable**, whereas you can plant crops, so they are **renewable**.

GOVERNMENT

The government can **add to the flow of income** by spending on infrastructure. The payment of wages to state employees (nurses, doctors, army, gardaí, teachers) and social welfare payments creates a demand for goods and services.

The government **can reduce the flow of income** by taxation. Taxation takes money out of the economy.

Taxation

Income tax reduces the income of households and as a result reduces the amount a household can spend on goods and services. Households have less money to spend.

VAT increases the price of goods and services and therefore reduces the purchasing power of households.

Corporation tax reduces firms' profits and therefore reduces the factors of production that they can buy. Firms will pay less wages.

As you continue to learn about our economy, you will notice that economic decisions have effects on:

- People – individuals, households, consumers, employees
- Profits – for both for-profit and not-for-profit organisations
- Government
- Our economy
- Our planet

Human resources are people with various skills, for example teachers.

THE FACTORS OF PRODUCTION

In order to grow economically, our country must produce goods and services. The more goods and services that are produced, the more jobs are created. Workers will have an income and be able to support themselves. They will also pay tax, creating additional income for the government.

To produce goods and services successfully, our country must make the best use of our economic resources or **factors of production** or **inputs**.

There are **four factors of production**: land, labour, capital and enterprise.

It is good for the Irish economy when we have enough economic resources to fulfil our needs and wants and additional resources to trade with other countries. A challenge happens when a country has limited resources.

1. LAND

Land is a country's main natural resource. Land includes agricultural land, rivers, sea, deserts, forests, minerals, metals, natural gas, oil, coal, water, weather and crops. Some of those resources are renewable. This means that they can be replaced by the environment over a relatively short time, for example forests. Others are non-renewable, for example oil and coal.

2. LABOUR

Labour is the human labour available. Even in a highly technological society people are still needed to produce goods and services.

3. CAPITAL

Capital can refer to money used to run a business or to items that are used to produce goods and provide services, for example machinery, equipment, technology, tools.

4. ENTERPRISE

An entrepreneur takes a risk by investing their money or other people's money to start an enterprise with the hope of making a profit. The entrepreneur brings together land, labour and capital.

EXAMPLE

Factors of production for baking bread

Land	Labour	Capital	Enterprise	Self-service bakery
Wheat	Farmer, baker	Tractor, oven, bakery	Ms Baker	Ms Baker's bakery

FACTORS OF PRODUCTION IN DIFFERENT COUNTRIES

Some countries, including Ireland, have fertile agricultural land while some countries, for example Saudi Arabia, have little fertile land but lots of oil.

We are fortunate in Ireland to have a highly educated, English-speaking labour force. These factors attract lots of companies into our country. Large companies such as Apple, PayPal and Microsoft have bases in Ireland.

Some countries, for example the USA, have numerous factors of production, while poorer countries, for example Mali, have scarce resources and few factors of production.

Remember, whoever provides the **factor of production** usually receives an **income**.

SUMMARY

The **circular flow of income** connects different sectors of an economy.

Businesses produce goods and services and in the process, **incomes are generated** for factors of production, for example wages and salaries are paid to employees.

LEAKAGES FROM THE CIRCULAR FLOW

Not all income will flow directly from households to businesses.

1. **Savings:** households might decide to save money with a financial enterprise in a deposit account
2. **Government:** raises taxation, e.g. income tax and national insurance
3. **Imports:** buying foreign goods and services

INJECTIONS INTO THE CIRCULAR FLOW

These are additions to investment, government spending or exports, which boost the circular flow of income, leading to greater output.

1. **Businesses:** capital expenditure, for example on new technology
2. **Government:** expenditure, for example on health
3. **Exports:** foreign countries buying Irish goods and services

Time to think

If you were to set up a business producing smartphones, you would find it challenging to compete with giant organisations like Apple in terms of unit cost (the cost of producing one item). Why would it be challenging?

ECONOMIES OF SCALE

When organisations increase in size they benefit from **economies of scale**. This allows an organisation to benefit from mass production. The more they produce, the cheaper the unit cost.

Larger for-profit organisations can buy bigger and **automated machinery** (such as robots) which is only justified by large-scale production, known as mass production. These organisations can afford the **capital expenditure**.

They can invest in **large trucks** to make deliveries, which saves time and transport costs, rather than using a small van doing numerous trips.

Larger firms can divide labour and have **workers specialise**, so that they can concentrate on a specific job and become skilled and quicker at doing that job.

If you were to set up a small business you would have to do all the jobs: dealing with suppliers, promoting and marketing the business, preparing the accounts, dealing with production.

If you ran a large organisation you would have enough money to employ an accountant. You could also employ an IT specialist.

Larger institutions buy in **bulk** and suppliers give them **discounts**, so they can sell cheaper. A large supermarket buying 100,000 cans of cola will get them at a lower cost per can than the small supermarket that only buys 1,000 cans.

Financial institutions are often willing to lend to large organisations. They are seen as less of a risk. The same paperwork is involved in arranging a **loan** of €10,000 as a loan of €1,000. The lender will get more interest on the larger loan.

A large organisation can afford to spend more on **marketing**. Costs can be spread over a larger scale; for example, big business can afford more expensive advertising, such as TV. Smaller businesses could not justify these costs.

As a result of large-scale production, the unit cost is cheaper. Companies can sell goods cheaper or make larger profits.

However, there are times when a company gets too big and we encounter **diseconomies of scale**. This is the opposite of economies of scale: the unit cost increases as the organisation expands. This can happen when workers lack motivation and production is not as efficient. Communication might become a challenge as the organisation expands and this may affect the business.

ECONOMIC SYSTEMS

An **economic system** is the way a government organises a country's economy. It is used to control the factors of production: land, labour, capital and enterprise.

Economic systems are divided into three types: free, centrally planned and mixed.

1. FREE ECONOMY

A **free economy** is where citizens are free to make all the decisions about the production of goods and services. Companies and individuals (the private sector) are free to operate without government interference. The **USA** is a good example of a free economy.

Good points: entrepreneurship is encouraged

Not so good points: damage to environment; inferior goods

2. CENTRALLY PLANNED ECONOMY

In a **centrally planned economy** the government or state controls and makes all the decisions about economic activity (this is known as the public sector). Citizens of the country have very little involvement in business; they are employees rather than entrepreneurs. Examples of this type of economy in the past were Russia and China; **North Korea** is a modern example.

Good points: everyone is treated the same

Not so good points: no motivation to do better and sometimes shortages of goods and services

3. MIXED ECONOMY

A mixed economy is a combination of both the first two types, a mixture of privately owned and state-owned enterprises. People are free to establish businesses and the government also sets up and/or controls businesses. Ireland is a mixed economy.

Good points: government can provide services/products that may not be profitable

Not so good points: inefficiencies, as profit is not necessarily a motive

THE IRISH ECONOMY

The Irish economy is moving more towards **free enterprise** with the **privatisation** and selling off of state enterprises and the encouragement of **entrepreneurship**. More and more services are being provided by the private sector, from telecommunications to waste disposal, building motorways and even building schools.

Regardless of the type of economy, you will always have **not-for-profit organisations** to help the less well-off and underprivileged.

SEMI-STATE/STATE-SPONSORED BODIES

Ireland is a mixed economy. The Irish government runs business, sometimes known as semi-state or state-sponsored bodies. These businesses are set up and funded by the government, and the government employs managers to run the businesses.

WORKING WITH OTHERS

Working together, either as pairs or squares (two pairs), look at the following logos. Name each organisation and say what it does. Name as many more state-sponsored bodies as you can.

- ervia
- An Post
- Met Éireann
- coillte
- CIE
- Enterprise Ireland — where innovation means business
- DART
- epa — Environmental Protection Agency
- ESB
- LUAS
- daa
- Bord na Móna — Naturally Driven
- IDA Ireland
- RTÉ

CIRCULAR FLOW OF INCOME 3.2

Why State-owned?
1. Some necessary businesses need a lot of **funding** to get started, for example the Luas
2. Some businesses develop our **natural resources**, for example Bord na Móna (peat) and Coillte (forests)
3. Some businesses supply **essential services** such as electricity (ESB)
4. Some businesses **promote our country** in terms of trade and entrepreneurship (Enterprise Ireland, IDA)
5. Some businesses **promote Irish tourism**, for example Fáilte Ireland

Financing State-owned Businesses
The government can borrow from banks – both Irish and foreign banks.

Some semi-state businesses charge for their services, for example the annual TV licence fee.

Time to think

Can you think of other semi-state businesses that charge for their services?

CHECKING IN...

1. Can you identify four factors of production for DESIGN K, a modern wooden kitchen designer and manufacturer? Copy and complete the following table.

Factors of production for DESIGN K wooden kitchens		
Factors	**Explain**	**Picture/Design**
Land		
Labour		
Capital		
Enterprise		

2. Copy the grid below and match each function (1–5) with the correct semi-state body (A–E).

1	Forestry	A	Enterprise Ireland
2	Peat resources	B	RTÉ
3	Grants and support for Irish businesses	C	Fáilte Ireland
4	National TV and radio	D	Coillte
5	Promotes tourism	E	Bord na Móna

1	2	3	4	5

3.2 BE BUSINESS: OUR ECONOMY

3. Copy the table below and insert a tick ✓ to indicate whether each statement is true or false.

	True	False
A semi-state company is run by the government		
An Post operates the postal service in Ireland		
Semi-state bodies don't charge for their services		
CIÉ is privately owned		
The government runs Met Éireann		
Shell runs Ireland's gas semi-state body		

4. What do the following acronyms (sets of initials) stand for?
   CIÉ   RTÉ   DART   EPA   VHI

5. Write a short, informative note on a semi-state body of your choice for a local newspaper.

PRIVATISATION

Privatisation is the transfer of ownership and control of government or state assets, firms and organisations to private investors.

The enterprises may be sold to another company or the government may decide to issue shares and have the enterprises listed on the stock exchange.

A business on the stock exchange will have **PLC** (or **plc**) after its name. PLC stands for **public limited company**.

An example of an Irish PLC is Aer Lingus plc.

REASONS TO SELL

1. The semi-state body may be **losing money**. It may need private enterprise to make it more profitable.
2. The business may have potential for growth but needs **additional investment** (finance). This could be achieved by selling the business.
3. The government **needs finance** and may sell a semi-state that is profitable to raise money to pay off government debt or even to reduce taxation.
4. The government may have **no interest** in a particular service and therefore it makes sense to sell.

Examples of semi-state bodies that were privatised are Eircom and Aer Lingus.

Time to think

Who benefits from the privatisation of semi-state bodies? The government receives money for the sale. Who else might benefit?

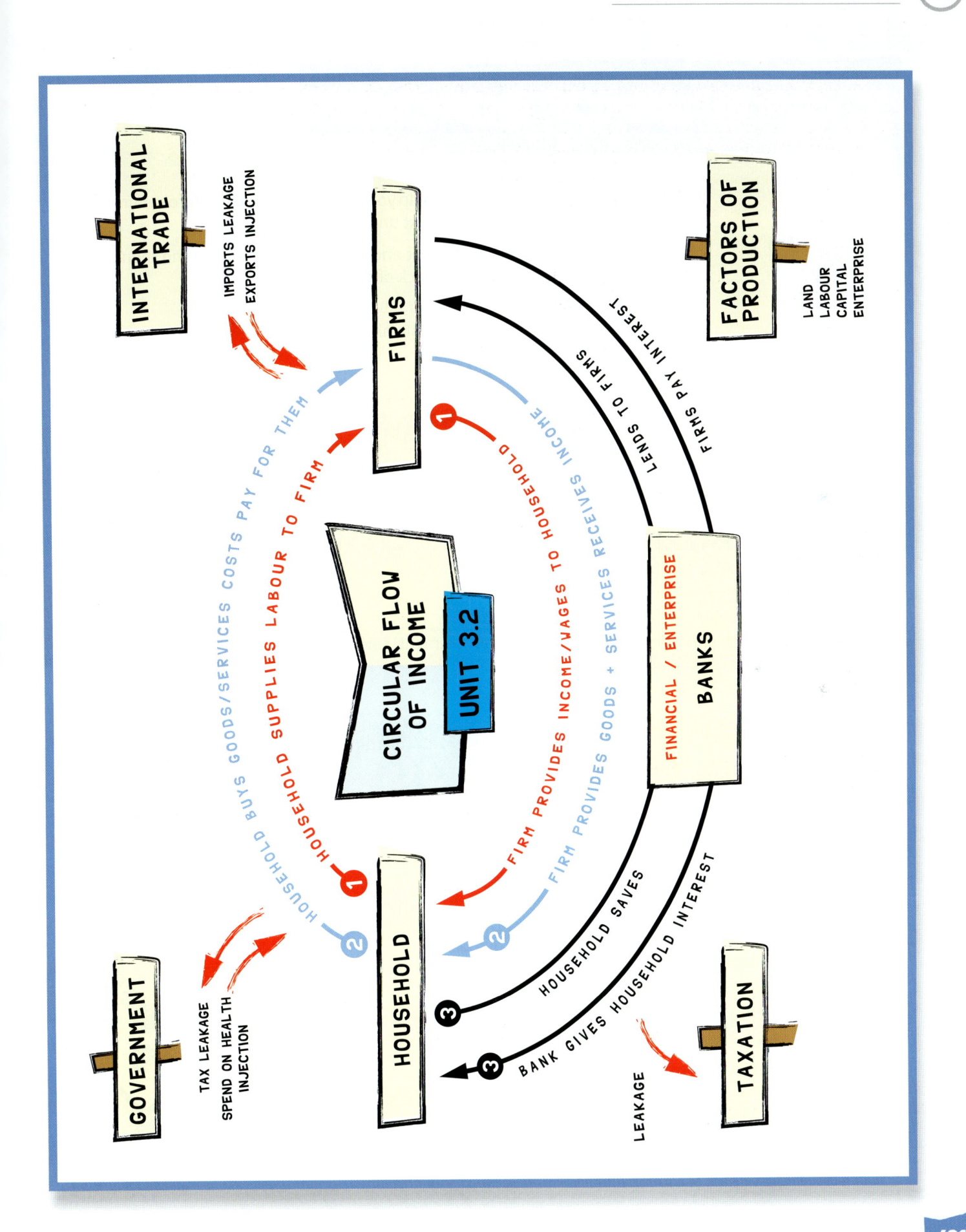

CIRCULAR FLOW OF INCOME 3.2

CIRCULAR FLOW OF INCOME — UNIT 3.2

INTERNATIONAL TRADE
IMPORTS LEAKAGE
EXPORTS INJECTION

FACTORS OF PRODUCTION
LAND
LABOUR
CAPITAL
ENTERPRISE

FIRMS

HOUSEHOLD

FINANCIAL / ENTERPRISE — BANKS

GOVERNMENT
TAX LEAKAGE
SPEND ON HEALTH INJECTION

TAXATION
LEAKAGE

Flows:
- ① HOUSEHOLD BUYS GOODS/SERVICES COSTS PAY FOR THEM
- ② HOUSEHOLD SUPPLIES LABOUR TO FIRM
- ① FIRM PROVIDES INCOME/WAGES TO HOUSEHOLD
- ② FIRM PROVIDES GOODS + SERVICES RECEIVES INCOME
- ③ HOUSEHOLD SAVES — LENDS TO FIRMS — FIRMS PAY INTEREST
- ③ BANK GIVES HOUSEHOLD INTEREST

421

Be Prepared: My Support Sheets

Completing the activities below will help you to reflect on and reinforce your learning before you move on to the next unit.

- Write down the **key terms** in this unit and make sure you understand them. See if they match the ones at the back of the book.
- List the **key concepts/themes** in this unit.
- List the **three most interesting points** about this unit.

THE SIZZLING SEAT

One student sits facing the rest of the class. This student must pretend to **be the government**.

a. Class groups think up challenging questions they would put to the government on the running of semi-state enterprises.
b. Students ask the government questions for five minutes.
c. Students take turns being the government.
d. Cross-examine after the event:
   1. What did you learn?
   2. What did you find fascinating and useful?
   3. Would you challenge anything that 'the government' said?

Economics in Action Idea!

Create a blog explaining the circular flow of income.

Success criteria:
- Know your target readers.
- Be yourself; a blog is personal.
- Include images.
- Include three different points of information.

QUESTION TIME

1. Explain circular flow of income.
2. Define economic resources.
3. Explain economies of scale.
4. List the three types of economy. Which one do you think is the best? Why?
5. Give three reasons why the government might be involved in businesses.
6. Write a brief note explaining privatisation.
7. In your own words, explain how the flow of income works.
8. Compare a mixed economy with a centrally planned economy.
9. Compare a free economy with a centrally planned economy.

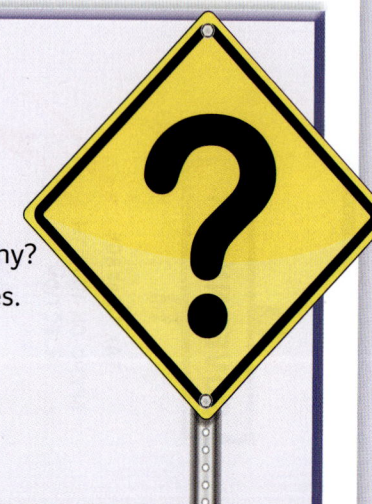

EVALUATE MY LEARNING: DAR

Describe
- Did I/we meet my/our learning intentions?
- What went well? What are my/our strengths?

Assess
- How did I/we work with others?
- Were there challenges?

Recommend
- How might I improve?
- What skills and learning might I apply to new situations?

Do your **Key Check** in the workbook for this unit and then mark your learning position on the following rating scale:

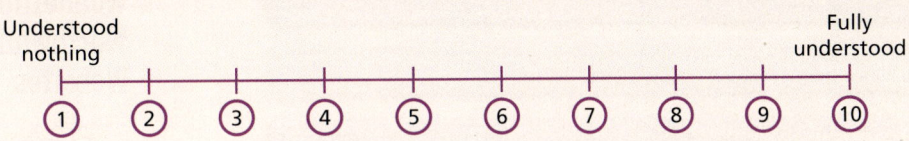

Understood nothing ① ② ③ ④ ⑤ ⑥ ⑦ ⑧ ⑨ ⑩ Fully understood

How can you move up the rating scale? What can you **say**, **make**, **write** and **do** to illustrate your learning?

CBA 1 Business in Action:
Will I use this unit for my topic for my **Economics in Action** and **Finance in Action**?

CBA 2 Presentation:
Will I use this unit for my topic for my **Presentation**?

Stop and think

Do I have any questions or concerns?
What are the mistakes or errors I made in this unit?

3.3 SUPPLY AND DEMAND

Evaluate how changes in the supply and demand of goods and services in different markets can affect prices.

Learning Intentions

At the end of this unit I will:
- Know about and understand demand and supply for goods and services
- Understand markets, how price and other factors will affect demand and supply
- Understand elasticity
- Be able to apply my understanding of graphs
- Value the concepts of demand and supply

Making the links with other LOs:

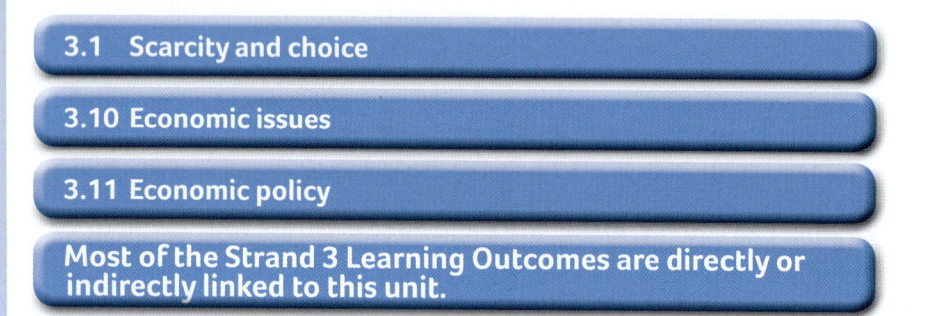

- 3.1   Scarcity and choice
- 3.10   Economic issues
- 3.11   Economic policy
- Most of the Strand 3 Learning Outcomes are directly or indirectly linked to this unit.

Are there other LOs?

Key Concepts
- ✓ Supply and demand
- ✓ Elasticity

Wonderful Worthwhile Websites
www.businesseducation.ie
www.tutor2u.net/economics

> **'3Ts' = Think, Turn, Talk**
> Can you name a type of market?
> Have you ever visited a market?
> What might be the advantages for a local farmer of selling his or her produce at a local market?

WHAT IS A MARKET?

A **market** is a setting where potential sellers and potential buyers come together to trade.

Historically, markets were physical meeting places where buyers and sellers met. Although physical markets are still dynamic, we now have virtual markets supported by IT networks such as the internet.

Some markets are very competitive, with a number of businesses selling the same kinds of products or services. Other markets have little or no competition.

TYPES OF MARKET

There are many **different types of market**. The following are some examples:

1. Farmers' markets
2. Festival markets, for example at Electric Picnic
3. National markets, for example DoneDeal
4. International markets, for example Christmas markets
5. Global markets, for example eBay
6. Stock exchange, where the shares of companies are bought and sold
7. Black market, where goods and services are sold illegally

Global market

Stock exchange

Farmers' market

Black market

FACTORS THAT AFFECT DEMAND AND SUPPLY

Many factors affect demand and supply, here we will look at:

1. Price   2. Income   3. Population   4. Fashion   5. Laws   6. The economy

1. PRICE

- **Be the Seller:** the seller always looks for the **highest** price. The seller has to cover all their costs while at the same time making a **profit** for the business.
- **Be the Buyer:** the buyer will be looking for the **lowest** price. The prices for products and services don't remain constant and prices can increase as well as decrease.

The prices charged depend on another concept in economics: the **supply** of goods and services and the **demand** for goods and services.

Economists call this **the law of supply and demand**.

3.3 BE BUSINESS: OUR ECONOMY

The demand for goods and services is the amount of those goods and services that consumers are willing to purchase at a given time for a given price.

When prices are low: **demand** for the product or service **increases**.

When prices are high: **demand** for the product or service **decreases**.

Of course, this is from the consumer's point of view. The consumer is always looking for a bargain.

The supply of goods and services is the amount that the supplier is willing to sell at a given time for a given price.

When prices are high: **supply** of the product or service will **increase**.

When prices are falling: **supply** of the product or service will **decrease**.

Of course, this is from the seller's point of view. The seller is looking for the highest price, to cover costs and to make a profit.

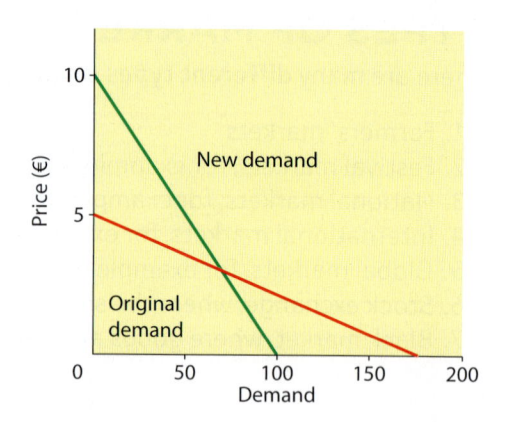

Demand is from the consumer's point of view.

Supply is from the seller's point of view.

WORKING WITH OTHERS

Working in pairs or small groups, can you think of other factors that affect demand?

2. INCOME

When **income increases**, this generally leads to an **increase in demand** for goods.
When **income decreases**, this generally leads to a **decrease in demand** for goods.
However, sometimes when income increases the consumer may demand higher-quality products and the demand for lower-quality products decreases.

3. POPULATION

If there were to be an increase in the number of babies born in Ireland, this would increase the demand for baby products, baby facilities and baby services.

However, the demands would change as the babies grew up, as children have different demands at different stages of their development. Age profile can affect demand and supply.

4. FASHION

Consumers are very fickle about style and tastes. Goods that are extremely popular one year may not be in demand the following year. It may be skinny jeans one year and flares the following year!

5. LAWS

When a new law is introduced (legislation) it can decrease the demand for some products and increase the demand for others. When the building regulations in Ireland changed to encourage sustainability, it resulted in an increase in demand for insulation for houses.

6. OUR ECONOMY

When our economy is in a recession (a time of economic decline), income falls, house prices fall and the demand for houses decreases.

Time to think

Can you think of any other factors that might affect demand and supply?

Demand and supply affects everything. The powers of demand and supply are everywhere. Look at this case study.

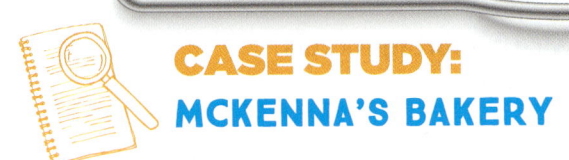

CASE STUDY: MCKENNA'S BAKERY

McKenna's Bakery supplies bread, cakes and pastries in a small village. They make a special recipe cake called the Strawberry Surprise.

Scenario 1

McKenna's Bakery bakes 100 Strawberry Surprise cakes: this is their **supply**.

150 people in the town want one of these special cakes: that is the **demand**.

The owner of McKenna's Bakery is aware that the people really want the cakes and he thinks that they will pay extra to get one. People end up paying **higher prices** until more cakes are baked to meet the demand. The bakery **loses out on potential sales** by not having enough.

Also, people get annoyed with higher prices and having to wait for supply so some people say they won't return to the bakery.

Scenario 2

McKenna's Bakery bakes 200 cakes: this is their **supply**.

150 people in the town want one of these special cakes: that is the **demand**.

Having made too many cakes the bakery **reduces the price** to try to get rid of them before the end of the day. They are still left with **excess stock** (cakes) and so they have to be thrown out at the end of the day and the bakery **loses money** overall.

You can see that it is essential for a business to match their supply with what the demand will be, while ensuring they make a profit.

Our daily life presents us with countless examples of supply and demand. You can come up with numerous examples of supply and demand and pose the question 'What if …?'.

> ### WORKING WITH OTHERS
>
> What might happen if the cocoa bean crop was wiped out in Brazil? Cocoa is the most important ingredient in chocolate making. Working in pairs or small groups, consider:
> - What might happen to the **supply** of chocolate?
> - What might happen to the **price** of chocolate? Why?
> - What might you do?

MARKET DEMAND SCHEDULE

When demand is greater than supply of a product or service, a **shortage** occurs.

Prices will increase.

When supply is greater than demand for a product or service, there is a **surplus**.

Prices will decrease.

A market demand schedule for a product indicates that there is an opposite relationship between price and quantity demanded. It is a table that lists the quantity of a good that consumers in a market will buy at each price.

EXAMPLE 1: CIARA'S DEMAND SCHEDULE

Ciara Carew runs a mini-enterprise called Ciara's Cupcakes. Ciara produces and sells quality cupcakes. Her cupcakes range in price from €1 to €3.50.

Before Ciara started her mini-company she did some research and found that as price increases the demand decreases, which is the law of demand. After completing extensive research she had enough information to draw up a **market demand schedule**.

We can also demonstrate Ciara's demand schedule using a demand curve.

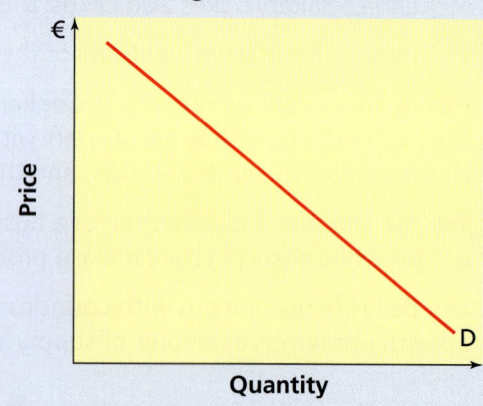

| CIARA'S DEMAND SCHEDULE FOR CUPCAKES ||
Price (y-axis)	Quantity of cupcakes (x-axis)
€1	100
€1.50	90
€2	70
€2.50	65
€3	30
€3.50	10

SUPPLY AND DEMAND 3.3

Be Numerate

Draw a demand curve

Let's look at the market for miniature chocolate eggs in Kilkenny. The following demand schedule shows the different quantities that customers are willing to buy at each price.

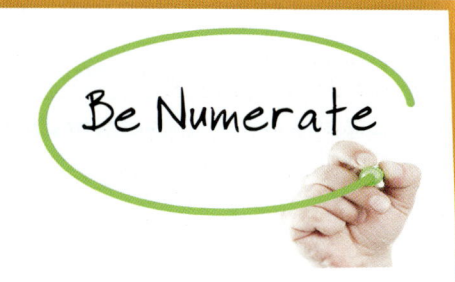

Price per miniature chocolate egg (y-axis)	Quantity: Number of miniature chocolate eggs per day (x-axis)
20 cents	30
40 cents	25
60 cents	20
80 cents	15
100 cents	10

The demand schedule table shows that at 20 cents, 30 consumers will demand the miniature eggs, but at €1 there is only a demand for 10. When presented in a graph form it is a demand curve.

Present the above information in a graph to show the demand curve.

Success criteria for demand curve:
- Use graph paper, if possible
- Label your graph: Demand curve, showing daily demand for miniature chocolate eggs
- Draw an L shape
- Fill in the x-axis with prices per miniature eggs
- Fill in the y-axis with quantity of eggs demanded
- Fill in the dots for each price
- Join the dots and you have your demand curve

429

EXAMPLE 2: CIARA'S SUPPLY SCHEDULE

Just as you have movements in demand you can also have changes in supply – supply can increase or decrease.

Ciara's supply of cupcakes:

Ciara's Supply Schedule	
Price (y-axis)	Quantity of cupcakes (x-axis)
€1	10
€1.50	20
€2	70
€2.50	80
€3	90
€3.50	100

We can also demonstrate Ciara's supply schedule using a supply curve.

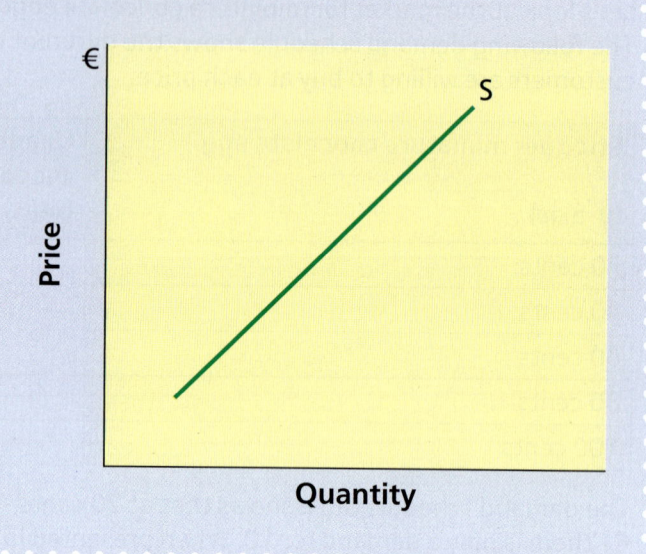

Excess supply is when quantity supplied is greater than quantity demanded.

Excess demand is when quantity demanded is greater than quantity supplied.

Where supply equals demand this is **equilibrium**.

EXAMPLE 3: CIARA'S EQUILIBRIUM

For Ciara, equilibrium is 70 cupcakes at €2, where demand equals supply.

At any price above €2, she will have excess supply. That is, the number of cupcakes supplied is greater than the demand for the cupcakes.

At any price below €2, she will have excess demand. That is, the number of cupcakes demanded is greater than the supply of Ciara's cupcakes.

From the supply curve graph, we can see that equilibrium is €2 and the equilibrium quantity is 70 cupcakes.

So price is determined by demand and supply.

You can draw a demand curve D, then the supply curve S. Where the two curves meet is where price settles. The graph resembles an X.

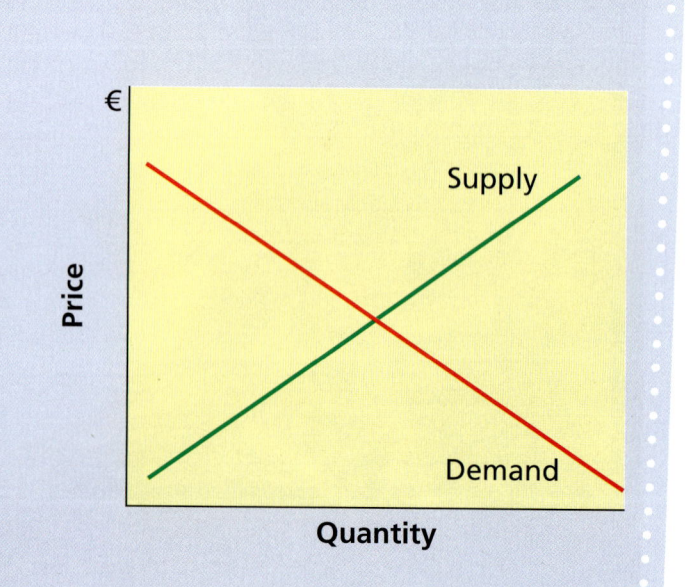

SUPPLY AND DEMAND 3.3

Be Numerate

Draw a supply curve

Let's look again at the market for miniature chocolate eggs in Kilkenny. The following supply schedule shows the different quantities that suppliers are willing to sell at each price.

Price per miniature chocolate egg (y-axis)	Quantity: Number of miniature eggs per day (x-axis)
20 cents	11
40 cents	16
60 cents	18
80 cents	22
100 cents	25

The table shows that at 20 cents, 11 miniature eggs can be supplied; however at €1, 25 eggs can be supplied. When presented in a graph form this is the supply curve.

Present the above information in a graph to show the supply curve.

Draw equilibrium

Equilibrium is where demand equals supply. You show demand and supply on the one graph like an **X**.

Draft the graph again, using the demand chart and the supply chart, and show equilibrium.

Success criteria for supply curve:
- Use graph paper, if possible
- Label your graph: Supply curve, showing daily supply of miniature chocolate eggs
- Draw an L shape
- Fill in the x-axis with prices per miniature eggs
- Fill in the y-axis with quantity of eggs supplied
- Fill in the dots for each price
- Join the dots and you have your supply curve

EXAMPLES OF PRICE INCREASE

- Tickets for the **All-Ireland final sold out**. Demand was greater than supply.
- **Emigrants returning** back to Dublin increase the price of houses in Dublin as there is a shortage of supply of houses in Dublin.
- A **cold winter** increases the need for oil, electric heaters and blankets, and insulation. Demand may be greater than supply and prices will increase.
- Demand for a particular **fashion label** increases and the price will go up.

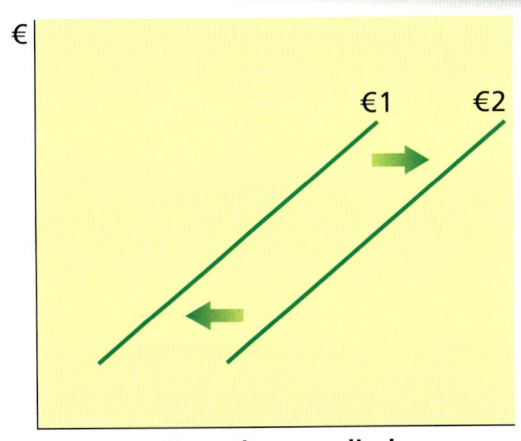

EXAMPLES OF PRICE DECREASE

- A concert for which **tickets did not sell** had an excess supply.
- Some **rural parts of Ireland** had an excess of houses built during the boom; now there is excess supply.
- During a **cold summer** with lots of rain, shops may have an excess supply of garden furniture and accessories for good weather.
- Some items in shops may **not be fashionable** next season, so shops with excess supply will have to reduce prices.
- **Other factors** such as **taxation** (less to spend), **inflation** and **interest rates** can also affect supply and demand.

ELASTICITY

> Elasticity refers to the degree of reaction in supply or demand in relation to changes in price.

Elasticity is a concept which involves examining how responsive demand (or supply) is to a change in another variable such as price or income.

If a curve is **more elastic**, small changes in price will cause large changes in quantity consumed.

If a curve is **less elastic**, it will take large changes in price to effect a change in quantity consumed.

What elasticity refers to is the **responsiveness** of demand or supply to changes in price or income.

Elastic demand is very responsive to price.

Inelastic demand is not very responsive to price.

ELASTIC DEMAND

If a change in price causes a large percentage change in demand, then we say demand is price elastic.

For example, if the price of Ballygowan mineral water increases, you would switch to other brands of mineral water. Therefore a change in price causes a bigger percentage change in demand and your demand is quite elastic.

Other Elastic Goods

1. **Tayto:** if the price of Tayto crisps increases, people will switch to an alternative brand of crisps.
2. **Dunnes Stores bread:** this is highly price elastic because there are many other alternatives. If the price of Dunnes Stores bread rises, customers will switch to alternatives.

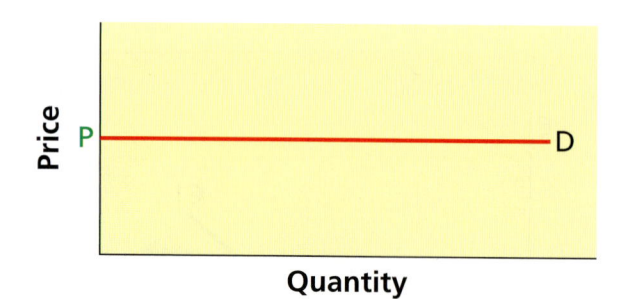

The term **perfectly elastic** is sometimes used where any change in price will cause demand to fall to zero.

INELASTIC DEMAND

If a change in price causes a smaller percentage change in demand, then we say demand is price inelastic.

For example, if the price of petrol increased by 10%, demand may only fall by 1%.

> **Time to think**
> Do you think a life-saving drug is an elastic or an inelastic good?

Other Inelastic Goods

1. **Apple iPhones and iPads:** the Apple brand is so strong that many customers will pay premium prices for Apple products. If the price of an Apple iPhone rises, many people will continue to buy them.

2. **Cigarettes:** if the government increases tax on cigarettes and as a result the price of all cigarettes increases, demand will be inelastic. Why? Most smokers are addicted and will continue to buy cigarettes.

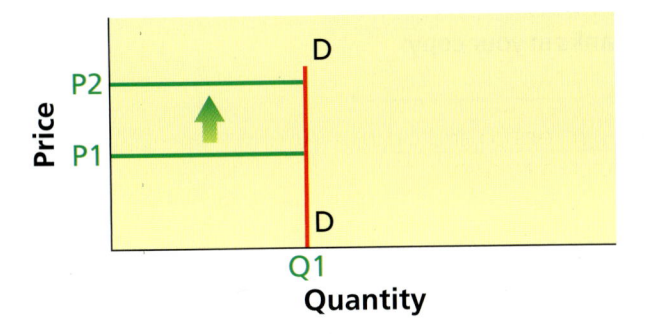

The term **perfectly inelastic** is sometimes used where any change in price, from P1 to P2, will have no effect on the amount demanded.

EXAMPLE 4: CIARA AND ELASTICITY

If a change in price causes a large percentage change in demand, then we say demand is price elastic.

For example, if the price of Ciara's cupcakes increases by 10% you would probably switch to another brand of cupcakes. Therefore a change in price causes a bigger percentage change in demand for Ciara's cupcakes and her demand is quite elastic.

If a change in price causes a smaller percentage change in demand, then we say demand is price inelastic.

For example, if Ciara's cupcakes were low in calories, sugar free and different from most cupcakes on the market, then a change in price of 10% might result in a fall in demand of only 2%. We would describe this demand as inelastic.

SUMMARY OF ELASTICITY

Inelastic	Elastic
A 10% increase in price might lead to a 6% decrease in quantity demanded	A 10% increase in price might lead to a 25% decrease in quantity demanded
Example: diesel	Example: holidays
Price increase will lead to total revenue increase	Price decrease is needed to increase total revenue

CHECKING IN...

1. What is your understanding of the word 'supply'?

2. Consider the following statements and fill the blanks in your copy:
   If the price of a good rises, supply of the good _____.
   If the price of a good falls, supply of the good _____.

3. Consider the following statements and fill in the blanks in your copy:
   If the price of a good rises, demand for the good _____.
   If the price of a good falls, demand for the good _____.

4. Complete the following sentences in your copy based on your understanding of demand curves. Use the word bank below.

   The demand curve slopes _____ from _____ to _____ as price _____. When price rises, demand _____.

   > rises   right   downward   left   falls

5. When might you change your mind when purchasing an item, deciding to buy one product over a different one?

6. The price of a school lunch is €3. A new catering company, Roll and Wok, has received the tender and have increased lunches to €4. Why might a business increase price? How might the students respond? What if the lunches were increased to €5?

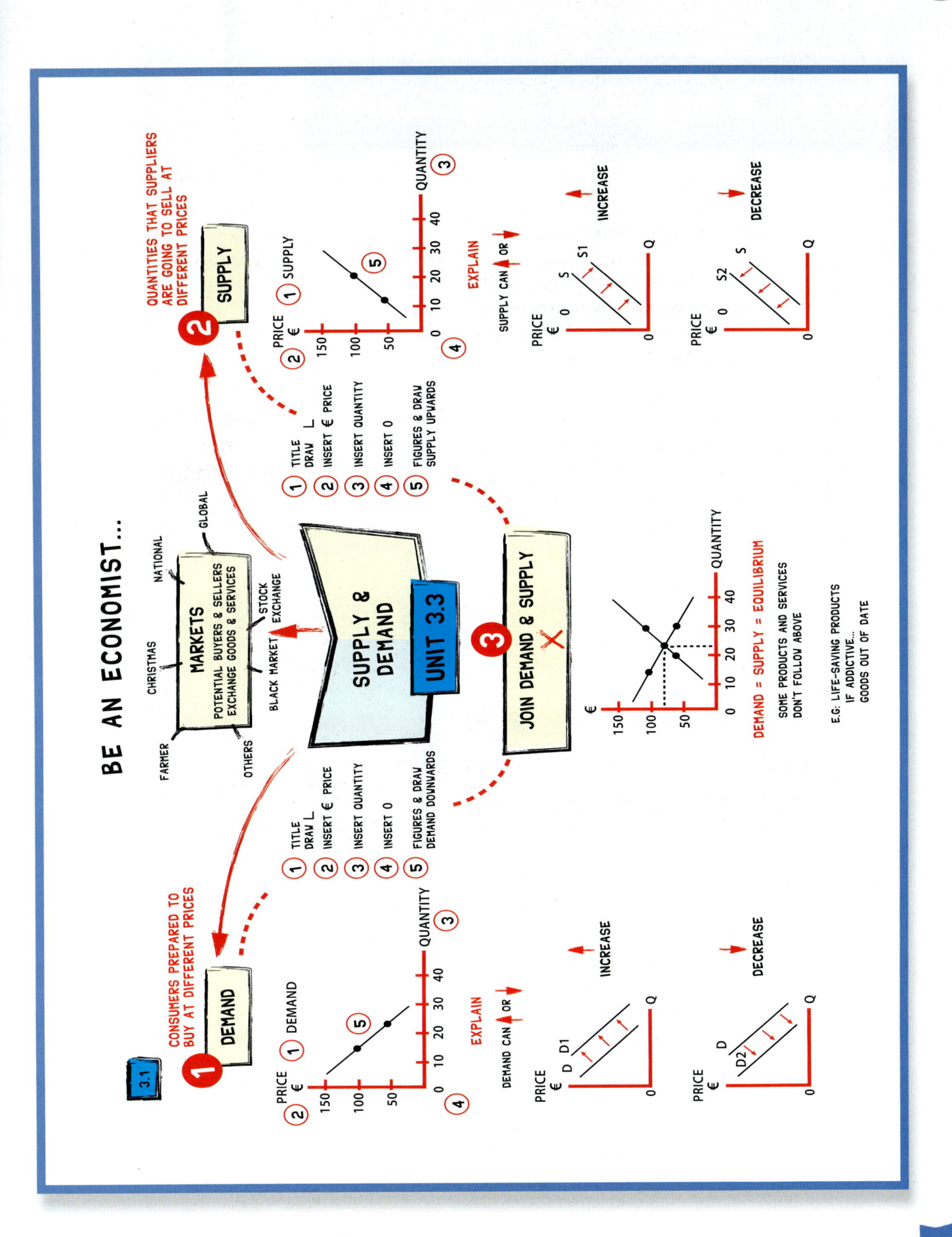

SUPPLY AND DEMAND 3.3

BE AN ECONOMIST...

MARKETS — POTENTIAL BUYERS & SELLERS EXCHANGE GOODS & SERVICES
- GLOBAL
- NATIONAL
- CHRISTMAS
- BLACK MARKET
- STOCK EXCHANGE
- FARMER
- OTHERS

SUPPLY & DEMAND — UNIT 3.3

① DEMAND
CONSUMERS PREPARED TO BUY AT DIFFERENT PRICES

1. TITLE — DRAW L
2. INSERT € PRICE
3. INSERT QUANTITY
4. INSERT 0
5. FIGURES & DRAW DEMAND DOWNWARDS

EXPLAIN — DEMAND CAN ↑ OR ↓

- INCREASE: D → D1
- DECREASE: D → D2

② SUPPLY
QUANTITIES THAT SUPPLIERS ARE GOING TO SELL AT DIFFERENT PRICES

1. TITLE — DRAW L
2. INSERT € PRICE
3. INSERT QUANTITY
4. INSERT 0
5. FIGURES & DRAW SUPPLY UPWARDS

EXPLAIN — SUPPLY CAN ↑ OR ↓

- INCREASE: S → S1
- DECREASE: S → S2

③ JOIN DEMAND & SUPPLY ✗

DEMAND = SUPPLY = EQUILIBRIUM

SOME PRODUCTS AND SERVICES DON'T FOLLOW ABOVE

E.G.: LIFE-SAVING PRODUCTS, IF ADDICTIVE... GOODS OUT OF DATE

435

3.3 BE BUSINESS: OUR ECONOMY

Be Prepared: My Support Sheets

Completing the activities here will help you to reflect on and reinforce your learning before you move on to the next unit.
- Write down the **key terms** in this unit and make sure you understand them. See if they match the ones at the back of the book.
- List the **key concepts/themes** in this unit.
- List the **three most interesting points** about this topic.

Do a role play

In pairs, create a role play on the effects of an increase in the price of Tayto crisps. One person should be the buyer, the other the seller. Then exchange roles. When you have completed your role play, exchange roles and see it from the other point of view.

Economics in Action Idea!

Create a poster explaining demand and supply.

Success criteria:
- Title
- Two different points of information
- An accurate graph
- Clear and consistent letters
- The Wow Factor!

Design a cartoon

Design a cartoon to explain demand and supply. Alternatively, see if you can source one from a local newspaper. Ask your class to vote on the best cartoon. Why was this cartoon chosen?

SUPPLY AND DEMAND 3.3

QUESTION TIME

1. Explain the term 'market'.
2. List the different types of market.
3. Discuss demand and give an example.
4. Discuss supply and give an example.
5. Draft a demand and supply curve and show equilibrium.
6. Explain elasticity and inelasticity.
7. Discuss what affects price decreases and price increases.
8. Create a fishbone summary of this unit using your fishbone template (p. 546).

EVALUATE MY LEARNING: DAR

Describe
- Did I/we meet my/our learning intentions?
- What went well? What are my/our strengths?

Assess
- How did I/we work with others?
- Were there challenges?

Recommend
- How might I improve?
- What skills and learning might I apply to new situations?

Stop and think
Do I have any questions or concerns? What are the mistakes or errors I made in this unit?

Do your **Key Check** in the workbook for this unit and then mark your learning position on the following rating scale:

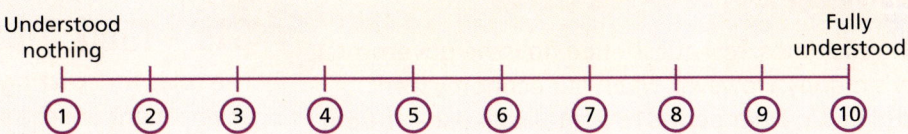

Understood nothing — 1 2 3 4 5 6 7 8 9 10 — Fully understood

How can you move up the rating scale? What can you **say**, **make**, **write** and **do** to illustrate your learning?

CBA 1 Economics in Action:
Will I use this topic for my **Economics in Action** project?

You need to be preparing for your CBAs

- Exceptional
- Above expectations
- In line with expectations
- Yet to meet expectations

437

3.4 GOVERNMENT REVENUE AND GOVERNMENT EXPENDITURE

Differentiate between different sources of government revenue and government expenditure.

Learning Intentions

At the end of this unit I will:
- Be able to list and explain sources of income for the government
- Be able to list and explain sources of expenditure for the government
- Apply my information to decide what to do with deficits and surpluses in a government budget
- Value financial planning

Making the links with other LOs:

1.2	Personal income and expenditure
1.4	Key personal taxes
1.12	Budgeting
3.5	Taxation
3.10	Economic issues
3.11	Economic policy

Are there other LOs?

Key Concepts
- ✓ Government finances, government income and government expenditure
- ✓ State-sponsored bodies
- ✓ National budget, deficits and surplus

Wonderful Worthwhile Websites
www.budget.gov.ie

GOVERNMENT FINANCES

During good economic times, few questioned how the government spent the country's money. However, when our economy went from the successful Celtic Tiger period to a total collapse – **'boom to bust'** – we became more aware of how governments and people manage money and finance. We discovered how the government's actions affected everyone in the country.

Just like individuals, households, for-profit organisations and not-for-profit organisations, the government must create and control its **budgets**. Budgeting is an important part of the planning process. The government needs to budget to identify anticipated (expected) **incomes** and anticipated **expenditures**. The government will also have to make **decisions** and control and monitor spending. The budget created by the government, which is known as the **national budget**, will help in decision-making.

'3Ts' = Think, Turn, Talk

The rules for creating a budget for a government are the same as creating an individual, household or organisation budget. What do you think some of the differences might be?

Can you name the current Minister for Finance?

GOVERNMENT REVENUE AND GOVERNMENT EXPENDITURE 3.4

You studied budgeting in **Unit 1.12**. In this unit you will learn to identify government revenue (income) and expenditure (spending), which can be clearly seen in the budget.

The importance of having a budget cannot be overstated. Creating a budget will provide the government with a guideline for expected income and expected expenses. Creating a budget using anticipated figures also enables the government to **compare** those figures with the actual ones later on.

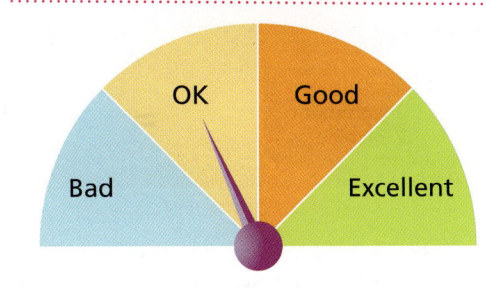

This can serve as a gauge for how the country is performing. It will also enable the government to plan ahead and to decide what changes should be considered.

The national budget is like a gauge to show how our country is doing

WHAT IS A BUDGET?

A budget comprises income and expenditure
- **Income** is money that the government receives.
- **Expenditure** is money that the government spends.

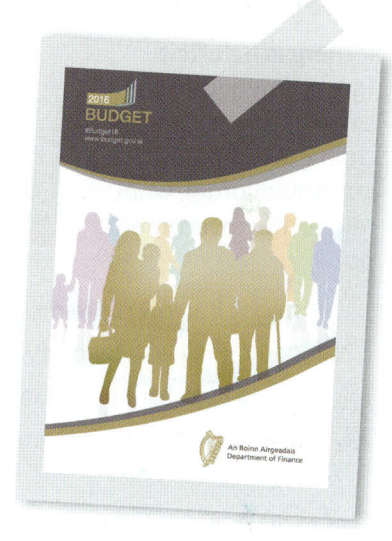

CREATING THE NATIONAL BUDGET

The **Minister for Finance** is responsible for preparing the national budget.

The Minister for Finance asks all the other ministers to send in **estimates** for spending in their departments. The Minister for Education and Skills sends in the estimates of spending of the Department of Education and Skills. The Minister for Health sends in the estimates of the spending of the Department of Health, etc.

The Minister for Finance then prepares the national budget, listing **all income and all expenditure**.

When there is a deficit (shortfall), the budget will show how much the government will have to borrow and therefore how much debt the country has.

The government also has to take factors such as unemployment, population, birth rate, etc. into consideration. When preparing a budget the Minister has three options; the budget can be balanced, deficit or surplus.

Balanced budget: planned revenue = planned expenditure
Deficit budget: planned revenue < planned expenditure
Surplus budget: planned income > planned expenditure

You won't have to calculate a government budget, but understanding it will help you to understand government revenue and government expenditure.

EXAMPLE 1: NATIONAL BUDGET 2016

Total Income	Total Spending
€50,385 million	€51,477 million

Deficit (shortfall) = government expenditure is greater than government income

Surplus (extra) = government income is greater than government expenditure

This budget has a shortfall of €1,092 million.

439

Balanced Budget

The Minister for Finance tries to balance the budget (government current income is equal to government current expenditure).

Government income = Government expenditure — Income is equal to expenditure

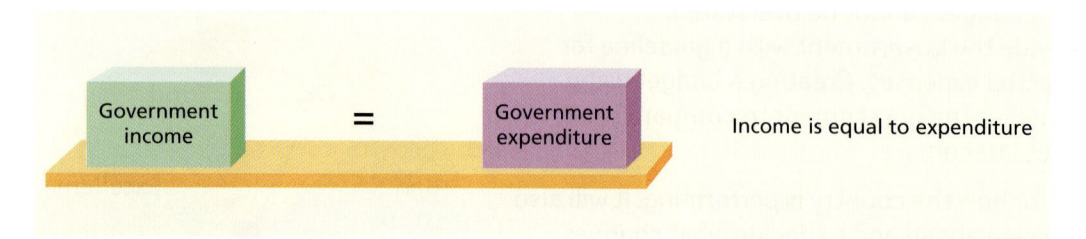

Budget Deficit

If there is a **deficit** (government current expenditure is greater than government current income), what might the government do?

Government income < Government expenditure — Income is less than expenditure

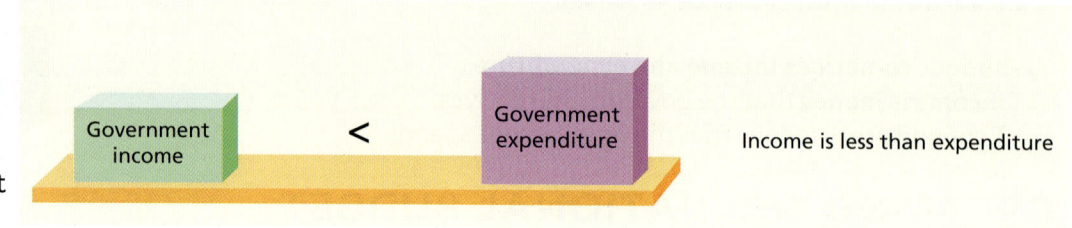

1. It might borrow more money. (Where could it borrow this money from?)
2. It could increase taxes. (What taxes might it increase?)
3. It could look for additional funding from the EU.
4. It might consider selling off state-sponsored bodies.

Budget Surplus

If there is a **surplus** (government current income is greater than government expenditure), what might the government do?

Government income > Government expenditure — Income is greater than expenditure

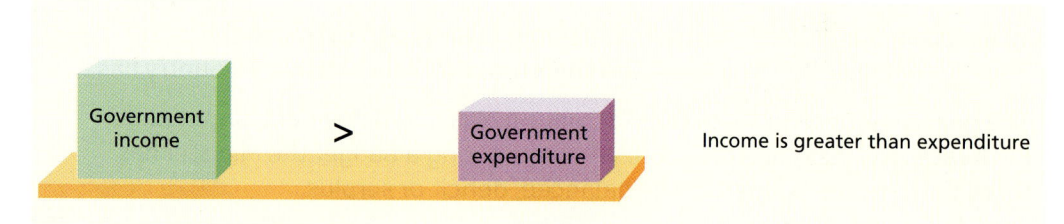

1. It could reduce some taxes. (What taxes might it reduce?)
2. It could pay off some of its loans (national debt).
3. It could give grants to encourage entrepreneurship and create new businesses and new jobs.
4. It could invest in new schools, hospitals and infrastructure (roads, rail, etc.).

WORKING WITH OTHERS

Working in pairs or small groups, consider the following questions.
- What might you do if you were Minister for Finance and there was a surplus in the national budget?
- What might you do if you were Minister for Finance and there was a deficit in the national budget?

DEPARTMENT SPENDING

Government departments need funding to provide services to the public. Some departments need more money than others, but all provide necessary services:

- **Security**, e.g. the army and the Gardaí
- **Essential services** and public utilities, e.g. education and health services
- **Services that are too expensive for private companies**, e.g. hospitals
- **Employment**, e.g. the public and civil service

WORKING WITH OTHERS

Source additional information on the following departments. Find out the name of the minister for each department and source the departments' logos. Copy and fill in the table.

Department	Services	Minister	Logo
Agriculture, Food and the Marine			
Arts, Heritage, Regional, Rural and Gaeltacht Affairs			
Children and Youth Affairs			
Communications, Climate Action and Environment			
Defence			
Education and Skills			
Finance			
Foreign Affairs and Trade			
Health			
Housing, Planning, Community and Local Government			
Jobs, Enterprise and Innovation			
Justice and Equality			
Public Expenditure and Reform			
Social Protection			
The Taoiseach			
Transport, Tourism and Sport			

3.4 BE BUSINESS: OUR ECONOMY

CHECKING IN...

1. In your opinion, what are the three most important government departments? Explain your choices.
2. Which, do you think, are the least important departments? Why?

GOVERNMENT REVENUE (INCOME)

The government receives revenue from many sources that can be categorised as taxation income and non-taxation income.

TAXATION INCOME

The following taxes are explained in more detail in Unit 3.5. Taxation revenue accounts for over 90 per cent of the Irish government's overall revenue.

- Income tax (PAYE, PRSI and USC)
- VAT (value added tax)
- DIRT (deposit interest retention tax)
- Corporation tax (tax on companies' profits)
- Capital gains tax (tax on the profit from a sale of an asset)
- Capital acquisition tax (tax on gifts and inheritance)
- Customs duties (tax on goods coming into the country)
- Excise duties (tax on cigarettes, alcohol and diesel/petrol)
- Stamp duty (tax on legal documents)
- Water tax
- Tax on property
- Carbon tax

NON-TAXATION INCOME

- TV and dog licences
- Court fines
- Passports
- Interest on loans
- Levies (e.g. the plastic bag levy)
- Fees for prescriptions

OTHER SOURCES OF INCOME

- EU grants and loans
- Selling off state-sponsored bodies (companies owned by the government)
- Profits from state-sponsored bodies

Be an Employee: when the government takes tax, from the employee's perspective it is an expense.

Be the Government: however, from the government's perspective it is income.

GOVERNMENT REVENUE AND GOVERNMENT EXPENDITURE 3.4

We can further categorise **income** and **expenditure** into **current** and **capital**.
1. **Current** is regular day-to-day income or expenditure.
2. **Capital** is long-term or once-off income or expenditure.

Current Income	Capital Income
Taxes – day to day	EU grants – large amounts
Current Expenditure	**Capital Expenditure**
Wages for doctors, nurses, teachers, etc.	Building new roads, schools, hospitals, etc.

GOVERNMENT EXPENDITURE (SPENDING)

Government expenditure refers to public spending on goods and services. Over **€51,400 million in the 2016 budget** was allocated to be spent by government departments.

INTERESTED PARTIES

Everyone has an interest in government income and expenditure.

Be a consumer: interested in any increase in VAT or duties

Be an employee: interested in any changes in PAYE, PRSI, USC and other taxes

Be an employer: interested in any changes in PRSI (the employer has to pay a percentage of employees' PRSI) and corporation tax

Be unemployed: interested in any changes in social welfare

Be a pensioner: interested in any changes in pensions

Be a financial institution: interested in how healthy the economy is and how government spending will affect them from a borrowing perspective

Be the EU: interested to see if the economy has improved, as this affects our ability to pay back debt and keep to any conditions

Be a trade union: interested in improved conditions for employees

Be a non-profit organisation: interested in whether government spending will help the less fortunate

Be a student: interested in spending on education and ensuring a secure country for the future

EXAMPLE 2: PREPARING A BUDGET

The following estimated figures were presented on Budget Day for the year 2019.

Revenue and Expenditure for Government	Estimated Figures in Millions €
Education and skills	2,000
Corporation tax	1,675
Agriculture and marine	1,000
Health services	4,500
USC	1,000
PAYE	3,925
Social protection	1,750
Debt servicing	1,250
VAT	3,150
Excise duties	335

Show the revenue and expenditure figures in graphical form.

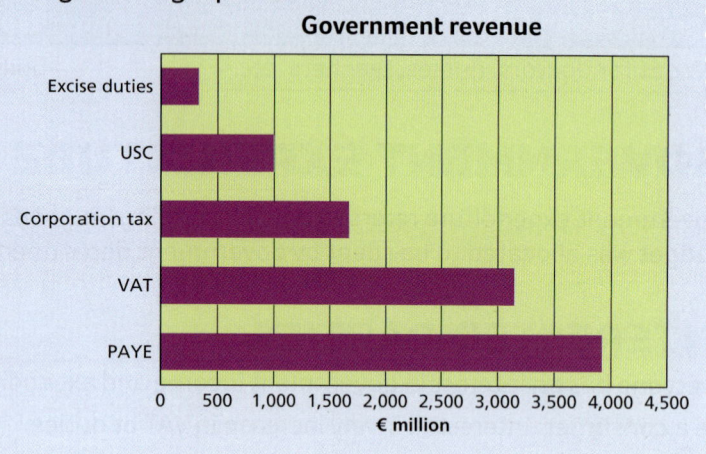

Government revenue

Government expenditure

Calculate the government's budget for 2019.

National Budget 2019		
Revenue	€ million	€ million
Corporation tax	1,675	
Excise duties	335	
PAYE	3,925	
USC	1,000	
VAT	3,150	
		10,085
Expenditure		
Health services	4,500	
Social protection	1,750	
Education and skills	2,000	
Debt servicing	1,250	
Agriculture and marine	1,000	
		10,500
Budget Deficit		**(415)**

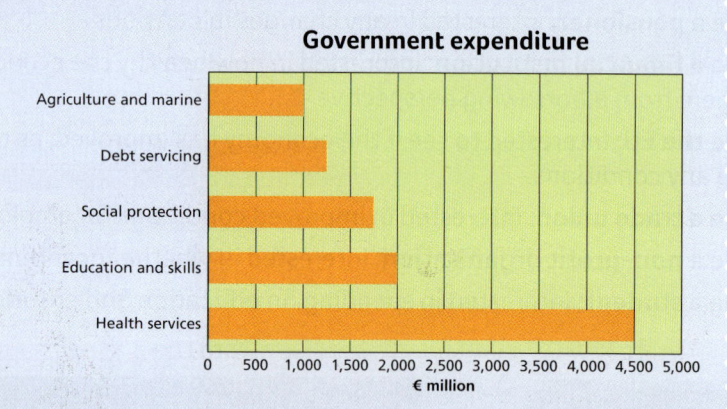

GOVERNMENT REVENUE AND GOVERNMENT EXPENDITURE 3.4

Make a pie chart

1. Present the information in Example 2 in a pie chart.

2. The Minister for Finance, having received all the estimates from the various ministers, presented the following figures for the National Budget of 2020. Answer the questions below the table.

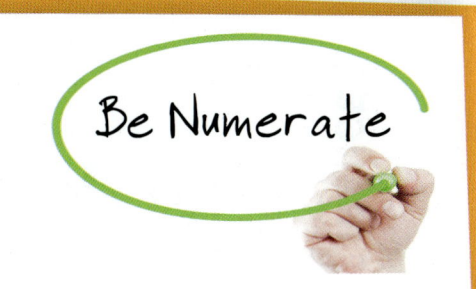

National Budget 2020

Revenue and Expenditure for Government	€ millions	Income or Expenditure
Education	10,250	
PRSI	3,580	
Health services	19,750	
Social welfare	15,500	
USC	6,600	
Justice	9,500	
Transport	4,500	
PAYE	16,750	
DIRT	3,750	
Excise duties	7,500	
VAT	17,250	
Corporation tax	8,750	
Other income: fines, licences, levies	1,430	

Be the Government:

Check whether each figure is income or expenditure
For example, PRSI is a tax:
For the government it's income
For an employee it's expenditure
Remember: we are looking at the figures from the point of view of the government

You are the Minister for Finance:

1. Draft the National Budget for 2020 from the above information.
2. Indicate whether it is a surplus or a deficit budget.
3. Every year the Irish government spends large sums of money on education. Give three examples of government spending on education.
4. Present the budget using graphs/diagrams to demonstrate income.
5. Present the budget using graphs/diagrams to demonstrate expenditure.
6. Write a tweet, using the Twitter template on p. 546, about the national budget.
7. What might the social welfare estimates include?
8. What might the health estimates include? Can you identify three expenditures?

3.4 BE BUSINESS: OUR ECONOMY

BE THE GOVERNMENT... BE THE MINISTER OF FINANCE...

ALL SHOULD/MUST BUDGET!
- INDIVIDUALS
- HOUSEHOLDS
- ORGANISATIONS — FOR-PROFIT / NOT-FOR-PROFIT
- GOVERNMENT
  * RUNS THE COUNTRY
  * LARGEST EMPLOYER
  * RUNS ENTERPRISE
  * LAWS TO PROTECT
  * SUPPORT

NATIONAL BUDGET = GOVERNMENT BUDGET

EXPENDITURE

CURRENT * DAY TO DAY
CAPITAL * LONG-TERM

- HEALTH
- EDUCATION
- ENTERPRISE
- FOREIGN
- TRANSPORT
- TOURISM
- AGRICULTURE
- FOOD
- CHILDREN
- ENVIRONMENT
- LOCAL COMMUNITY
- ENERGY
- FINANCE
- ENVIRONMENT
- ETC
- *SOCIAL WELFARE

GOVERNMENT REVENUE & EXPENDITURE — UNIT 3.4

NATIONAL DEBT — 3.9

DEFICIT
- GOVERNMENT BORROWS
- TAXATION ← → SPENDING
- EU
- SELL OFF SEMI-STATE BODIES

SURPLUS
- TAX
- PAY OFF SOME OF OUR DEBT ← → SPENDING
- GRANTS – ENTERPRISE

BUDGET
* INCOME
* EXPENDITURE

REVENUE

TAXATION: INCOME, VAT, DIRT, CORPORATION TAX, CAPITAL ACQUISITION TAX, CUSTOMS DUTIES, STAMP DUTIES, WATER TAX, TAX ON PROPERTY, CARBON TAX

NON-TAX: FEES FOR SERVICES, PASSPORTS, MEDICINE, TV LICENCE, DOG LICENCE

EU: GRANTS, BORROWING

SEMI-STATE: PROFITS, INTEREST/DIVIDEND

PRIVATISATION: SALE OF STATE-SPONSORED BODIES — 3.10, 3.11

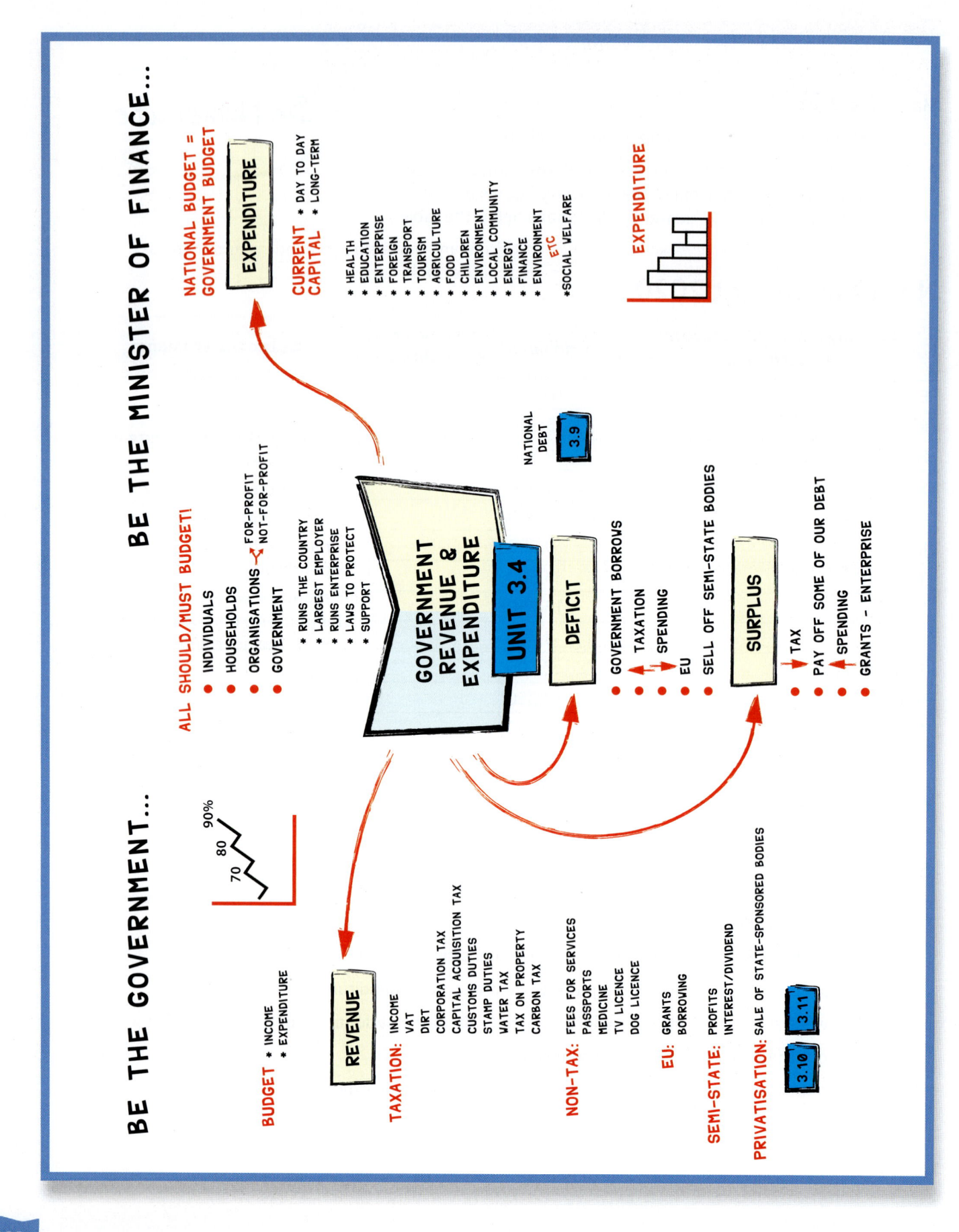

446

GOVERNMENT REVENUE AND GOVERNMENT EXPENDITURE 3.4

Be Prepared: My Support Sheets

Completing the activities here will help you to reflect on and reinforce your learning before you move on to the next unit.

- Write down the **key terms** in this unit and make sure you understand them. See if they match the ones at the back of the book.
- List the **key concepts/themes** in this unit.
- List the **three most interesting points** about this unit.

THE SIZZLING SEAT

A chair is placed facing the class and a student is given a character.

In this case: **Be the Minister for Finance**.

Class groups spend five minutes thinking up challenging questions to ask the minister. Each student or group will represent a different government department.

Students ask the minister their questions and the minister attempts to answer them.

Afterwards the class consider the following questions:

1. What did you learn from this exercise?
2. What did you find fascinating and helpful?
3. Would you challenge anything the minister said? Give reasons.
4. Has this exercise changed your opinion? Give reasons.

Economics in Action Idea!

Source an Irish newspaper, e.g. *The Irish Times*, the *Sunday Business Post* or the *Independent*.

Skim read the headings. Do any relate to the units in Our Economy?

Can you source new information?

Success criteria:
- Your information should be dated
- Information must be current and relevant

QUESTION TIME

1. Explain government income.
2. Explain government expenditure.
3. What is a deficit and how might the government deal with this?
4. What is a surplus and how might the government deal with this?
5. List all the different types of government income and government expenditure.
6. Compare and contrast the government budget with a household budget.
7. Discuss the various stakeholders that are interested in government spending.

EVALUATE MY LEARNING: DAR

Describe
- Did I/we meet my/our learning intentions?
- What went well? What are my/our strengths?

Assess
- How did I/we work with others?
- Were there challenges?

Recommend
- What skills and learning might I apply to new situations?
- How might I improve?

Stop and think
Do I have any questions or concerns?
What are the mistakes or errors I made in this unit?

Do your **Key Check** in the workbook for this unit and then mark your learning position on the following rating scale:

Understood nothing 1 2 3 4 5 6 7 8 9 10 Fully understood

How can you move up the rating scale? What can you **say**, **make**, **write** and **do** to illustrate your learning?

CBA 1 Business in Action:
Will I use this unit for my **Economics in Action**?

You need to be preparing for your CBAs

- Exceptional
- Above expectations
- In line with expectations
- Yet to meet expectations

3.5 TAXATION

Examine the purpose of taxation from a financial, social, legal and ethical perspective.

Learning Intentions
At the end of this unit I will:
- Know about the characteristics of a tax system
- Be able to make arguments for and against tax
- Understand the results of choices from different perspectives
- Value the importance of taxation from a financial, social, legal and ethical perspective

Making the links with other LOs:

- 1.4 Key personal taxes
- 1.9 Ethics and sustainable consumption
- 3.4 Government revenue and government expenditure
- 3.9 Economic indicators
- 3.10 Economic issues
- 3.11 Economic policy

Are there other LOs?

Key Concepts
- ✓ Taxation
- ✓ Water tax, property tax, USC
- ✓ Tax avoidance and evasion
- ✓ Tax as a social duty
- ✓ Tax on sugar

Wonderful Worthwhile Websites
www.revenue.ie
www.citizensinformation.ie

WHY PAY TAX?

Taxation is a **compulsory payment** to the government. Individuals and organisations pay tax on income earned as well as on the purchase of goods and services, on savings and on property they own.

1. The government needs money and taxation is a really important **source of income/revenue**.
2. The government **provides lots of services** to run a country and it needs money to pay for this (see Unit 3.4).
3. From a social perspective, it is important to tax the wealthy and **redistribute income/wealth** to the less well off. Taxation is a way of bridging the gap between the well off and the less well off.
4. Taxation can **influence consumption** (what consumers use). For example, if the government wants to discourage people buying cigarettes, it can increase the tax on cigarettes. If the government wants people to spend more in a particular industry, it can reduce value added tax (VAT) on that industry's products.
5. Taxation can even **encourage savings**. If the government decreased deposit interest retention tax (DIRT: a tax on the interest on savings), individuals might be more inclined to save.
6. Taxes on imports can **protect goods produced in a country**. Import tax on non-EU goods can encourage consumers to buy European-made goods.

'3Ts' = Think, Turn, Talk
Do you have any savings in a savings account? Did you know that you pay DIRT on your savings?
What might happen if the government reduced DIRT?

As with all areas of business, there are financial, social, legal and ethical issues when it comes to taxation.

CHARACTERISTICS OF A TAX SYSTEM

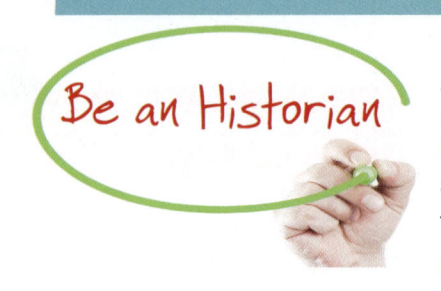

Be an Historian

Adam Smith (1723–1790) was a Scottish economist who is known as the Father of Modern Economics. According to Smith, there are four canons or principles of taxation.

To Smith, a good tax system is one which provides:

1. Equality or equity
2. Certainty
3. Convenience
4. Economy

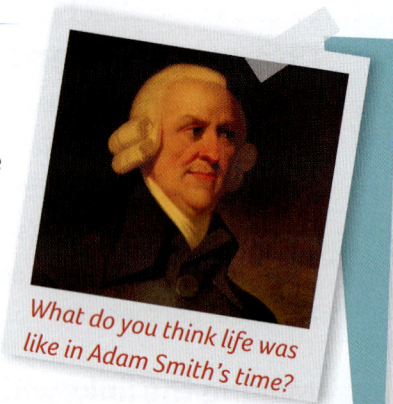

What do you think life was like in Adam Smith's time?

A tax system should have the following characteristics:

- It should be **equitable** – the more you earn the more tax you pay.
- It should be **certain** – each taxpayer should know how much tax they have to pay.
- It should be **convenient** for the taxpayer. A good example is PAYE, where the tax is deducted from pay each week/month.
- It should be **economical**. The cost of collecting the tax should only be a proportion of the tax revenue.

E
C
C
E

DIRECT AND INDIRECT TAXATION

Taxes can be divided into two basic types:

- **Direct taxation**: tax on income or wealth
- **Indirect taxation**: tax on goods and services

Direct tax is considered a **progressive tax** as it is linked to income earned; so it takes a larger percentage from high-income earners than it does from low-income earners.

Indirect tax is considered a **regressive tax** because everyone, regardless of income level, pays the same amount; so lower-income earners pay a larger share of their income than wealthier earners.

DIRECT TAXATION

A direct tax is a tax on income or wealth and is paid by the income earner. The more earned, the more tax is paid. Some would argue that this is a disincentive to work longer hours.

Direct taxes include the following:

- Income tax (PAYE)
- Universal Social Charge (USC)
- Pay Related Social Insurance (PRSI)
- Corporation tax
- Deposit interest retention tax (DIRT)
- Water charges
- Local property tax (LPT)

See Unit 1.4 for more information on PAYE, USC and PRSI.

Corporation Tax

Corporation tax is a tax paid by companies that are making a profit. In Ireland the rate has been kept low over recent years to encourage companies to set up here. Some would say that this gives Ireland an unfair advantage over other countries.

DIRT (Deposit Interest Retention Tax)

DIRT is tax paid on the interest you receive on your savings.

If you have savings of €1,000 and interest is 10% you will receive €100 interest on your savings. However, this interest is **income** and liable to DIRT. If the rate of DIRT is 33%, you will receive €67 in interest.

Interest from savings	€100
DIRT	€33
Interest received after DIRT	€67

DIRT is taken directly from your interest and forwarded to the exchequer. It is additional income for the government. DIRT affects the better off more than the less well off.

Water Charges

Water charges were introduced in 2013 to provide money for each county council (local government). Water charges were not new for businesses but had never been charged directly to householders.

In 2016, water charges were suspended while a commission looks into ways of funding the water system. The commission will have to take into account, among other things, these pros and cons of a water charge:

Pros
- It's a source of **income** for the government.
- The income can be used for **maintaining** the water supply and **improving** the quality of water.
- It will encourage households to be innovative, environmentally friendly and to **reduce water usage**. (While it's currently a flat rate, it may in the future be based on usage.)
- It brings Ireland in line with all **other EU countries** who already have this tax.

Cons
- It is an additional expense for consumers so they have **less money to spend** in the economy.
- Larger families pay more as they use more water – it is a considerable **extra expense** for this kind of household.
- It is **inequitable**, as householders' earnings are not taken into account. High earners and low earners pay the same.

Time to think

Do you think water charges are equitable, certain, convenient and economical?

Local Property Tax

Property tax came into effect in 2013 and is charged on the market value of all residential properties in the State.

Pros
- It's a source of **income** for the government.

Cons
- It **reduces consumer spending** as more money is spent on tax.
- It is **inequitable**, as householders' earnings are not taken into account. High earners and low earners pay the same.

WORKING WITH OTHERS

Debating is an excellent way to view both perspectives or sides of an argument. Debate the following motion: 'Property tax should be avoided.'

INDIRECT TAXATION

Indirect taxation is tax on goods and services. Unlike direct tax, it is not paid directly to Revenue. It is paid to the seller, who in turn pays it to Revenue.

Indirect taxes include the following:
- Value added tax (VAT)
- Import tax
- Motor registration tax
- Excise tax (for example on alcohol and cigarettes)

WORKING WITH OTHERS

What's your view? Be the Government, Be the Individual, Be the Business. Look at the USC, water charges and DIRT and give reasons for and reasons against having these taxes.

CHECKING IN...

1. Why does the government collect taxes?
2. What is direct taxation? Give two examples.
3. What is indirect taxation? Give two examples.

CASE STUDY:
THE BITTERSWEET TRUTH – TAX ON SUGAR

Governments and beverage producers across the world are in conflict over taxes on sugary drinks. Some countries impose a tax on them; for example, Hungary introduced a sugar tax in 2011.

Why might a government tax sugar consumption?

It has to do with promoting good health and preventing diseases such as diabetes and cancer. There is a direct link between excessive sugar consumption, leading to obesity, and developing life-threatening diseases. The healthcare costs associated with treating these diseases must be funded by the government. The more obesity-related diseases there are, the more expensive it is for the government.

However, taxing sugary drinks may not necessarily lead to a change in consumption. We have seen a similar situation in Ireland, with tax increases on cigarettes not necessarily leading to a decrease in the consumption of cigarettes.

WORKING WITH OTHERS

- Research the amount of sugar in the drinks your class consumes on a weekly basis. Are you surprised? Present your information in a visual form.
- Will any of your class change drinks as a result of the findings? Should there be a tax on these drinks, with extra tax on the ones that contain the most sugar?
- What might be the results of consuming excessive amounts of sugar?

TAX AVOIDANCE

Some organisations go to great lengths to avoid paying tax – this is known as **tax avoidance**.

A for-profit enterprise aims to make a profit. Taxation is an extra cost/expense. It will be recorded in the **Income Statement**. Just like any other expense, a business will try to reduce its tax costs by availing of any government incentives, such as tax allowances, deductions, rebates (tax back) and exemptions (valid reasons not to pay tax). Another example of tax avoidance is the use of overseas tax havens (countries where tax rates are low).

Tax avoidance is legal, but it can be seen as bending the rules. So organisations can **avoid** tax and comply with the law, but is this really the **ethical** (right) thing to do?

Time to think

What are your thoughts on tax avoidance?

If you found out a company was avoiding paying tax, would it put you off the company?

PAYING A FAIR SHARE

Some very successful and highly profitable multinational businesses pay little or no local **corporation tax**. Corporation tax is a tax on profits, so the greater a company's profits, the more tax they should pay.

When our government is reducing spending and making cutbacks because of a lack of money, is it fair that some multinational businesses **avoid paying** their fair share of taxes?

Tax avoidance can make a company appear greedy and even damage its reputation. Paying a fair amount of tax in the country where it operates is the **socially responsible** thing for a company to do. After all, the tax a company pays is income to our government to pay for the infrastructure that they need to run the company, and for healthcare and education for their employees. Companies benefit directly and indirectly. You can understand why some argue that the practice of tax avoidance is wrong and **unethical**.

On the other hand, one could argue that businesses have a responsibility to **maximise profit** and to provide a return to shareholders. Businesses pay many other taxes, such as PRSI, rates, water charges, etc.

TAX EVASION

Tax avoidance is legal, but it can be seen as bending the rules. In contrast, **tax evasion** means using illegal methods of not paying tax. It could involve under-declaring or not declaring income to Revenue.

Tax evasion is a **criminal offence**.

Revenue has powers to tackle tax evaders and can secure information about taxpayers from third parties and financial institutions. **Tax clearance certificates** (which prove that you have paid tax) were introduced in the 1980s as a measure to combat tax evasion.

> **Did You Know?**
>
> Revenue has an online service known as **ROS** (Revenue Online Service).
>
> ROS is an internet facility that allows taxpayers a quick and secure way to file their tax returns and to access information and details about their tax. ROS is available 24 hours a day, 7 days a week, 365 days a year.
>
> ROS won a prestigious EU award for developing this online system.
>
> You can take a look at ROS on **www.revenue.ie**

IMPORTANCE OF TAXATION

Be Financial: we need to be aware of taxation. Taxation is money/income the government uses to provide resources for everyone. For the individual and for-profit organisations, tax is an **expense**; for the government, it is **income**.

Be Social: we need taxation to ensure a better society. Tax revenue is used to provide for the less well off, to support the young and the old, to help people with special needs, the unemployed, etc. Taxation helps the government to deal with areas causing social problems, for example taxes on cigarettes, sugar and alcohol.

Be Legal: we have to pay our tax by law. If we are liable for tax it must be paid. We have looked at tax evasion and tax avoidance. While tax avoidance is legal, we can ask whether it is ethical. There are penalties and even prison sentences for tax evasion.

Be Ethical: paying our taxes helps everyone in our country. Some of our taxes help protect the environment and ensure sustainability, for example carbon tax. Remember, all of our decisions have a moral and an ethical element.

TAXATION 3.5

Be a Researcher

Copy and fill in this personal taxation learning sheet.

Define, **r**ate and **d**escribe the drift (whether it is going up or down) (**DRD**). Use websites to source information.

www.revenue.ie

www.finfacts.ie

Can you find any other websites?

Personal Taxation Learning Sheet

PAYE (Pay As You Earn)
- Define:
- Rate (%):
- Describe the drift.
- Is it increasing or decreasing?

PRSI (Pay Related Social Insurance)
- Define:
- Rate (%):
- Describe the drift.
- Is it increasing or decreasing?

USC (Universal Social Charge)
- Define:
- Rate (%):
- Describe the drift.
- Is it increasing or decreasing?

VAT (Value-Added Tax)
- Define:
- Rate (%):
- Describe the drift.
- Is it increasing or decreasing?

DIRT (Deposit Interest Rate Tax)
- Define:
- Rate (%):
- Describe the drift.
- Is it increasing or decreasing?

Capital Gains Tax
- Define:
- Rate (%):
- Describe the drift.
- Is it increasing or decreasing?

Evaluate your findings:

CHECKING IN...

1. What is tax avoidance? Do you think it's ethical?
2. What is tax evasion? Is it legal?
3. Why is taxation important?

3.5 BE BUSINESS: OUR ECONOMY

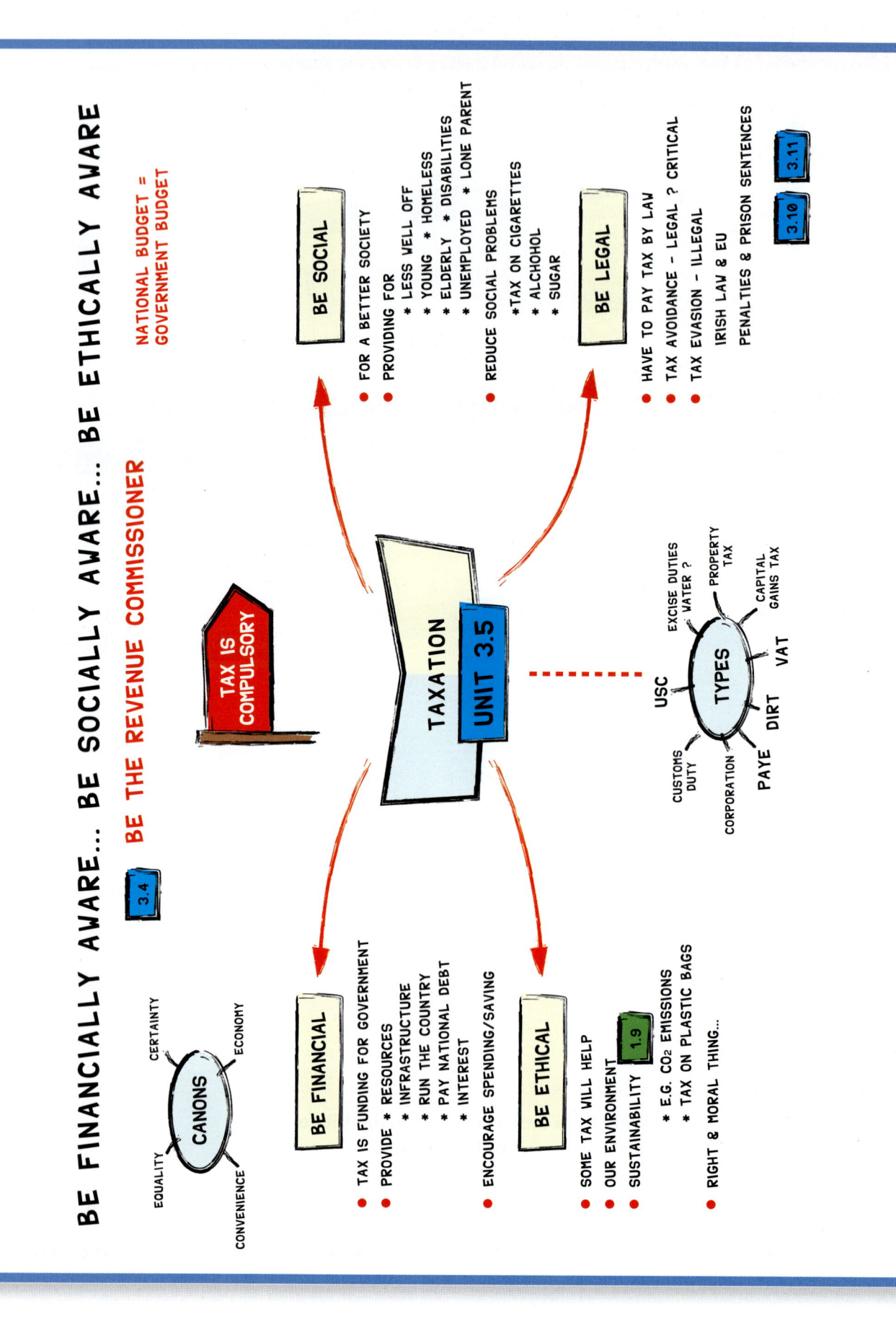

BE FINANCIALLY AWARE... BE SOCIALLY AWARE... BE ETHICALLY AWARE

BE THE REVENUE COMMISSIONER

NATIONAL BUDGET = GOVERNMENT BUDGET

TAXATION — UNIT 3.5

TAX IS COMPULSORY

CANONS
- EQUALITY
- CERTAINTY
- ECONOMY
- CONVENIENCE

TYPES
- EXCISE DUTIES
- WATER ?
- PROPERTY TAX
- CAPITAL GAINS TAX
- VAT
- DIRT
- PAYE
- CORPORATION
- CUSTOMS DUTY
- USC

BE SOCIAL
- FOR A BETTER SOCIETY
- PROVIDING FOR
  * LESS WELL OFF
  * YOUNG   * HOMELESS
  * ELDERLY   * DISABILITIES
  * UNEMPLOYED   * LONE PARENT
- REDUCE SOCIAL PROBLEMS
  * TAX ON CIGARETTES
  * ALCOHOL
  * SUGAR

BE LEGAL
- HAVE TO PAY TAX BY LAW
- TAX AVOIDANCE – LEGAL ? CRITICAL
- TAX EVASION – ILLEGAL
- IRISH LAW & EU
- PENALTIES & PRISON SENTENCES

BE FINANCIAL
- TAX IS FUNDING FOR GOVERNMENT
- PROVIDE   * RESOURCES
  * INFRASTRUCTURE
  * RUN THE COUNTRY
  * PAY NATIONAL DEBT
  * INTEREST
- ENCOURAGE SPENDING/SAVING

BE ETHICAL
- SOME TAX WILL HELP
- OUR ENVIRONMENT
- SUSTAINABILITY
  * E.G. CO_2 EMISSIONS
  * TAX ON PLASTIC BAGS
- RIGHT & MORAL THING...

Be Prepared: My Support Sheets

Completing the activities here will help you to reflect on and reinforce your learning before you move on to the next unit.
- Write down the **key terms** in this unit and make sure you understand them. See if they match the ones at the back of the book.
- List the **key concepts/themes** in this unit.
- List the **three most interesting points** about this unit.

Do a role play

In groups of four, prepare your thoughts for and against increasing the rate of VAT. Each member of the group chooses one of the following roles:
- An individual taxpayer
- A for-profit organisation
- A not-for-profit organisation
- A pensioner

What did you discover from your role play?

Be the Minister

Write a tweet explaining why taxation is good. Use the Twitter template on p. 546.

Add a graph as an attachment to your tweet.

Success criteria:
- Informative graph attached
- Write in a personal way – Twitter is about person-to-person communication
- Readability – make it easy to read
- Retweetability – people should want to share it

QUESTION TIME

1. Discuss the costs and the benefits of taxation.
2. Why do we have to pay taxes? List the taxes an individual has to pay.
3. During Ireland's period of austerity VAT was increased to 23%. Outline the effects of this increase.
4. USC increases as income increases. Might this discourage you from working extra hours? Explain your opinion.
5. Discuss taxation from the taxpayer's perspective and the government's perspective.
6. Compare tax evasion and tax avoidance.

EVALUATE MY LEARNING: DAR

Describe
- Did I/we meet my/our learning intentions?
- What went well? What are my/our strengths?

Assess
- How did I/we work with others?
- Were there challenges?

Recommend
- What skills and learning might I apply to new situations?
- How might I improve?

Do your **Key Check** in the workbook for this unit and then mark your learning position on the following rating scale:

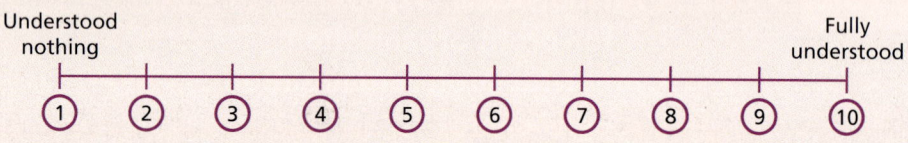

Understood nothing — 1 2 3 4 5 6 7 8 9 10 — Fully understood

How can you move up the rating scale? What can you **say**, **make**, **write** and **do** to illustrate your learning?

CBA 1 Business in Action:
Will I use this unit for my **Economics in Action/Finance in Action**?

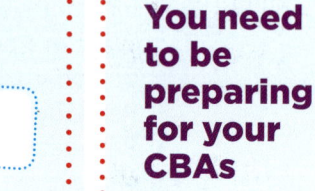

You need to be preparing for your CBAs
- Exceptional
- Above expectations
- In line with expectations
- Yet to meet expectations

CBA 2 Presentation:
Will I use this unit for my **Presentation**?

Stop and think

Revisit this unit in Third Year to document any major changes.

It's a good idea to write the date on any research material you use. Why might you date research material?

Have you changed your opinions on taxation after studying this unit?

Do I have any questions or concerns?
What are the mistakes or errors I made in this unit?

3.6 POSITIVE AND NEGATIVE ECONOMIC GROWTH AND SUSTAINABILITY

Explain how economic growth can impact positively and negatively on society and the environment and justify the promotion of sustainable development.

Learning Intentions

At the end of this unit I will:
- Know and understand the good points and the not so good points about economic growth
- Know and understand the importance of sustainable development
- Know the choices we have to make about sustainable development
- Value sustainable development

Key Concepts
- ✓ Economic growth
- ✓ Sustainable development

Making the links with other LOs:

- 1.9 Ethics and sustainable consumption
- 3.9 Economic indicators
- 3.10 Economic issues
- 3.11 Economic policy

Wonderful Worthwhile Websites

www.un.org
www.globalgoals.org

Are there other LOs?

ECONOMIC GROWTH

One of the ways to measure the health of an economy is by looking at gross domestic product (GDP). The government uses GDP as the best indicator of economic health because it represents the **total market value of all goods and services** during a given year. Unlike gross national product (GNP), it does not include income from overseas investment.

Economic **growth** occurs when there is an **increase in GDP**. If there is growth, it shows that an economy is improving. By economic growth we mean an increase in output per person in the economy. This topic is covered in more detail in Unit 3.9.

A lot of businesses have been accused of only thinking about profit and not about the people around them, such as their employees, customers, young people and people living in their local community.

We need to be aware that economic growth can have both positive and negative effects on society and in particular on our environment, all of which affects people.

IMPACT ON SOCIETY

Economic growth can have positive and negative impacts on society.

Positive

- Improves **living standards** – people have more money to spend
- Creates demand for more goods and services and so more **employment**
- Creates confidence and so **more businesses** are set up
- Government receives **more income** through taxes
- Government pays **less social welfare**
- With more income the government can afford to **improved public services**

Negative

- Even when an economy is growing there may still be **inequalities**, many of the gains from growth may only go to a few people
- Increased demand can lead to **inflation** (higher prices)
- People can get caught up in working and the need to buy more material goods and forget to take care of their **wellbeing**

WELLBEING

Human wellbeing is a complex and varied concept, determined by a wide range of factors including a person's income, health, education, living situation and the quality of their environment.

We need to be aware of how we can improve our wellbeing. We must look after ourselves and also our friends, families and local communities and in doing so we will create a positive impact on our society. In the midst of economic growth and an increase in how busy we are, the following can help our wellbeing:

> Staying well is one of the key skills in your Junior Cycle courses.

1. Be Connected

Developing relationships with other people is really important. Relationships with family, school, local community and friends can give support and a sense of meaning in our lives.

2. Be Active

Experts have shown that exercising releases endorphins in our brains that make us feel good. There are numerous ways that we can exercise, from playing sports to surfing, swimming, mountain climbing, dancing and walking.

3. Be Mindful

We can all get caught up in the busy-ness of modern life. We are all constantly on social media, Instagram, Twitter and Facebook. We need to focus our awareness on what is going on within us and what is going on around us. Taking time to be mindful can work wonders for our mental health – and it's free!

POSITIVE AND NEGATIVE ECONOMIC GROWTH AND SUSTAINABILITY 3.6

4. Be Positive
Positivity can make a difference. Surround yourself with positivity and positive people. Have a **can do** rather than a **can't do** attitude. Set yourself achievable goals.

5. Be Generous
Always be generous with things, money and time. Help your friends, family and classmates. Think about getting involved in a not-for-profit organisation.

6. Be Curious
Continue to learn and be engaged. This can boost confidence. It's not all about books and lectures – learning can take place in many ways. New learning can happen all the time if we are open to it.

Time to think

What have you learned or tried out for the first time recently?

IMPACT ON THE ENVIRONMENT

Economic and environmental performance must go hand in hand. The natural environment is central to economic activity and growth, providing the resources we need to produce goods and services, and absorbing and processing unwanted by-products in the form of pollution and waste.

Economic growth can have positive and negative impacts on the environment.

Positive
- If companies are making more money, they may choose to **invest in environmentally friendly technologies** (e.g. low carbon) as a way of making them more attractive to consumers.
- When economies are doing well, governments may have the time and resources to **address environmental concerns** such as climate change.

Negative
- When more goods are being made it can cause the **depletion** (reduction) of **natural resources** (e.g. wood and fish stocks).
- Rapid growth can create **pollution**, for example noise and air pollution
- There can be an **increase in waste** from businesses and households
- Increased production can lead to a loss of **non-renewable resources** (e.g. gas and coal).

CHECKING IN...
1. What is economic growth?
2. Name four positive and four negatives results of economic growth.
3. What is wellbeing? How can economic growth affect wellbeing?

3.6 BE BUSINESS: OUR ECONOMY

Not everyone benefits from the decision to improve a public transport system. Take a look at this next case study.

CASE STUDY:
SOCIAL COST OF THE NEW LUAS ROUTES

The Luas light rail system is extending its routes to provide a better public transport system in Dublin.

This expansion is not without its drawbacks. The following are some examples of the price the local communities have to pay:

- Increased pollution while the new lines are put in place
- Disruption, traffic congestion and loss of trade for local businesses
- Upsetting the infrastructure that is already in place, for example damage to roads, surrounding buildings, etc.

SOME WORLD ISSUES
POVERTY AND WEALTH

We are all aware of the extreme poverty that exists around the world. We know that money isn't always equally distributed. In Ireland, we often complain about not having everything we want, but when compared with other countries we are actually a lot better off than we sometimes think.

The countries of the world are not equal. Some underdeveloped countries experience extreme poverty. The poorest countries have poor healthcare, high child mortality (deaths of young children), limited access to education, a high rate of HIV and increasing slum populations. The gap between rich and poor is rising, particularly in southern Asia and parts of Africa. Many people do not have access to clean water or enough affordable food and malnutrition is widespread.

POSITIVE AND NEGATIVE ECONOMIC GROWTH AND SUSTAINABILITY 3.6

Trócaire provides humanitarian assistance and long-term support to help underprivileged communities in 20 countries across Africa, Asia, Latin America and the Middle East.

CLIMATE CHANGE

According to the **World Meteorological Organisation**, carbon emissions are at their highest in history and continue to rise. Climate change is already having a serious impact: we are experiencing more frequent and more intense extreme weather events; and agriculture and water supplies all around the world are being affected. Factories have been blamed for climate change and environmental destruction, due to the large amount of fossil fuels they burn and how they treat their local environment.

Now and in the future, businesses will have to think about how they produce goods and services and finding more sustainable ways of doing business.

We need to be enterprising to create jobs!

GLOBAL JOBS CRISIS

In many parts of the world we see increasing unemployment rates, especially among young people. Global employment figures show that world unemployment is edging towards 200 million, and that developing countries (and, in particular, young people) suffer the highest unemployment rates.

THE UNITED NATIONS

In 2012 the **United Nations Conference on Sustainable Development**, also known as **Rio+20**, was held in Rio de Janeiro in Brazil.

Over 1,000 executives from more than 100 countries gathered at the Rio+20 Corporate Sustainability Forum and gave their support to priority issues, including sustainable development. The conference focused on building a green economy and creating an effective institutional framework for sustainable development. Rio+20 had three objectives:

- Secure renewed political **commitment to sustainable development**
- Assess the progress and implementation gaps in **meeting already agreed commitments**
- Address new and **emerging challenges**

The conference looked at the need to agree at all levels – local, national and international. Everyone needs to prioritise sustainability and to find ways of moving more quickly to low-carbon and sustainable economies and societies.

463

SUSTAINABLE DEVELOPMENT GOALS

In 2015 the UN General Assembly accepted a set of 17 measurable Sustainable Development Goals. These range from ending world poverty to achieving gender equality by 2030. The 17 goals replace the eight Millennium Development Goals, which were agreed in September 2000.

The 17 Sustainable Development Goals are:

1. No poverty
2. No hunger
3. Good health
4. Quality education
5. Gender equality
6. Clean water and sanitation
7. Renewable energy
8. Good jobs and economic growth
9. Innovation and infrastructure
10. Reduced inequalities
11. Sustainable cities and communities
12. Responsible consumption
13. Climate action
14. Life below water
15. Life on land
16. Peace and justice
17. Partnership for the goals.

WORKING WITH OTHERS

- Working in pairs, discuss these 17 Sustainable Development Goals. What can you do to help reach these goals?
- Look at each goal from the perspectives of people, profit and our planet.
- You studied not-for-profit organisations as part of Enterprise. What role do you think these organisations play in sustainable development?

SUSTAINABLE DEVELOPMENT

Sustainable development is development that meets the needs of the present without risking the ability of future generations to meet their needs.

POSITIONS AND NEGATIVE ECONOMIC GROWTH AND SUSTAINABILITY   3.6

You have studied this as part of Personal Finance and you looked at interesting ideas to be more sustainable (revisit sustainability in Unit 1.9).

Governments and citizens need to find a balance between ensuring that people have a good quality of life and enough money to meet their needs (and hopefully wants), and at the same time making sure that economic development does not harm society and the environment.

The three main goals of sustainable development are:

- to eliminate poverty
- to protect our planet
- to maintain economic growth

Moving to a **sustainable economic growth path** will not happen overnight, but it is essential if we are to secure long-term economic growth and make the economy strong enough to deal with risks in the future.

Free Trade Ireland

Free Trade Ireland is an interesting example of people coming together to help the environment. Its motto is **don't rubbish it, reuse it**.

People register on the Free Trade Ireland website and post a photo of an item they don't want. Someone who does want the item then makes contact and the product is passed on. No money is exchanged.

Some of the benefits of this service are:

- Reduces waste disposal costs
- Encourages better use of household and business resources by extending the lifespan of products
- Gives a great sense of community
- Environmentally friendly
- It's free!

Check out the Free Trade Ireland website on www.freetradeireland.ie

CHECKING IN...

1. Do you know any other examples of sustainable development?
2. How would you promote sustainability in your school and your community?

WORKING WITH OTHERS

Debate the following statement: 'Economic growth has more negative impacts than positive impacts'.

3.6 BE BUSINESS: OUR ECONOMY

CASE STUDY: BOTTLED WATER

Bottled water is extremely popular. You can buy everything from 'purified spring water' to flavoured water and even water enriched with vitamins and minerals. The growth of the bottled water industry has had an effect on our environment.

Some water is taken from reserves, which can create droughts.

Water is sold in bottles made from polyethylene terephthalate (PET), which uses materials derived from crude oil and natural gas. But PET does not decompose; and even though it can be recycled, it often isn't.

As a result, bottled water is now a cause of plastic waste!

Did you know that a lot of bottled water is actually processed water?

Remember, tap water is free and available in our kitchens!

- Is bottled water tastier than tap water?
- Is it sustainable?

View bottled water through the lens of People, Profit and our Planet.

People: think about employment, income

Profit: for-profit organisations creating jobs, profits, taxation

Planet: carbon emissions, the ozone layer, health issues

CHECKING IN...

Copy and fill in this 'Not-for-profit and Sustainability Learning Sheet'. You can use websites to source information. Make a note of any websites used and the date you used them.

Not-for-profit and Sustainability Learning Sheet

Name of **not-for-profit organisation**	
Aims of organisation	
Website	
Local, national or International	
Examples of how this organisation promotes/encourages and helps sustainable development	
Develop ideas it might use to help sustainable development	
Evaluate the costs and benefits	

POSITIVE AND NEGATIVE ECONOMIC GROWTH AND SUSTAINABILITY 3.6

BE AWARE...

WELLBEING

OUR WORLD: POSITIVE, MINDFUL, GENEROUS, ACTIVE, CURIOUS, EQUAL, CONNECTED

UNIT 3.6 — POSITIVE/NEGATIVE ECONOMIC GROWTH & SUSTAINABILITY

TOTAL PRODUCTION → GDP

ECONOMIC GROWTH

NOT SO GOOD POINTS
- POLLUTION
  - HOUSES
  - ORGANISATIONS — FOR-PROFIT – NOT-FOR-PROFIT
  - WASTE
- SUSTAINABILITY (1.9)
- INEQUITY

ALL HAVE A PART TO PLAY
- PEOPLE
- PROFIT
- PLANET...

OUR PLANET: SUSTAINABLE DEVELOPMENT, POVERTY, CLIMATE CHANGE → CLIMATE WARMING / CO_2, SUSTAINABLE ENERGY, GLOBAL JOB CRISIS, INJUSTICE, INEQUALITY (1.9)

GOOD POINTS (3.4)
- IMPROVES LIVING STANDARDS
- EMPLOYMENT
- BUSINESSES
- GOVERNMENT ↑ TAX ETC

GLOBALISATION (3.7 / 1.10)
AS THE WORLD SHRINKS AND BECOMES ONE BIG MARKET

FOR ALL COUNTRIES

SOLUTION → CARBON FOOTPRINT (1.9)

THE GLOBAL GOALS
For Sustainable Development

1. NO POVERTY
2. ZERO HUNGER
3. GOOD HEALTH AND WELL-BEING
4. QUALITY EDUCATION
5. GENDER EQUALITY
6. CLEAN WATER AND SANITATION
7. AFFORDABLE AND CLEAN ENERGY
8. DECENT WORK AND ECONOMIC GROWTH
9. INDUSTRY, INNOVATION AND INFRASTRUCTURE
10. REDUCED INEQUALITIES
11. SUSTAINABLE CITIES AND COMMUNITIES
12. RESPONSIBLE CONSUMPTION AND PRODUCTION
13. CLIMATE ACTION
14. LIFE BELOW WATER
15. LIFE ON LAND
16. PEACE AND JUSTICE
17. PARTNERSHIPS FOR THE GOALS

THE GLOBAL GOALS

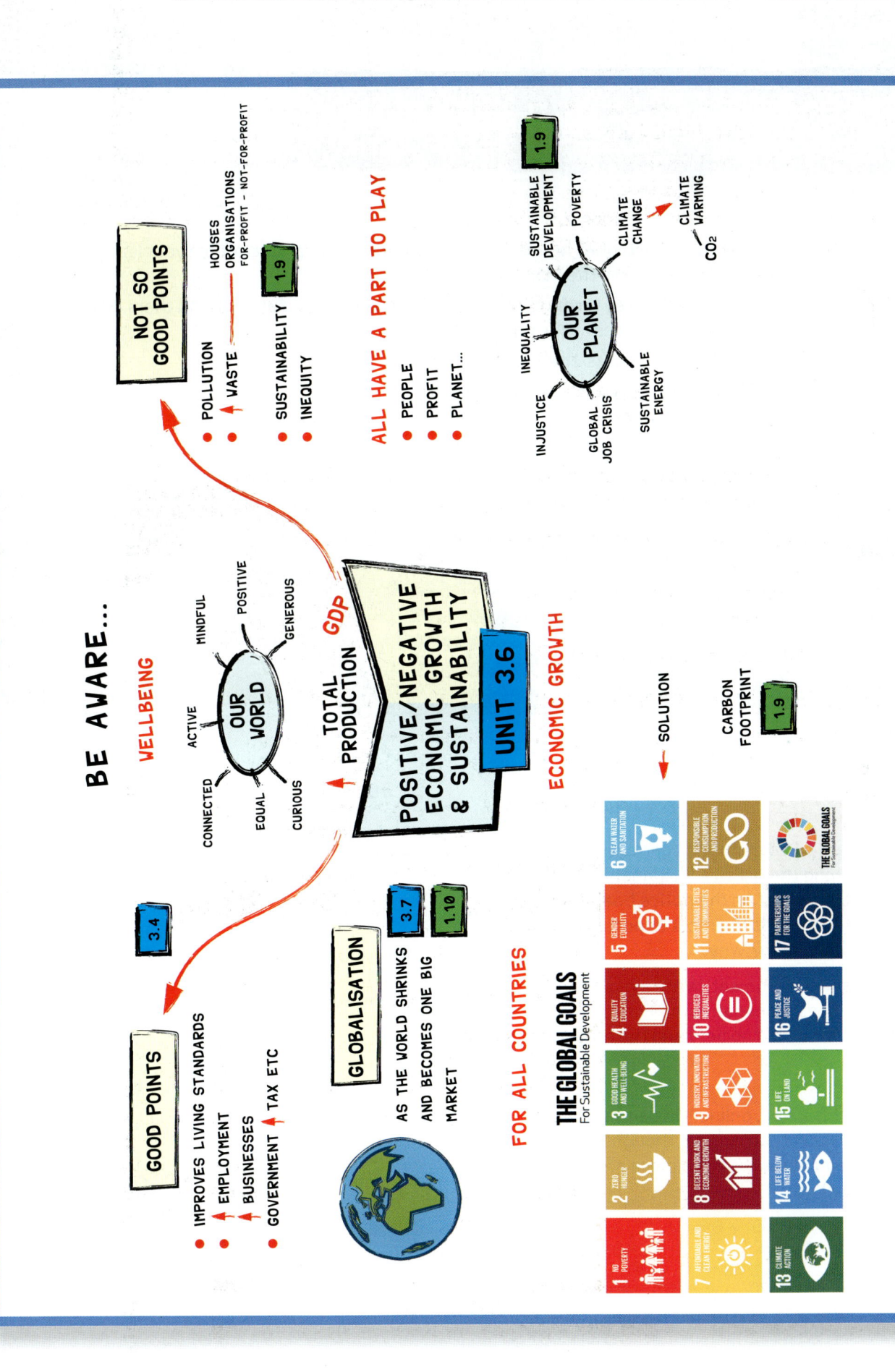

467

Be Prepared: My Support Sheets

Completing the activities here will help you to reflect on and reinforce your learning before you move on to the next unit.

- Write down the **key terms** in this unit and make sure you understand them. See if they match the ones at the back of the book.
- List the **key concepts/themes** in this unit.
- List the **three most interesting points** about this unit.

Use placemats

Individually write down all you know on economic growth and sustainability. Working together in groups of four (A, B, C and D), and using the placemat template on p. 82, write down a consensus (what you all agree on) in the middle. Prioritise the three most important areas.

Economics in Action Idea!

1. Create a Padlet notice board (www.padlet.ie) showing the UN's 17 Sustainable Development Goals. Reflect on the notice board. Which do you think is the most important goal for sustainability? Why?
2. Be the government. Write a report on the positive and negative impacts of economic growth on our society and the environment.

Padlet is a free, online 'virtual wall' tool where users can express thoughts on topics of their choice. It's like a piece of paper, but on the Web.

Success criteria:
- Title and introduction
- Appropriate background
- Link to relevant information
- Clear purpose and focus
- Three positive and three negative
- Conclusion – summarise main points
- Information from a variety of sources

Success criteria:
- Title and introduction
- Clear purpose and focus
- Three positive and three negative
- Conclusion – summarise main points
- Information from a variety of sources

QUESTION TIME

1. Discuss the impact of economic growth on our society.
2. Discuss the impact of economic growth on our environment.
3. Illustrate your understanding of wellbeing.
4. Describe how a not-for-profit organisation can be sustainable.
5. Is our government addressing sustainability? Discuss.

EVALUATE MY LEARNING: DAR

Describe
- Did I/we meet my/our learning intentions?
- What went well? What are my/our strengths?

Assess
- How did I/we work with others?
- Were there challenges?

Recommend
- How might I improve?
- What skills and learning might I apply to new situations?

Stop and think
Do I have any questions or concerns?
What are the mistakes or errors I made in this unit?

Do your **Key Check** in the workbook for this unit and then mark your learning position on the following rating scale:

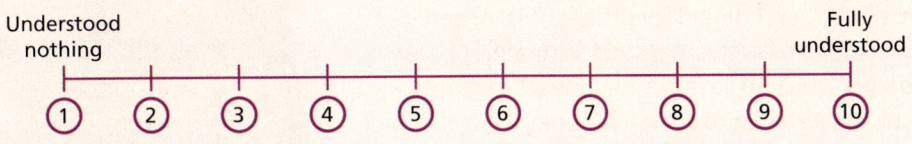

Understood nothing ① ② ③ ④ ⑤ ⑥ ⑦ ⑧ ⑨ ⑩ Fully understood

How can you move up the rating scale? What can you **say**, **make**, **write** and **do** to illustrate your learning?

CBA 1 Business in Action:
Will I use this unit for my topic **Economics in Action**?

You need to be preparing for your CBAs

- Exceptional
- Above expectations
- In line with expectations
- Yet to meet expectations

3.7 GLOBALISATION OF TRADE

Debate the implications of globalisation of trade, including the benefits and challenges of international trade.

Learning Intentions

At the end of this unit I will:
- Know about globalisation
- Understand the benefits and challenges of globalisation
- Know about the balance of trade and the balance of payments
- Value international trade

Making the links with other LOs:

1.9	Ethics and sustainable consumption
1.10	Globalisation and technology
3.6	Positive and negative economic growth and sustainability
3.8	European Union: benefits and challenges
3.10	Economic issues
3.11	Economic policy

Are there other LOs?

Key Concepts
- ✓ Globalisation
- ✓ International trade, imports and exports
- ✓ Balance of trade and balance of payments
- ✓ Currency conversions

Wonderful Worthwhile Websites
www.businesseducation.ie
www.cso.ie
www.tutor2u.net/economics

INTRODUCTION

Thousands of years ago people used a **bartering** system. Goods or services were directly exchanged for other goods or services without using a medium of exchange, such as money. In order for bartering to work, you had to find someone who wanted your product, but you also had to want what they were offering!

After bartering came **trade**. Trade is when goods and services are exchanged for payment. There is local trade, national/domestic trade (within a country) and international trade.

> **Did You Know?**
> Bartering hasn't been consigned to history. A community in Clonakilty, County Cork have set up their own bartering system. It's called the Clonakilty Favour Exchange.
>
> You can find out more about the Clonakilty Favour Exchange at www.clonakiltyfavourexchange.ie

GLOBALISATION OF TRADE 3.7

You looked at an introduction to globalisation in Unit 1.10. We will now investigate globalisation in more detail.

GLOBALISATION

Economic globalisation describes how countries are coming together to create one global economy, making international trade easier. National economies can develop into international economies.

National companies can develop into multinational companies with subsidiaries all over the world. This expansion of international markets can allow the free movement of goods, services, labour and capital, resulting in a very **large, single world global market**.

In Strand 1 you learned about the good points and the not so good points of globalisation. Economic globalisation has also created winners and losers.

BENEFITS

It is argued that economic globalisation can be beneficial to developing countries. As countries improve economically, it creates the conditions for human rights to improve: for example women's rights, enabling children to go to school instead of having to work, and the reduction of poverty.

Globalisation increases income and in turn improves the standard of living in a country. India and China were opened up to trade and direct foreign investment in the 1980s and this has led to a dramatic reduction in poverty in those countries.

CHALLENGES

Critics of economic globalisation believe that the world free market is undesirable and also unrealistic. They say that it is the more powerful and richer countries that make the rules of economic globalisation and that get all the benefits, at the expense of the poorer countries.

WHY HAS GLOBALISATION EXPANDED?

The speed of globalisation has increased for a number of reasons:

1. Improvements in **technology and communications** have helped the development of globalisation. The internet enables global communication 24 hours a day, seven days a week, 365 days a year.
2. Improvements in **transportation** and the introduction of standardised containers in shipping (see box) allows huge quantities of goods to be shipped around the world at very low cost.
3. Sophisticated **online payment methods** have increased the speed of trade.
4. The growth of **multinational companies** (MNCs) and the increase in global brands like Apple, Microsoft and McDonald's has been central to the development of globalisation.

> Multinational companies such as Apple and McDonald's are also known as **transnational companies** (TNCs) as they produce and sell goods in more than one country.

> **Containerisation** is a system that uses standard-sized containers to transport goods. These containers can be loaded and unloaded between ships, trains and trucks using mechanical lifting equipment. The containers don't need to be opened or stored in expensive warehouses and are numbered and tracked using computer programs. Containerisation has reduced the cost of transportation and helped globalisation.

ECONOMIC ADVANTAGES

1. Globalisation is an incentive for countries to **specialise** and benefit from **comparative advantage** (being able to produce goods more efficiently than another country).
2. Access to larger markets means that businesses may experience greater demand for their products. They should benefit from **economies of scale** (the more units produced, the cheaper the unit cost), which in turn leads to a reduction in production costs and more profits for the business.
3. Globalisation gives businesses access to cheap raw materials, and this enables firms to be more **competitive**.
4. An increase in trade and production should lead to an **increase in employment** in all the countries involved.
5. **Shareholders** will be happy. As businesses make more profits they will pay higher dividends. (Remember, a dividend is the interest that shareholders receive on their investment.)

ECONOMIC DISADVANTAGES

1. One of the biggest risks of globalisation is that countries become **too dependent** on each other. A negative economic impact in one country can quickly spread to other countries. In the 1990s an economic crisis in Japan spread across East Asia and many countries went into recession (a period of economic decline).
2. The increased **power and influence of MNCs** can be seen as a disadvantage. For example, large MNCs can switch their investments between countries. This can have a huge impact on the country they leave. There is also no guarantee that MNCs will reinvest their profits in the countries where the goods are produced. Profits are sent back to the countries where the MNCs are based.
3. **Over-specialisation** – producing only a limited range of goods for the global market – is another risk. A sudden downturn in world demand for one of these products can drop an economy into a recession. Many developing countries suffer by over-specialising in areas such as agriculture and tourism.
4. MNCs and their **economies of scale** (see above) could drive local companies out of business.
5. A **lack of international laws** means that MNCs might operate in developing countries in a way they would not be allowed to at home. For example, working conditions, wage rates and environmental policies may not be strictly followed.
6. The growth in trade has **increased pollution** and helped contribute to CO_2 emissions and global warming. Trade growth has also decreased our non-renewable resources, such as oil and gas.
7. Globalisation generates **winners and losers**, and for this reason it is likely to increase inequality, as richer nations benefit more than poorer ones.

ARE ALL GLOBAL PRODUCTS IDENTICAL?

Global businesses sell standardised products. This provides the opportunity for mass production and economies of scale, which lowers costs and therefore increases profitability.

However, not all global products are identical. Some elements are changed to reflect culture, language, values, currency and legislation.

1. Products may need to be adjusted to reflect **technical differences**, for example a left-hand-drive car.
2. Different countries may have **different laws** about packaging and labelling.
3. **Tastes** differ in different parts of the world. Starbucks modifies its menu to fit local tastes. In Hong Kong, for example, they sell Dragon Dumplings.
4. **Prices** may vary, as taxes and duties can vary. Exchange rates can also impact on prices, as currencies can fluctuate (change).

INTERNATIONAL TRADE

Ireland is an open economy and to prosper and maintain growth it needs to export and attract oversees companies to locate in Ireland. This will ensure job creation.

The following organisations work to promote Ireland overseas:
- IDA Ireland (Industrial Development Authority)
- Enterprise Ireland
- Bord Bia
- Tourism Ireland
- Science Foundation Ireland

> An **open economy** is an economy where goods and services are traded with other countries without rules or limits.

When Ireland trades with other countries this is known as **foreign trade** or **international trade**. We can divide Ireland's trade into exports and imports.

The following are some important definitions of national and international trade:

> **Domestic trade** is buying and selling goods and services in our own country.

> **International trade** means selling goods and services to, and buying goods and services from, other countries.

> **Exporting** is when goods and services are sold to other countries.

> **Importing** is buying goods and services from other countries.

Trade can be further divided into visible and invisible trade:

> **Visible trade** is trade in physical goods.

> **Invisible trade** is trade in services.

IMPORTS

Imports are made up of **visible imports** and **invisible imports**. The important thing to remember, whether an import is invisible or visible, is that the **money is leaving** our country.

> Think of an import as money leaving the country.

EXAMPLE 1

If Ireland imports BMWs from Germany it is a **visible import**. Why?
- The BMWs come into Ireland (physical goods)
- Money leaves Ireland and goes to Germany to pay for the BMWs

EXAMPLE 2

If Irish people holiday in New York it is an **invisible import**. Why?
- Nothing physical comes into Ireland
- Money leaves Ireland as Irish money is spent in New York

3.7 BE BUSINESS: OUR ECONOMY

Other visible imports	Other invisible imports
Citrus fruits from Spain	Irish people holidaying in Cuba
Cars from Germany	Irish people using British Airways

Why Import?

1. There are **raw materials** that we don't have in Ireland, for example oil.
2. Our **climate** isn't suited to growing certain products, for example oranges and bananas.
3. We **don't produce** all the products we need, for example cars.
4. Irish people like to **travel** and explore the world.
5. It's really easy to buy goods **online** and import goods from other countries.

Benefits of Importing

1. It gives consumers a greater **variety** of goods.
2. It provides **taxation** for the government, known as customs duty.
3. Consumers can **obtain goods** that would not otherwise be available, for example oil.
4. We import essential **raw materials** which help production and in turn help the economy.

We're used to buying goods and services from all around the world. Our **circular flow of income** is also affected by international trade (see Unit 3.2).

Time to think

Think about where you buy your clothes and accessories. Are any of your clothes or accessories produced in Ireland?

Consider doing an audit of where all the clothes and accessories you bought over the last year were produced.

EXPORTS

Exports are made up of visible exports and invisible exports. The important thing to remember, whether an export is invisible or visible, is that the **money is coming in to** our country.

Think of an export as something good for the country in terms of money.

EXAMPLE 3

If Ireland exports beef to Poland it is a **visible export**. Why?
- Irish beef goes to Poland (physical goods)
- Money (euros) leaves Poland and comes into Ireland to pay for the goods

EXAMPLE 4

If French people holiday in Ireland it is an **invisible export**. Why?
- Nothing physical leaves Ireland
- The French tourists come to Ireland with their money and they spend it in hotels, restaurants, shops, etc., which helps the Irish economy

474

GLOBALISATION OF TRADE 3.7

Other visible exports	Other invisible exports
Irish beef	English tourists in Ireland
Chemicals	Canadians travelling with Aer Lingus

Why Export?

Ireland is a small open economy and we need to export to create employment and to increase our **GDP** (gross domestic product (see **Unit 3.6**)).

1. We don't want to **depend** entirely on the home market (Irish products).
2. We benefit from **economies of scale** – the more a business produces the cheaper the costs.
3. We earn **foreign currency** from non-eurozone areas that we trade with.

Benefits of Exporting

1. The increased levels of production create **employment**.
2. There are **additional taxes** for the government as businesses make more profits.
3. Companies are **less dependent on the home market** and therefore reduce their risk.

The eurozone is all the countries that are part of the European single currency and have the euro as their currency.

Currently 19 member countries of the EU are in the eurozone.

Non-eurozone countries are all the other countries of the world.

Time to think

Have you ever had to exchange your euros for British pounds when visiting the UK?

What happened? What is the current euro–sterling exchange rate?

CHECKING IN...

1. Copy and complete the sentences below by selecting the two correct terms from the word bank.

   visible exports   invisible exports   visible imports   invisible imports

   Post-primary students taking a skiing holiday in Salzburg, Austria are shown under _____ _____.

   Winnings by the Irish horse, Bacon and Cabbage, racing in Dubai are shown under _____ _____.

2. Copy the table and place a ✓ in the correct box.

	True	False
Ireland is an open economy		
Eurozone countries all have the same currency		
Visible exports are services we sell to other countries		
An export is something bad for a country		

475

THE BALANCE OF TRADE

The **balance of trade** is the difference between the value of **visible exports** and the value of **visible imports**.

Balance of Trade = Visible Exports – Visible Imports

The following is an example of a healthy balance of trade.

Balance of Trade (BOT) € millions	
Total visible exports	€300
Less total visible imports	€250
Balance of Trade **Favourable**	€50

If the value of visible exports is greater than the value of visible imports = **surplus**

If the value of visible exports is equal to the value of visible imports = **balanced**

If the value of visible exports is less than the value of visible imports = **deficit**

CHECKING IN...

Look at the transactions in the chart below and put a ✓ in the correct box to indicate whether each transaction is a visible export, invisible export, visible import or invisible import.

Transaction	Visible Export	Invisible Export	Visible Import	Invisible Import
John and Aoife Smart from Waterford go on holiday in Austria				
An Irish business person buys a Ferrari				
Irish football fans travel to France for the Euros				
An Irish café buys chocolates from Belgium				
Tourists from Italy have a holiday in Belmullet				
Justin Bieber plays at a concert in the O2 Arena in Dublin				
A French rugby team travel by Aer Lingus for a match in the Aviva				
A restaurant in London buys alarms from Netwatch in Carlow to improve security				
A US restaurant buys Irish beef				

GLOBALISATION OF TRADE 3.7

> **WORKING WITH OTHERS**
> - Source the top three products that Ireland imports.
> - Source the top three products that Ireland exports.
> - Source the top three countries that Ireland imports from.
> - Source the top three countries that Ireland exports to.

BALANCE OF PAYMENTS

The balance of payments is the difference between the total value of **all** goods and services that Ireland exports and imports. This is both visible and invisible trade.

Balance of Payments = Total Exports – Total Imports
(Visible plus invisible exports) – (Visible plus invisible imports)

Balance of Payments BOP €million		
Total Exports		
Visible Exports	300	
Invisible Exports	350	650
Less Total Exports		
Visible Imports	250	
Invisible Imports	200	450
Surplus 😊		200

The balance of payments can have a surplus, be balanced or be a deficit.

What can our country do to improve on a balance of payments **deficit**?

1. Try to **grow exports**
2. **Reduce imports**
3. Encourage a '**buy Irish**' campaign
4. Encourage government agencies (e.g. Bord Bia and Fáilte Ireland) to **promote Irish products** and services

What can our country do with a balance of payments **surplus**?

1. The extra money can be used to **pay off some of our national debt** or to reduce taxes
2. More money can be spent on **services and infrastructure**, creating jobs and a better standard of living for Irish people

3.7 BE BUSINESS: OUR ECONOMY

EXAMPLE 5: BALANCE OF TRADE AND BALANCE OF PAYMENTS

From the following figures calculate the balance of trade and the balance of payments. State whether it is a deficit or a surplus. Show your workings.

- Visible exports €800m
- Invisible exports €400m
- Visible imports €650m
- Invisible imports €500m

Balance of Trade (BOT) € millions	
Visible exports	€800
Less visible imports	(€650)
BOT Surplus	€150

BOT is a surplus as visible exports are greater than visible imports.

Balance of Payments (BOP) € millions	
Total exports	€1,200
Less total imports	(€1,150)
BOP Surplus	€50

Total exports = visible + invisible exports (€800 m + €400 m).

Total imports = visible + invisible imports (€650 m + €500 m).

BOP is a surplus as total exports are greater than total imports.

WORKING WITH OTHERS

Be the Minister for Finance. What might you do with the surplus?

CHECKING IN...

1. You are given the following information for a country called Bistia.
   Visible exports €9,785 m
   Visible imports €358 m
   Invisible imports €704 m
   Invisible exports €345 m

   From the above figures, calculate the following:
   (a) Total exports
   (b) Total imports
   (c) The balance of trade
   (d) The balance of payments
   State whether each is a deficit or a surplus. Show your workings.

2. From the following figures, calculate the balance of trade and the balance of payments for a country called Youty. State whether there is a deficit or a surplus in each case. Show your workings.

   Visible exports €875 m
   Invisible exports €400 m
   Visible imports €350 m
   Invisible imports €604 m

   If it is a surplus, what might the government of Youty do?

   If it is a deficit, what might the government of Youty do?

Import substitution occurs when a country tries to reduce imports by encouraging domestic producers to provide the same goods or services, for example Irish strawberries instead of Spanish strawberries.

FACTORS IN INTERNATIONAL TRADE

A business will have to consider a number of factors when trading with other countries.

1. **Language barriers:** English is commonly used in the EU and the USA, but there may be an added cost of translation when trading with non-English-speaking countries.
2. **Cost of transport:** Ireland is an island so we have to use sea and air to transport goods – this increases costs.
3. **Insurance costs:** as goods will be at ports and airports and at additional risk, there may be additional premiums on insurance.
4. **Adjusting products** for different standards worldwide: measures may differ, standards for quality may differ, etc.
5. **Currency:** countries outside the eurozone use different currencies. Currencies can go up or down and these fluctuations can add a considerable cost to trade.

WORKING WITH OTHERS

- Working in groups of four or five, write a script for your own economics show, called *The JC Business Economics Fix*. The topic of the show is 'International Trade'.
- What would make the best possible show: content, communication skills, visuals, research …?
- You might decide to present your show to your classmates.

CURRENCY

We refer to currency conversions as exchange rates.
The following are the rules for converting currencies.

1. Going from euro to foreign currencies, you multiply by the 'sell at' rate **x**
2. Going from foreign currency to euro, you divide by the 'buy at' rate **÷**

EXAMPLE 6: SAMPLE EURO EXCHANGE RATE

	Sell	Buy
British Pound £	0.80	0.90
US Dollar $	1.28	1.32

Remember, if you're converting from euros to a foreign currency – multiply.

If I have €100 to convert to pounds = €100 x £0.80 = £80
If I have $500 to convert to euros = $500 ÷ 1.32 = €378.79

It is a good idea for businesses to trade with countries that use the same currency. However, this is not always possible.

3.7 BE BUSINESS: OUR ECONOMY

CHECKING IN...

Be a holidaymaker. You must decide on three destinations where you would like to go on holiday and the amount of euros you want to convert. Use the sample Bank Sell Rates in the chart below to help you make your decision. You have €300 to take with you on holiday.

	USA Dollar	UK Pound	Australian Dollar	Canada Dollar	South African Rand	New Zealand Dollar	Japanese Yen	Chinese Yuan
Euro (€1)	1.36688	0.87202	1.41868	1.40737	9.53923	1.85189	114.727	9.22687

Destination	Amount €	Foreign Currency
1.		
2.		
3.		

Be a Researcher

1. Research the exchange rates for ten countries that are not in the eurozone. Remember to date your research as currency values can change. Can you source an online currency converter? Do you know of any apps for currency conversions?
2. Use websites to source information on Ireland's current imports and exports. Copy and fill in this 'Trade Learning Sheet 1'. Make a note of the websites you used and the date you used them.
3. Use websites to source information on Ireland's current Balance of Trade and Balance of Payments. Copy and fill in this 'Trade Learning Sheet 2'. Make a note of the websites you used and the date you used them.

Trade Learning Sheet 1

Imports
Define:
Top five products we import:
1.
2.
3.
4.
5.
Amount this year: €
Top five countries we import from:
1.
2.
3.
4.
5.

Exports
Define:
Top five products we export:
1.
2.
3.
4.
5.
Amount this year: €
Top five countries we export to:
1.
2.
3.
4.
5.

Invisible Exports
Define:
Examples:

Invisible Imports
Define:
Examples:

Visible Exports
Define:
Examples:

Visible Imports
Define:
Examples:

Trade Learning Sheet 2

Balance of Trade
Define:
Example:

Balance of Payments
Define:
Example:

Import Substitution
Define:
Example:

Exchange Rates
Define:
Example:

Demonstrate using graphs/bar charts where appropriate

Revisit your Learning Sheets in Third Year to document any major changes.

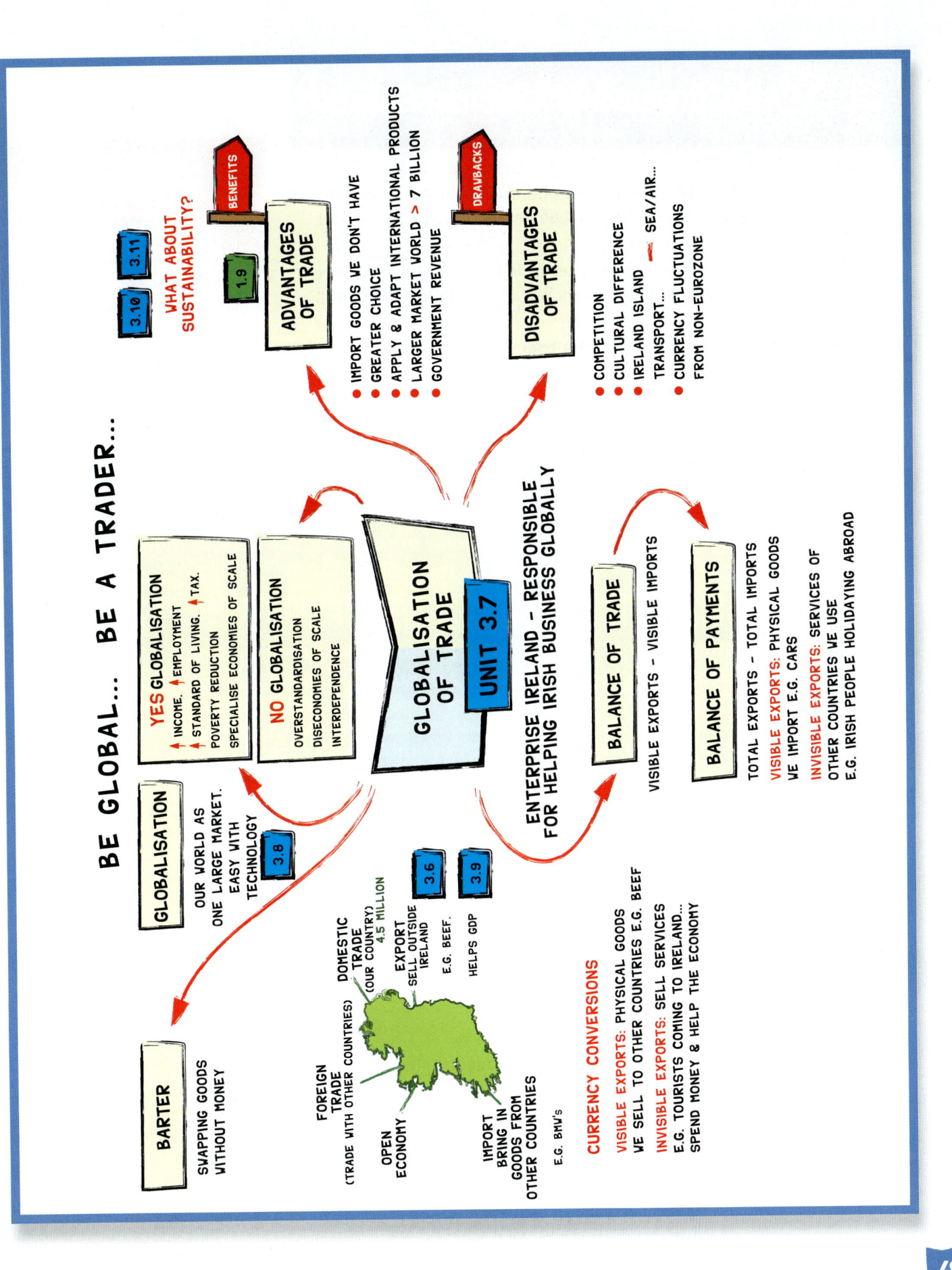

GLOBALISATION OF TRADE   3.7

BE GLOBAL... BE A TRADER...

UNIT 3.7 — GLOBALISATION OF TRADE

ENTERPRISE IRELAND – RESPONSIBLE FOR HELPING IRISH BUSINESS GLOBALLY

BARTER
SWAPPING GOODS WITHOUT MONEY

GLOBALISATION
OUR WORLD AS ONE LARGE MARKET. EASY WITH TECHNOLOGY

YES GLOBALISATION
- ↑INCOME, ↑EMPLOYMENT
- ↑STANDARD OF LIVING, ↑TAX.
- POVERTY REDUCTION
- SPECIALISE ECONOMIES OF SCALE

NO GLOBALISATION
- OVERSTANDARDISATION
- DISECONOMIES OF SCALE
- INTERDEPENDENCE

ADVANTAGES OF TRADE (BENEFITS)
- IMPORT GOODS WE DON'T HAVE
- GREATER CHOICE
- APPLY & ADAPT INTERNATIONAL PRODUCTS
- LARGER MARKET WORLD > 7 BILLION
- GOVERNMENT REVENUE

WHAT ABOUT SUSTAINABILITY? (1.9, 3.10, 3.11)

DISADVANTAGES OF TRADE (DRAWBACKS)
- COMPETITION
- CULTURAL DIFFERENCE
- IRELAND ISLAND — SEA/AIR... TRANSPORT...
- CURRENCY FLUCTUATIONS FROM NON-EUROZONE

BALANCE OF TRADE
VISIBLE EXPORTS – VISIBLE IMPORTS

BALANCE OF PAYMENTS
TOTAL EXPORTS – TOTAL IMPORTS

VISIBLE EXPORTS: PHYSICAL GOODS WE IMPORT E.G. CARS

INVISIBLE EXPORTS: SERVICES OF OTHER COUNTRIES WE USE E.G. IRISH PEOPLE HOLIDAYING ABROAD

FOREIGN TRADE
(TRADE WITH OTHER COUNTRIES)

OPEN ECONOMY

IMPORT
BRING IN GOODS FROM OTHER COUNTRIES
E.G. BMW'S

DOMESTIC TRADE
(OUR COUNTRY) 4.5 MILLION

EXPORT
SELL OUTSIDE IRELAND
E.G. BEEF
HELPS GDP

CURRENCY CONVERSIONS

VISIBLE EXPORTS: PHYSICAL GOODS WE SELL TO OTHER COUNTRIES E.G. BEEF

INVISIBLE EXPORTS: SELL SERVICES E.G. TOURISTS COMING TO IRELAND... SPEND MONEY & HELP THE ECONOMY

481

Be Prepared: My Support Sheets

Completing the activities here will help you reflect on and reinforce your learning before you move on to the next unit.

- Write down the **key terms** in this unit and make sure you understand them. See if they match the ones at the back of the book.
- List the **key concepts/themes** in this unit.
- List the three most **interesting points** about this topic.

Top Tip!

Working with others is really important for your Economics in Action and individually for your Presentation.

Have a debate

Have a class debate on globalisation. The motion is: Globalisation is a necessity. Check the guidelines on debating on p. 130.

a. Do your research – prepare for the debate thoroughly.
b. Make sure data is correct.
c. Working in pairs, write a pro (for) and a con (against) list on the motion. Ensure you have four key points for each side.
d. Use visual stimuli, for example graphs, photographs or even a prop.
e. You could also have a walking debate. As you put forward your points, the students who agree move to one side of the classroom and the students who disagree move to the other side of the classroom. Any student might be asked why they agree or disagree with the motion.

Economics in Action/Presentation Idea!

1. Create a Facebook page using the template on p. 546. You are the government and the topic is International Trade. Add appropriate comments, likes, friends.

Success criteria:
- Title
- Visuals
- Relevant friends/likes

2. **Be the Minister for Foreign Affairs and Trade.**

Explain how you plan to maximise trade for Ireland. Give three main points.

Share any good ideas with your class.

Success criteria:
- Title
- Three points
- Visual(s)
- Accurate research and statistics
- Good communication skills

QUESTION TIME

1. Explain globalisation.
2. Explain what is meant by the balance of trade and the balance of payments.
3. Explain currency exchanges. Give four examples.
4. What are the differences between visible and invisible trade?
5. 'Globalisation is really good for our world.' Do you agree or disagree with this statement? Give reasons for your answer.
6. When trading with other countries, what might be the challenges? Take one challenge and discuss it in detail.
7. If you were the Irish government, how would you create and expand import substitution?

EVALUATE MY LEARNING: DAR

Describe
- Did I/we meet my/our learning intentions?
- What went well? What are my/our strengths?

Assess
- How did I/we work with others?
- Were there challenges?

Recommend
- How might I improve?
- What skills and learning might I apply to new situations?

Stop and think
- Do I have any questions or concerns?
- What are the mistakes or errors I made in this unit?

Do your **Key Check** in the workbook for this unit and then mark your learning position on the following rating scale:

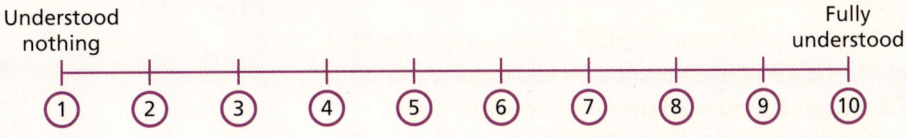

Understood nothing 1 2 3 4 5 6 7 8 9 10 Fully understood

How can you move up the rating scale? What can you **say**, **make**, **write** and **do** to illustrate your learning?

CBA 2 Presentation:
This unit is related to Globalisation **Unit 1.10**, which is an important Learning Outcome for your **Presentation**.

Revisit this unit in Third Year to document any major changes.

It's a good idea to write the date on any research material you use. Why might you date research material?

3.8 EUROPEAN UNION – BENEFITS AND CHALLENGES

Discuss the economic and social benefits and challenges of Ireland's membership of the European Union (EU).

Learning Intentions

At the end of this unit I will:
- Know about the EU and understand how it works
- Understand the benefits and challenges of the EU
- Value EU polices
- Apply my skills to researching the EU

Making the links with other LOs:

- 1.10 Globalisation and technology
- 3.7 Globalisation of trade
- 3.10 Economic issues
- 3.11 Economic policy

Are there other LOs?

Key Concepts
- ✓ European Union
- ✓ Eurozone

Wonderful Worthwhile Websites

www.ec.europa.eu

THE EUROPEAN UNION

Ireland is a member of the **European Union (EU)**. The EU is like a club of countries whose governments work together. It is an economic and political union that works towards common goals on all economic, political and monetary matters.

The European Economic Community (EEC), now the EU, was established in March **1957** with six countries. Ireland joined the EU in **1973**. There are now 28 member countries with more countries waiting to join. The UK has voted to leave the EU but it is a member until it is legally separated from the EU. When it leaves, there will be 27 members.

The countries that make up the EU (**member states**) remain independent nations, but they pool their power in order to gain a strength and world influence none of them could have on their own. The EU is now the **world's largest economic area**.

The EU is based on a number of international treaties (agreements) between the member states and has its own institutions to run its affairs.

The number of members of the EU may change.

Can you find out what the current EU budget is? Log on to www.ec.europa.eu.

EUROPEAN UNION – BENEFITS AND CHALLENGES 3.8

MEMBER STATES

The EU has 28 member countries. Most of them are in the eurozone, which means they have a common currency, the euro. Some have not joined the eurozone. The table shows the member countries of the EU with the year they joined and the currency they use

The EU will continue to grow as an increasing number of countries express interest in membership.

Country	Year of Entry	Currency	Country	Year of Entry	Currency
Austria	1995	euro	Latvia	2004	euro
Belgium	1958	euro	Lithuania	2004	euro
Bulgaria	2007	Bulgarian lev	Luxembourg	1958	euro
Croatia	2013	Croatian kuna	Malta	2004	euro
Cyprus	2004	euro	Netherlands	1958	euro
Czech Republic	2004	Czech koruna	Poland	2004	Polish Zloty
Denmark	1973	Danish krone	Portugal	1986	euro
Estonia	2004	euro	Romania	2007	Romanian Leu
Finland	1995	euro	Slovakia	2004	euro
France	1958	euro	Slovenia	2004	euro
Germany	1958	euro	Spain	1986	euro
Greece	1981	euro	Sweden	1995	Swedish krona
Hungary	2004	Hungarian Forint	United Kingdom	1973	pound sterling
Ireland	1973	euro			

*The UK voted to leave the EU in June 2016

485

3.8 BE BUSINESS: OUR ECONOMY

EUROPEAN INSTITUTIONS

The EU is governed by a number of bodies and institutions.

EU Commission	Drafts legislation and represents EU internationally. Promotes the common interests of EU members
EU Parliament	Discusses proposals and is the voice of the people
EU Council of Ministers	Makes decisions and is the voice of the member states
EU Commission	Implements legislation
EU Court of Justice	Interprets the laws
EU Court of Auditors	Monitors the management of finance
EU European Central Bank	Central Bank for all member states – sets the EU interest rates
European Ombudsman	Deals with any complaints about the EU's institutions

DECISION-MAKING IN THE EU

Decision-making in the EU can be quite complex, but if you follow the steps you will see that the sequence is quite logical.
See the diagram below.

5 steps

1. Draft proposed law
Drafted by the EU Commission and sent to the EU Parliament

2. Pass or amend
EU Parliament discusses proposal and passes it or suggests amendments, which are returned to the EU Commission

3. Redraft
EU Commission redrafts the proposal and submits it to the EU Council of Ministers

4. Agree or reject
Council of Ministers accepts or rejects the proposal

5. If rejected ...
Conciliation Committee comprising members of EU Parliament and EU Council of Ministers tries to achieve a compromise

Time to think

Would you be interested in studying or working in other EU member states? Why/why not? Learning European languages will make it easier for you to travel between countries when studying or working.
Look at www.eujobs.ie for more information.

Did You Know?
Young people can study or pursue personal development in other European countries with the support of the EU's Erasmus+ programme for education, training, youth and sport.

Erasmus+

EU POLICIES

A **policy** is a course of action. The EU has many policies, which are aimed at benefiting or protecting member countries. For example, the EU's policies on the Irish language, consumer and employee rights, and improving sustainability are all **social** policies.

The following two policies are of interest to Ireland, as we are an island and agriculture plays an important role in our country.

1. **Common Agricultural Policy** (CAP): a system of subsidies (grants) and support programmes for agriculture. For example, the Basic Payment Scheme is a payment to farmers and is linked to meeting environmental and health standards.
2. **Common Fisheries Policy** (CFP): with this policy quotas (maximum amounts) are set for member states in terms of the amounts of each type of fish they are allowed to catch.

THE EU AND SUSTAINABILITY

We have already studied **sustainability** and the importance of a greener planet. The EU plays a significant role in supporting a green environment. Through legislation, the EU has introduced some very important changes:

- Cleaner bathing water
- Reduction in acid rain
- Lead-free petrol
- Free and safe disposal of old electronic equipment
- Strict rules on food safety
- More organic and better-quality farming
- More effective health warnings on cigarettes
- Registration and control of all chemicals (REACH)

THE FUTURE OF THE EU

Europe 2020 is the EU's jobs and growth strategy. It was launched in 2010 with the aim of creating a **smart**, **sustainable** and **inclusive** economy.

Achieving **smart growth** will entail **educating** the population and a greater use of **communication** technologies.

Sustainability must become a priority, leading to **sustainable growth** with a resource-efficient, greener and efficient economy.

In addition the EU aims to have **inclusive growth**. This means additional and improved jobs, investment in skills and training, modernisation of the labour market and welfare systems and spreading the benefits to all member states.

Each member state has its own **national targets** in each of these areas. They must achieve concrete goals and targets.

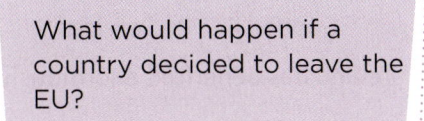

> What would happen if a country decided to leave the EU?

> Gaeilge is an official EU language. Follow EU tweets as Gaeilge on @Europarl_GA

> When is Europe Day?

CHECKING IN...

1. What is the European Union?
2. What is the eurozone?
3. Name an EU policy and say how it might affect Ireland.

3.8 BE BUSINESS: OUR ECONOMY

Be a Researcher

Use websites to source information on one EU country. Copy and fill in this 'EU Learning Sheet'. Make a note of the websites you used and the date you used them.

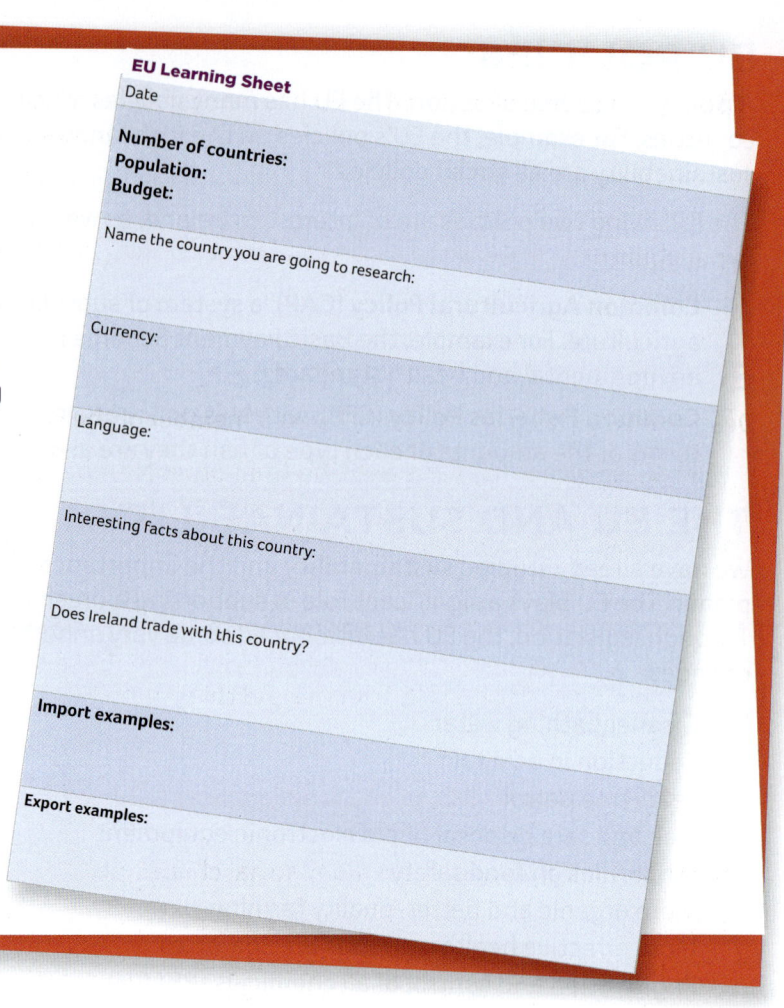

EU Learning Sheet
Date
Number of countries:
Population:
Budget:
Name the country you are going to research:
Currency:
Language:
Interesting facts about this country:
Does Ireland trade with this country?
Import examples:
Export examples:

IRELAND AND THE EU

The EU is a **single market,** which means that people and products can move freely between EU countries. The four freedoms of the single market are the free movement of:

1. Goods   2. Services   3. People   4. Capital (money)

Ireland has benefited enormously from being a member of the EU.

ECONOMIC BENEFITS

1. We have access to a market of over **500 million people** and 25% of world trade. (The population of Ireland is only 4.7 million.)
2. Ireland has received **funding** (subsidies) from the EU, for example funding to improve infrastructure. A subsidy is a financial support given to a particular sector, institution, business or individual. There are many forms, from student loans to farm subsidies. For example, the EU subsidises agriculture to help small farmers.
3. The EU is a free trade area where **goods, services, labour and capital** can move freely without obstacles. It is much easier for Ireland to trade and Irish people can live and work in EU member states.
4. To ensure consistency and equality, all **legislation is harmonised** (the same) throughout the EU. This has made it easier for Irish firms to do business within the EU.
5. Trading in the **eurozone** removes the uncertainty linked with foreign trade and eliminates the cost of converting currencies. As Ireland uses the euro, it is easier for Ireland to trade internationally.

EUROPEAN UNION – BENEFITS AND CHALLENGES 3.8

SOCIAL BENEFITS

1. The EU has taken various measures to **protect the citizens** of member states and to afford members equal rights and conditions, for example consumer rights, product safety and employee rights.
2. The Irish **language** is recognised as an official language of the EU. This helps to protect the future of our first official language.
3. The freedom of movement allowed within the EU gives Irish people the **opportunity to travel, live, work and study** in other EU countries.

ECONOMIC CHALLENGES

Despite all the positive aspects of being a member of the EU, there are also challenges.

1. Irish companies face **competition** from other member states. It can be challenging for new, small Irish businesses to compete in the EU market.
2. Complying with all EU legislation is **expensive** and can add to a company's costs. Some companies may decide to leave Ireland due to high costs and relocate to a different member state where wages and costs are cheaper, leading to company closures, redundancies and additional costs to the government.
3. The Irish government has to **give up** some of its **independent powers** to the EU so that the EU can act on behalf of all states. We experienced this during the Irish financial crisis of 2007–8 and the financial restructuring that followed.

SOCIAL CHALLENGES

The EU, including Ireland, faces many social challenges.

1. With high levels of unemployment, poverty and an uneven distribution of wealth, there is a need to create jobs and encourage entrepreneurship right across Europe.
2. The EU has an aging population, so issues of health and wellbeing have to be addressed.
3. With the increased number of terrorist attacks across Europe there needs to be an emphasis on protecting all citizens.
4. Immigration needs to be managed well to be successful.

Other Benefits of EU Membership	Other Challenges of EU Membership
The eurozone simplifies imports and exports	Dealing with non-eurozone fluctuations in currencies
Interest rates set by EU, so inflation is kept low	Greater competition
Increased markets	Additional laws and standards, which can increase costs
Funds and grants	Language differences
Many international firms locate in Ireland because we are in the EU	Additional transport costs – Irish businesses have to use sea or air, extra insurance

CHECKING IN...

1. Name three economic benefits and three economic challenges for Ireland as a member of the EU.
2. Name three social benefits and three social challenges for Ireland as a member of the EU.

3.8 BE BUSINESS: OUR ECONOMY

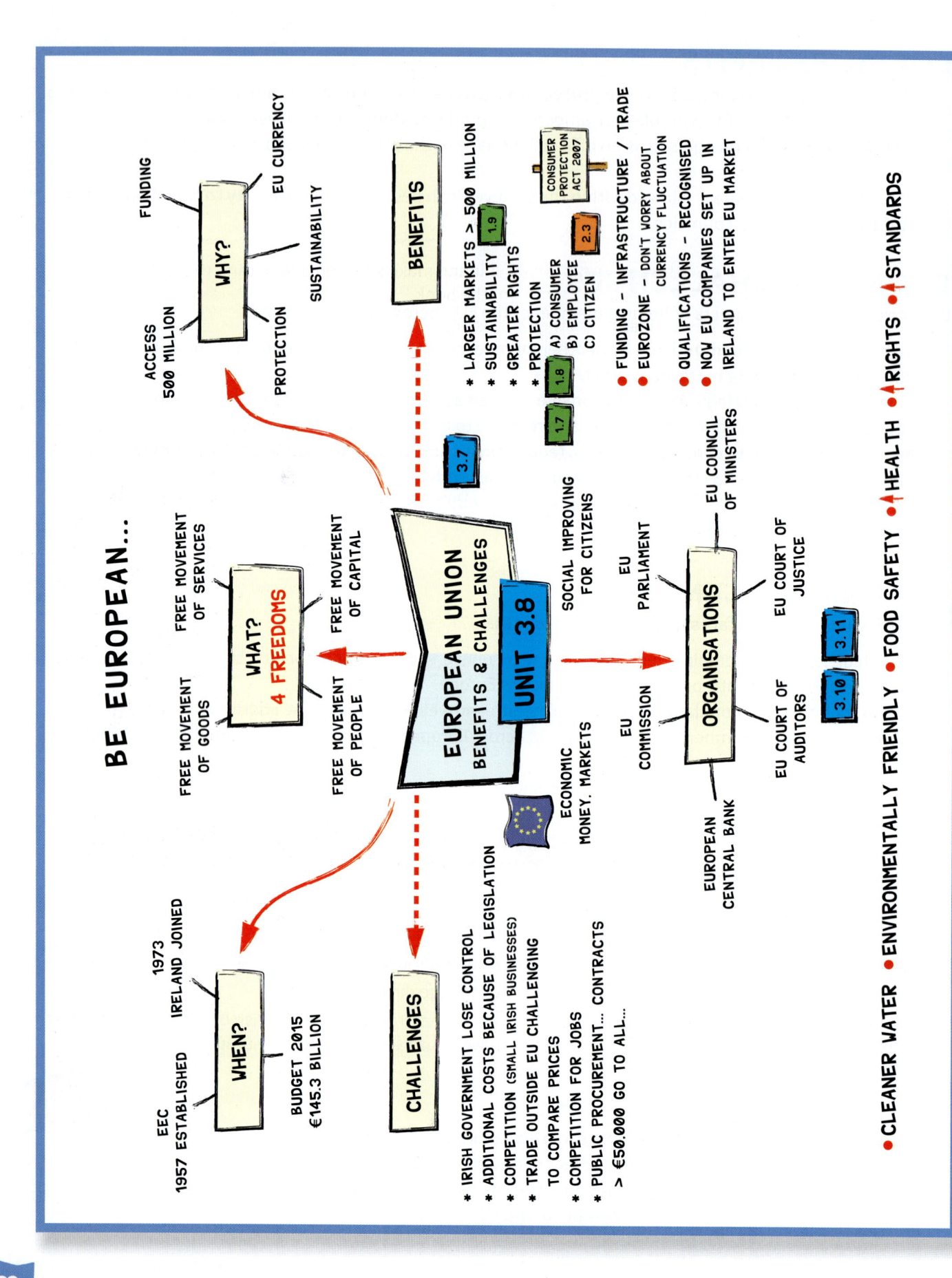

BE EUROPEAN...

EUROPEAN UNION — Benefits & Challenges (UNIT 3.8)

WHEN?
- EEC 1957 ESTABLISHED
- 1973 IRELAND JOINED
- BUDGET 2015 €145.3 BILLION

WHAT? 4 FREEDOMS
- FREE MOVEMENT OF GOODS
- FREE MOVEMENT OF SERVICES
- FREE MOVEMENT OF CAPITAL
- FREE MOVEMENT OF PEOPLE

WHY?
- ACCESS 500 MILLION
- FUNDING
- EU CURRENCY
- SUSTAINABILITY
- PROTECTION

BENEFITS
* LARGER MARKETS > 500 MILLION
* SUSTAINABILITY
* GREATER RIGHTS
* PROTECTION
  - A) CONSUMER
  - B) EMPLOYEE
  - C) CITIZEN

- CONSUMER PROTECTION ACT 2007
- FUNDING – INFRASTRUCTURE / TRADE
- EUROZONE – DON'T WORRY ABOUT CURRENCY FLUCTUATION
- QUALIFICATIONS – RECOGNISED
- NOW EU COMPANIES SET UP IN IRELAND TO ENTER EU MARKET

CHALLENGES
* IRISH GOVERNMENT LOSE CONTROL
* ADDITIONAL COSTS BECAUSE OF LEGISLATION
* COMPETITION (SMALL IRISH BUSINESSES)
* TRADE OUTSIDE EU CHALLENGING
* TO COMPARE PRICES
* COMPETITION FOR JOBS
* PUBLIC PROCUREMENT... CONTRACTS > €50,000 GO TO ALL...

ORGANISATIONS
- EU COUNCIL OF MINISTERS
- EU PARLIAMENT
- EU COMMISSION
- EUROPEAN CENTRAL BANK
- EU COURT OF AUDITORS
- EU COURT OF JUSTICE

ECONOMIC MONEY. MARKETS
SOCIAL IMPROVING FOR CITIZENS

- CLEANER WATER
- ENVIRONMENTALLY FRIENDLY
- FOOD SAFETY
- HEALTH
- RIGHTS
- STANDARDS

EUROPEAN UNION – BENEFITS AND CHALLENGES 3.8

Be Prepared: My Support Sheets

Completing the activities here will help you to reflect on and reinforce your learning before you move on to the next unit.

- Write down the **key term**s in this unit and make sure you understand them. See if they match the ones at the back of the book.
- List the **key concepts/themes** in this unit.
- List the **three most interesting points** about this topic.

Have a debate

Have a class debate on the EU. The motion is: Should Ireland remain in the EU? Check the guidelines for debating on p. 130

a. Do your research – prepare for the debate thoroughly.
b. Make sure your data is correct.
c. Working in pairs, write a pro (for) and a con (against) list on the motion. Ensure you have four key points for each side.
d. Use visual stimuli, for example graphs, photographs or even a prop.
e. You could also have a walking debate. As you put forward your points, the students who agree move to one side of the classroom and the students who disagree move to the other side of the classroom. Any student might be asked why they agree or disagree with the motion.

Presentation Idea!

Draft a poster showing the benefits and challenges of being a member of the EU.

Success criteria:
- Title
- Three benefits and three challenges
- Accurate information and statistics
- An appropriate visual
- Grammar, spelling and layout

3.8 BE BUSINESS: OUR ECONOMY

QUESTION TIME

1. What are the advantages of Ireland trading within the eurozone?
2. List the economic benefits of being a member of the EU. What do you think is the most important benefit? Why?
3. List the economic challenges of being a member of the EU. What is the most important challenge? Why?
4. Sustainability is an important concept for your future and the future of our planet. How does the EU contribute to ensuring sustainability?
5. Trading with other countries is really important for Ireland. How does being a member of the EU help?
6. Write a newspaper article on the social benefits of being a member of the EU.

EVALUATE MY LEARNING: DAR

Describe
- Did I/we meet my/our learning intentions?
- What went well? What are my/our strengths?

Assess
- How did I/we work with others?
- Were there challenges?

Recommend
- How might I improve?
- What skills and learning might I apply to new situations?

Do your **Key Check** in the workbook for this unit and then mark your learning position on the following rating scale:

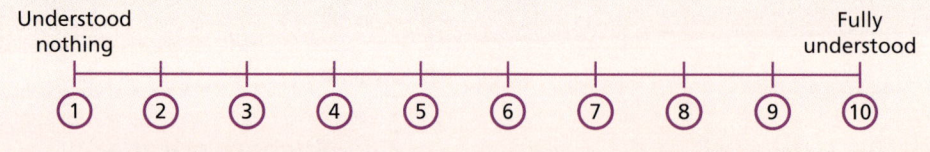

Understood nothing — 1 2 3 4 5 6 7 8 9 10 — Fully understood

How can you move up the rating scale? What can you **say**, **make**, **write** and **do** to illustrate your learning?

The information in this unit can be applied to many of the units in the course, from rights and responsibilities to trade, globalisation and sustainability.

Stop and think

Do I have any questions or concerns?
What are the mistakes or errors I made in this unit?

3.9 ECONOMIC INDICATORS

Explain the relevance of economic indicators such as inflation, employment rates, interest rates, economic growth, national income and national debt for individuals and the economy.

Learning Intentions

At the end of this unit I will:
- Know about and understand inflation
- Understand employment and unemployment
- Understand interest rates, the cost of borrowing
- Apply the concepts of national income and national debt
- Value the importance of economic indicators to individuals and our economy

Making the links with other LOs:

- 1.10 Globalisation and technology
- 3.4 Government revenue and government expenditure
- 3.6 Positive and negative economic growth and sustainability
- 3.8 European Union: benefits and challenges
- 3.10 Economic issues
- 3.11 Economic policy

Are there other LOs?

Key Concepts
- ✓ Inflation
- ✓ Employment and unemployment
- ✓ Interest rates
- ✓ Economic growth
- ✓ National income and national debt

Wonderful Worthwhile Websites

www.finfacts.ie
www.cso.ie
www.ntma.ie
www.centralbank.ie
www.revenue.ie

INTRODUCTION

We refer to the economy of Ireland as our **national economy**. In this unit we will investigate the **factors** that affect our national economy. These factors are called **economic indicators**.

An **indicator** is a measure. It can help individuals, households and organisations (for-profit and not-for-profit) to make decisions. Indicators are also known as variables and factors.

3.9 BE BUSINESS: OUR ECONOMY

In a perfect world, we would like to have growth in our **economy**, with every business (for-profit organisation) booming, making profits and encouraging **entrepreneurship**. Ideally, everyone would be **employed** and there would be **no unemployment**. We would have low interest rates and low inflation. Ireland would export more than it imports and the government would have a surplus in its budget account.

This ideal would only be found in a really **successful economy**, or probably a perfect economy. There are numerous economic indicators that affect our economy and make such an ideal economy an unrealistic fantasy.

ECONOMIC INDICATORS

The following are the eight most important economic indicators affecting our economy:

- Inflation
- Employment rates
- Interest rates
- Economic growth
- National income
- National debt
- Exchange rates
- Taxation

We have already discussed some indicators such as **taxation** (Unit 3.5) and **exchange rates** (Unit 3.7). We will now look at the other indicators in more detail.

They may seem challenging at first, but take each indicator one by one. First you must **understand** the term and **apply** it. Then try to understand the concepts from **different perspectives**, or points of view.

The rates associated with the indicators will vary over time, so when you complete your economic indicators learning sheet at the end of this unit, make a note of the date, and **keep this information as up to date as possible**. It's a good idea to work in pairs and divide the work between you before you present your findings to your class. Remember, always date your information.

Source relevant information in the business supplements of Irish newspapers such as *The Irish Times* on Friday, the *Irish Independent* on Thursday and the *Sunday Business Post*.

INFLATION

EMPLOYMENT

INTEREST RATES

ECONOMIC GROWTH

EXCHANGE RATES

TAXATION

NATIONAL INCOME

NATIONAL DEBT

INFLATION

> **Inflation** is rising prices over a period of time, usually one year.

The price of a Curly Wurly in 1970 was approximately 5 cents; the price of a Curly Wurly in 2016 was approximately €1. Nearly 50 years later, the Curly Wurly tastes the same, but our money does not go as far!

This increase in prices is called **inflation**.

This increase applies not only to the Curly Wurly chocolate bar but to all products and services.

The **rate of inflation** is calculated as follows:

$$\text{Rate of inflation (\%)} = \frac{\text{Price difference}}{\text{Original price}} \times \frac{100}{1} = \%$$

EXAMPLE 1

A chocolate bar cost €1.00 in 2015 and €1.05 in 2016.

This is inflation of 5%. We calculate this as follows:

$$\frac{\text{Difference}}{\text{Original}} \times \frac{100}{1}$$

$$\frac{5}{100} \times \frac{100}{1} = 5\%$$

Inflation causes a rise in prices and therefore your **purchasing power** (what you can afford to buy) decreases. If you only have one euro in 2016, you won't be able to purchase that chocolate bar, as it now costs €1.05.

Is inflation bad? No, unless our economy encounters **extreme** rates – then it is bad.

CASE STUDY: TAYTO PACKS FROM THE 1970s

In the 1970s a bag of Tayto crisps would have cost you 3 pence (or 8 cents in euros).

In 1990 a bag cost in the region of 14 pence (or 18 cents).

Seven years later, the same size bag would have set you back 22 pence (28 cents) and the price climbed to 28 pence (36 cents) by the end of 2001, just before the euro was introduced.

What is the price of a bag of Tayto crisps today?

Can you draw a graph of the price increases?

> Did you know that you can get married in Tayto Park? Now that's diversification!

3.9 BE BUSINESS: OUR ECONOMY

Be Savvy

In order to keep the value of our money, especially our **savings**, we need to choose our investments wisely, ensuring that our money holds its purchasing power.

If inflation is 5% we would need **at least** 5% interest on savings for our savings to have the same value.

Time to think

Do you think interest of 5% would match inflation of 5%? What about DIRT? Remember, taxes on savings reduces our interest.

INFLATION: DIFFERENT PERSPECTIVES

BE AN ECONOMIST...

Economists use a tool to measure **inflation** called the **Consumer Price Index (CPI)**. The CPI measures the overall change over time in the prices of products and services that people typically buy. An economist will take the average price of products and services that a person buys. It is like the cost of an imaginary basket of these products and services.

EXAMPLE 2

The basket of products and services costs **€1,000** in 2019.
The same basket of products and services costs **€1,100** in 2020.
The rate of inflation is 10%.

$$\frac{\text{Difference}}{\text{Original}} \times \frac{100}{1}$$

$$\frac{100}{1,000} \times \frac{100}{1} = 10\%$$

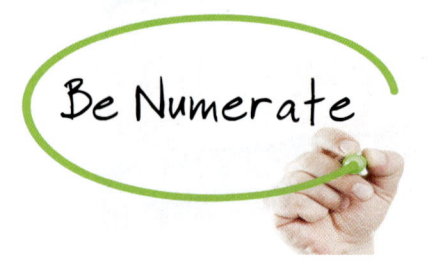

Be Numerate

A basket of products and services costs €100 in 2017.
The same basket of products and services costs €105 in 2018.
Calculate the rate of inflation.

$$\frac{\text{Difference}}{\text{Original}} \times \frac{100}{1} = \underline{\quad}\%$$

BE AN INDIVIDUAL: A SAVER
You will want to ensure that your savings and investments will at least keep in line with inflation.

If **interest rates are 1%** and **inflation is 2%**, as a saver you are worse off. You have less **purchasing power**. You will spend rather than save.

BE A BANKER
If inflation is rising, you will have to ensure that the **interest** charged on money lent will cover inflation as well as other costs.

BE AN ENTREPRENEUR/BE A BUSINESS
It may be more expensive to borrow, so it may limit your business expansion. Inflation increasing pushes up the prices of wages and materials and as a result the cost of production rises.

BE A UNION
An increase in inflation means that employees will need higher wages.

BE AN EXPORTER
If products become more expensive, this will make it more challenging to compete. Exports will decrease and imports will increase.

BE THE ECONOMY
How the economy is affected depends on whether inflation is high or low.

- **High inflation:** Borrowing expensive, exports expensive, increase in imports, decrease in employment, increase in welfare, and additional expenses for government.
- **Low inflation:** Borrowing cheap, greater spending, exports increase, increase in employment, decrease in unemployment.

Don't forget that interest is liable for DIRT too!

Be a Researcher
Research, using a search engine, what the price of certain products were ten years ago. Compare the prices with the price of the same products today.

CHECKING IN...

This graph shows the rate of inflation in Ireland for the years 2011–2016.

1. Explain the term inflation.
2. Identify the year that had the highest rate of inflation.
3. Identify the year that had the lowest rate of inflation.
4. Calculate the average rate of inflation over the five years.

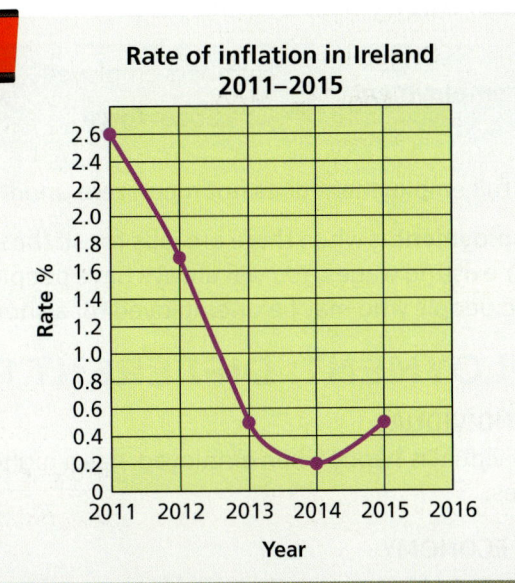

Rate of inflation in Ireland 2011–2015

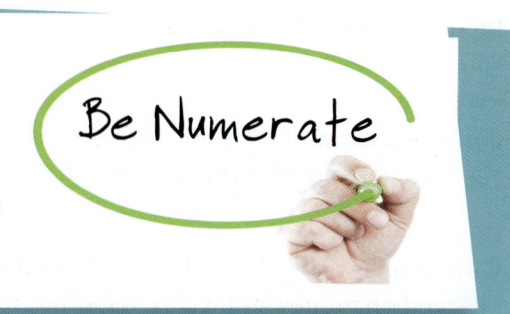

3.9 BE BUSINESS: OUR ECONOMY

Be Numerate

If your pocket money is €20 per week now, and the rate of inflation is 1%, calculate how much you would need to receive per week in the next year to keep up with inflation.

Show your answer and workings.

Find out the current inflation rate and compare it with the rate for the last ten years. Describe the drifts (whether it's gone up or down) and present the information using an appropriate graph or chart.

EMPLOYMENT RATES

The government is always concerned about creating jobs and making Ireland an attractive location for industry.

Foreign firms see Ireland as a good place to locate. Some of the reasons for this are:

- Ireland has a low taxation rate (corporation tax – tax on companies' profits, see p. 451)
- Ireland has a highly educated, English-speaking workforce
- As a member of the EU, Ireland has access to the European market (EU)

Ideally, we would like to have **full employment**, but not everyone is available for employment.

Those available for employment are known as the labour force.

The **labour force** is all those between the ages of 16 and 65 who are available for work. People who are physically unable to work, retired or in full-time education are excluded from the labour force.

The labour force is made up of the **total employed** and those unemployed who are **available** to work.

The **rate of employment** is calculated as follows:

$$\text{Rate of employment} = \frac{\text{Numbers employed}}{\text{Labour force}} \times \frac{100}{1} = \%$$

Having full employment does not mean zero unemployment.

Full employment is when there are jobs for all those willing to work for existing wages. You will always have people changing jobs and people who may be unemployed for a short time.

Time to think

Can you think of people who might not be available to work?

WORKING WITH OTHERS

Source the following figures (use www.finfacts.ie). Present the information visually.

- What is the population of your nearest town/city?
- What is the population of Ireland?
- What is the population of the EU?
- What is the population of the world?
- What is Ireland's unemployment rate?

EMPLOYMENT: DIFFERENT PERSPECTIVES

BE AN INDIVIDUAL

The individual is happy when employed: has a higher standard of living, can borrow, buy goods and services and pay taxes.

BE THE ECONOMY

The government receives additional income in tax and a reduction in expenditure on social welfare payments.

When you have unemployment, the opposite occurs.

UNEMPLOYMENT

When members of the labour force cannot find employment this creates unemployment.

> People who are not in work, but who are available for and actively seeking work, are known as **unemployed**.

Just like full employment, a country will never have zero unemployment, even when an economy is thriving. This is due to many factors, such as skills and education levels and the degree of labour movement. For this reason, a **full rate of employment** is generally considered to exist when unemployment is **approximately 4%**.

The government gives employable people, who are currently unemployed, payments in the form of the Jobseeker's Benefit (for those who paid PRSI when employed) or Jobseeker's Allowance (means tested). To receive these benefits they must **register as being unemployed** and prove that they are currently seeking work. While the benefits sum is small, it allows the unemployed to continue to pay for necessary items while searching for a new job.

The **Live Register** contains the names of those in receipt of the Jobseeker payments. The Live Register is not a precise measure of unemployment because it includes people who are working part-time and signing on part-time.

The **rate of unemployment** is calculated as follows:

$$\text{Rate of unemployment} = \frac{\text{Numbers unemployed}}{\text{Labour force}} \times \frac{100}{1} = \%$$

WORKING WITH OTHERS
Be the Government: If you were the government, what might you do to reduce unemployment?

After the downturn and crash in the Irish economy in 2008, Ireland had high levels of unemployment.

Unemployment is a huge cost to the government. Spending on welfare payments goes up and taxation goes down. When an economy improves, jobs are created and unemployment decreases.

INTEREST RATES

> **Interest rate** is the rate which is charged or paid for the use of money. An interest rate is often expressed as an annual percentage of the amount borrowed or saved.

If we **save** money, we receive **income** called interest.
If we want to **borrow** money we have to pay a **fee** and this fee is called interest.
The **rate of interest** on a loan is calculated as follows:

$$\text{Rate of interest} = \text{Loan amount}/100 \times \text{Percentage rate}/1 = €$$

EXAMPLE 3: INTEREST ON A LOAN

If the interest on a €100,000 loan is 7%, how much interest do you pay every year?

$$\frac{€100{,}000}{100} \times \frac{7}{1} = €7{,}000$$

We can borrow from **financial institutions** (banks, building societies, credit unions, etc.) and pay interest. We can save money with financial institutions and receive interest.

Banks charge borrowers a **higher** interest rate for borrowing than they pay savers for that same money on deposit. This is how the banks make a **profit** for providing these services.

Interest rates are charged not only for personal loans, but also for mortgages, credit cards and unpaid bills. The interest rate is applied to the total unpaid portion of your loan or bill.

3.9 BE BUSINESS: OUR ECONOMY

An increase in interest rates increases the cost of living.

A bank must quote the **annual percentage rate** (APR) when lending money. This takes into account fees and charges. It also makes it easier for the consumer to compare the cost of different financial products.

INTEREST RATES: DIFFERENT PERSPECTIVES

BE A DEPOSITOR

If interest rates are low then the interest/income you get on your savings will be low. 😕

If interest rates are high then the interest/income you get on your savings will be high. 😃

BE A BORROWER

If interest rates are low then the interest/expenditure you pay on your borrowings will be low. 😃

If interest rates are high then the interest/expenditure you pay on your borrowings will be high. 😕

> Banks are businesses whose objective is to make money, just like any other business. Interest is the fee they charge for money.

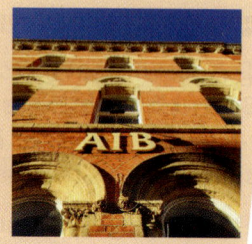

EXAMPLE 4: FLAT RATE VS APR

Derek Ryan wants to borrow €15,000 over three years.

He will repay €5,000 plus interest at the end of each year.

Carter Finances Ltd offered Derek a flat rate of 10% (a fixed amount of 10% every year on the original amount of the loan) and English Finances Ltd offered him 11% APR.

Calculate the interest.

Carter Finances Ltd	English Finances Ltd
Year 1 €15,000 @ 10% = €1,500	Year 1 €15,000 @ 11% = €1,650
Year 2 €15,000 @ 10% = €1,500	Year 2 €10,000 @ 11% = €1,100
Year 3 €15,000 @ 10% = €1,500	Year 3 €5,000 @ 11% = €550
Total interest €4,500	Total interest €3,300

The flat rate of 10% is lower than the 11% APR.

However, the 10% flat rate works out more expensive and Derek would pay €1,200 more interest.

ECONOMIC INDICATORS 3.9

Be Numerate

Steve and Róisín want to borrow €20,000 over three years.

They will repay €5,000 plus interest at the end of each year.

BOI Finances offered a flat rate of 10% and AIB finances offered 11% APR.

Calculate the interest.

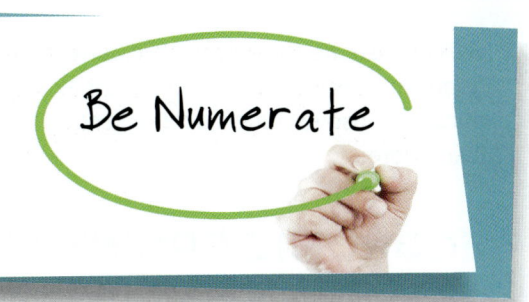

ECONOMIC GROWTH

As we saw earlier, one of the ways to measure the health of an economy is by looking at the gross domestic product (GDP), as it represents the **total market value of all goods and services** during a given year. Economic growth occurs when there is an increase in the GDP.

When a country experiences economic growth, employment increases and unemployment decreases. The **standard of living** improves and people have more money to spend.

The government also has **more money to spend** on health, education, social services and infrastructure. It also has more money to help the less well off in our economy.

In order for growth to happen, all the economic variables must be controlled, for example low inflation and interest rates.

Look back at **Unit 3.6** for a reminder of the impact of economic growth on society and the environment.

EXAMPLE 5: ECONOMIC GROWTH AS AN AMOUNT

	€ billion
Last year GDP	80
This year GDP	88
Economic growth	8

The **percentage change in GDP** is calculated as follows:

$$\frac{\text{Change in amount}}{\text{Original amount}} \times \frac{100}{1} = \%$$

$$\frac{\text{Plus}}{\text{Increase}} = \text{Growth} \qquad \frac{\text{Minus}}{\text{Decrease}} = \text{Recession}$$

EXAMPLE 6: ECONOMIC GROWTH AS A PERCENTAGE (INCREASE)

In 2020 €200 million is produced in Ireland
In 2021 €220 million is produced in Ireland

$$\frac{20}{200} \times \frac{100}{1} = \text{Plus/Increase 10\%}$$
= **Growth**

EXAMPLE 7: ECONOMIC GROWTH AS A PERCENTAGE (DECREASE)

In 2020 €200 million is produced in Ireland
In 2021 €195 million is produced in Ireland

$$\frac{-5}{100} \times \frac{100}{1} = \text{Minus/Decrease 5\%}$$
= **Recession**

We can also measure economic performance using **gross national product (GNP)**. GNP is also the total value of goods and services produced, but it excludes income coming into Ireland that has been earned by Irish people living abroad. It also excludes income sent to other countries that has been earned by people from those countries who are living here.

ECONOMIC GROWTH: DIFFERENT PERSPECTIVES

BE AN INDIVIDUAL
If there is growth: Higher employment, banks will lend, people will buy new products, there is an increase in demand for houses and standard of living improves.

If there is a fall: Emigration, decrease in employment, decrease in spending and standard of living disimproves.

BE THE ECONOMY
If there is growth: Extra income for the government, higher tax revenue, pay off part of government debt.

If there is a fall: Brain drain – emigration, rise in unemployment, very little investment and even business closures.

CHECKING IN...

1. In 2019 €180 million is produced in Ireland
   In 2021 €220 million is produced in Ireland
   a. Calculate GDP in money terms.
   b. Calculate GDP as a percentage.
   c. In relation to the above figures, is Ireland experiencing a recession or growth?
2. In 2020 €150 million is produced in Ireland
   In 2021 €125 million is produced in Ireland
   a. Calculate GDP in money terms.
   b. Calculate GDP as a percentage.
   c. In relation to the above figures, is Ireland experiencing a recession or growth?
3. What happens when we have growth in our economy?
4. What happens when we have recession in our economy? What might the government do if there is a recession?
5. Present the above information in a visual format.

NATIONAL INCOME

National income is the total value of all income in a nation during a given period. This includes wages from employment and self-employment, profits to firms, interest to lenders and rents to owners of land.

An individual receives income for the production of goods and services. Just as a person's income reflects the value of goods and services he or she produces in a year, the **national income** reflects the total value of goods and services produced by the residents of our country during the year.

ECONOMIC INDICATORS 3.9

There are three ways to calculate national income:
1. **The income method:** add up all incomes received in the country during a year.
2. **The output method:** add up the value of goods and services produced in the country during a year.
3. The **expenditure method**: add up all spending in the economy by households and firms on new and final goods and services.

See **Unit 3.2**, Circular Flow of Income, for how income flows through the economy.

NATIONAL INCOME: DIFFERENT PERSPECTIVES

BE AN INDIVIDUAL
When the national income increases, the standard of living improves, there are more opportunities and individuals are better off.

BE THE ECONOMY
When the national income increases, more goods are produced, employment goes up and there is extra revenue for the government.

When national income falls, it has the opposite effect in both cases.

NATIONAL DEBT

> **National debt** is the total amount of money borrowed by the government. Just like individuals and businesses, there is a cost to the government for borrowing money.

2015 national debt = €203.2 billion

Interest, which is known as debt servicing, on €203.2 billion was €8.457 billion.
If the government had no debt, imagine what they could spend this €8.457 billion on!

NATIONAL DEBT: DIFFERENT PERSPECTIVES

BE AN INDIVIDUAL
Increase in national debt: Taxes have to increase, which means individuals don't have as much **money to spend**. There is a reduction in the amount and **quality** of **services** such as transport, health and education. **Unemployment** increases.

Decrease in national debt: Taxes can be reduced, which means individuals have **more money** to spend. **Better services** can be provided. There are **more jobs** available.

BE GOVERNMENT
Increase in national debt: As taxes are increased, costs go up, there is less spending in the economy.
Decrease in national debt: There is more money to go around.

Revise the government budget scenarios in **Unit 3.4**. If the government decides to build new schools, health may lose out. The government may have to borrow more, pay repayments and interest, and therefore have to cut back in other areas. It's a really interesting circle.

Remember, it is always good to look at things from a different perspective and be able to switch your roles. Be an individual or be a business or be the government.

3.9 BE BUSINESS: OUR ECONOMY

Be a Researcher

Use websites to source information on Ireland's economic indicators. Copy and fill in this 'Economic Indicators Learning Sheet'. Make a note of the websites you used and the date you used them.

Economic Indicators Learning Sheet

Employment www.cso.ie	**Unemployment** www.cso.ie
Define: Rate (%): Describe the drift: Is it increasing or decreasing?	Define: Rate (%): Describe the drift: Is it increasing or decreasing?
Interest Rates www.centralbank.ie	**Inflation** www.cso.ie
Define: Rate (%): Describe the drift: Is it increasing or decreasing?	Define: Rate (%): CPI: Describe the drift: Is it increasing or decreasing?
National Income www.cso.ie	**National Debt** www.ntma.ie
Define: Total: GNP and GDP: List main sources: Describe the drift: Is it increasing or decreasing?	Define: Total in billions: Total interest in billions: Describe the drift: Is it increasing or decreasing?
Population www.cso.ie	**Taxation** www.revenue.ie
Define: Ireland: Europe: The world: Trend: is it increasing or decreasing?	List the different types of taxes and rates:

The key interest rates in Ireland are controlled by the European Central Bank (ECB), which sets the main rates for all of the eurozone countries. Find out what the current ECB rates are.

CHECKING IN...

1. Create a fishbone summary of this unit using your fishbone template (p. 546).
2. Copy this octopus template and write down the eight main economic indicators.

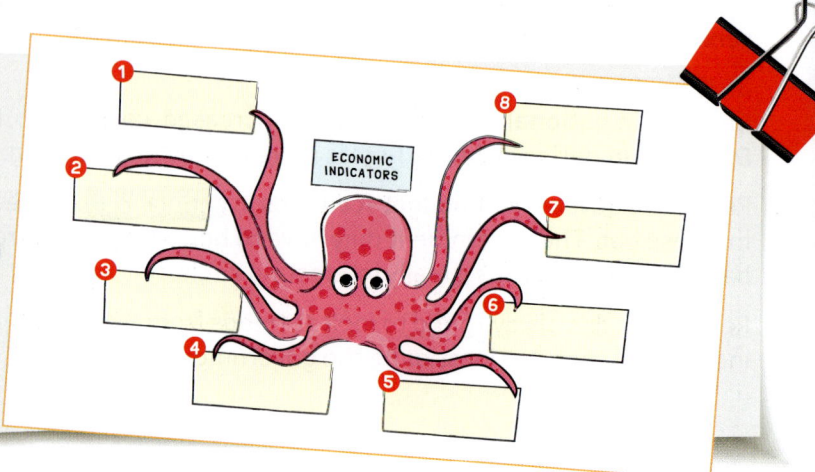

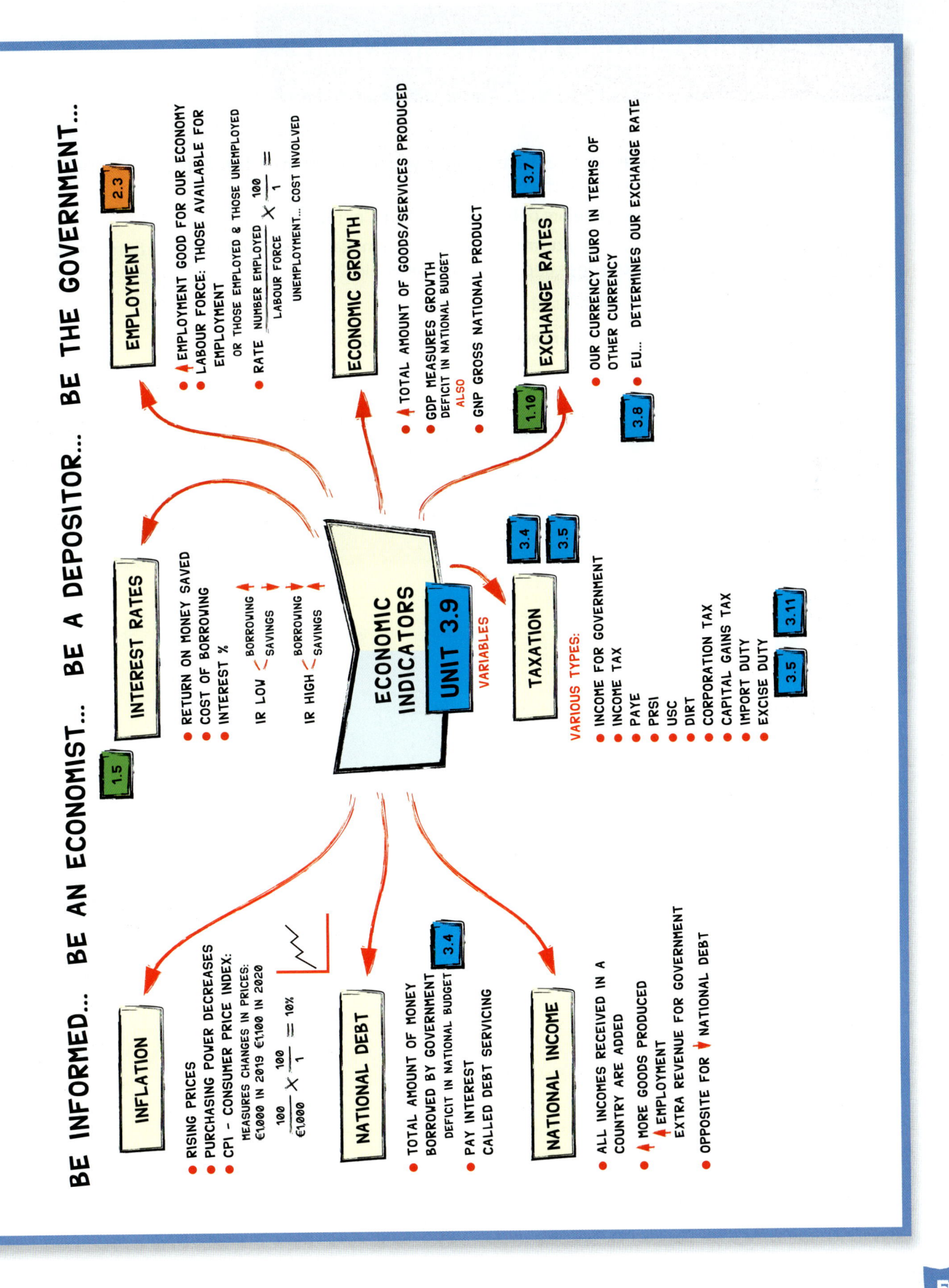

ECONOMIC INDICATORS 3.9

BE INFORMED... BE AN ECONOMIST... BE A DEPOSITOR... BE THE GOVERNMENT...

EMPLOYMENT [2.3]
- ↑EMPLOYMENT GOOD FOR OUR ECONOMY
- LABOUR FORCE: THOSE AVAILABLE FOR EMPLOYMENT OR THOSE EMPLOYED & THOSE UNEMPLOYED
- RATE = NUMBER EMPLOYED / LABOUR FORCE × 100/1 =
- UNEMPLOYMENT... COST INVOLVED

ECONOMIC GROWTH
- TOTAL AMOUNT OF GOODS/SERVICES PRODUCED
- GDP MEASURES GROWTH DEFICIT IN NATIONAL BUDGET
- ALSO
- GNP GROSS NATIONAL PRODUCT

EXCHANGE RATES [3.7]
- OUR CURRENCY EURO IN TERMS OF OTHER CURRENCY
- EU... DETERMINES OUR EXCHANGE RATE
- [1.10] [3.8]

INTEREST RATES [1.5]
- RETURN ON MONEY SAVED
- COST OF BORROWING
- INTEREST %
- IR LOW ↘BORROWING ↗SAVINGS
- IR HIGH ↗BORROWING ↘SAVINGS

ECONOMIC INDICATORS UNIT 3.9
VARIABLES

TAXATION [3.4] [3.5]
VARIOUS TYPES:
- INCOME FOR GOVERNMENT
- INCOME TAX
- PAYE
- PRSI
- USC
- DIRT
- CORPORATION TAX
- CAPITAL GAINS TAX
- IMPORT DUTY [3.11]
- EXCISE DUTY [3.5]

INFLATION
- RISING PRICES
- PURCHASING POWER DECREASES
- CPI – CONSUMER PRICE INDEX: MEASURES CHANGES IN PRICES: €1000 IN 2019 €1100 IN 2020
- $\frac{100}{€1,000} \times \frac{100}{1} = 10\%$

NATIONAL DEBT [3.4]
- TOTAL AMOUNT OF MONEY BORROWED BY GOVERNMENT DEFICIT IN NATIONAL BUDGET
- PAY INTEREST CALLED DEBT SERVICING

NATIONAL INCOME
- ALL INCOMES RECEIVED IN A COUNTRY ARE ADDED
- ↑MORE GOODS PRODUCED ↑EMPLOYMENT EXTRA REVENUE FOR GOVERNMENT
- OPPOSITE FOR ↓NATIONAL DEBT

505

3.9 BE BUSINESS: OUR ECONOMY

Be Prepared: My Support Sheets

Completing the activities here will help you to reflect on and reinforce your learning before you move on to the next unit.

Work by yourself, in pairs or in a team of three or four.
- Write down the **key terms** in this unit and make sure you understand them. See if they match the ones at the back of the book.
- List the **key concepts/themes** in this unit.
- List the **three most interesting points** about this topic.

Write a quiz

Write a quiz based on this chapter. Write three questions that relate to economic indicators. Pick one of your quiz questions and give your own answer in detail.

Economics in Action Idea!

Create a poster about the main economic indicators.

Success criteria:
- Title
- Accurate and up-to-date statistics
- Correct grammar and spelling
- Visual(s)

QUESTION TIME

Working in pairs, discuss and then document your answers.
1. List the eight economic indicators.
2. Which economic indicator might be the most important and why?
3. 'High and increasing interest rates keeps everyone happy.' Debate.
4. Explain the sources of income for our government.
5. Why does a country never achieve zero unemployment?
6. The total value of goods produced in Year 1 and Year 2 was €10,000 and €11,000 respectively. Calculate the rate of economic growth.

ECONOMIC INDICATORS 3.9

EVALUATE MY LEARNING: DAR

Describe
- Did I/we meet my/our learning intentions?
- What went well? What are my/our strengths?

Assess
- How did I/we work with others?
- Were there challenges?

Recommend
- How might I improve?
- What skills and learning might I apply to new situations?

Do your **Key Check** in the workbook for this unit and then mark your learning position on the following rating scale:

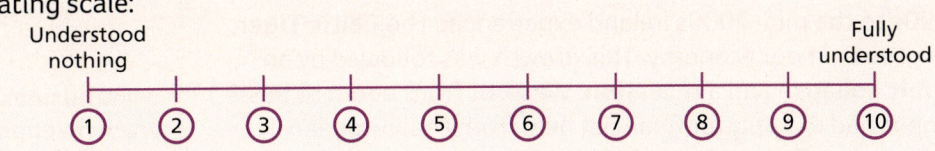

Understood nothing — 1 2 3 4 5 6 7 8 9 10 — Fully understood

How can you move up the rating scale? What can you **say**, **make**, **write** and **do** to illustrate your learning?

CBA 2 Presentation:
Will I use this unit for my **Presentation**?

You need to be preparing for your CBAs
- Exceptional
- Above expectations
- In line with expectations
- Yet to meet expectations

Revisit this unit in Third Year to document any major changes. Remember to date your research material.

Stop and think
Do I have any questions or concerns?
What are the mistakes or errors I made in this unit?

3.10 ECONOMIC ISSUES

Use knowledge and information from a range of media sources to discuss current economic issues and present an informed view.

Learning Intentions

At the end of this unit I will:
- Know how to discuss the Irish economy
- Apply information to different situations
- Understand the importance of researching information

This chapter has links with numerous **Learning Outcomes**. Choose an issue that you have an interest in and that you have researched and look at it from the perspective of economics.

Key Concepts
- ✓ The Irish economy
- ✓ Economic policies
- ✓ Economic issues

Wonderful Worthwhile Websites

www.businesseducation.ie
www.revenue.ie
www.finfacts.ie

OUR ECONOMY

From the mid-1990s to the mid-2000s Ireland experienced the **Celtic Tiger**, a period of record growth in our economy. This growth was followed by an enormous **economic collapse** and a **recession**. We went from boom to bust! The Irish government had to apply for financial help from the European Commission, the European Central Bank (ECB) and the International Monetary Fund (IMF), collectively called the **troika** (group of three).

Ireland went from being known as an excellent example of how a small, open economy could be successful in the modern global marketplace to a country on the edge of financial collapse.

The Irish economy has now started to recover. With very strict budgetary controls by the government, and under the watchful eye of the **EU**, measures have been put in place to encourage growth in our economy. The financial crisis made us realise how vulnerable our economy or any other economy is.

ECONOMIC ISSUES

During your study of Business Studies you have seen how economic issues affect us all in our daily lives. It is the work of the government to address these issues and it is our duty as citizens and voters to make sure they are doing a good job. To do that we need to understand the issues through research, understand them through evaluation and make informed judgments and recommendations.

Some Important Economic Issues

- Unemployment
- Housing shortage
- Emigration
- National debt
- Inflation
- Exchange rates
- Education costs
- Healthcare

SOURCING INFORMATION

Information is all around us and available in many different formats. We have access to books, newspapers, TV, radio, web pages, Facebook, Twitter, Instagram, videos, photographs, and lots more.

Social media has become a really powerful tool for you as a student, for consumers, for your family, for businesses and even for our government.

With so much information available it is important to be able to **evaluate** and **interpret** it correctly. We should not be complacent and just accept any information at face value.

ECONOMIC ISSUES 3.10

WORKING WITH OTHERS

Let's look at the issue of obesity as an example of an economic issue.

You have been asked to give advice to the government on how to tackle obesity in young people.

For your research you could use a range of media sources:
- Websites
- Newspapers
- Radio
- TV

Before deciding on your advice, look at the issue from a range of different viewpoints:
- Young people struggling with obesity
- Organisations that deal with obesity
- Teachers
- Parents/guardians
- For-profit and not-for-profit organisations
- Politicians

Top Tip: Debating

It's very important to set the **correct tone** and ensure you can influence the outcome.

When researching and preparing, look at lots of **different perspectives** – these can be your basic building blocks. Use different sources for your research.

When you're discussing an issue, the **way you use language** is really important. For example, 'How can we achieve X while also doing Y and Z?' (keeping everyone happy!) rather than 'We should …' or 'We must …'

Be confident: have evidence to back up your opinion.

It's a good idea to **practise arguing** for one side of the debate and then for the other side. Not only will this help your debating skills, it will also help you see and value issues from different perspectives.

CASE STUDY: OBESITY

Gateway School of Education is located on the outskirts of a town with a population of over 10,000. The school has 500 students and is growing. Wellbeing is a central policy of the school.

The school conducted some **research on obesity** in the school, and found that 30% of the girls and 10% of the boys were overweight. These figures showed an increase from the previous year, when 22% of girls and 9% of boys were overweight.

A **focus group** was established to **come up with a plan** to deal with this issue. Members of the focus group included students, staff, parents and representatives of the local communities, including not-for-profit organisations. After many meetings and discussions the group decided that the school should build a state-of-the-art gymnasium with a fitness centre to cater for all students. The gym would be available before school, at lunchtime and after school.

However, after a **cost-benefit analysis**, the group realised that this project would require substantial funding, not only to build the gym but to employ extra people, cover heating costs, insurance, etc. While they agreed that this was a **good long-term plan**, the group used a decision tree to come up with suggestions in the short term.

After numerous discussions it was decided to create a **walking path** around the sports pitch. All students would be supplied with a **pedometer**. The school would test students' weight and fitness at the beginning of the term and at the end of the term and document the results.

The above is an example of **problem-solving**. You must choose the best solution for the problem, taking into account the cost of the various options and what is achievable within existing constraints.

> **WORKING WITH OTHERS**
> - How might Gateway School of Education fundraise for a new gymnasium?
> - Are there other inexpensive strategies the school could employ to tackle lack of fitness and weight issues among students? (See www.getirelandactive.ie for ideas.)
> - How might the school encourage students to become more active?
> - What are the costs to the government of an increase in obesity?

EVALUATING INFORMATION

Once information has been gathered through research it is very important to **evaluate** it. Understanding the information allows you to make **better judgements** and decisions.

When you debate an issue, make sure you have evidence to back up your opinion!

Seven questions you should consider when evaluating information:
1. Who is sending this message/information?
2. Why are they sending the message?
3. What methods are used to attract attention, to create interest and desire, and to encourage action?
4. What points of view are represented?
5. Could the message be understood in different ways?
6. What is missing from the message?
7. What is the date of the information?

When we are looking at information we need to be aware that our own attitudes, experiences and beliefs might influence our interpretation of it.

ECONOMIC POLICIES

An economic policy is a **plan/rule/decision** made by our government to make changes to our economy. You will see in the next unit that there are different ways in which our government can achieve this.

EVALUATING GOVERNMENT POLICIES

The following are some important questions to address when evaluating government policies to deal with issues that arise.

1. **Define** the issue. Remember to carry out your research.
2. What **policy** (plan/rule) did the government introduce to solve the issue?
3. Be the government: What might **I** do to solve the issue?
4. Is this a **new** issue?
5. Do any **other countries** experience the same issue?
6. Has the issue been successfully **resolved** in another country?
7. **How much money** could the issue cost?
8. Who **benefits** from this policy?
9. Who might bear the **cost**?
10. How is the policy **operated** and what happens if it doesn't work?

*It is important to understand and value economic **issues** and the **policies** used to tackle them. Different policies can actually **conflict** with each other. The government needs to be decisive.*

ECONOMIC ISSUES 3.10

CHECKING IN...
1. List five questions you should ask yourself when evaluation information.
2. List five questions you should ask yourself when evaluating government policy.

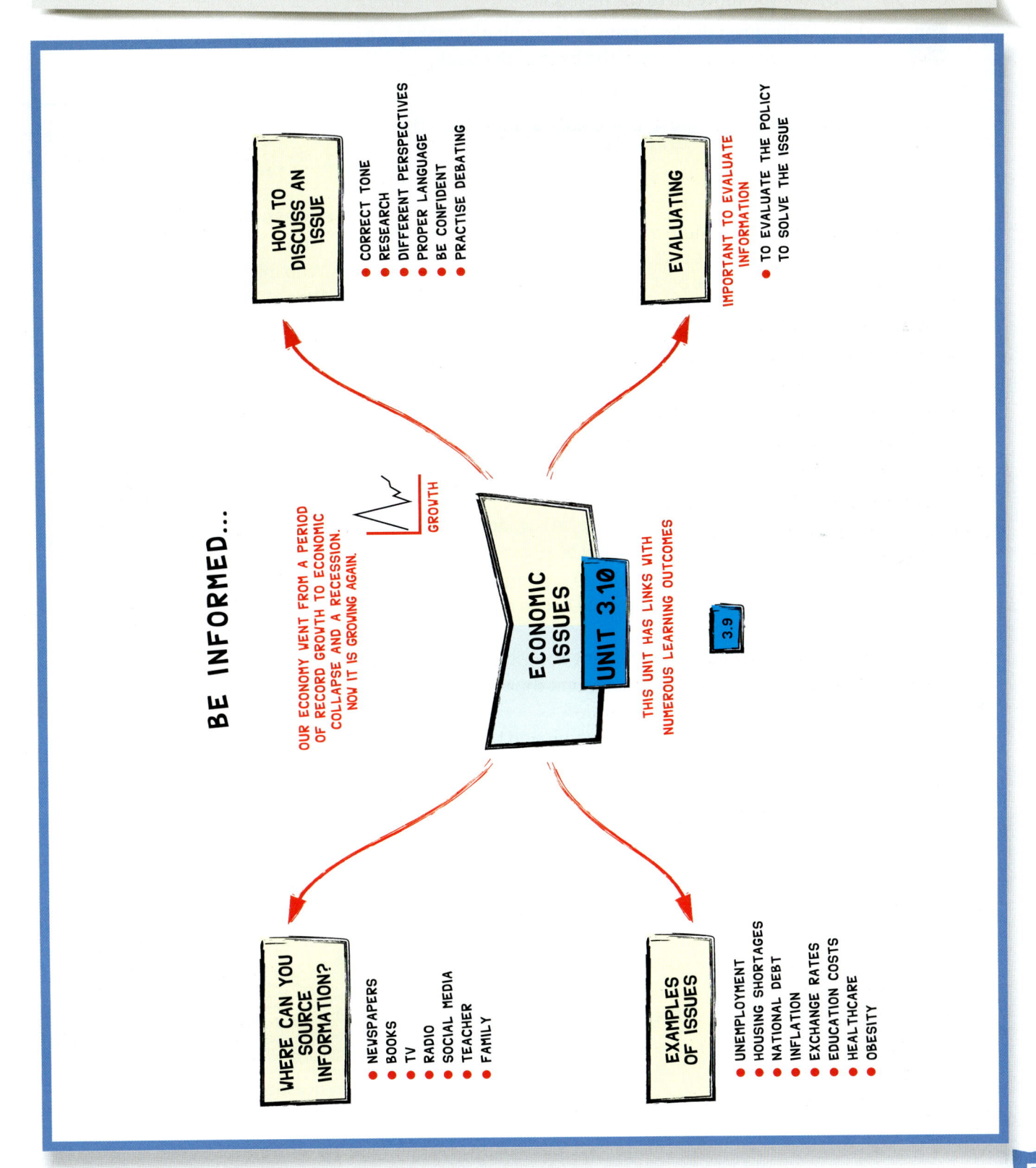

BE INFORMED...

ECONOMIC ISSUES — UNIT 3.10

Our economy went from a period of record growth to economic collapse and a recession. Now it is growing again.

This unit has links with numerous learning outcomes (3.9)

HOW TO DISCUSS AN ISSUE
- CORRECT TONE
- RESEARCH
- DIFFERENT PERSPECTIVES
- PROPER LANGUAGE
- BE CONFIDENT
- PRACTISE DEBATING

EVALUATING
- IMPORTANT TO EVALUATE INFORMATION
- TO EVALUATE THE POLICY TO SOLVE THE ISSUE

WHERE CAN YOU SOURCE INFORMATION?
- NEWSPAPERS
- BOOKS
- TV
- RADIO
- SOCIAL MEDIA
- TEACHER
- FAMILY

EXAMPLES OF ISSUES
- UNEMPLOYMENT
- HOUSING SHORTAGES
- NATIONAL DEBT
- INFLATION
- EXCHANGE RATES
- EDUCATION COSTS
- HEALTHCARE
- OBESITY

511

Be Prepared: My Support Sheets

Completing the activities here will help you to reflect on and reinforce your learning before you move on to the next unit.

- Write down the **key terms** in this unit and make sure you understand them. See if they match the ones at the back of the book.
- List the **key concepts/themes** in this unit.
- List the **three most interesting points** about this topic.

Enterprise in Action Idea!

Create an individual two-minute presentation entitled 'If nurse's wages increased as part of a government health policy'. Remember, the best presentations are well researched, provide evidence to support claims, display an interest in the topic and use variety, creativity and superb communication skills to hold the audience's attention.

Success criteria:
- Title
- Who might benefit?
- Who will bear the costs?
- Visual(s)

QUESTION TIME

1. Jot down five economic issues that are relevant to Ireland today. Take one issue and discuss it in detail.
2. If the government decided to increase VAT, what would the effects be?
3. What would be the costs and benefits of an increase in unemployment?
4. The price of cigarettes includes a large proportion of tax. Why do you think the government continues to increase tax on cigarettes? Who bears the costs and who benefits?
5. What might happen if the government abolished all hospital fees?

Do your **Key Check** in the workbook for this unit and then mark your learning position on the following rating scale:

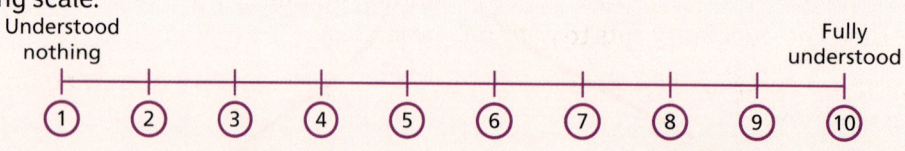

Understood nothing — 1 2 3 4 5 6 7 8 9 10 — Fully understood

How can you move up the rating scale? What can you **say**, **make**, **write** and **do** to illustrate your learning?

CBA 1 Business in Action:
Will I use this unit for my topic for **Enterprise in Action**?

CBA 2 Presentation:
Will I use this unit for my **Presentation**?

Stop and think

Do I have any questions or concerns?
What are the mistakes or errors I made in this unit?

3.11 ECONOMIC POLICY

Evaluate the benefits and costs of a government economic policy and assess who enjoys the benefits and who bears the costs

Learning Intentions

At the end of this unit I will:
- Know the meaning of government policy
- Understand the benefits of government polices
- Understand the costs of government polices
- Understand choices from different perspectives with regard to taxation
- Value the benefits of government policies
- Know how to apply my research skills

Key Concepts
- Fiscal policies and monetary policies
- Taxes on cigarettes
- Water charges, the Universal Social Charge, the property tax
- Carbon tax

Making the links with other LOs:

3.10 Economic issues

ECONOMIC POLICIES

An **economic policy** is a course of action taken by a government to influence its country's economy.

Here are two of the main types of economic policy:

- **Fiscal policy:** relates to public revenues (taxation) and public spending. Concerned with changes in taxation (increases or decreases) and decisions on government spending.
- **Monetary policy:** relates to how money is supplied to, and circulates in, an economy. Concerned with changes in interest rates. Being a part of the eurozone means that the Irish Central Bank needs the permission of the European Central Bank (ECB) to make such changes.

Wonderful Worthwhile Websites

www.publicpolicy.ie
www.revenue.ie
www.cso.ie

We can see the government's economic policies in the **national budget**. These policies can include anything from taxation and budgetary cuts to national ownership.

Governments **pay for the goods and services** they provide through taxation or borrowing from lending institutions, such as the ECB.

Government **departments make policies** that affect our everyday lives by providing services we use, for example education, health, social, defence and environmental services.

Some government policies try to **redistribute income** by providing the less well off with income through social welfare payments.

The cost of some government policies is sometimes greater than the benefits. This may happen when the government promises a policy as an incentive to voters. It can also happen if the government decides to do something that has a social benefit rather than an economic benefit.

WHERE DO TAXES GO?

Keep yourself informed about where taxes are going.

If your salary is **€50,000**, at 2016 **tax rates** you will pay tax of approximately **€15,130.80**.

Where is the **€15,130.80** spent and who benefits?

State Administration	€381.43
Security	€768.95
Education	€2,174.90
Community, Culture & Environment	€225.15
Infrastructure	€400.51
Social Programmes	€5,007.54
Foreign Affairs	€159.63
Health and Children	€3,513.83
Economic Supports	€522.47
Servicing Debt	€1,976.39

A portion of the price you pay goes to the government in taxation.

	Wine (bottle)	Beer (pint)	Petrol (tank)
Average Cost	€10.00	€5.00	€83.60
Average Tax	€5.58	€1.79	€51.55

SOME CONTROVERSIAL TAXES

Most people understand the need to pay personal taxes (Unit 1.4), but there are other taxes that cause controversy, such as taxes on water and property, and the carbon tax.

Water Charges

Water charges are income for the government. They are a positive step from an environmental and sustainable perspective as they make us more aware of our water usage.

There was a lot of opposition when the government introduced water charges. Does this mean that we're happy to spend money on bottled water but not to pay for the water in our homes? Or is it more complicated than that? What do you think? Remember the environmental effects and costs of plastic bottles too!

The debate over water charges continues. We must remember that water is a scarce resource. The government's view is that the best way to ensure that water is consumed and supplied economically and efficiently is to charge for it. Irish Water is the regulated utility for water. It was established and domestic water charges were introduced in 2015.

Did You Know?

The idea of selling bottled Irish water was first introduced by Geoff Read in the early 1980s.

Read created the Ballygowan brand, which is the leading bottled water in Ireland. Over 40 million litres of natural water are distributed from the plant each year. The source of the natural mineral water is Newcastle West in Co. Limerick.

The Ballygowan brand is owned and distributed by Britvic Ireland Ltd.

ECONOMIC POLICY 3.11

Property Ownership

Property prices in Ireland are very high and there isn't enough supply to meet the demand. This makes it very difficult for first-time buyers. Deposits are required for mortgages and it isn't always easy to get a mortgage. However, Irish people want to own their own homes.

Yet in many parts of Europe, such as France and Germany, renting is the norm. Renting is not necessarily cheap, but many Europeans are less concerned than the Irish about owning their own property.

There are good reasons for this difference. In most parts of Europe:

- Property prices don't really increase
- There is a very good supply of quality rental property and rent is very fair
- Rent contracts are controlled and there are limits to increases
- Lending for purchasing property is difficult to obtain
- Tax rules don't favour buying

Could renting be the future for the Irish property market?

Carbon Tax

The Green Party introduced a carbon tax in 2010. Carbon tax is income for the government. It also helps to reduce greenhouse gas emissions, ensuring a more sustainable environment.

WORKING WITH OTHERS

Have a class debate on environmental taxes and carbon emissions. Motion: 'The government should abolish the carbon tax'.

A government could abolish a tax in the hope that it will be re-elected. What tax or charge would you abolish if you were the government?

CHECKING IN...

If the government introduced a policy to create more rental accommodation, who might benefit? What might be the costs? Watch a current affairs programme on television, e.g. *Prime Time*. What government policy was discussed? What did you learn?

POLICY DECISIONS

Different policies can sometimes conflict with each other. The government needs to be decisive about what it wants to do and how best to do it. For example, after our EU bailout following the economic crash, the Irish government introduced the National Recovery Plan, which introduced very strict budget cuts: wages were cut, the minimum wage decreased, and the Universal Social Charge (USC) was introduced, along with VAT increases. Since then our economy has improved, with an increase in employment and much-needed growth in our economy.

It is important to know, value and understand economic policies.

When a government changes a policy, for example on taxation, who pays and who benefits? Let's look at an example.

CASE STUDY: TAX ON CIGARETTES

Tax on cigarettes is a valuable source of revenue for the government.

The government can raise up to €2 billion a year in taxation on cigarettes. That's a lot of money for the government.

However, roughly the same amount is spent by the government on treating illnesses caused by smoking, such as cancer and asthma.

Approximately 80 per cent of the price of a pack of cigarettes goes to the government through VAT and excise duty.

How does the government spend the income from taxing cigarettes?

A pack of 20 cigarettes costs approximately €10.50.

Of this amount, €8.13 goes to the government as tax.

The government spends tax received from cigarette sales to improve sectors of the economy such as social services, health and education.

This tax is spent as follows:

€2.69	Social services
€1.89	Health
€1.17	Education
€1.06	Repaying debt
€1.32	Other

A lot of smokers are addicted to nicotine and would like to quit smoking. Most want to quit for health reasons, but it's also a very expensive habit.

If you smoke a packet of 20 a day, your habit will cost you approximately **€3,832** a year. If you smoked for 40 years, your habit will have cost you **€153,300**. That's a lot of money gone up in smoke!

Anti-smoking groups always welcome additional tax on cigarettes.

Who wants price increases on cigarettes?

ASH (Action on Smoking and Health) Ireland (**www.ash.ie**) is an organisation that focuses on reducing the impact of tobacco use in Irish society. It does this through education and by running information campaigns on tobacco use. In Ireland, approximately 5,500 people die each year from the effects of tobacco-related disease. ASH Ireland is determined to reduce this number. It strives for a tobacco-free society.

Time to think

Be the Government: How would you choose to spend tax received from cigarette sales?

Be the Manufacturer: Would you be happy with the heavy tax on cigarettes and the work of organisations such as ASH Ireland?

ECONOMIC POLICY 3.11

Both the Irish Cancer Society and ASH Ireland welcome price increases on cigarettes. They believe it will be a disincentive for children to start smoking, and encourage current smokers to quit.

Who doesn't want price increases on cigarettes?

However, other agencies are not so happy. The National Federation of Retail Newsagents (NRFN) (representing shops that sell cigarettes) and tobacco companies feel that price increases will drive smokers out of the shops and into the arms of criminals who sell cigarettes on the **black market** at half the price they are in the shops – and the people who sell these cigarettes don't pay any tax on them. Selling cigarettes without a licence is a serious criminal offence.

> According to the HSE, 29% of the Irish population were smokers in 2003. By 2014 this had dropped to approximately 19.5%.
>
> See the HSE website at www.hse.ie

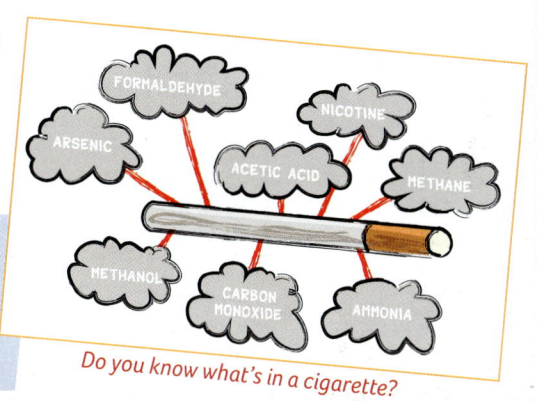

Do you know what's in a cigarette?

Be a Researcher

Use websites to source information on one of Ireland's economic policies. Copy and fill in this 'Government Economic Policy Learning Sheet'. Make a note of the websites you used and the date you used them.

Government Economic Policy Learning Sheet

- Name of Policy
- Define:
- Objectives:
- Sources of information:
- Research carried out:
- Evaluation of research from economic, social and environmental points of view:
- Costs and benefits:
- Skills I used and developed:

517

3.11 BE BUSINESS: OUR ECONOMY

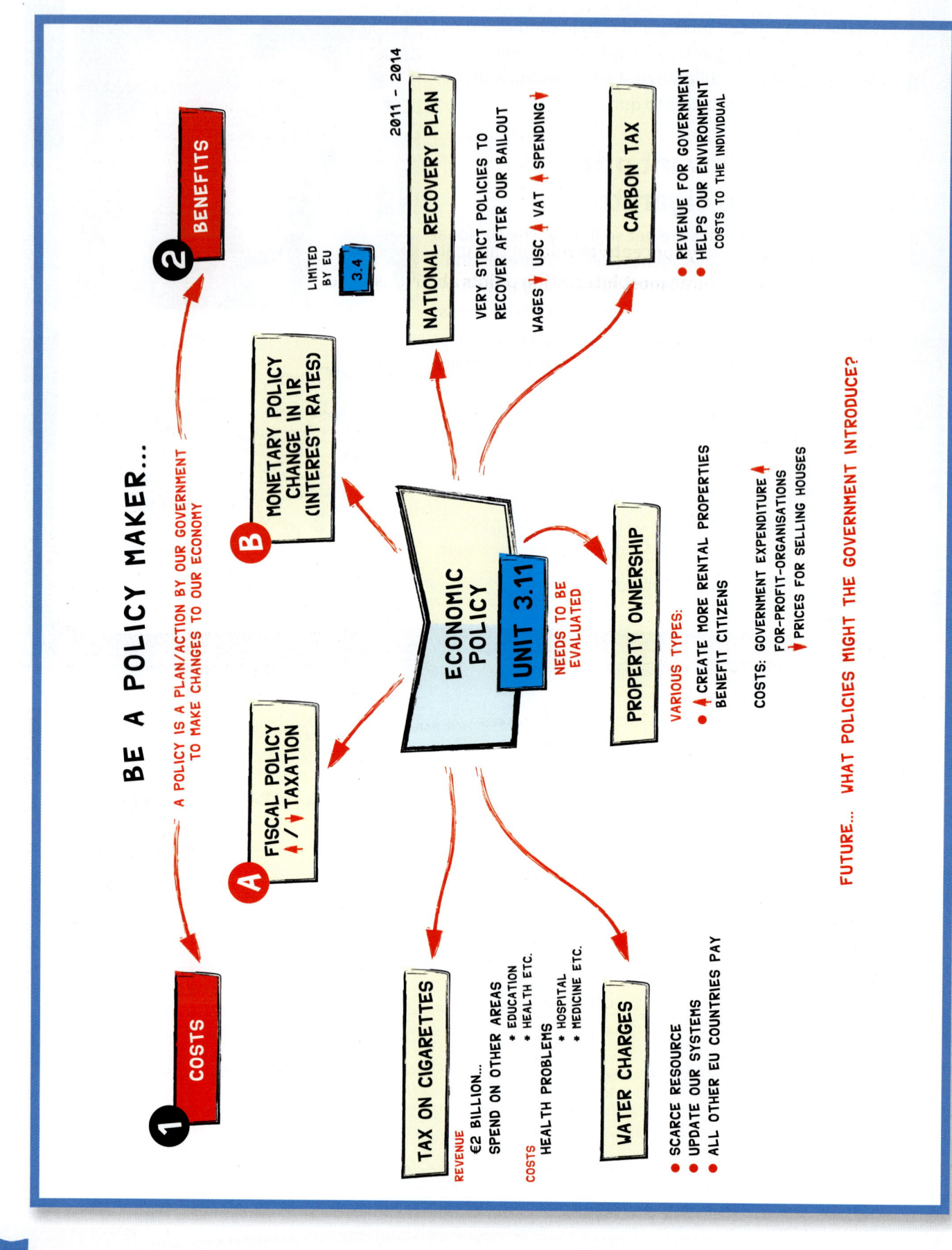

BE A POLICY MAKER...

A POLICY IS A PLAN/ACTION BY OUR GOVERNMENT TO MAKE CHANGES TO OUR ECONOMY

ECONOMIC POLICY — UNIT 3.11
NEEDS TO BE EVALUATED

1 COSTS

2 BENEFITS

A FISCAL POLICY ↑/↓ TAXATION

B MONETARY POLICY CHANGE IN IR (INTEREST RATES)
LIMITED BY EU

NATIONAL RECOVERY PLAN 2011 – 2014
VERY STRICT POLICIES TO RECOVER AFTER OUR BAILOUT
↓WAGES ↑USC ↑VAT ↓SPENDING

CARBON TAX
- REVENUE FOR GOVERNMENT
- HELPS OUR ENVIRONMENT
- COSTS TO THE INDIVIDUAL

PROPERTY OWNERSHIP
VARIOUS TYPES:
- ↑CREATE MORE RENTAL PROPERTIES BENEFIT CITIZENS

COSTS: GOVERNMENT EXPENDITURE ↑ FOR-PROFIT-ORGANISATIONS ↑
↓PRICES FOR SELLING HOUSES

TAX ON CIGARETTES
REVENUE
€2 BILLION...
SPEND ON OTHER AREAS
* EDUCATION
* HEALTH ETC.

COSTS
HEALTH PROBLEMS
* HOSPITAL
* MEDICINE ETC.

WATER CHARGES
- SCARCE RESOURCE
- UPDATE OUR SYSTEMS
- ALL OTHER EU COUNTRIES PAY

FUTURE... WHAT POLICIES MIGHT THE GOVERNMENT INTRODUCE?

Be Prepared: My Support Sheets

Completing the activities here will help you to reflect on and reinforce your learning before you move on to the next unit.

- Write down the **key terms** in this unit and make sure you understand them. See if they match the ones at the back of the book.
- List the **key concepts/themes** in this unit.
- List the **three most interesting points** about this topic.

Economics in Action Idea!

1. **Be the Minister:** Write a speech explaining how your view of a policy has changed after investigating an issue. Work together, in pairs and then in squares.

2. Imagine your school published a monthly newspaper called *The JC Business Studies Times*.

   Working with others, create a page for this newspaper representing the benefits and costs of government policies. Look back at the advice on discussing issues in Unit 3.10.

Success criteria:
- Title and introduction
- Name of policy
- Why your view has changed
- Relevant statistics
- Persuasive language

- Title and introduction
- Clear purpose and focus
- Add a visual, perhaps a cartoon
- Include statistics
- No mistakes in grammar, punctuation or spelling
- Conclusion – summarise main points

QUESTION TIME

1. List three government economic policies.
2. What do you think is the most important economic policy? Why?
3. Should cigarettes be taxed? How should this money be spent?
4. Discuss the costs and benefits of water charges.
5. Choose a tax of your choice and explain the pros and cons of this tax.
6. Draft a speech about where taxation is spent.
7. Name a government policy and discuss the pros and cons of this policy.

EVALUATE MY LEARNING: DAR

Describe
- Did I/we meet my/our learning intentions?
- What went well? What are my/our strengths?

Assess
- How did I/we work with others?
- Were there challenges?

Recommend
- How might I improve?
- What skills and learning might I apply to new situations?

Do your **Key Check** in the workbook for this unit and then mark your learning position on the following rating scale:

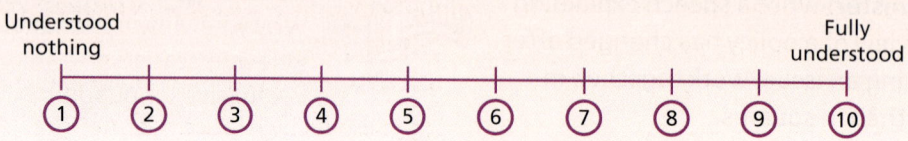

Understood nothing — 1　2　3　4　5　6　7　8　9　10 — Fully understood

How can you move up the rating scale? What can you **say**, **make**, **write** and **do** to illustrate your learning?

CBA 1 Business in Action:
Will I use this unit for my topic for **Enterprise in Action**? ☐

CBA 2 Presentation:
Will I use this unit for my **Presentation**? ☐

You need to be preparing for your CBAs
- Exceptional
- Above expectations
- In line with expectations
- Yet to meet expectations

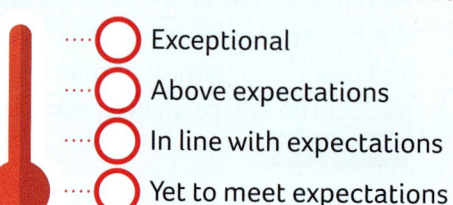

Revisit this unit in Third Year to document any major changes.

Remember to date your research material.

Stop and think

Do I have any questions or concerns?

What are the mistakes or errors I made in this unit?

KEY TERMS GLOSSARY

STRAND 1

UNIT 1.1

Assets Items of value that you own, e.g. your phone.

Careful spending Planning what you are going to spend your money on.

Debt The amount you owe.

Economic influences The state of the economy – this affects people's wants and their ability to meet their needs.

Environmental influences Being environmentally friendly.

Environmental responsibility Being aware of the planet's limited resources and acting responsibly to preserve them.

Environmental sustainability Looking after the planet and considering the impact of our actions on the environment.

Government influences Actions and policies decided by the government have an effect on how you spend your money.

Income The money you receive, e.g. your wage/salary, benefits.

Material resources Money and possessions.

Need A basic requirement, e.g. food.

Peer pressure Influence from your peers to persuade you to behave in a particular way.

People resources Friends, family, classmates and the local community.

Personal influences Personal factors that will determine your needs and wants. They include culture, age, gender, hobbies and attitudes.

Personal resources What you do well – your abilities, skills and talents.

Psychological influences Emotional factors in our behaviour.

Resources Anything that can help us to reach a goal.

Want Something you desire, e.g. an expensive smartphone.

Wealth What you own (assets) minus what you owe (debts).

UNIT 1.2

Bonus Extra income, usually paid for reaching a target or meeting a deadline.

Budget Planned income and expenditure.

Capital expenditure Money spent on durable items that will last a long time (e.g. car, washing machine).

Child benefit Paid every four weeks to the parent/guardian of each child under the age of sixteen.

Commission Extra pay for selling more: an incentive to encourage salespeople to sell.

Current expenditure Spending on day-to-day items that will last for a limited period only (e.g. food).

Discretionary expenditure Money spent on things you can live without (luxuries).

Expenditure The amount of money you spend.

False economy A purchase that seemed as though it would save money, but in the long term results in money being wasted.

Fixed expenditure Money spent at the same time each week, each month and/or each year (annually), e.g. rent, TV licence. The amount is normally the same every week/month/year.

Gross wage Total pay before tax and other deductions.

Impulse buying Unplanned buying.

Income Money and/or something of value that you receive.

Irregular expenditure Spending that varies in the amount and time paid, e.g. petrol, school supplies.

Irregular income Income that is only received now and again (e.g. a Christmas present). It is not certain that you will receive this income.

Opportunity cost When you make a financial decision to do without an item due to limited or scarce resources, the item not chosen is called the opportunity cost.

Overtime Working additional hours, for which you are paid extra.

Regular income Income that is usually paid at certain intervals (e.g. every Thursday, the last Friday of the month) and is always the same amount.

Time rate Payment for time worked (e.g. per hour, per day).

UNIT 1.3

APR Annual percentage rate – the true rate of interest.

Dependence stage The stage of your life when you are dependent on your parents or guardians.

Emerging stage The stage of your life when you can finance others, e.g. your family.

Entrepreneur A person who starts their own business.

Independence stage The stage of your life when you can finance yourself.

Jobseeker's allowance Money the government pays to people who are unemployed and seeking work.

Loan Borrowed money.

Pension Income you receive when you retire.

Personal financial life cycle plan Sets out your needs and wants at each stage of your life and matches them with sources of finance.

Pre-retirement stage The stage of your life when you are building up your finances again.

Retirement stage The stage of your life when you are spending your finances.

Sources of finance Where your money comes from.

SMART Specific, measurable, attainable, relevant and time-bound – a way of setting goals.

UNIT 1.4

Corporation tax Tax on companies' profits.

Customs duties Taxes on imported goods (goods brought into Ireland from abroad).

Excise duty Tax on home-produced goods (goods produced in Ireland).

Gross pay Total money earned *before* any deductions have been made.

Net pay Take-home pay after deductions have been made.

Non-statutory deductions Deductions from pay that are voluntary, i.e. you choose to pay them, e.g. health insurance.

PAYE Pay as you earn – income tax.

Property tax Tax on property you own. The rate depends on the value of the property.

PRSI Pay Related Social Insurance – paid to the Department of Social Protection and used to pay social welfare benefits and pensions.

Revenue Commissioners The state body responsible for collecting taxes in Ireland is known as the Office of the Revenue Commissioners (often called Revenue for short).

Statutory deductions Compulsory deductions from pay, i.e. you must pay them.

Tax allowances Reduce the amount of tax you have to pay. Unlike tax credits, tax allowances are subtracted from your gross pay *before* it is taxed.

Tax credit Reduces the amount of tax you have to pay and is deducted from your tax. Most people have a €3,300 annual tax credit.

Tax rates Always expressed as a percentage (%). Different rates apply to different levels or bands of income.

Taxation The taxes and charges collected by the state to pay for things that we all need as a country.

Union subscription Fee paid for membership of a trade union.

USC Universal Social Charge: a charge that is taken from your income. The rate varies according to your income.

VAT Value-added tax – a tax on goods and services.

Wage slip Gives details of gross pay, deductions and net pay.

UNIT 1.5

APR Annual percentage rate – the true rate of interest.

Borrowing Receiving money (a loan/overdraft) from a financial institution that you must pay back with interest.

CAR Compound annual rate. This means that the interest on your savings is added each year to the principal (the amount of money you save).

Collateral Property or other assets that a lender can take if you fail to repay the loan.

Credit card A card you use to buy goods/services. You are billed at the end of the credit period (usually one month). If you do not pay the bill on time, you will be charged interest.

Creditworthy Having a good track record of paying back loans and of being a regular saver.

Debit card A card you use to buy goods/services. The money is debited from your current account.

DIRT Deposit interest retention tax – tax on interest earned on savings.

Financial institutions Banks, building societies, credit unions, An Post.

Guarantee A promise. Financial institutions guarantee to protect customers' savings.

Interest Income on savings or the cost of borrowing.

Investment Putting your money/savings into a product or scheme that should make a profit (income).

Loan A fixed amount of money that you borrow and agree to repay with interest.

Mortgage Long-term loan used to buy a house. Mortgages are typically for 20 to 30 years. They are provided by financial institutions.

Overdraft Allows you to withdraw more money (up to a set limit) than you have in your current account.

Pension fund When you are working, you pay into a fund (similar to a savings account) to provide for your retirement (when you will receive an income known as a pension).

Risk Danger. When you invest money, there is a risk that you could lose your money.

Saving Keeping your money – not spending it.

Shares Money invested in a company, for which you receive a dividend out of the company's profits.

KEY TERMS GLOSSARY

UNIT 1.6

Assessor Works on your behalf to get you the money that your insurance policy entitles you to claim.

Average clause If you have under-insured your property and make a claim, your insurance company will not pay the full amount of the claim.

Comprehensive motor insurance Covers you for loss, theft or damage to your vehicle. It also covers you for accidental damage to another vehicle or to property.

Financial Services Ombudsman Deals with complaints about financial institutions.

Injuries Board A government body that assesses claims for compensation from anyone who has been in an accident and suffered an injury.

Insurance Protecting yourself from the costs that may arise from damage to your property or your health. It is a way of transferring risk.

Insurance actuary Calculates the premium to pay to the insurance company.

Insurance broker Works for many companies and will choose the best option for a fee.

Life insurance/assurance A policy that provides financial protection for your dependants when you die.

No claims bonus A discount in return for not claiming on an insurance policy.

Over-insured Paying too much for an insurance policy. If you claim, you will only receive the actual cost.

Premium Fee paid to the insurance company. The greater the risk, the higher the premium.

Principles/rules of insurance

1. You can only insure something you own (insurable interest).

2. You must always tell the truth on proposal forms and claims (utmost good faith).

3. You can't make a profit/financial gain from an insurance claim (indemnity).

Proposal form A form you fill in when taking out insurance. You must answer the questions truthfully (an underlying rule/principle of insurance).

Reinstatement value Insuring your home for the amount it would cost to rebuild it.

Third party, fire and theft motor insurance Covers you for damage to another person's vehicle or property, but not for damage to your own car. Also covers the risk of your car being destroyed by fire or being stolen.

Third party motor insurance Covers you for damage to another person's vehicle or property, but not for damage to your own car.

Under-insured Paying too little for an insurance policy. If you claim, you will only receive the actual cost.

UNIT 1.7

Caveat emptor 'Let the buyer beware'.

Choices Consumers have to make choices because they have limited resources.

Consumer A person who buys goods and services.

Contract A legally binding agreement. A seller and buyer enter into a contract when buying and selling goods.

Deposit A part payment made in advance when you order or reserve goods and services.

Electrical equipment If you buy electrical goods, the shop or manufacturer must collect your old equipment when they deliver the new goods to replace them.

Ethical consumer An ethical consumer knows the effects of consumption on society, the environment and the quality of life of people around the world.

Faulty goods If a product is faulty, you have a legal right to a repair, a replacement or a full refund.

Guarantee A legal promise from the manufacturer to offer a refund, repair or replacement for a faulty product.

Informed consumer An informed consumer budgets, shops around, knows their rights and responsibilities and keeps proof of purchase.

Labelling Food products must show a wide variety of information on their labels or packaging. This includes the name and address of the manufacturer or seller, the ingredients used and the product's use-by or best-before date.

Online contracts Contracts for goods and services bought online can be cancelled without penalty within fourteen days. This is known as the cooling-off period.

Rights Legal entitlements. Consumers have a right to expect goods that are of merchantable (good) quality and goods that are fit for purpose (do what they are supposed to do).

Sale items Consumers have the same rights when they buy items in a sale as they would if the item was not reduced.

Second-hand goods You have the same consumer rights if you buy a second-hand product as you have when you buy a new product.

Warranty A promise to repair or replace a faulty product. It is offered by the seller (usually for a fee) and lasts longer than a guarantee.

UNIT 1.8

Advertising Standards Authority for Ireland (ASAI) A body set up by the advertising industry to ensure that all commercial advertisements are legal, decent, honest and truthful.

Consumer redress Compensation for a problem with something you have purchased.

BE BUSINESS

Competition and Consumer Protection Commission (CPCC) A government body responsible for enforcing consumer protection and competition law in Ireland.

Financial Services Ombudsman (FSO) Deals with complaints about financial institutions.

Irish Health Trade Association (IHTA) Represents the interests of manufacturers, importers and distributors of specialist health products in Ireland.

Irish Travel Agents Association (ITAA) Represents travel agents and tour operators. It also offers consumer advice on holidays, air travel and information from the Department of Foreign Affairs.

Office of the Ombudsman Investigates complaints against government departments, the Health Service Executive (HSE), publicly funded third-level education bodies and local authorities.

Ombudsman for Children Protects the rights and welfare of children and young people up to 18 years old.

Small Claims Court A cheap, fast and easy way for consumers to resolve complaints without resorting to a solicitor. Maximum claim is €2,000.

Trade association An organisation that represents all the businesses that sell a particular type of product or service.

UNIT 1.9

Business ethics Doing the right thing in everything the company does.

Ethics Moral principles; a system that defines right and wrong and provides a guiding philosophy for every decision you make.

Global warming The rise in temperature on earth, caused by the 'greenhouse effect' of increased levels of CO_2 and other pollutants.

Sustainability Taking the environment into consideration in all economic activity.

Sustainable energy Energy provided by the sun, the wind, the earth's heat, waterfalls, tides and the growth of plants. It creates little or no waste or polluting emissions.

UNIT 1.10

Con Against the motion/idea.

Corporation tax The tax a company pays on its profits.

Globalisation The process of turning the world into one massive marketplace.

Information and communications technology (ICT) Using computers, phones and other electronic devices to transmit information.

Infrastructure The structures and facilities a society needs, e.g. roads, ports, air routes, power supplies, telephone, broadband.

Pro For the motion/idea.

Technology The machinery and other devices that have been developed by scientists and engineers to carry out tasks, solve problems, make life easier, etc.

TNCs Transnational companies.

UNIT 1.11

ATM Automated teller machine.

Current account Bank account for everyday use.

Deductions Total deductions are statutory (compulsory) deductions plus non-statutory (voluntary) deductions.

Employee A person who works for an employer in return for income.

Employer A person or organisation who employs people.

Gross pay Basic pay, plus any overtime earnings and in some cases commissions or bonuses.

Net pay The amount of pay you receive after all deductions have been made.

Paypath A system for transferring wages/salaries from the employer's bank account directly into the employee's bank account.

Personal Public Service (PPS) number Unique identifier issued by the state for use in any transactions you have with public bodies.

Wage slip A statement from an employer showing the employee's gross pay (before deductions), all deductions made and net pay (after deductions).

UNIT 1.12

Budget A written financial plan matching your expected income with your planned expenditure.

Budget deficit Planned income is less than planned expenditure.

Budget surplus Planned income is greater than planned expenditure.

Closing cash The money you expect to have at the end of the month. Your closing cash for January becomes your opening cash for February.

Discretionary expenditure Money spent on things you can live without (luxuries).

Excel A computer spreadsheet that can be used for accounts.

Expenditure The amount of money you spend.

Fixed expenditure Money spent at the same time each week, each month and/or each year (annually), e.g. rent, TV licence. The amount is normally the same every week/month/year.

Irregular income Income that is only received now and again (e.g. bonuses).

KEY TERMS GLOSSARY

Net cash Planned income minus planned expenditure.

Opening cash The money you expect to have at the beginning of the month.

Regular income Income that you receive every week or every month (e.g. wage, salary, jobseeker's benefits, student grant, pension) and is always the same amount.

UNIT 1.13

Analysed cash book A system of dividing recorded information into different categories to learn more about how cash was received and spent.

Analysing Breaking something down into parts.

ATM Automated teller machine.

Balance b/d Balance brought down – the money starting off next month/year.

Balance c/d Balance carried down – the difference between the two sides.

Bank charges Fees paid to the bank for using its services.

Bank statement A statement that shows your transactions and how much you have in the bank.

Cash account A way of monitoring your cash income and cash expenditure.

Contra entry A special entry that affects both sides of the cash book, e.g. 'Withdrew from bank for cash' or 'Lodged cash in bank'.

Credit side Right side.

CT Credit transfer – money transferred into a bank account.

DD Direct debit – money taken out of a bank account, e.g. to pay a bill.

Debit side Left side.

Electronic cash account Cash account drawn up using a spreadsheet package, e.g. Excel or Google Sheets.

Overdraft Money borrowed from the bank – a short-term source of finance.

STRAND 2

UNIT 2.1

Adding value The process of transforming inputs into outputs.

An Post A financial enterprise offering a range of services, in addition to postal services, e.g. insurance, savings.

Creativity Being innovative in how you approach or do something.

Credit unions Non-profit-making co-operatives that encourage saving and offer loans.

Current account An account used primarily for paying bills and expenses. You can apply for an overdraft on a current account.

Cultural enterprises Enterprises that promote the arts.

Deposit account A savings account; money can be lodged in the account and left until needed. Banks usually offer interest on savings accounts.

Enterprise The ability of a person, acting by themselves or working with others, to generate ideas, identify opportunities and turn them into businesses.

Entrepreneurship To turn opportunities and ideas into value for others. The value can be financial, cultural or social.

Financial enterprise A business that provides finance (money) and/or financial services, e.g. banks, building societies, credit unions, An Post, insurance companies.

Idea generation Coming up with ideas, e.g. by brainstorming.

Social enterprises Tackle social, economic and environmental issues and support the vulnerable in society. Quite a few are not-for-profit organisations.

Young Social Innovator (YSI) A programme that gives young people the opportunity to collaborate on innovative social projects.

UNIT 2.2

Adaptable Flexible, able to change to fit a situation.

Capitalism An economic system in which trade, industries, and the means of production are owned privately and operated for profit.

Characteristic Something you are born with.

Committed Willing to put energy into things.

Creative Able to use imagination to create new ideas.

Delegation Giving work/responsibility to others.

Franchise A licence agreement that allows a franchisee (person starting the business) to trade and sell goods/services of a franchisor (an existing business).

Gross domestic product (GDP) An indicator of the economic prosperity (wealth) of a country. The calculation is based on the total number of products and services produced in a country. The more products and services produced, the higher the GDP.

Initiative Willing to do, or to take charge, before anyone else.

Innovative Able to come up with new ideas.

Motivation Enthusiasm for doing something.

Multiplier effect When growth in one area of the economy causes growth in other related areas.

Networking Building good relationships with other people for mutual benefit.

Realistic Accepting things as they are.

Skill Something you learn to do over a period of time.

UNIT 2.3

Contract of employment A written statement of the terms and conditions of employment.

Employee Provides work in return for a wage or salary.

Employer Hires an employee and pays them a wage or salary in return for their effort.

Employment Equality Act, 1998/2004 All employees must be treated equally and not be discriminated against.

Health and Safety Act, 2005 The workplace must be safe. If required, workers must be supplied with protective gear and equipment.

Industrial action Conflict in the workplace, e.g. a strike.

Industrial relations Relationships between employers and employees.

Industrial Relations Act, 1990 Sets out legal requirements in disputes and industrial action.

Irish Second-Level Students' Union (ISSU) A union for post-primary students.

Labour force All the people who are available to work.

Payment When you are employed, you receive payment – income.

Trade union An organisation that is set up to protect workers, who pay a fee to the union, e.g. ASTI.

Unemployed People who are willing to work but are unable to find suitable work.

Unemployment A situation when there are people who are willing and able to work but don't have a job. People who are unemployed may receive Jobseeker's Allowance (JA).

Unfair Dismissals Act, 1977 People must be treated fairly in employment, promotion, etc.

Volunteering Doing something that will benefit others in society or the environment. It is carried out freely and by choice, with no financial payment.

Young Persons Act, 1996 A piece of legislation that protects young workers.

UNIT 2.4

Employees' responsibilities Honest and trustworthy, fair day's work, respect property of employer, be punctual.

Employees' rights Fair wage, equal pay, pay slip, safe and healthy workplace, holidays and leave.

Employers' responsibilities Pay a fair wage, follow tax regulations, maintain safe and healthy working conditions, obey the law.

Employers' rights Hire suitable staff, dismiss employees (provided it is done fairly), run a business.

Ethical responsibility Duty to do right and avoid doing wrong.

Ethics Principles, morals, values and standards that govern a person's behaviour.

Green energy Sources of energy that do not damage the environment, e.g. wind energy, solar energy, sea energy.

Legal responsibility The duty to obey the law – both Irish and European laws (EU).

Responsibility Something you have a duty to do.

Rights What every human being is entitled to, no matter who they are or where they are from, e.g. the right to live in a fair and just society, the right to food, clothing, education, freedom of speech.

Social responsibility Duty to members of society, including our family and community.

UNIT 2.5

Economic impact A financial impact, e.g. employment.

Environmental impact An impact on the environment, e.g. on air, water, wildlife, etc.

For-profit organisation Its aim is to make a profit, e.g. a business.

Impact An effect or influence on someone or something. An impact can be positive or negative.

Negative impact An unfavourable influence or effect.

Not-for-profit organisation Its aim is to improve people's lives and communities, e.g. ALONE.

Positive impact A good influence or effect.

Social impact An impact on society, e.g. sponsoring a local sports team.

UNIT 2.6

Broadband High-speed internet access.

Digital technology Tools and resources (e.g. computers, tablets, smartphones and apps) used to create, store, manage, view and share information in electronic formats.

Environmental costs Negative effects on the environment.

Globalisation Businesses and organisations that operate on an international scale.

Information and communications technology (ICT) Using technology to send, receive, gather, store, analyse, distribute and communicate information.

Redundancy Losing your job due to a company restructuring, closing or reducing the number of staff.

Redundancy payment A lump sum paid to an employee who is made redundant.

Social costs Negative effects on society, e.g. unemployment, data being hacked.

Technology Applying knowledge and skills to practical purposes, e.g. making a task easier, solving a problem.

KEY TERMS GLOSSARY

Video conferencing A way of holding meetings with people in different locations.

UNIT 2.7

Closed-ended questions Questions that can be answered yes or no.

Consumer satisfaction research Following up customers to see if they were happy with the product or service they purchased.

Desk research Finding information that has already been published. Sources may include social media, newspapers, magazines, trade journals, reports, the Central Statistics Office (CSO), other government agencies.

Direct observation Watching consumers, without them knowing, to see how they behave.

Field research Going out into the marketplace and interviewing prospective customers. Research tools include questionnaires, observation, interviews (personal, telephone, online), consumer panels, retail audits, postal surveys.

Market research Collecting and analysing information related to a product or service and using the information to make business decisions.

Market segmentation Dividing consumers into different categories based on socio-economic groups, religion, geographic location, age, gender, etc.

Networking Creating business opportunities by talking to people, striking up a conversation, etc.

Niche market A small targeted market. A business might produce a specialised product/service that meets the need of the niche.

Open-ended questions Questions that require a more detailed answer than yes or no.

Primary research Field research.

Product testing Giving out free samples to see what customers' reactions are. A good way of testing people's reactions to new food products.

Psychological profiling Studying consumers' lifestyle, income, etc. and using data analysis to link types of consumer to their consumption patterns.

Questionnaire A list of questions that can be written or asked person-to-person, either face to face, by telephone, or online.

Research Gathering information on a topic.

Secondary research Desk research.

UNIT 2.8

4Ps Product, price, place, promotion. Each P is like an ingredient in the marketing mix.

Advertising Paid-for promotion of a product or service with the aim of informing and influencing potential customers.

Marketing Identifying what a customer wants, producing the right products to satisfy the customer and making a profit.

Marketing mix Getting the 5Ps right: the right product at the right price, in the right place and with the right promotion and the right packaging, in order to effectively sell the product or service.

Packaging Some products (e.g. food) have to packaged in a certain way. The packaging of a product can make it look appealing and add to the product.

Place Where a product is sold. It needs to be available in a location convenient to the customer at the right time.

Price The cost to the customer. The business needs to make a profit but sell at a price the customer will pay.

Product The item that the business produces. It needs to be something that people will buy.

Promotion Getting the attention of the customer and creating a positive image of the product.

Public relations (PR) Creating a positive image of the product, e.g. Supermac's sponsors the Galway hurling team.

Sales promotion Offering free gifts and loyalty cards.

Slogan A catchy phrase that advertisers use to help people remember their product or company.

UNIT 2.9

Business plan A plan that should help you decide whether you should or shouldn't pursue your business idea.

Capital Money used to start a business.

Cash flow Cash in and cash out.

Flexible Allowing for changes.

Income statement Shows the net profit for the year.

Mission statement Outlines what the business does and its values.

Patent The exclusive right to make, use or sell a product or process.

Production process Once-off, batch or mass production.

Sole trader An individual who runs the business.

Sources of finance Capital, loans, overdrafts, hire purchase, leasing.

Statement of financial position Shows the assets and liabilities at a particular date.

Unique selling point (USP) Something that makes your product/service different from your competitors'.

UNIT 2.10

Credit note A document that is sent to correct a mistake. Seller sends this document to the buyer.

Debit note Seller sends this when the buyer has been undercharged. It shows the extra amount due.

E&OE Errors and omissions excepted. If the seller makes a mistake over the price, the buyer still has to pay the right amount.

eStatement An electronic statement. More environmentally friendly than paper statements

Invoice A bill: the seller sends it to the buyer.

Letter/email of enquiry Potential buyer sends this document to the seller asking about products the buyer wants to buy.

Order Buyer sends to seller to place an order for the exact quantity and models required.

Delivery docket Buyer of the goods signs this document to confirm receipt of goods.

Quotation Seller sends to buyer. A quotation lists prices and terms and conditions.

Receipt Seller sends this to the buyer to confirm that payment has been received.

Statement of account Sent from seller to buyer. It lists all the transactions between the seller and a buyer over a given period, normally a month. The statement of account will include details of invoices, payments received and the total amount payable by the customer.

UNIT 2.11

Cash A business needs cash to pay bills, buy materials and cover delays in payments from suppliers (debtors). It is very important to have enough cash.

Cash budget Shows all the projected (planned/likely) cash coming in to a business and all the projected (planned/likely) cash going out. This is usually shown on a month-by-month basis.

Credit Buying on credit is when a business purchases items and pays for them later.

Creditor Someone we buy goods from on credit. We owe them. Our business will pay them at a later date. They are a liability – something that we owe.

Debtor Someone we sell goods to on credit – they owe us. They are an asset – something of value.

Loan Money that is borrowed for a given period and has to be repaid with interest. Sometimes the lender may ask for security in case the business runs into financial difficulty. This is called a secured loan.

Grant A sum of money given to an organisation for a particular purpose. Businesses can receive grants from Local Enterprise Offices (LEOs), Enterprise Ireland, the government, the European Union (EU). Grants often have certain conditions attached to them, e.g. to create jobs.

Hire purchase A method of buying over a period of time. You pay a deposit on an item and then pay off the rest in instalments. When the last instalment has been paid, you own the item.

Leasing Hiring something, usually equipment. This saves having to pay out large sums of money to purchase the items. Leasing could be used for motor vehicles, machines and equipment.

Overdraft A facility provided by a bank. The borrower is given permission to take out more from their bank account than they have put in. The bank will set a maximum limit (an agreed amount) for the overdraft. Interest is charged on the overdraft daily.

Stock control Ensuring that the business has the right amount of stock. Too much stock is a waste of cash, as stock can become damaged and out of date. Too little stock could lose the business customers.

UNIT 2.12

Analyse Break down into different parts.

Cash account credit Money paid out is entered on the right-hand side or credit side of the account (*minus*).

Cash account debit Money received is entered on the left-hand side or debit side of the account (*plus*).

Cash book A record of all the cash that comes into and goes out of an organisation on a daily basis.

Double entry Every debit entry has a corresponding credit entry.

General ledger If it's on the debit side in the cashbook it's on the credit side in the ledger. If it's on the credit side in the cashbook it's on the debit side in the ledger.

T accounts Accounts are often called T accounts because they are shaped like a capital T.

Trial balance An account that lists all the ledger balances. You work from the trial balance to prepare your final accounts.

VAT Value-added tax – a tax on spending.

UNIT 2.13

Asset Something of money value, e.g. motor vehicles, premises/buildings, equipment, cash, stock.

Closing stock The stock left over; it reduces cost of sales.

Current assets Short-term assets that will vary during the year, e.g. stock – because you sell stock.

Creditor Someone we buy goods from on credit. We owe them. Our business will pay them at a later date. They are a liability – something that we owe.

Current liabilities Owed by the business and must be paid within a year, e.g. bank overdraft.

Debtor Someone we sell goods to on credit – they owe us. They are an asset – something of value.

Depreciation A decrease in the value of an asset.

Dividend Interest paid to shareholders.

Expenses Money a business spends, e.g. insurance, rent, rates, wages, allowing discounts, depreciation. Expenses decrease your profit.

Final accounts Accounts prepared at the end of an accounting period, usually a year.

Fixed assets Assets that remain relatively unchanged, e.g. buildings.

Gross profit The difference between sales and the cost of sales. If sales is less than the cost of sales the business would have a gross loss.

Income statement (IS) Shows the profit for the year.

Liability Money a business owes and will have to pay back, e.g. loan, overdraft, creditors.

Net profit Gross profit minus expenses.

Sales The money value of stock that a business sells.

Shareholders People who invest money (shares) in a business.

Statement of financial position (SFP) Shows assets and liabilities at a particular date.

Stock Products the business sells, e.g. a garage's stock is cars.

Trial balance A list of ledger balances.

STRAND 3

UNIT 3.1

Economics The study of the production, consumption and transfer of wealth.

Financial costs The price that has to be paid for goods and services.

Limited resources We only have a certain amount of income to spend, which limits us in terms of our needs and wants. People, organisations and governments have limited resources.

Non-renewable resource A finite resource. It cannot be replaced when it is used up.

Need A basic requirement we have to have to survive, e.g. food.

Opportunity cost The benefit or value of something that must be given up to acquire or achieve something else. Every choice has an associated opportunity cost.

Rational behaviour Making choices that result in desired outcomes. Assumes that people would prefer to be better off rather than worse off, have more rather than less.

Scarcity When our needs and wants are greater than our resources.

Want Something we would like to have.

UNIT 3.2

Capital Money used to run a business or to buy items that are used to produce goods and provide services, for example machinery, equipment, technology, tools.

Centrally planned economy The government or state controls and makes all the decisions about economic activity. Citizens of the country have very little involvement in business; they are employees rather than entrepreneurs, e.g. North Korea.

Circular flow of income How money flows through our economy.

Corporation tax Tax on a company's profits. It reduces a firm's profits and therefore reduces the factors of production that they can buy. Firms will pay less wages.

Economic systems The way governments distribute resources and trade goods and services

Economies of scale Producing more at a lower unit cost.

Economy A system of organisations involved in the production and distribution of goods and services.

Entrepreneur An entrepreneur takes a risk by investing their money or other people's money to start an enterprise with the hope of making a profit. The entrepreneur brings together land, labour and capital.

Factors of production Land, labour, capital and enterprise.

Free economy An economy where citizens are free to make all the decisions about the production of goods and services. Companies and individuals operate without government interference, e.g. the USA.

Income tax Tax paid on income. It reduces the total income of households and as a result reduces the amount a household can spend on goods and services.

Injections Additions to the circular flow of income, e.g. government spending on education.

Labour The human labour available. Even in a highly technological society people are still needed to produce goods and services.

Land The main natural resource. Includes agricultural land, rivers, sea, deserts, forests, minerals, metals, natural gas, oil, coal, water, weather and crops.

Leakages Withdrawals from the circular flow of income, e.g. savings.

Mixed economy A combination of a free economy and a centrally planned economy – a mixture of privately owned and state-owned enterprises. People are free to establish businesses and the government also sets up and/or controls businesses, e.g. Ireland.

Privatisation The transfer of ownership and control of government or state assets, firms and operations to private investors.

VAT Value-added tax is a tax on spending. It increases the price of goods and services and therefore reduces the purchasing power of households.

UNIT 3.3

Demand The amount of goods and services that consumers are willing to purchase at a given time for a given price.

Demand curve Graph showing quantities that consumers will buy at different prices.

Elasticity How responsive demand (or supply) is to a change in another variable such as price or income.

Elastic demand A change in price causes a large percentage change in demand.

Equilibrium When supply equals demand.

Inelastic demand A change in price causes a small percentage change in demand.

Market A setting where potential sellers and potential buyers come together to trade.

Price The cost of a product or service.

Supply The amount that the supplier is willing to sell at a given time for a given price.

Supply curve Graph showing the quantities that a seller will supply at different prices.

UNIT 3.4

Balanced budget Planned revenue = planned expenditure.

Budget planned income and expenditure.

Capital acquisition tax Tax on gifts and inheritance.

Capital gains tax Tax on the profit from the sale of an asset.

Capital income/expenditure Long-term or once-off income or expenditure.

Corporation tax Tax on companies' profits.

Current income/expenditure The government regular day-to-day income or expenditure.

Customs duties Tax on goods coming into the country.

Deficit budget Planned revenue < planned expenditure.

Excise duties Tax on cigarettes, alcohol and diesel/petrol.

Income tax PAYE, PRSI and USC: income for the government.

National budget The government's budget, prepared by the Minister for Finance.

Non-tax revenue Revenue the government receives from sources other than taxation, e.g. the EU.

Stamp duty Tax on legal documents.

Surplus budget Planned income > planned expenditure.

Tax revenue All the income from taxation that the government receives.

VAT Value-added tax: income for the government.

UNIT 3.5

Deposit Interest Retention Tax (DIRT) Tax paid on the interest you receive on your savings.

Local property tax A tax on property you own.

Tax avoidance Avoiding paying tax by legal means, e.g. by using overseas tax havens.

Tax evasion Avoiding paying tax by illegal means, e.g. under-declaring or not declaring income to Revenue.

Taxation A compulsory payment made to the government. It is a source of income and is used to pay for services.

Universal social charge (USC) A tax on income.

Water charges Introduced in 2013 to provide money for each county council (local government). Water charges are not new for businesses but had never been charged directly to householders.

UNIT 3.6

Climate change A change in climate patterns, mainly due to increased levels of greenhouse gases. Carbon emissions are at their highest in history and continue to rise. Climate change is already having a serious impact: we are experiencing more frequent and more intense extreme weather events.

Economic growth Measured as the percentage growth in gross domestic product (GDP). Economic growth occurs when there is an increase in the total production and consumption of goods and services in a country.

Sustainable development Development that meets the needs of the present without risking the ability of future generations to meet their needs.

UNIT 3.7

Balance of payments Total exports minus total imports.

Balance of trade Visible exports minus visible imports.

Comparative advantage Being able to produce goods more efficiently than another business/country.

Containerisation A system that uses standard-sized containers to transport goods. These containers can be loaded and unloaded easily, don't need to be opened or stored in warehouses and are numbered and tracked. Containerisation has reduced the cost of transportation and helped globalisation.

Domestic trade Buying and selling goods and services in our own country.

Eurozone Countries in Europe that use the euro as their currency (19 members). This makes trade between eurozone countries easier and eliminates the cost of converting currencies.

Exporting Selling goods and services to other countries, e.g. selling Irish beef to Poland.

Exports The things we sell to other countries.

KEY TERMS GLOSSARY

Globalisation The process of turning the world into one massive marketplace.

Importing Buying goods and services from other countries, e.g. buying BMWs from Germany.

Imports The things we buy from other countries.

International trade Selling goods and services to, and buying goods and services from, other countries.

Invisible trade Trade in services.

Multinational companies (MNCs) Companies that produce and sell goods in more than one country, e.g. Apple and McDonald's. Also known as transnational companies (TNCs)

Visible trade Trade in physical goods.

UNIT 3.8

EU Commission Drafts legislation, represents the EU internationally and promotes the common interests of EU members.

EU Council of Ministers Makes decisions and is the voice of the member states.

EU Court of Auditors Monitors the management of finance.

EU Court of Justice Interprets the laws.

EU Parliament Discusses proposals and is the voice of the people.

European Central Bank (ECB) Central Bank for all member states. Sets the EU's interest rates.

European Ombudsman Deals with any complaints about the EU's institutions.

European Union (EU) A group of countries whose governments work together. It is a single market, which means that people and products can move freely between EU countries.

Eurozone Countries in Europe that use the euro as their currency (19 members). This makes trade between eurozone countries easier and eliminates the cost of converting currencies.

UNIT 3.9

Consumer Price Index (CPI) Measures the change over time in the prices of products and services that people typically buy. It's a tool to calculate inflation.

Economic growth The increase in the total amount of goods and services produced in a country over a period of time, usually one year.

Full employment When there are jobs for all those willing to work.

Gross domestic product (GDP) An indicator of the economic prosperity (wealth) of a country. The calculation is based on the total number of products and services produced in a country. The more products and services produced, the higher the GDP.

Gross national product (GNP) The total amount of goods and services produced in a country, less income earned by people from abroad living in our country and sent back to their home countries, plus income earned by Irish people living abroad and sent home to Ireland.

Inflation Rising prices over a period of time, usually one year. It is measured by the Consumer Price Index (CPI).

Live register A publication containing a count of all those under 65 who are in receipt of Jobseeker's Benefit and Jobseeker's Allowance.

National debt The total amount of money borrowed by the government. Just like individuals and businesses, there is a cost to the government for borrowing money.

National income Total amount of income earned by residents in our country in a given year from the production of goods and services.

Unemployment The number or percentage of people who are not in work, but who are available for and actively seeking work.

UNIT 3.10

Celtic Tiger A period of record growth in the Irish economy.

Recession A period of economic decline.

Troika 'Group of three': the European Commission, European Central Bank (ECB) and International Monetary Fund (IMF). The Irish government had to apply for financial help from the troika following the country's economic collapse.

UNIT 3.11

Carbon tax A tax on fossil fuels, which provides income for the government and helps to reduce greenhouse gas emissions.

Economic policy Economic plans and decisions made by the government.

Fiscal policy Decisions the government makes about spending.

Monetary policy Government decisions to change interest rates.

National budget The government's budget, prepared by the Minister for Finance.

CLASSROOM-BASED ASSESSMENT GUIDELINES

BUSINESS IN ACTION (CBA 1)

Business in Action gives students an opportunity to actively engage in a practical and authentic learning experience that reflects activities undertaken regularly in the business environment.

Business in Action is a **group project**.

Students will engage in four areas of activity that contribute to the generation of their evidence of learning and achievement.

1. Conduct **research**
2. **Evaluate** your information
3. Develop **action plans**
4. **Report** findings

The teacher and students decide which Business in Action project they wish to undertake. From the outset, you should be familiar with the Features of Quality (see p. 542) used to judge the quality of their work.

Below is a suggested scaffold to support you with **Project option 1. Enterprise in Action**; an opportunity to engage in an enterprise activity.

What might be the difference if this was a for-profit activity?

Project option 1: An enterprise activity for a not-for-profit organisation

Decide on a project

Which enterprising activity?	Students can organise an enterprise event or activity (for-profit or not-for-profit). It can be a once-off event or one that is organised over a longer period of time. It can be undertaken for economic, social or cultural purposes.
Event	Running an enterprise activity for a non-profit organisation (charity) for social purposes.
Group activity	*Five members in the group.
Process	Be the team!

* It is recommended that the number of students in a group should be between three and five students to allow each group member to make a meaningful contribution and to facilitate work being distributed and shared more easily among group members.

Decide on a name

Our organisation/team name	Students can organise an enterprise event or activity (for-profit or not-for-profit). It can be a once-off event or one that is organised over a longer period of time. It can be undertaken for economic, social or cultural purposes.
Our logo	Running an enterprise activity for a non-profit organisation (charity) for social purposes.

Choose the activity

> In groups, students begin to gather data and information from different sources. Students should undertake some field (primary) research and some desk (secondary) research.

We decided to use our creativity skills and **brainstormed** ideas on how to fundraise for our not-for-profit organisation. Initially we were being as **creative** as possible, however we had to be **realistic** and ensure that we could run the event within time and financial constraints. Working together, the following ideas were presented:

- 'Strictly Come Dancing' event
- Fashion show
- 'Come Dine With Me'
- Table quiz
- Sell tickets

After discussion and debating we agreed on an idea. We also needed to choose an activity that would give a **return** and one with the least amount of challenges.

Our event	A table quiz fundraiser with a difference! It will be based on a theme.
Our chosen charity	We opted for the LauraLynn children's hospice. One of our team members has a cousin who is currently availing of the services. After listening to the story we wanted to support this charity.

What other fundraising ideas might they have come up with?

Conduct research

> In groups, students begin to gather data and information from different sources. Students should undertake some field (primary) research and some desk (secondary) research.

We completed research on this idea. Research involved gathering, recording and analysing information about the idea to make informed decisions on how to put it into practice.

Desk research

1. We researched online, using search engines, to source information about suitable quiz questions and how to organise a table quiz.
2. We interviewed our history teacher who has an interest in quizzes.
3. We researched online about raising money for charities
4. We interviewed our principal to get some advice on representing the school.

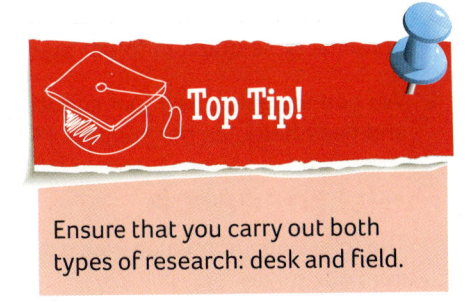

Top Tip!
Ensure that you carry out both types of research: desk and field.

Field research

1. We sent the following survey about our idea to four local post-primary schools. We used closed questions to ensure it was easy to analyse. We kept to four short questions and printed out the questionnaire.

> Charmone is an organisation running an entrepreneurial event to raise money for a charity. Please fill in the following questionnaire to help us make the event a success.
>
> 1. Are you
>
>   male ☐   female ☐
>
> 2. Would you be interested in attending a fundraiser table quiz for LauraLynn?
>
>   Yes ☐   No ☐
>
> 3. How much would you be willing to pay to participate in the quiz?
>
>   €10 ☐   €5 ☐   Other ☐
>
> 4. Which of the following types of quiz would you prefer to attend?
>
>   General Knowledge ☐   Sports ☐   Business Studies ☐
>
> Thank you for taking time to respond to our questionnaire.
>
> *Charmone*

2. We went to the local hotels to talk about booking a room and organising an event like this.

Evaluate information

Desk research

1. There was so much information online that we asked our business teacher to show us how to filter and manage the information.

2. Our history teacher gave us invaluable tips on the role of the quizmaster, rules and regulations, and how to ensure the smooth running of the quiz. He also offered to be our quizmaster, or support whomever we choose to be our quizmaster.

3. We researched how others have raised money for charity and found information on how best to present the idea to potential table quizzers to get maximum attendance.

4. We had a meeting with our school principal, who was really supportive. She agreed that it could be a school event and has offered us her support. However, she wants us to send her regular updates.

Field research

1. The following information was extracted from the 100 student responses we received from our survey:

   - 40% male and 60% female
   - 95% were interested in attending
   - 65% were willing to pay €10; 30% were willing to pay €5; and 5% were willing to pay other
   - 10% opted for general knowledge; 5% opted for sports; and 85% chose Business Studies

Which type of research is most expensive?

In groups, students will evaluate their research in order to assess the feasibility of their enterprise in terms of its finances, its marketability and its viability.

Ensure to analyse your information.

The team decided to run a Business Studies theme and chose seven topics, representing seven rounds for the table quiz. This is an ideal opportunity to learn and revisit these themes:

- Sustainability
- Finance and Budgeting
- Taxation
- EU
- Globalisation and technology
- Consumer
- Insurance

2. The manager of The Broadhaven Bay kindly offered the hall **free of charge**, including **insurance** for the event.

Viability

Finances

Given the interest from schools in attending, the willingness to pay €10 per table and the fact that we have a venue free of charge, this event is financially viable.

Marketability

As the theme will be Junior Cycle Business, our target market is clearly defined (Junior Cycle Business Studies students) and the event is easily marketed to them.

It should be noted that the free use of the room and many volunteers help to make it viable – this might not be the case if running an event of this type again.

Develop action plans

Business action plan

Objectives

1. To run a successful entrepreneurial not-for-profit activity for social purposes.
2. To raise funds for LauraLynn children's hospice.
3. To work together as a team, developing our Junior Cycle skills.

> Students will develop a business action plan that will describe elements of the marketing mix to be applied and financial information for the enterprise.

Marketing Plan

Marketing mix: 4Ps

Product/service	A fundraiser; a Business Studies table quiz. Raising finance for LauraLynn. The themes are extremely relevant for Junior Cycle Business Studies. USP: learning event as well as fundraiser.
Price	€10 per table. Tickets will be sold on the night for raffle prizes. Prize for each of the teams that score the highest in each round. If there is a tie, a challenging question will be asked.
Place	Local hotel.
Promotion	Advertise in the local newsletter. LauraLynn will send a representative and promote the event. Local financial enterprises have offered to advertise the event. Advertise using social media, including Twitter. Contact the local radio station.

BE BUSINESS

Financial Plan

Here is our planned cash budget to ensure our income is more than our expenditure and that we make a profit for the charity.

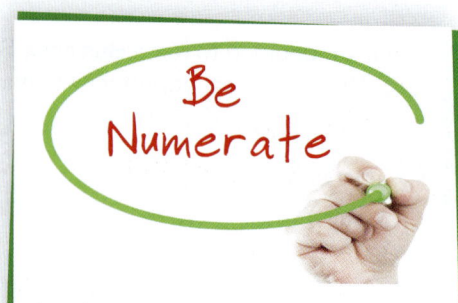

> **Be Numerate**
>
> Are there other accounts that might be useful?

Cash Budget for Charmone			
	August	**September**	**Total**
	€	€	€
Cash In			
Capital	50		50
Tickets for the table quiz		500	500
Sponsorship from the credit union	500		500
Sponsorship from Bank of Ireland	500		500
1. Total receipts	**1,050**	**500**	**1,550**
Cash out			
Advertising	40		40
Photocopying and printing		100	100
Posters	55		55
Internet	10		10
Markers/accessories/tickets	15		15
2. Total payments	**120**	**100**	**220**
Net cash (1 – 2)	930	400	1,330
Opening cash	10	940	10
Closing cash	**940**	**1,340**	**1,340**

	€
Revenue from tables €10 × 50	500
Sponsorship	1,000
Total revenue	1,500
Less expenses:	220
Profit	**1,280**

Advance planning

Working together we decided to distribute the workload as follows:

> **Working with others. Think of the best team. Advantages/ challenges of team work**

> They will endeavour to provide their chosen product, service, enterprise event or activity to their target market, where possible.

Team member Jane	Lobby local for-profit organisations for spot prizes. Lobby local financial enterprises – banks, building societies and the credit union – for sponsorship.
Team member Jimmy	Write copy for advertising. Arrange and pay for advertising as agreed. Buy raffle tickets.
Team member James	Link with Business teachers and prepare the questions on the seven themes from the new Junior Cycle Business Studies course.
Team member Jenny	Decorate the room with information on LauraLynn and liaise with their representative on the day.
Team member Joseph	Design and print the quizmaster's question sheet and a number of answer sheets. Organise a method of recording and presenting the results.
Each team member	Set up the room. Sell raffle tickets on the night and assist with distributing and gathering answer sheets. Use this as an opportunity to practice key skills and at the same time ensure an individual contribution for the assessment task.

Actions and resources

Layout	All tables will be given an answer sheet with space for the name of the team and for responses to ten questions for each of the seven rounds. While using paper was probably not a sustainable choice, we had concerns about doing it digitally given the opportunity for students to do online searches. No phones or devices were allowed to be used during the quiz.
Tables	The number of tables will be limited to 50, to ensure the smooth running of the event. With four students per table that is 200 students. We also need seats for volunteers, helpers, the quizmaster and the sponsors.
Volunteers	Both parents and staff are volunteering to collect answer sheets and correct them. The hotel and parents council are providing security and someone to control the car park.
Literacy and accuracy	Questions will be checked by the team and a Business teacher, to ensure all answers are accurate and avoid any disputes.
Food and refreshments	Food is being sponsored by the local pizzeria, with a free pizza per table. The local convenience store will supply bottled water and minerals. These businesses need to be thanked on the night.
Spot prizes	There will a raffle for various spot prizes provided by local businesses. These businesses need to be thanked on the night.
Technology	An online spreadsheet, using Excel, will be compiled to allow the team to present the results digitally on the night.
Venue	Need to email the hotel with regards to room arrangements. IT requirements, refreshments and room decoration.

Action plan for the night

5.30 p.m.	The team arrive at the hotel and meet with the manager, Mr Brennan, to go through the action plan.
6.00 p.m.	Set up and number the 50 tables and place an answer sheet on each. Ensure data projector is working for presentation of results and do a microphone check. Put up posters/signage about LauraLynn and the project. Set up a top table for quizmaster.
7.00 p.m.	Doors open. Brief all the volunteers. #Charmone is the Twitter tag.
7.30 p.m.	Team member practises communication skills by welcoming everyone. Table quiz commences.
8.30 p.m.	Break for refreshments (pizza and drinks) and raffle for spot prizes.
9.00 p.m.	Presentation of results and prizes.
9.30 p.m.	After the event, counting of money from spot prizes and revenue.

What might you recommend to others if they were to organise this event?

Record inputs/outputs

Inputs	Outputs
Our team	Successful fundraising event
Sponsorship from local businesses	Revision of Business Studies topics
Help from volunteers	Team used and improved various skills
Assistance from the hotel	Money raised for LauraLynn

If you were to organise this event again, would you do anything differently?

Conclusions and recommendations

The event was a really successful entrepreneurial activity. It generated a feel-good factor from local organisations, parents, teachers and students, as well as significant funds for LauraLynn. Business Studies students had fun and were amazed at their learning from the night.

1. When compiling research, we should have used survey monkey or Google forms, which makes collating the results much easier.
2. We have been asked to hold this event in other venues; when demand increases so too might price.
3. We might now collate the questions and answers to provide a Junior Cycle resource for the school.

What might you recommend to others if they were to organise this event?

This enterprising event reinforces the learning of lots of learning outcomes.

CLASSROOM-BASED ASSESSMENT GUIDELINES

Reporting findings

To complete the work related to the classroom-based assessment, each group of students must submit evidence of their project. One project is submitted per group. Students will present their evidence in a written report.

The project report should be approximately 1,200–1,500 words in length. This is not a specific requirement but a guideline for teachers and students. The evidence submitted in the report will be judged against the relevant Features of Quality set out on p. 542.

The written project report should provide the following information:

1. Title
2. Group and student's name
3. Introduction to the project
4. Explanation or rationale for the project
5. An explanation of the research methods
6. An evaluation of the research findings
7. An action plan for implementing the findings of the project
8. Conclusion and recommendations
9. The Student Reflection form of each group member (see the next page). Completion of the reflection is the student's specific declaration of the part that he or she has played in the work of the group on the project.
10. Appendix: prototypes or artefacts, graphic representations, financial accounts, images, photographs, a storyboard and infographics where appropriate.

One report per group. Remember to divide the workload when writing the report.

The innovative use of different means of representing information should be promoted and encouraged. This may impact on the final word count of the report. Depending on the chosen format, some project reports may involve fewer words but nonetheless present all the research and findings comprehensively. All evidence submitted will be used to judge the student's level of achievement.

BE BUSINESS

Business in Action – Template for Student Reflection

All team members must complete an individual reflection.

Project option:	Enterprise in Action	✓
	Economics in Action	
	Finance in Action	

Title of your project

Student name

Introduction: Provide a brief outline of your project

Roles and responsibilities: Describe your key role and your main responsibilities

1.3 Summary: Give a brief summary of how you contributed to your project during the following activities:

(a) How I contributed to researching the project

(b) How I contributed to analysing the research information

(c) How I contributed to developing the action plan

(d) How I contributed to writing up the report

1.13 Review: Describe how you got on as a team and any difficulties you overcame while working as a team *or* Describe the advantages and challenges of working on this group project as an individual

Teacher feedback

Features of quality that your project will be assessed on

Exceptional
- The students use a range of well-considered research methods, some of which show ingenuity, to collect data.
- The students' evaluations of the research findings are of excellent quality, demonstrating a consideration of different points of view and fully supporting the proposed action plan.
- Action plan demonstrates ambition and creativity and is based on a sound, evidence-based judgement of all the information available to the students. It is completed to a very high standard.
- The individual Student Reflection describes clearly and in detail how the student engaged at an exceptional level in all stages of the project. It presents a meaningful reflection on his/her experience of group work.
- The project report is completed to a very high standard, is very comprehensive and represents information in a variety of different formats, e.g. visual, written, with little scope for improvement.

Above expectations
- The students use a range of well-considered research methods to collect data.
- The students' evaluations of the research findings are of very good quality, demonstrating some critical and creative thinking, and supporting the proposed action plan.
- The action plan demonstrates an evidence-based judgement of the information available to the students. It is completed to a high standard.
- The individual Student Reflection demonstrates how the student engaged fully in all stages of the project. It presents some reflection on his/her experience of group work.
- The project report is complete and presented in a clear and organised manner, with some scope for improvement.

In line with expectations
- The students use a range of research methods to collect data.
- The students' evaluations of the research findings generally support the proposed action plan, although there is limited evaluation of other points of view.
- The action plan is completed to a good standard, displaying a reasonably sound judgement of the evidence.
- The individual Student Reflection provides some evidence of how the student engaged at some stages of the project. Reflections on his/her experience of group work are limited.
- The project report has some omissions, but overall is complete and is presented in an organised manner.

Yet to meet expectations
- The students use a very limited range of research methods to collect data.
- The students' evaluation of the research findings are poor, providing little evidence to support the proposed action plan.
- The action plan demonstrates a judgement of the evidence, though the evidence on which it is based is flawed in places.
- The individual Student Reflection demonstrates poor engagement by the student in the project. There is very limited reflection on his/her experience of group work.
- The project report provides a very basic summary of information, omits important elements and lacks clarity in its presentation

CLASSROOM-BASED ASSESSMENT GUIDELINES

THE PRESENTATION (CBA 2)

> Students are given opportunities to develop **communication skills** as they realise various learning outcomes. These communication skills include an ability to discuss and debate, to listen to and express an opinion, to use language and numbers to communicate, and to communicate using digital technology.
>
> The presentation is an **individual** project.
>
> As a guideline, the presentation should last up to **three minutes** per student. Each student will present orally on what they have learned having examined a business-related topic. The information should be presented in their own words to demonstrate personal understanding of the knowledge and ideas relevant to the chosen topic.
>
> Over the course of **three weeks** the student will engage in three areas of activity that contribute to the generation of their evidence of learning and achievement in the classroom-based assessment:
>
> - Investigating
> - Reflecting on learning
> - Communicating

You can of course develop and prepare for this assessment over the first two years. From the outset, you should be familiar with the Features of Quality (see below) used to judge the quality of their work in this area.

Remember that you will complete **an assessment task (AT) based on this CBA**, which is sent to the SEC for marking.

Below is a suggested scaffold to support you with your presentation.

PRESENTATION: TO INVESTIGATE AND PRESENT ON A BUSINESS-RELATED TOPIC

Decide on a project

The chosen topic may be directly related to specific course content, or you may decide to study an issue of personal or local relevance, provided it is related to the business environment.

Potential topics are:

- Field visit to a local enterprise
- Investigation of a business-related story in the media
- Leaders in the Irish business field
- Investigation of the impact of an organisation on a community
- Consumerism
- Investigation of a current economic issue
- Careers in business

You can't present on what you have already submitted in your Business in Action CBA.

Investigating

> Once the student has decided on their topic of interest, he/she will undertake some original investigative work in order to find out more about the topic.

543

Begin to gather information from primary and/or secondary sources, e.g. organising a meeting/interview or online research. As the topic options are very broad, you should focus on one aspect of the topic.

Document the source of all the information gathered in order to be able to assess its reliability and quality. Many business-related topics can be looked at from different perspectives and you should consider differing viewpoints.

Reflecting on learning

> Having undertaken some original investigative work on the business-related topic, the students should:
>
> - Evaluate what they have learned about the business environment as a result of the investigation
> - Reflect on whether/how they see the world differently and whether/how their behaviour has changed having engaged with this topic.

This will include, for example:

- Exploring the importance of the topic for personal, local, social or environmental relevance
- Applying knowledge, understanding and ideas relevant to the chosen topic
- Explaining different opinions related to the chosen topic where appropriate
- Reflecting on what you thought about the topic before the investigation and what you think now
- Reflecting on whether/how your behaviour or attitudes have changed having found out more about the topic.

Develop a **personal opinion** in relation to the business-related topic that you can back up with evidence from your investigative work.

Communicating

> Each student will present orally on what they have learned having examined a business-related topic. The information should be presented in their own words to demonstrate personal understanding of the knowledge and ideas relevant to the chosen topic.

A priority for this assessment is to show confidence in your presentation and communication skills. Experiment with and practise your presentation.

The Presentation: Individual – 3 minutes

1. Identify and provide a brief overview of the business-related topic.

2. Explain your interest in the topic.

3. Evaluate what you have learned about the business environment as a result of your investigation of the topic.

4. Reflect on whether/how you see the world differently and how your behaviour has changed having engaged with the project.

5. Present an opinion on the business-related topic.

6. Demonstrate the development of communication skills.

Note: You may speak with or without notes, and a reading of a prepared script is permissible.

You can use a range of different support materials and tools, such as stimulus material, digital technology, tabular or graphic representations, posters or storyboards – whatever you feel confident using. The use of suitable support materials to support the oral presentation is rewarded (see Features of Quality below).

Features of quality that your project will be assessed on

Exceptional
- The student shows an eloquence and confidence in oral communication, displaying a very comprehensive knowledge of the topic, and the presentation is very well structured.
- The chosen support material displays creativity and is used very effectively to captivate the target audience.
- The student's reflections on the topic are of excellent quality, clearly demonstrating how the student's point of view has developed or evolved over time.

Above expectations
- The student communicates clearly, competently and with confidence, displaying a very good knowledge of the topic, and the presentation is well structured.
- The support material is well chosen to interest the audience, displaying some creativity and supporting the oral presentation.
- The student's reflections on the topic are of very good quality.

In line with expectations
- The student communicates well, displaying a good knowledge of the topic but lacks some confidence and the presentation is unclear in places.
- The support material chosen is appropriate but not used to its full potential.
- The student displays an ability to reflect on their own perspective of the topic.

Yet to meet expectations
- The student doesn't communicate clearly or confidently, displaying a very limited knowledge of the topic, and the presentation lacks structure.
- The chosen support material is used in a basic manner.
- The student's reflections on the topic are narrow and of poor quality.

Ten Tips for the Presentation

1. Choose a topic that you are interested in.
2. Find and select information from reliable sources; you must reference all sources of information, images and video clips (this will be useful when completing the AT).
3. Once you have the content, choose a presentation tool that is most suitable to convey your message.
4. Use a combination of words, images, links and videos if possible. Support the presentation with suitable materials: digital technology, tabular or graphic representations, posters, storyboard, etc.
5. The content needs to be accurate and, of course, you will require evidence.
6. Know the learning outcomes you are covering.
7. Have a story to tell. Keep all presentations short and interesting.
8. Draft and redraft your presentation, checking grammar, punctuation and spelling each time. Your work must be error-free!
9. Communicate clearly in any text you use and when you speak. Practise presenting and get feedback from family and friends until you feel confident.
10. Be creative and, most importantly, enjoy the experience!

TEMPLATES

1. FACEBOOK

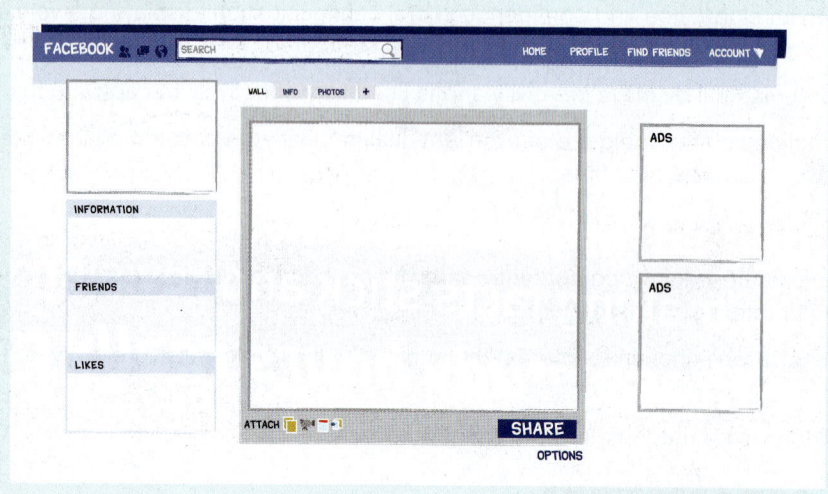

2. DECISION TREE

3. FISHBONE DIAGRAM

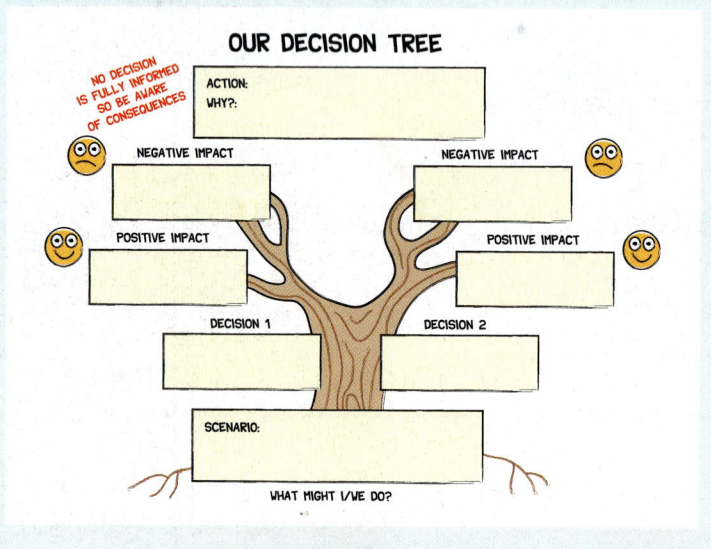

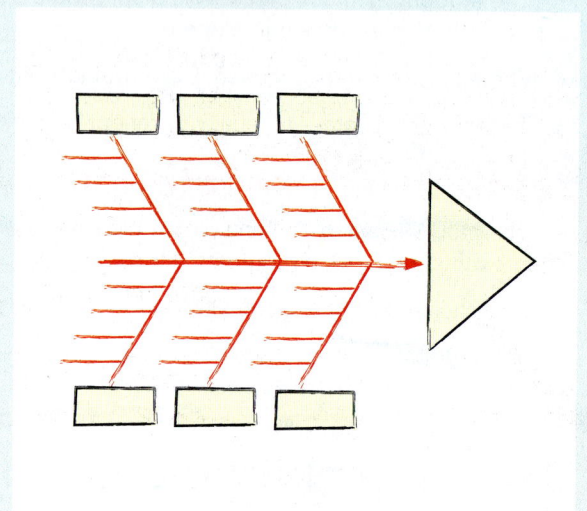

4. TWITTER

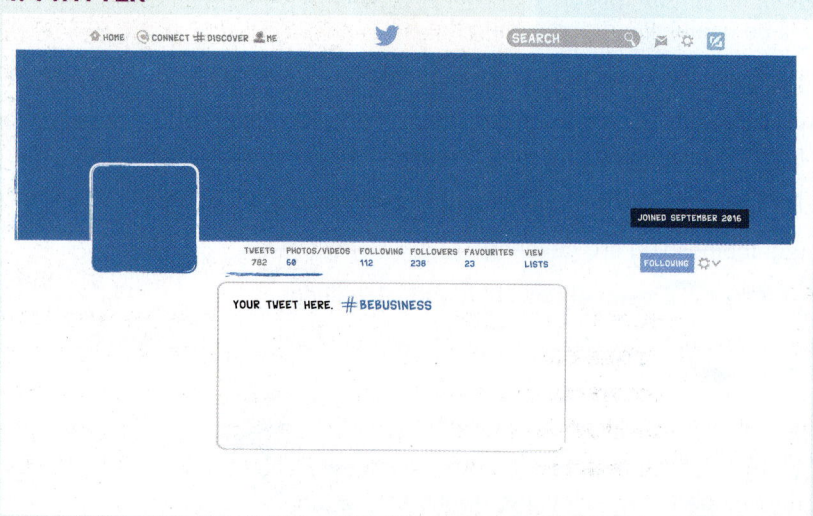